CARIBBEAN ACCESS®

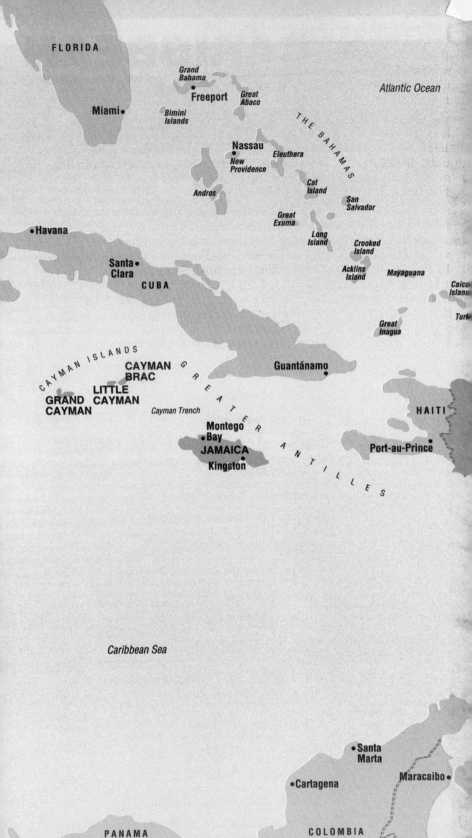

Orientation

Gently swaying palm trees, deserted sandy beaches, turquoise waters, and the soft rhythms of a steel band—these are the images conjured up by one lyrical word: Caribbean. It's a sun-splashed tropical playground where the average temperature ranges from 78 to 90 degrees year-round, the sea is peaceful, the trade winds blow calmly, and life is truly a day at the beach.

Inland treasures lie hidden beyond the surf and sand. Rain forests are rich with exotic flowers and birds, hot springs, and waterfall-fed swimming ponds. Hiking trails climb to volcanic craters or cross salt flats to flamingo nesting grounds. Riding stables, golf courses, tennis courts, and bicycles provide plenty of diversion for landlubbers. Spectator sports range from cricket to cockfights.

The Caribbean islands have a long history of war, domination, and intermingling of cultures. The indigenous Arawak are thought to have been the area's first settlers. They were later joined by the fierce, warlike Carib, who drove the Arawak from some of the islands. However, when Columbus arrived in the Caribbean, most of the islands were still inhabited by Arawak, who were enslaved and eventually wiped out by Spanish, British, French, Dutch, and Danish colonizers. The colonial powers then brought in African slaves to work the plantations. Their eventual emancipation was followed with the import of Asian laborers. Traces of all these groups remain throughout today's Caribbean, though each island has its own distinct heritage.

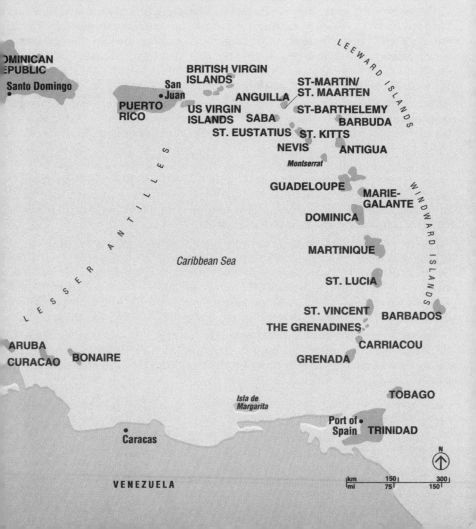

Local legends are populated by royalty and rogues, pirates and cannibals. Their footprints remain in historic forts and colonial architecture, most notably the 16th-century Spanish capitals of **San Juan** on **Puerto Rico** and **Santo Domingo** in the **Dominican Republic.** The 18th century lives on in the nautical British atmosphere of **Nelson's Dockyard** on **Antigua,** **Brimstone Hill** fortress on **St. Kitts,** and in trim European-style villages on **Curaçao** (Dutch), **St. Croix** (Danish), and **St-Barthélemy** (Swedish and Breton). Moody old plantation manors and sugar mills also grace the island landscapes, especially on **Barbados** and **Martinique.**

Shoppers will find bargains on French perfumes, Swiss watches, crystal, and other imports as well as local handicrafts, fine fabrics, jewelry, and art. High rollers can spend their time (and money) in glittering casinos, most prevalent in **Aruba,** the Dominican Republic, Puerto Rico, and **St. Maarten.** Nightlife also abounds in cosmopolitan **Trinidad,** the throbbing heart of Carnival and hometown of steel bands, limbo, and calypso. World-weary mainlanders in search of quieter pursuits will love unspoiled **Anguilla, Dominica, Saba, St. Eustatius,** and **St. Lucia.** And then there's **Jamaica,** famous for its charismatic islanders, smooth rum, and reggae music.

That's just scratching the surface. Head for the water and you'll find outstanding dive sites scattered throughout the Caribbean Basin. Undersea visibility extends well beyond 100 feet in a dazzling seascape of lava flows and sand spills, caves and mountains, coral forests and ancient shipwrecks. Divers and snorkelers come from around the globe to explore the **Cayman Islands,** the **Grenadines,** Aruba, Antigua, and the **British Virgin Islands.** Curaçao is surrounded by more than a hundred dive sites and a 12-mile marine park; **Bonaire** boasts over 80 sites and a kaleidoscope of coral and fish.

After you work up an appetite, head for a feast at a beachfront seafood shack or a romantic continental restaurant. From the "Spice Island" of **Grenada** to **Guadeloupe,** with its celebrated Creole cooks, the Caribbean offers a mélange of international styles and flavors.

In addition to English, many languages (Dutch, French, Spanish, and several dialects) are spoken throughout the Caribbean islands. But don't fret about potential communication barriers. Tourism is the number one industry, and most islanders will go to great lengths to understand your needs and make you feel *wilkommen, bienvenus,* or *bienvenidos.*

Whether you choose to mingle with the people or hibernate in your resort, however, is up to you; tropical vacations are meant to be easygoing, with T-shirts, shorts, and swimsuits the order of the day (along with a mai tai and a basket of conch fritters). So kick off your shoes (they're optional on most Caribbean islands) and dig your toes into the silky sand—life doesn't get much better than this.

Note: Because of the devastation caused by volcanic eruptions in **Montserrat,** the island is not covered in this edition of ACCESS® CARIBBEAN. For current information on the island, contact **Montserrat Tourism Information** at the **Caribbean Tourism Organization** (see page 8).

How To Read This Guide

ACCESS® CARIBBEAN is arranged by island so you can see at a glance where you are and what is around you. The numbers next to the entries in the chapters correspond to the numbers on the maps. The text is color-coded according to the kind of place described:

Restaurants/Clubs: Red   **Hotels:** Blue

Shops/ ⦿ Outdoors: Green   **Sights/Culture:** Black

Rating the Restaurants and Hotels

The restaurant star rating takes into account the quality of the food, service, atmosphere, and uniqueness of the restaurant. An expensive restaurant doesn't necessarily ensure an enjoyable evening, while a small, relatively unknown spot could have good food, professional service, and a lovely atmosphere. Therefore, on a purely subjective basis, stars are used to judge the overall dining value (see star ratings below). Keep in mind that chefs and owners often change, which can drastically affect the quality of a restaurant, for better or for worse. The ratings in this guidebook are based on information available at press time.

The price ratings, as categorized below, apply to restaurants and hotels. These figures reflect general price ranges among other restaurants and hotels in the area; they do not represent specific rates.

Restaurants

★	Good
★★	Very Good
★★★	Excellent
★★★★	An Extraordinary Experience
$	The Price Is Right
$$	Reasonable
$$$	Expensive
$$$$	Big Bucks

Hotels

$	The Price Is Right
$$	Reasonable
$$$	Expensive
$$$$	Big Bucks

Map Key

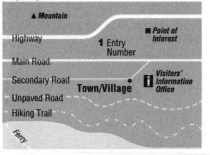

▲ Mountain

Highway

Main Road

Secondary Road

Unpaved Road

Hiking Trail

Ferry

1 Entry Number

Town/Village

■ Point of Interest

ℹ Visitors' Information Office

Getting to the Islands

By Air

The Caribbean islands are served by international carriers through hubs in San Juan, St. Maarten, and Antigua. For more airline information and local phone numbers, see the "Getting to the Island" section at the beginning of each chapter.

Airlines

Air Canada	800/776.3000
Air Jamaica	800/523.5585
American Airlines	800/433.7300
BWIA International Airways	800/538.2942
Cayman Airways	800/422.9626
Continental Airlines	800/231.0856
Delta Air Lines (Comair)	800/241.4141
Northwest Airlines	800/447.4747
Pan American	800/824.7386
Trans World Airlines	800/892.4141
United Airlines	800/241.6522
US Airways	800/428.4322

Interisland Carriers

In addition to the following airlines, **Air Jamaica**, **BWIA**, and **Cayman Airways** (above) also provide interisland service.

Air Anguilla	264/497.2643
Air Aruba	800/882.7822
Air Guadeloupe	590/824700
Air Jamaica Express	809/952.5401
Air Martinique	596/421660
Air St. Thomas	800/522.3084
Airlines of Carriacou	473/444.3549, 473/444.1475
ALM (Antillean Airlines)	800/327.7230
American Eagle	800/433.7300
Cardinal Air	767/448.7432
Carib Express	212/694.3990
LIAT (Leeward Islands Air Transport)	800/468.0482
Mustique Airways	800/526.4789
Tyden Air	800/842.0261
WINAIR (Windward Island Airways)	5995/54237

By Ship

The Caribbean is the world's premier cruise destination. Each year, hundreds of thousands of passengers board the dozens of luxurious floating resorts that sail into Caribbean ports. They disembark at each destination in search of beaches, bargains, and natural beauty, then reboard for more food, fun, and relaxation.

Cruise Lines

American Canadian Caribbean Line 800/556.7450

Carnival Cruises 800/327.9501

Celebrity Cruises 800/437.3111

Clipper Cruise Line 800/325.0010

Commodore Cruise Line 800/237.5361

Costa Cruises 800/462.6782

Crystal Cruises 800/446.6645

Cunard 800/221.4770

Holland America Line 800/426.0327

Norwegian Cruise Line 800/327.7030

Premier Cruise Line...........................800/356.5566

Princess Cruises 800/421.0522

Radisson Seven Seas Cruises 800/333.3333

Renaissance Cruises 800/525.5350

Royal Caribbean International 800/327.6700

Royal Olympic Cruises 800/872.6400

Seabourn Cruise Line 800/929.9595

Star Clippers 800/442.0551

Windjammer Barefoot Cruises 800/327.2600

Windstar Cruises...............................800/258.7245

Ferries

Although going by seacraft from island to island might seem like the ideal way to explore the Caribbean, flying is usually more efficient—many of the islands are more than 100 miles apart, and sea currents can be rough. In addition, there is no regular passenger ferry service to some islands. Your best bet is to call or stop by the local tourist office to determine which are the best available connections. For more ferry information and local phone numbers, see the "Getting to the Island" section at the beginning of each chapter.

Getting Around the Islands

Car Rental

Don't count on getting a modern car in the Caribbean (though you'll have better luck on the larger islands), as available rentals can be old and in poor condition. For the names of individual car-rental companies, see the "Getting Around the Island" section at the beginning of each island chapter. Also check the individual chapters for license information (US and Canadian driver's licenses are valid on *most* islands) and car-rental age restrictions. If the countryside is mountainous, ask for a four-wheel-drive vehicle; on the British islands, be prepared to drive on the left side of the road. If the roads are poorly maintained or badly marked, you might be better off touring by bus or taxi.

Driving

Giving or getting directions in the Caribbean can sometimes be confusing. Communities generally spread out from the boat docks; consequently, islanders may direct befuddled motorists to "the third building after the dilly tree" or "the shop in front of

the yellow hibiscus." Some islands list areas, or beaches and bays, instead of street addresses, though most have a major roadway fronting the sea that provides access to hotels, restaurants, and other attractions. At any rate, expect to get lost a few times; you can always ask again for directions.

FYI

Accommodations

Caribbean lodgings range from simple guest houses to swank resorts. Condominiums and time-share apartments rent by the day or week, and posh villas feature service staffs, chefs, and private pools. Some islands offer central reservation offices for picturesque country inns through umbrella organizations such as Puerto Rico's **Paradores Puertorriqueños.**

On many of the islands, notably Jamaica, couples-only resorts have grown in popularity over the past several years. Another trendy option is the all-inclusive program that covers room, meals, sports, entertainment, liquor, and wine for one prepaid price. Other resorts offer packages that combine accommodations, ground transportation, and airfare.

Room rates can drop as much as 60 percent in the off-season (late spring, summer, and early fall); some major hotels close for maintenance or renovation in September and October.

To arrange home stays or meetings with Caribbean families, get in touch with the following nonprofit international organization:

United States Servas Committee
11 John St, Suite 407
New York, NY 10038
212/267.0252; fax 212/267.0292

To rent a house, condominium, or private island in the Caribbean, contact one of the following booking agencies:

At Home Abroad
405 East 56th St, Suite 6H
New York, NY 10022-2466
212/421.9165; fax 212/752.1591

Caribbean Connection Plus
PO Box 261
Trumbull, CT 06611
203/261.8603

Creative Leisure
951 Transport Way
Petaluma, CA 94954
707/778.1800, 800/426.6367; fax 707/763.7786

Hideaways International
767 Islington St
Portsmouth, NH 03801
603/430.4433, 800/843.4433; fax 603/430.4444

La Cure Villas
275 Spadina Rd
Toronto, Ontario, CANADA M5R 2V3
416/968.2374, 800/387.2726; fax 416/968.9435

Rent a Home International
200 34th Ave NW
Seattle, WA 98117
206/789.9377; fax 206/789.9379

Villa Leisure
PO Box 30188
Palm Beach, FL 33420
561/624.9000, 800/526.4244; fax 561/622.9097

Villas and Apartments Abroad Limited
420 Madison Ave, Suite 1003
New York, NY 10017
212/759.1025, 800/433.3020; fax 212/755.8316

Villas International Ltd.
950 Northgate Dr, Suite 206
San Rafael, CA 94903
415/499.9490, 800/221.2260; fax 415/499.9491

Villas of Distinction
PO Box 55
Armonk, NY 10504
914/273.3331, 800/289.0900; fax 914/273.3387

WIMCO (West Indies Management Company)
PO Box 1461
Newport, RI 02840
401/849.8012, 800/932.3222; fax 401/847.6290

Also see the "Reservations Services and House Rentals" section at the beginning of each chapter.

Clothes

The tropics can get pretty muggy, so your best bet for Caribbean resortwear is anything made of cool cotton. Synthetic fabrics and dark colors absorb heat, while whites and pastel shades are cooler.

On a number of Caribbean islands, vacationers virtually live in their swimsuits. But if you plan to go out on the town, the basic evening attire is lightweight cotton sport shirts and slacks for men, and cotton sundresses or dressy blouses and pants for women. The dress codes are fairly relaxed, although a few hotels on Barbados require men to wear jackets in the evenings. Some hotels or restaurants in the region require ties, however. Many tourist publications recommend that you wear "elegantly casual" attire, which can mean a dress or a stylish T-shirt and pants for women, and a long-sleeve sport shirt for men.

Customs

In general, US citizens who have spent 48 hours outside the country can bring $400 worth of duty-free, tax-exempt goods back home with them, provided this allowance hasn't already been met within a 30-day period. When the exemption is exceeded, a flat 10-percent duty is assessed on the next $1,000 worth of merchandise; additional items are taxed at varying rates, depending on the type of article. Families traveling together can pool their purchases and their exemptions. (A family of 4, for instance, could run up a shopping tab of $1,600 duty-free and pay a 10 percent duty on an additional $4,000 in purchases.)

Each US citizen over the age of 21 may bring home one carton of cigarettes, 100 non-Cuban cigars, and a liter of alcohol duty-free. There are no limits on the number of antique goods (which must be certified as being at least 100 years old), foreign-language books, or original works of art that may be brought into the country.

The rules are a little different for US citizens visiting the US Virgin Islands. The limit is $1,200 worth of merchandise every 30 days; this may include 5 bottles of liquor (6 if one is locally produced), 5 cartons of cigarettes, and a carton of cigars. The next $1,000 in goods is taxed at 5 percent; additional items are taxed at varying rates, depending on the type of article.

The duty-free limit has been raised to $600 on many of the Caribbean islands covered in this book, including Antigua and **Barbuda,** Aruba, Barbados, the British Virgin Islands, Dominica, the Dominican Republic, Grenada, Jamaica, the **Netherlands Antilles** (Bonaire, Curaçao, Saba, St. Eustatius, and St. Maarten), St. Kitts and Nevis, St. Lucia, St. Vincent and the Grenadines, and Trinidad and **Tobago.** Because Puerto Rico is a US commonwealth, US visitors do not have to go through customs.

In addition, the Generalized System of Preference (GSP), passed by the US in 1976 to aid developing nations, assigns duty-free status to some 3,000 items, including baskets, photographic equipment, china, silverware, earthenware, unset precious or semiprecious stones and pearls, certain jewelry, musical instruments, and much more. Request the pamphlet, *GSP and The Traveler,* from the US Customs Service (address below).

Gifts mailed from abroad need not be declared and will not count toward your duty-free exemption, but you are limited to one $100 item each day per recipient (the limit rises to $200 from the US Virgin Islands). Be sure to enclose a receipt. Again, for details and restrictions, request the brochure, *Buyer Beware: International Mail Imports,* from the US Customs Service.

If you plan to bring along a camera, computer, or other electronic gear, be sure to register such items with the US Customs Service or you might get stuck with duties coming and going.

If you fail to declare dutiable goods or try to import restricted products (drugs, plants, black coral, tortoise shell, anything made from endangered animals or made in Cuba), you will be breaking the law. This could lead to confiscation of the items, stiff fines, or even a prison sentence for smuggling. Don't risk it.

For more about these regulations, call the Customs Office listed in the government pages of your telephone directory or contact the **US Customs Service** (PO Box 7407, Washington, DC 20044, 202/927.6724).

Canadian citizens may bring back $50 (Canadian currency) worth of duty-free merchandise every time they leave their country for more than 24 hours or $200 worth of duty-free merchandise after 48 hours. Once a year, they may return with $500 in duty-free goods. Canadians over the age of 18 may bring back 200 cigarettes, 50 cigars, and 400 grams of tobacco duty-free. They may also return with 40 ounces of wine or liquor or two dozen 12-ounce cans of beer or ale.

Entry Requirements

Proof of citizenship and a return plane ticket are commonly required to gain entry onto a Caribbean island, although some officials may request an additional photo ID, documented room reservations, or evidence of adequate funds. Don't expect a driver's license to satisfy the citizenship requirement. In most cases a voter's registration card or a birth certificate with an official raised seal will do just fine, but a passport is your safest bet. Some islands also require a tourist card, which should be obtained before departure from a consulate, government tourist office, or travel agent. Check for specifics listed under "Entry Requirements" at the beginning of each chapter.

Passports and passport information are available at main post offices and federal and state courthouses. The US maintains passport offices in Boston, Chicago, Honolulu, Houston, Los Angeles, Miami, New Orleans, New York City, Philadelphia, San Francisco, Seattle, Stamford, CT, and Washington, DC.

Most airlines check for proof of citizenship before issuing a boarding card. Since cruise ships hold on to passports until the cruise ends, passengers are issued identity cards when ships call at island ports. A ship identity card may also be required to reboard.

Health or vaccination certificates are not necessary to enter (or leave) any of the islands featured in this guide, but inoculations and other preventive measures may be advised in certain circumstances. For the latest information contact the **Caribbean Tourism Organization** (see "Tourist Offices," below) or the **US Centers for Disease Control,** which maintains the **International Health Requirements and Recommendations Information Hotline** (404/332.4559).

Hours

Opening and closing times for shops and attractions in this book are listed just by day(s) when a place opens between 8 and 11AM and closes between 4 and 7PM. In all other cases, specific hours are given (e.g., 6AM-2PM, daily 24 hours, noon-5PM).

Money

Eastern Caribbean islands use the Eastern Caribbean dollar (EC$), but the US dollar and major credit cards are widely accepted throughout the region. For specific currencies of the various islands, see the "Money" section in each chapter.

Telephones

See chapter introductions for each island's area code and information on calling each country from the US.

Time Zones

Jamaica is on Eastern Standard Time (EST), the same as New York and Florida, as are the Cayman Islands, except during Eastern Daylight Saving Time (EDST), when the Caymans are one hour earlier.

All of the other islands featured in this book are on Atlantic Standard Time, which coincides with EST during EDST and is one hour later the rest of the year.

Tipping

As a general rule, service charges are part of hotel bills, eliminating the need to tip individual housekeepers (although you may always leave an additional gratuity for *service extraordinaire*). On larger islands, 15 percent is also added to restaurant tabs. If you're not sure whether a tip has been included in your bill, don't hesitate to ask.

Tour guides are generally tipped about US$2 per person. Those who hail a cab or unload your luggage usually get US$1 or US$2 (regardless of the number of bags), and taxi drivers receive 10 to 15 percent of the fare.

Cruise lines make their tipping policies clear for passengers by posting details in each cabin on the proper amounts to leave for the staff.

Tourist Offices

Free information on the islands may be obtained by writing (allow at least four weeks for a response) or calling these major New York–area offices:

Caribbean Tourism Organization
20 East 46th St, Suite 400
New York, NY 10017
212/682.0435; fax 212/635.9511

Anguilla Tourist Information and Reservations Office
c/o Caribbean Tourism Organization (see above)

Antigua & Barbuda Department of Tourism
610 Fifth Ave, Suite 311
New York, NY 10020
212/541.4117; fax 212/757.1607

Aruba Tourism Authority
1000 Harbor Blvd
Weehawken, NJ 07087
201/330.0800, 800/TOARUBA; fax 201/330.8757

Barbados Tourism Authority
800 Second Ave, Second floor
New York, NY 10017
212/986.6516, 800.221.9831; fax 212/573.9850

Bonaire Tourism Corporation
10 Rockefeller Plaza, Suite 900
New York, NY 10020
212/956.5912, 800/BONAIRE; fax 212/956.5913

British Virgin Islands Tourist Board
370 Lexington Ave, Room 1605
New York, NY 10017
212/696.0400, 800/835.8530; fax 212/949.8254

Cayman Islands Department of Tourism
420 Lexington Ave, Suite 2733
New York, NY 10170
212/682.5582; fax 212/986.5123

Curaçao Tourist Board
475 Park Avenue South, Suite 2000
New York, NY 10016
212/683.7660, 800/270.3350; fax 212/683.9337

Dominica Division of Tourism
c/o Caribbean Tourism Organization (see page 8)

Dominican Republic Tourist Information Center
1501 Broadway, Suite 410
New York, NY 10036
212/768.2482; fax 212/768.2677

French Government Tourist Office
444 Madison Ave, 16th floor
New York, NY 10022
212/838.7800, 900/990.0040

Grenada Board of Tourism
820 Second Ave, Suite 900D
New York, NY 10017
212/687.9554, 800/927.9554; fax 212/573.9731

Guadeloupe Department of Tourism
c/o French Government Tourist Office (see above)

Jamaica Tourist Board
801 Second Ave, 20th floor
New York, NY 10017
212/856.9727, 800/233.4582; fax 212/856.9730

Martinique Tourist Board
c/o French Government Tourist Office (see above)

Puerto Rico Tourism Company
575 Fifth Ave, 23rd floor
New York, NY 10017
212/599.6262, 800/223.6530; fax 212/818.1866

Saba Tourist Office
c/o Caribbean Tourism Organization (see page 8)

St-Barthélemy Department of Tourism
c/o French Government Tourist Office (see above)

St. Eustatius Tourism Office
c/o Caribbean Tourism Organization (see page 8)

St. Kitts & Nevis Tourism Office
414 East 75th St, 5th floor
New York, NY 10021
212/535.1234, 800/582.6208; fax 212/734.6511

St. Lucia Tourist Board
820 Second Ave, Suite 900E
New York, NY 10017
212/867.2950, 800/456.3984; fax 212/867.2795

St. Maarten Tourist Office
675 Third Ave, Suite 1806
New York, NY 10017
212/953.2084; 800.786.2278; fax 212/953.2145

St-Martin Department of Tourism
c/o French Government Tourist Office (see above)

St. Vincent & the Grenadines Tourist Office
801 Second Ave, 21st floor
New York, NY 10017
212/687.4981, 800/729.1726; fax 212/949.5946

Trinidad & Tobago Tourist Board
247 Cedar Ave
Long Branch, NJ 07740
732/728.9426, 800/748.4224; fax 732/728.9428

United States Virgin Islands Department of Tourism
1270 Avenue of the Americas, Room 2108
New York, NY 10020
212/332.2222, 800/372.USVI; fax 212/332.2223

Tourist Seasons

In recent years the Caribbean region has enjoyed year-round tourism, but traditionalists consider late fall and winter the prime time to visit.

Hotel rates are generally lower on the islands from 15 April through 15 November, with many of the more expensive resorts offering special rates from Easter to Thanksgiving. The best values are often available May through October, when off-season travelers will also find reduced rates on sports, shopping bargains, more European tourists, relaxed service staffs, and smaller crowds.

Weather

Because the Caribbean is warm in the winter, many people mistakenly believe that summers must be unbearably hot. On the contrary: The temperature seldom varies by more than 10 degrees throughout the entire year. And while the summer months can be humid, some vacationers find that hotel bills slashed by 60 percent (and perhaps a few extra rum punches) help to ease the stickiness of July afternoons.

The hurricane season runs from June through November, with greatest activity concentrated in August and September. Modern technology makes it much easier to predict storms these days. Anyone traveling in the Caribbean after June should stay informed of the latest forecasts by radio, television, or newspaper.

The West Indies Federation, established in 1959 by 10 former British possessions, broke up in 1962 because of economic disparities between its members. In 1967, some of the participants formed the West Indies Associated States, a British-sponsored federation, but they left it one by one as they achieved full independence in the 1970s and early 1980s.

"I come from a place that likes grandeur; it likes large gestures; it is not inhibited by flourish; it is a rhetorical society; it is a society of physical performance; it is a society of style."

Derek Walcott, West Indian poet and playwright

The Caribbean's Famous Festivals

Holidays and fiestas crowd the Caribbean calendar, celebrating everything from crop harvests to the end of hurricane season, from international jazz and classical music festivals to patron saints' days. Islands that still have colonial ties often celebrate the special holidays of the mother country: The **Netherlands Antilles** salute the coronation day of Queen Beatrix (30 April); British islands join Queen Elizabeth's birthday party (early June); and **Bastille Day** (14 July) means high times in the **French West Indies.** And just before **Ash Wednesday, Carnival** is the biggest show of all (see "Come Celebrate Carnival," page 308).

Hundreds of special events are scheduled throughout the region every year; contact the individual islands' tourist offices (see page 8) for details, as the dates may vary from year to year. Meanwhile, read on for a sampling of the best.

January

The **Festival de Musique** in **St-Barthélemy** imports international performers for two weeks of classical and jazz music and dance.

February

Jamaicans celebrate **Bob Marley's Birthday** in **Kingston** on 6 February with everything from reggae concerts to academic symposia.

Holetown Festival in **Barbados** commemorates the island's European discovery in 1627 at mid-month, with a week of street fairs, music, dancing, and tattoo shows.

Just before **Ash Wednesday,** the parks and streets of **Port of Spain, Trinidad** are crammed with steel bands and spectacular masqueraders. Though **Carnival** is celebrated throughout the Caribbean, this is the center ring of the circus.

March

In Barbados, **Holder's Opera Season** at **Holder's House, St. James,** features big-name opera, music, and theater performances.

April

BVI Spring Regatta on **Tortola** attracts an international crowd of yachts and spectators.

Buccoo, Tobago separates the sheep from the goats, and the crabs too, in a tournament of goat and crab races held the first Tuesday after **Easter.**

Antigua Sailing Week, at the end of the month, brings seven days of ocean races and shoreside parties, ending with a **Dockyard Day** of fun nautical competitions (greased pole climbing, spinnaker flying) and **Lord Nelson's Ball.**

May

St. Lucia Jazz Festival imports internationally known performers at mid-month.

June

Aruba High-Winds Pro-Am Windsurfing Tournament is a colorful spectacle that takes place in the month's first week.

Festival Pablo Casals, Puerto Rico, begun in 1957 by the late cellist-composer, features musical performances during the month's first two weeks in **San Juan, Ponce,** and **Mayagüez.**

Jamaica Jazz Festival, in the second week of the month, features international and Jamaican performers at venues in **Ocho Rios,** Kingston, and **Montego Bay,** plus jazz teas, jazz barbecues, and jazz feasts on the river.

July

St. Vincent Carnival is a weeklong celebration of parades, steel bands, calypso competitions, and feasting in the first week of the month.

Antigua Summer Carnival brings 10 days of music, parades, calypso contests, and parties near the end of the month.

Barbados Crop Over is a two-week festival marking the sugar harvest (though not much sugar has been harvested here for many years), with parades, crafts displays, plantation fairs, and concerts culminating in a lively all-day jump-up known as the **Grand Kadooment.**

Carnaval de Merengue (Merengue Festival) in the **Dominican Republic** is celebrated on the dance floors, streets, and tabletops of the **Malecón** in **Santo Domingo** at month's end and early August.

Statia Carnival brings food, steel bands, and the **Last Lap Pyjama Jump-Up,** all preludes to the traditional burning in effigy of King Moumou.

Culturama brings calypso shows, dances, and parties to **Nevis.**

Tobago Heritage Festival features folk dancing and storytelling, a reenactment of a traditional island wedding, and other picturesque events, along with the consumption of plenty of traditional curried crab and dumplings. It takes place during the last two weeks of the month.

Tours des Yoles Rondes is a colorful week of yawl racing in the traditional sailboats of **Martinique.**

August

Anguilla Carnival is a one-week festival of boat races, costume parades, music contests, and parties that climaxes on the first Monday of the month.

BVI Summer Festival brings two weeks of beauty contests, parades, and dancing in the streets.

La Fête des Cuisinières in **Guadeloupe** honors the island's famed women chefs, who parade through the streets in national costume in preparation for a huge feast.

Grenada Carnival in the early part of the month features more than a week of calypso, steel bands, parades, and pageantry.

Reggae Sunsplash International Music Festival draws top reggae and rock bands (and big crowds) to a different Jamaica location each year.

Fête Patronale de St-Barthélemy (the Feast of St. Bartholomew, 24 August) is a country fair with feasting and fireworks. The next day, the feast of France's patron St. Louis is observed with a blessing of the sea in the tiny fishing village of **Corossol.**

October

Bonaire International Sailing Regatta brings six days of races (both working and pleasure boats), steel-band music, dancing, and feasting.

Cayman Islands Pirates' Week is a swashbuckling celebration starting with the reenactment of a landing of pirates and their wenches and ending with their trial, when the islands' governor banishes them for another year.

Buildings and gardens in **Trinidad** are illuminated with millions of twinkling lanterns for **Divali,** the Hindu Festival of the Lights. Especially moving are the **Divali Nagar** ceremonies in **Chaguanas.**

Hurricane Thanksgiving Day in the **US Virgin Islands** celebrates the end of hurricane season on the third Monday of the month (the beginning of the season is marked with **Hurricane Supplication Day** in late July).

Dominica Creole Day is on the last Friday of the month, when all Dominicans wear national dress to work and school, and restaurants feature local dishes. The **World Creole Music Festival,** featuring the best in cadence, zouk, soukous, and bouyon music, is held on the weekend immediately following.

An **International Deep-Sea Fishing Tournament** lures throngs of sport fishers and fans from the US and South America to the chase for white marlin and other game fish off **Aruba.**

November

Concordia Day (11 November) celebrates Dutch/French friendship on the multinational island of **St-Martin/St. Maarten.**

Pan Jazz Festival in Trinidad features steel-pan and other music that is part of the black heritage of the Americas and Europe.

Statia Day (16 November) commemorates the first official salute to the US flag in 1776 with islandwide parades and parties.

December

Saba Days in the first weekend of the month feature greased-pole and spearfishing contests, swimming and donkey races, Maypole dances, and other small-town fun.

Nine Mornings on **St. Vincent** is a series of pre-dawn parades from the streets of **Kingstown** to the town's dance halls on each of the nine mornings before **Christmas.**

St. Kitts Carnival (23 December to 2 January) is the island's biggest festival, with parades, music, and dancing.

Christmas on St. Croix is a two-week fiesta that lasts until the **Feast of the Epiphany** (6 January).

Hatillo Festival of the Masks in **Puerto Rico** commemorates King Herod's massacre of the innocents with a masked musical parade reenacting a house-to-house search for children through the town of **Hatillo** on the 28th.

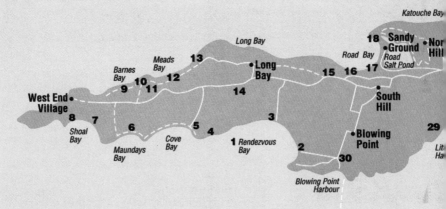

Prickly
Pear Cays

Dog Island

Sandy
Island

Croc

Katouche Bay

Long Bay

18 Sandy
•Ground
Road
Salt Pond

•Nor
Hill

Road Bay

Barnes
Bay

Meads
Bay

13

•Long
Bay

15 16 17

10
9   12
11

14

West End
Village

•South
Hill

8   7

3

5
6   4

•Blowing
Point

29

Shoal
Bay

1 Rendezvous
Bay

2

Maundays
Bay

Cove
Bay

30

Lit
Ha

Blowing Point
Harbour

to Marigot, St-Martin

N

| km | | 2 | | 4 |
| mi | | 1 | | 2 |

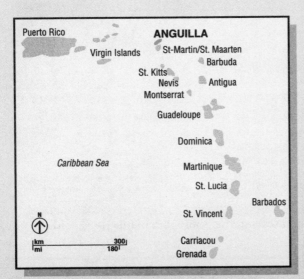

Puerto Rico

ANGUILLA

St-Martin/St. Maarten

Virgin Islands

Barbuda

St. Kitts

Nevis   Antigua

Montserrat

Guadeloupe

Dominica

Caribbean Sea

Martinique

St. Lucia

Barbados

St. Vincent

N

| km | | 300 |
| mi | | 180 |

Carriacou

Grenada

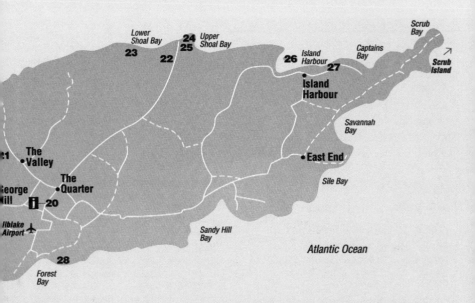

Anguilla

If the first British settlers had brought along a French-English dictionary when they arrived on Anguilla (pronounced An-*gwil*-a) in 1650, it might be known as Eel Island today. The name was given to the island by French explorer Pierre Laudonnaire, who sailed by in 1565 and christened the long landmass *Anguille* after the creature it resembled.

This 35-square-mile getaway is most famous for its beaches of soft, glittering white "powdered sugar" sand, which gently slope into crystalline waters ranging in color from royal blue to aquamarine. The low-lying island is surrounded by 33 beaches and coves, coral reefs, and 7 islets and cays that are excellent for swimming and snorkeling.

Anguilla's beaches are ranked among the prettiest in the world. Favorites include **Shoal Bay** on the east end of the island, where day-trippers from St-Martin/St. Maarten often take a dip before ferrying back; **Island Harbour**; **Road Bay** at **Sandy Ground; Maundays Bay, Barnes Bay,** and **Meads Bay** on the west end; and **Rendezvous Bay** (where a French soldier from St-Martin once tried to invade the island), **Little Harbour,** and **Sandy Hill Bay** on the southern coast.

Water sports are the top activity on this island of just 10,000 people. If you want to hire a craft for deep-sea fishing, overnight cruising, or a romantic sunset sail, this is the place to do it. Fishing is an important source of local revenue, and boat racing is the national sport, so charter operations abound.

Divers can poke through eight shipwrecks at various depths just offshore—but don't expect to find any gold doubloons or pieces of eight. The retired ships were scuttled by the government (beginning in 1985) to create an artificial reef system. The latest, sunk in 1993, is the *Cathely H,* a 150-ton freighter built in Denmark in 1951, which now rests 60 to 80 feet below the surface.

Thanks to Anguilla's spectacular beaches, ultraluxurious resorts, moderately priced inns, and cosmopolitan restaurants, tourism remains the island's leading industry.

Area code 264 unless otherwise noted.

Getting to the Island

Airlines

Interisland Carriers

Air Anguilla	497.2643
American Eagle	497.3500, 497.3501, 800/433.7300
LIAT (Leeward Islands Air Transport)	497.2238, 800/468.0482
Tyden Air, Inc	497.2719, 800/842.0261
WINAIR (Windward Island Airways)	497.2748

Airport

Wallblake Airport (497.2514), located just south of **The Valley,** offers connections to St. Maarten, Puerto Rico, Antigua, St. Kitts, St. Thomas, and St. Croix.

Ferries Regular daily powerboat service links Marigot on St-Martin with Anguilla's **Blowing Point.** The trip takes about 20 minutes one way. Call 497.6853 or 497.6403 for schedules and fares.

Getting Around the Island

Bicycles and Motorbikes

Boo's Cycle Rental	497.2323
MultiScenic	497.5810

Car Rental

Apex	497.2642
Budget	497.2217, 800/472.3325
Connor's Car Rental	497.6433, 497.6541
Island Car Rental	497.2723
Triple "K" Car Rental	497.2934

Driving To obtain a temporary Anguillan driver's permit present a valid driver's license and US$6 at any car-rental agency. Driving is on the left side of the road; yield to traffic when entering a roundabout. Anguilla's roads are fairly well paved and maintained, but they are not well marked, so bring a good map.

Taxis

Bennie's Tours	497.2788, 497.2360
Malliouhana Travel and Tours	497.2431

Tours **Bennie's Tours** and **Malliouhana Travel and Tours** (phone numbers above) offer full- and half-day island tours. Several boat charter companies (see "Great Escapes," page 18) visit offshore cays, sail into the sunset, or carry anglers into deep waters. **Tyden Air, Inc.** (497.2719) schedules "flightseeing" excursions.

FYI

Electricity The current is 110 volts/60 cycles, the same as in the US and Canada.

Entry Requirements US and Canadian visitors must present a valid passport or proof of citizenship (birth certificate, voter's registration card) plus a picture ID, as well as a return or onward ticket.

Language The official language is English.

Money The official currency is the Eastern Caribbean dollar (EC$), but American dollars are accepted islandwide. Banking hours are generally Monday through Thursday from 8AM to 3PM and Friday from 8AM to 5PM.

Personal Safety Crime isn't a big problem on Anguilla, but keep an eye on your belongings on the beaches. The possession of drugs, other than prescription medications, is illegal on the island.

Publications The *Chronicle* and the *Herald,* both dailies from St. Maarten, and the *Light,* an Anguillan weekly, are available on newsstands. Although international papers are generally not sold at newsstands, arrangements can be made with **Tyden Air** (497.2719) for delivery of major American and British newspapers to the airport, where you can pick them up. *What We Do in Anguilla,* revised annually, and *Anguilla Life,* published three times a year, are tourist information guides available islandwide.

Reservation Services and House Rentals

Anguilla Vacations	703/534.8512
Inns of Anguilla	497.3180; fax 497.5381
International Travel Resorts	212/251.1800, 800/223.9815; fax 212/545.8467

Reservations can also be made by contacting the **Anguilla Tourist Board** (497.2759, 800/553.4939; fax 497.2710).

Taxes There is an eight-percent hotel tax. Departure taxes are US$10 if you leave by air, US$2 if you travel by ferry.

Tipping Both hotels and restaurants tack on a 10- to 15-percent service charge to your bill. Cab drivers expect a 10- to 15-percent tip.

Visitors' Information Office The **Anguilla Tourist Board** (497.2759; fax 497.2710) is located between **Wallblake Airport** and **The Quarter.** It's open Monday through Friday from 8AM to 5PM.

Phone Book

Ambulance	911
Directory Assistance	118
Diving Emergencies/ Decompression Chambers	911
Emergencies	911
Fire	911
Hospital	497.2551
Police	497.2333
Post Office	497.2528

1 Rendezvous Bay This sweeping beauty is fringed by one of the island's loveliest beaches, a long stretch of white sand that attracted some of Anguilla's earliest resort development. Water sports, food, and drink are available at nearby hotels. ◆ Southwest shore

2 Rendezvous Bay Resort $$ One of Anguilla's first tourist resorts, this hotel offers 20 rooms cooled by sea breezes and 24 air-conditioned villas (8 of which have full kitchens). Two tennis courts, an exercise room, a dining room, and a lovely white-sand beach add to the appeal. ◆ Rendezvous Bay. 497.6549, 800/274.4893; fax 497.6026

3 Anguilla Great House $$$ This beachfront property has the atmosphere of a turn-of-the-century plantation home. The 27 rooms, all elegantly furnished with traditional mahogany furniture, are within gingerbread-trimmed beachside cottages. Meals are served at an open-air restaurant near the beach. The staff is friendly and the atmosphere is casual. All-inclusive packages include meals, drinks, nonmotorized water sports, and snorkeling excursions. There are "room only" rates as well. Nonguests are welcome at the restaurant. ◆ Rendezvous Bay. 497.6061, 800.345.0356; fax 497.6019

4 Sonesta Beach Resort Anguilla $$$$ Splurge on a few "Arabian Nights" at this Moorish extravaganza of ornate pink buildings complete with fountains, archways, and mosaics. Formerly the **Casablanca Hotel,** the property was purchased by Sonesta International in late 1995. The 100 rooms and suites all have private patios with views of the sea and St-Martin, ceiling fans, air-conditioning, TV sets, telephones, and safes. Situated on three miles of white-sand beach, the resort also boasts a health club with sea views, a freshwater pool, water sports, and two lighted tennis courts; there's a children's program, **Just Us Kids,** too. The **Casablanca Restaurant** (which retains its old name) serves dishes that fuse Floridian, Caribbean, and South American flavors; casual fare is available at **Restaurant Ici;** and the **Casablanca Bar** serves cocktails and hors d'oeuvres in the evening. ◆ Rendezvous Bay West. 497.6999, 800/SONESTA; fax 497.6899

5 Paradise Cove $$$ Spend your days lounging around an Olympic-size pool or in one of the 14 spacious suites (8 2-bedroom and 6 1-bedroom) at this elegant retreat. The suites are packed with all the amenities needed for a home away from home—a fully equipped kitchen, air-conditioning, cable TV, and even a washer and dryer. For an extra charge, the hotel will arrange for a West Indian cook to prepare your meals. Other features include two Jacuzzis, a children's pool, a pool bar and restaurant, and beautiful gardens. If you get the urge to venture beyond the resort's boundaries, Cove Bay and Rendezvous Bay beaches are just short walks away. ◆ The Cove. 497.6603; fax 497.6927

CAP JULUCA

6 Cap Juluca $$$$ With views of Maundays and Cove Bays that will knock your sandals off, and a guest-to-staff ratio of two to one, this elegant resort with a casual sand-in-your-shoes ambience offers 58 rooms, 17 suites, and 6 private villas. The Moroccan-style complex, named for the rainbow god of Anguilla's Arawak Indians, was nearly five years in the making. All guest rooms are air-conditioned and have telephones as well as enormous bathrooms that are grandly outfitted in beige marble. The deluxe tubs with white leather headrests accommodate two and are framed by glass walls that overlook private sunbathing terraces. TV sets and VCRs are available for rent. Tennis and water sports are included in the rates, and for an extra charge, the hotel will arrange for guests to tee off at the **Mullet Bay Golf Course** on nearby St. Maarten (a 15-minute boat ride takes golfers door-to-door). There's also a fitness center and a croquet lawn. But perhaps the resort's most impressive features are the 1,800-square-foot swimming pool and the several secluded sunbathing areas, where guests merely raise a red flag for beachside service. During the summer months, the resort offers a complimentary activities program for kids age three and older; during the winter season, however, no children under six are allowed. ◆ Maundays Bay. 497.6666, 497.6779, 800/323.0139; fax 497.6617

Within Cap Juluca:

Eclipse ★★★$$$ Fine food is served alfresco at this gracious restaurant overlooking Maundays Bay, where diners view the curved beach and illuminated Moorish buildings after dark. Managed by chef Bernard Erpicum of LA's Eclipse, the dining spot features such specialties as striped bass fillet with eggplant risotto, and breadfruit salad. Pizza and fish are baked in the bar's wood-burning oven. ◆ Californian/Provençal ◆ Daily lunch and dinner. Reservations required for dinner. 497.6666

George's ★★$$$ The hotel's executive chef George Reid makes his own goat cheese at a nearby farm for the goat cheese pancakes served at this beachside eatery. Other recommended dishes: baked tomato and basil tart, and braised chicken sausage stuffed with crayfish, ginger, leeks, and fresh herbs. On Monday nights there's a West Indian buffet, while Friday features what's billed as a

"Beach Bonfire Seafood Extravaganza."
♦ Mediterranean ♦ Daily lunch and dinner.
497.6666

7 Leduc's Restaurant ★★$$$ French and island specialties are in the spotlight at Veronica and Maurice Leduc's latest Anguillan eatery. The menu changes seasonally, but might include conch fritters, escargot, or a terrine of goat cheese for starters, and filet of snapper with Caribbean spices or duck with red currant wine sauce as main courses. ♦ French/Caribbean ♦ Daily dinner. Reservations recommended. Shoal Bay. 497.6393

8 Covecastles $$$$ *Architectural Digest,* among others, raved about these futuristic "sandcastles" created by award-winning New York architect **Myron Goldfinger.** The 12 posh white villas are attractively and elegantly furnished, with details like hand-embroidered bed linens and hand-crafted glassware. Amenities include cable TV, VCRs, CD players, and telephones, but no air-conditioning. Four of the units are three-bedroom luxury villas; the remainder are two-bedroom town houses with fully equipped kitchens. All have verandas with hammocks. Complimentary snorkeling and tennis equipment is available, and the fine restaurant on the premises will deliver meals to the guest rooms. ♦ Closed September. Shoal Bay. 497.6801, 800/223.1108; fax 497.6051

9 Mango's ★★$$$ This open-air eatery is one of the hottest spots on the island and *the* place to go for lobster cakes. Chef Claudine Dallam also whips up great French and Caribbean cuisine, with dishes like marinated sesame snapper and blackened grouper. Don't leave without trying the coconut cheesecake with a raspberry puree. ♦ French/Caribbean ♦ M, W-Su lunch and dinner; closed in August. Reservations required. Barnes Bay. 497.6479

10 Coccoloba $$$$ Straddling the white sands of Meads and Barnes Bays, this resort was completely renovated after substantial hurricane damage in 1995. Part of the international Club Valtur chain of all-inclusive resorts, the Mediterranean-style property offers 51 individual villas with terraces, air-conditioning, ceiling fans, mini-bars, hair dryers, TV sets, telephones, and safes. The rate includes buffet breakfast and lunch, sit-down or buffet dinner, wine with lunch and dinner, sports and instruction, and entertainment. There's plenty to keep guests amused—in addition to the long white beach the resort offers a pool, saunas, two tennis courts, a gym, aerobics classes, windsurfing, sailing, snorkeling, kayaking, paddleboats, and beach volleyball. There's also a spa (treatments are available for an additional fee)

and a disco. At press time a great house with seven guest rooms and a pool was in the works. ♦ Barnes Bay. 497.6871

11 La Sirena $$$ The flat tropical setting couldn't be less alpine, but those special touches of personal service for which Swiss hoteliers are famous are evident here, thanks to manager Rolf Masshardt. The 20 rooms and 2 air-conditioned villas are set amid lush foliage, and a milelong beach is only minutes away. All units have a balcony or terrace and are furnished with wicker furniture; bougainvilleas are scattered throughout the rooms and terraces. Two freshwater pools and shops round out the amenities. The popular on-site restaurant is best known for its beautiful view. ♦ Meads Bay. 497.6827, 800/331.9358; fax 497.6829

12 Blanchard's ★★★$$$$ One of the island's best restaurants, this intimate, candle dining room blends Southwestern, Cajun, and Creole influences to present a unique menu. Although dishes change often, you could find gumbo ya-ya soup, lemon-glazed lobster dumplings, or chili-crusted sea scallop salad. ♦ Eclectic ♦ M-Sa lunch and dinner. Reservations required. Meads Bay. 497.6100

Frangipani Beach Club

12 Frangipani Beach Club $$$$ Built in Spanish Mediterranean style, this luxury retreat on a white-sand beach has 8 luxury suites and 15 1-, 2-, and 3-bedroom suites with large terraces, full kitchens, and washe dryers. Decorated in light colors and rattan furniture, each unit features ceiling fans as well as air conditioners. Private cooks are available to prepare West Indian dinners in suites, and there's also a waterfront gourme restaurant (see below). Guests can enjoy the pool, and water sports are available for an additional fee. ♦ Meads Bay. 497.6442, 800.892.4564; fax 497.6440

Within Frangipani Beach Club:

Restaurant Frangipani ★★$$$ On the waterfront at Meads Bay, this large resort dining room offers both indoor and outdoor tables. The menu created by chef Claude Jani is also large and it includes gourmet French dishes both classic and island-inspired. Amor the many mouth-watering choices are crayfis in a Marsala wine and pink peppercorn sauce and veal, mushrooms, and bacon in puff pastry, flamed with Cognac and served in a light cream sauce. ♦ French ♦ Daily breakfas lunch, and dinner; closed September and October. Reservations recommended. 497.6442

Malliouhana

13 Malliouhana Hotel $$$$ Mediterranean in design, this exotic hideaway run by British entrepreneur Leon Roydon and his son Nigel is for those who seek the very best. **Malliouhana** (the original Arawak name for Anguilla) boasts 53 elegant rooms and suites, 4 tennis courts, 3 beaches, 2 swimming pools, a Jacuzzi, an exercise hall, and some of the most tastefully designed public areas in the Caribbean. Guest rooms are fitted with pedestal beds topped with beige cotton spreads and at least a dozen pillows, and the spacious bathrooms are equipped with every imaginable amenity. Three of the villas do not have air-conditioning, but their louvered windows do catch the continuous breezes. There's an excellent restaurant (see below) and the poolside bar, with its large white couches and brightly hued pillows, is a marvelous destination for a late-afternoon drink. A supervised children's playground includes a paddling pool and a small basketball court. And just in case you never make it off the premises, there's also a shop that offers a tasteful selection of jewelry, wallets, and other gift items to bring home. ◆ Closed September and October. No credit cards accepted. Meads Bay. 497.6111, 800/835.0796; fax 497.6011

Within the Malliouhana Hotel:

Malliouhana Restaurant ★★★★$$$$ This outstanding dining experience was formerly directed by the late Jo Rostang (of **La Bonne Auberge** in Antibes, France, and **Le Regence** at the **Hotel Plaza Athénée** in New York); his son Michel now runs the show. And what a production: The wine cellar is renowned, and the Limoges china could be graced with anything from a classic foie gras with wild mushrooms to spicy roasted triggerfish with peppercorn sauce. Tropical fruits star in the mango tart and soursop sorbet. ◆ Continental/Caribbean ◆ Daily breakfast, lunch, and dinner. Reservations required. 497.6111

14 Cheddie's Carving Studio Whether you come to buy or just to watch native Anguillan Cheddie Richardson carve sculptures from mahogany, driftwood, and coral, visiting his studio/gallery is a delight. Cheddie's rendering of a driftwood dolphin mounted on stone was presented to Queen Elizabeth. Ask about his recent venture into bronze casting. ◆ Daily. The road to West End Village. 497.6027

15 Arlo's Place ★★★$$ Great pizza draws locals and tourists alike to this beachfront restaurant. Other menu favorites include fettuccine with lobster, cheese tortellini, and roasted red pepper stuffed with scallops and served with angel-hair pasta and vodka sauce. ◆ Italian ◆ M-Sa dinner. Reservations recommended. Lower South Hill. 497.6810

16 Sandy Ground Although this is one of Anguilla's most developed beaches, it remains clean and uncrowded. The small harborside village of Sandy Ground is a picturesque charmer located between Road Salt Pond and the sea. Water sports, restaurants, and bars are abundant.

16 Mariners Cliffside Beach Resort $$$ Single rooms, doubles, suites, and cottages (67 in all, 6 with air-conditioning) dot the grounds of this beachfront hotel, a classic example of West Indian architecture. Also on the premises are a popular bar/restaurant (see below), a pool, a tennis court (with lighting for night play), and water sports facilities and equipment. TV sets are available for rent. ◆ Sandy Ground. 497.2671, 497.2615, 800/848.7938; fax 497.2901

Within Mariners Cliffside Beach Resort:

Paw Paw Beach Grill ★★★$$$ A hangout for yachters, local dignitaries, and expatriates, this friendly poolside bar /restaurant serves salads, soups, and sandwiches for lunch and fresh grilled fish, seafood salads, and chicken for dinner. ◆ Daily breakfast, lunch, and dinner. 497.2671

17 Riviera ★★★$$$ The French-accented seafood dishes and desserts are as good as you'll find in some of the best restaurants in Paris, and a selection of sashimi adds Japanese flavor to the menu as well. This beachside spot also has a bar and a boutique. ◆ French ◆ Daily lunch and dinner. Sandy Ground. 497.2833

18 Johnno's Beach Bar ★★$ This well-loved and well-worn watering hole is frequented by both visitors and locals (look for martial artist Chuck Norris, who owns a house on the island). Barbecued chicken and ribs are served on wooden picnic tables at the tin-roofed beach shack, as are grilled snapper and lobster that Johnno catches himself. Dumpa and the Anvibes, a local band, draws lively crowds on Wednesday, Saturday, and Sunday evenings. Another local band plays Friday nights. Keep an eye on the sky for the fabled green flash at sunset. ◆ American ◆ Tu lunch; W, F-Su lunch and early dinner. No credit cards accepted. Sandy Ground. 497.2728

18 The Dive Shop Here's the place to rent snorkel or scuba-diving equipment or even take a **PADI** course in scuba diving. Day and night dives are also available. ◆ Daily. Sandy Ground. 497.2020

19 Devonish Gallery Browse among paintings, wood carvings, and ceramics by local and foreign artists in this airy gallery owned by Courtney Devonish, who also displays her own paintings. Don't miss the collection of antique Caribbean maps, prints of which are available for sale. ◆ M-Sa. George Hill. 497.2949

20 New World Gallery What's an African and Asian antiques gallery doing in Anguilla? The owners say their low overhead costs and the favorable Anguilla tax structure help them compete successfully with similar galleries in New York and Paris. The offerings change constantly at this no-frills place, but you may find African tribal masks and ceremonial chairs, and centuries-old jade jewelry. ◆ M-Sa. The Quarter. 497.5950

21 Koal Keel Restaurant ★★$$$$ One of Anguilla's best-known restaurants, this romantic charmer is housed in an 18th-century West Indian home. Specialties include curried chicken and shrimp, grilled seafood with fresh roasted vegetables, lobster bisque, and conch chowder. ◆ Caribbean/ Continental ◆ Daily breakfast and dinner. Reservations recommended. The Valley. 497.2930

22 The Fountain Excavation continues in this cave, where researchers have found a 16-foot stalagmite carved into what they believe is Jocahu, a Taino Indian God. Hundreds of fragments of pottery and some petroglyphs have also been found in the cave, a dome-shaped limestone sinkhole that descends from a ridge about 70 feet above sea level. Anguilla is planning to create a 3.5-acre national park around the site and open it as a tourist attraction, but at press time no completion date had been set. ◆ The road to Shoal Bay

23 Shoal Bay Not to be confused with the Shoal Bay on Anguilla's west end, this beach, often called Shoal Bay East, is located on the northeastern shore of Anguilla and is as perfect as they get. The beach—which is divided into two sections, Upper and Lower Shoal Bay—has abundant offshore coral gardens populated by schools of iridescent fish, while the drop-off and reef that lie beyond are a big draw for experienced divers. Unfortunately, most of the shade trees in this area are gone now, devastated by Hurricane Luis in 1995. Snorkeling equipment is available for rent, as are chairs and beach umbrellas. Food and drink are for sale at nearby beach bars. ◆ East end

23 Fountain Beach $$$ This beachfront hotel's 10 studio and 1-bedroom units offer Mediterranean style and a sense of seclusion on the western end of Shoal Bay. Much of the action here centers around the freshwater pool. Rooms are furnished with island antiques, but the kitchenettes are modern. There's also a restaurant for those who would prefer not to cook themselves (see below). ◆ Lower Shoal Bay. 497.3491; 800.342.3491; fax 497.3493

Within Fountain Beach:

La Fontana ★★$$ Chef Morris Brooks is best known for preparing traditional fare (grilled fish, T-bone steaks, Italian standards), but he'll prepare whatever guests request, given advance notice. ◆ Italian ◆ M-Tu, Th-Su breakfast, lunch, and dinner; W breakfast. Reservations recommended. 497.3491

Great Escapes

Travelers come to Anguilla to avoid crowds, but the most determined hermit crabs can escape to one of these offshore hideouts, where they'll find even fewer people and less activity than on the main island.

Sandy Island is a coconut palm–shaded circle. Ringed by reefs, it's a good destination for snorkelers. Come up for air, lunch, and drinks at the beach barbecue bar. Powerboats and sailboats make the two-mile trip from **Road Bay** hourly.

Prickly Pear Cays, the tip of a six-mile chain of reefs, is well known in the scuba world for its spectacular underwater canyon carved with ledges and caverns. Landlubbers can scramble along the shoreline to hear the so-called whistling rocks, but be sure to wear sturdy shoes (the rocks are sharp). Catamarans and sloops sail the six miles from Road Bay, and several packages include snorkel gear and lunch at the beach barbecue bar.

Scrub Island, two square miles of solid peace and quiet, lies just off Anguilla's east end. The snorkeling is great, and amateur archaeologists can explore the ruins of a deserted tourist resort or the carcass of an airplane abandoned at the old dirt airstrip. Weather

and sea conditions permitting, chartered yachts or powerboats will take you here from either Road Bay or **Island Harbour.**

Scilly Cay is home to the very popular watering hole/restaurant known as **Gorgeous Scilly Cay** (see page 19). It can be noisy when the bands heat up, but snorkelers can find an underwater respite. There's also plenty of coral sand and tropical landscape to explore. Just stand on the floating rubber pier at Island Harbour to hitch a free ride— a quick two-minute crossing.

Dog Island is a bit of a misnomer, as the population runs more to wild goats and sea birds. Most charter companies that run trips here include scenic cruising along Anguilla's spectacular **Long Bay, Meads Bay,** and **Barnes Bay.** Set aside a full day for this trip, as the flat little island lies 10 miles west-northwest of Road Bay.

For more information on the wide variety of packages available (and about sunset cruises and trips to Anguilla's secluded coves), contact one of the charter companies listed in "Getting Your Feet Wet in Anguilla" on page 19.

24 **Uncle Ernie's** ★★★$ This beachside bar/restaurant is one of the most popular hangouts on Shoal Bay East, offering barbecued chicken, ribs, and the catch of the day. Live music adds to the island ambience on Sundays between 2 and 7PM. ◆ Daily lunch and dinner. No credit cards accepted. Upper Shoal Bay. No phone

25 **Shoal Bay Beach Resort Hotel** $$$ Set along 2 miles of one of Anguilla's prettiest beaches are 26 1-bedroom suites with kitchen facilities and terraces or balconies overlooking the bay. The spacious units features bamboo furniture, tile floors, ceiling fans, TV sets, and telephones. There's no pool, but it's just steps from the beach. A range of water sports is offered. Although there's no restaurant on the premises, many are nearby, several within walking distance. ◆ Upper Shoal Bay. 497.2011, 800/869.5827; fax 497.3355

25 **Shoal Bay Villas** $$$ This charming complex offers a unique "pick-a-package" system, which allows vacationers to choose among different water-sports programs. Accommodations consist of 13 units (studios and 1- or 2-bedroom apartments with fully equipped kitchens), each with a patio or balcony. There's a freshwater pool, and the beach is outstanding. ◆ Upper Shoal Bay. 497.2051, 800/722.7045; fax 497.3631

26 **Gorgeous Scilly Cay** ★★★★$$$ Climb aboard the boat at the Island Harbour dock for a two-minute ride to this private island restaurant, where swimsuited diners feast on grilled chicken, lobster and prawns marinated in the eatery's signature "secret" sauce. The mood is always fun and casual, but Sundays are best, when the crowd is peppered with residents and local restaurateurs. Live music is a big attraction on Wednesday, Friday, and Sunday. Customers from St. Maarten touch down at the heliport, where there's no landing charge. It's not only the most unusual dining place on Anguilla, for island ambience and spectacular food, it's the best! ◆ American ◆ Tu-Su lunch and early dinner. No credit cards accepted. Island Harbour. 497.5123

27 **Hibernia** ★★$$$ Overlooking the water in a pleasant fishing village, this small, off-the-beaten-path eatery serves continental cuisine with a strong Caribbean and Thai flavor that's inspired by the travels of chef-owner Raoul Rodriquez. A Thai seafood soup, lobster medaillons with celery–star anise cream, and crayfish with basil and coconut milk are three of the restaurant's innovative dishes. ◆ French/Thai/Caribbean ◆ Tu-Su lunch and dinner; closed September and October. Reservations required. Island Harbour. 497.4290

28 **Straw Hat** ★★$$ Set on the old fishing wharf on Forest Bay and decorated (appropriately enough) with lots of straw hats, this restaurant has something for everyone. The eclectic menu includes Thai ginger lemongrass shrimp (in varying intensities), bouillabaisse, vegetable tortilla, Jamaican jerk pork and chicken, and New York strip steak. ◆ International ◆ Daily dinner. Forest Bay. 497.8300

29 **Cinnamon Reef Beach Club** $$$ Personalized service is the hallmark of this impressive seaside hotel, owned by Richard and Carol Hauser since 1993. There are 22 rooms, and amenities include a quiet beach, a huge freshwater pool, 2 tennis courts, a Jacuzzi, water sports, and a restaurant (see below). Morning coffee and tea are complimentary, as is afternoon tea. ◆ Little Harbour. 497.2727, 800/346.7084; fax 497.3727

Within the Cinnamon Reef Beach Club:

Palm Court ★★★★$$$$ One of the most celebrated restaurants in the Caribbean showcases the creativity of Zeff Bonsey and Vernon Hughes, whose multicultural cuisine is regularly voted the best on Anguilla. Settle in at this airy spot for yellowfin tuna tartare with marinated black beans, or pumpkin seed–crusted grouper with carrot-tamarind sauce. ◆ American/Caribbean ◆ Daily breakfast, lunch, and dinner. Reservations recommended. 497.2727, 497.2781

30 **El Rancho del Blues** This horse ranch offers two-hour beach rides, so pack your bathing suit in those saddlebags. Western and English saddles are available, as are riding lessons. ◆ Daily. Blowing Point. 497.6164

Getting Your Feet Wet in Anguilla

Anguilla is known for its beautiful beaches, but the sea provides more to explore. Here are a few organizations that can help get you afloat:

Boating
Caribbean Concepts Ltd. Sandy Ground. 497.2671

Sandy Island Enterprises Sandy Ground. 497.5643

Scuba Diving
The Dive Shop Sandy Ground. 497.2020

Sportfishing
Mike's Glass-Bottom Boat Cruises The road to Fountain Beach, Lower Shoal Bay. 497.2051, 497.4155

Windsurfing
Sandy Island Enterprises Sandy Ground. 497.5643

Antigua

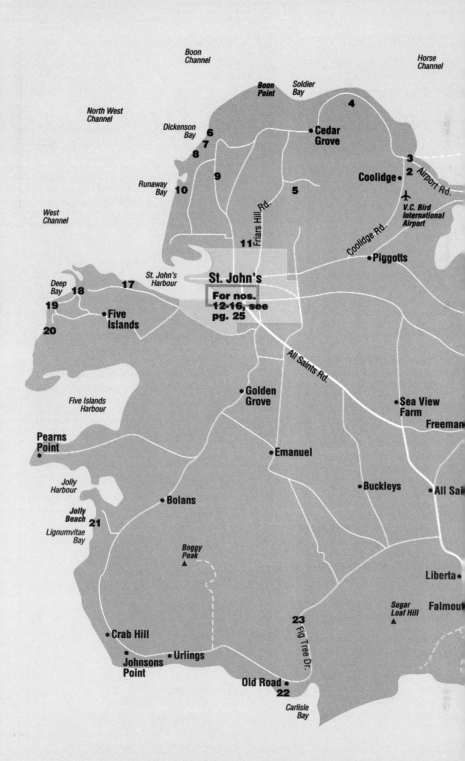

Boon
Channel

Horse
Channel

**Boon
Point**

Soldier
Bay

4

North West
Channel

Dickenson
Bay

6

7

8

● **Cedar
Grove**

3

2

Coolidge

Airport Rd.

9

Runaway
Bay

10

5

**V.C. Bird
International
Airport**

West
Channel

11

Friars Hill Rd.

Coolidge Rd.

● **Piggotts**

Deep
Bay

18

17

St. John's
Harbour

St. John's

For nos.
12-16, see
pg. 25

19

● **Five
Islands**

20

All Saints Rd.

Five Islands
Harbour

● **Golden
Grove**

● **Sea View
Farm**

Freeman

**Pearns
Point**

● **Emanuel**

Jolly
Harbour

● **Buckleys**

● **All Sai**

Jolly
Beach

21

● **Bolans**

Lignumvitae
Bay

Boggy
Peak
▲

Liberta

Sugar
Loaf Hill
▲

Falmou

23

Fig Tree Dr.

● **Crab Hill**

● **Johnsons
Point**

● **Urlings**

Old Road ●

22

Carlisle
Bay

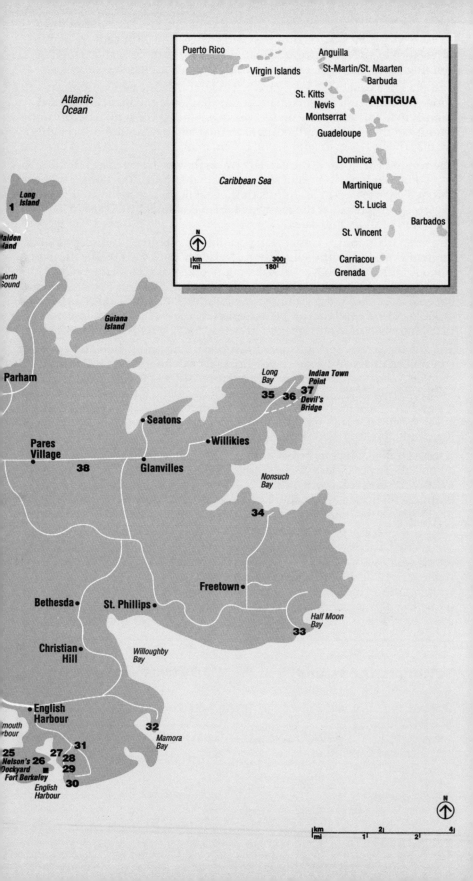

Antigua

Imagine England with sunshine, a countryside of picture-postcard villages and 18th-century harbors, where former seaside fortresses are now used for barbecues and Georgian buildings stand in stark contrast to white sands and cloudless blue skies.

Antigua's 365 beaches, cooling trade winds, and exotic trees and plants will entice the most resistant mainlander. The largest of the **British Leeward Islands** (63,000 people live on its 108 square miles) is a gem of beauty and serenity in the Eastern Caribbean. Each inlet and bay around this roughly circular isle has its own white-sand beach, many fronted by a hotel or resort.

The region of **St. John's,** the capital city on the northwest coast, is home to 24,000 residents and a host of shops, restaurants, and attractions. The twin Baroque-style towers of **St. John's Cathedral** dominate the local skyline. Lighter spirits prevail at the renovated arsenal of **Redcliffe Quay,** a lively collection of shops and cafes.

The other main tourist center is the beautifully preserved 18th-century port of **English Harbour** on the south shore. **Nelson's Dockyard** recalls the days when Admiral Horatio Nelson was stationed here as commander of the Leeward Islands Squadron. The restored waterfront taverns and chandleries have served as stomping grounds for centuries of mariners, both ancient and modern. **Shirley Heights** and **Fort Berkeley,** the high-perched lookouts built to defend the port against French invasion, today offer fine sunset views.

The French weren't the only ones interested in the rolling hills and graceful contours of this island. Ever since Christopher Columbus, on his second trip to the New World, named Antigua (pronounced An-*tee*-ga, with a hard "g") for Santa María de la Antigua (the miracle-working saint at the Seville Cathedral), it was caught in a territorial tug-of-war among Spain, France, Holland, and Great Britain. It wasn't until the 1630s that colonists from St. Kitts claimed the island and its crops of tobacco and sugarcane for the English crown.

It took another 350 years before Antigua gained independence and tourism became the major industry. One reason for the island's popularity is its central location, with easy access to other Caribbean destinations. The little island of **Barbuda,** for instance, is readily accessible from Antigua's north shore. A day trip to this quiet sister island may include such diverse activities as cave climbing, bird watching, and hunting—not to mention lounging on the pink beaches.

Meanwhile, back on Antigua, active types will find plenty of opportunity for tennis, golf, riding, and all water sports. Divers and snorkelers can explore shallow reefs, deep coral canyons, caves, and wrecks at dozens of sites scattered along the coast. Antiguans are internationally known for their flashy fast bowling and big-hit batting in cricket, and visitors will find the game everywhere—from formal test matches to street-corner "knockabouts."

Area code 268 unless otherwise noted.

Getting to the Island

Airlines

Air Canada	462.1147, 800/776.3000
Air Jamaica	800/523.5585
American Airlines	462.0950, 800/433.7300
BWIA International Airways	462.3102,
	800/538.2942
Continental	462.5355, 800/634.5555

Interisland Carriers

LIAT (Leeward Islands Air Transport)	462.0700,
	800/468.0482

Airport

V.C. Bird International Airport (462.4672), the main port of entry to the island, this airport is located on the northeast shore, about four miles from St. John's.

Getting Around the Island

Bicycles and Motorbikes Antigua's roads are rough and bumpy, but if you still want to give cycling here a try, you can rent a bicycle or motorbike from one of the following:

Bike Plus	462.2453
Sun Cycles	461.0324

Buses Inexpensive, but undependable, the island's buses run on an extremely irregular schedule. They can be boarded at the **East Bus Station** (Independence Dr and Factory Rd, St. John's, no phone) or the **West Bus Station** (Market St, south of Tanner St, St. John's, no phone). Buses can also be hailed on the road.

Car Rental

Avis	462.2840, 800/331.1212
Budget	462.3009, 800/472.3325
Dollar	462.0362, 800/800.4000
Huntley Car Rental	462.1575
Jonas Rent-a-Car	462.3760
National Car Rental	462.2113, 800/328.4567
Rent-a-Car Association	462.4600

Driving You can obtain a temporary Antiguan license with a valid driver's license for US$20 from any police station and most car-rental offices. Driving is on the left side of the road. Antigua's famously rugged roads have undergone significant improvements in recent years. Because parking is almost impossible in St. John's, instead of renting a car to visit the capital, stick to taxis.

Taxis

Reliable Taxi	462.1510
Taxi Stand	462.0711
Twenty Four Hour Taxi	462.5190/1

Taxis are unmetered, but the fares for specific routes (including the trip from the airport to most hotels) are regulated by the government. Confirm the fare before taking off, and make sure it's quoted in US$, not EC$. Hotels and the **Antigua Tourist Board** (see below) can provide a list of taxi fares to and from major points on the island; fares are also posted at the airport.

Tours

Alexander Parish Travel Agency	462.0187
Antours	462.4788

FYI

Electricity The current is 110 volts in some places and 220 volts in others. If you depend on plug-in gadgets, ask when making hotel reservations or bring along a converter.

Entry Requirements US and Canadian citizens must present a valid passport or other proof of citizenship (such as a birth certificate or voter's registration card) plus a photo ID, along with a return or onward ticket.

Gambling There is a charming, European-style casino at **St. James's Club** at **Mamora Bay** (see page 29) with both table and machine play. It opens daily at 8PM; closing times vary. The **King's Casino** at **Heritage Quay** in St. John's (462.1727) also offers baccarat, blackjack, craps, poker, roulette, and slot machines. It's open Monday through Saturday from 10AM to 4AM, Sunday from 6PM to 4AM. The minimum age for gambling is 18.

Language English is the official language.

Money The Eastern Caribbean dollar (EC$) is the Antiguan currency, but US dollars are widely accepted, as are major credit cards. Banking hours are typically Monday through Thursday from 8AM to 1PM, and Friday from 8AM to noon and 3 to 5PM.

Personal Safety Drugs are very common on the island, so avoid dark, isolated areas.

Publications The *Daily Observer, Outlet, Antigua Sun,* and *Sentinel* are newspapers published in St. John's. *What's Happening* comes out four times a year. The *Trinidad Guardian, Jamaican Gleaner, E.C. News,* and *Caribbean Week* are also available, along with *The New York Times, USA Today,* and other US and London newspapers.

Reservation Services and House Rentals

Caribrep	462.0818

Taxes An 8.5-percent tax is added to all hotel bills and some restaurant checks. Plan on a US$14 departure tax.

Tipping Most restaurants add a 10-percent service charge to the tab. Other tipping is discretionary.

Visitors' Information Offices The **Antigua Tourist Board** has an office on Long Street in St. John's (462.0480; fax 462.2483); it's open Monday through Thursday from 8AM to 4:30 PM, Friday from 8AM to 3PM. Additional information centers are at **V.C. Bird International Airport** (462.3082 ext. 121), open when flights are scheduled to arrive, and at **Heritage Quay** (no phone) in St. John's, open when cruise ships are scheduled to call.

Phone Book

Ambulance	Call hospital or 911
Directory Assistance	411
Diving Emergencies/ Decompression Chambers	911
Emergencies	999, 911
Fire	462.0044
Hospital	462.0251
Police	462.0125
Post Office	462.0023

JUMBY BAY
ISLAND

1 Jumby Bay Resort $$$$ This ultraposh getaway is set on a 300-acre private island less than 2 miles off the northeast coast of Antigua (access is by ferry). Guests may choose from 24 cottages, 14 rooms in a Mediterranean-style villa, 12 2- and 3-bedroom luxury villas, or 3 private homes. All meals (served in two restaurants) and drinks, as well as water sports (except for scuba diving) and the use of the three tennis courts are included in the rates. Free laundry service is available. At press time, **Jumby Bay** was closed with a November 1998 reopening date. ♦ Long Island (off the northeast coast). 462.6000, 800/421.9016; fax 462.6020

2 Antigua Beachcomber Hotel $ This budget hotel on Winthorpes Beach offers 36 rooms, a pool, and a restaurant. ♦ Airport Rd (just east of Coolidge). 462.3100, 800/223.6510; fax 462.4017

3 Lord Nelson Beach Hotel $ A windsurfing center and other water sports attract an informal clientele to this quiet 17-room hotel. The family-operated beachfront property is one mile north of the airport. After a long day on the water, guests can relax in the hotel's restaurant. Continental breakfast is included in the rate. ♦ Closed September through October. Dutchman Bay (just east of Coolidge). 462.3094; fax 462.0751

4 Le Bistro ★★★$$$$ One of Antigua's most acclaimed restaurants, this French country–style dining spot features French-Caribbean fare. Chef Patrick Gauducheau's menu changes twice a year, but there is always a superb selection of soups, pastas, seafood, and meat dishes, as well as an extensive dessert tray. Try the crispy roasted duck with honey and orange sauce or the medaillons of lobster—both superb. The wine list features selections from Australia, France, Germany, and Italy. ♦ French/Caribbean ♦ Tu-Su dinner. Hodges Bay. 462.3881

5 Cedar Valley Golf Club This 6,077-yard, par-69, 18-hole course is on Dickenson Bay, a few minutes from hotels. It hosts the Antigua Open every November. ♦ Greens fees. Daily. East of Friars Hill Rd. 462.0161

6 Dickenson Bay This l-o-n-g stretch of glistening white sand is perhaps the greatest beach on an island of great beaches. There are no public changing facilities, but water sports and restaurants abound at the many hotels that share the strand. ♦ Northwest coast

6 Rex Halcyon Cove Beach Resort and Casino $$$ Water sports, tennis, volleyball, and shuffleboard are among the activities here, and golf is available nearby. If all you want is to relax, there's a wonderful beach area, and all 210 rooms and suites feature either balconies or patios. ♦ Dickenson Bay. 462.0256, 800/255.5859; fax 462.0271

Within the Rex Halcyon Cove Beach Resort and Casino:

Warri Pier ★$$ Snacks, salads, complete meals, and drinks are served at this peaceful and breezy waterfront restaurant. ♦ American ♦ Daily lunch and dinner. 462.0256

Arawak Terrace ★★$$$ The menu changes daily, but there's always plenty of local seafood available at this dining spot. There's also a fine breakfast buffet, and on Sunday night the activity moves down to the beach for the weekly barbecue. ♦ Seafood ♦ Daily breakfast, lunch, and dinner. Reservations required. 462.0256

7 Sandals $$$ Like its sister properties throughout the Caribbean, this 191-room all-inclusive resort offers a superb beach, non-stop activity, and endless amenities. Mahogany furniture fills the pastel-painted guest rooms. Beautiful landscaping surrounds five freshwater pools—including the hallmark swim-up bar—and five Jacuzzis. Among the various restaurants are the **O.K. Coral**, a Western-style grill, and **Il Palio**, an Italian eatery. Water sports and spa services are available all day. There's also a fitness center and wedding gazebo. ♦ Dickenson Bay. 462.0267, 800/SANDALS; fax 462.4135

7 Antigua Village $$$ All of the 100 studio and 1- and 2-bedroom apartments at this property are on the beach and have kitchen facilities, but only 55 are for rent. The others are privately owned. Water sports, a pool, and a minimarket are among the amenities; golf and tennis are available nearby. ♦ Dickenson Bay. 462.2930; fax 462.0375

7 Spinnakers ★★$$ Next door to **Antigua Village** is a casual beachside restaurant with a friendly staff and a menu featuring salads, seafood, snacks, and burgers. The joint jumps on Wednesday afternoons when a beachside barbecue takes place; there's live entertainment on Monday, Wednesday, Friday, Saturday, and Sunday evenings. ♦ American ♦ Daily breakfast, lunch, and dinner. Dickenson Bay. 462.4158

8 Siboney Beach Club $$$ This intimate 12-suite hotel was named for the island's early Indian residents (also called Ciboney). Relics from their times can be found in the **Antigua and Barbuda Museum** in St. John's. The guest rooms are air-conditioned and outfitted with ceiling fans and mahogany and rattan furniture. There's a pool and a popular seaside restaurant (see below) on the premises, and golf and tennis are nearby. ♦ Dickenson Bay. 462.0806, 800/533.0234; fax 462.3356

Restaurants/Clubs: Red   **Hotels:** Blue

Shops/♥ Outdoors: Green   **Sights/Culture:** Black

Within Siboney Beach Club:

Coconut Grove ★★★$$$ Owner Paddy Costeloe provides personalized service at this open-air beachfront dining spot. The menu features seafood (try the lobster), steaks, Mexican fare, and a few vegetarian dishes. There's also live entertainment some evenings. ◆ Continental/Caribbean/Mexican ◆ Daily breakfast, lunch, and dinner. 462.1538

9 The Island Inn $ Owner/manager Doreen Barnard has created a delightful 2-story hotel with 10 modern 1-bedroom studios and a swimming pool. She calls it a "friendly family resort," and it is just that. The restaurant caters mostly to guests. ◆ Anchorage Rd. 462.4065; fax 462.4066

10 Barrymore Beach Club $$ This complex has 32 beach- and garden-view hotel rooms and 1- or 2-bedroom apartments. There's no restaurant or pool on the premises, but water sports are available nearby. ◆ Runaway Bay. 462.4101; fax 462.4101

11 Home ★★$$$$ Located in the boyhood home of owner and chef Carl Thomas, this cozy restaurant offers traditional Antiguan food, including molasses pepper steak, duck with pineapple rum sauce, and lamb chops. On Saturday, an outdoor bar offers snacks and drinks. ◆ West Indian ◆ M-Sa dinner. Gambles Terrace (between Friars Hill and Fort Rds). 461.7651

12 Heritage Quay Everything from T-shirts to designer luggage and pricey diamond watches can be found somewhere among the dozens of shops at this brightly decorated open-air mall. ◆ M-Sa. Thames St (between Redcliffe and Church Sts), St. John's. No phone

At Heritage Quay:

Heritage Hotel $ This 20-room hotel caters to the business traveler, yet it's close to casinos, restaurants, shops, the beach, and tennis courts. ◆ 462.1247; fax 462.1179

13 Redcliffe Quay Architect **William Fraser** retained the traditional Redcliffe-style facades when he transformed the original dockside warehouses and shops here into a fine modern-day shopping center. Those early shops tempted British sailors with a variety of wares. Today's boutiques are attractive and equally eclectic, filled with goods from around the islands and the world. Fun places include **Jacaranda** (Antiguan handicrafts and clothing; 462.1888), **A Thousand Flowers** (batik sundresses and sportswear; 462.4262), **The Toy Shop** (toys; 462.1041), and **Pizzas on the Quay** (462.2621). At **Noreen Phillips Couturiere** (462.3127), Noreen herself will take your measurements and design something exclusively for you. ◆ Daily. Thames and Redcliffe Sts, St. John's. No phone

14 Antigua and Barbuda Museum Housed in a former courthouse built in 1750, this museum is funded by the Canadian International Development Agency, UNESCO, and private donors. It exhibits the best finds unearthed at archaeological digs on the islands; some artifacts date back to about 2000 BC. There's a collection of ancient utensils, relics from the islands' seafaring past, and a large Arawak Indian house. You'll find some of the best souvenirs on the island in the museum's gift shop. ◆ Donation requested. M-Sa. Long and Market Sts, St. John's. 462.1469, 462.4930

Julian's

15 Julian's ★★$$$ This intimate restaurant features indoor and patio seating. The menu includes both local and international dishes, including fresh seafood, tenderloin of beef stuffed with stilton and bacon, and a good

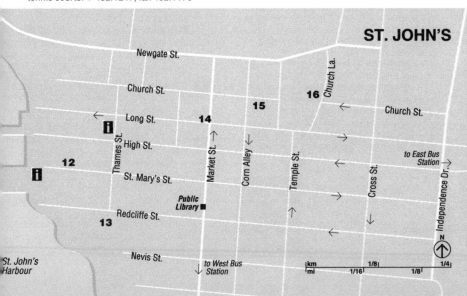

selection of vegetarian dishes. A jazz band plays on Saturday nights. ♦ Continental/Caribbean ♦ Tu-Su dinner. Church St and Corn Alley. 462.4766, 461.3868

16 St. John's Cathedral
First built in 1683, this Anglican cathedral was rebuilt in 1745 and again in 1845 following earthquakes. The current structure has a stone exterior and a pitch-pine interior that has proved more resistant to quakes—the most recent one to damage the building occurred in 1974. The gates date from 1789. ♦ Church La (between Long and Newgate Sts), St. John's. 462.4686

17 Yepton Beach Resort $$ These 38 beachfront studios and 1-bedroom apartments occupy a quarter-mile of private white-sand beaches. Each unit has a balcony or patio and a fully equipped kitchen. The **Patio Carib** serves continental and Creole fare. ♦ Yeptons (west of St. John's). 462.2520, 800/361.4621; fax: 462.3240

18 Royal Antiguan $$$ Here historic forts, sunken schooners, and a spectacular white-sand beach are combined with the comfort of a modern resort. The 282 guest rooms have an island motif. Amenities include three restaurants, four bars, an electronic casino, eight tennis courts, a swimming pool, a shopping arcade, and live entertainment nightly. The array of complimentary water sports—snorkeling, windsurfing, kayaking, and Sunfish sailing—is an added attraction. Snorkelers can explore the sunken shipwreck *Andes,* located just offshore. All-inclusive plans are available. ♦ Deep Bay. 462.3733, 800/345.0356, 561/994.5640 in Florida; fax 462.3732

Within the Royal Antiguan:

Barrington's ★★$$$ Named after the fort that overlooks the **Royal Antiguan,** this restaurant offers an international menu with a Caribbean flair. Menu selections include roasted duck in orange-and-raisin sauce, grilled chicken in fresh fruit sauce, and shrimp kebabs in red-pepper jelly. ♦ Continental ♦ Daily dinner. Reservations recommended. 463.3733

19 Galley Bay $$$$
Antigua's most exclusive hideaway sits on a secluded, three-quarter–mile white-sand beach. The architecture is an eclectic mix of West Indian

and Polynesian styles; among the 61 guest rooms are romantic thatch-roofed bungalows that face a bird sanctuary and luxurious beachfront rooms that are only three seconds from bed to sea. Among the abundant amenities are a landscaped swimming pool, a tennis court, bicycles, indoor and outdoor games, a library, water sports, and two beachfront bars. The oceanfront **Sea Grape** restaurant serves Euro-Caribbean cuisine. The all-inclusive rate includes all meals and drinks, water sports and instruction, taxes, service charges, and gratuities. Other pluses: an unpretenious but elegant atmosphere and perhaps the most helpful and pleasant service on the island. ♦ Five Islands. 462.0302, 800/345.0356, 561/994.5640 in Florida; fax 561/994.6344

20 Hawksbill Beach Resort $$$$ Set on the site of an old sugar plantation, this 39-acre resort bumps up against 4 beaches, including Antigua's only clothing-optional strand. The 99 rooms are modern, with great views and lots of natural breezes (the lack of air-conditioning is no problem). Some rooms have one stone wall, like those in old plantation houses. Families favor the three-bedroom great house—complete with a spacious living room, kitchen, and four bathrooms—since it can accommodate up to eight people. There are also two restaurants, two bars, a tennis court, and a boutique in the old sugar mill. Water sports include windsurfing and snorkeling—there's a coral reef nearby. ♦ Five Islands. 462.0301, 800/223/6510; fax 462.1515

21 Jolly Harbour Villas $$ Surrounding the marina here are 150 2-bedroom, 2-bath waterfront villas. Perks include six restaurants, a squash court, four lighted tennis courts, golf, and water sports. Ask about special packages that include the use of facilities at the adjacent **Club Antigua,** an all-inclusive resort with four restaurants, six bars, and a nightclub with nightly entertainment. Long-term rentals are also available. ♦ Jolly Beach. 462.6166, 800/777.1250; fax 462.6167

Within Jolly Harbour Villas:

Jolly Harbour Golf Club This 18-hole, par 71 golf course, designed by Karl Litton, offers lessons, motorized and pull carts, and rental clubs. ♦ Greens fees. Daily. 480.6950

22 Curtain Bluff Resort $$$$ An elegant resort on the island's southwest coast, this 63-room property boasts 2 beaches, one with plenty of waves, another with calm waters. Guests can enjoy sailing, waterskiing, snorkeling, and scuba diving or check out the swimming pool, fitness center, putting green, squash court, and four lighted tennis courts. Although the rooms are not air-conditioned, the ceiling fans and breezes keep you comfortable. There's a formal dining room and a casual lunch spot, the **Beach Club.** Rates include three meals a day, as well as afternoon tea, all drinks, nightly entertainment, and water sports. Tennis is a big draw; the annual Antigua Tennis Week is held here in the spring. Note: Men must wear jackets in the evening for most of the season (mid-December to mid-April). ♦ Closed May through mid-October. Old Road. 462.8400, 462.8401, 462.8402, 212/289.8888 in NY, 800/67BLUFF; fax 462.8409

23 Fig Tree Drive A bit rough but worth the bumps, Antigua's prettiest country drive winds through the southwestern region of the island. The green hillsides are dotted with old sugar mills and lovely churches. ♦ Between Old Road and Liberta

24 Harbour View Apartments $$ These six split-level, two-bedroom apartments offer great views of the water. Each unit has its own kitchen, but there is no restaurant. The complex is set near Antigua's only national park, **Nelson's Dockyard** (see below). Watersports equipment can be rented. ♦ Falmouth. 460.1762; fax 460.1762

25 Falmouth Harbour Beach Apartments $$ These fully equipped studio apartments—22 in all—dot a beautiful white-sand beach and the hillside west of English Harbour. Although there's no restaurant, each unit has a full kitchen and maid service. The complex is owned and operated by the **Admiral's Inn** (see page 28) in **Nelson's Dockyard.** ♦ Falmouth Harbour. 460.1813; fax 460.1534

26 Nelson's Dockyard Lord Horatio Nelson first arrived at English Harbour in 1784, when he was 26 and in command of the *Boreas,* a 28-gun frigate of the Royal Navy. He used this dockyard during numerous Caribbean wars with the French, Spanish, and Dutch in the late 18th century. Today it is a national park, with shops, inns, and restaurants built to harmonize with the original architecture. Look for **Fort Charlotte** and **Fort Berkeley,** standing guard over the harbor entrance. A 15-minute walk from the dockyard up to **Fort Berkeley** is an ideal way to see the area. ♦ Admission. Daily. English Harbour. 460.1053, 460.1379, 460.1380

Within Nelson's Dockyard

Admiral's House Artifacts of more than 200 years of dockyard history are displayed at this museum. (The house was not in fact Lord Nelson's; it was built in 1855, 50 years after Nelson's death.) ♦ Free. Daily. 460.1053, 460.1379, 460.1380

Beautiful Barbuda

One of the last frontiers of the Caribbean lies 27 miles north of Antigua, a beautifully undeveloped island where there are no paved roads, few hotels, only a handful of restaurants, and just 1,200 full-time residents. Renowned for its pink-tinged beaches, the most famous of which stretches more than 17 miles long the Atlantic coast, **Barbuda** is a tranquil escape.

Nature-lovers flock to the **Frigate Bird Sanctuary** (no phone) at **Codrington Lagoon,** accessible only by boat, where *Fregata magnificens* nest in miles of mangrove bush. Also known to old-time sailors as the man-o'-war bird" or "hurricane bird," frigate birds have an eight-foot wingspan that powers flight to 9,000 feet. Visitors can observe the birds year-round, but mating season runs from September through February, and chicks hatch from December through March. The baby giants remain in the nest for up to eight months before they're strong enough to fly.

Bird-watchers on Barbuda will also spot pelicans, snipes, ibis, herons, kingfishers, tropical mockingbirds, oyster catchers, and cormorants. Other wildlife ranges from deer to donkeys, wild boar to red-footed tortoises.

Darby Sink Caves on the Atlantic Coast is a cavern where deep pools of clear water extend a mile underground, and Arawak drawings deck the walls of the caves at **Two Feet Bay.** Historic attractions include the remains of the **Highland House,** the former estate of Sir William Codrington, and the ruins of the seaside fortress known as **Martello Tower.** Divers can explore approximately 89 shipwrecks off these shores.

Several Antigua-based companies offer day trips and package tours to Barbuda by air and sea; ask at any hotel. For those wanting to stay a while, get in touch with **K Club Barbuda** (460.0300, 800/223.6800; fax 460.0305) for luxurious accommodations. Several private homes and guest houses offer basic bed and board at modest prices; contact **Claudia Richards** (462.5647) for more information.

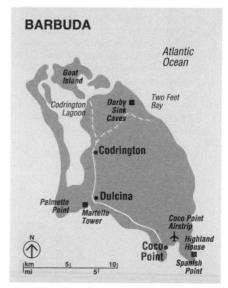

BARBUDA

Atlantic Ocean

Goat Island

Codrington Lagoon

Darby Sink Caves

Two Feet Bay

Codrington

Dulcina

Palmetto Point

Martello Tower

Coco Point Airstrip

Highland House

Coco Point

Spanish Point

N

km 5 10
mi 5

Copper and Lumber Store Hotel $$$
This former warehouse is now a delightful
hideaway with Georgian elegance. Each of the
14 suites is named after one of Lord Nelson's
ships engaged in the Battle of Trafalgar.
There's fine dining in the **Wardroom** daily,
and meals are also served in the courtyard.
♦ 460.1059, 800/275.0877; fax 460.1529

Art Centre Lou Cottage, an American who
has spent more than 12 years on the island,
operates a lovely gallery featuring works by
many local artists. ♦ Daily. 460.1380

Admiral's Inn $$ This charming waterfront
inn has 13 twin-bedded rooms, and a 2-
bedroom loft with kitchen facilities. The 17
pillars outside were brought from England as
ballast, and the royal palms were planted in the
1960s by Queen Elizabeth II. ♦ Closed in
September. 460.1027, 800/223.5695; fax
460.1534

Within the Admiral's Inn:

Admiral's Inn Restaurant ★★$$ Dine
on such local favorites as curried chicken and
grilled seafood in a beautiful outdoor setting
at the water's edge. ♦ Caribbean ♦ Daily
breakfast, lunch, and dinner; closed
September. Reservations recommended for
dinner in season. 460.1027

27 Clarence House Built in 1786 for Prince
William (later King William IV), this 4-
bedroom house is filled with British-style
furniture. Maintained by the Antiguan
government, it was used by Winston Churchill
for a nap during one of his visits and by
Princess Margaret and Lord Snowdon on their
Caribbean honeymoon in 1962. During state
visits in 1966, 1975, and 1985, Queen
Elizabeth II stopped here to freshen up. The
view out back of English Harbour will take
your breath away. At press time, the home
was closed for renovations, and no date had
been set for reopening. ♦ Donation. Hours
vary. English Harbour. No phone

28 The Inn at English Harbour $$$$ This
property features 22 rooms on the beach and
6 up on the hillside, with a shuttle running
guests back and forth. All guest rooms have
ceiling fans and either a balcony or veranda.
Windsurfing and snorkeling are among the
water sports available here. The terrace
restaurant serves international cuisine and
offers a stupendous view of English Harbour.
Meal plans are available. ♦ Closed September
through mid-October. English Harbour.
460.1014, 800/223.6510; fax 460.1603

29 Galleon Beach Club $$$ One of the
prettiest settings on Antigua, this hotel is
situated on the south coast, below Shirley
Heights. The 35 cottages have full kitchens
and private sundecks overlooking Freeman's
Bay, the entry to English Harbour. There are
shops on site, and water sports, fishing,
boating, and tennis are available. ♦ Freemans
Bay (south of The Inn at English Harbour),
English Harbour. 460.1024; fax 460.1450

Within the Galleon Beach Club:

Colombo's Italian Restaurant ★★$$$
The first Italian restaurant on Antigua, this
place is popular with tourists and locals alike
Chef Peter Smit prepares the pasta, seafood,
and veal specialties. ♦ Italian ♦ Daily lunch
and dinner. Reservations recommended on
weekends. 460.1452

30 Shirley Heights Lookout Drive to the top
for an eagle's-eye view of English Harbour,
Falmouth Harbour, and **Nelson's Dockyard.**
There's a rustic restaurant that serves lobster
and such familiar standbys as burgers and
fries at lunch and dinner. A gift shop is open
daily. Sunday barbecues at the lookout are
lively affairs, with steel-band music in the
afternoon and a reggae band in the evening.
♦ Shirley Heights. 460.1785

31 Dow's Hill Interpretation Center For an
overview of island history, take in *Reflections
of the Sun,* a multimedia trip through six
eras, including those dominated by early
Amerindians, colonial planters, and the British
military. The complex also houses a shop, bar
and restaurant. ♦ Admission. Daily. English
Harbour. 460.2777

32 St. James's Club $$$$ Recently
refurbished, this glamorous, upscale resort
set on a hundred acres has 178 2-bedroom
villas, suites, and guest rooms, all facing the
brilliant blue ocean. The rooms are spacious
and comfortable, and the villas are perfect for
families. Activities include tennis on seven
courts, croquet, non-motorized water sports,
fishing, and boat charters. There are also 3
restaurants, a beach bar and grill, a full-
service casino, a yacht club, a dive shop,
horseback riding, and an 18-slip marina. All-
inclusive plans are available. ♦ Mamora Bay
460.5000, 800/345.0356, 561/994.5640 in
Florida; fax 460.3015

33 Half Moon Bay There's something for
everyone at this Atlantic beach: One end
shelters a clear and calm swimming pool, and
the other is rough enough for the most
adventurous bodysurfers. The crescent of
powder-pink sand stretches for nearly a mile.
♦ Southeast coast

34 Harmony Hall ★★★$$ Set in an old
sugar mill, this hotel restaurant is quite
possibly the island's most perfect spot for
lunch. Dinner here is also an exceptional

event. Service is first-rate, and owners Marilisa and Ricardo Parisi have created a fabulous menu with a selection of Italian and Caribbean dishes. The hotel also houses six delightful guest rooms overlooking Nonsuch Bay, and a gallery featuring Caribbean arts and crafts, with a special emphasis on local works. Monthly shows offer visitors the opportunity to meet well-known regional artists. There's a pool on the premises, and boat trips are available. ♦ Italian/Caribbean ♦ M-Sa lunch and dinner; Su lunch. Nonsuch Bay. 460.4120, 463.8657; fax 460.4406

35 Long Bay Sheltered by offshore reefs, this pretty beach is great for snorkeling and swimming in the Atlantic. Coconut palms provide plenty of shade, while three nearby hotels offer water-sports equipment and restaurants. ♦ East end

35 Pineapple Beach Club $$$ This laid-back all-inclusive resort on the island's east end is a favorite among repeat guests. Recently refurbished, the property boasts four tennis courts, an air-conditioned fitness center, non-motorized water sports, an oceanfront pool, two restaurants, three bars, nature trails, reef fishing, and shopping trips to St. John's. Rattan furniture, tropical pictures, and pastel colors decorate the 135 guest rooms. The **Outhouse** (yes, that's the name) is a popular gathering spot for snacks and drinks at sunset. ♦ Long Bay. 463.2006, 800/345.0356, 561/994.5640 in Florida; fax 463.2452, 561/994.6344 in Florida

36 Long Bay Hotel $$ A lovely beach is the prime attraction for guests staying at the 20 rooms (with verandas), 5 self-catering cottages, and fully equipped 2-bedroom bayfront villa. This family-owned and -operated hotel has a restaurant and water sports, including scuba diving. Regular live entertainment is another plus. ♦ Closed June–mid-October. Long Bay. 463.2005, 800/448.8355; fax 463.2439

37 Devil's Bridge Seawater shoots through the "blow holes" at this dramatic rock formation, which was pounded into shape by the Atlantic surf. A small (usually deserted) beach nearby is great for picnics. ♦ East of Long Bay

38 Betty's Hope Sugar Plantation These ruins are all that's left of one of the largest sugar plantations in the Caribbean, which was owned in the 17th century by Christopher Codrington. Following the self-guided tour, visitors can still see two restored working windmills and arches of the boiling house. There's also an interpretive center. ♦ Free. Daily. Between Glanvilles and Pares Village. 462.4930

Getting Your Feet Wet in Antigua

The seas around Antigua—most of which are calm—offer plenty to do, and most hotels and resorts offer water sports and beachfront boat and equipment rentals. Some other organizations that can get you afloat are:

Boating
Catamaran Club (yachts only) Catamaran Hotel, Falmouth Harbour. 460.1036

Jolly Roger Pirate Cruises St. John's. 462.2064

Nicholson Yacht Charters (yachts only) Nelson's Dockyard. 463.1530, 800/662.6066

Sun Yacht Charters 460.2615, 800/772.3500

Wadadli Watersports Dickenson Bay. 462.4792

Snorkeling and Scuba Diving
Aquanaut Divers St. James's Club, Mamora Bay. 460.5000, 800/345.0356

Dive Antigua Rex Halcyon Cove Beach Resort, Dickenson Bay. 462.3483

Dive Runaway Runaway Bay. 462.2626

Dockyard Divers Nelson's Dockyard. 460.1178

Jolly Dive Club Antigua, Jolly Beach. 462.0061

Long Bay Hotel Long Bay. 463.2005, 800/448.8355

Pirate Divers Lord Nelson Beach Hotel, Dutchman Bay. 462.3094

Sportfishing
Catamaran Club Catamaran Hotel, Falmouth Harbour. 460.1036

Frankie Hart *Overdraft*, Falmouth Harbour. 462.0649

Long Bay Hotel Long Bay. 463.2005, 800/448.8355

Windsurfing
Paradise Watersports Spinnakers (restaurant), Dickenson Bay. 462.4158

Patrick's Windsurfing School Lord Nelson Beach Hotel, Dutchman Bay. 462.WIND

Wadadli Watersports Dickenson Bay. 462.4792

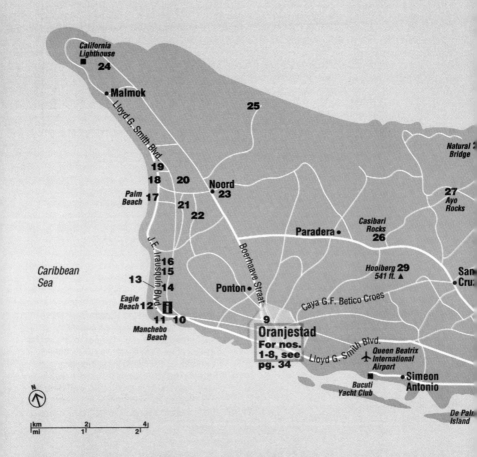

Aruba

When the Spanish came upon Aruba in 1499, they declared it an insignificant find, not particularly beautiful (vegetation is sparse), an *isla inutil* (useless island). Little did the navigators realize what a delightful spot they'd passed up.

Modern tourists have changed the scene on this windswept island, which has become a major destination for water sports and cruise ships. More than 7 miles of palm-shaded white beaches line clear turquoise seas, where visibility extends up to 100 feet. Scuba divers can explore the Caribbean's largest sunken wreck just off the northwest coast or join a reef excursion, and anyone can get a close-up look at the undersea world with **Atlantis Submarines**.

Although Aruba lies outside the hurricane belt, the island enjoys strong breezes year-round, a feature that attracts hordes of windsurfers. There's even sailing across land at **Eagle Beach**, where three-wheeled carts rigged with sails speed riders across the dunes. The trade winds sculpt divi-divi trees into twisted natural art, splayed low against a wild backdrop of cacti, aloe, and ancient rock formations. In fact, the arid landscape bears a striking resemblance to the US Southwest—except for the lighthouses and windmills.

Today tourism is the number one industry in Aruba, but earlier years saw gold mining (beginning in 1824) and oil refining (100 years later) as the leading moneymakers. In fact, **Lloyd G. Smith Boulevard** was named for one of the oil company's first managers. Now it's better known as "Resort Row."

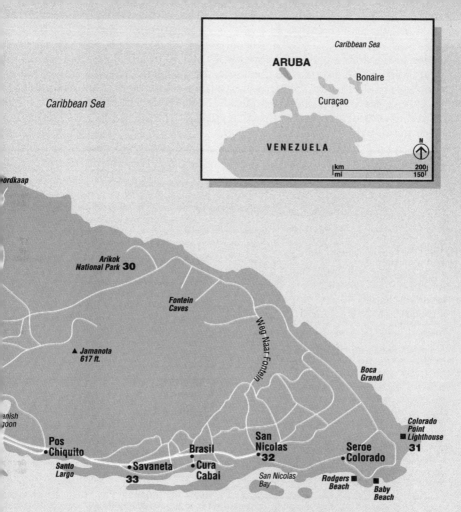

The first deluxe resort to develop on the island's west coast debuted in 1959,
and others quickly followed. Dozens now line the boulevard along the lovely
stretch of sandy coast between Eagle Beach and **Palm Beach** just west of
Oranjestad (pronounced O-*ran*-yeh-stat). But development came so fast and
furious that at press time there was a standing moratorium on new hotel
construction.

Just 15 miles off the coast of Venezuela, Aruba is about 20 miles long and
barely 6 miles wide. The whole island could be explored in a day, although
one could spend at least that long in Oranjestad, the picturesque Dutch-
influenced capital. The main shopping street is **Caya G.F. Betico Croes**, but
fashionable boutiques and restaurants are also housed in vibrant colonial-
style complexes at **Port of Call** and **Seaport Village**. Oranjestad's lovely Old
World architecture is another attraction, best seen when exploring on foot.
The grandest historic buildings line the street called **Wilhelminastraat**.

The earliest known settlers on the island were Arawak Indians, and ancient
tribal drawings can still be seen on cave walls in **Arikok National Park** on the
northeastern coast. Aruba's European ties date to the early 17th century,
when the Dutch took over the island. Since 1986 Aruba has been an
autonomous member of the Kingdom of the Netherlands, which also includes
Holland and the five other islands of the Netherland Antilles (Bonaire,
Curaçao, Saba, St. Eustatius, and St. Maarten).

Indian and Dutch are only 2 of the more than 40 nationalities that season the local melting pot. One way to meet some of the island's 85,000 residents and sample its multicultural spirit is to go to the weekly celebration of Aruba's folklore, crafts, dance, music, and food. It's held every Tuesday in the courtyard of the historical museum at **Fort Zoutman**, and named for the Papiamento word of welcome: *bon bini*.

To call from the US, dial 011 (international access code), 297 (country code), and the 6-digit local number. On Aruba, dial only the 6-digit local number unless otherwise noted.

Getting to the Island

Airlines

Air Aruba 836600

American Airlines 822700, 800/433.7300

Interisland Carriers

ALM (Antillean Airlines)........838080, 800/327.7230

Avensa 827779

Airport **Queen Beatrix International Airport** (848000), located just east of Oranjestad on Lloyd G. Smith Boulevard, is known for its quickly moving lines for immigration inspection; baggage claim and customs clearance have been experiencing delays, however, because of ongoing airport expansion. Travelers who arrive during the day are often greeted with island music and an official *bon bini* stamped on passports by Aruba's customs officers. Transportation to island hotels and rental cars can be found just outside the door. The **Aruba Tourism Authority** has a desk in the arrivals hall.

Getting Around the Island

Bicycles and Motorbikes

Caribbean Cycle Rental..................................870356

George's Cycle and Jeeps.............................825975

Nelson Motorcycle Rental 866801

Ron's Motorcycle Rental 862090

Semver Cycle Rental 866851

Buses Yellow public buses run every 20 to 30 minutes between Oranjestad and the hotels on Eagle and Palm Beaches, except on Sunday and holidays. The one-way fare is $1 (payable in US or local currency); round-trip "yellow cards" can be purchased from the driver for $1.60.

Car Rental Some car-rental agencies require drivers to be at least 23 years old.

Avis 825496, 800/331.1212

Budget 828600, 800/527.0700

Caribbean Car Rental.....................................822515

Economy...830200

Hertz 824545, 800/654.3131

National................................821967, 800/328.4567

Optima 836263

Topless 875236

Toyota Car Rental 834832

Driving Roads are good and clearly marked. US and Canadian driver's licenses are valid on the island.

Taxis

Central Dispatch Office 822116, 821604

Tours Choices include land tours on air-conditioned buses, four-wheel-drive-vehicle excursions over rocky countryside and along seaside cliffs, and snorkeling and sailing trips. Contact **DePalm Tours** (824400), **Eagle Jeep Tours** (839469), **Explore Aruba Tours** (822228), **Octopus Sailing and Snorkeling** (833081), or **Pelican Watersports** (831228). Most taxis also offer tours.

FYI

Electricity The current is 110 volts/60 cycles, the same as in the US and Canada.

Entry Requirements US and Canadian visitors must present a valid passport or other proof of citizenship (birth certificate, voter's registration card) plus a photo ID.

Gambling Hours vary seasonally at the island's 11 casinos, but gaming usually begins at 11AM and continues through the wee hours. The **Aruba Sonesta Resorts** casino (see page 34) is open 24 hours a day. All offer baccarat, roulette, blackjack, and slots.

Language Dutch is the official language, but everyone speaks English and, usually, Spanish. Islanders communicate with each other in Papiamento, a mixture of French, Spanish, Dutch, Portuguese, English, and African dialects.

Money The Aruban florin (Afl) is the local currency but US dollars are accepted everywhere. Banks are generally open Monday through Friday from 8AM to noon and from 1:30 to 4PM; some remain open during lunch.

Personal Safety Crime is minimal on Aruba, but caution is advised when entering dark areas or remote neighborhoods. Know where you're going. Don't wear tempting jewelry or leave belongings unattended. In other words, use the same common sense you practice at home.

Publications *Aruba Events* and *Aruba Nights* are ad-driven tourism magazines (published monthly or quarterly) distributed free at the tourist bureau, airport, and most hotels. *Experience Aruba* is another free mini-magazine, published annually.

Aruba Today and The News, both published Monday through Saturday, are free English-language newspapers available at hotels. The New York Times and the Miami Herald hit the newsstands daily.

Reservation Services and House Rentals The **Aruba Tourism Authority** (see below) can help with hotel reservations.

Taxes There is a five-percent hotel room tax. Visitors must pay a $20 departure tax at the airport.

Tipping An 11-percent (or higher) service charge is added to hotel bills. A 10- to 15-percent service charge is usually tacked on to restaurant checks. Additional tips may be offered at your discretion.

Visitors' Information Office The **Aruba Tourism Authority**'s main office is located across the street from the hotel strip on Manchebo Beach (172 Lloyd G. Smith Blvd, 823777; fax 834702). It is open Monday through Friday from 8AM to 5PM. The office at the **Queen Beatrix International Airport** (829041) is open daily when flights arrive.

Phone Book

Ambulance	
Oranjestad	821234
San Nicolas	845050
Directory Assistance	118
Diving Emergencies/ Decompression Chambers	825520
Emergencies	115
Fire	115
Hospital	874300
Police	100
Post Office	821900

"TALK OF THE TOWN"

1 **Talk of the Town** $$ This property was built as a hotel in 1942, but 20 years later was being used as an office building. Restored to its original use in 1964 by Ike and Grete Cohen of Jacksonville, Florida, who were among the first to recognize Aruba's potential as a vacation spot, the hotel is now part of the Best Western chain. The 63 nicely done rooms are favorites of business travelers on a budget and tourists who don't need all the extras offered by the big resorts. The atmosphere is basic, but homey. A courtyard, with a bar and small, simple restaurant, surrounds the freshwater pool and whirlpool, and a beach is across the street. ♦ 2 Lloyd G. Smith Blvd (at Vondellaan), Oranjestad. 823380, 800/223.1108; fax 833208

2 **Caya G.F. Betico Croes** It wasn't so long ago that Caribbean travelers dashed to this street for the best bargains in the region—and every day looked like Christmas here. Once called Nassaustraat, this street was renamed Caya G.F. Betico Croes after the late leader of Aruba's independence movement. Although shopping malls have lured away some trendier boutiques, there are still plenty of good buys. For duty-free electronics and cameras, stop at **Boolchand's** (No. 10, 830147). **Little Switzerland** (No. 14, 821192) carries duty-free jewelry, crystal, and watches. The **Aruba Trading Company** (No. 12, 823950), a landmark since 1930, is one of the best spots to buy perfume. ♦ Between Adriaan Laclé Blvd and Emmastraat, Oranjestad

Also on Caya G.F. Betico Croes:

Art and Tradition This shop offers visitors the option of taking home something unusual. Featured here are intricately decorated mopa mopa masks and decorative figures. Mopa mopa items are created through a complicated process in which plant resin is boiled, stretched, and adhered to wood. ♦ M-Sa. No. 30. 836534

3 **Boonoonoonoos** ★★$$ The name means "good times" and the "ooh" sound gets quite a workout here, with a menu rich in island specialties such as Jamaican jerk ribs (made from a 300-year-old recipe), sea terrine, and roast chicken Barbados (topped with plantains and coconut). Traditional continental items are offered as well. ♦ Caribbean/Continental ♦ M-Sa lunch and dinner; Su dinner. Reservations recommended for dinner. 18A Wilhelminastraat (east of Oranjestraat), Oranjestad. 831888

4 **Numismatic Museum** Even visitors indifferent to coin collecting will find themselves astonished at the variety of this private museum's coins and currency, which include a souvenir Chinese bill with Richard Nixon's image on it, coins from Nazi camps, and even coins used in leper colonies. Mario Odor, who has been amassing the collection for more than a half-century, claims his favorite coin is a copper "bonk bar"—a rectangular bar of metal cast in Ceylon 150 years ago, stamped with the emblem of the United East India Co., and once used in trade. ♦ Admission. M-F; Sa-Su by appointment. 7 Zuidstraat (north of Lagoenweg), Oranjestad. 828831

ORANJESTAD

5 Fort Zoutman Aruba's oldest building was completed in 1796 to protect the new capital from invasion. Since then it has functioned as police headquarters, a prison, and a government building. The tower that marks the entrance was constructed in 1868 and bears the initials "WIII," for William III, the king of the Netherlands at the time. It has served as a lighthouse as well as a public clock. The fort's **Historical Museum** displays antique furniture, farm equipment from colonial days, and musical instruments brought over by European settlers. One display is dedicated to the processing of aloe, once an important source of revenue for the island. On Tuesday evenings from 6:30 to 8:30PM, a *bon bini* celebration features Aruban music, dance, food, crafts, and folklore. ◆ Admission. M-F. Zoutmanstraat and Oranjestraat, Oranjestad. 826099

6 Port of Call Market Place This bustling waterfront center features duty-free shops selling fragrance, liquor, and jewelry; one-hour photo development places; souvenir stores; and more. Among the familiar fast-food eateries you'll find here are **Subway, Dunkin' Donuts,** and **Domino's Pizza.** ◆ M-Sa. 17 Lloyd G. Smith Blvd (at Werfstraat), Oranjestad. 836706

7 Aruba Sonesta Resorts $$$$ This 2-part property offers 250 fully equipped 1-bedroom waterfront suites—each furnished in elegant tropical style with a kitchenette and balcony—as well as a 300-room hotel across the street. The 2 facilities share 3 restaurants, a 24-hour casino, 2 spas, 2 fitness centers, 3 pools, the beach, and access (via regular boat shuttles) to the resorts' 40-acre private island on the bay (with 6 beaches, tennis courts, a health club, a restaurant and bar, and a full water-sports program). There are two marinas for guests, as well as a private yacht (fishing and sailing charters available). The numerous and well-supervised children's activities are a draw for family vacationers. The two **Seaport Village** arcades adjoining and facing the hotel feature convenient shopping, dining, and entertainment, including a cineplex. ◆ 82 Lloyd G. Smith Blvd (between Arnold Schuttestraat and Weststraat), Oranjestad. 836000, 800/766.3782; fax 834389

7 Seaport Village Aruba's largest shopping complex is actually two shopping centers: **Seaport Marketplace,** with an eclectic collection of 85 high-fashion stores, fragrance shops, a bevy of restaurants, the elegant **Crystal Casino,** and even a **McDonald's,** and, across the street, the smaller **Seaport Mall,** with about 50 stores and a 6-theater cinema. ◆ Restaurants, casino, cinema: daily. Shops: M-Sa. 82 Lloyd G. Smith Blvd (between Arnold Schuttestraat and Weststraat), Oranjestad. No phone

Within Seaport Village:

Little Holland Dutch treats here emphasize delft blue tiles and linens. ♦ 836752

Colombian Emeralds International Despite the name, emeralds are not the only precious gems sold at this duty-free jewelry store. ♦ 836238

Eva's Boutique Shop here for a wide variety of women's swimwear in outstanding international designs. ♦ 838038

 LES ACCESSOIRES

Les Accessoires Neckties, exclusive design swimsuits, and handmade leather purses are just the beginning of the chic inventory at this delightful boutique that also features Italian sweaters, elegant blouses from the Far East, and beaded dresses by Fabrice and Oleg Cassini. ♦ 837965

Scuba Aruba Water-sports fans flock here for equipment, and landlubbers love it for the souvenirs. Colorful top-grade T-shirts, snorkeling gear, swimwear, vibrant beachwear, and sunglasses are among the attractions. ♦ 834142

Zzapp Music For the latest in island music, this is the place. In addition to tapes and CDs of Aruban music groups and singers, the store carries other regional music, including reggae, salsa, merengue, steel band, and even Latin pop. ♦ 838010

L'Escale ★★★$$$ How about French cuisine, a Hungarian string orchestra, and a view of a Caribbean harbor? All three await at one of the island's most romantic restaurants. Start with Singapore shrimp or jerk quail appetizers, then move on to baked Caribbean grouper or rack of lamb. ♦ French ♦ Daily dinner. Reservations recommended. 836000 ext 1791

The Waterfront ★★★★$$$ This wonderful seafood restaurant is run by buddies Roger Coster, Michael Jordan (not the basketball star), and Roy Leitch, who worked together at Divi hotels in the Caribbean for two decades before joining forces to open this popular establishment. The garlic crabs are great, the escargots are wonderful, and the Maine lobster *fra diablo* is really hot stuff. Try the crusted shrimp—it's baked with a light coating of fine herbs, bread crumbs, and parmesan cheese, and served with a marmalade-horseradish sauce. The meal in itself is worth the trip to Aruba. ♦ Seafood ♦ Daily breakfast, lunch, and dinner. Reservations recommended. 835858

8 Atlantis Submarines A narrative in Spanish and English describes the beauty of life in the depths of the sea and on nearby natural reefs. The sub takes visitors on a 2-hour, close-up tour of the spectacular reefs, submerging 140 feet below sea level to view the subterranean mountains. It also stops at the wreck of the retired vessel *MiDushi*, and sometimes at a sunken plane. There are 5 to 8 voyages each day, with up to 46 passengers on each trip. One caveat: The price is a bit steep. ♦ Admission. M-F, Su. Yacht Basin, Lloyd G. Smith Blvd (southeast of Weststraat), Oranjestad. 836090

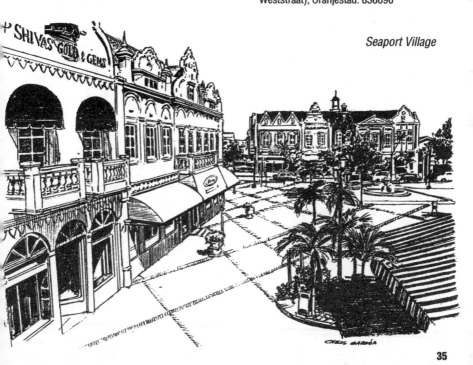

Seaport Village

9 Archaeology Museum Previously located on Zoutmanstraat, this museum is now housed in the **Maria Convent**. Artifacts taken from Tanki Flip, an archaeological site believed to be the remains of an entire Indian village, are the newest attraction here. Also on display are other Amerindian relics, including burial urns, farm equipment, cooking utensils, and the clay stamps the early island residents used for body painting. There are also skeletons from the pre-Columbian period as well.
♦ Free. M-F. 2A J.E. Irausquínplein (off Boerhaavestraat), Oranjestad. 828979

10 Divi Dutch Village $$$ Set in sleek, modern town houses, the 97 studios and 1- and 2-bedroom apartments feature satellite TV, Jacuzzis, and other luxuries. Additional perks include a swimming pool, two tennis courts, shops, a restaurant, and a bar. ♦ 39 J.E. Irausquín Blvd (off Lloyd G. Smith Blvd). 823300, 800/367.3484; fax 820501

10 Tamarijn Aruba Beach Resort $$$ All 236 rooms (including those in a 70-room annex) at this all-inclusive resort have a sea-view balcony or terrace and all are only a few barefoot steps from the 2,000-foot beach. Appealing Andalusian decor (red-tile roofs, white walls) is found inside and out. Other pluses: a pool, two Jacuzzis, a small fitness center, five eateries, and four bars, including one right on the beach featuring nightly music by local groups. All-inclusive rates cover meals and drinks (even alcoholic beverages), a sunset cruise, tennis, windsurfing, sailing, and snorkeling, plus lessons. ♦ 41 J.E. Irausquín Blvd (off Lloyd G. Smith Blvd). 824150, 800/554.2008; fax 834002

Divi Aruba Beach Resort

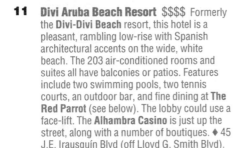

11 Divi Aruba Beach Resort $$$$ Formerly the **Divi-Divi Beach** resort, this hotel is a pleasant, rambling low-rise with Spanish architectural accents on the wide, white beach. The 203 air-conditioned rooms and suites all have balconies or patios. Features include two swimming pools, two tennis courts, an outdoor bar, and fine dining at **The Red Parrot** (see below). The lobby could use a face-lift. The **Alhambra Casino** is just up the street, along with a number of boutiques. ♦ 45 J.E. Irausquín Blvd (off Lloyd G. Smith Blvd). 823300, 800/554.2008; fax 834002

Restaurants/Clubs: Red   Hotels: Blue

Shops/♟ Outdoors: Green   Sights/Culture: Black

Within the Divi Aruba Beach Resort:

The Red Parrot ★★★$$$ Tantalizing island fare mates with international cuisine at this lovely restaurant. Try the coconut shrimp served with mango-banana chutney, or one of the chef's specialties, such as the "Captain's Medley," which features lobster, shrimp, and swordfish. ♦ Creole/Continental ♦ Daily lunch and dinner. 823300

11 Best Western Manchebo Beach $$ We situated on one of the island's best and wide stretches of beach, this informal resort attracts an international clientele. Each of the 71 large rooms has a balcony or patio, and there's an on-site restaurant (see below). Th mood is casual and friendly and guests get t know one another at weekly cocktail gatherings around the pool with live dance music. ♦ 55 J.E. Irausquín Blvd (off Lloyd G. Smith Blvd), Manchebo Beach. 823444, 800/223.1108; fax 833667

Within the Best Western Manchebo Beach:

French Steak House ★★$$ Although quality cuts of North and South American beef are the lure here, French cuisine—including chateaubriand, escargots, and filet mignon— figures on the menu at this candlelit dining establishment. This place is an Aruban landmark, with good food, a soothing and romantic ambience, and some of the friendliest staff on the island. ♦ French ♦ Tu-Su dinner. Reservations recommended. 823444

12 Eagle Beach These beautiful sands are at the southern end of the so-called "Turquoise Coast," which stretches northward to **Palm Beach** (see page 37). Along this picturesque expanse, thatch-roofed shelters are provided for picnicking, while water sports and restaurants are abundant at area hotels. ♦ J.E Irausquín Blvd (north of Manchebo Beach)

12 Costa Linda Beach Resort $$$ This family-oriented, five-story oceanfront resort debuted in the early 1990s with 155 2- and 3 bedroom suites. Features include kitchenett in the suites, four whirlpools, two swimming pools (one for kids), two lighted tennis cour a fitness center, a restaurant, a nightclub, a shopping arcade, and water sports. ♦ 59 J.E Irausquín Blvd. 838000, 800/992.2015; fax 836040

13 Mi Cushina ★★$$ The family-run "My Kitchen" features Aruban fare in a setting filled with antique collectibles representing local history, especially Aruba's role in oil refining. The tools, cooking implements, musical instruments, and old photos on display are as notable as the food. Be sure to try some of the special local dishes such as *pan bati* (pancake-shaped bread made from cornmeal) and *funchi* (cornmeal bread served with fried fish). Turtle and stewed lamb are other popular entrées. ♦ Aruban ♦ M-W, F-Su lunch and dinner. Reservations recommended. 221 J.E. Irausquín Blvd, Eagle Beach. 872222

14 La Quinta $$ This cozy, family-oriented resort offers 54 rooms, a pair of swimming pools, a tennis court, plenty of water sports, a lovely beach just across the road, 2 eateries, 2 bars, a minimarket, and a night club. ♦ 228 J.E. Irausquín Blvd, Eagle Beach. 874133, 800/223.9815; fax 876263

15 Chalet Suisse Restaurant ★★$$ The scenic Alps are a continent away, but the Aruban-accented European fare is pretty dramatic at this chalet-style restaurant. The fondue and veal dishes are excellent, and the US prime meats are flown in daily. End your meal with the restaurant's trademark Toblerone chocolate fondue. ♦ Swiss ♦ M-Sa dinner. Reservations recommended. 246 J.E. Irausquín Blvd, Eagle Beach. 875054

16 La Cabana All-Suite Beach Resort and Casino $$ This ultramodern and ultralarge resort is conveniently located near several restaurants and along a public bus route. The beach and huge pool area emphasize water sports, but five tennis courts, racquetball and squash courts, and a fitness center also help guests keep in shape. Each of the 803 apartments features a fully equipped kitchen, balcony or patio, and Jacuzzi. There are five restaurants and a shopping arcade on the premises. A supervised children's program and video arcade for teens makes this place appealing to families. Its **Royal Cabana Casino** is the island's largest gaming house. ♦ 250 J.E. Irausquín Blvd, Eagle Beach. 879000, 800/835.7193; fax 870834

16 Amsterdam Manor $$$ This luxurious all-suite resort is a Dutch treat, boasting a tropical setting along Eagle Beach and 72 apartments with fully equipped kitchenettes. Every unit faces either the ocean or a garden. A swimming pool, restaurant, pool bar, and minimarket are also on the premises. ♦ 252 J.E. Irausquín Blvd, Eagle Beach. 871492, 800/766.6016; fax 871463

17 Palm Beach Convenient to Oranjestad, this glittering strand is lined with hotels and resorts that offer water sports, restaurants, and other comforts. The calm waters and gentle slope into the sea are easy on kids and less adventurous swimmers. There are no public facilities, but nonguests can use the facilities of most hotels, though sometimes for a price. ♦ Northwest coast

17 Wyndham Aruba Palm Beach Resort $$$ Formerly a member of the Hilton chain, the island's tallest hotel has 478 rooms, all with tropical-motif furnishings, mini-bars, safes, and balconies overlooking the sea. Lush landscaping sets off a free-form pool, and a sauna and water sports lure guests to the beach. Other draws include four restaurants (including **Pago Pago,** see below), a nightclub, several lounges, and a lively casino. Geared more toward adults than families, this is the top choice in its price category for discriminating travelers. ♦ 77 J.E. Irausquín Blvd, Palm Beach. 864466, 800/WYNDHAM; fax 861941

Within the Wyndham Aruba Palm Beach Resort:

Pago Pago ★★★$$$ Polynesian cuisine meets Caribbean scenery at this new restaurant. "Chef Tanoa's Feast" is a tasty six-course dinner, but there are also plenty of tantalizing options on the à la carte menu (like the Tahitian baked shrimp). Live piano music accompanies dinner. ♦ Polynesian ♦ M-Sa dinner. Reservations recommended. 864466

17 Aruba Palm Beach $$$ This striking and recently renovated high-rise with 200 oversized rooms—all with private balconies—has a lovely pink color scheme and beautiful gardens. It boasts a 1,200-foot

beach, 2 lighted tennis courts, a gorgeous pool area, water sports, 2 restaurants, a theater, a small ballroom, and a casino. ♦ 79 J.E. Irausquín Blvd, Palm Beach. 863900, 800/345.2782; fax 861941

18 Hyatt Regency Aruba Resort and Casino $$$$ Aruba's top deluxe resort, this $57-million property has 365 luxurious rooms along 12 acres right on Palm Beach. It boasts an elegant lobby decorated with stunning Oriental rugs and seven chandeliers, and a magnificently landscaped multilevel pool and lagoon area, complete with black swans. Steps lead out to the stunning beachfront on Aruba's northwest coast. The all-inclusive hotel offers exclusive **Regency Club** accommodations, the **Casino Copacabana,** a health spa, water sports, two lighted tennis courts, and three restaurants (see below). ♦ 85 J.E. Irausquín Blvd, Palm Beach. 861234, 800/554.9288; fax 865478

Aruba's drinking water comes from the world's second-largest desalination plant.

Aruba is completely outside of the hurricane belt.

Within the Hyatt Regency Aruba Resort and Casino:

Ruinas del Mar ★★★$$$ This romantic restaurant offers fine dining amid the re-created ruins of a gold mine, with stone pillars, candlelit tables, waterfalls, and a lagoon stocked with black swans and goldfish. Reserve a table on the terrace and let the ambience enchant you. Mediterranean specialties—including grilled lamb, beef, chicken, and fish—are featured at dinner. The incredible Sunday seafood brunch buffet overflows with fresh shrimp, oysters, clams, calamari, smoked salmon, caviar, and more. ◆ International ◆ M-Sa breakfast and dinner; Su brunch. Reservations required. 861234

Cafe Piccolo ★$ Northern Italian favorites, fresh pasta, and gourmet pizza from a brick oven are featured in this casual eatery. Italian wines are available by the glass. ◆ Italian ◆ M-Sa dinner. 861234

18 Playa Linda $$$ A stylish time-share resort with a clublike atmosphere and full hotel services, this property offers 191 luxurious studios and 1- and 2-bedroom apartments. Also on site are a restaurant, a minimarket, indoor and outdoor cocktail lounges, and various shops along a white-sand beach. ◆ 87 J.E. Irausquín Blvd, Palm Beach. 861000, 800/346.7084; fax 863479

19 Holiday Inn Aruba Beach Resort & Casino $$$$ Right on aptly named Palm Beach, this resort offers 600 air-conditioned rooms, day and night tennis on 6 courts, non-motorized water sports (including scuba diving and windsurfing), a fitness center, a casino, a pool, 4 restaurants, and a seaside boardwalk. The 200-room **Curacao Wing,** which was renovated in 1996 and sits apart from the rest of the complex, functions as an all-inclusive resort operated jointly by Holiday Inn and Bounty Resorts. ◆ 230 J.E. Irausquín Blvd, Palm Beach. 863600, 800/HOLIDAY, 800/GO-BOUNTY for all-inclusive vacations; fax 865165

19 Aruba Marriott $$$$ Here's a stunning 413-room hotel that exudes polish and class. Luxury is the word here, from the spectacular eight-story atrium lobby to the extra-large guest rooms, all with balconies offering Caribbean views. The pool is next to a lagoon that features a waterfall, palm trees, and a wooden bridge. Guests can dine in any of three restaurants, including the family-style **Seaview** and the Italian eatery **Tuscany.** A pool, a health club, a sauna, water sports, a lobby bar, and the **Stellaris Casino** are other highlights. ◆ Lloyd G. Smith Blvd, Palm Beach. 869000, 800/223.6388; fax 860258

20 The Steamboat Buffet and Deli ★$ This deli offers more than 20 different types of salads, as well as pizza, vegetables, and entrées (including roast beef, fish, Virginia ham, roast turkey, and barbecued ribs). The mouthwatering desserts beckon locals and tourists alike. Open around-the-clock, the place features an all-you-can-eat breakfast buffet. ◆ Deli ◆ Daily breakfast, lunch, and dinner. 370 Lloyd G. Smith Blvd, Palm Beach. 866700

20 Old Cunucu House Restaurant ★$$ Savory Aruban fare and international dishes are skillfully prepared by chef Ligia Maria in a restored, early-1900s *cunucu* (country) house. Delicacies include coconut fried shrimp, fish soup, and veal dishes. Be prepared to linger—service can be leisurely. There's musical entertainment Saturday nights. ◆ Aruban/International ◆ M-Sa dinner. Reservations recommended. Palm Beach. 861666

21 Gasparito Restaurant and Art Gallery ★★$$ Much of the island art on display here is for sale. Dine on local foods, including fish soup, conch stew, chicken breast topped with pineapple sauce, and shrimp in coconut milk and brandy. ◆ Aruban ◆ M-Sa dinner. Reservations recommended. Gasparito. 867040

22 Papiamento ★★★$$ A garden patio contributes herbs to the kitchen and adds extra romance to this family-run restaurant set in a restored 19th-century house. Fresh lobster, shrimp, and snapper are grilled tableside on hot marble. Other good choices are Dover sole meunière, lamb chops, and classic chateaubriand for two. Lovers can dine in a secluded, delicately lit alcove known as the **Honeymoon Room.** There is also dining poolside on the patio and in the bar. ◆ Continental/Caribbean ◆ Daily dinner. Reservations recommended. Washington. 864544

23 La Paloma Restaurant ★★$ Northern Italian dishes are the specialty here; try the veal cacciatore, *pollo alla parmigiana* (chicken topped with eggplant and mozzarella), pasta, or fresh seafood. ◆ Italian/Seafood ◆ M, W-Su dinner. Reservations recommended. Noord. 862770

23 Mama's and Papa's ★★★$ Dine indoors or out at this typical Aruban cafe, where authentic local specialties include *bakijow stoba seroe patrishi* (stewed cod), *kreeft di cay reef* (broiled lobster), and *keshi yena* (stuffed cheese). There's also live music and dancing. ♦ Aruban ♦ M-Sa dinner. Reservations recommended. Noord. 867913, 860633

23 Santa Anna Church Built by Spanish missionary Domingo Antonio Silvestre around 1772, this is the second-oldest church on Aruba. Its hand-carved oak altar by Dutch sculptor Hendrik van der Geld won an award in Rome in 1879. ♦ Noord

24 Tierra del Sol Designed by Robert Trent Jones Jr., this stunning 18-hole, par-71, 6,811-yard championship golf course incorporates the island's desert terrain, including cacti, sand, and boulders. The 5th fairway hugs a saltwater marsh favored by wild egrets; the 12th hole—the most challenging—sits on a rock cliff above the ocean. Managed by Hyatt hotels, the course is first-class all the way. The clubhouse's **Ventanas del Mar** restaurant (see below) is a perfect spot to dine after a round. ♦ Greens fee. Daily. North of Malmok. 860978

Within Tierra del Sol:

Ventanas del Mar ★★$$$ Almost in the shadow of the **California Lighthouse** on the northwesternmost tip of the island, this elegant eatery in the golf course clubhouse offers seafood and Caribbean specialties, including whole roasted red snapper and crab cakes. The lunchtime menu features lighter fare such as salads, sandwiches, and jerk-chicken quesadillas. The view is dramatic and there is live jazz at night. ♦ Caribbean/Seafood ♦ Daily lunch and dinner. Reservations recommended for dinner. 867800

25 Alto Vista Chapel White wooden crosses line the roadway to this hilltop chapel built on the site of the island's first mission, where in the early 1700s prayer meetings took place under a tree or in a hut. The original chapel, built in 1750 by Spanish missionary Domingo Antonio Silvestre, fell to ruins within the next century. It was replaced in 1952 with this small church; the original altar remains intact. Regular masses are not held here, but it is a favorite spot for weddings. The church is kept open during the day for visitors and the devout. ♦ Northeast of Noord

26 Casibari Rocks Some geologists think these building-sized diorite rocks and those at Ayo (see below) might be the result of earthquakes or volcanic eruptions, and that they were originally part of the South American mainland. Although their origin is still a mystery, these several-ton boulders are quite interesting. If you're wearing good walking shoes, climb to the windy top of the rock pile for an impressive panoramic view of the area. ♦ Northeast of the road between Santa Cruz and Paradera

27 Ayo Rocks This fascinating and beautiful collection of rock formations, like that at Casibari (see above), provides great photo opportunities. These diorite boulders are also gigantic, but you can climb only halfway up here. ♦ East of Casibari Rocks

28 Natural Bridge There are two bridges on Aruba that have been carved out of coral rock over the years by the wind and sea. The one to see (illustrated on page 40) is on the jagged northern edge of the island near Noordkaap. It stretches dramatically for more than 100 feet and rises 25 feet above sea level. ♦ Northeast of Ayo Rocks

29 Hooiberg (Haystack Mountain) Aruba's most visible natural landmark sits smack in the center of the island. There's a stairway to the top—541 feet high—and a spectacular view. (On clear days, you can see Venezuela.) It's definitely worth the trek. ♦ Northwest of Santa Cruz

30 Arikok National Park This park, which covers nearly a fourth of the island, boasts interesting nature trails and a restored *cunucu* cottage. It is also home to the caves with the island's best-preserved Indian drawings, a sight-seeing must. One of the most fun and unusual ways to explore the park is on horseback with guides from **Rancho del Campo** (850290). ♦ Southeastern coast and interior

Within the Arikok National Park:

Fontein Caves These caves—cool, wide subterranean caverns with low ceilings and dripping water—feature intriguing 1,000-year-old Arawak Indian paintings still undeciphered by modern scientists (and, unfortunately, marred by graffiti in some spots). The larger, more open, and more popular **Guadirikiri Cave** is named for the wife of an Indian chief; openings above allow the sunlight to enter and dapple the Indian paintings. **Huliva Cave,** 100 steps down into a tunnel, is sometimes called the "Tunnel of Love." Follow its winding pathways to an exit on the other side of the hill. Good walking shoes and a flashlight are a must here (flashlights are available for rent at the entrance to the caves). ♦ Free. Daily.

Cacti far outnumber palms on arid Aruba.

Restaurants/Clubs: Red   **Hotels:** Blue
Shops/ Outdoors: Green   **Sights/Culture:** Black

Natural Bridge, Aruba

31 Colorado Point/Seroe Colorado The **Colorado Point Lighthouse** here marks the southeast point of the island. It is also where Seroe Colorado, once the private residential compound for foreign executives working at Esso's Lago Oil refinery, is located. When Venezuela stopped sending heavy crude to Aruba for refining, the operation was downsized and the homes put up for sale. Today the area is public, and provides access to the lighthouse and to Baby and Rodgers Beaches (see below). ♦ Southeastern corner

At Seroe Colorado:

Baby Beach The name of this beach comes from the gentle, shallow water that's free of undertow and perfect for little swimmers. The beach was once used almost exclusively by the families of foreign executives stationed at the oil refinery. Now it's open to anyone who loves swimming, sunning, and snorkeling in clear, surf-free waters. The only facility is a refreshment stand, so wear your suits and bring a picnic lunch. On a clear day, you can spot Venezuela (15 miles away) from here. Not far from the beach is a sandy hill dotted with wooden crosses—the local pet cemetery.

Rodgers Beach Protected by reefs, but with enough surf to provide lots of fun, this is a favorite swimming spot for Arubans. A white-powder beach is lapped by clear aquamarine water. Accessible only by car or taxi, the beach has little shade and no changing facilities. A refreshment stand is open on weekends only.

32 Charlie's Bar and Restaurant ★★$$ This casual watering hole has been popular for more than 50 years. Charlie and Marie Brouns opened the hangout for seafarers, contractors, and refinery and harbor workers in 1941. Their son, Charlie Jr., and his wife operate the place today. Specialties include local fish in hot curry sauces and giant shrimp and calamari in butter-and-parsley sauce. Lots of island memorabilia and artifacts of the oil-rush days are on display here, along with license plates, T-shirts, and flotsam left by tourists. Come prepared for a wait; there aren't many tables and no reservations are taken. ♦ Aruban/Seafood ♦ M-Sa lunch and dinner. 56 Zeppenfeldstraat (at Rodgersstraat), San Nicolas. 845086

33 Brisas Del Mar ★★★$$ With its homey atmosphere, friendly service, and superb local cuisine, this seafood restaurant has become popular with locals and tourists alike. The many Aruban specialties served include conch, grouper, fish cakes, and shrimp dishes. Fried plantains and *pan bati* (pancake-shaped bread made from cornmeal) go well with any entrée. Best of all, as the name implies, the restaurant is right on the sea. ♦ Seafood ♦ M dinner; Tu-Su lunch and dinner. Reservations recommended for dinner. Savaneta. 847718

34 Balashi Gold Mine The ruins of this 19th-century mine are a testimony to the island's gold rush. At nearby Spanish Lagoon, formerly a pirates' hideaway, visitors can see Aruba's desalination and power plants. ♦ Free. Daily. North of Pos Chiquito. No phone

Getting Your Feet Wet in Aruba

The waters along the western coast of the island are the calmest. Most hotels and resorts offer water sports and beachfront boat and equipment rentals. Here are some other outfits that can get you afloat:

Boating

Aruba Nautical Club Marina Spanish Lagoon (just northwest of Pos Chiquito). 823022

Bucuti Yacht Club 31 Bucutiweg (northwest of Simeon Antonio). 823793

Snorkeling and Scuba Diving

Aruba Pro Dive Ponton. 825520

De Palm Tours 824400

Mermaid Sports Divers 55 J.E. Irausquín Blvd, Manchebo Beach. 835546

Pelican Watersports 66 Lloyd G. Smith Blvd, Oranjestad. 831228

Red Sail Sports 83 Lloyd G. Smith Blvd, Palm Beach. 861603, 800/255.6425

Scuba Aruba Seaport Village, 82 Lloyd G. Smith Blvd (between Arnold Schuttestraat and Weststraat), Oranjestad. 834142

Sportfishing

De Palm Tours 824400

Pelican Watersports 66 Lloyd G. Smith Blvd, Oranjestad. 831228

Red Sail Sports 83 Lloyd G. Smith Blvd, Palm Beach. 861603, 800/255.6425

Windsurfing

Pelican Watersports 66 Lloyd G. Smith Blvd, Oranjestad. 831228

Red Sail Sports 83 Lloyd G. Smith Blvd, Palm Beach. 861603, 800/255.6425

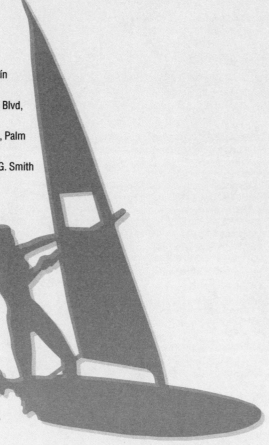

Barbados

Portuguese explorers and traders who arrived on the easternmost Caribbean island in the early 500s decided the lush tropical trees that covered this spot of land looked a t like bearded men, and so Barbados—Portuguese for "bearded men"—was ristened. The name stuck, lasting through British colonization, African and merican cultural influences, and more than 30 years of independence. But e original meaning of the name is mostly forgotten, as the island, which njoys one of the highest standards of living in the Caribbean, promotes urism with dozens of posh resorts and grand estates. Today, for most eople, "Barbados" means "tropical vacation."

ghty miles east of its nearest neighbor, this compact isle—just 21 miles long nd 14 miles wide—is ideally suited to tourism. It offers a mix of land and ater sports, lively nightlife, and plenty of opportunities to explore historical tes and natural beauty.

arbados also offers a tropical getaway with a distinctly British accent. Thanks the islanders' fondness for afternoon tea, cricket, and driving on the left de of the road, the island has been called more British than Britain herself. he **Scotland District** to the north looks much like its namesake, with rolling een hills ("bonnie braes") and a mist about which Scottish poet Robert irns would surely have rhapsodized. In contrast, the inland roads pass rough thick tropical forests and fields of sugarcane. The island's eastern ore is harsh, with spectacular rocky shores, while the west, shielded from e Atlantic trade winds, is lined with powdery coral beaches.

nder British rule for more than 350 years (until 1966), the island has its own **rafalgar Square** in **Bridgetown**, the capital city; the square's statue of Lord elson predates the London version by 36 years. Even the villages bear such nglish names as **Hastings**, **Vauxhall**, and **Brighton**. And like the famous ub crawlers of England, the Bajans (pronounced *Bah*-jahns and used terchangeably with "Barbadians" to denote residents) have a tradition of ociable drinking—except that rum, not ale, is the alcohol of choice. Barbados as the first country to export rum; in fact, the word was coined on the land, probably derived from the original Bajan word for the liquor, *mbullion.*

oday the island is home to about a quarter-million citizens, most of whom ve in the urban area that stretches along the Caribbean side from **peightstown** through **Oistins.** Nearly 100,000 people reside in **St. Michael** arish, most in the capital city. As a rule, they're a congenial people and xtend a warm welcome to the more than one million vacationers who visit eir island each year.

---

rea code 246 unless otherwise noted.

etting to the Island

rlines

r Canada	428.5077, 800/776.3000
nerican Airlines	428.1684, 800/433.7300
VIA International Airways	
	426.2111, 800/538.2942

terisland Carriers

r Martinique	431.0540
AT (Leeward Islands Air Transport)	436.6224,
	800.253.5011

rport Grantley Adams International Airport (28.5570) serves international and interisland flights. Located at the southeast corner of **Christ Church** parish, the airport is 18 kilometers (11 miles) east of Bridgetown.

Getting Around the Island

Bicycles and Motorbikes

Fun Seekers	435.9171
Irie Mountain Bike	424.4730
M.A. Williams Bicycle Rentals	427.3955

Buses Buses are comfortable, reliable, and inexpensive. Board at marked bus stops after flagging down the driver. Several hotels operate mini-van shuttles to and from Bridgetown for their guests.

Car Rental There are dozens of car-rental companies in Barbados, including:

Barbados Rent a Car 425.1388

Courtesy Car Rentals...............................431.4160,
....431.4161, 431.4162

Drive-A-Matic...422.4000

L.E. Williams Tour Co 427.1043

National Car Rentals 426.0603, 800/328.4567

Regency Car Rentals 427.5666, 427.0909

Sunny Isle Motors 435.7979

Driving Visitors with a current US or Canadian license may obtain an island license from a car-rental agency at **Grantley Adams International Airport** or at police stations in larger towns such as Oistins, Hastings, **Worthing**, and Speightstown. The roads in Barbados are well paved and marked. Driving is on the left side. The maximum speed limits are 60 kilometers (37 miles) per hour in the country and 34 kilometers (21 miles) per hour in town—but no one adheres to them.

Taxis Cab fares between major attractions on the island and to **Grantley Adams International Airport** are fixed and posted in the airport; the list also is available at the front desk of hotels or from cab drivers. Taxis are readily accessible at most tourist sites.

Barbados Transport Coop Society 428.6565

Belmont Taxi & Car Service 429.2659

Paramount Taxi Service 429.3718

Tours The **Transport Board** public buses and smaller, privately operated minibuses are both very inexpensive ways to tour Barbados. For a bird's-eye view of the island, contact **Bajan Helicopters** (The Wharf, west of Trafalgar Sq, Bridgetown, 431.0069). An 80-mile bus tour of the coast that includes lunch, drinks, and entrance fees is offered by **L.E. Williams Tour Co. Ltd.** (427.1043; fax 427.6007). The **Barbados National Trust** (426.2421) offers free five-mile Sunday hikes to historic plantation houses, sugar factory yards, and other local landmarks; young Bajans and National Trust members trek along, offering observations on geography, history, geology, and agriculture. Day tours are available to the Grenadines (a chain of islands extending from St. Vincent to Grenada) from Barbados hotels; call **Grenadine Tours** (435.8451; fax 435.6444). Day or evening party cruises offer passengers the opportunity to snorkel or swim in the lovely turquoise waters offshore and to dance to the music of local bands; for more information, call **Bajan Queen** (436.6425) or **Jolly Roger** (436.6424).

FYI

Electricity The current is 110 volts/50 cycles. Most US and Canadian appliances are compatible, though they run slowly, and many hotels provide converters.

Entry Requirements US and Canadian visitors must present a valid passport or proof of citizenship (birth certificate, voter's registration card) plus a photo ID, along with a return or onward ticket.

Language The official language is English.

Money The official currency is the Barbados dolla (Bd$) but US dollars and traveler's checks are wide accepted. Larger hotels and restaurants take credit cards. Banks are open Monday through Thursday from 9AM to 3PM, and Friday from 9AM to 1PM an from 3PM to 5PM. **Barclay's Bank** (Broad St, Bridgetown, 431.5151) and the **Royal Bank of Canada** (Broad St, Bridgetown, 426.5200) open ar hour earlier, and on Friday both are open from 8AM to 5PM. The **Caribbean Commercial Bank** (Broad Bridgetown, 431.2500) is also open from 9AM to noon on Saturday. The **Barbados National Bank** ru an exchange bureau at the airport that's open daily from 8AM to 9:30PM. Many banks have automatic teller machines (ATMs).

Museum Passes The **Barbados National Trust** (426.2421) sells a "Heritage Passport" that grants the holder discounted admission to 16 of the island historic attractions. The trust also offers three mini passports that allow entry to five properties each. A press time, the passport cost US$40; the mini-passports were US$21.

Personal Safety Barbados is a relatively safe island, but visitors should exercise common sense all times. Don't venture into areas where you don't feel comfortable; use hotel safe-deposit boxes to store valuables; and don't take anything extraneou to the beach.

Publications The two daily papers are the *Advocate* and the *Nation*. On weekends, the latter appears as the *Sunday Sun* and includes *Pelican Magazine*. *The Bajan* comes out monthly; it's a glos magazine with a mix of articles on island politics, culture, and personalities. Among the local tourist publications are the monthly *What's On* and the twice-monthly *Sun Seeker*. Every Monday, the *Nat* puts out *The Visitor*, a tourist-oriented tabloid. Brit and US papers are also available.

Reservation Services and House Rentals
Barbados Hotel Association 800/462.252

Taxes A 10-percent service sales tax is applied to most hotel bills, while a 15-percent value-added ta (VAT) is added to the price of restaurant meals, sightseeing tours, boat cruises, and car rentals. There is a Bd$25 (US$12.50) departure tax.

Tipping Tip waiters 10 to 15 percent of the tab, hotel maids $1 or $2 (US) per day, taxi drivers 10 percent of the fare, porters and bellhops $1 per bag

Visitors' Information Offices The main tourisr office is on **Harbour Road,** next to the **Harbour Industrial Park** near **Deep Water Harbour** in Bridgetown (427.2623/4). It's open Monday throuc Friday from 8:15AM to 4:30PM. Other information centers are located at **Grantley Adams Internation Airport** (428.0937) and on the cruise-ship pier at **Deep Water Harbour** (426.1718); their schedules vary according to plane and ship arrivals.

Phone Book

1 Divi Southwinds Beach Resort $$ Towering cathedral ceilings in the lobby herald a gracious facility where you can kick back and enjoy yourself without the onus of dressing for dinner. The dress code, such as it is, is relaxed. The 150 air-conditioned guest quarters—28 bedroom suites and 122 rooms—feature tropical decor, and there are 2 lighted tennis courts, 3 freshwater pools, a beautiful white-sand beach, and a restaurant. The suites feature fully equipped kitchens—ideal for vacationing families. ◆ Hwy 7, Maxwell. 428.7181, 800/367.3484; fax 428.4674

2 Dover Cricket Club Bajans take the game of cricket very seriously, and there's always a match going on weekends at the field across from pretty **Dover Beach.** Nonmembers can participate in pick-up games but the real matches are reserved for team members. Spectators are always welcome. Practice games occasionally take place weekdays. ◆ Daily; schedules available from the **National Sports Council.** Dover. 436.6127

3 Pisces Restaurant ★★$$ The menu may focus on Caribbean seafood specialties, but there's nothing fishy about the superlative view of the ocean from this cute (but hardly upscale) latticework house-turned-eatery. Snapper caribe is a must. Meat, chicken, and vegetarian dishes are good, too. And the wine list is a broad one, offering labels from Europe and South America. ◆ Seafood ◆ Daily dinner. Reservations required. St. Lawrence. 435.6564

3 Church of St. Lawrence This beautiful old Anglican church is located right on the beach. The very English interior has high ceilings, a mahogany altar, and mahogany pews. You can catch a wedding here almost every weekend. ◆ St. Lawrence

3 Witch Doctor ★★$$ A casual spot with jungle decor, this eatery features tasty island cookery. Shrimp in garlic sauce, lobster thermidor, and spicy chicken *piri piri* are among the house specialties. The latter is a recipe from Mozambique—chicken marinated in lime and baked with garlic and chili. ◆ African/Caribbean ◆ Daily dinner. Reservations recommended. St. Lawrence. 435.6581

3 Josef's Restaurant ★★★$$$ This romantic and stylish establishment serves excellent fish (especially the barracuda in hollandaise sauce) and steak dishes. ◆ Continental ◆ M-F lunch and dinner; Sa dinner. Reservations required. St. Lawrence. 435.6541

3 The Steak House ★$$ Since this lovely, old, plant-filled house was converted into a cozy eating spot in the 1970s, it has become a Barbados institution. Specialties include steak St. Lawrence (grilled sirloin with sweet peppers) and fillet Karen (tenderloin with sautéed onions, mushrooms, and green peppers)—named for the manager's daughter. Both are served with a baked potato and all the salad you can eat. ◆ Steaks/Seafood ◆ Daily dinner. St. Lawrence. 428.7152

3 Chattel House Shopping Village A collection of tourist boutiques and souvenir shops is set up in brightly painted historic re-creations of slave homes. The attractions include **Summer Scents, Best 'n the Bunch, Friendlies Delicatessen and Bar, Finecrafts,** and **Biddy's Information Centre** (the latter offering car rentals, tours, and entertainment reservations). ◆ M-F; Sa-Su morning. St. Lawrence. 428.2474

3 Luigi's ★$$$ This cozy Italian restaurant has a delightful ambience. Try the shrimp in garlic butter and the stuffed pepper and manicotti specialties. More than 15 pasta dishes grace the menu, and grilled pizza is a house favorite. ◆ Italian ◆ Daily dinner. St. Lawrence. 428.9218

3 David's Place ★★$$ Bajan food is prepared with a flair at this casual spot overlooking St. Lawrence Bay. Recommended choices: pumpkin fritters to start, curried shrimp or pepper pot (a meaty stew)

as your main course, and coconut cream pie for dessert. ◆ Caribbean ◆ Daily dinner. St. Lawrence. 435.9755

4 Ile de France Restaurant ★★$$$
Grilled seafood is given a continental accent by an award-winning French chef at this elegant dining spot. Try the tournedos Rossini, stuffed with foie gras and truffles in Madeira, and the onion soup gratinée. Desserts include banana flambé, nougat glacé, and lemon tart. The more casual **Bistro** dining room serves snacks and light meals. ◆ French ◆ Tu-Su dinner. Windsor Arms Hotel, Hastings. 435.6869

4 Caribbee Beach Hotel $ A modest beach hotel, it offers 55 air-conditioned rooms (some with kitchenettes) right on the beach. There's also a restaurant on the premises. ◆ Hastings. 436.6232, 800/223.6510; fax 436.0130

4 Ocean View $ This hotel features Old World atmosphere, sea views, and a fine restaurant that serves traditional Bajan fare. Not all of the 31 rooms are air-conditioned. Snorkelers will enjoy the reef-rimmed beach. ◆ Hastings. 427.7821, 800/441.7087; fax 427.7826

4 Coconut Court Beach Hotel $ Charlie Blades and his family own and operate this pleasant 92-unit beachfront hotel with a restaurant. Facilities include a pool and dive shop, and Sunfish and Windsurfers are available for rent. Conveniently located just outside the capital, this place is within walking distance of restaurants, nightclubs, banks, and shops. ◆ Hastings. 427.1655; fax 429.8198

4 Champers Wine Bar ★★$$ This lively wine bar draws a congenial local crowd for snacks or creative dishes featuring seafood. Be sure to try the fish pie, a savory blend of local fish, mashed potatoes, and cheese. There's live jazz or guitar music on some Saturdays. ◆ Seafood ◆ Daily lunch and dinner; closed in September. Chattel Plaza, Hastings. 435.6644

5 Barbados Museum and Historical Society Housed in an old military prison (part of which dates from 1820), the museum's collection spans the history of this multicultural island—from Arawak and Carib Indians to Africans and Europeans. Dolls, household items, and clothing are displayed. Exhibits also spotlight Barbados's natural history and the island's architecture. Don't miss the collection of fine maps, prints, and other Caribbean historical documents in the **Cunard Gallery**. A cafe, library with current and historical publications, and gift shop (with T-shirts) are also on the premises. This is a Heritage Passport site. ◆ Admission. Museum M-Sa, Su afternoons. Library: M-F mornings, and by appointment. Gift shop: M-Sa. East of Hwy 7, Garrison Savannah. 427.0201

Within the Barbados Museum and Historical Society:

1627 and All That A real toe-tapper, this exuberant musical dinner-theater offers a lively overview of the island's history. Dinner features traditional foods: peas 'n' rice, sweet potatoes, pumpkin fritters, fried flying fish, calypso chicken, and various salads. One price covers the dinner, show, and transportation to and from your hotel. ◆ Tu-Su. 428.1627

6 Garrison Historic Area This collection of buildings of historical and architectural interest is set around a modern-day racecourse outside of Bridgetown. British military barracks that housed troops stationed in the West Indies from 1780 to 1905 are interspersed with gravestones from the mid-17th century. The **National Cannon Collection** is reputed to be one of the world's finest. Horse races take place on the track Saturday afternoons, but there's no set schedule, so check with your hotel. ◆ East of Hwy 7, Garrison Savannah. No phone

Within the Garrison Historic Area:

Bush Hill House In 1751, 19-year-old George Washington and his older brother Lawrence came to Barbados so Lawrence could recuperate from tuberculosis in a warm climate. Lawrence's father-in-law's third wife was the sister of a prominent Barbadian, Gedney Clarke—a connection that probably influenced the brothers' travel plans. It wasn't until 1983 that this house was identified as the place where the Washington brothers stayed. ◆ Admission. Daily. No phone

7 Brown Sugar ★★$$ Enormous portions of traditional Bajan specialties are offered at this charming restaurant in a Bajan home. Dinner is served by candlelight in a fern-filled patio banked by cascading water. The Sunday buffet brunch is a great way to sample local dishes from *cou cou* (cornmeal pudding) to Creole-style flying fish. ◆ Caribbean ◆ M-Sa lunch and dinner; Su brunch and dinner. Hilton Rd (west of Hwy 7). 426.7684

When George Washington slept here (at the Bush Hill House on the outskirts of Bridgetown) he regarded the rent of 15 pounds a month, exclusive of liquors and laundry, to be exorbitant.

Tropical Texts

Find out more about the Caribbean islands and the colorful culture of some of the countries by flipping through the pages of the following titles.

Nonfiction

The Caribbean: Culture of Resistance, Spirit of Hope edited by Oscar Bolioli (Friendship Press, 1993)

The Caribbean: The Lands and Their Peoples by Eintou Pearl Springer (Silver Burdett Press, 1988)

Caribbean Ways: A Cultural Guide by Chelle Koster Walton (Riverdale Press, 1992)

The Conquest of Paradise by Kirkpatrick Sale (Alfred A. Knopf, 1990)

Democracies and Tyrannies of the Caribbean by William Krehm (Lawrence Hill and Company, 1984)

The Modern Caribbean by Franklin W. Knight and Colin A. Palmer (University of North Carolina Press, 1989)

On the Trail of the Arawaks by Irving Rouse (University of Oklahoma Press, 1974)

The "Redlegs" of Barbados, Their Origins and History by Jill Sheppard (KTO Press, 1976)

A Short Account of the Destruction of the Indies by Bartolomé de las Casas (16th century; Penguin, repr. 1992)

A Short History of the West Indies by J.H. Parry and P.M. Sherlock (St. Martin's Press, 1971)

When I Was Puerto Rican by Esmeralda Santiago (Addison Wesley, 1993)

Fiction

Arkansas Testament by Derek Walcott (Farrar, Straus & Giroux, 1987)

The Autobiography of My Mother by Jamaica Kincaid (Farrar, Straus & Giroux, 1996)

The Bounty by Derek Walcott (Farrar, Straus & Giroux, 1997)

Caribbean by James A. Michener (Random House, 1989)

Caribbean Poetry Now edited by Stewart Brown (Routledge Chapman & Hall, 1992)

The Collected Short Stories by Jean Rhys (W. W. Norton, 1992)

Como el Aire de Abril by Arturo Echavarria (University of Puerto Rico Press, 1994)

Crick Crack Monkey by Merle Hodge (Heinemann, 1981)

Finding the Center by V.S. Naipaul (Alfred A. Knopf, 1984)

A House for Mr. Biswas by V.S. Naipaul (Penguin Books, Ltd., 1969)

The House on the Lagoon by Rosario Ferre (Farrar, Straus & Giroux, 1995)

In the Time of the Butterflies by Julia Alvarez (Plume, 1995)

Lucy by Jamaica Kincaid (Farrar, Straus & Giroux, 1991)

Miguel Street by V.S. Naipaul (Penguin Books, Ltd., 1971)

My Brother by Jamaica Kincaid (Farrar, Straus & Giroux, 1997)

Omeros by Derek Walcott (Farrar, Straus & Giroux, 1990)

Un plat de porc aux bananes verts by Simone Schwarz-Bart and André Schwarz-Bart (Editions du Soleil, 1967)

Pluie et vent sur Télumée-Miracle by Simone Schwarz-Bart (Editions du Soleil, 1972)

Praisesong for the Widow by Paule Marshall (Plume, 1983)

A Small Place by Jamaica Kincaid (NAL/Dutton, 1989)

Ti-Jean l'horizon by Simone Schwarz-Bart (Editions du Soleil, 1979)

A Way in the World by V.S. Naipaul (Alfred A. Knopf, 1994)

Wide Sargasso Sea by Jean Rhys (W. W. Norton, 1992)

Youngest Doll by Rosario Ferre (University of Nebraska Press, 1991)

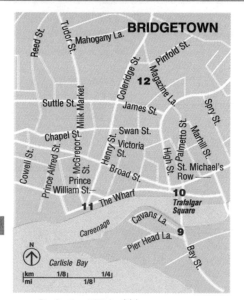

BRIDGETOWN

7 Barbados Hilton $$$ The 185 rooms here are complemented by 3 restaurants (including the **Veranda**, see below), a swimming pool, tennis courts, and a wide range of water sports. ♦ Hilton Rd (west of Hwy 7), Needham's Point. 426.0200, 800/HILTONS; fax 436.8946

Within the Barbados Hilton:

Veranda Restaurant ★★$$$ Bajan specialties—including flying fish, cornmeal and okra fritters, and curried stews—are served in a picturesque setting designed to

Trafalgar Square

resemble a Barbados street, with chattel houses and island architecture. Guests may dine inside or out. ♦ Caribbean ♦ Daily breakfast, lunch, and dinner. 462.0200

8 Harbour Lights Dine and dance beneath the stars at this open-air beachfront nightclub above Carlisle Bay. Locals and tourists alike mix it up on the dance floor to live Caribbean music. Monday is Beach Party night. ♦ Admission. Daily. Marine Villa, Bay St, Bridgetown. 436.7225

8 Grand Barbados Beach Resort $$$ This beautifully redecorated and landscaped 133-room resort has everything a vacationer could possibly require. Two restaurants (one with live entertainment nightly) and a coffee shop are on the premises, and a pool, horseback riding, and tennis are nearby. ♦ Bay St, Bridgetown. 426.4000, 800/814.2235; fax 436.2400

Within the Grand Barbados Beach Resort:

The Boardwalk Cafe ★★★$$$$ Perched on a pier in the heart of Carlisle Bay, this lovely restaurant with attentive service is known for its popular theme buffets: barbecue on Monday nights, Italian on Friday, and West Indian on Sunday. The à la carte menu ranges from Caribbean to continental; favorite entrées include mahimahi topped with a spicy onion-and-butter Creole sauce, and perfect roast lamb chops. ♦ International ♦ Daily lunch and dinner. 426.0890

9 Waterfront Cafe ★$$ Caribbean appetizers, curries, vegetarian entrées, and seafood specialties are served at this friendly diner overlooking the yachts moored in the Careenage. The nightly live entertainment—usually jazz—is extremely popular. ♦ Caribbean/American ♦ M-Sa lunch and dinner. Cavans La and Bay St, Bridgetown. 427.0093

9 Colors of de Caribbean Jewelry, bright flowing cotton clothing, and souvenir collectibles designed by local artists come together at this boutique housed in a historic warehouse building on the marina. ♦ Waterfront Marina, Cavans La, Bridgetown. 436.8522

9 Bajan Helicopters Barbados can be uplifting in more ways than one. For a real bird's-eye view of the island, take an aerial tour aboard a five-passenger chopper. You'll see coral reefs through the crystalline ocean, view the island's cliffside villas (one belonged to the late actress Claudette Colbert), and marvel at the difference between Barbados's calm western side and the rough and risky (for swimmers) Atlantic coast on the east. ♦ Fee. Reservations required. Bridgetown Heliport, Waterfront Marina, Cavans La, Bridgetown. 431.0069

10 Trafalgar Square A statue of Lord Nelson marks this central square located opposite the parliament building. Like its counterpart in London, this 1813 memorial honors the admiral's naval victory in 1805. ♦ At St. Michael's Row and Broad St, and Bay and High Sts

11 Atlantis Submarines Visit the ocean depths to view the living world of coral reefs and colorful sea life up close. The sub ride takes an hour and is a perfect opportunity for photographers. You can also take a trip on *Atlantis*'s sister vessel, the 40-passenger *Seatrec*, a cross between a submarine and a glass-bottom boat. ♦ Admission. Daily. Reservations required. Horizon House, McGregor St (between The Wharf and Princess Alice Hwy), Bridgetown. 436.8929

12 Barbados Synagogue and Cemetery The original synagogue on this site, built in 1654, was destroyed by a hurricane in 1831. The current synagogue, a small, simple building, was constructed two years later, but fell into disuse in the early 1900s. After the Barbados National Trust restored the building, it was reopened as a house of worship in 1992. Three Torahs donated by communities in the US, England, and Israel are interesting, but even more fascinating than the building and its treasures is the cemetery. It is filled with gravestones—inscribed in Hebrew, Portuguese, Spanish, and English—dating back to the mid-17th century. ♦ M-F; Sa-Su by appointment. Synagogue La (between Magazine La and Coleridge St), Bridgetown. 436.8043

13 Tyrol Cot Heritage Village The centerpiece here is the home of Sir Grantley Adams, the island's first premier. Constructed in 1854, the mansion is filled with antiques and memorabilia that once belonged to Adams and his wife. Around the white stone home with pink trim is the "village"—a group of colorful reconstructed chattel houses, all

serving as studios/galleries for artists and craftspeople. ♦ Admission. M-F. Hwy 2, Grazettes. Barbados National Trust 424.2074

14 Mount Gay Distillery Barbados's famous rum has been refined, blended, and bottled here for nearly three centuries, despite English archbishop and longtime island resident Thomas Tenison's assertion that rum is "destructive to nature, wasting to vitals, and an enemy of propagation." Take a 45-minute tour or book a luncheon tour that includes a buffet of Bajan food. Both end with a rum tasting. ♦ Admission. M-Sa. Spring Garden and ABC Hwys, Batts Rock Bay. 425.9066

15 Koko's ★★$$$ Owners Stephen and Sandra Toppin have attracted a loyal following of locals and visitors alike to their casual, cliff-side restaurant. The menu features unusual and creative Bajan dishes such as *koq-ka-doo* (chicken stuffed with banana and topped with rum sauce) and seafood. ♦ Caribbean/Seafood ♦ Daily dinner Dec-Apr; Tu-Su dinner May-Nov. Reservations recommended. Hwy 1, Prospect. 424.4557

15 Coconut Creek Club Hotel $$ This cottage colony is a sophisticated little property offering lush gardens, water sports on 2 beaches, 53 rooms (each with a patio or balcony), a freshwater pool, and **Cricketers**, an English pub with a first-rate chef and good entertainment (see below). ♦ Hwy 1, Prospect. 432.0803, 800/223.6510; fax 432.0272

Within the Coconut Creek Club Hotel:

Cricketers ★★$$ There's something different every day of the week at this congenial pub/restaurant. In addition to the à la carte menu, it offers a lunchtime barbecue on Tuesday and Thursday, island specialties on Sunday, and Wednesday-night buffets with a wide variety of dishes. But the most popular night is Saturday, which features a sizzling barbecue, an offbeat list of exotic tropical cocktails, and a live steel band. ♦ International ♦ Tu-Su lunch and dinner. Reservations recommended. 432.0803

Pirate Sam Lord died in England under strange circumstances. His coachman reported that he last saw his master enter a strange house. When he did not return, the coachman questioned a porter, who told him, "I would never wish you to be as your master is now. You will never see him again." Apparently the house belonged to the surviving captain of the *Wanderer*, one of the ships that Lord had wrecked against Cobblers Reef.

Restaurants/Clubs: Red   **Hotels:** Blue
Shops/♥ Outdoors: Green   **Sights/Culture:** Black

15 La Cage aux Folles ★★★$$$$ This tiny spot is one of the island's hottest dining destinations. Owned by Nick Hudson and Suzie Blandford, the restaurant is in a fine old Barbadian great house. The menu is à la carte, with an emphasis on French haute cuisine with a Caribbean accent. Start with sesame prawn pâté, then follow with the spicy curried chicken or fish in banana sauce. There are also creative vegetarian dishes. ♦ French-Caribbean ♦ M, W-Su dinner. Reservations required. Hwy 1, Prospect. 424.2424

16 Carambola ★★★★$$$ Possibly the best restaurant on the island, this open-air cafe, with a dramatic cliffside location, serves creatively prepared seafood. Standouts include yellowfin tuna in a crisp potato crust and a satay trio—chicken, pork, and shrimp kabobs on a bed of rice with a spicy peanut sauce. The extensive wine list features many French labels. ♦ Seafood ♦ M-Sa dinner. Reservations required. Derricks. 432.0832

17 Tamarind Cove Hotel $$$$ Luxury is everywhere at this 117-room hotel, which boasts 500 feet of sand on St. James Beach, water sports, and 3 pools. The open-air lobby is decorated in soothing peach and gray marble, with lovely Spanish arches and fountains. Dining options include **Neptunes**, a seafood restaurant (see below), and an eatery featuring US and Bajan staples. ♦ Paynes Bay. 432.1332, 438.4680, 800/223.6510; fax 223.6510

Within the Tamarind Cove Hotel:

Amazone The fashion-forward women's clothing found here is perfect for tropical days and evenings, as well as to wear back home. ♦ M-F; Sa mornings. 432.2358

Neptunes ★★$$$ This stylish restaurant is considered one of the island's most innovative. The restaurant's dark walls and the saltwater aquarium in the center of the room give diners the impression that they're dining underwater. Shrimp, lobster, and swordfish specialties—in particular the garlic shrimp and the blackened snapper—are the best choices. ♦ Seafood ♦ Daily dinner. Reservations required. 432.1332, 432.6999

In 1809 pirate Sam Lord married heiress Lucy Wighwich (against her family's will) and sailed with his bride for Barbados. The union lasted less than three years. Eventually Lucy, imprisoned by her husband in the castle dungeon, bribed a slave jailer with jewels and escaped.

17 Smugglers Cove $ This 20-room hotel has a pool and a small restaurant. It's a good choice for families, as all the units have either full kitchens or kitchenettes with small refrigerators and microwave ovens. They're also equipped with air-conditioning, but not TV sets. ♦ Paynes Bay. 432.1741; fax 432.1749

17 The Coach House ★$$ It's a proper English pub, with a posted dress code that asks patrons to "please dress nicely" and a real British phone booth on the grounds. But the nightly live calypso music reminds you that you're in Barbados. The eclectic menu ranges from Bajan beef stew to *cou cou* (cornmeal pudding) with codfish gravy to steak and kidney pie. ♦ British/Caribbean ♦ M-F, Su lunch and dinner; Sa dinner. Reservations required for dinner. Paynes Bay. 432.1163

17 Fathoms Seafood and Bar ★★$$$ Shrimp and crab étouffée is a great starter here, and sautéed conch cutlets an ideal main course, but there's a wide selection of meat dishes (including some with local rabbit), too. The beachfront setting is casually elegant; patrons may dine inside or out. This place, a favorite of locals, is owned by the same folks as **Koko's** (see above). ♦ Seafood ♦ Daily lunch and dinner. Paynes Bay. 432.2568

BARBADOS' PREMIER
ALL-INCLUSIVE RESORTS

18 Almond Beach Club $$$$ A deluxe complex overlooking the beach, this all-inclusive resort features a fitness center, 3 freshwater pools, a squash court, a tennis court, 151 guest rooms, and a good continental restaurant. All-inclusive means just that—the rates here cover all meals and drinks (including alcoholic beverages), water sports, nightly live entertainment, island tours, taxes and tips, and transportation to the airport for departure. Guests can also dine at several Bajan restaurants at no additional charge. The children's program keeps young ones ages six and older happily occupied; no children under six are allowed. ♦ Sandy Lane. 432.7840, 800/4ALMOND; fax 432.2115

18 Sandy Lane Hotel $$$$ One of the best-known hotels in the Caribbean and the poshest in Barbados, this hostelry sits on a 380-acre former sugarcane plantation. There are 90 ultra-elegant guest rooms (each with a patio or balcony) and another 30 suites. The public areas all have marble and terrazzo floors. Other highlights: a half-mile crescent of beach, an 18-hole championship golf course, 5 tennis courts, a saltwater pool, a fitness center, and 2 restaurants (see below).

The room rate includes two meals per day. This is the place to rub elbows with the jet set; a Rolls-Royce will meet you at the airport, free of charge. ♦ Sandy Lane. 432.1311, 800/225.5843; fax 432.2954

Within the Sandy Lane Hotel:

Sandy Bay Restaurant ★★★$$$$ Fine cuisine is served in a luxurious setting at the more formal of the hotel's two restaurants. Chef Hans Schweitzer is famous for bringing such specialties to the menu as sautéed red snapper in a salt crust, and a "crown of asparagus" filled with lobster, shrimp, caviar, fresh vegetables, and herbs (the latter dish is taught at cooking classes held for resort guests in season). Honey and guava cheesecake and hot mango soufflé both make for a nice finishing touch to a meal. The restaurant also features a large wine list. There's a floor show on Tuesday nights. ♦ Continental ♦ Daily breakfast, lunch, and dinner. Reservations recommended. 432.1311

Seashell Restaurant ★★★$$$ Superlative service complements the well-prepared fare at this homey Italian restaurant. Entrées make good use of local seafood: There's manicotti stuffed with fresh crabmeat, and pasta primavera with grilled tuna. The scrumptious lunch buffet features homemade pasta, fruit and vegetable salads, fritters, and tropical desserts like Key lime and coconut cream pie. ♦ Italian/Seafood ♦ Daily lunch and dinner Dec-Apr; daily lunch May-Nov. Reservations required. 432.1311

19 Raffles Old Towne ★★★★$$$$ Outstanding island cuisine is served in a cozy dining spot with an exotic African decor. Dishes featuring local seafood spiked with homemade curries and chutneys are specialties. Don't miss the coconut pie for dessert. ♦ Caribbean ♦ Daily dinner. Reservations required. First St, Holetown. 432.6557

19 La Maison ★★★★$$$$ Popular with residents, this attractive seafood spot is set in a coral stone building on the beach. All the tables are outdoors, but don't worry about rain—white tents protect diners and their food. Specialties include panfried lobster in Sherry sauce and grilled dolphinfish with white wine and pesto. If you're not looking for an expensive dinner, stop for a drink at the elegant bar, fashioned of rich green Guyanese hardwood. ♦ Seafood ♦ Tu-Su lunch and dinner. Reservations recommended. Main Rd, Holetown. 432.1156

20 St. James Parish Church Built in 1630, this is one of the oldest churches in the Caribbean. Set on a cliff, it offers a dramatic view of the surf below. The exterior is especially striking when the poinsettia hedge is in bloom; the interior has a stone floor and lots of mahogany. Some of the headstones in the cemetery behind the church date from the 1600s. Ronald and Nancy Reagan attended Easter services here during an island visit in 1982. ♦ Hwy 1, Holetown. 422.4117

20 Monument to Holetown Settlers Captain John Powell landed the ship *Olive Blossom* here on 14 May 1625 and claimed the island for King James. This obelisk commemorates the event. The British settled here two years later. ♦ Hwy 1, Holetown

20 Discovery Bay Hotel $$$ A lovely beach setting and casual but elegant appointments distinguish this property, which has 88 rooms and 2 villas. There are also water sports and two tennis courts. Breakfast and dinner are served at the main restaurant, lunch at the poolside restaurant. ♦ Hwy 1, Holetown. 432.1301, 800/233.6510; fax 432.2553

Within the Discovery Bay Hotel:

Best of Barbados Shop Souvenirs and locally made goods are sold here, including prints by Jill Walker. Several other branches of this chain are located on the island. ♦ M-Sa. 422.3060

20 Settlers Beach Hotel $$$$ This resort gains a little cachet from its location near the point where the first British settlers set foot on Barbados. The 22 villas, set around a swimming pool, are popular with visitors from the UK. Each villa has two bedrooms, a living room/dining room, and kitchen. Lunch and dinner are available at the beach restaurant. ♦ Hwy 1, Holetown. 422.3052; fax 422.1937

20 Coral Reef Club $$$ Privacy is a major plus at this sister resort to the **Sandpiper Inn** (see below): Well-designed terraces, patios, and balconies are intimate outdoor hideaways. Set in a plantation-style building, the hotel is both beautiful and comfortable. There are 69 units of various sizes, including 6 deluxe suites and 4 superior rooms. Pool and water-sport facilities are quite good, and guests can use the two lighted tennis courts across the road at the **Sandpiper Inn.** Cocktail cruises aboard the club's 30-foot catamaran are another favorite activity. The restaurant offers a view of the sea and the hotel's garden. ♦ St. James Beach, Holetown. 422.2372, 800/223.1108, 800/ELEGANT; fax 422.1776

20 Colony Club Hotel $$$$ Here's a 98-room hotel that simply exudes tropical elegance. Casuarina trees shade the pretty beach and there's a swimming pool on the premises; snorkeling, waterskiing, and windsurfing, as well as Sunfish and catamaran rides are among the activities available. A meal plan is included in the rates from mid-December through early April; it is optional the rest of the year. ◆ St. James Beach, Holetown. 422.2335, 800/223.6510; fax 422.0667

Within the Colony Club Hotel:

Orchids ★★★$$$ An elegant chandelier-lit ambience and an attentive staff add to the charm at this restaurant, which has garnered rave reviews. Award-winning chef Sylvan Hervochon specializes in light *cuisine naturelle,* deftly employing local fruits, seafood, and vegetables to turn out international dishes served in view of tropical gardens and the ocean. Tableside flambés add excitement. ◆ Continental ◆ Daily dinner. 422.2335

20 Folkstone Marine Park A place for recreation and scientific study, this park is divided into four activity-specific zones: a popular picnic area, a snorkeling trail on nearby Dottins Reef, an aquarium, and exhibits of marine antiques including maps, logs, and compasses. Stop by the **Visitors' Center** to see displays of shells and marine life as well as films and videos about the park. ◆ Admission. Daily. Hwy 1, Holetown. 422.2871

20 Sandpiper Inn $$$ Tennis, complimentary water sports, and access to the nearby **Sandy Lane Hotel Golf Course** make this 45-room hotel a perfect getaway for active vacationers. The restaurant (see below) prepares local foods with finesse. ◆ Hwy 1, Holetown. 422.2251; fax 422.1776

Within the Sandpiper Inn:

Sandpiper Inn Restaurant ★★★$$$ This restaurant has won awards in annual competitions sponsored by the Caribbean Hotel Association and the Caribbean Culinary Federation. Sample such specialties as stuffed eggplant; potato pancakes topped with smoked salmon, caviar, and sour cream; Caribbean fish soup; and, for dessert, a wonderful walnut and coconut tart. ◆ Caribbean ◆ Daily lunch and dinner. 422.2251

21 Château Créole ★★$$$ Seasonings and spices get great play here in shrimp remoulade (cold shrimp, mayonnaise, mustard, and pickles), crab *diablo* (seasoned with hot spices and stuffed back into the crab shell), pumpkin soup, and a variety of mouthwatering Creole and island specialties. ◆ French/Creole ◆ M-Sa dinner. Reservations recommended. Hwy 1, Alleynes Bay. 422.4116

21 Glitter Bay $$$$ The name of this 89-suite resort says it all. Lots of white marble sets off all that glitters (and there's plenty that does), but lovely watercolor paintings soften the decor, and the landscaping is spectacular. The property once belonged to Sir Edward Cunard of the shipping family, and his estate's guest house now contains five luxury suites for those who seek posh privacy. Afternoon tea is a daily ritual at this property nestled along a gentle beach and boasting a swimming pool, two tennis courts, and lovely boutiques. ◆ Hwy 1, Alleynes Bay. 422.4111; fax 422.1367

Within Glitter Bay:

Piperade ★★★$$$ This open-air restaurant features nightly entertainment and a European and Bajan menu. Try the chef's pâté, a roti (curried chicken wrapped in an Indian pancake), callaloo, or even a thin-crust pizza. ◆ West Indian/Continental ◆ Daily breakfast, lunch, and dinner. Reservations recommended. 422.4111

21 Royal Pavilion $$$$ The sister resort and next-door neighbor to **Glitter Bay** has plenty of its own glitz and glamour. In addition to 75 oceanfront guest rooms, there are 2 tennis courts, a pool, a restaurant (see below), and a snack bar. Water sports are included in the rate. ◆ Hwy 1, Alleynes Bay. 422.4444; fax 422.0118

Within the Royal Pavilion:

Palm Terrace ★★$$$ This casually elegant restaurant serves British-inspired Caribbean dishes such as veal stuffed with panfried crab, and passion-fruit pudding. A fashionable spot, it often attracts celebrities. ◆ Continental ◆ Daily breakfast, lunch, and dinner. Reservations recommended. 422.4444

22 Mullins Beach Bar & Restaurant ★$ Lunch on flying fish and salad niçoise at this outdoor eatery overlooking the bay. Then shell out an extra Bd$5 for a beach chair and plop down on the sand right outside for a siesta. ◆ Continental/Caribbean ◆ Daily breakfast, lunch, and dinner. Mullins. 422.1878

23 Kings Beach Hotel $$$ This attractive beachfront hotel has 57 rooms, each boasting a terrace or patio. There's a restaurant serving continental and Bajan specialties on the premises, and guests can enjoy the pool and variety of water sports. ◆ Road View, Speightstown. 422.1690; fax 422.1691

24 Sandridge Beach Hotel $$ Popular with visitors from the UK, this hotel's 58 units range from single rooms to deluxe 1-bedroom suites, all with balconies or patios. Some duplexes have kitchenettes and TVs. Amenities include a restaurant, a white-sand beach, a beach bar, a pool, a children's pool, and complimentary water sports. There are two tennis courts, and matches can be arranged. ♦ Road View, Speightstown. 422.2361; fax 422.1965

24 Cobblers Cove $$$$ Owned by a British couple, Hamish and Linda Watson, this 40-suite hotel is a member of the tony Relais & Châteaux group. Reminiscent of a quaint hotel in the British countryside, complete with a charming lounge for tea or reading, it's perfect for a romantic getaway. Three of the suites offer such deluxe extras as marble floors, four-poster beds, whirlpool baths, and a small private rooftop swimming pool. The beautiful beach is just steps away from the red-tile pool and bar, and the property also offers a complete water-sports program, a lighted tennis court, and guest privileges at the **Royal Westmoreland** golf course. Although all rooms have kitchenettes, most guests prefer to enjoy fine continental and Bajan specialties in the hotel dining room (see below). ♦ Road View, Speightstown. 422.2291, 800/890.6060; fax 422.1460

Within Cobblers Cove:

Cobblers Cove Restaurant ★★★$$$ Dine on *fritto misto* (dorado, shrimp, flying fish, and calamari, lightly breaded, fried, and served with a tangy tomato sauce) or sautéed leeks wrapped in puff pastry with leek sauce in this elegant dining room with a terrace overlooking the sea. Live music accompanies dinner on Tuesday, Thursday, and Saturday. ♦ Continental/Bajan ♦ Daily breakfast, lunch, and dinner. 422.2291

25 Almond Beach Village $$$ Formerly known as **Heywoods,** the name of the owners of the sugar plantation that once stood on this site, this 288-room luxury resort is located on the island's scenic northern end. The original mill remains, and the 30-acre complex is beautifully landscaped with tropical gardens. Set on a milelong white beach with water sports, it boasts nine swimming pools, five lighted tennis courts, a crafts market, beachfront shopping arcade, and a wide range of bars and restaurants. ♦ Speightstown. 422.4900, 800/4ALMOND; fax 422.0617

26 Farley Hill National Park Just across from the **Barbados Wildlife Reserve,** this giant park contains ruins of an old great house, which was the location of the filming of the movie *Island in the Sun*. Don't forget

to bring a camera—the breathtaking views from here extend all the way to the wild and rocky east coast and also reach due north to the island's Scotland District. ♦ Admission. Daily. Hwy 1 (southeast of Portland). 422.3555

27 Barbados Wildlife **Reserve** Monkeys, tortoises, iguanas, and other animals native to Barbados and other Caribbean islands roam freely through four acres of mahogany forest. A few are caged—parrots and pythons, for example—but otherwise visitors are cautioned to keep alert as they walk through the grounds. ♦ Admission. Daily. Hwy 1 (southeast of Portland). 422.8826

28 Harrison's Cave These vast subterranean caverns are served by a tram (no twisted ankles in these caves, thank you). The fabulous waterfalls, streams, pools, and stalagmites and stalactites in the limestone caverns will leave you awestruck. ♦ Admission. Daily. Reservations recommended. South of Hwy 2, Welchman Hall. 438.6640

29 Flower Forest The flowers on this old sugar plantation provide a feast for the eyes as well as the soul. See more than a hundred species in the forest, including ginger lilies, puffball trees, and a variety of ferns, orchids, and palm trees spread over eight acres. Follow the signs to **Harrison's Cave,** then follow "Flower Forest" signs from there to where the St. Thomas, St. Joseph, and St. Andrew parishes meet. ♦ Admission. Daily. Richmond Rd, Melvin Hill. 433.8152

30 Barclay's Park Named for the British bank folks who created this charming and scenic picnic area right along the wild, wave-lashed coast, the 50-acre park commemorates the island's independence in 1966. For an extra treat, take along a gourmet lunch and a bottle of Champagne. ♦ East Coast Rd (between Bathsheba and Hwy 2)

Within Barclay's Park:

Barclay's Park Snackette $ Snacks and cold drinks are refreshing, and the view is unbeatable. Casuarina trees bent almost in half by strong coastal winds make a dramatic setting for photographers. ♦ Snacks ♦ Daily. 422.9976

31 Kingsley Inn ★★$ Enjoy cool drinks on the veranda at this former private club for plantation owners. Now the congenial little restaurant welcomes everyone, and the fixed-price lunches are a delicious deal. Baked yam casserole and coconut meringue pie are among the specialties. ♦ Caribbean ♦ Daily breakfast, lunch, and dinner. East Coast Rd, Cattlewash. 433.9422

Getting Your Feet Wet in Barbados

Everyone who comes to Barbados should take advantage of the beautiful blue waters. Most hotels and resorts offer water sports and beachfront boat and equipment rentals. Some other organizations that can get you afloat are:

Boating

Barbados Yacht Club Bay Street (south of Trafalgar Sq), Bridgetown. 427.1125

Harbor Master Cruises The Wharf (west of Trafalgar Sq), Bridgetown. 430.0900

Tiami Catamaran Cruises Bridge House, Cavans La (west of Bay St), Bridgetown. 427.7245

Snorkeling and Scuba Diving

Dive Boat Safari Barbados Hilton, Hilton Rd (west of Hwy 7), Needham's Point. 427.4350, 429.8216 evenings

The Dive Shop Hwy 7 (south of Bridgetown). 426.9947, 426.2031 evenings

Exploresub Barbados St. Lawrence. 435.6542

Hightide Watersports Sandy Lane Hotel, Sandy Lane. 432.0931

Reefers & Wreckers Kings Beach Hotel, Road View, Speightstown. 422.5450

Underwater Barbados Scuba Diving Shop
Bay St (south of Trafalgar Sq), Bridgetown. 426.0655; Coconut Court Beach Hotel, Hastings. 435.6415

Willie's Water Sports Holetown. 432.5980

Sportfishing

Blue Jay Charters Waterfront Cafe, Cavans La and Bay St, Bridgetown. 422.2098

Blue Marlin Charters 1 Golf Club Rd, Christ Church. 436.4322

Windsurfing

Club Mistral Barbados Butterfly Beach, Christ Church. 428.7277

Silver Rock Silver Sands Beach, St. Lawrence. 420.8558

32 Bathsheba This broad beach, a favorite with Bajan surfers, is pounded by Atlantic waves. Visitors will enjoy the dramatic view, but there are no lifeguards on duty, so this is no place to swim alone. ♦ Bathsheba

32 Edgewater Hotel $ There's a Spanish feel to this once-private home. The building is more than a hundred years old, and the old furniture recalls earlier times. There are 20 rooms, some with remarkable views of the island's east coast. The restaurant serves breakfast, lunch, and dinner. ♦ Bathsheba. 433.9900; fax 432.9902

32 Bonito Bar and Diner ★★$ Owned by Enid Worrell, this second-floor establishment overlooking the beach and boulders offers a superb value. Flying fish, potato pie, rice and peas, and *cou cou* (cornmeal pudding with okra) are among the house specialties. ♦ Caribbean ♦ Daily lunch. Reservations recommended. Bathsheba. 433.9034

33 Andromeda Botanic Gardens These gardens on a coral cliff were created in the mid-1950s by Iris Bannochie on land her family had owned for more than two centuries. Among the thousands of plants on six terraced acres are tropical bougainvillea, hibiscus, heliconia, orchids, palms, cacti, and succulents. Bannochie created a wild and wonderful world of flora that anyone—especially shutterbugs and those with green thumbs—can enjoy. ♦ Admission. Daily. St. Elizabeth. 433.9261

33 Atlantis Hotel $$ Once a simple family guest house, this 15-room inn dates back to

1882. Some rooms have private balconies overlooking the flower gardens or the ocean. ♦ St. Elizabeth. 433.9445

Within the Atlantis Hotel:

Atlantis Restaurant ★★$$ This seaside establishment is best known these days for its outstanding West Indian buffet on Sunday, including pepper pot, fried fish, okra, pumpkin fritters, fried plantains, and pickled bananas. At other times the restaurant serves fried fish and baked chicken seasoned with West Indian spices. ♦ Seafood/Bajan ♦ Daily breakfast, lunch, and dinner. Reservations required on Sunday. 433.9445

34 St. John's Parish Church The beautiful Bajan/Anglican architecture of this church, built in the mid-1600s, is complemented by a spectacular view of the east coast. The pulpit contains six kinds of wood: ebony, locust, mahogany, manchineel, oak, and pine. In the cemetery outside, look for the gravestone of the man who has gone to "dance again in Heavy to a Bajan beat." There's a souvenir and refreshment shop on the grounds. ♦ Hwy 3B, Glebe Land. No phone

35 Barbados Zoological Park and Oughterson Plantation A combination zoo and botanical garden set on an old sugar plantation, this place is populated by monkeys, birds, and goats. There's also a petting zoo for children. At the center of the park is a great house containing antiques and other interesting items. ♦ Admission. Daily. Hwy 4B (east of Church Village). 423.6203

36 Marriott's Sam Lord's Castle $$$
Notorious pirate Sam Lord built the 19th-century castle that is the centerpiece of this full-service complex—at 72 acres, the largest resort on Barbados. Set on a cliff overlooking the Atlantic, the National Trust House is a shady legacy from the "Regency Rascal." It's filled with his personal collection of art, antiques, and other loot valued at over $1 million—much of the castle was financed and furnished from the 22 ships Lord lured onto Cobblers Reef below. According to legend, Lord ordered his slaves to string lanterns among the palm trees, so that passing captains would think they had arrived at the entrance to Carlisle Harbor in Bridgetown. As the reef tore into the ships' hulls, Lord's pirates would swarm aboard to claim their booty. Today, guests may book one of the castle's 10 bedrooms (perhaps Sam's own suite, with his four-poster bed and massive wardrobe), all furnished with the original mahogany antiques from England. Thoroughly modern facilities are just a few steps away (shielded from castle views), including 233 contemporary guest rooms and suites, a milelong beach, 7 lighted tennis courts, 3 pools, a health club, movie room, and 4 restaurants. Sightseers are welcome to visit the castle's public areas, and the entire resort is open to nonguests for a small admission fee. ♦ Long Bay. 423.7350, 888/765.6737; fax 423.5918

Within Marriott's Sam Lord's Castle:

The Wanderer ★★$$ Buffet breakfasts are served here, and Sam's Sunday Feast is an island favorite. There's music every night except Monday and Thursday. ♦ American ♦ Daily breakfast, lunch, and dinner. 423.7350

The Sea Grille ★★$$$ Local fishers sell their daily catch to this large restaurant, which also offers fine service. Selections depend upon what's been hooked or netted, but usually include grouper, snapper, and local lobster. ♦ Seafood ♦ Daily dinner. 423.7350

36 Castle Grill ★$$ The place is popular with locals and tourists, who come for the local fare. Menu highlights include pumpkin fritters, codfish cakes, roti, fried chicken with herbs, Bajan flying fish, and island seafood curry (with flying fish, kingfish, and shrimp). ♦ Caribbean ♦ Daily breakfast, lunch, and dinner. Long Bay. 423.5674

37 Crane Beach Frequently named among the world's best, this southern beach is lined with pink-tinged coral sand and floodlit at night. The long-range ocean views are breathtaking. The Atlantic waves are big, but lifeguards stand watch. Water sports, chaises, food, and drink are available at the Crane Beach Hotel. ♦ Southeast coast

37 Ginger Bay Beach Club $$$ The hotel has 16 rooms, all washed by delightful ocean breezes that cool things down even during the summer. Much of the furniture is Barbadian mahogany. The atmosphere is wonderfully laid-back and social life centers around a pool and tennis court. There are even signs to remind you that you are a million miles from home and 35 kilometers (22 miles) from the closest traffic jam. ♦ Crane Beach. 423.5810, 800/223.9815; fax 423.6629

Within the Ginger Bay Beach Club:

Ginger's Restaurant ★$$ Flying fish tops the list of Bajan specialties on the menu at this pretty open-air restaurant. A Caribbean buffet is featured Sunday. ♦ Caribbean ♦ Daily breakfast, lunch, and dinner. 423.5810

38 Crane Beach Hotel $$$ The 25 rooms and apartments have views and breezes that are the envy of most Caribbean properties. The sand is like sugar and the ocean is an indescribable blue; the water is much wilder here. The hotel opened its doors in 1867, so guests can enjoy its history as well as beauty. Don't miss the fabled Roman pool, a swell backdrop for photographers. The entire setting is magnificent. ♦ Crane Beach. 423.6220; fax 423.5343

Within the Crane Beach Hotel:

The Panoramic Restaurant ★★★$$$ They say this is the most romantic location in Barbados—it's certainly one of the most beautiful. Set high above the same waters in which lobster and other seafood are caught daily for the hotel's chef, the restaurant also overlooks Crane Beach. ♦ Seafood ♦ Daily breakfast, lunch, afternoon tea, and dinner. Reservations recommended. 423.6220

Bests

Professor Henry Fraser
President, Barbados National Trust/Professor, University of the West Indies/Author

Any of the 15 places in the Barbados Heritage Passport, because this passport provides "cut-price" entry into the best of the uniquely rich historic pageantry of Barbados.

Harrison's Cave—the subterranean wonder of the Caribbean, with awesome caverns, stalactites, streams, and waterfalls.

The **Barbados Museum and Historical Society,** in an ancient garrison building, and the restored **Barbados Synagogue** in **Bridgetown** (1658, rebuilt in 1833) are astonishing gems.

Bathsheba—the nearest place to perfection in this sad world. Eat kingfish cutters at **Kingsley Inn** or have a sumptuous buffet at the **Atlantis Hotel.**

All of the beautiful bays and cliffs along the designated **East Coast National Park.**

St. John's Parish Church—holy of holies, high on **Hackleton's Cliff,** surveying the entire east coast.

A wander through Bridgetown, from the bustle of the markets to the cool comfort of the **Waterfront Cafe.**

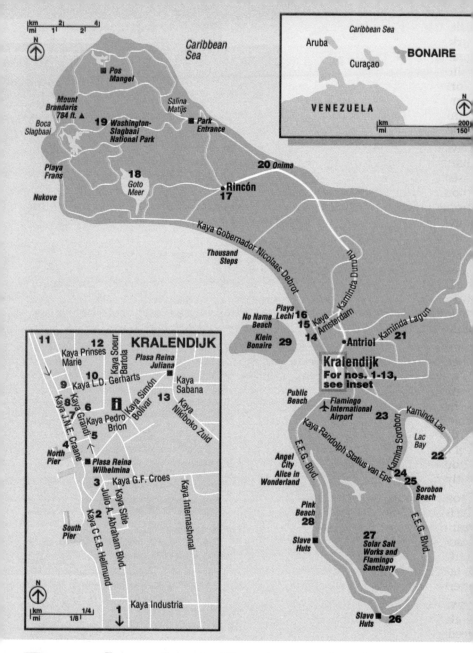

Bonaire

Created millions of years ago by volcanic eruptions, the boomerang-shaped island of Bonaire is actually the crest of a submerged mountain, fringed by sloping reefs that remain unscarred by pollution or poachers. Island license plates read "A Diver's Paradise" and that's not just local boosterism. Here, expert divers and first-time snorkelers can wade right into one of the world's premier underwater environments, an award-winning marine sanctuary lush with undisturbed coral and bursting with brilliant jewel fish, red-lip blennies, and parrot fish.

Long before "eco-tourism" was even a gleam in some marketing specialist's eye, Bonaireans drafted laws to protect their natural habitat, both above and beneath the sea. In 1971, all surrounding waters were designated a marine preserve, with strict industrial regulations and bans on spearfishing and coral collecting. At the island's northwest corner, **Washington-Slagbaai National Park** sprawls over 13,500 acres, home to wild goats, indigenous blue lizards, iguanas, and 190 species of birds. Down at the southern tip of the island, visitors can observe "eco-friendly" solar salt production at the **Solar Salt Works and Flamingo Sanctuary**, owned by the Antilles International Salt Company, a major local moneymaker that shares turf with some 11,000 flamingos that use the area as their nesting grounds. The flamingo head count peaks at around 15,000 during breeding season (March through May).

Arawak Indians inhabited this arid landscape for centuries before it was charted in 1499 by Amerigo Vespucci; he gave the island its name, which is based on the Indian word *bojnay* (low land). Spain made several attempts to colonize Bonaire before it was claimed by the Dutch in 1634 as a military stronghold; two years later it officially became a Dutch colony. Soon after, the Dutch West India Company imported 100 African slaves to work on salt, corn, and livestock enterprises here.

For the next two centuries, French and British pirates plied the coast, repeatedly raiding the island. The British took over Bonaire for a time until the Dutch reclaimed it permanently in 1816. Slavery was abolished in 1863 and as a result Bonaire's economy suffered. Without free slave labor, government-run salt production became unprofitable, and by the beginning of this century many locals left to work in neighboring islands.

But the sleepy little island finally found its most valuable resource—diving—when its first hotel opened in 1951. Though only 24 miles long and 7 miles at its widest point, Bonaire boasts more than 80 dive spots. Here beyond the hurricane belt there are no big storms to damage the reefs and, with only 12 inches of rain annually, no freshwater runoff to cloud undersea visibility—which averages 100 feet and frequently is more than 150 feet. Less than a mile offshore, the tiny island of **Klein Bonaire** (Little Bonaire) acts like a barrier reef to create calm leeward seas. Excellent walk-in dive sites are located at **Thousand Steps** and farther north at **Nukove**. The average boat trip to outlying sites takes 15 minutes, with the most remote reachable in an hour.

Those who prefer land-based adventures can rent a bicycle or moped to visit the island's lighthouses, colorful obelisks, and slave huts; go see the 500-plus-year-old Arawak inscriptions at **Onima**; sunbathe at the clothing-optional beach at **Sorobon**; or sample cactus soup at local eateries. Other possible activities include going to the **Green Parrot** to watch the green flash at sunset or taking an excursion aboard the *Samur,* an exotic 56-foot Siamese junk that offers sunset, moonlight, snorkeling, and barbecue sails.

All visitors should set aside a few minutes for shopping and sight-seeing in **Kralendijk** (pronounced *Krawl*-in-dike). But a few minutes is really all that's needed—the tiny capital is made up of just a handful of streets.

To call from the US, dial 011 (the international access code), 5997 (the country code), and the 4-digit local number. On Bonaire, dial only the 4-digit number unless otherwise indicated.

Getting to the Island

Airlines
Air Aruba 7880, 800/882.7822
ALM (Antillean Airlines)..8300, 8500, 800/327.7230
American Airlines 800/433.7300
KLM Royal Dutch Airlines.............................
................................5352, 5350, 800/374.7747

Interisland Carriers
Air Aruba 7880, 800/882.7822
ALM (Antillean Airlines)..8300, 8500, 800/327.7230

Airport Flamingo International Airport (5600), a 5-minute drive from the main city of **Kralendijk**, has an 8,100-foot runway that services international jets.

Getting Around the Island

Bicycles and Motorbikes
Avanti Scooters 5661
Cycle Bonaire 7558

Car Rental

A.B. Car Rentals	8980
Avis	5795, 800/331.1085
Budget	7424, 8315, 800/472.3325
Island Car Rentals	5111
Tropical Car Rental	8313

Driving US, Canadian, and European driver's licenses are valid; drivers must be at least 21 years old. Roads are in good condition, but narrow.

Taxis Prices are fixed, but agree on a fare in advance. To order a cab, call the **Central Dispatcher** (8100).

Tours A variety of island tours are offered by **Ayubi's Tours** (5338), **Baranka Tours** (2200), and **Bonaire Sightseeing** (8778).

FYI

Electricity The current is 127 volts/50 cycles. US appliances will work—slowly—but a converter is recommended.

Entry Requirements US and Canadian citizens must present a valid passport or other proof of citizenship (birth certificate, voter's registration card) and a photo ID, plus a return or onward ticket.

Gambling The **Plaza Resort Bonaire** (80 Julio A. Abraham Blvd, between Kayas Internashonal and Industria, Kralendijk, 2500) opens its casino at noon each day and the fun around the slot machines and blackjack tables continues until 2AM. The **Divi Flamingo Beach** resort (40 Julio A. Abraham Blvd, at Kaya Industria, Kralendijk, 8285) also has a casino, but at press time both the resort and casino were closed and no reopening date had been announced.

Language The official language is Dutch, but most islanders speak English, Spanish, and Papiamento, the local patois.

Money The official currency is the Netherlands Antilles florin (NAf or guilder), but US dollars and credit cards are widely accepted. Banks are open Monday through Friday from 8:30AM to 4PM.

Personal Safety There's no reason for concern, but exercise normal precautions; i.e., don't leave valuables lying around the beach.

Publications *Bonaire Holiday* is published three times a year; designed for visitors, it lists lodging, restaurant, and shopping information, and is available at the tourist office, the airport, and hotels. Two small magazines, *Bonaire Affair* and *Bonaire Nights,* with information on entertainment and attractions, are also distributed free at hotels, restaurants, and the airport They are both published annually.

Reservation Services and House Rentals The **Tourism Corporation of Bonaire** (see "Visitors' Information Office" below) has a list of hotels and rental properties.

Shopping Hours Most stores on the island are closed from noon to 2PM each day. Shops in Kralendijk stay open until 9PM on Friday; on other nights they close at 6PM.

Taxes A government room tax will increase your hotel bill by US$4.50 per person per night. Car rentals are taxed at $3 per day. A $10 departure tax must be paid at the airport.

Tipping Most hotels and restaurants add a service charge of 10 to 15 percent of the bill to cover staff tipping. Unless some special service has been provided, it's not necessary to leave an additional tip Give porters and bellhops 50¢ per bag (but never les than $1 total). Tipping cab drivers is not mandatory, but up to 10 percent of the fare is appreciated.

Visitors' Information Office The **Tourism Corporation of Bonaire** (12 Kaya Simón Bolívar, between Kaya Hermandad and Plasa Reina Juliana, Kralendijk, 8322, 8649; fax 8408) is open Monday through Friday from 8AM to 1PM and 1:30 to 5PM.

Phone Book

Ambulance	11
Directory Assistance	19
Diving Emergencies/Decompression Chambers	14
Emergencies	11
Fire	11
Hospital	14
Police	11
Post Office	8508

Kralendijk

The town's name (it means "coral dike") comes from its setting on a dike of coral rock in a natural harbor. Most evenings, residents can be found strolling the waterfront promenade. Except for the fashionable shops and restaurants that have sprung up along its main streets, this tiny capital city looks much as it did when it was founded in 1810. The streets are narrow and the Dutch Colonial buildings are still painted a distinctive mustard yellow or in the bright pastels that are so popular throughout the Caribbean.

1 Plaza Resort Bonaire ★★★★$$$
Guests can choose between accommodations facing the ocean or off a beach-lined lagoon at this Dutch-owned complex featuring 224 rooms, suites, and 1- and 2-bedroom villas. The Mediterranean-style resort is casual, but that doesn't mean no-frills. All the guest rooms are well stocked with amenities—cable TV, air-conditioning, in-room safes, and telephones—and the villas have full kitchens, complete with dishwashers and microwaves. A swimming pool, four tennis courts, water-sports facilities, a fully licensed dive shop, and a fitness center are available for the athletically inclined. Three restaurants and a casino complete the picture. ♦ 80 Julio A.

Abraham Blvd (between Kayas Internashonal and Industria). 2500, 800/766.6016; fax 7133

Within the Plaza Resort Bonaire:

Caribbean Point ★★★$$$ This elegant restaurant specializes in French cuisine with a Caribbean twist and boasts a tantalizing array of seafood dishes. It's a perfect stop before trying your luck at the hotel casino or strolling along the beach at the resort. ◆ French ◆ Daily dinner. Reservations recommended. 2500

1 Carib Inn $ Bruce Bowker, one of the first expats to crash the local scuba scene, expanded his dive operation in this former private home to include an easygoing complex of seven simple rooms (five with full kitchens), one large one-bedroom suite with sea view and kitchen, and one two-bedroom suite. Predictably, the guests are mostly divers. This congenial inn, complete with pool and patio, is one of the island's best buys. ◆ Julio A. Abraham Blvd (between Kayas Internashonal and Industrial). 8819; fax 5295

1 Richard's ★★$$ Boaters tie up at the pier out front and go inside for a seafood fix. Locals love the shrimp primavera, the hands-down favorite at this indoor/outdoor bistro enhanced with tropical landscaping. While waiting for a table, consider stopping for a drink or two at the bar. ◆ Seafood ◆ Tu-Su dinner. Reservations recommended. 60 Julio A. Abraham Blvd (between Kayas Internashonal and Industria). 5263

2 Klein Bonaire Restaurant ★★$ With a veranda facing the ocean, this funky eatery is right in the middle of the action (such as it is) in sleepy Kralendijk. Situated in an old home, the restaurant is perfumed with rich cappuccino when it opens each morning. Lunch and dinner options range from sumptuous vegetarian platters to succulent seafood. It's also a good place to stop in for an icy beer between swimming and shopping. ◆ American/Caribbean ◆ Daily breakfast, lunch, and dinner. 5 Kaya Charles E.B. Hellmund (south of Plasa Reina Wilhelmina). 8617

3 Fundashon Arte Boneriano Support local crafters by sending home a few souvenirs from this not-for-profit workshop and gallery. The post office is right next door. ◆ M-Sa. Julio A. Abraham Blvd (just south of Plasa Reina Wilhelmina). No phone

4 Fish Market Directly on the waterfront, this is a popular place for locals and visitors alike. As its now-dated name suggests, the open-air market surrounded by Romanesque stone arches was once used to sell local fish. But some years back, the fish were replaced by fresh fruits and vegetables (and sometimes crafts) brought over from Venezuela. The best day to come is Tuesday, when the most boats are in and the greatest variety of merchandise is on display. ◆ Daily. Kaya J.N.E. Craane (north of Plasa Reina Wilhelmina)

A Birder's Paradise

Best known for its flamingos, Bonaire is also home to 189 other feathered species. The abundance of birds here makes the annual Bonaire Birdwatching Olympics and Nature Week, established in 1992, a fun event for both experienced and fledgling birders.

Held in late September—a peak bird migration period for the region—the weeklong competition gives participants access to private property and extended hours at the 13,500-acre **Washington-Slagbaai National Park.** Sightings often include the rare Caribbean elania, the Amazona parrot, and Bonaire's unique Caribbean parakeet. Top spotters are presented with gold, silver, and bronze medals at a special awards dinner. Eco-tours and other special events are scheduled islandwide throughout the week.

At the island's southwest tip, visitors can usually view the island's famous pink flamingos near their home at the **Solar Salt Works and Flamingo Sanctuary.** When conservation efforts began here, there were only four nesting grounds for flamingos in the world and about 1,500 of these birds on Bonaire. Today the sanctuary remains one of the world's few flamingo breeding sites, but the local bird population soars to 15,000 during some periods of the year. Another place to spot this beautiful species is on **Goto Meer,** in the northwestern part of the island.

5 Best Buddies Caribbean fashions in tropical prints for men, women, and children are the big sellers at this delightful local shop. There are two locations on the same street. ♦ M-Sa. 13 Kaya Grandi (between Kayas Simón Bolívar and Pedro Brion). 7570 Also at: 32 Kaya Grandi (north of Plasa Reina Wilhelmina). 7570

6 Dalila Indonesian carvings star in a colorful inventory of local and imported clothing and crafts. ♦ M-Sa. Just east of Kaya Grandi (between Kayas Pedro Brion and L.D. Gerharts). No phone

7 Caribbean Arts & Crafts Here's another opportunity to help fund the local arts scene: Black-coral crafts are a specialty, along with sterling silver jewelry and stone carvings. You'll also find some Mexican onyx and Peruvian tapestries. Note: If you want a black-coral souvenir, buy one at this certified shop—it's against the law for nonauthorized divers to gather it themselves. Be sure to obtain an exporting permit, as you may be prevented from bringing your purchase into the US without one. ♦ M-Sa. 38A Kaya Grandi (north of Plasa Reina Wilhelmina). 5051

7 Karel's Beach Bar The bar is always active, but this waterfront hangout really comes alive with reggae, soca, and dance bands on Friday and Saturday nights. ♦ Daily. Kaya J.N.E. Craane (north of Plasa Reina Wilhelmina). 8434

8 Little Holland Beachwear, blue delft, and linens imported from Europe abound here, but the big lure is the cedar cigar room where stogies from around the region—including Cuba—are on sale. You'll have to smoke the Cuban cigars here, as it is illegal to bring them into the US. ♦ M-Sa. Harborside Mall, Kaya Grandi (north of Plasa Reina Wilhelmina). 5670

9 Croccantino ★★★$$ Have a craving for pasta? Head straight to this charming Italian eatery, where homemade linguine and fettucine serve as the base for tantalizing sauces. A good wine list complements the menu, which also includes a fine selection of seafood options. ♦ Italian ♦ Daily lunch and dinner. Reservations recommended. 48 Kaya Grandi (north of Plasa Reina Wilhelmina). 5025

10 Rendez-Vous ★$ Vegetarians will find a good selection at this relaxed cafe, which also serves grilled seafood, steak, salads, and desserts. All meals begin with freshly baked French bread and garlic butter. For a quick reviver, step up to the bar for a fresh-steamed espresso or cappuccino. ♦ American ♦ M-Sa lunch and dinner. Reservations recommended. 3 Kaya L.D. Gerharts (between Kayas Prinses Marie and Grandi). 8454, 7261

11 Club Nautico Bonaire $$$$ The historic home that now serves as this hotel's clubhouse was once the residence of the Dutch governor in Bonaire. Situated right on the downtown waterfront and boasting its own pool, marina, and private pier (making it a favorite with water-sports fans and fisherfolk), the small complex of buildings houses 16 airy suites with balconies and kitchens. For those not inclined to do their own cooking, there's a restaurant and a coffee shop, as well as a bar for guests. ♦ 29 Kaya J.N.E. Craane (at Kaya Den Tera). 5800; fax 5850

12 Blue Iguana $ In keeping with the name, a giant blue lizard is painted on the entrance to this cozy bed-and-breakfast. West Indian antiques adorn the seven guest rooms, all thoughtfully equipped with ceiling fans and mosquito netting; none, however, have private bathrooms. Breakfast is included in the rate, and guests are free to use the kitchen to cook other meals (clean-up is de rigueur!). The hammocks in the courtyard are also nice perks. The yellow, two-story building dates back at least 100 years, and the charming owner loves to regale visitors with tales of Bonaire past. ♦ 6 Kaya Prinses Marie (between Kayas L.D. Gerharts and Grandi). 6855; fax 6855

13 Mi Poron ★★★$ Local dishes, including stewed goat, conch, and fresh fried fish are served in the breezy courtyard of this historic Bonairean home. On the way in or out of the restaurant, take a peek at the area set aside as a countryside "museum." It is graced with Bonairean furniture and artifacts from days gone by; souvenirs and postcards are for sale. ♦ Caribbean ♦ Tu-Sa lunch and dinner; Su dinner. No credit cards accepted. 1 Kaya Caracas (at Kaya Nikiboko Zuid). 5199

Slavery was finally abolished in Britain's Caribbean colonies in 1833, in the French colonies in 1848, in the Dutch colonies in 1863, in Puerto Rico in 1873, and in Cuba in 1880.

Restaurants/Clubs: Red   **Hotels:** Blue
Shops/♥ Outdoors: Green
     Sights/Culture: Black

Elsewhere on the Island

14 Harbour Village Beach $$$$ The top property on the island, this resort boasts posh accommodations, a pool, a spa, a tennis court, a marina, and its own beach. The 64 rooms and suites are air-conditioned, with white ceramic tile floors, telephones, and cable TV. French doors open onto balconies or patios that overlook either the beach or the full-service marina. The spa offers everything from Bonaire salt exfoliation to massages (with special packages for divers) and facials. There are also mountain bike excursions and water aerobics. The property has three restaurants (including **Kasa Coral**) and a bar. ◆ Kaya Gobernador Nicolaas Debrot (just south of Kaya Amsterdam). 7500, 800/424.0004; fax 7507

Within Harbour Village Beach:

Kasa Coral ★★$$$ The alfresco break-fast buffet is much like those you'll find back home, but the lunch menu is big on local favorites. Fixed-price dinners include a familiar assortment of dishes, ranging from fresh seafood to rack of lamb. ◆ American/ Caribbean ◆ Daily breakfast, lunch, and dinner. Reservations recommended. 7500

14 Sunset Beach $$ A member of the Golden Tulip chain, this comfortable old two-story hotel offers 145 rooms and suites, a superb beach (with a pavilion for lunch), a swimming pool, 3 whirlpools, 2 lighted tennis courts, mini-golf, a playground, boutiques, a restaurant (see below), 2 bars, and a coffee shop. **Dive-Inn** (8761) administers the on-site water- sports program. This is a popular overnight stop for tour groups. ◆ Kayas Gobernador Nicolaas Debrot and Amsterdam. 8291, 800/328.2280; fax 5320

Within Sunset Beach:

Playa Lechi ★★$$ Stop by any Saturday for the weekly "Bonairean Night," when guests can sample a buffet of local specialties while enjoying a floor show and live music. Otherwise, this open-air beachfront restaurant is known for surf-and-turf standards and barbecues on Thursday and Friday nights. ◆ American/Caribbean ◆ Daily dinner. Reservations recommended on weekends. 5300

15 Den Laman ★★$$ The aquarium decor is calming, the bar is congenial, and local seafood is fresh off the boat. Choose your victim from the lobster tank or order one of the four types of local fish prepared each night. The housemade cheesecake and salad bar are noteworthy, too. A special menu of criollo cuisine is offered Wednesday and Sunday; dance bands and other entertainment are scheduled on Saturday. ◆ Seafood ◆ M, W-Su dinner. Reservations recommended. Kaya Gobernador Nicolaas Debrot (just north of Kaya Amsterdam). 8955

15 Sand Dollar Condominium Resort $$$ The beach disappears at high tide, but this cheerful place is still very popular, especially with young families. The 72 air-conditioned apartments have full kitchens and from 1 to 3 bedrooms. Also on the premises are the **Green Parrot** cafe (see below), the **PADI** five-star **Sand Dollar Dive and Photo Shop** (5252), a tennis court, a pool, a grocery store, and water-sports facilities. ◆ Kaya Gobernador Nicolaas Debrot (just north of Kaya Amsterdam). 8738, 617/821.1012, 800/228.4773; fax 8760

Within the Sand Dollar Condominium Resort:

Green Parrot ★★$$ Watch for the fabled green flash at sunset from this beachfront cafe, where you can also enjoy burgers, seafood, steaks, native dishes, and "Giant Green Salads." Amble over on Saturday night for live entertainment and a buffet featuring salads, fish, barbecued chicken and beef, and rice and beans. ◆ American/Caribbean ◆ Daily lunch and dinner. Reservations recommended for dinner. 5454

16 Buddy Beach and Dive Resort $ The original 10 tiny oceanfront apartments here have kitchenettes, showers, and twin beds—only 5 are air-conditioned and none are equipped with telephones or TV sets. A second building, built in 1993, has 15 units with 1 to 3 bedrooms, and a third 15-unit complex recently opened. The best rooms are in the newer additions (they're set up like apartments with full kitchens, air-conditioning, and telephones) and are well worth the extra few dollars they cost per night. All units offer ocean views. Guests have access to scuba diving and other damp adventures through the **Buddy Watersports Center.** ◆ Kaya Gobernador Nicolaas Debrot (between Kaya Amsterdam and Kaminda Santa Barbara). 5080, 800/786.3483, 800/359.0747; fax 8647

16 Captain Don's Habitat $$$ On the oceanfront with a beach and a pool, accommodations at this spot are spread among 11 2-bedroom cottages, 24 oceanfront suites with balconies, and 13 villas with air-conditioning and terraces. All of the villas and cottages have kitchens; some of the villas feature rooftop solariums. Don Stewart's complex is also home to the popular **Rum Runners** restaurant, the **Deco Stop Bar,** and **Captain Don's Habitat Dive Center.** ♦ Kaya Gobernador Nicolaas Debrot (between Kaya Amsterdam and Kaminda Santa Barbara). 8290, 305/373.3341, 800/327.6709; fax 8240

17 Rincón The oldest town on Bonaire, this sleepy burg was selected by Dutch colonizers as its base because it was ringed by hills that made it invisible to pirates plying the island's coast. (The buccaneers sailed on, thinking Bonaire was uninhabited.) It was also the place where slaves from Africa were housed. Today the town's streets are lined with low, pastel-colored homes. In the *cunucu* (countryside) goats roam fields bounded by cactus fences. ♦ Northwest interior

In Rincón:

Rose Inn This huge outdoor patio is a local hangout, where the open-air bar serves up cold Amstel beers and local musicians get the crowd dancing on Saturday nights. On weekends, they pull out grills and pots and cook up a criollo feast, including such local treats as savory goat stew. After buying their food tickets, folks line up at the long table where grandmotherly women fill up their plates, then find seats at one of the handful of picnic tables or plastic lawn chairs and dig right in. ♦ Daily. E.E.G. Blvd. 6420

Prisca's Ice Cream Homemade frozen treats in unusual tropical fruit flavors attract crowds of regulars to this little shop that opens "whenever Prisca feels like it." ♦ Kaya Komkomber. 6334

18 Goto Meer Bonaire's most beautiful inland region is also a good place to watch flamingos, who have only two breeding spots left in the Caribbean—in Venezuela, and at this saltwater lake with its own island. During mating season as many as 15,000 of the striking pink birds live on the island. They fly from this marshy lake—designated a bird sanctuary—to Venezuela every evening at sunset, but return the next day. They can be seen striding across the lake or resting with one leg tucked under them. The gray birds are the babies. Be sure to bring along a camera and binoculars. ♦ West of Rincón

---

The Bonairean government allows controlled harvesting of black coral by authorized Bonaireans, for sale in island shops. Collecting the rare marine life is otherwise illegal.

---

19 Washington-Slagbaai National Park  This 13,500-acre game preserve, the first of its kind in the Netherlands Antilles, spreads across the entire northwestern corner of the island. Although hunting, fishing, and overnight camping are forbidden here, the unspoiled paradise has much to offer visitors. Hikers can explore the miles of well-marked hiking trails and dirt roads that crisscross the park, while swimmers and divers can enjoy the secluded beaches and rocky caves. Bird-watchers flock to Salina Matijs, a salt flat popular with flamingos; the pond at Pos Mangel; and Bronswinkel Well at the bottom of Mount Brandaris, where you'll also see the 20-foot-high cacti that locals use to make cactus soup. Boca Slagbaai (Slaughter Bay) is a good spot for picnics, and there's a lighthouse at Seru Bentana (Window Hill), so called because the boulders form a natural window through which you can look out to sea. Throughout the park, watch for iguanas, goats, and donkeys. An excursion guide booklet is sold at the entrance for $6; it's well worth the price, with details on the park's flora, fauna, topography, and history. Here's the story behind the name of the park, which was established in 1974. The land was once a plantation called "America." The most important place in America—where the workers got their pay—was called "Washington." Hence the original name, **Washington National Park.** It became **Washington-Slagbaai National Park** in 1978. There's a small museum at the entrance. ♦ Admission. Daily. Northwestern corner. No phone

20 Onima Just beyond Bonaire's oldest village of Rincón on the eastern coast is a 50-foot volcanic cliff at Boca Onima, carved into elaborate patterns by centuries of wind and water. Follow the "Indian Inscription" signs to shallow caves, where you can see Caiquetio petroglyphs at least 500 years old. Archaeologists have still to decipher the messages that appear here and in other caves around the island, but one popular theory holds that Indians left them before they set out on long sea journeys. ♦ Northeast of Rincón

21 Bonaire Lagoen Hill Bungalows $ Ideal for families or travelers who want some space at bargain prices, these seven air-conditioned, two-bedroom bungalows are nestled in a peaceful rural spot halfway between Kralendijk and the beach. Each unit has a kitchen nook, a living room area with a TV set, and a spacious bathroom. Outside there's a covered terrace and a small garden area. The complex is part of a new hillside housing development. ◆ Kaminda Lagun (east of Antriol). 2840; fax 7440

22 Cai Windsurfers flock to landlocked Lac Bay and this remote, laid-back waterfront settlement. Things get lively here on Sunday afternoons, when islanders gather to hear local bands play, snack on the offerings of the little food stalls, and dance. ◆ Kaminda Lac (east of Kaminda Sorobon)

23 Kunuku Warahama This ranch is the place to experience the *cunucu* the old-fashioned way. Among its many offerings are guided horse rides through Bonaire's rough countryside, a landscape dominated by cactus fences, water-spurning foliage, and iguanas. Also available are carriage rides and post-excursion lunches and dinners. There are two playgrounds on the premises. ◆ Admission. Daily. Southwest of Kaminda Sorobon. 7537

24 Lac Bay Resort & Spa $$$ Windsurfing is the thing at this deluxe nature-lover's resort on the southeast (windward) coast. The breezes are steady and the water is shallow (a plus for beginning windsurfers) at the complex, which is nestled on a five-square-mile protected lagoon and nature reserve. Guests are lodged in 19 studio, 1-, or 2-bedroom apartments and 2 luxury villas, all with patios or balconies. There's also a restaurant (see below), and guests can arrange meal plans. Those who get tired of the white-sand beach can go horseback riding, biking, or hiking, or just sign up for a massage at the spa. ◆ Kaminda Sorobon (just north of E.E.G. Blvd). 8198, 800/253.6573; fax 5686

Within the Lac Bay Resort & Spa:

Oasis Bar and Grill ★★$$ International cuisine is featured at this restaurant and sports bar. The seafood is always a good choice. ◆ International ◆ Daily lunch and dinner. 8198

25 Sorobon Beach $$$ Don't try to go "sight-seeing" at this clothing-optional hideaway on Lac Bay; peepers will be turned away at the front door. However, "naturists" are welcome at this uncommon resort, where 30 1-bedroom cottages with kitchenettes (but no air-conditioning) share a restaurant and private beach. Day-trippers can hit the beach for a fee ($15 a day); drop in just long enough to take home an all-over tan. ◆ North of E.E.G. Blvd, Lac Bay. 8080, 800/828.9356; fax 6080

26 Willemstoren Lighthouse Built in 1837, this is Bonaire's oldest lighthouse. Though the building is not open to the public, the well-landscaped grounds are a good place to stop for a picnic or photo opportunity. The lighthouse is now operated by solar power. ◆ E.E.G. Blvd (south of Solar Salt Works and Flamingo Sanctuary)

27 Solar Salt Works and Flamingo Sanctuary
After being abandoned for many years, these historic salt ponds have been reactivated for eco-friendly solar salt production by the Antilles International Salt Company. White pyramids of sea salt resembling snow-covered hills sit in dazzling contrast to the plain of ponds, whose colors vary depending on how much seawater has evaporated. Nearby, thick-walled huts dating from around 1850 still stand. Barely waist high, they were used as crude shelters for slaves who labored in the salt works and were allowed to make the long walk back to their family homes in Rincón only on weekends. (Slavery was abolished here in 1863.)

Within the facility is a 135-acre bird sanctuary, the exclusive breeding ground for the entire southern Caribbean flamingo population. Entering the sanctuary is strictly prohibited, but the nesting area is visible from the slave huts at Oranje Pan. The birds usually nest in the spring. ◆ E.E.G. Blvd (south of Kaya Randolph Statius van Eps)

"Total physical and mental inertia are highly agreeable, much more so than we allow ourselves to imagine. A beach not only permits such inertia but enforces it, thus neatly eliminating all problems of guilt. It is now the only place in our overly active world that does."

John Kenneth Galbraith, US economist

Getting Your Feet Wet in Bonaire

The warm (78 to 84 degrees F), crystal-clear waters surrounding Bonaire are a diver's and snorkeler's dream, and the underwater photography is superb. Boating, fishing, and windsurfing are great, too. Here are a few outfits that can set you afloat:

Boating

Samur Sand Dollar Condominium Resort, Kaya Gobernador Nicolaas Debrot (just north of Kaya Amsterdam). 5433

Snorkeling and Scuba Diving

Bruce Bowker Carib Inn, Julio A. Abraham Blvd (between Kayas Internashonal and Industrial), Kralendijk. 8819

Buddy Watersports Center Buddy Beach and Dive Resort, Kaya Gobernador Nicolaas Debrot (between Kaya Amsterdam and Kaminda Santa Barbara). 5080, 800/786.3483, 800/359.0747

Captain Don's Habitat Dive Center Captain Don's Habitat, Kaya Gobernador Nicolaas Debrot (between Kaya Amsterdam and Kaminda Santa Barbara). 8290, 305/373.3341, 800/327.6709

Dee Scarr 133 Kaya Gobernador Nicolaas Debrot. 8529

Dive-Inn Sunset Beach, Kayas Gobernador Nicolaas Debrot and Amsterdam. 8761

Great Adventures Bonaire Harbour Village Beach, Kaya Gobernador Nicolaas Debrot (just south of Kaya Amsterdam). 7500, 800/424.0004

Neal Watson Undersea Adventures Coral Regency, Kaya Gobernador Nicolaas Debrot (between Kaya Amsterdam and Kaminda Santa Barbara). 5580

Sand Dollar Dive and Photo Shop Sand Dollar Condominium Resort, Kaya Gobernador Nicolaas Debrot (just north of Kaya Amsterdam). 5252, 800/934.DIVE

Sportfishing

Captain Bob Harbour Village Beach, Kaya Gobernador Nicolaas Debrot (just south of Kaya Amsterdam). 7070

Club Nautico Bonaire 29 Kaya J.N.E. Craane (at Kaya Den Tera), Kralendijk. 5800

Piscatur Charters Kralendijk. 8774

Windsurfing

Windsurfers Castle Lac Bay Resort & Spa, Kaminda Sorobon (just north of E.E.G. Blvd). 8198, 800/253.6573

Windsurfing Bonaire Lac Bay. 5363

Jibe City Bonaire Lac Bay. 5233, 800/252.1070

28 **Pink Beach** Escape to the island's softest white sands—named for the rosy hue at the waterline—during the week if you're seeking solitude. Don't expect the same open expanses on weekends, however. Hordes invade on the weekends to enjoy swimming, snorkeling, and scuba diving. ♦ E.E.G. Blvd (south of Kaya Randolph Statius van Eps)

29 **Bonaire Marine Park** The coasts of Bonaire and Klein Bonaire that make up this park are protected from the high-tide mark out to a depth of 200 feet. Strict laws prohibit removal of anything from this spectacular undersea world, one of the most successful marine conservation efforts in the Caribbean since its 1979 inauguration. The best reefs are along Bonaire's protected leeward side, where the sloping terrace extends seaward with a drop-off at 33 feet, followed by a slope varying from 30 feet to a vertical wall of 100 to 200 feet. The best walk-in sites are at **Nukove** and **Thousand Steps** (not really that many steps but it feels that way if you're walking up them with a dive tank or two). The most popular destinations for boat dives are **Alice in Wonderland**, a double-reef complex divided by a sand channel, and **Angel City**, final resting place of the 1,000-ton sunken freighter *Hilma Hooker*. In all, the park boasts over 80 dive sites. Anyone planning to dive here must purchase a dive tag (good for one year of unlimited use), available from any scuba shop or the park headquarters (Klein Bonaire, 8444).

Within Bonaire Marine Park:

 Klein Bonaire There are no facilities, little shade, and no fresh water on this little island, but that doesn't diminish its appeal.

Snorkelers flock here to test the coral- and fish-rich waters, and families come from the mainland on weekends to picnic. The best spot for picnicking and swimming is a gentle spot dubbed "No Name Beach," located at the island's northern point. For those with a sense of adventure, Kralendijk dive shops rent kayaks for the milelong trip from the main island. Tour operators in town will drop-off and pick-up passengers on the island; a picnic lunch is usually included in the arrangement.

Bests

Ralph Stewart and Larry Thorne
Kunuku Band, a combo specializing in Caribbean music

Mi Poron restaurant and the **Blue Iguana** bed-and-breakfast: Here you can see, feel, and experience a little bit of old Bonaire.

No Name Beach at **Klein Bonaire**: Great place to spend the day snorkeling and having a barbecue.

Kunuku Warahama: A horse ranch with an ambience of the past.

Climb **Brandaris**—the highest hill in Bonaire—and see the entire island.

Goto Meer: The best place to see the flamingos, and to us, it's the prettiest spot. To go there is like going back in time.

Dee Scarr
Dive Guide/Naturalist/Photojournalist

Year-round: Scuba diving anywhere around the leeward coasts of Bonaire, or anywhere at all around **Klein Bonaire** (Little Bonaire).

Year-round: Watching the sunset, watching for the green flash from oceanfront bars and restaurants.

Spring: Attending Karnaval (same dates as Mardi Gras) and especially Kid's Karnaval (the weekend before Karnaval).

Year-round: Watching flamingos fly to Venezuela for the night, around sunset.

The Fifth of December is St. Nicolaas's Day; the Sunday before, St. Nicolaas and his helpers, the Swartze Peters (Black Peters), arrive on Bonaire by boat. Children and adults gather to greet St. Nicolaas and celebrate his arrival. Many St. Nicolaas celebrations take place the week following St. Nicolaas's arrival. My favorite is that hosted by the wives of Bonaire's Rotary Club members (assisted by their husbands) for underprivileged children. Fifty to 100 children and their parents are bused to this very special party; the children are entertained with stories, dancing, and singing, until St. Nicolaas and Swartze Peters arrive by horse-drawn carriage. Each child receives a beautifully gift-wrapped present courtesy of the Rotarians.

Captain Don Stewart
Caribbean Pioneer and Renowned Reef Ecologist, Captain Don's Habitat

Today Bonaire is a leader in reef ecology, the worldwide drawing board for reef conservation, and is at the same time one of the world's top ranking scuba-diving destinations.

However, other outstanding attractions are being discovered by the sporting crowd, such as windsurfing at **Lac Bay,** and fat-tire mountain biking over untold miles of virgin outback trails.

From aloft, a more daring person can soar several hundred feet above the surface in a parasail.

For the nondiver, there is glass-bottom boating and snorkeling, a much more personal method of viewing the corals, fish, and the underwater terrain.

From the depths to aloft, the in-between is fishing, both deep-sea and bone fishing in Lac Bay; canoeing among the mangroves in Lac Bay; jet skiing and waterskiing (some of which, as a diver, scare me half to death) and other plastic motor-driven contrivances of speed and skill. Ask around the waterfront in town.

A more tranquil sport, yet thrilling, are the boards—Sunfish for the older, and windsurfing for the kids. FYI: The wind is from the east, blowing due west; next stop to the west is Curaçao. If you miss that, then it's Mexico.

Speaking of sailing, there are several great boats available for the sunset sailing crowd. The *Samur* offers great sunset cruises, rum punch and all. Hey! Thinking of rum, don't overlook the **Klein Bonaire** (Little Bonaire) beach parties that are offered by this charter boat.

Here is another thing not to be overlooked, a Klein Bonaire exploring trip on your own. Your hotel can arrange for you to be dropped off at one of the beaches there, picnic lunch and all, then pick you up whenever. The snorkeling is terrific.

Bonaire's solar salt is a natural product of seawater, sunshine, and wind. The Caribbean flows into the Pekelmeer (salt lake), where it is pumped into condenser ponds, then crystallizers. About once a year, the salt in each crystallizer is harvested and transported to a wash plant, where it is slurried with brine and cascaded over curved grates to remove impurities. Afterward, it is conveyed to a double-wind stacker and windrowed onto long stock-piles to drain and dry for several months. Finally, it is loaded by conveyor belts onto ships—at the rate of 2,000 tons per hour—bound for ports in the Caribbean, US, and New Zealand.

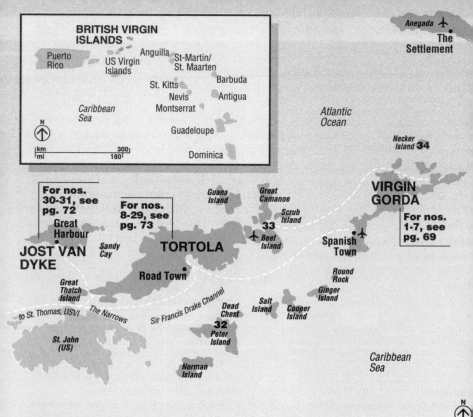

British Virgin Islands

The British Virgin Islands (BVI) probably started out as one large island, formed by volcanic activity a million years ago. The original island subsequently splintered, and now the BVI number from 40 to 60, depending on how many of the tiny islets and cays you care to include in your survey of this 59-square-mile area. Green-sheathed mountains (dormant volcanoes) descend from the islands' centers to water that's as clear as glass, creating a paradise for sailors and divers.

Although many travelers anchor themselves to the onshore hotels, which range from simple inns to some of the world's top luxury resorts, the most popular activity here is boating. The steady trade winds and scores of sheltered harbors are ideal for sailing; in fact, more than half of the visitors to the British Virgin Islands stay aboard private or charter boats. **Tortola** is frequently referred to as the yacht-charter capital of the world.

Settled and fought over by the Ciboney, and then the Arawak and Carib tribes, the islands were later claimed in turn by the Spanish (Columbus "discovered" and named Tortola, **Virgin Gorda,** and **Anegada**), Dutch, and French, until the British finally annexed Tortola in 1672.

Today the British Virgin Islands are still part of the British Commonwealth, with a governor appointed by Queen Elizabeth. The queen's portrait on stamps, the customary afternoon tea, and the popularity of cricket all reveal the islands' links to Merry Olde England.

Tourism developed here later than on other Caribbean islands. It began in 1964 when Laurance Rockefeller opened the **Little Dix Bay** resort on Virgin orda, and accelerated when Charlie and Ginny Cary created a resort called he **Moorings** on Tortola in the 1970s. Getting to these islands isn't easy; sually it requires a flight to San Juan or St. Thomas, then another short hop r ferry ride. But that very inaccessibility has helped keep the British Virgin lands from being inundated by tourists, as many other Caribbean estinations are. There's a serenity here that's often missing elsewhere.

he most developed islands are Virgin Gorda and Tortola, but several others re worth exploring, especially by boat. Anegada, the BVI's only coral island, as a population of 180 and lies about 20 miles northeast of Tortola. The andscape is flat (the highest point is a mere 28 feet), but what lies below sea vel beyond its 20 miles of sandy beaches draws plenty of divers. Extensive efs, including the third-largest barrier reef in the Western Hemisphere, and 00 shipwrecks are the island's prime attractions. **Norman Island,** believed to e the original site of Robert Louis Stevenson's *Treasure Island,* has three caves t **Treasure Point.** Rumors of buried pirate treasure persist, and visitors often oke around by rowboat or dive here.

1 the past, **Salt Island** was a stopping point for ships, which loaded on the land's salt to preserve food. Today it is best known for the sunken wreck of he *Rhone,* a Royal Mail Steam Packet Company ship that went down in an 867 hurricane. The two sections lying in 80 feet of water provide great norkel and scuba adventures (*The Deep* was filmed here). It's arguably the est dive site in the Western Hemisphere, and its numerous boat moorings revent anchor damage to the fragile coral beds. For an outstanding history of he *Rhone* and drawings of the ship, whether or not you plan to dive, consult he *Cruising Guide to the Virgin Islands* (Cruising Guide Publications; 00/330.9542). The book contains reams of good information about the other lands as well.

'eter Island is home to Amway's **Peter Island Resort and Yacht Harbour** nd a lovely, palm-lined beach. Tiny **Beef Island** lures visitors with dinner nd shows at **The Last Resort** in **Trellis Bay,** where owner Tony Snell regales achters with off-color songs about the pitfalls of sailing. And the island of ost **Van Dyke,** named for a Dutch pirate, has mountains and a few rustic nns. But don't expect high-tech amenities—telephones only arrived on the land in 1990. For local cuisine and calypso music, kick off your sandals and o as the islanders do at such spots as **Foxy's Bar** at **Great Harbour.** At the ther extreme, **Necker Island** boasts an ultra-elegant 10-bedroom villa for up o 24 people, with a pool, tennis courts, lots of privacy, and a staff of 19 to see o guests' every need. Princess Diana vacationed on the island, and for around 15,000 a day, you can too.

---

 call from the US, dial 284/49 before the five-git local number unless otherwise noted. In the itish Virgin Islands, dial only the local five-digit mber.

etting to the Islands

irlines

merican Eagle	52559, 800/751.1747
ly BVI	51747, 800/I.FLY.BVI

terisland Carriers

aribAir	787/791.1240
IAT (Leeward Islands Air Transport)	51187,
	800/468.0482

Airports Beef Island International Airport (52525), seven miles from **Road Town,** is where interisland flights arrive and depart. Beef Island is connected to Tortola by a one-lane toll bridge. **Virgin Gorda Airport** (55220), just east of the **Virgin Gorda Yacht Harbour,** has a light-aircraft landing strip.

Ferries To travel from St. Thomas, USVI, to Road Town or **West End** in Tortola, take **Smith's Ferry** (42355) or **Native Son** ferry (54617). **Dohm's Water Taxi** (340/775.6501) also operates between the US Virgin Islands and the BVI. The trip from Red Hook Bay, St. Thomas, to West End, Tortola, takes 45 minutes; the trip from Charlotte Amalie, St. Thomas, to West End takes an hour and 15 minutes. The ferry ride from West End to Road Town takes 15 minutes.

Getting Around the Islands

Bicycles and Motorbikes

Denully's, Wickhams Cay 1, Road Town, Tortola......
....46819

Last Stop Sports, Nanny Cay, Tortola.............40564

Car Rental

On Virgin Gorda:

Andy's Taxi & Jeep Rental 55511

L&S Jeep Rental..55297

Mahogany Rentals 55469

On Tortola:

Avis 43322, 42193, 800/331.1084

Budget.........42639, 42531 evenings, 800/472.3325

Caribbean Car Rental.....................................42595

Hertz Car Rental 54405, 800/654.3131

International Car Rentals 42516, 42517

Driving The roads here are full of hairpin curves and deep plunges that are best left to calm and skillful drivers. To further complicate matters, driving is on the left, British style. Most of the rentals here are four-wheel-drive vehicles, which make it easier to negotiate the tricky terrain. A British Virgin Islands driver's license, available at car-rental agencies for about $10, is required.

Ferries **Smith's Ferry** (42355) and **Speedy's** (55240, 55235) both make the 30-minute trip from Road Town in Tortola to the **Virgin Gorda Yacht Harbour.** To go from Beef Island to the **Bitter End Yacht Club, Leverick Bay,** or **Gun Creek** on Virgin Gorda, take the **North Sound Express** (52271). To get from Road Town to **Peter Island Resort and Yacht Harbour,** take the **Peter Island Boat** (52000). Call for ferry schedules; reservations are required in season.

Taxis

On Virgin Gorda:

Andy's Taxi...55511

Mahogany Taxi Service 55469

On Tortola:

BVI Taxi Association.......................................42322

Style's Taxi Service......42260 days, 43341 evenings

Tours Taxis or open-air, canvas-topped safari buses provide tours, with drivers often supplying the narrative.

On Virgin Gorda:

Andy's Taxi...55511

Mahogany Taxi Service 55469

On Tortola:

Nature's Secret Adventure Company 52722

Style's Taxi Service.............42260, 43341 evenings

Travel Plan Tours 42872

FYI

Electricity The current is 110 volts/60 cycles, the same as in the US and Canada.

Entry Requirements US and Canadian visitors mu present a valid passport or other proof of citizenship (voters' registration card or birth certificate) and a picture ID, along with a return or onward ticket. Be aware that local laws bar entry to Rastafarians (reportedly due to concerns about drug smuggling) and officials have been known to turn away visitors who wear dreadlocks or other Rasta styles.

Language English is the official language.

Money US currency is used on the islands. Banks are generally open Monday through Thursday from 9AM to 3PM, and Friday from 9AM to 4PM.

Personal Safety Crime is rare here—the British Virgin Islands are among the safest destinations in the Caribbean—but exercise ordinary precautions and don't leave valuables unguarded on the beach.

Publications The *Welcome* is a free bimonthly tourist guide. The *Island Sun* and *BVI Beacon* are island weeklies.

Reservation Services and House Rentals

Travel Solutions 800/832.4509

Taxes A seven-percent tax is levied on hotel rates. The departure tax is $10 per person when leaving by air; when leaving by sea, a $5-per-person tax is included in the ferry price. There is no sales tax.

Tipping A service charge of 10 to 15 percent is adde to hotel bills. In restaurants, leave 10 to 15 percent of the tab. Tip cabbies 10 to 15 percent of the fare.

Visitors' Information Offices The **British Virgin Islands Tourist Board** on Tortola is in Road Town (Joseph Joshua Smith Social Security Building, Waterfront Dr, between Nibbs and Decastro Sts, 43134; fax 43866). It is open Monday through Friday from 9AM to 5PM, Saturday from 9AM to 2PM. Another good source of information is the **National Parks Trust** in Road Town (Fishlock Rd, between Fleming and Main Sts, 43904), open Monday throug Friday from 8AM to 5PM. In Virgin Gorda, the tourist office is at the **Virgin Gorda Yacht Harbour** (55181); it's open Monday through Friday from 8AM to 5PM.

Phone Book

Ambulance 999

Directory Assistance 119

Diving Emergencies/
Decompression Chambers 999

Emergencies 999

Fire...43473

Hospitals

Virgin Gorda..57310

Tortola...43497, 45268

Police...43822

Post Office 43701

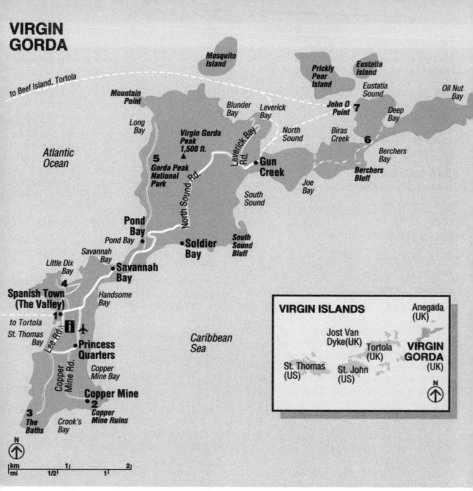

VIRGIN GORDA

Mosquito Island

Prickly Pear Island

Eustatia Island

to Beef Island, Tortola

Mountain Point

Blunder Bay

Leverick Bay

John O Point 7

Eustatia Sound

Deep Bay

Oil Nut Bay

Long Bay

Virgin Gorda Peak 1,500 ft. ▲

North Sound

Biras Creek

6

Atlantic Ocean

Gorda Peak National Park

Leverick Bay Rd.

North Sound Rd.

●**Gun Creek**

Berchers Bay

Berchers Bluff

Joe Bay

South Sound

Pond Bay

Pond Bay

●**Soldier Bay**

South Sound Bluff

Savannah Bay

Little Dix Bay

●**Savannah Bay**

4

Caribbean Sea

Spanish Town (The Valley)

Handsome Bay

1●

to Tortola
St. Thomas Bay

ℹ ✈

Lee Rd.

●**Princess Quarters**

Copper Mine Rd.

Copper Mine Bay

Copper Mine
●2
Copper Mine Ruins

3
The Baths

Crook's Bay

N ⊕

km
mi
1/2
1
1
2

VIRGIN ISLANDS

Anegada (UK)

Jost Van Dyke(UK)

Tortola (UK)

VIRGIN GORDA (UK)

St. Thomas (US)

St. John (US)

N ⊕

Virgin Gorda

Named by Christopher Columbus, who thought the island's skyline resembled an overweight woman lying on her back, today the "Fat Virgin" appeals to tourists with fat purses. The southern part of the 10-milelong island offers **The Baths,** a spectacular site of huge granite boulders, along with a bit of commercialism at **Spanish Town.** All land higher than a thousand feet in the island's mountainous midsection is designated a national park and is filled with hiking trails. The northeastern section, by contrast, looks like a geological afterthought; its many spits and islets harbor numerous sailing vessels, both private and for hire.

In colonial times Spanish Town was the capital of the British Virgin Islands. Virgin Gorda's population peaked in 1812 at 8,000, and has steadily declined to its current count of about 2,500 residents. The second-largest of the British Virgins (after Tortola, which has more hotels and marinas), Virgin Gorda is the home of several luxurious resorts, yet even these are casual in style. Many of the resorts spilling down the hills to the sparkling beaches are accessible only by boat.

1 Virgin Gorda Yacht Harbour Developed by multimillionaire Laurance Rockefeller to accommodate his **Little Dix Bay** luxury resort nearby, the harbor is now managed by Rosewood Hotels & Resorts. Up to 150 boats can be docked at this boating and shopping nucleus, where many visitors go through customs. A commissary and ship's store are on the premises. ◆ Daily. Lee and Millionaire Rds, Spanish Town. 55500

Within the Virgin Gorda Yacht Harbour:

The Bath and Turtle ★★★$$ Meals are served either outdoors or in the pub-like dining room with a polished wood bar, beveled glass, and brass railings that were purchased from New York's Carnegie Hall. The fare ranges from hamburgers and pizza to lobster and steaks, with a few local dishes

69

such as conch fritters and soup. Crowds gather Wednesday and Sunday to hear local bands play calypso, reggae, and soul music. ♦ American/West Indian ♦ Daily breakfast, lunch, and dinner. Reservations required Wednesday and Sunday. 55239

Euphoric Cruises If you want to try out your sea legs in something small, rent a Boston whaler here. Then graduate to one of the outfit's 50-foot yachts, which can certainly induce a state of euphoria. All may be chartered for half-day, full-day, and weeklong sails. ♦ Daily. 55542; fax 55818

Spirit of Anegada Set sail on this traditional gaff-rigged schooner for full-day excursions to Anegada and half-day trips around Virgin Gorda's North Sound. Skipper Nick Voorhoeve takes guests to protected reefs for snorkeling and spins entertaining yarns about local island history, while his wife, chef Lyndsay Voorhoeve, serves gourmet Caribbean fare. ♦ Daily; closed September. 55937, 66825; fax 55937

Virgin Gorda Craft Shop Look for great local handiwork such as island paintings, Anegada pottery, straw items, and jewelry. ♦ M-Sa. 55137

Dive BVI Ltd. Those who can't resist taking the plunge can buy or rent snorkel and dive equipment here. Men's and women's sportswear and various necessities, such as the requisite sunblock, are also for sale. ♦ Daily. 55513, 800/848.7078; fax 55347

Pelican's Pouch Boutique Casualwear made of cotton, along with swimsuits and plenty of cool, comfortable T-shirts, fill the racks of this small store. ♦ Daily. 55477

2 Copper Mine Ruins Remains of chimneys, a boiler house, a cistern, and stone walls from 19th-century miners' quarters run along a bluff overlooking the sea. The mines themselves—modeled after those in Cornwall, England—still exist. A trail leads to an information board. Warning: Remain on the pathways—the open shafts are dangerous. ♦ Free. Daily. Copper Mine Rd (south of Church Hill Rd). 43904

3 The Baths A spectacular natural sight awaits at the southwestern end of Virgin Gorda. Here, pools of water have created "baths" between gigantic rocks and boulders that were created by volcanic pressure millions of years ago. Some of the rocks come together to form cave-like "rooms" and A-shaped grand

entrances to grottoes and shaded pools. One path over the rocks and through the tidal pools leads to the gorgeous Devil's Bay.

Many boaters drop anchor nearby— snorkeling is excellent here—but landlubbers can reach this phenomenon by taxi. Ask the cab driver to pick you up later at the information center, a gazebo with a posted map. From there, it's a 350-foot descent via either of two trails, so wear sneakers or hiking shoes. The **Mad Dog** beach bar offers frosty piña coladas, bathrooms, and the ubiquitous souvenir T-shirts. ♦ Southwest end. 43904

Next to The Baths:

Toad Hall $$$$ Owners Steve and Marie Green rent this 6.5-acre estate (with 3 pavilion suites and a fully equipped kitchen) to a single family or group. Built into and around the stone formations near The Baths, the highly original villa, designed by Steve's brother, architect **Christopher Green,** has rock-faced showers with living plants for curtains, and boulders incorporated into a swimming pool with its own cave. A private boardwalk crosses the beach to The Baths. The rental rate includes the services of a housekeeper, who will also cook or baby-sit for an additional fee. ♦ 55397; fax 55708

LITTLE DIX BAY

4 Little Dix Bay $$$$ Want to vacation like a Rockefeller? This 98-room Rockresort opened in 1964 after years of planning by Laurance Rockefeller, who envisioned a wilderness beach resort that would provide privacy and solitude. The property, which is now owned by Caribbean Resort Holdings, a subsidiary of Bankers Trust Co., and managed by Rosewood Hotels & Resorts, still fulfills Rockefeller's goal. The epitome of laid-back luxury, it is a place where room keys are not needed, and the only television is in the central activities room. Honeymooners flock here, and the swank lodgings are popular with the rich and famous (Dick Cavett is a regular). *Condé Nast Traveler* magazine has ranked it among the top 20 tropical resorts in the world.

Refurbished in 1995 after Hurricanes Luis and Marilyn, the rooms are casually elegant, with custom-designed, handmade furniture. More than half the units are air-conditioned and all have telephones, which are removed for those guests who want to get away from it all. Some units are a few steps off the beach; others are perched on stilts, like opulent octagonal tree houses. The magnificent white-sand beach stretches for a half mile along an almost heart-shaped cove, once the major fishing harbor for locals. The 500-acre grounds are lushly planted, and botanical tours are offered. Other hallmarks are the outstanding service (the staff-to-guest ratio is three-to-one) and excellent food. Rates include tennis on seven courts, waterskiing, water taxis to nearby beaches, aerobics classes, Sunfish sailing lessons, movies, and a guided snorkel tour. A children's program offers both indoor and outdoor activities six days a week. ♦ North of Little Rd, Spanish Town. 55555, 800/928.3000; fax 55661

Within Little Dix Bay:

The Pavilion ★★★★$$$$ The interlaced, silver-shingled peaks of a Polynesian-style pavilion shelter this open-air dining room. All of the tables, especially those on the terrace, provide stunning, unimpeded views. Try the warm lobster taco with yellow tomato salsa and jicama salad, or the roasted duckling breast with raspberry and Port wine sauce. The bourbon pecan crème brûlée with milk chocolate sauce makes a memorable dessert. ♦ American/Caribbean ♦ Daily breakfast, lunch, and dinner. Reservations required. 55555

The Sugar Mill ★★★$$$$ The remains of an early sugar mill have been transformed into a casual dining room and lounge. The set menu offers light Mediterranean and Italian fare, including pizza fresh from the wood oven and various pasta dishes. ♦ Mediterranean/ Italian ♦ Daily lunch. Reservations recommended. 55555

5 Gorda Peak National Park On the road leading to North Sound, a brown and white sign marks the park entrance where hikers will find a number of trails, including one along an old dirt road on the northwest side of the island. Signs direct visitors to Virgin Gorda Peak, where there's an observation tower and picnic area. The easy hike takes about 30 minutes. Standing on the peak, the island's highest spot (1,359 feet), it's possible to see the points where Virgin Gorda narrows so dramatically that the Atlantic Ocean and Caribbean Sea practically meet. ♦ North Sound Rd (between Leverick Bay Rd and Pond Bay). 43904

6 Biras Creek Resort $$$$ Perched atop a breezy hill on a narrow neck of land and commanding a 360° view of the Atlantic, Caribbean, and North Sound, this complex of native-stone and wood-shingle buildings has pampered those seeking privacy and gourmet cookery since 1973. In 1995, a loyal guest,

Bert Houwer, purchased the resort and conducted a major renovation that included an overhaul of the furnishings in the 33 beachside suites and the 2-bedroom villa. As before, the rooms are tastefully free of such modern intrusions as TV and telephones, although all have air-conditioning. Amenities include a gorgeous beach, a freshwater pool, two tennis courts, bicycling, hiking trails, and every water sport, including sportfishing. The dock—completely rebuilt after Hurricanes Luis and Marilyn passed through in 1995— accommodates 11 yachts up to 60 feet. Guests "de-sand" their feet just outside their rooms in individual foot baths garnished with floating hibiscus blooms and shower outdoors in private garden enclosures. All meals are included in the rate. Every Monday morning the gardener leads botanical tours of the grounds. ♦ Biras Creek. 43555, 43556, 800/223.1108; fax 43557

Within the Biras Creek Resort:

Biras Creek Restaurant ★★★★$$$$ Many guests choose this hotel because of its justly celebrated dining room, where chefs hold credentials from such prestigious institutions as Cordon Bleu, Culinary Institute of America, and the Ritz in London. Try the grilled chicken with papaya vinaigrette or the pan-seared snapper with yogurt citrus sauce. The talented staff will also prepare fish caught by guests, vegetarian dishes, or other special meals. Desserts include Key lime pie with raspberry sauce and a warm chocolate brownie with a rich chocolate sauce. The restaurant has an extensive wine list. ♦ Continental ♦ Daily breakfast and lunch for hotel guests only; daily dinner for guests and the public. Reservations required for dinner; jackets and tie required for dinner. 43555, 43556

7 The Bitter End Yacht Club $$$$ Once a rustic hangout for barefoot sailors, this North Sound resort has upgraded and now offers a variety of  accommodations in wooden buildings. Digs range from 60 simple, breezy, beachfront rooms with ceiling fans and no telephones to 40 more luxurious air-conditioned chalets with phones as well as marble baths and tiled outdoor showers. The rooms have no TV sets, but CNN is broadcast at the open-air video theater, along with nightly movies.

This area was originally called the Bitter End because it was the easternmost point in the Virgin Islands before ships struck out into the ocean, and the focus here is still on the salty life. The fine location on a protected harbor with proximity to the open sea is ideal for

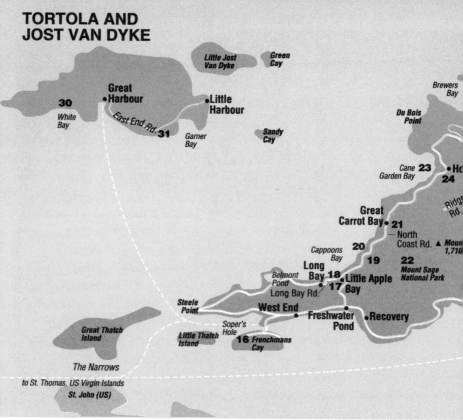

TORTOLA AND JOST VAN DYKE

Little Jost Van Dyke

Green Cay

Brewers Bay

Great Harbour

30

White Bay

East End Rd.

Little Harbour

31

Garner Bay

Sandy Cay

Du Bois Point

Cane Garden Bay **23**

Ho 24

Ridg Rd

Great Carrot Bay **21**

North Coast Rd. ▲ Moun 1,710

Cappoons Bay

20

Long Bay 18

19

22

Belmont Pond

Little Apple Bay

Mount Sage National Park

Long Bay Rd.

17

Steele Point

West End

Freshwater Pond

Recovery

Soper's Hole

Great Thatch Island

Little Thatch Island

16 Frenchmans Cay

The Narrows

to St. Thomas, US Virgin Islands

St. John (US)

---

sailors. Action centers around a marina with 100 yachts and other craft available for charter, including 10 live-aboards. Room rates cover unlimited use of the resort fleet (several dozen sailboats, 20 Boston whalers, plus Sunfish and sailboards) and introductory courses at the **Nick Trotter Sailing School** on the premises. One program teaches kids ages seven and older. The milelong waterfront is augmented by a pool; there's also a conference center. All meals are included in the rate. ♦ North Sound. 42746, 800/872.2392; fax 312/944.2860

Within The Bitter End Yacht Club:

Clubhouse Steak and Seafood Grille ★★★$$$ Seafood, steaks, and ribs are the specialties here. Chef Angus Bowen's tropical seafood salad with lemon vinaigrette is also a good choice. For those who can't decide on one dish, there's a nightly dinner buffet. The popular beachfront spot offers both indoor and outdoor dining, and a steel-drum band plays in the evenings. ♦ Steaks/Seafood ♦ Daily breakfast, lunch, and dinner. 42746

English Carvery ★★$$$$ Smaller and more elegant than the **Clubhouse** (above), this British-style restaurant serves traditional carving-board fare: roast beef, pork, chicken, and lamb. ♦ English ♦ Daily dinner Dec-May; W, F-Su dinner June-Nov. 42746

Tortola

Home to **Road Town,** capital of the BVI, Tortola is th largest—both in area and population (more than 13,500)—of the colony's 50 or so islands and islets. A dock built in 1996 on **Wickhams Cay 1** allows thre cruise ships to berth at a time, swelling the island's population on the two to three days a week that cruise ships are in port.

The atmosphere in Road Town is somewhat businesslike, despite the fact that most of the wooden West Indian–style buildings are painted pink green, or aqua with red-tin roofs. This is primarily a provisioning stop for boaters, because prices here are lower than on the other islands. (Note: Swimsuit without cover-ups are prohibited in town.)

One unusual element of Tortola's history is that it was at one time the home of a Quaker community. Quaker moved here in the early 18th century after leaving England and then Barbados because of religious persecution. Since they refused to carry firearms and were opposed to slavery, the Quakers' way of life conflicted with Caribbean culture at the time. The Quaker community here died out by the 1780s, when many of its members moved on to Pennsylvania.

8 Fort Wines & Spirits Find a large and excellent selection of beer, wine, and spirits at this amply stocked retail outlet. Delivery to your hotel or boat is free of charge. ♦ M-Sa. Port Purcell. 42388, 41580

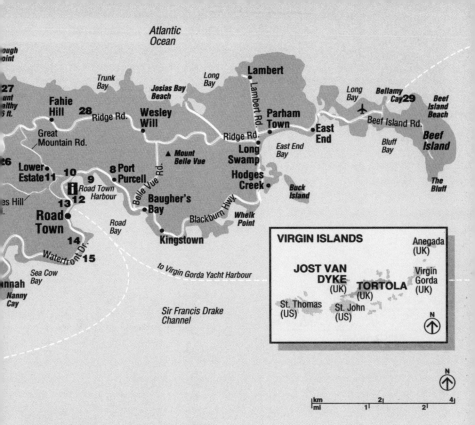

Atlantic Ocean

Lambert

Trunk Bay
Long Bay
Josias Bay Beach
Fahie Hill
28 Ridge Rd.
Wesley Will
▲ Mount Belle Vue
Lambert Rd.
Parham Town
Ridge Rd.
East End
East End Bay
Long Bay
Bellamy Cay 29
Beef Island Rd.
Beef Island Beach
Beef Island
Great Mountain Rd.
Long Swamp
Bluff Bay
Lower Estate 11
10
8 Port Purcell
9
Road Town Harbour
Hodges Creek
Buck Island
The Bluff
13 12
Baugher's Bay
Road Town
14
Road Bay
Kingstown
Blackburn Hwy
Whelk Point
Belle Vue Rd.
Waterfront Dr.
15
Sea Cow Bay
to Virgin Gorda Yacht Harbour
Nanny Cay
Sir Francis Drake Channel

VIRGIN ISLANDS

JOST VAN DYKE (UK)

TORTOLA (UK)

St. Thomas (US)

St. John (US)

Anegada (UK)

Virgin Gorda (UK)

N

km
mi
1
2
2
4

N

9 The Moorings Even if you don't plan to sail away, you've got to see this operation. In 1969 Charlie and Ginny Cary began a yacht-chartering business with six sailboats. Today the facility operates 140 yachts ranging from 32 feet to 60 feet, available bareboat or with crew. In addition to the 72-slip charter dock, there's a 70-slip visitors' dock. Just stroll along the boards and you're bound to meet interesting people with colorful sea stories to tell. ◆ Wickhams Cay 2, Road Town. 42332, 813/535.1446; fax 42226

Within The Moorings:

Underwater Safaris Four-day **PADI**-certified diving courses and resort courses are offered here, along with two half-day completion courses for those with previous training. Guided half-day dive tours are available twice weekly, and divers may rent boats and equipment, including tanks, regulators, and wet suits. ◆ Daily. 43235, 43965, 800/537.7032; fax 45322

The Mariner Inn $$$ Geared primarily to charterers from **The Moorings** who want to extend their stays, this dockside hotel's 40 air-conditioned rooms are also available to landlubbers. The property offers a pool, a tennis court, water sports, a full-service marina, a gourmet food shop, a restaurant, and a bar. ◆ 42332, 800/535.7289; fax 42226

10 Treasure Isle Hotel $$$ Built on a hill above the harbor, these pleasant gingerbread-trimmed buildings offer 42 air-conditioned rooms and three suites with kitchenettes; all have ocean views. There's entertainment Saturday nights during the high season, and a large swimming pool adjoins the **Lime 'n' Mango** restaurant (see below). ◆ Waterfront Dr and Treasure Isle Rd, Road Town. 42501, 800/437.7880; fax 42507

Within Treasure Isle Hotel:

Lime 'n' Mango ★★★$$$ The casual open-air atmosphere of this dining spot beckons, as does the eclectic menu of Mexican food with West Indian touches. Try the grilled tandoori scallops or a Caribbean chicken roti—thin flat bread wrapped around a spicy chicken filling. On Saturday in high season, there's a barbecue with entertainment provided by a steel-drum band. ◆ Mexican/ West Indian ◆ Daily breakfast, lunch, and dinner. 42501

According to local legend, the harm less, three-quarter-inch-long Virgin Gorda dwarf gecko enters only pregnant women's homes.

11 **J.R. O'Neal Botanic Garden** Curious about the identities of all those tropical flowers or the origins of exotic herbs? Visit this four-acre garden, named after a BVI businessman, where horticulturists give guided tours. Highlights include a fern house and a simulated rain forest with waterfalls. ♦ Admission. Daily. Main St (between Lower Estate and Huntums Ghut Rds), Lower Estate. 44557

12 **The Ample Hamper** This is just the place to stock up on food and wine for a secluded beach picnic or a boating trip. Baked quiches, pâtés, Fortnum & Mason jams, sliced meats, wine, and liquor are among the goodies sold. ♦ Daily. Wickhams Cay 1, Road Town. 42494. Also at: Soper's Hole Marina, Soper's Hole Wharf, West End. 54684

SEA URCHIN SHOPS

12 **Sea Urchin** Forgot your swimsuit? Want some new summer clothes? This shop outfits men, women, and children. Brand names include Alegre and Catalina. ♦ M-Sa. Mill Mall, Wickhams Cay 1, Road Town. 44108. Also at: Waterfront Dr (between Customs Rd and Hallwell St), Road Town. 42044

13 **Pusser's Outpost** ★★$$$ The first of the four **Pusser's** now in the BVI, this store and eatery faces the waterfront. Oceans of nautical memorabilia cover the walls, which are trimmed in Victorian-style carved woodwork. Upstairs a more formal dining room serves beef Wellington, healthful "Heart Smart" dishes (including steamed mussels), and Tex-Mex fare. The downstairs pub dishes up meat pies and sandwiches. The ground floor also houses a store featuring nautical souvenirs. ♦ Continental/Tex-Mex ♦ Daily dinner. Main St, Road Town. 43897

13 **Post Office** Here's the place to pick up colorful BVI stamps, thought by many collectors to be the prettiest in the Caribbean. ♦ M-F; Sa until noon. Sir Olva Georges Plaza, Main St, Road Town. 43701

13 **Kids in de Sun** Stylish duds for children include Java Wraps for kids, plus items by Jungle Rags and Pacific Coast Highway. ♦ M-Sa; Su when cruise ships are in port. Main St, Road Town. 43343

13 **Sunny Caribbee Spice Company** Flavor your memories with a visit to this West Indian–style building where apothecary jars are filled with exotic seeds and powders. The company, founded in 1982 by former Maine residents

Bob and Susan Gunter and their son Greg, packages its own herbs, tea, coffee, spices, preserves, hot sauces, and herbal cosmetics. The West Indian "Hangover Cure" tea could come in handy. The shop also stocks original handmade crafts, including pottery and papier-mâché accessories. The **Sunny Caribbee Gallery** next door sells island paintings, sculpture, and ceramics. ♦ M-Sa; Su when cruise ships are in port. Main St, Road Town. 42178

13 **Little Denmark** This store has a little of everything, with Denmark represented by a modest selection of silver jewelry and cutlery and Royal Copenhagen china. There are also straw baskets, Cuban cigars (smoke them here, it's illegal to bring them into the US), and fishing and snorkeling equipment. ♦ M-Sa. Main St, Road Town. 42455

13 **Serendipity** Housed in a colorful wooden home, this shop is chock-full of clothes, souvenirs, and accessories from everywhere from Antigua to Zululand. Check out the selection of sarongs, said to be the largest on the island. ♦ M-Sa. Main St, Road Town. 55865

13 **J.R. O'Neal Ltd.** Amidst the woven rugs, baskets, and hardware items at this home-accessories store are hand-painted Italian dishes and blown Mexican glassware. ♦ M-Sa. Main St, Road Town. 42292

14 **Fort Burt Hotel** $$ The remains of a 300-year-old Dutch/English fort add a sense of history to this 12-room, 5-suite property. The fort was apparently rebuilt in 1776 and named after William Burt, governor of the Leeward Islands. The hotel, which extends beyond the original structure, offers modern guest rooms with air-conditioning, televisions, telephones, and ocean views. Two suites have their own private pools. Other amenities include a restaurant, lounge, and swimming pool. ♦ Waterfront Dr (south of McNamara Rd), Road Town. 42587; fax 42002

15 **Prospect Reef Resort** $$$ Located on its own harbor, this low-rise resort has 130 units ranging from fan-cooled rooms to air-conditioned suites, some with kitchenettes. Some units have TVs, rental is available in others. For vacationers who want to do more than loll in a hammock or stroll among the lush gardens, there are six tennis courts (two lighted), a junior Olympic-size pool, a stone-inlaid sea pool, a variety of water sports, a health and fitness center, and a nine-hole pitch-and-putt golf course. **Baskin in the Sun** operates a dive center here and a shuttle bus takes guests to the beach and Road Town. For little guests, there are two children's pools and a kids' program that focuses on nature. Children under 12 stay free with their parents in deluxe rooms. A conference center is also on the premises. ♦ Fisher. 43311, 800/356.8937; fax 45595

Within the Prospect Reef Resort:

Callaloo ★★★$$$ Lights twinkling from the harbor below make for a romantic dinnertime ambience. Try trendy local dishes like spicy grilled shark, Caribbean-style beef Wellington, and a to-die-for coconut crème brûlée. There's live music nightly. ♦ Continental/West Indian ♦ Daily breakfast, lunch, and dinner. Reservations required. 43311

Scuttlebutt ★★$$ Light and informal meals are served here on a sheltered harborfront terrace, a good place to relax and watch all the boating activity. The menu emphasizes seafood and healthful fare. ♦ American/West Indian ♦ Daily breakfast, lunch, and dinner. 43311

16 Soper's Hole Marina This 18-slip marina on tiny Frenchmans Cay also harbors a few shops in pastel West Indian buildings. ♦ Soper's Hole Wharf, West End. 54553

Within the Soper's Hole Marina:

BASKIN IN THE SUN

Baskin in the Sun In business since 1969, this outfit offers diving lessons with **PADI**-certified instructors, equipment sales, and scuba or snorkel trips on a three-boat fleet (docked here at the tin-roofed headquarters or at the **Prospect Reef Resort**). There are two-tank dives every morning and a one-tank dive each afternoon. Dive packages with unlimited daytime dives and stays at the **Long Bay Beach Resort, Prospect Reef Resort, Sebastian's on the Beach,** or the **Sugar Mill Hotel** can also be arranged. ♦ Daily. 45854, 42858, 800/233.7938; fax 45853

Island Treasures West Indian oil paintings, watercolors, and sculptures are showcased here, along with silk-screen prints and books. ♦ Daily. 54787

Pusser's Landing ★★$$$ Part of the **Pusser's** chain, which has expanded throughout the BVI, this eatery serves seafood and steaks in a dining room filled with decorative wood and nautical doodads. Try the beef Wellington and conch fritters anytime, or all-you-can-eat shrimp on Tuesday nights.

Next door, **Pusser's Company Store** sells ship models, "adventure" clothing, and jewelry. ♦ American/Seafood ♦ Daily lunch and dinner. 54554

Sea Lion This small store has brand-name resortwear for men, women, and children. It's run by the same folks who own the **Sea Urchin** shops in Road Town. ♦ Daily. 54850

Zenaida Tired of shell jewelry? Here's a shop that specializes in antique and modern accessories from India, Africa, and Mexico, along with batik fabrics and the Java Wraps clothing line. ♦ Hours are erratic; call ahead. 54867

Sunsail A young and energetic crew enlivens the professional charters offered by this international chain, which debuted in Greece in 1983. Some 60 sailboats are available for hire at this location. ♦ 54740, 800/327.2276

17 Long Bay Beach Resort $$$$ Snuggled between the verdant hills and a milelong beach is this 50-acre resort with a full range of accommodations. There are 20 deluxe oceanfront rooms and villas and 62 hillside or beachfront rooms and cabanas. If you tire of surf and sand, move on to the freshwater pool, fitness center, tennis courts (three, with lighting), or the nine-hole pitch-and-putt golf course. You'll also get plenty of exercise from the uphill climb to many of the rooms. Make up for all that activity at the resort's two restaurants (see below). Children under 12 room with their parents for free. ♦ Long Bay Rd (west of Zion Hill Rd), Long Bay. 54252, 800/729.9599; fax 54677

Within the Long Bay Beach Resort:

Beach Cafe ★★$$ Sample West Indian favorites—including roti and curried chicken—in the authentic stone sugar mill of a 200-year-old rum distillery. There's a "Taste of Tortola" dinner buffet on Tuesday and a West Indian dinner buffet on Friday—try the salt fish, curried goat, or barbecued ribs. ♦ West Indian/American ♦ Daily breakfast, lunch, and dinner. 54252

Garden Restaurant ★★★$$$ Men are requested to wear slacks and shirts—but certainly not jackets and ties—at this somewhat formal restaurant set amid romantically lit gardens. West Indian flavor enlivens the continental fare—the dinner menu changes nightly, but might include conch fritters and curry sauce, red snapper in a ginger sauce, or linguine with goat cheese. A vegetarian dish is also available, and the chef is happy to cater to special dietary requirements. Manager James Hawkins is justly proud of his extensive wine list. ♦ Continental ♦ Daily dinner. 54252

Restaurants/Clubs: Red   **Hotels:** Blue
Shops/♥ Outdoors: Green   **Sights/Culture:** Black

Idyllic Islands

In addition to the most-frequented British Virgin Islands covered in this chapter, several others deserve mention.

Anegada is a limestone and coral atoll that would probably be more at home in the South Pacific or Indian Ocean. Though 15 square miles, it's easy to miss—the highest point is only 28 feet above sea level. And, as mariners both ancient and modern can attest, the coral shelf that extends beyond the shoreline is treacherous. More than 300 ships have sunk here, the greatest number of wrecks in any one site in the Caribbean. Though little of the sunken ships remain, they have made this one of the region's top destinations for divers. Landlubbers who visit the island will have miles of sandy beach to themselves: The local population is about 180; the biggest hotel has only 16 rooms; and the entire island offers fewer than a dozen restaurants. The natural splendor is carefully guarded by the BVI National Parks Trust; most of the island is reserved for birds and other wildlife and is off-limits to settlement. Nonsailors can reach Anegada by plane from **Beef Island** or **Tortola.**

According to local legend, **Norman Island** was the setting of Robert Louis Stevenson's *Treasure Island.* Today, sailors can anchor at **The Bight** to climb a rough cattle track up a sloping hilltop for a panoramic view of the anchorage; dinghy over to the caves at **Treasure Point;** or toss back a few grogs aboard the **William Thornton,** a Baltic trader converted into a floating restaurant and bar.

Salt Island was once a regular stop for ships along the trade route; they took on salt here for food preservation. Now divers flock to the island to explore the famous wreck of the *Rhone,* which sank offshore during an 1867 hurricane. Moorings are provided at **Lee Bay,** just to the northeast of the wreck to minimize anchor damage.

Sandy Cay, south of **Little Jost Van Dyke,** is a true desert isle, accessible only by boat. The water is deep almost to shore—a long and lovely stretch of white beach. There are no signs of civilization here at all—just the sand and a palm tree or two.

17 Sunset House $$$ With the intimate atmosphere of a private home and spectacular views from its hillside perch, this modern hideaway is a real treasure. It offers just 5 rooms (each with a balcony, 1 with air-conditioning) in the main house, which is rented out in its entirety to up to 10 people. The pool area features a bar and Jacuzzi (but don't forget the insect repellent). A staff chef cooks in the common kitchen or at the pool; meal programs are arranged in advance of the stay. **Sunset Villa,** another home under the same ownership, with two bedrooms housing up to four visitors, is right on Long Bay beach and can be rented separately or along with this house. ◆ Long Bay Rd (west of Zion Hill Rd), Long Bay. 45864; fax 47626

18 Sebastian's on the Beach $$$ Originally a beach bar, this spot now has 26 rooms—some air-conditioned, all with refrigerators—and offers a wide range of water sports. Rattan furnishings and angled wood ceilings add an island touch. ◆ Long Bay and Zion Hill Rds, Little Apple Bay. 54212, 800/336.4870; fax 54466

Within Sebastian's on the Beach:

Sebastian's Restaurant ★★$$$ Dine on the fresh fish of the day, conch from Anegada, barbecued chicken, or filet mignon while enjoying the ocean breezes and fabulous scenery from the restaurant's open windows. Try the lobster at least once—that's what this place is known for. Vegetarian dishes are also available. Stop by Saturday or Sunday night for live West Indian music. ◆ Seafood/Continental ◆ Daily breakfast, lunch, and dinner. 54212 ext 1313

19 Sugar Mill Hotel $$$$ On the site of the **Appleby Plantation,** which is more than 350 years old, former California food writers Jinx and Jeff Morgan have created a deluxe resort. The circular pool is located where oxen once marched in circles to provide power for the mill, but the decor is far from rustic and the service is impeccable. There are 21 rooms and a villa, all with air-conditioning. The beach is stone's throw away. Children under 10 stay free from May through November; no children are allowed December through April. ◆ Closed August and September. North Coast Rd (east of Zion Hill Rd), Apple Bay. 54355, 800/462.8834; fax 54696

Within the Sugar Mill Hotel:

Sugar Mill Restaurant ★★★★$$$
Considered by many to be the best on the island, this picturesque dining room is set within the plantation's 17th-century stone sugar-boiling house. Vibrant Haitian paintings complement the cobblestones and slabs that were brought from Liverpool as ballast on ships that would leave the island carrying rum and sugar. Elegant four-course dinners may feature Jamaican jerk pork roast or scallops in puff pastry with roasted red pepper sauce; there's also a daily vegetarian selection. Skillfully created desserts include piña colada cake and creole banana crepes. ◆ Californian/West Indian ◆ Daily dinner; closed August and September. Reservations required. 54355

Islands Restaurant ★★★$$ Located on the beach, the hotel's less-formal dining spot offers island fare prepared with a decidedly gourmet touch. Try the roti—East Indian flat bread filled with curried chicken. "Jump up," another house specialty, tops grilled, marinated fresh fish with a salsa of chopped tomatoes, green onions, olives, and capers. ◆ West Indian ◆ Daily breakfast, lunch, and dinner; closed August and September. 54355

20 **Apple Bay** The waves are higher and the winds are stronger here than anywhere else on the island, especially between October and March. This bay is known as *the* surfing spot on Tortola. ◆ West end

21 **Mrs. Scatliffe's Bar and Restaurant**
★★$$ For a special treat, try West Indian cuisine prepared and served by Una Scatliffe and her family on the open-air second floor of her yellow-and-white residence. Everything is fresh, including the homegrown fruits and vegetables. Don't miss the curried goat and chicken, a stew served over rice in a coconut shell. Monday through Saturday nights, family members jam on the guitar, marimba box, and squash. ◆ West Indian ◆ Daily lunch and dinner. Reservations required. Great Carrot Bay. 54556

22 **Mount Sage National Park** Tortola's highest peak rises to 1,710 feet, providing spectacular views of Jost Van Dyke, Virgin Gorda, and St. John. The air is cooler here, so bring along a sweater. The 92-acre preserve offers hikers 3 trails through rain forest and mahogany forest, the latter the remains of a mahogany plantation created 20 years ago. Pick up a copy of a self-guided tour at the **Tourist Board** or **National Parks Trust Office** (see "Visitors' Information Offices," on page 68); it will help you identify the trees and plants as you traipse through the junglelike rain forest. From the bottom, the climb to the summit takes about an hour; it is also possible to drive halfway and continue the ascent on foot. Because it's so steep, this land was not cleared by the British in the 18th century when they laid out their cotton and sugarcane plantations. Today the towering trees still droop with vines as they did when the first European settlers arrived. ◆ Sage Mountain Rd (south of Ridge Rd)

23 **Cane Garden Bay** The bay is edged by one of Tortola's loveliest beaches, 1.5 miles of white sand dotted with coconut palms and spots for snacks and changing. It's also one of the BVI's top anchorages, so you're bound to spot fleets of sailboats moored here. Several casual eateries with bars dish up local goodies. ◆ West coast

24 **Ole Works Inn** $$ Just across the road from lovely Cane Garden Bay beach, a 300-year-old sugar factory has been converted into a hostelry with 8 simple air-conditioned rooms; another 10 air-conditioned rooms are in an adjacent newer building. Some rooms have televisions and telephones, and all are equipped with small refrigerators. ◆ Hodge. 54837; fax 59618

Within the Ole Works Inn:

Quito's Gazebo ★★★$$$ Casual eats (burgers, roti) are very good at this beach-side watering hole, but the entertainment definitely rates four stars. The main attraction is loquacious owner Quito Rymer, who regales his guests with stories and music (he's known for his exuberant renditions of Jimmy Buffet tunes). Look for Quito on Tuesday and Thursday through Sunday nights. There are buffet dinners on Tuesday and Sunday nights and a fish fry on Friday nights. ◆ American/West Indian ◆ Tu-Su lunch and dinner. 54837

25 **Brewers Bay Beach** Renowned throughout Tortola for its excellent snorkeling, this secluded beach is reached by a series of switchback mountain roads. There are more varieties of tropical fish under the surface here than anywhere else on the island. There's a bar and a campground, too. ◆ Brewer's Bay Rd (north of Cane Garden Bay Rd)

The *RMS* (Royal Mail Ship) *Rhone* made its movie debut in *The Deep*, but the sunken wreck is much more impressive in person. The 310-foot steamer went down in an 1867 hurricane off Salt Island. Today she lies broken in two on the sandy bottom, her steel hull encrusted with coral. The bow section is about 75 feet below the surface, where divers are greeted by colorful parrotfish, snappers, grunts, and soldierfish. The stern half lies at a depth of 30 feet, but the enormous rudder juts up to within 15 feet of the surface. Because the water is so remarkably clear, snorkelers can also enjoy the view from above. The area surrounding the *Rhone* is a national park.

26 Skyworld ★★$$$ On a hill about a quarter-mile above Road Town, this scenic restaurant is furnished in rattan, the walls hung with Haitian and local oil paintings and prints. Diners can view both the Atlantic and the Caribbean through large windows—sunsets are spectacular. Best bets are the rack of lamb and baked stuffed chicken breast. Save room for the rich "chocolate suicide" dessert, made with dark and white chocolates. Diners are offered free round-trip transportation from Road Town. ♦ Continental ♦ Daily lunch and dinner; closed September. Reservations required; jacket and tie required. Ridge Rd (between Joes Hill and Great Mountain Rds). 43567

27 Mount Healthy A stone windmill and a few other historical ruins that date from the sugar-plantation era can be found at this peaceful spot above Brewer's Bay. It's a perfect place for an afternoon picnic. ♦ North of Brewers Bay Rd

28 The Cloud Room ★★★$$$ This is an experience not to be missed, but don't try to get here on your own—the ascent is so steep and precarious that guests are picked up and transported to the mountaintop aboard an open-sided, canvas-topped bus (the trip is included in the price of dinner). At one point, the driver must turn the vehicle around and back up the switchback road. After a safe arrival, relax over cocktails on the veranda or inside the 10-table dining room, where a sliding roof rolls back in good weather. Continental and island dishes are served, including filet mignon, local fish, and curried shrimp. ♦ Continental/West Indian ♦ M-Sa dinner. Reservations required. Ridge Rd (between Belle Vue and Great Mountain Rds). 42821

29 The Last Resort ★★$$ Join the crowds who trek to tiny Bellamy Cay off Beef Island for British-style buffet dinners and bawdy shows by a one-man band, owner/entertainer Tony Snell. Sail over by dinghy or call and they'll send one for you. ♦ British ♦ Daily lunch and dinner. Reservations required. Bellamy Cay, Trellis Bay. 52520; VHF Ch 16

Tortola is named for the turtle dove, the official bird of the British Virgin Islands.

Jost Van Dyke

Telephones finally arrived on this tiny unspoiled island in 1990, and there's only one taxi. Only about 200 people live here year-round, and the main street (actually, the *only* street) is a sandy lane lined with two-story houses, the police station, the Customs Department, and **Christine Chinnery's Bakery** (known for great home-baked local breads and pastries). A ferry from **West End** in Tortola makes the trip here four times daily.

30 Sandcastle $$$ Here's a family-run haven for folks who want to get far, far away from it all. Four modern 1-bedroom octagonal cottages are surrounded by hibiscus and bougainvillea, and there's a pleasant outdoor restaurant, a bar, and 200 feet of lovely beach. All meals, windsurfing, and snorkeling are included in the rates. The owner picks up guests by boat at Red Hook Bay on St. Thomas. ♦ White Bay. 66109, 340/690.1611; VHF Ch 16

31 Foxy's Bar ★★$$$ Here's a fun spot for good sports who don't mind being the subject of jest in the musical tales of the guitarist/owner. The ceiling of this open-air joint is plastered with business cards from visitors who have flocked here since 1968. Come for live music Friday and Saturday nights. Sandwiches and snacks dominate the menu, but chicken roti, *soca* (spicy steamed shrimp), and Caribbean lobster are available too. ♦ West Indian ♦ M-F lunch and dinner; Sa-Su dinner. Reservations required by 5PM for dinner. East End Rd (between Garner Bay and Great Harbour). 59258; VHF Ch 16

Elsewhere in the British Virgin Islands

32 Peter Island Resort and Yacht Harbour $$$$ The A-frames that house this private island's 30 original guest rooms were shipped from Norway and reassembled here on Sprat Bay, creating sleek and luxurious accommodations with a surprising Scandinavian accent. More recent additions include 20 luxurious beachfront units faced in redwood and native stone, and 4 villas on lovely Deadman Bay (ask about the one called **Crow's Nest**, which has a private pool). All share a clubhouse, fitness center, freshwater swimming pool, marina, four Laykold tennis courts, abundant water sports, and a helipad (a ferry from Road Town can also bring you here). Honeymooners love the seclusion of White Bay Beach, with drop-off and pickup provided by hotel staff. Guests dine well at the **Tradewinds** and the less formal **Deadman's Bay Beach Bar.** Meal-plan packages are available. A band comes over from Road Town several nights a week for dancing. ♦ Peter Island. 52000, 800/346.4451; fax 52500

PUSSER'S®

33 Pusser's Marina Cay $$$ In the 1930s, Marina Cay was the home of writer Robb White, the author of *Two On The Isle*, which later became a 1950s movie starring Sidney Poitier and John Cassavetes. Today the island is the site of this Pusser's outpost, which offers accommodations for 16 guests in 2 villas and 4 guest rooms—all rattan-furnished—overlooking the Sir Francis Drake Channel and the BVI beyond. **Dive BVI** has an operation on the premises, and the restaurant serves up steaks, seafood, and frosty cold drinks in an open-air setting. A free ferry makes the 10-minute trip from Beef Island 9 times daily. ♦ Marina Cay. 42174; fax 44775

34 Necker Island $$$$ Princess Diana vacationed here, but each and every guest gets the royal treatment on this 74-acre private island. The plush hideaway is owned by Richard Branson, founder of Virgin Records and Virgin Atlantic Airways, but when he's not in residence, paying guests are pampered by a staff of 19. The island comes complete with a 10-bedroom Balinese-style villa, 2 separate guest houses, 3 white-sand beaches, and a virgin coral reef. The villa, set on the summit of Devil's Hill, is encircled by terraces with great views. Its magnificent open living area, a masterwork of native stone and wood, is built around a tropical garden; above it is a gallery library filled with books and games. Hedonists will love the dining room with its slide-back roof and fine wine cellar. Other perks include an exercise room, freshwater pool, two Jacuzzis, tennis, water sports, snooker, and meeting facilities. For groups of up to 24, the daily tab also covers an open bar, all meals, and transfers to the island from Beef Island and Virgin Gorda by launch or helicopter. ♦ Necker Island. 42757, 800/557.4255; fax 44396

Among the endangered species protected on the limestone and coral atoll of Anegada is the rarely seen rock iguana, a fierce-looking, but quite harmless, reptile that grows to a length of 5 feet and weighs up to 20 pounds.

Dr. John Lettsom, born on Jost Van Dyke, founded the Medical Society of London. Another native of the British Virgin Islands, Dr. William Thornton, designed the US Capitol building in Washington, DC.

Getting Your Feet Wet in the British Virgin Islands

Everyone who comes to the British Virgin Islands should take advantage of the beautiful blue waters. Here are some organizations to get you afloat:

Boating

Euphoric Cruises Virgin Gorda Yacht Harbour, Spanish Town, Virgin Gorda. 55542.

The Moorings Wickhams Cay 2, Road Town, Tortola. 42332, 813/535.1446

Offshore Sail & Motor Yachts Nanny Cay Resort & Marina, Nanny Cay, Tortola. 800/582.0175

Sun Yacht Charters Hodges Creek Marina, Hodges Creek, Tortola. 800/772.3500

Virgin Islands Sailing Ltd. Tortola. 800/233.7936

Snorkeling and Scuba Diving

Baskin in the Sun Prospect Reef Resort, Fisher, Tortola, and Soper's Hole Marina, Soper's Hole Wharf, West End, Tortola. 45854, 42858, 800/233.7938; fax 45853

Caribbean Images Prospect Reef Resort, Fisher, Tortola. 41147

Dive BVI Ltd. Virgin Gorda Yacht Harbour, Spanish Town, Virgin Gorda. 55513, 800/848.7078

Kilbride's Underwater Tours Bitter End Yacht Club, North Sound, Virgin Gorda. 59638, 800/932.4286

Patouche II Wickhams Cay 1, Road Town, Tortola. 46300

Underwater Safaris The Moorings, Wickhams Cay 2, Road Town, Tortola. 43235, 43965, 800/537.7032

White Squall II Village Cay Marina, Road Town, Tortola. 42564

Surfing

Sebastian's on the Beach Long Bay and Zion Hill Rds, Little Apple Bay, Tortola. 54212, 800/336.4870

Cayman Islands

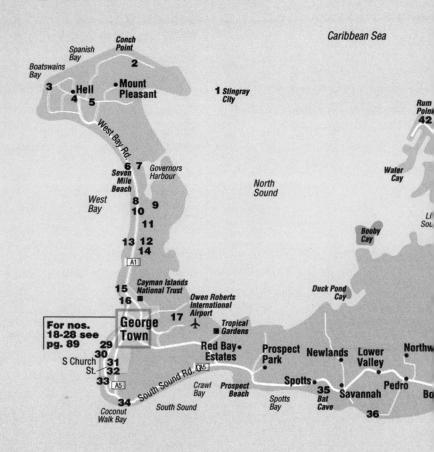

Caribbean Sea

Conch Point

2

Spanish Bay

Boatswains Bay

3

• Hell
4
5

• Mount Pleasant

1 Stingray City

Rum Point
42

Water Cay

West Bay Rd.

6 7
Seven Mile Beach

Governors Harbour

North Sound

West Bay

8
10   9

11

Booby Cay

Li Sou

13   12
14

A1

Cayman Islands National Trust

Owen Roberts International Airport

Duck Pond Cay

15
16

17

For nos. 18-28 see pg. 89

George Town

Tropical Gardens

Red Bay Estates

Prospect Park

Newlands

Lower Valley

Northw

29
30
S Church St.   31
32
33   A5
34

Coconut Walk Bay

South Sound Rd.

Q5

Crawl Bay

South Sound

Prospect Beach

Spotts Bay

Spotts

35
Bat Cave

Savannah

Pedro

Bo

36

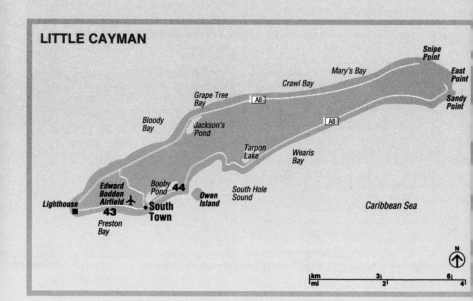

LITTLE CAYMAN

Snipe Point

Mary's Bay

East Point

Crawl Bay

Grape Tree Bay

A8

Sandy Point

Bloody Bay

Jackson's Pond

A8

Tarpon Lake

Wearis Bay

Edward Bodden Airfield

Booby Pond   44

Owen Island

South Hole Sound

Caribbean Sea

Lighthouse

43

• South Town

Preston Bay

N

km
mi

3

6

2

4

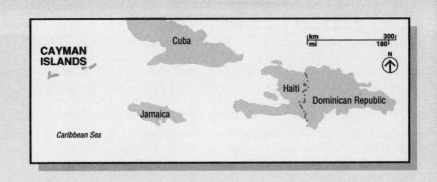

CAYMAN ISLANDS

Cuba

Haiti

Dominican Republic

Jamaica

Caribbean Sea

km 300
mi 180

N

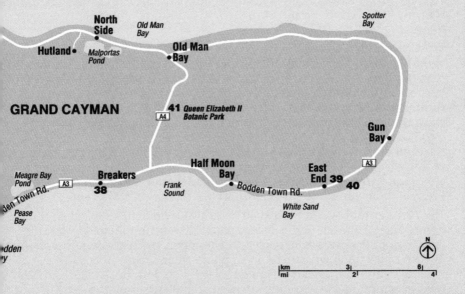

North Side

Old Man Bay

Spotter Bay

Hutland

Malportas Pond

Old Man Bay

GRAND CAYMAN

41 Queen Elizabeth II Botanic Park

A4

Gun Bay

A3

Half Moon Bay

Meagre Bay Pond

Breakers

A3

38

Frank Sound

East End

39

40

Bodden Town Rd.

Pease Bay

White Sand Bay

dden ry

km 3 6
mi 2 4

N

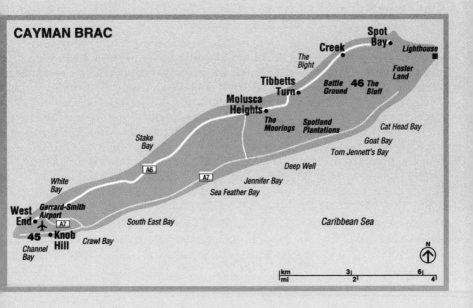

CAYMAN BRAC

Spot Bay

Creek

Lighthouse

The Bight

Tibbetts Turn

Battle Ground

46 The Bluff

Foster Land

Molusca Heights

The Moorings

Spotland Plantations

Cat Head Bay

Goat Bay

Stake Bay

Tom Jennett's Bay

A6

A7

Deep Well

White Bay

Jennifer Bay

Sea Feather Bay

West End

Gerrard-Smith Airport

A7

South East Bay

Caribbean Sea

45 • **Knob Hill**

Channel Bay

Crawl Bay

km 3 6
mi 2 4

N

Cayman Islands

Until the 1960s, the few tourists who requested vacation information from the Cayman Islands received a rather tentative welcome—a single mimeographed sheet that warned of bad roads, rampant insects, and a capricious electrical system. But in the last few decades this tiny chain of three coral-covered mountaintops—**Grand Cayman**, **Little Cayman**, and **Cayman Brac**—has become one of the top five scuba diving destinations on earth, as well as the fifth-largest financial center in the world.

In fact, 1997's million-plus visitors outnumbered the island population (31,000) over 30 to one. More than 500 banks conduct business in **George Town**, the capital of the island chain on Grand Cayman, which has more financial institutions per capita than anywhere in the world, including Switzerland. The islands are politically stable, and the employment rate here is nearly 100 percent. Result: virtually zero crime, and unfailingly pleasant locals.

Most of Grand Cayman's resort action is concentrated to the north, along **West Bay Road** and **Seven Mile Beach**. Winding roads that hug the coastline (you can't get lost) lead to districts like **West Bay**, **North Side**, and **East End**, where traditional wood-frame Caymanian cottages are trimmed with pink shutters, white picket fences, and raked sand lawns. On the East End, waves crash through blowholes etched by nature into limestone caves, spraying water 60 feet high in a spectacular show of force. Sea turtles propagate by the thousands at the **Turtle Farm** in West Bay, also the home of a bizarre geological attraction known as **Hell**. Islanders and travelers alike gather for afternoon barbecues under the feathery branches of Australian pines at **Rum Point** and for sunset cocktails on the eastern shores of **North Sound**.

The 20th century officially dawned on Little Cayman in 1990, when the 27 homes and businesses of this divers' paradise were illuminated by electric light. Until the arrival of electricity, the residents (who now number about 50) depended upon gas generators to power their refrigerators, ovens, and fans. Telephones arrived soon after, replacing the four radios that had been used to communicate with the outside world. Planes from the sister islands still touch down on a grassy airstrip, but the word is that condo and hotel developers are eyeing the island with lust. Should these shores someday be overrun with tourists, there's always **Owen Island**, a quarter-mile out in **South Hole Sound,** whose residents swear their 11-acre patch of sand and palm trees will never be sullied by civilization.

Meanwhile, the Braccers of Cayman Brac tend to their yellow, pink, and white homes with care and devotion, planting periwinkles, bougainvillea, and palms in their sand yards, which are carefully raked of debris every day. Villagers gather to sweep and rake the cemetery each Saturday evening and to celebrate special occasions by cooking pots of coconut stew in outdoor kitchens called cabooses. Visitors tend to congregate along the southwest coast for easy access to the more than 50 spectacular dive sites. The north coast's limestone and coral beaches are best for beachcombing, while those near the hotels to the south are perfect for sunning and snorkeling. Once you've chosen whether to dive, swim, hike, or hang out in a hammock, you've pretty much made all your decisions for the day, which illustrates Brac's most endearing attribute—utter tranquillity.

The Cayman Islands lie 150 miles south of Cuba and 140 miles northwest of Jamaica near the **Cayman Trench**, the deepest part of the Caribbean at 24,720 feet. In 1503 Christopher Columbus came upon the islands and christened them *Las Tortugas* for the large turtle population here. The modern name is an anglicized version of *caymanas,* the Spanish-Carib word for alligators, although the closest indigenous cousins are actually iguanas.

A British possession since 1670, the Caymans were granted freedom from taxation and wartime conscription by George III, a status they still enjoy. And though Caymanians embrace their West Indian heritage, their home remains a British crown colony, with all the pomp and circumstance intact.

Area code 345 unless otherwise noted.

Getting to the Islands

Airlines

American Airlines 800/433.7300

Cayman Airways................949.8200, 800/422.9626

Northwest ....
  in the Cayman Islands 800/225.2525,
  in the US 800/447.4747

Interisland Carriers

Air Jamaica 949.2309, 800/523.5585

Cayman Airways................949.8200, 800/422.9626

Island Air..949.5252

Airports Owen Roberts International Airport
(949.3603) on Grand Cayman is two miles east of George Town and five miles southeast of Seven Mile Beach. **Gerrard-Smith Airport** (948.1222) on the southwestern end of Cayman Brac is served by **Cayman Airways** and **Island Air** flights from Grand Cayman. **Edward Bodden Airfield** (no phone) on the southwestern end of Little Cayman is served by **Cayman Airways** and **Island Air** from Grand Cayman.

Getting Around the Islands

Bicycles and Motorbikes

Eagle's Nest Cycles 949.4866

Soto Scooters, Bikes, Car Rentals 945.4652

Buses Flag down one of the private minivans that make the trip from George Town to Seven Mile Beach.

Car Rental

Avis....................................949.2468, 800/331.1084

Budget 949.5605, 800/527.0700

Coconut...................949.4037, 949.4377, 949.7703

Hertz 949.2280, 949.7861, 800/654.3131

Just Jeeps 949.7263

Driving Influenced by British custom, cars have steering wheels on the right and are driven on the left side of the road. It's considered a discourtesy to honk your horn unless necessary. Air-conditioned sedans, jeeps, and motor scooters are available for rent. A permit to drive any rental vehicle is available from rental companies for $5 with a valid driver's license. By law, require motorcyclists must wear helmets.

Taxis Cabs are plentiful on Grand Cayman and Cayman Brac, and they are a reasonably priced option for traveling along Seven Mile Beach and in George Town. Farther out on Grand Cayman, the fares become quite steep—as much as a day's car rental. However, a taxi gives you the chance to pick up some local lore from a charming Caymanian driver, and to imbibe at your destination without worrying about getting home safely. Although there are no taxis on Little Cayman, pickups and drop-offs can be arranged through the hotels.

Tours Arrange tours through the **Cayman Island Taxi Cab Association** (947.4491) or one of the following companies on Grand Cayman:

Evco Tours, Ltd 949.2118

Majestic Tours 949.7773

Reid's Premier Tours 949.6531

Rudy's Travellers Transport 949.3208

Tropicana Tours 949.0944

Vernon's Sightseeing 949.1509, 949.1193

FYI

Electricity The current is 110 volts/60 cycles, the same as in the US and Canada.

Entry Requirements US and Canadian citizens must present a valid passport or other proof of citizenship (birth certificate, voter's registration card) plus a photo ID, and a return or onward ticket.

Language The official language is English.

Money Cayman currency was introduced in 1972 and includes 6 bills and 4 coins. US currency is accepted at most establishments. Banks are open Monday through Thursday from 9AM to 4PM, and Friday from 9AM to 4:30PM.

Personal Safety Caymanians are justifiably proud of their islands' reputation for being virtually crime free; they boast about leaving their cars and homes unlocked. Still, don't tempt fate: Exercise normal precautions with valuables and belongings. Cayman gendarmes have no patience with drunk drivers and drug users, who are immediately taken to jail. Sentencing by a local magistrate, at its lightest, will include an order to leave immediately.

Publications *The Caymanian Compass* is the local daily newspaper. *Key to Cayman,* published twice yearly, is an excellent magazine with information on restaurants, shopping, and nightlife. The monthly *What's Hot* also provides visitor information and is available free at major hotels. US dailies, including *USA Today,* the *Miami Herald,* and *The New York Times,* are sold at most hotels.

Reservation Services and House Rentals

Cayman Islands Hotel and Condo Association..........
....947.4057; fax 947.4143

Cayman Islands Reservation Service........................
....800/327.8777

Taxes There is a 6-percent government tax on accommodations; the departure tax is US$12.50.

Tipping Some hotels add a service charge of 10 to 15 percent. If yours does not, give chambermaids $1 to $2 per room per day, and bellhops 50¢ per bag, but no less than $1 total. In restaurants, 15 percent is usually added to the bill.

Visitors' Information Office The **Cayman Islands Department of Tourism** has an office at **Cricket Square** in George Town (Elgin Ave, between Thomas Russell Way and Shedden Rd, 949.0623, 949.7999) that's open Monday through Friday from 9AM to 5PM. There's also a booth at the airport (949.2635) that's open only when flights arrive, and another at the cruise ship pier (no phone) that operates Monday through Friday whenever a ship is in port. Another good source of information is the **Cayman Islands National Trust** (Courts Rd, east of Eastern Ave, George Town, 949.0121), which is open Monday through Friday from 8:30AM to 5PM. The tourism telephone hotline (949.8989; 800/346.3313 in the US) offers information on events, attractions, and activities, plus free assistance with booking tours.

Phone Book

Ambulance	911
Directory Assistance	411
Diving Emergencies/ Decompression Chambers	555
Emergencies	911
Fire	911
Hospitals	
Grand Cayman	949.8600
Cayman Brac	948.2243
Police	911
Post Office	George Town 949.2474, Seven Mile Beach 949.4177

Grand Cayman

Most bankers in the Caribbean conduct business on Grand Cayman; at 20 miles long and 4 to 8 miles wide, it's the largest of the three Cayman islands. **George Town,** the capital city, consists of six "major" streets (most only one or two blocks long) and is the site of government and civic buildings, banks, and many duty-free shops—most of which are located on **Cardinal Avenue** and **Fort Street.** **George Town Harbour** at **Hog Sty Bay** is where cruise-ship passengers arrive by the thousands, and where adventurers in smaller numbers descend beneath the moored sailboats on submarine sightseeing rides.

Most of the island's hotels and condos lie just north of George Town, lining **West Bay Road** and the misnamed **Seven Mile Beach**, actually a five-mile stretch of coconut palms, well-populated sands, and endless aquamarine horizons. A few smaller resorts catering to divers are scattered along the **South Sound.** Beyond these two clusters of commerce lies the real Grand Cayman, which is found in the tiny districts simply named **West Bay, North Side,** and **East End.**

1 Stingray City Imagine kneeling on white sand 12 feet underwater, stroking the silken underbelly of a stingray that has a six-foot wingspan, while other rays affectionately nuzzle you. Dangerous? Not at all. The rays that congregate at this spot are so accustomed to human attention that they swim toward dive boats with anticipation, knowing they'll be fed, petted, and loved.

Three local divemasters discovered this hangout for Southern stingrays (*Dasyatis americana*) in 1986 on their trips to the North Sound. They realized the rays were drawn to a shallow area where boat crews habitually cleaned their catch of fish and conch for lunch. The divers began visiting the rays regularly, feeding them bits of squid and dodging their whiplike, venomous tails—the source of their reputation as fearsome, dangerous creatures. Gradually, a community of 20 or so stingrays (mostly female) took up residence in the area and learned to get along with humans—they virtually never sting even the most inexperienced divers.

Over the years stingrays have come and gone, but their numbers stay fairly stable; the number of human visitors, however, has multiplied. Almost all of Grand Cayman's dive operators offer trips to this truly unique little paradise, and as many as 200 divers and snorkelers visit the underwater city each day during the high season. Even if you don't scuba dive, it's worth the trip to view these graceful creatures with a mask and snorkel. The water is just 2 to 3 feet deep on the sandbar; 12 to 16 feet deep elsewhere. ◆ North Sound

2 Ristorante Pappagallo ★★$$$$ A-frame peaks of palm thatch jut out at angles from the roof of this romantic Polynesian-style restaurant, set on a natural lagoon in the midst of a bird sanctuary. Parrots, cockatoos, and macaws preen within the glass cages in the air-conditioned **Pappagallo Room,** while tropical breezes stir the palm fronds in the lakefront **Flamingo Room.** Start with the mouthwatering swordfish carpaccio, followed by lobster and shrimp flamed with Armagnac or chicken breast sautéed with sausage and garlic. Dress is casually elegant for this special spot. ◆ Northern Italian ◆ Daily dinner. Reservations recommended. Palmetto Dr (south of Conch Point Rd). 949.3479, 949.1119

3 Cayman Turtle Farm Thousands upon thousands of green sea turtles in various stages of development flop about on top of each other in circular blue cement tanks and pools at the only green sea turtle breeding farm in the world. Sea turtles were once a staple of the Caymanian diet, but they have been hunted nearly into extinction and are considered endangered in many parts of the world. A marine biologist on Grand Cayman came up with the idea of establishing a green sea turtle farm in 1968 as both a commercial and ecological venture. In 1978, when the United States banned the import of turtle products, the emphasis was switched to research and release programs (although annually about 3,000 of the turtles raised here are sold for local consumption). The farm is a fascinating venture well worth touring. A large gift shop sells just about everything you can imagine with a turtle theme—but remember, tortoise-shell products are not allowed into the US. A snack shop sells turtle soup and steaks, perhaps your only guilt-free chance to sample these chewy delicacies. ♦ Admission. Daily. North West Point Rd (just south of Boatswains Bay Rd). 949.3893, 949.3894

4 Hell With jagged, blackened rock peaks that are thought to look like the charred remains of a fire in Hades, this is the ultimate tourist curiosity. The tiny post office stamps your postcards from Hell, gift shops offer T-shirts with predictable slogans, and a boardwalk overlooks the stygian formations. They are made of ironshore rock, a hard limestone that looks like black volcanic rock because its coating of algae secretes acid, eroding it into devilish shapes. A nearby bar, the **Club Inferno** (949.3263), is operated by a family appropriately named McDoom. ♦ Hell Rd (between Town Hall and Water Course Rds), Hell

5 Liberty's ★★★$ Barbara and Grayson Liberty serve hefty portions of Caymanian dishes to crowds of locals and tourists willing to trek out to their small cottage in West Bay. You can get a good overview of the local cuisine at the Wednesday, Friday, and Sunday night buffets, where diners enjoy some of the most memorable conch fritters in the Caribbean, plus boiled cassava, breadfruit, rice and beans, curried chicken, and irresistible coconut cream pie. ♦ Caymanian ♦ Daily lunch and dinner. Reverend Blackman Rd (between Church St and Town Hall Rd), Water Ground. 949.3226

6 Seven Mile Beach Most of Grand Cayman's tourist accommodations are clustered along this five-mile stretch of white-sand beach running north from George Town along West Bay. (No one seems to know the reason for the discrepancy between the beach's name and its real length.) Locals point out that the beaches all belong to the queen, meaning they're open to the public. There is a wonderful absence of vendors here, but a preponderance of jet skis and other noisy water toys. Many dive boats leave from this area. ♦ West Bay Rd (between N Church St and Boggy Sand Rd)

INDIES SUITES

7 Indies Suites $$$ One of the Caymans' most respected fishermen, Ronnie Foster created the islands' first (and only) all-suite hotel in 1990 and met with nearly instant success. Popular with divers, anglers, families, and business travelers, the complex is spread over 20 tropical acres and has 38 suites with living rooms, complete kitchens (with microwave ovens), and storage space for diving and fishing gear. Foster chose a wonderful stretch of nearly secluded beach for his hotel, and designed it to harmonize with the island's natural colors, using blue tile on the roof and soft peach and periwinkle in the decor. All rooms face the courtyard pool and hot tub. Fishing and dive packages are available. There's no restaurant, but continental breakfast is included in the rate. ♦ West Bay Rd, Governors Harbour. 945.5025, 800/654.3130; fax 945.5024

8 Westin Casuarina $$$ Surrounded by hundreds of date and coconut palms, this $50-million resort is laden with amenities. Grand Cayman's largest hotel, the glittering 5-story structure houses 341 rooms and 4 suites—all airily decorated in tropical garden colors and featuring oversized marble bathrooms. Most units boast balconies overlooking Seven Mile Beach. There are three restaurants, including a casual open-air eatery, and three bars, including a swim-up pool bar. Other highlights include two pools, two whirlpools, two tennis courts, a fitness center, a dive shop, boutiques, and business meeting rooms. Guests have privileges at the **Links at Safehaven** (see below). ♦ West Bay Rd, Seven Mile Beach. 945.3800, 800/228.3000; fax 949.5825

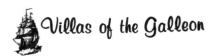

Villas of the Galleon

8 Villas of the Galleon $$$ These 74 fully equipped 1- and 3-bedroom luxury villas feature all the comforts of home on one of the Caribbean's best beaches. Each unit has either a patio or a balcony from which to enjoy the view, and a kitchen (handy, as there's no restaurant on the premises). Golf can be arranged at **Links at Safehaven** across the road (see below). ◆ West Bay Rd, Seven Mile Beach. 947.4433, 947.4311, 800/327.8777; fax 947.4705

9 Links at Safehaven The islands' only true 18-hole golf course, this par-71, 6,519-yard layout is windy and quite challenging. The complex includes a relaxing clubhouse, a seafood restaurant, a bar, a pro shop, and a driving range floodlit for evening practice. ◆ Fees. Daily. West Bay Rd, Seven Mile Beach. 949.5988

10 Holiday Inn $$$ In recent years this 213-room beachfront property has been given a $6-million renovation and a new, lively look. Guest rooms shine in tropical greens, blues, and mauves, and the works of local artists line the long hallways. There are three restaurants, including a poolside lunch eatery and a coffee shop with a breakfast buffet that is renowned among locals and visitors for its made-to-order omelettes and abundance of food—meats, potatoes, pancakes, waffles, and tropical fruits. A fun, festive place, the hotel offers plenty of water-oriented activities by the beach and at the large freshwater pool. **The Ten Sails,** an English pub by day and a comedy club at night, provides entertainment. There's also dancing under the stars to the music of the famed local singer Barefoot Man and his band at the poolside tiki hut Wednesday through Saturday nights. Other amenities include a coin-operated laundry and a hot tub. ◆ West Bay Rd, Seven Mile Beach. 945.4444, 800/421.9999; fax 945.4213

Within the Holiday Inn:

Don Foster's Dive Cayman The Cayman Islands have more than 30 dive operators, and this shop is one of the best: a **PADI** 5-star operation with **NAUI, SSI,** and **YMCA** licenses, a fleet of first-rate dive boats, excellent divemasters, and a full range of instruction, including underwater photography. Dive packages include unlimited shore diving and discounts on rental cars and film processing. There's a maximum of 20 divers per boat/dive. ◆ Daily. 945.4786, 945.5132, 800/83.DIVER; fax 945.5133, in the US 305/438.4220

11 Clarion Grand Pavilion Hotel $$$$ Queen Elizabeth II slept here on her first trip to the Caymans in 1983, but the teal-and-blue property has changed a lot since then. It now boasts 93 rooms decorated in West Indian style and equipped with everything from mini-bars to hair dryers and trouser presses. There are also two restaurants (including the celebrated **Ottmar's,** see below), water sports, scuba facilities, a fitness center, a sauna, a pool, and a Jacuzzi situated under a waterfall. The beach is just across the road, and service here is excellent. ◆ West Bay Rd, Seven Mile Beach. 947.5656, 800/CLARION; fax 947.5353

Within the Clarion Grand Pavilion:

Ottmar's ★★★★$$$$ Veteran chef and owner Ottmar Weber, who has been pleasing the palates of Cayman diners for more than two decades, dazzles with his own brand of classic cooking at this formal restaurant. Continental dishes often feature rich sauces, and portions are generous. Start off with baked Gulf shrimp or sherried crabmeat chowder; recommended main courses include the panfried catch of the day and the chicken with orange rum sauce. The Sunday brunch is delightful. ◆ Continental ◆ M-Sa breakfast, lunch, and dinner; Su breakfast, brunch, and dinner. Reservations recommended for dinner. 947.5879

12 Hyatt Regency Grand Cayman $$$$ Regal, serene, and luxurious, this periwinkle-blue hotel sits amid the emerald lawns of the **Britannia Golf Course** like a colonial British baron's Caribbean hideaway. Stately white columns, multipaned French doors, perfectly pruned palms, and an abundance of blossoms will make you feel as though you should be dressed for a garden party—or even a bit part in a film (several scenes of *The Firm* were shot on the sprawling property).

The hotel has a fully equipped beach club on a 266-foot stretch of talcum-powder sand, with water-sports equipment, a pool, restaurants, and an excellent dive shop. A second pool on the hotel grounds has a swim-up bar. A color scheme that reflects the island's sunsets gives the 236 rooms and suites and 55 villas a calm, cool ambience. ◆ West Bay Rd, Seven Mile Beach. 949.1234, 800/233.1234; fax 949.8528

Within the Hyatt Regency Grand Cayman:

Britannia Golf Course Designed by Jack Nicklaus, the island's first golf course has its own style of ball, lighter than normal to match the half-length fairways. The course is reminiscent of Scotland's Royal Troon and Turnberry courses, with grassy mounds and rolling dunes along the shores of lakes and the Caribbean. This course can be played 3 ways: as a 9-hole par-35 championship course, as an 18-hole par-58 executive course (by playing the 9 holes twice), or as an 18-hole par-72 course using the Nicklaus-created "Cayman ball," a lightweight golf ball with convex dimples that flies about half the distance of a standard ball and requires a shorter course. The **Golf Club** restaurant is a pleasant spot for a leisurely lunch. ◆ Greens fees. Daily. 949.8020

Hemingway's ★★★$$ Set in a white pavilion at the center of the hotel's beach club overlooking the ocean, this is a pretty spot for lunch or dinner. Start with the Papa Doble, a daiquiri supposedly just like those favored by Ernest Hemingway in Havana, with white and spiced rum and orange, pineapple, grapefruit, and lime juice. (Rumor has it Hemingway could down 16 of the potent concoctions in a single sitting—challenges to his record are not encouraged.) For a light lunch, have a Key West salad with crabmeat and palm hearts and a bowl of fish tea (herb bouillon with mussels, scallops, lobster, and shrimp). For dinner, try such regional specialties as beer-batter coconut shrimp served with steamed yucca, macadamia-crusted pork with sweet potatoes, or spicy jerk chicken with coconut rice and fried plantains. ♦ West Indian/Continental ♦ Daily lunch and dinner. Reservations recommended. 949.1234

Red Sail Sports Top-notch boats with shade, showers, tropical fruit snacks, and plenty of room are trademarks of this dive operation, as are the accomplished and personable dive masters. Those planning to get certified on Grand Cayman are well cared for, and everyone—be they gung-ho, cowardly, physically challenged, elderly, or youthful novices—is guided into the underwater world with ease. Experienced divers can take specialty courses in night, wall, and wreck diving, as well as underwater navigation. Beginners can take a resort course that gives them a brief introduction to the wonders below, or stay above water on Hobie Cats, water skis, Windsurfers, and parasails. Anglers can go after blue marlin on air-conditioned yachts. There's also a small shop with a gorgeous selection of T-shirts, dive gear, books, and cards—all with an underwater theme, of course.

Do treat yourself to a sunset cruise on *The Spirit of Ppalu,* a 65-foot catamaran named after the Polynesian god of navigation. The best seats are on the hull, where the water rushes beneath six glass viewing panels. The warm breezes will lull you into a complacent glow. Drinks and hors d'oeuvres are served inside the teak cabin—try the Blue Ppalu, made with curaçao, and you'll feel at one with the sea. Snorkel trips to Stingray City and dinner cruises are also available. ♦ Daily. 945.5965, 947.5965, 800/225.6425; fax 947.5808

12 Cracked Conch ★★$$ The rustic, nautical decor, brightened by colorful murals of the island, and the low-key, friendly mood make this a good spot for a scrumptious and reasonably priced steak, fish, turtle, or lobster dinner. Drive your cholesterol into oblivion with the coconut stew, or choose from the "heart-wise" selection of fat-free dishes. The luncheon buffet is one of the island's best

values. ♦ Caribbean ♦ M-Sa lunch and dinner; Su dinner. West Bay Rd, Seven Mile Beach. 947.5217

12 Lone Star Bar and Grill ★★$ *Newsweek* rated it "one of the world's Top 100 Bars," and the cooks are past winners of the Great Caribbean Chili Cook-Off, so it's no wonder the place is popular. Mean barbecued ribs, grilled steaks, spicy Cajun dishes, good fajitas, and a fun-lovin' attitude are served up around wooden tables; drinkers catch major sporting events on the bar's satellite TV. This is a good place to meet those permanently tanned expats from all over the world who work as divemasters, waiters, and the like so they can live in paradise. ♦ Tex-Mex ♦ Daily lunch and dinner. West Bay Rd, Seven Mile Beach. 945.5175

13 Colonial Club $$$ This pretty-in-pink complex features 24 2- and 3-bedroom apartments furnished with everything a vacationer could need. There's no restaurant, but each unit has a fully equipped kitchen. Also on site are two tennis courts, a pool, a Jacuzzi, and that unbelievably beautiful Seven Mile Beach practically outside your door. ♦ West Bay Rd, Seven Mile Beach. 945.4660; fax 945.4389

13 Lacovia $$$$ Of the many condominium complexes on Seven Mile Beach, this one earns high praise for its luxury and tranquillity. White 2-story buildings with Spanish-style wood arches house 45 apartment units (1-, 2-, or 3-bedroom) with kitchens, air-conditioning, TVs, and telephones. The complex has a swimming pool, hot tubs, tennis courts, saunas, and water-sports facilities, but no restaurant. ♦ West Bay Rd, Seven Mile Beach. 949.7599, 800/223.9815; fax 949.0172

13 Lantana's Restaurant and Bar ★★★★ $$$ When Austrian-born chef Fred Schrock opened this restaurant in 1991, he brought a taste of the US Southwest to Cayman, creating such dishes as grilled lamb smothered in a red-onion marmalade, pork tenderloin coated with jerk spices, and shrimp served with cilantro pasta. Leave room for the apple pie—it's to die for. The restaurant, located at the **Caribbean Club,** is decorated with cacti, terra-cotta pottery, and North American Indian weavings. ♦ American/

Caribbean ♦ M-F lunch and dinner; Sa-Su dinner. Reservations required on weekends. West Bay Rd, Seven Mile Beach. 947.5595

14 Golden Pagoda ★★★$$ Chinese favorites and the more subtly flavored Hakka cuisine (similar to hibachi-grilled dishes) are available in the dining room and for takeout (ideal for sunset picnics on the beach). Try the shrimp in hot spicy sauce or the Mongolian beef. The daily luncheon buffet is a bountiful feast. The service is gracious at this restaurant, which is known for catering grand banquets. ♦ Chinese ♦ M-F lunch and dinner; Sa-Su dinner. West Bay Rd, Seven Mile Beach. 949.5475

14 Galleria Plaza Several strip malls line West Bay Road between the clusters of hotels and restaurants. Most have branches of familiar fast-food chains, plus liquor stores and gift shops. This is one of the largest of these centers, with plenty of parking and diversions for everyone. ♦ M-Sa. West Bay Rd, Seven Mile Beach. No phone

Within Galleria Plaza:

Chests of Gold Artist Kristin Anderson does gorgeous things with cloisonné and gold—her glittering angelfish with emerald green inlays are worth a splurge. The shop also has an impressive display of ancient coins (sold with certificates documenting their authenticity) and heavy gold chains for wearing your new treasure. ♦ M-Sa. 949.7833. Also at: Hyatt Regency Grand Cayman, West Bay Rd, Seven Mile Beach. 949.8846; Westin Casuarina, West Bay Rd, Seven Mile Beach. 949.5330

The Book Nook This shop offers a superb choice of fiction for the beach, as well as children's and travel titles, and books about the Caribbean—including a wide range of fiction and nonfiction by regional authors. Divers come here for the generous selection of scuba books; visitors enamored with the local food pick up Caribbean cookbooks. The shop also sells souvenir cards, toys, and T-shirts. ♦ M-Sa. 945.4686

Street vendors, called "higglers" by the locals, are outlawed on the Cayman Islands.

Restaurants/Clubs: Red   **Hotels:** Blue
Shops/♟ Outdoors: Green   **Sights/Culture:** Black

15 The Wharf ★★★★$$ One of the few restaurants right on the sands of Seven Mile Beach, this romantic spot also boasts the **Ports of Call** bar, the perfect place for a sunset daiquiri before dinner under the swaying coconut palms. Choose from Caribbean turtle, conch, and seafood dishes, or such traditional continental fare as French onion soup and lamb chops *Provençale;* be sure to order the seafood paella if it's offered as a special. Chef Werner Meyer, a native of Austria, has a nice touch with seafood, stuffing dolphinfish (also known as dorado and mahimahi) with scallops, and serving red snapper with a mango sauce. Don't miss his *Mohr Im Hemd,* a killer Austrian chocolate soufflé. Try to be here at 9PM, when huge tarpon leap around the edge of the wharf as they wait to be fed by the restaurant's staff. Prices are more reasonable at lunch, when you can relax under a blue-and-white-striped umbrella and watch the boats sail by. Air-conditioned dining is available, but it's a shame to miss the stunning view. ♦ Caribbean/Continental ♦ M-F lunch and dinner; Sa-Su dinner. Reservations recommended. West Bay Rd, Seven Mile Beach. 949.2231

16 The Almond Tree ★★★★$$$ Marinated as an appetizer or baked as a steak, conch is prepared with finesse here; the turtle steak is another rare and flavorful treat. This dining spot is also known for its exotic rum drinks (try the Hurricane, a blend of light and dark rum, vodka, gin, triple sec, grenadine, and lime) and its inexpensive all-you-can-eat twice-weekly lunch buffets. There's outdoor dining on a garden patio surrounded by almond, breadfruit, and poinciana trees, or inside the big thatch-roofed restaurant filled with artifacts and memorabilia from Africa, South America, and the South Pacific. ♦ Seafood/Steaks ♦ M, Tu, Th, Sa dinner; W, F lunch and dinner. N Church St (south of West Bay Rd), George Town. 949.2893

17 Tortuga Rum Company In 1990, Carlene and Robert Hamaty started making and selling scrumptious rum cakes using an old family recipe. Their cottage industry has grown enormously, its products deservedly popular among visitors. Cakes can be shipped to the US and Canada. Stop in for a free sample. Local rum is also on sale. ♦ M-Sa. Industrial Park, Dorcy Dr (south of North Sound Rd), George Town. 949.7701

18 Hog Sty Bay Café ★★★$$ You name it, this place has it. The varied menu offers everything from Belgian waffles and salads to more exotic Indian curries, barbecued alligator, and jerk burgers. The large Caesar salad topped with marinated conch is a satisfying meal in itself, especially when followed by a West Indian sundae (vanilla ice cream with banana fritters and rum-raisin sauce). More substantial entrées include seafood pasta with a tangy citrus sauce and snapper topped with tomatoes and feta cheese. There's also a fine selection of beers, including Tennant's on draft. A good choice for lunch or dinner during a tour of George Town, the cafe has nine tables on a wooden deck perched over the water. Much of the interior is taken over by dart players challenging each other to hit bull's-eyes on the boards lining one wall. This is one of the few places near George Town that's open for lunch on Sunday. ♦ Caribbean/Eclectic ♦ Daily breakfast, lunch, and dinner. N Church St (north of Harbour Dr), George Town. 949.6163

19 Fort George The fort built by the British around 1790 to protect Grand Cayman from Spanish invasion no longer exists, but a monument and plaque stand in its place. The cliff-top site affords great views of the sea. Next door is the **Old Fort Building,** a complex of gift shops. ♦ N Church St and Harbour Dr, George Town. No phone

20 Legislative Assembly Building This government structure is noteworthy for its architecture, which is more modern than most Cayman buildings. Visitors may watch island law being created from a gallery over the **Legislative Hall.** (But don't wear shorts or bathing suits here, or in other government buildings or churches—it's considered disrespectful.) ♦ Free. M-F. Fort St (between Mary and N Church Sts), George Town. 949.4236

21 Black Coral and . . . Even if you're not in a buying mood, stop by this gallery to see the work of sculptor Bernard Passman, one of the island's most famous black-coral artists, with commissions from the Cayman government, the British royal family, and tourists who enjoy his exotic work. If you do choose to make a purchase, ask for a certificate, as you may not be able to take your new sculpture back into the US without one. (Black coral is a protected species and only authorized persons can

harvest it.) Also make sure the work is signed by Passman, whose shop offers a money-back guarantee that all coral pieces will appreciate in value. ♦ M-Sa. Fort St (between Albert Panton and N Church Sts), George Town. 949.0123

22 Elmslie Memorial Church Captain Rayal Bodden, a prominent shipbuilder on Grand Cayman Island in the 1800s, designed this wood-frame, steepled church as the waterfront center of downtown. The timber work in the ceiling is said to resemble that in the hulls of Bodden's sailing ships. Caymanians are respectful, decorous people, so don't wear shorts or bathing suits in the church or in the legal and government buildings of George Town. ♦ Open only during services: Su 11AM, 7PM. Harbour Dr (between Cardinal Ave and N Church St), George Town. 949.7923

23 Kirk Freeport Plaza Duty-free shopping is one of Grand Cayman's major attractions, particularly for cruise-ship passengers. At this large complex are several small shops specializing in imported perfumes, jewelry, china, and crystal (including Lalique, Waterford, and Baccarat). ♦ M-Sa. Cardinal Ave and Albert Panton St, George Town. 949.7477

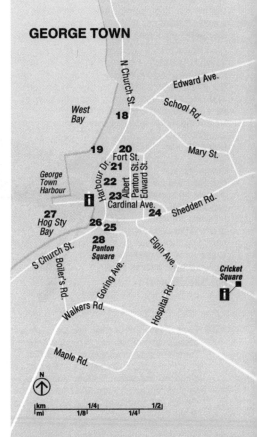

GEORGE TOWN

Diving in the Deep

The Cayman Islands are to scuba divers what Disneyland is to kids, except here the attractions are walls of extraordinary coral formations, abundant fish, and dozens of shipwrecks, all in comfortable 82-degree water with visibility at 100 to 150 feet.

Diving in the Caymans is sure to be a memorable experience—one against which all subsequent dives will be measured. As you float toward the sunken hull of one of the islands' 60 shipwrecks, look for elephant-ear sponges and gorgonian fans in the coral gardens just a few feet from shore. Stingrays accustomed to human antics sometimes rub their silky underbellies against divers, while silvery barracudas hover just out of touch. Meanwhile, French angelfish, nurse sharks, Creole wrasses, pufferfish, moray eels, spotted drums, rainbow parrotfish, blue-striped grunts, eagle rays, giant grouper, and green turtles pose for underwater portraits as if modeling for a tourist brochure.

Dive gear can be rented everywhere; if you bring your own, **Cayman Airways** allows three pieces of luggage per passenger to accommodate the load. Hotels and resorts routinely offer packages with dive excursions, and more than two dozen dive operators provide everything from beginner's certification courses to advanced deepwater and wreck diving, underwater photography classes, and nitrox diving.

Grand Cayman's dive boats generally leave from **Seven Mile Beach** or the south shore to sites just minutes away. Some companies have boats on the **North Side** for trips to **Stingray City** and the **North Wall.** Most operators are members of the **Cayman Islands Watersports Operators Association,** which emphasizes safety, education, and conservation. Grand Cayman has decompression chambers and full medical emergency services. The following are some of Grand Cayman's most established dive shops; most also offer snorkeling equipment and excursions.

Bob Soto's Diving Five island locations. 949.2022, 800/262.7686

Crystal Clear Divers Grand Cayman. 949.3730

Don Foster's Dive Cayman Holiday Inn, West Bay Rd, Seven Mile Beach, Grand Cayman. 945.4786, 945.5132, 800/83DIVER

Eden Rock George Town, Grand Cayman. 949.7243

Parrots Landing S Church St (south of Harbour Dr), George Town, Grand Cayman. 949.7884, 800/448.0428

Red Sail Sports Hyatt Regency Grand Cayman, West Bay Rd, Seven Mile Beach, Grand Cayman. 945.5965, 800/255.6425

Sunset Divers Sunset House, S Church St (south of Harbour Dr), George Town, Grand Cayman. 949.7111, 800/854.4767

Treasure Island Divers Seven Mile Beach, Grand Cayman. 949.4456, 800/872.7552

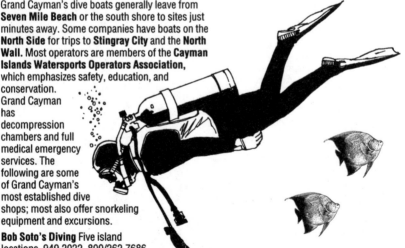

24 Post Office The circular, cement-block post office, built in 1939, is a gathering spot since there is no mail delivery on the island. The islanders' 2,000 mailboxes are on the outside of the building, which is strung with colored lights. The Caymans' beautiful postage stamps make great souvenirs. ♦ M-F. Edward St and Cardinal Ave, George Town. 949.2474

25 Cayman Islands National Museum The **Old Courts Building,** a national treasure and landmark since the early 1800s, was transformed into a museum in 1990. The two-story Cayman colonial building is an architectural delight, with porches, green shutters, and a flagpole once used to hold the lighthouse lantern. The museum's exhibits chronicle the island's shipbuilding, turtling, and rope industries, as well as its history as a harbor for explorers, pirates, and shipwrecked sailors. There is a snack bar and gift shop. ♦ Admission. M-Sa. S Church St and Shedden Rd, George Town. 949.8368

26 Atlantis Submarines If you're not keen on scuba diving, check out the underwater scenery from a porthole of a submarine traveling 50 to 150 feet beneath the surface. Gliding past the Cayman Wall, you'll see brilliant orange and yellow coral, and schools of colorful tropical fish. These submarine tours are popular, albeit rather pricey, so make reservations early. (If you're claustrophobic, think twice.) ♦ Fee. Daily. Children under four are not allowed on board. S Church St (just south of Harbour Dr), George Town. 949.7700, 800/253.0493

26 Nautilus Submarine Now here's something you don't see every day: Murder-mystery dinner theater performed aboard a semi-submersible vessel. During the day, the 78-foot *Nautilus* takes 100 passengers at a time on underwater tours; at night, it becomes the venue for hors d'oeuvres, drinks, and a show. Three large TV monitors allow the 60 guests aboard to see "clues" that are "hidden" underwater during the 90-minute show. The undersea landscape, lit by giant lights that reveal its true colors, is spectacular. ♦ Admission. Call for schedule. S Church St (just south of Harbour Dr), George Town. 945.1355; fax 945.3739

27 Hog Sty Bay Home of the less colorfully named George Town Harbour, this is Grand Cayman's main bay. Cruise ships dock outside the bay, and thousands of passengers are tendered to shore to splurge in the duty-free shops, submerge themselves along the island's world-famous reefs, or take a trip to **Hell** (see page 85). Many visitors just enjoy a small park at the harbor; others head for the tourist information booth that's open when cruise ships are docked. The National Trust has established a self-guided walking tour of the harbor area's historic sites; it's all explained in the trust's map and brochure, available at most hotels.

28 Panton Square The Caymans' version of Victorian architecture is exquisitely preserved in the homes around this grassy square. Note the frilly latticework along the upstairs porches, which is set off by the simplicity of the shuttered windows and plain porch railings. ♦ S Church St (between Goring Ave and Boiler's Rd), George Town

29 Seaview Hotel $ One of the oldest inns on the island, this is also one of the few low-priced lodging spots. Built in 1952 and later renovated, the aqua-colored hotel has 15 simple, air-conditioned rooms (with telephones, but no TV sets) set in 2-story buildings around a freshwater swimming pool. There's a seaside restaurant and an indoor/outdoor lounge. The on-site **Seaview Dive Center** offers resort and certification courses, dive trips, equipment rentals, and dive packages. ♦ S Church St (south of Harbour Dr), George Town. 949.8804, 800/327.8777; fax 949.8507

30 Parrots Landing Although it's billed as a water-sports park, visitors won't find splashy rides here. The fun comes from snorkeling at four excellent spots just offshore, diving the North Wall from shore, parasailing over the South Sound, or riding in a glass-bottom paddleboat. On an island where divers are often crammed into crowded "cattle-boats," this complex's dive shop specializes in trips for small groups. Hammocks hang between feathery pines, tables and grills are scattered about the raked-sand beach, and Caymanian and Honduran parrots provide the appropriate background squawks for picnics and barbecues. The large gift shop offers skimpy swimsuits, neon-bright scuba gear, and T-shirts emblazoned with purple and green designs. ♦ Daily. S Church St (south of Harbour Dr), George Town. 949.7884, 800/448.0428; fax 949.0294

30 Sunset House $$ Even if you don't stay here, stop by this friendly, award-winning divers' resort one evening to toast the setting sun. The view is particularly spectacular from the seaside deck of **My Bar**—and the tropical cocktails aren't bad either. The complex offers 59 simple rooms and 2 apartments set in 2-story, peach-colored cottages, all within 100 feet of the ocean and one of the island's best-run dive operations. The waterproof and sandproof decor is more serviceable than picturesque, but the rooms do have air-conditioning and telephones. There's an indoor/outdoor restaurant (see below), but the favorite gathering spot is the bar, where sandwiches and snacks as well as drinks are served.

A limestone shelf extends from the hotel grounds over the water; stairs cut into the stone and ladders hung from the shelf give divers and snorkelers easy access to the living reefs just offshore. The proximity to even larger reefs makes this a good spot for night dives. Most guests are divers on package plans, though the rates are reasonable for nondivers. The dive shop (with four boats) and staff come highly recommended by scuba experts and publications in the US. ♦ S Church St (south of Harbour Dr), George Town. 949.7111, 800/854.4767; fax 949.7101

Within Sunset House:

Seaharvest ★★$$ An unexpected Cajun zing spikes the fresh seafood at this casual restaurant with lovely ocean views. Dine in the air-conditioned indoors or outside on the patio. Try the Cayman medley (lobster tail, dolphinfish, and shrimp) or stop by for the Friday barbecue specials. The steaks are just as tasty as the seafood. ♦ Seafood/Caribbean ♦ Daily breakfast, lunch, and dinner. 945.1385

Sunset Underwater Photo Centre
Professional underwater photographer, author, and teacher Cathy Church has a full-scale darkroom/classroom/rental operation here. She provides daily film processing; half-day, full-day, and weeklong underwater-photography classes; and rental of high-quality cameras and video recorders, including the Nikonos underwater camera. Amateur photographers can arrange for a "photo buddy" (an underwater photography instructor) to go along on a dive, and it's possible to learn more just by studying the incredible photos on the walls. Slides and prints taken by pros are sold. ♦ Daily. 949.7415; fax 949.9770

31 Eldemire's Guest House $ Budget accommodations with character are in short supply on Grand Cayman, but charming Erma Eldemire has done an admirable job of providing low-cost rooms with style for nearly three decades. Her Caymanian cottage, within walking distance of downtown and the ocean, has seven rooms, one studio, and one apartment, all simply furnished and air-conditioned. No meals are available. ♦ Glen Eden Rd and S Church St, George Town. 949.5387; fax 949.6987

32 Pure Art This pretty Cayman cottage houses the island's best display of paintings, prints, sculptures, clothing, and crafts by local artists. Souvenirs with a Caymanian flair include handmade thatch brooms (some small enough to hang on a Christmas tree), rosewood and purpleheart *waurie* boards used in a local marble game, Caymanian honey and preserves, rum cakes, and postcards and stationery with drawings of the local scenery by the shop's owner, Debbie van der Bol. ♦ M-Sa; evenings by appointment. S

Church St (south of Glen Eden Rd), George Town. 949.9133. Also at: Hyatt Regency Grand Cayman, West Bay Rd, Seven Mile Beach. 947.5633

33 Chef Tell's Grand Old House ★★$$ Chef Tell Erhardt, a former Philadelphia television personality who has been cooking since he was 14, has created one of the most popular tourist restaurants on the island in a colonial-style plantation house by the sea. Start with a drink in the restaurant's **Clown Bar,** then move to the screened veranda or seaside gazebos for a candlelit dinner of crepes, crab, or lobster. The tenderloin steak Diane and deep-fried grouper beignets are also good choices. ♦ Seafood ♦ M-F lunch and dinner; Sa dinner. Reservations required. S Church St (south of Harbour Dr), George Town. 949.9333

34 Crow's Nest Restaurant ★★★$$ A veranda wraps around this traditional Caymanian house facing a secluded beach lined with palms and pines. All that's visible from the road is a dirt parking lot; walk to the beach side to find tables draped in bright cloths on decks over the sand. This informal eatery stays busy even during the low season, thank to a chef who does wonderful things with loc flavors and seafood. Notable are the spicy, deep-fried, coconut-battered shrimp with pineapple plum sauce; grilled swordfish with jerk mayonnaise; and turtle steak with vermouth sauce. The filet mignon with spicy jerk sauce is superb. Try to arrive before sunset, or take advantage of the sea view at lunchtime. ♦ Seafood/Caribbean ♦ M-Sa lunch and dinner; Su dinner. Reservations recommended. South Sound Rd (east of Walkers Rd). 949.9366

35 Bat Cave Off the main road on the way to Bodden Town, spelunkers can climb down a 10-foot cliff that leads to the sea and look inside the cave to see—you guessed it—bats Watch your step, as the guano deposits can be slick, as well as pungent. ♦ South of Bodden Town Rd

36 Pedro St. James Castle Commonly known as **Pedro's Castle,** this is the oldest existing structure in the Cayman Islands. Constructed in 1780 as the home of plantatio owner William Eden, five decades later the house served as a meeting site for the residents who formed the first elected parliament in the Cayman Islands. A $6-million-plus restoration project transformed the then-abandoned waterfront structure in 1996. The original two-story building and its wide verandas were rebuilt, and new outbuildings were constructed in the style of their 18th-century neighbor. Slated to open at press time: a visitor's center featuring a laser show, exhibits, a cafe, and a gift shop. ◆ South of Bodden Town Rd. 947.3329

37 Bodden Town The island's original capital is named after **Captain Rayal Bodden,** a shipbuilder and architect who influenced much of Grand Cayman's development in the 1800s. Two cannons mark the entrance to the town, which sits at a good vantage point on a limestone bluff above the sea; a monument to Queen Victoria and a colorful cemetery overlook the water at the historic and picturesque spot. ◆ Bodden Town Rd

In Bodden Town:

Pirates' Cave These privately owned underground tunnels, allegedly once used by pirates to hide their loot, now house artifacts and (fake) treasure chests. Locals believe many real treasures are still buried along the coast here. Ask anyone in town to direct you to the souvenir shop that houses the entrance to the caves. ◆ Admission. Daily. 947.3122

38 Lighthouse at Breakers ★★★$$ This cobblestoned lighthouse set on a solitary beach now serves as a first-class, but informal, restaurant that attracts discerning diners from all over the island. Chef David Chambers varies his offerings, mixing West Indian dishes with Italian fare. Seafood Sorrento (cold poached salmon, lobster, and shrimp served with a variety of sauces) shares space on the menu with jerk shrimp, conch chowder, vegetarian dishes, and seven gourmet burgers. Guests eat at tables made from tree trunks; the best seats in the house are at the banquettes along the screened windows overlooking the beach. ◆ Italian/West Indian ◆ Daily lunch and dinner. Bodden Town Rd, Breakers. 947.2047

39 East End The rugged coastline of the island's East End is pockmarked with caverns and caves, creating dramatic blowholes where geysers of seawater spray 60 feet into the air. Only one road runs along this part of the island, so it's impossible to get lost. The town of East End was the first settlement on Grand Cayman. ◆ Bodden Town Rd

40 Cayman Diving Lodge $$ Dedicated divers with little need for shopping and bar hopping are perfectly content at this small hotel far from the crowds in town. With only 10 air-conditioned rooms, the lodge is the kind of place where guests and staff are on a first-name basis, sharing family-style meals, playing cards on the communal patio, and exploring the underwater scenery along the shallow, horseshoe-shaped reef that's so close you can see it from shore. The lodge is located on the southeasternmost point of Grand Cayman in East End, a quiet community

with more churches than restaurants or bars. The water is equally uncrowded, and there are more than 100 dive sites along the East Wall—a nearly virgin territory where other boats rarely appear. ◆ Bodden Town Rd, East End. 947.7555, 800/852.3483; fax 947.7560

41 Queen Elizabeth II Botanic Park These ecologically (and aesthetically) correct gardens in the center of the island cover 60 acres of manicured wilderness and ponds. Interpretive signs direct visitors to rare orchids; rare blue iguana live in a walled compound; and the bright-green Cayman parrot may fly by. ◆ Admission. Daily. Frank Sound Rd (between Bodden Town Rd and Old Man Bay). 947.9462

42 Rum Point Considered by many to be the loveliest spot on the island, this point pokes into the North Sound above Booby Cay on a limestone shelf nearly buried with needles from the windswept Australian pines. Aqua-colored picnic tables dot the soft sand beaches, where crystalline water laps lazily. A reef just offshore creates a natural wind-and-wave break, so the bays are as calm as fish tanks. This is a wonderful spot for escaping the crowds.

An animal sanctuary and environmental-protection zone that border this spot help keep it unspoiled. There are a few hotels and resorts in the area, and many condos and private homes. Some snorkel and dive tours to Stingray City and the North Wall stop here for lunch. ◆ East shore of North Sound

At Rum Point:

Rum Point Club ★$ This tiny eatery in a pine grove gets major points for ambience and attitude—it's about as tropically languid as any place anywhere on the islands. An outdoor jukebox plays reggae and calypso tunes, regulars lounge about at the aptly named **Wreck Bar,** and first-timers spend as much time snapping photographs as eating their conch sandwiches (not a bad idea, since the setting is far more pleasing than the cuisine). If you've got wheels, come for the Wednesday, Friday, or Saturday barbecues. Most of the island's expats and citizens gather here on Sunday, away from outsiders on the more tourist-oriented beaches; join them and imagine what it would be like to stay forever. ◆ West Indian ◆ M-Tu, Th, Su lunch and early dinner; W, F-Sa lunch and dinner barbecues. 947.9412

The group of Caribbean islands known as the Lesser Antilles consists of Anguilla, Antigua and Barbuda, Barbados, Dominica, Grenada, Guadeloupe, Martinique, Montserrat, St. Kitts and Nevis, St. Lucia, St. Vincent and the Grenadines, and the Virgin Islands.

Getting Your Feet Wet in the Cayman Islands

Though the Cayman Islands are famous for world-class snorkeling and scuba diving (see "Diving in the Deep" on page 90), you'll also find plenty of water sports that allow visitors to just skim the sea's surface—or fly above it. Some outfitters that will set you afloat:

Boating

Aqua Delights Holiday Inn, West Bay Rd, Seven Mile Beach, Grand Cayman. 947.4444, 947.4786

Cayman Delight Cruises, West Bay, Grand Cayman. 949.8111

Gerry Kirkconnell Seven Mile Beach, Grand Cayman. 949.7477

Ron Ebank's Charter Boat Headquarters Coconut Place Shopping Center, West Bay Rd, Seven Mile Beach, Grand Cayman. 945.4340

Parasailing

Cayman Skyriders Seven Mile Beach, Grand Cayman. 949.8745

Sportfishing

Chuckie Ebanks Black Princess Charters Coconut Place Shopping Center, West Bay Rd, Seven Mile Beach, Grand Cayman. 949.0400, 949.3821

Crystal Clear Divers Grand Cayman. 949.3730

Ron Ebank's Charter Boat Headquarters Coconut Place Shopping Center, West Bay Rd, Seven Mile Beach, Grand Cayman. 945.4340

Windsurfing

Sailboards Caribbean Seven Mile Beach, Grand Cayman. 949.1068

Surfside Watersports The main office for this dive operation is in George Town, and a boat leaves from the west side of the island with the rest of the scuba flotilla. But the Rum Point shop is a great launching spot for excursions to Stingray City and the sites along the North Wall, including Tarpon Alley, where you'll likely encounter several four-foot tarpon floating in a coral canyon. Manager Bob Carter is on a first-name basis with the eels and rays in the area, and is an expert underwater photographer; bring your camera or rent one here. The divemasters and shop staff are amiable, amusing, and given to grinning at the slightest provocation—probably because they know they've got the jobs everyone else just dreams about. ♦ Daily. 947.7330. Also at: Indies Suites, West Bay Rd, Seven Mile Beach. 945.5025, 800/654.3130; fax 945.5024

Little Cayman

Eleven miles long and only a mile wide, Little Cayman is a spit of limestone, coral, and salt marsh 65 miles northeast of Grand Cayman. More parrots and iguanas than sunbathers populate Little Cayman; the island is more than 98 percent undeveloped, making it a refuge for rare native and migrating birds, including West Indian whistling ducks, which favor **Tarpon Lake.** People come here for refuge too—and for spectacular diving and sportfishing. Anglers find tarpon and bonefish in abundance. Divers marvel at 200-foot visibility around **Bloody Bay Wall,** which plunges 1,000 feet and which Jacques Cousteau called one of the 10 best dive sites in the world.

43 Pirate's Point Resort $$$ Expatriate Texan Gladys Howard (the self-described "Mouth from the South") is your host at this easygoing 10-room lodge spread over 5 acres of beachfront property secluded enough to feel like a private retreat. The rooms are simply furnished and airy; not all are air-conditioned. The scuba packages include two dives daily and meals at Howard's terrific restaurant (see below). Deep-sea fishing excursions can be arranged. ♦ Rte A8 (west of Edward Bodden Airfield). 948.1010, 800/327.8777; fax 948.1010

Within Pirate's Point Resort:

Pirate's Point Restaurant ★★★★$$$ Resort owner Gladys Howard is a Cordon Bleu chef who trained with Julia Child and James Beard, and her wonderful restaurant reflects her culinary expertise. On Monday, "Island Night," local food is in the spotlight; choices include steamed triggerfish, *cho cho* (stuffed Caribbean squash), and spinachlike callaloo. Deftly seasoned and sauced pork, chicken, conch, and vegetable dishes are on the menu the rest of the week. ♦ West Indian ♦ Daily dinner. Reservations required. 948.1010

The five largest Caribbean islands are: Cuba (44,218 square miles); Hispaniola, encompassing the Dominican Republic and Haiti (29,371 square miles); Jamaica (4,244 square miles); Puerto Rico (3,435 square miles); and Trinidad (1,864 square miles).

44 Southern Cross Club

$$ This hospitable 10-room property sits on a thousand feet of white-sand beach. In the 1960s, it was the first hotel on the island to cater to adventurous anglers and divers seeking isolation; that's still its reputation and focus today. The large guest rooms are decorated in bright white and yellow, and are cooled by ceiling fans and sea breezes. (Guest rooms have no air-conditioning, telephones, or TV sets.) Meals are included in the room rate; fishing and scuba diving packages are available. ♦ Rte A8, Booby Pond. 948.1099, 800/327.877

Cayman Brac

Endangered Cayman parrots squawk in uninhabited woods, and green sea turtles lumber to familiar beaches to lay their eggs in this natural paradise. Cayman Brac, 80 miles northeast of Grand Cayman, is only 12 miles long and 1 miles wide, with a population of some 1,700 die-hard Braccers. In the spring a canopy of bright-orange royal poinciana tree blossoms covers every road and trail, and rare orchids bloom beside mangoes and papayas. A few modern hotels and shops are clustered along the southwest end of the island near the international airport, and electricity, telephones, and satellite TVs are common commodities. But, for the most part, the Brac remains classically, quietly Caymanian.

45 Brac Reef Beach Resort $$ Braccer

Linton Tibbets combines the best of the island's culture, natural beauty, and hospitality with accommodations designed to captivate outsiders accustomed to certain luxuries. The 40 rooms are air-conditioned, for example, though it's far more romantic to open the windows and feel the sea breezes. The favorite gathering spot is a two-story, thatch-roofed bar and deck at the end of a wooden pier—but the pool and hot tub have their devotees as well. Caymanian specialties are regular offerings at the **Coral Gardens** restaurant and are sometimes served buffet style on the beach. **Reef Divers,** the resort's full-service dive shop, has a luxurious dive boat that makes trips to remote, uncrowded reefs. ♦ West of Rte A7. 948.1323, 800/327.3835; fax 948.1207

45 Divi Tiara $$$ A hideaway with creature

comforts galore, this is first and foremost a diver's destination, though honeymooners find it idyllic as well. Expansions have transformed the formerly rustic inn into a full-scale resort with 59 air-conditioned rooms, satellite TV, and telephones. Also here is **Club Tiara,** a luxury time-share condominium with 12 units. Amenities include a freshwater pool just off the white-sand beach, two tennis courts, a hot tub, a restaurant, and a bar. The resort has a top-notch dive operation, **Dive Tiara,** with six high-speed boats and an underwater-photo and -video center. ♦ West of Rte A7. 948.1553, 800/367.3484; fax 948.1316

46 The Bluff The name "Brac" is said to be

Middle English or Gaelic for bluff, referring to this 140-foot-high limestone plateau. Historians say the gray-white cliff was probably the first land spotted by Christopher Columbus when he arrived at the Caymans in 1503. Pirates later found the caves here to be natural safe-deposit boxes for their loot. Today, the Braccers use the deep, solid caves as refuges from hurricanes and tropical storms, while treasure hunting and spelunking are popular pastimes for curious tourists. Wear sneakers or sturdy shoes to climb about the bluff's slippery, steep paths, and stay away from the sheer cliffs to the north and south. More than 150 kinds of resident and migratory birds can be seen here; dedicated bird-watchers spot peregrine falcons and white barn owls. ♦ Northeast end

Bests

Barbara Currie Dailey

Writer and Longtime Expatriate Resident

The Sister Islands! Even if you can only take a day trip via **Island Air** to **Cayman Brac** or **Little Cayman,** do so! These islands are tiny (fewer than 12 square miles) and very different from the "sophisticated big sister," **Grand Cayman.** The people of the Sister Islands are what you'll remember most.

On Little Cayman: Visit Gladys Howard and her **Pirate's Point Resort.** A raconteuse and Cordon Bleu chef, Gladys devotes her spare time to environmental crusades as chairman of the Little Cayman National Trust chapter. Don't miss Sunday morning—Gladys takes guests on a milelong nature walk along the "pirates trail" through the tropical woodland, pointing out crabs, orchids, iguanas, and birds on a tour laced with folklore.

If you have the time for only one "big activity" during your stay, make it a **North Sound** snorkeling trip (by boat), including **Stingray City**—an absolute must. Ron and Eugene Ebanks are two of the best to ask for.

Memories are made of this: At least one morning, get up at dawn to walk along **Seven Mile Beach** when few will be out. Or drive around the island very early on a Sunday morning.

Eat conch: It's the traditional dish of Cayman. Fritters, stew, marinated, cracked—it's a delicacy you can't find done as well anyplace else. If you're in the islands during Pirates' Week (October), be sure to try something from the pots stewing at the district Heritage Day fairs. Otherwise, try **Liberty's** or the **Cracked Conch.**

Noordpunt

26

25 **Westpunt**

Weg naar Westpunt 27 *Boca Tabla Grotto*

Westpuntbaai

■ *Landhuis Savonet*

Christoffelpark (Christoffel National Park) 28

Bartolbaai

▲ *Christoffelberg 1,230 ft.*

• **Lagún**

• **Santa Krus**

• **Barber**

• **Soto**

Boca Ascención

Santa Martabaai

24

Weg naar Santa Krus

29

Weg naar Westpunt

Weg naar

23

San • *San Willibrordus*

Willibrordus

22

Caribbean Sea

Bullenbaai

• **Bullenbaai**

Weg naar Bullenbaai

• **Sint Mich**

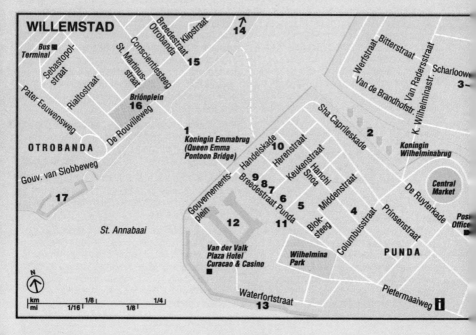

WILLEMSTAD

Bus ■
Terminal

Sebastopol-straat

Pater Eeuwensweg

Rialtostraat

St. Martinus straat

Conscientiesteeg

Breedestraat Otrobanda

Klipstraat

↑
14

15

Briónplein

16

De Rouvilleweg

OTROBANDA

Gouv. van Slobbeweg

17

St. Annabaai

1
Koningin Emmabrug (Queen Emma Pontoon Bridge)

Gouvernements-plein

Handelskade

Herenstraat

Sha Caprileskade

Werfstraat

Bitterstraat

Van de Brandhofstr.

Van Radersstraat

K. Wilhelminastr.

Scharloow

3-

2

Koningin Wilhelminabrug

10

Keukenstraat

Hanchi Snoa

9 8 7

Breedestraat Punda

6

5

Middenstraat

Blok-steeg

De Ruyterkade

Central Market

4

Columbusstraat

Prinsenstraat

Post Office

12

11

Van der Valk Plaza Hotel Curacao & Casino
■

Wilhelmina Park

PUNDA

Pietermaaiweg
ℹ

Waterfortstraat
13

N
↑

km
mi

1/16

1/8

1/8

1/4

Curaçao

Caribbean Sea

Aruba

Bonaire

CURAÇAO

N

VENEZUELA

km 200
mi 150

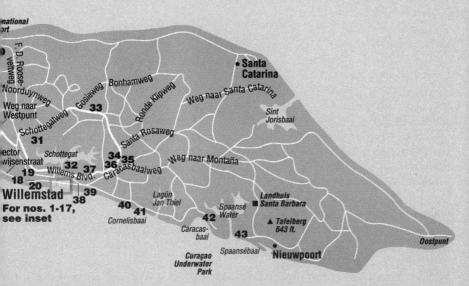

Caribbean
Sea

*national
ort*

F. D. Roose-
veltweg

Noorduynweg

Weg naar
Westpunt

Schottegatweg

Gosieweg

Bonhamweg

Ronde Klipweg

33

Santa Rosaweg

31

*ector
wijsenstraat*

Schottegat

32 **37**

34 35
36

Willems Blvd.

Caracasbaaiweg

19

18
20

39

Willemstad

38

**For nos. 1-17,
see inset**

40

41

Cornelisbaai

*Lagún
Jan Thiel*

*Spaansé
Water*

42

*Caracas-
baai*

43

*Curaçao
Underwater
Park*

Spaansébaai

Weg naar Santa Catarina

• **Santa
Catarina**

*Sint
Jorisbaai*

Weg naar Montaña

Landhuis
■ Santa Barbara

▲ *Tafelberg
643 ft.*

Nieuwpoort

Oostpunt

N

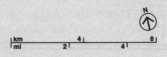

km 4 8
mi 2 4

Curaçao

People in Curaçao claim that the glare of the sun against whitewashed walls once provoked a colonial governor's migraines, so 200 years of tradition dictate that the citizens of **Willemstad**, the capital and port of this 38-mile-long island, paint their houses in vibrant pastels. One of the architectural stars of the Caribbean, Willemstad is Amsterdam's tropical cousin, nestled among a tidy maze of inland waterways. In this storybook town, rows of fanciful buildings right out of a Vermeer painting are trimmed with elaborate cupolas, dormers, and curving gables. In December 1997, UNESCO declared Willemstad a World Heritage Site because of its historic architecture.

Since 1888, the two sides of Curaçao's port city have been linked by the **Koningin Emmabrug** (Queen Emma Pontoon Bridge), "The Swinging Lady" that opens wide to welcome boats into the central harbor. Nearby, Venezuelan schooners tie up at a floating market where shoppers crowd the shore to haggle over imported fish and produce.

Scattered about the countryside, tidy thatch-roofed huts still shelter millers, weavers, and other craftspeople. Well-maintained island roads loop past the Dutch plantations, known as *landhuizen,* that were built on hilltops in sight of one another for protection and communication in wilder days. Traditional windmills creak incongruously in an arid landscape colored not by tulips and dairy cows, but by cacti, goats, and iguanas. Tenacious divi-divi trees are splayed low by the trade winds.

Blessed with an outstanding deepwater port (now the seventh-largest and the fifth-busiest in the world), Curaçao has long been a prized target for empire builders, industrialists, and other entrepreneurs. Following the initial discovery by Spanish explorers in 1499, it was occupied variously by Britain, Holland, Spain, and independent islanders before being returned to Dutch rule in 1816.

Just 40 miles off the Venezuelan coast, the island was probably first settled by seafaring Caiquetio Indians (close relatives of the Arawak) fleeing the ferocious Carib tribes of South America. Since then, a steady flow of refugees has found asylum here, including freedom fighters Simón Bolívar and Francisco de Miranda from Venezuela, and Juan Pablo Duarte and Buenaventura Báez from the Dominican Republic.

Jews who had endured persecution in Latin nations established a local community in 1651, which still thrives. In 1732 they built the **Synagoge Mikve Israel-Emanuel,** the oldest existing synagogue in the Western Hemisphere. The island's religious tolerance also drew Muslims, English Pilgrims, and other religious exiles.

The developing international population exploded with the discovery of oil in Venezuela in 1914. Eventually the Royal Dutch Shell Company built a huge refinery near Willemstad that, coupled with worldwide traffic through Curaçao's booming port and financial center, stirred more than 50 different nationalities into the local mix. Now leased by a Venezuelan corporation, the renamed **ISLA-Raffinaderij** (ISLA Oil Refinery) is a local landmark that represents jobs and economic security for the islanders, who now number about 145,000.

Today the shoreline of volcanic sand, ringed by submerged lava caves and coral reefs, attracts both serious divers and confirmed beach potatoes. At the **Curaçao Sea Aquarium,** landlubbers can walk among huge glass tanks to view the sea life that populates the *HMS Oranje Nassau,* which sank off these shores in 1906. Or adventurous nondivers can opt for the aquarium's "Animal Encounter," donning a wet suit to venture (with dive guides) into 12-foot waters to feed sharks and play with stingrays.

When the sun goes down, a multicourse Indonesian feast (known to Dutch colonials as rijsttafel, literally "rice table") is the perfect excuse to toss back a few of the Amstel beers brewed on the island with distilled sea water. Just be sure to finish with a taste of that world-famous liqueur, curaçao. It's still produced at the 17th-century Chobolobo estate and is fragrant with the oranges that grow only here.

To call from the US, dial 011 (international access code), 5999 (country code), and the 7-digit local number. On Curaçao, dial only the 7-digit local number unless otherwise indicated.

Getting to the Island

Airlines

Air Aruba.........868.3777, 868.3659, 800/88.ARUBA
ALM (Antillean Airlines).....461.3033, 800/327.7230

Airport Hato International Airport (868.1719) is home base for **ALM,** Curaçao's national airline. The airport services international and interisland flights, and is about a 25-minute drive from Willemstad.

Getting Around the Island

Buses Bright yellow public buses (called "konvoys" by the locals) travel from downtown Willemstad throughout the island. There are two terminals: at the central market in **Punda,** and at Sebastopolstraat in the **Otrobanda.** For more information, call 868.4733. Look on the front of the buses or ask the driver to find out its destination.

Private vans with a capacity of up to 14 people also pick up passengers at bus stops. Before you board, check the windshield for the destination and the license plate for the word "BUS."

Car Rental

Avis 461.4700, 461.1255, 800/331.1212
Budget..............868.3466, 868.3420, 800/527.0700
Caribe...461.3089
Hertz 465.8585, 800/654.3131
Holiday...560.3297
National............869.4433, 868.3489, 800/328.4567
Star 462.7444
Rista...737.8873, 737.8871

Driving US and Canadian driver's licenses are valid on the island.

Taxis

Central Taxi Office 869.0747

Tours Half- and full-day bus tours are run by Altino Tours (461.4888) and **Taber Tours** (767.6637). Taxis also offer tours at a set hourly rate. **Old City Tours** (461.3554) conducts walks through old residential neighborhoods and plantation houses led by a local architect and an art historian; customized itineraries are available for groups of four or more. Local amateur historian **Jopie Hart** (767.3798) guides groups on walks that focus on the socioeconomic development of different neighborhoods.

FYI

Electricity The current is 110 to 130 volts/50 cycles, with US-style outlets, fine for razors and most hair dryers. For other appliances, hotels can usually supply converters.

Entry Requirements US and Canadian citizens must present a valid passport or other proof of citizenship (birth certificate, voter's registration card) plus a photo ID, along with a return or onward ticket.

Gambling Curaçao's 10 casinos are open daily from 2PM until 5AM. To try your luck, visit the **Porto Paseo** complex (47 De Rouvilleweg, at Kijkduinstraat, 462.7007), or casinos located in the following hotels: **Coral Cliff** (see page 104), **Curaçao Caribbean** (see page 104), **Van der Valk Plaza Hotel Curaçao** (see page 102), **Holiday Beach** (see page 103), **Hotel Holland** (524 Franklin D. Rooseveltweg, just east of the airport, 869.2961), **Otrobanda** (see page 102), **Princess Beach Resort and Casino** (see page 108), **San Marco Hotel** (7 Columbusstraat, between Breedestraat Punda and Hanchi Snoa, 461.6628), and **Sonesta Beach Hotel and Casino** (see page 108).

Language The official language is Dutch, but most islanders also speak English and Spanish. The native tongue is Papiamento—a blend of Dutch, French, English, Portuguese, and Spanish, spiked with Caribbean and Indian dialects.

Money The official currency is the Netherlands Antilles florin (NAf or guilder), but US dollars and major credit cards are widely accepted. Banks are open Monday through Friday from 8AM to 3PM. The airport bank exchange office is open Monday through Saturday 8AM to 8PM, and Sunday 8AM to 4PM.

Personal Safety Crime is not a big problem on Curaçao, but exercise normal precautions. Don't leave valuables in an unlocked car or unguarded on the beach.

Visitors to Curaçao arrive in the greatest numbers from the Netherlands and Germany. South Americans are the second-largest group, and travelers from the US make up approximately 15 percent of visitors to this island.

The Caribbean islands have two, rather than four, seasons: a long rainy season from May through October, and a dry season the rest of the year.

Publications *Curaçao Holiday* is a useful English-language guide to attractions, shopping, special events, restaurants, and other subjects of interest to visitors. The magazines *Now . . . Curaçao!* (published by the hotel association), and *Curaçao Nights* also have information on attractions, shops, and restaurants. A twice-monthly Dutch-English newspaper, *The Beach Herald*, focuses on tourist attractions and events. All four publications are free and are available at the airport, tourist office, and most hotels. Willemstad bookstores carry *The New York Times,* the *Wall Street Journal,* and the *Miami Herald.*

Reservation Services and House Rentals The **Curaçao Tourist Board** (see below) has listings of places to stay and will help make arrangements.

Taxes There is a seven-percent tax on hotel rooms. In addition, a US$12.50 departure tax is paid at the airport.

Tipping Hotels add a 12-percent service charge to each bill; it takes care of bartenders, bellhops, chambermaids, and waiters. Add an extra five percent for special services. Most restaurants tack on a 10-percent service charge to the tab. Tip cab drivers only if they help with bags or perform other extra chores. Porters expect 50¢ per bag, but not less than US$1 total.

Visitors' Information Offices The **Curaçao Tourist Board** has an office in Willemstad (19 Pietermaaiweg, just east of Pietermaaiplein, 461.6000) and a branch at the airport (868.6789). The Willemstad office is open Monday through Friday from 8AM to 5PM and Saturday from 9AM to noon. The airport unit is open until the last flight of the day has arrived during peak season, and Monday through Friday from 8AM to 5PM during the off-season.

Phone Book

Ambulance	112
Directory Assistance	121
Diving Emergencies/ Decompression Chamber	462.4900
Emergencies	114
Fire	114
Hospital	462.4900
Police	114
Post Office	737.6666

Most of the fish on display at the Curaçao Sea Aquarium were caught personally by Dutch Schear, the aquarium's designer and manager.

In Curaçao, ice water is known as "Eskimo Punch."

Willemstad

Curaçao's capital (also the capital of the Netherlands Antilles) is a lovely pastel-tinted city on **St. Annabaai** (St. Anna Bay), just 40 miles from the coast of Venezuela. One of the world's busiest ports, Willemstad is also a picturesque collection of Dutch colonial architecture and historic forts. The canal that leads into the harbor separates the city's two distinct neighborhoods, which are connected by the **Koningin Emmabrug** (Queen Emma Pontoon Bridge). The main part of town—**Punda**—is home to most of the restaurants, shops, and other visitor attractions. The **Otrobanda,** or "other side," was created 300 years ago as a drop-off point for criminals and lepers. It came into vogue as an artists' colony during the 1950s and 1960s, and is now the target of some historic-building renovation and tourist development.

1 **Koningin Emmabrug (Queen Emma Pontoon Bridge)** Curaçao's signature landmark and the favorite starting point for any tour of Willemstad, this bridge swings open more than 30 times a day to admit the more than 8,000 ships that enter the harbor canal annually. The original "Swinging Lady" was built in 1888 by entrepreneur and US Consul Leonard Burlington Smith. The current (and third) model was completed in 1939. In the early days, barefoot pedestrians crossed for free, while those wearing shoes paid a sort of "rich man's tax"—a 2¢ toll. Today this largest floating pedestrian bridge in the world is free to everyone. (If the bridge is closed, walk down the street to the ferries that shuttle passengers across the canal.) Look north to see the 1974 Koningin Julianabrug (Queen Juliana Bridge), the Caribbean's tallest bridge. The 1,625-foot span stands 185 feet high to allow big ships to pass beneath it. ♦ Between Breedestraat Punda and De Rouvilleweg, Otrobanda

2 **Drijvende Markt (Floating Market)** Venezuelan schooners tie up here and form a vibrant marketplace of tropical fruit and vegetables, dried meats, fish, spices, fabrics, handicrafts, and other colorful wares. Don't be afraid to bargain—it's an acceptable practice. ♦ M-Sa. Sha Caprileskade (between Koningin Wilhelminabrug and Handelskade), Punda

3 **Scharloo** This once-elegant district is being pulled out of disrepair thanks to an ambitious historic-building rescue effort. The best way to get a sense of the transformation is to cross the Koningin Wilhelminabrug (Queen Wilhelmina Bridge), which joins the two parts of the Punda and turn right onto Scharlooweg. At first you'll pass mansions in ruins, but just beyond the post office you'll see the magnificent results of the face-lifts. This is a great outing for photographers and architecture buffs. ♦ Scharlooweg (between Borneosteeg and Koningin Wilhelminastraat), Punda

4 Joods Cultuur Historisch Museum (Jewish Historical and Cultural Museum) Displays of religious articles used by one of the oldest Jewish communities in the Western Hemisphere include Torah scrolls said to date from 1492, replicas of 17th-century gravestones, utensils for kosher butchering, scales, and intricate silverwork. Once a rabbi's house, later a Chinese laundry, this 1728 building next to the **Synagoge Mikve Israel-Emanuel** was restored when a centuries-old *mikvah* (ritual bath) was discovered in the courtyard. ♦ Admission. M-F; closed Jewish and public holidays. 29 Hanchi Snoa (between Columbusstraat and Middenstraat), Punda. 461.1633

4 Synagoge Mikve Israel-Emanuel The oldest continually operating synagogue in the Western Hemisphere was built in 1732 by a congregation founded here in 1651 by 12 families from Amsterdam. A beautiful example of colonial Dutch architecture, the stately gabled building features a central courtyard and rich interior appointments of mahogany and silver. Three of the 24-candle brass chandeliers are more than 250 years old, replicas of those in Amsterdam's Portuguese Synagogue. Floors are covered with white sand, a reminder of God's promise that Abraham's descendants would be "countless as the sands of the sea," as well as of the Jews' journey through the desert to the Promised Land. The custom also may be a throwback to the days of the Spanish Inquisition, when sand was used to muffle the sound of services held in Spanish and Portuguese synagogues. ♦ Donation. M-F. English and Hebrew services: F evening, Sa morning. 29 Hanchi Snoa (between Columbusstraat and Middenstraat), Punda. 461.1067

5 La Perla This chic boutique features an exclusive line of swimwear, beach clothing, lingerie, and hosiery, including the shop's signature "Le Rose" pantyhose. ♦ M-Sa. 4 Gomezplein (between Breedestraat Punda and Hanchi Snoa), Punda. 465.3955

6 Little Switzerland With branches scattered throughout the Caribbean, this well-known shop offers excellent prices on fine jewelry, Swiss watches, china, crystal, and flatware. ♦ M-Sa. 44 Breedestraat Punda (at Keukenstraat), Punda. 461.2111

7 Yellow House Step into this fragrant boutique, a local landmark since 1887, for perfume, cosmetics, and accessories. ♦ M-Sa. 46 Breedestraat Punda (at Keukenstraat), Punda. 461.3222

8 Boolchand's If you're in the market for a computer, the ones on sale here are duty-free. There are also well-priced electronic goods and cameras, also duty-free. ♦ M-Sa. 50 Breedestraat Punda (between Keukenstraat and Herenstraat), Punda. 461.6233

9 J.L. Penha & Sons Men's and women's clothing from European designers, French perfume, Italian leather goods, and cashmeres from Great Britain are the stock in trade at this Willemstad shop, which is housed in one of the city's oldest buildings. ♦ M-Sa. 1 Herenstraat (at Breedestraat Punda), Punda. 461.2266

10 Gallery 86 The island's largest art gallery focuses on the works of local and Dutch artists. It also affords a lovely view of the harbor. ♦ M-F; Sa morning. Trompstraat and Handelskade, Punda. 461.3417

11 Gandelman Jewelers Here you'll find intricate gold jewelry in contemporary designs and settings, crafted by local artists. ♦ M-Sa. 35 Breedestraat Punda (between Wilhelmina Park and Gouvernementsplein), Punda. 461.1854. Also at: Sonesta Beach Hotel & Casino, John F. Kennedy Blvd (just south of Piscaderaweg). 462.8386

12 Fort Amsterdam Directly behind the **Waterfort** (see below), the current seat of government is home to the yellow-and-white **Paleis van de Gouverneur** (Governor's Palace), the ministry, and several national offices. From 1648 to 1861 walls surrounded what was then all of Willemstad; visitors who step through the archway into the lovely courtyard will be transported back to the 18th century. The old Dutch church here is beautifully preserved, right down to the English cannonball still embedded in its southwest wall, which was fired in 1804 by Captain William Bligh of *Mutiny on the Bounty* fame. One corner of the fort is near the intersection of Handelskade and Breedestraat Punda, the beginning of Curaçao's main shopping district. The fort buildings are not currently open to the public, but visitors may stroll around the courtyard and grounds. ♦ Gouvernementsplein (just southwest of Breedestraat Punda), Punda

13 Waterfort The original 1634 structure was replaced in 1827 by this turreted bastion that once guarded the mouth of the harbor canal on the Punda side and served as a holding place for slaves. During World War II, troops were quartered here, and a steel net was stretched across the bay to Riffort on the Otrobanda (opposite bank) as a barrier to enemy submarines. You can still see the heavy iron links embedded in the outer walls. Today restaurants and shops are housed in the fort's "arches," which were formerly used as brigs. ♦ Waterfortstraat (west of Batterijstraat), Punda

Within Waterfort:

Van der Valk Plaza Hotel Curaçao & Casino $$$ Watch ships squeeze perilously close by here as they enter the harbor canal and you'll see why this is one of the very few hotels in the world to carry marine collision insurance. The original hotel, built within the fort in 1957, blends well with the historic ramparts, while the addition of a modern 15-story tower has brought the total number of air-conditioned rooms to 254. The hotel is ideally located for exploring Willemstad and the shops and restaurants tucked into the **Waterfortboogjes** (Waterfort Arches) just below. Other perks include a casino, a parapet, a swimming pool with snack bar, and the romantic **Waterfort Restaurant & Terrace** (stop by any Monday for Curaçao Night, complete with limbo show, steel band, and local food). Full breakfast is included in the room rates. ♦ 461.2500, 800/223.1588; fax 461.6543

La Pergola ★★$$$ Homemade pasta, veal chops, and local seafood are the stars of the Northern Italian menu at this indoor/outdoor *ristorante*. There's also a good wine list. Ask for a seaside table. ♦ Italian ♦ M-Sa lunch and dinner; Su dinner. Reservations recommended. Waterfortboogjes. 461.3482

The Grill King ★★$$ Pause for a casual meal of grilled seafood, steaks, or chicken at this convenient rest stop for waterfront explorers. There's the added bonus of live music on weekends. ♦ American ♦ M-Sa lunch and dinner; Su dinner. Reservations recommended. Waterfortboogjes. 461.6870

14 Arawak Craft Products Plunked right on the waterfront beside the cruise-ship dock, this combination workshop/store offers a lovely selection of pottery, charcoal drawings, watercolor paintings, wind chimes, T-shirts, and, most notably, reproductions of some of the historic buildings on the island. ♦ M-Sa; open Su when cruise ships are in port. 1 Mattheywerf (at Kijkduinstraat), Otrobanda. 462.7249

15 Otrobanda Hotel & Casino $ Great views of port traffic and the old Dutch architecture of the opposite bank are a special attraction at the first harborfront hotel in the Otrobanda. A popular stop for business travelers, this scenic property offers 45 guest rooms, a casino, a coffee shop, and an open-air bar and restaurant overlooking the harbor entrance (see below). Breakfast is included in the rates. ♦ Breedestraat Otrobanda and De Rouvilleweg, Otrobanda. 462.7400, 800/328.7222, 800/448.8355; fax 462.7299

Within the Otrobanda Hotel & Casino:

Bay Sight Terrace ★★$$ Cruise- and cargo-ship traffic is an important facet of life on Curaçao, and this casual, open-air restaurant is the spot to watch the big ships go by. Sunset is the best time to enjoy a cocktail, fish dinner, or conch soup; the sight is impressive as the sun goes down and the lights come on. ♦ Continental/Creole ♦ Daily lunch and dinner. 462.7400

16 Briónplein This plaza is named for Pedro Luis Brión (1782-1821), the national hero whose battle skills helped repel English invaders. Following the island militia's successful occupation of Curaçao in 1800, Brión (then chief of the militia) led the resistance movement that eventually forced the Brits to withdraw in 1803. The square is dominated by a statue of Brión, unveiled in 1956. ♦ De Rouvilleweg and Conscientiesteeg, Otrobanda

17 Riffort Heavy chains or steel nets were sometimes stretched from this fort to the **Waterfort** on the opposite bank to prevent enemy ships from entering the harbor. Over the years, it has served as headquarters for the Harbor Authority, the police, and the Boy Scouts, among others. ♦ Gouverneur van Slobbeweg (just southwest of Pater Euwensweg), Otrobanda

Within the Riffort:

Bistro Le Clochard ★★$$$ Splurge on continental cuisine in a beautifully furnished jail cell or perhaps in the former cistern of this old fortress. Interior dining rooms have few windows, but you can drink in the seaside view over cocktails and hors d'oeuvres on the **Harbor Side Terrace**. Swiss fondue, local seafood, veal dishes, and rich desserts are fine here. Not surprisingly, this is one of the island's most popular restaurants. ♦ French/Swiss ♦ M-F lunch and dinner; Sa dinner. Reservations recommended. 462.5666

Restaurants/Clubs: Red   **Hotels:** Blue

Shops/ Outdoors: Green   **Sights/Culture:** Black

Elsewhere on Curaçao

18 Curaçaosch Museum The museum gardens show off plants and trees native to the island. Step inside to view artifacts of the Caiquetio Indians, the cockpit of the *Snipe* (a Fokker F-XVIII trimotor that made the first commercial crossing of the southern Atlantic in 1934), sculptures, antiques, and other treasures. The re-creation of a colonial kitchen is painted red with white polka dots, an old trick used to conceal spatters and confuse flies—and some say to ward off evil spirits. The 1853 building was originally a seamen's hospital. ◆ Admission. M-F; Su. Van Leeuwenhoekstraat (east of Van Eyckstraat). 462.3873

19 Fort Waakzaamheid Besieged for 26 days in 1804 by Captain William Bligh of *Bounty* fame, this fort, now in ruins, was also used for barracks and as an observation post by US forces during World War II. ◆ Free. Daily. Gouverneur van Lansbergeweg (off Willems Blvd). No phone

Within Fort Waakzaamheid:

Fort Waakzaamheid Bistro ★★$ Built atop the hillside fort, this Dutch-style country tavern, rich with native stone and wood, affords great views of the harbor and the Otrobanda. Fish, steaks, and other barbecued meats are good here. ◆ Continental/Caribbean ◆ M, W-Su dinner. Reservations recommended. 462.3633

20 Holiday Beach Hotel & Casino $$$ This resort on the Rifwater lagoon is active night and day, with the island's biggest casino and a lively schedule of beach barbecues, steel-band performances, and other entertainment. The airy lobby, beach bar, and restaurant complement the 200 guest rooms, all with balconies and tropical rattan and bleached-wood furnishings. The half-moon–shaped beach is outlined by an artificial "reef" that creates protected shallows for swimming and water sports. Other sports facilities include a big pool, two lighted tennis courts, and a dive shop. ◆ 31 Pater Euwensweg (at Boerhavenstraat). 462.5400, 800/444.5244; fax 462.4397

21 Sonesta Beach Hotel & Casino $$$$ The island's most luxurious and expensive resort, this lovely complex boasts an excellent beach with water sports, a dive operation, a health spa and fitness center, a free-form pool with swim-up bar, two tennis courts, three restaurants (including **Portofino**, featuring Northern Italian cuisine), supervised children's programs, a 5,000-square-foot casino, and a shopping arcade. Arrangements can be made for guests to play nine holes at the island's only golf course. The 248 elegantly furnished guest rooms feature balconies or patios. Located right across the street from the **Curaçao International Trade Center**, the hotel also has its own meeting facilities. ◆ John F. Kennedy Blvd (just south of Piscaderaweg). 736.8800, 800/SONESTA; fax 462.7502

Yuletide Customs

US residents who visit Curaçao during the Christmas holidays may be in for a surprise. Though islanders do celebrate Christmas with many of the same religious and family customs as in North America, the jolly old man with the white beard will have come and gone long before 25 December.

Here, as in Holland, St. Nicholas (the inspiration for our Santa Claus) makes his rounds on 5 December. Aided by his assorted helpers, all known as "Black Pete," he travels from house to house, where children have left their shoes stuffed with grass for his horse. In turn, he fills the shoes with gifts.

Like Santa Claus, St. Nicholas usually puts in several personal appearances before the big night, arriving by boat at **St. Annabaai** in late November to officially open the season, then visiting schools and special events for a couple of weeks.

When 31 December rolls around, Curaçaoans set off fireworks to chase away the ghosts of the year gone by. Locals wear yellow underwear on New Year's Eve for good luck. They spend the hours before midnight with their families, enjoying a traditional feast that always includes *ayacas* (ground meat or fish with vegetables, raisins, nuts, and prunes wrapped in corn-flour dough and then in a banana leaf, much like Mexican tamales). At midnight, they leave their homes to gather in their backyards, as all houses must be empty for their evil spirits to be effectively banished. Afterward, everyone meets for public celebrations with neighbors and friends.

21 Curaçao Caribbean Hotel & Casino
$$$$ Modern and comfortable, this 181-room link in the Golden Tulip chain offers a small beach with water sports on Piscaderabaai, a dive center, a pool, 2 tennis courts, 3 restaurants, its own shopping arcade, and a shuttle to downtown. Nighttime action centers around the casino, dining, and dancing. ♦ John F. Kennedy Blvd (just south of Piscaderaweg). 462.5000, 800/44.UTELL; fax 462.5846

21 Seaworld Explorer Now docked beside the **Curaçao Caribbean Hotel**, this semi-submersible craft allows nondivers to see the undersea world off the island's coast during a one-hour tour. ♦ Admission. Tours daily 11:30AM and 3:30PM. John F. Kennedy Blvd (just south of Piscaderaweg). 462.8833, 462.8986

22 Martha Koosje Cafe ★★$ Goats once roamed on this old plantation on the west side of the island, which dates from the first half of the 19th century. Today it's the site of a family-run restaurant set on the patio of a house filled with antique furniture. Local fare is featured; the house specialty is *La Costeña*, red snapper served with rice and coconut. ♦ Caribbean ♦ M-F dinner; Sa-Su lunch and dinner. 10 Martha Koosje (southwest of Weg naar Westpunt). 864.8235

23 Landhuis Jan Kok (Jan Kok House) Curaçao's oldest continuously inhabited building is said to be haunted. Built in 1650, it was originally the manor house for a salt-producing operation. Today it's a private home, but call ahead and owner Jeannette Leito will lead you on a one-hour tour—complete with ghost stories. She also serves homemade Dutch pancakes at the **Fungi Pot** restaurant out back, which is open only on Sunday from 11AM to 7PM. ♦ Admission. Tours by appointment. Just north of Weg naar San Willibrordus, Jan Kok. 864.8087

24 Coral Cliff Resort & Beach Club $ Snorkeling and scuba diving are big attractions at this simple low-rise complex with a complete **PADI** dive shop and access to prime underwater sites. The 46 air-conditioned apartments are comfortably furnished and have kitchenettes and telephones. There's no pool, but guests will find plenty of water sports on the 600-foot private beach, along with a tennis court, a restaurant, a bar, and playgrounds for both children and adults (the small casino offers slots, blackjack, and roulette). Free shuttles

make the 22-kilometer (14-mile) trip to downtown Willemstad. ♦ Southwest of Weg naar Santa Krus, Santa Martabaai. 864.1610, 800/223.9815; fax 864.1781

25 Westpunt If you want to meet Curaçaoans, join the weekend crowds who head for the small beaches and secluded coves along Westpuntbaai, about an hour's drive from Willemstad. Local fisherfolk work this shoreline during the week, when you can watch as they cast their nets into the surf and clean their catch on the sand. The beaches (framed by huge cliffs from which daredevils dive) are natural and unspoiled—in other words, be prepared to hide behind a rock to change your clothes or ask to use the rest room at one of the small area restaurants. ♦ Weg naar Westpunt and Weg naar Santa Krus

At Westpunt:

Jaanchie's Restaurant ★★$ Call ahead if you want to sample iguana soup (rumored to be a powerful aphrodisiac) at this outdoor spot that specializes in local fare and fresh seafood. The family-run eatery near **Christoffelpark** (Christoffel National Park) has been a local favorite since 1930, when it was established by the current owner's father. ♦ Caribbean/Seafood ♦ Daily lunch. No credit cards accepted. 15 Weg naar Westpunt. 864.0126

Playa Forti ★★$ Get ready for breathtaking views of Westpuntbaai from this hilltop restaurant, where specialties of the house include conch stew, lamb, and red snapper. ♦ International ♦ Daily lunch. Weg naar Westpunt. 864.0273

26 Kadushi Cliffs $$$$ If you've traveled down to the far edge of the Caribbean to escape the workaday world, here's a real hideaway. Located on Curaçao's undeveloped northwestern tip, this complex is set in a verdant, undulating landscape on a bluff overlooking a tiny beach. There's a restaurant and pool on the premises, and the management will set up scuba or fishing trips, but that's about it for entertainment. The 12 2-bedroom, 2-bath luxury villas with kitchens are modern and well-equipped, but you'll definitely need a rental car. ♦ Northwest of Westpunt. 864.0200, 800/448.8355, 800/KADUSHI; fax 864.0282

27 Boca Tabla Grotto This is the most famous of the hundreds of coral and limestone grottoes marking the island's shoreline. The thundering Atlantic waves of the north coast have chiseled this into an earthly moonscape where beachcombers can scramble along the sharp rocks (wear sturdy sneakers) and climb into the caves. Be sure to keep an eye on the tide and watch your footing, as some areas are under water. ♦ Weg naar Westpunt (east of Westpunt)

28 Christoffelpark (Christoffel National Park) Twisted divi-divi trees, cacti, and rare sabal palms are brightened by the occasional orchid, while sharp eyes are rewarded with sightings of several bird species, iguanas, rabbits, and shy Curaçao deer. This 4,500-acre preserve is crisscrossed by a 20-mile network of roads and trails that lead to caves with ancient Indian paintings, hillside lookouts, the summit of **Christoffelberg** (Mount Christoffel; see below), and the ruins of **Landhuis Zorgvliet** (Zorgvliet Plantation House), where a whipping post still stands. Inexpensive guide booklets, souvenirs, and refreshments are sold at the park's visitors' center, set in an outbuilding of the 18th-century **Landhuis Savonet** (Savonet Plantation House; see below). The plantation's main house is privately owned and closed to the public. Bird-watching expeditions, guided Jeep trips, and other special tours are available by appointment. From Willemstad take the Westpunt bus, which leaves from the Otrobanda terminal every two hours. No one is admitted to the park after 2PM—the circuit takes about 3.5 hours by car. ♦ Admission; children under six free. Daily. Weg naar Westpunt (between Barber and Westpunt). 864.0363

Within Christoffelpark:

Christoffelberg (Mount Christoffel) The highest point in the Netherlands Antilles, this 1,230-foot peak can be seen for miles rising out of the flat *cunucu* (countryside).

Museum Christoffelpark Savonet (Savonet Museum of Natural and Cultural History) Pre-Columbian artifacts, 500-year-old Caiquetio cave drawings, and modern environmental displays are among the exhibits at this former plantation *magazina* (storeroom), one of the **Landhuis Savonet**'s outbuildings. ♦ Fee included in park admission. Daily. 864.0363

29 Landhuis Ascención (Ascension Plantation House) This stately manor house was built in 1672, restored in 1963, and today is a recreation center for Dutch marines stationed on the island.

An open house is scheduled the first Sunday of each month, when the public is invited for live music, folk dancing, and island handicrafts and food. ♦ Free. First Sunday of each month. Off Weg naar Westpunt (southeast of Barber). 864.1950

30 Grotten van Hato (Hato Caves) Though the geological formations took centuries to develop, these ancient caves have been open to the public only since 1992. One-hour tours by local guides go past 1,500-year-old Indian petroglyphs and active stalagmites and stalactites; gravel walkways wind through an eerie network of white limestone caverns illuminated by hidden lights. The snack bar serves local fare. ♦ Admission. Tu-Su. Franklin D. Rooseveltweg (east of Hato International Airport). 868.0379

31 Beth Haim Cemetery The oldest Caucasian burial ground still in use in the Western Hemisphere dates back to 1659. Its three acres contain some 2,500 graves, and many of the 17th- and 18th-century headstones are beautifully carved. ♦ South of Schottegatweg, Gasparitu

32 Fort Nassau Originally built (ca. 1796) to defend St. Annabaai and the city of Willemstad, this old fortress has served for years as the signal and control tower that regulates the opening and closing of the pontoon bridge. Today it also offers visitors a

Grotten van Hato

fine restaurant and panoramic views of Willemstad from 200 feet above the inner harbor. ♦ Free. Daily. North of Presidente Rómulo Betancourt Blvd. No phone

Within Fort Nassau:

Restaurant Fort Nassau ★★★$$$$
The 360° view is the main attraction at this glass-enclosed dining room decorated in 18th-century style. Wild game is the specialty here, with some Indonesian-inspired dishes as well as local seafood and rib-sticking beef. The outdoor terrace bar is a popular meeting spot, especially at sunset. ♦ International ♦ M-F lunch and dinner; Sa-Su dinner. Reservations recommended. 461.3450, 461.3086

33 **El Marinero Seafood Restaurant & Cocktail Lounge** ★★★$$ Be sure to arrive hungry when you come here. Giant seafood platters are laden with red snapper, Caribbean lobster, Basque-style sea bass, shrimp-stuffed avocado, or a mixed grill of squid, octopus, shrimp, conch, and lobster. Paella and other Spanish dishes are specialties. The decor is appropriately nautical, with hanging fishing nets and other maritime objects. ♦ Seafood/Spanish ♦ Daily lunch and dinner. Reservations recommended. 87-B Schottegatweg (between Emancipatie Blvd and Gosieweg), Emmastad. 737.9833

34 **De Taveerne** ★★★$$$$ The red octagonal **Landhuis Groot Davelaar,** former private residence of a Venezuelan president, is now home to one of the island's premier restaurants. Dutch and colonial antiques furnish a white-stucco interior trimmed with polished wood, terra-cotta tiles, and copper, reminiscent of an Old World roadside inn. The menu is revised every five weeks, but the beef and seafood dishes are always outstanding here. ♦ Continental/Caribbean ♦ M-Sa lunch and dinner. Reservations required. Schottegatweg and Santa Rosaweg. 737.0669

34 **Landhuis Zeelandia** ★★$$$ Entering this 150-year-old mansion decorated with antiques and other remnants of centuries past is like stepping into colonial Curaçao. Continental beef, chicken, lamb, and seafood dishes are complemented by a wide-ranging wine list. ♦ Continental ♦ M-Sa dinner. Reservations recommended. Polarisweg (west of Schottegatweg). 461.4688

Seven types of cactus grow on Curaçao. Some are used in cooking, and soup made with the *kadushi* cactus is said to be an aphrodisiac for women. Men swear by iguana soup (it tastes like chicken).

RYSTTAFEL
RESTAURANT

35 **Rysttafel Restaurant Indonesia** ★★$$
Don't miss this local favorite, where Javanese cooks prepare ancient recipes with spices and herbs imported from their homeland. For a memorable blowout, order the house specialty, rysttafel (also spelled rijsttafel). The name means "rice table," and the dish is actually a buffet of 16 to 25 items served from warming trays that surround your table. For a lighter midday meal, try one of the typical Javanese lunches, which often include vegetables cooked with coconut milk, and fish or poultry in peanut sauce with Indonesian spices. The restaurant's **Holland Club Bar** is a traditional meeting spot for drinks and appetizers. ♦ Indonesian ♦ M-Sa lunch and dinner; Su dinner. Reservations recommended. 13 Mercuriusstraat (between Saturnusstraat and Schottegatweg). 461.2606, 461.2999

35 **Curaçao Liqueur Distillery** The celebrated after-dinner drink, known locally as *chobolobois,* is made in this 19th-century *landhuis,* owned by the Senior family since 1948. The liqueur gets its distinctive flavor from the sun-dried unripened peel of the *laraha* (an orange that grows only on Curaçao), blended with herbs according to a secret family recipe passed down for generations. The 1-room distillery turns out 200 gallons each week. Visitors are treated to complimentary tastings following the self-guided tour. ♦ Free. M-F. Landhuis Chobolobo, Schottegatweg (just north of Caracasbaaiweg). 461.6946

36 **Autonomy Monument** Created by local artist J. Fresco, the six stylized birds spreading their wings in this sculpture represent the six islands of the Netherlands Antilles, which were released from colonial rule in 1955. Unveiled that same year, it bears the motto, "Trusting in our own strength, but ready to support each other." (Aruba has since declared independence from the other five islands, but remains in the Dutch realm.) ♦ Fokkerweg and Rijkseenheid Blvd

36 **Amstel Brouwerij (Amstel Brewery)** This modern facility fills 40,000 bottles per hour, and is the only brewery in the world to make beer from distilled seawater. The water is provided by Curaçao's desalination plants, which have produced the island's drinking water since 1929. Come for a tour and a tasting. ♦ Free. Tours: Tu, Th 9:30AM; closed mid-June–early August. Rijkseenheid Blvd (just north of Fokkerweg). 461.2944

37 **Roosevelt House** Flapping stars and stripes stand out against the black-tile roof of the US

Consul General's home, a gift from the Dutch in gratitude for US assistance during World War II. Part of the surrounding US Consulate complex, the gray building on Ararat Hill overlooks Willemstad and the harbor. This building is not open to the public.
♦ Presidente Rómulo Betancourt Blvd (just west of Fokkerweg)

38 Wine Cellar ★★$$ As the name implies, the wine list is a big draw at this award-winning restaurant furnished with Victorian antiques. Eight wooden tables lit by candles make for an intimate scene. Chef/owner Nico Cornelisse, who has served as official caterer to the Dutch royal family on their state visits to Curaçao, is known for his fresh takes on regional seafood, especially lobster.
♦ Continental/Caribbean ♦ Tu-F lunch and dinner; Sa-Su dinner. Reservations

recommended. Concordiastraat (between Julianaplein and Abraham Mendez Chumaceirokade). 461.2178

39 Bolívar Museum Exiled freedom fighter Simón Bolívar cooled his heels here at his sisters' seaside home during the Venezuelan wars of independence. Also known as the **Octagon-huisje** (Octagon House), the eight-sided mansion exhibits a small collection of Bolívar's personal belonging. It also features displays tracing South America's liberation from the Spanish, and restored rooms furnished in 19th-century antiques. Note: At press time the museum was closed for renovation and no reopening date had been announced; call the **Curaçao Tourist Board** (461.6000) for current information. ♦ Admission. Daily. 126-8 Penstraat (east of Julianaplein)

Saving the Reefs

Blessed with spectacular coral reefs and superior underwater conditions, Curaçaoans are determined to protect their natural resources from "overdiving" and reckless exploitation. Reef Care Curaçao is a nonprofit organization that sponsors research and preservation, public awareness programs, seminars, lectures, and children's snorkeling courses. Their "Code for Reef Visitors" is good advice for offshore explorers of any Caribbean island:

Don't touch, rest on, or kick live coral. Corals are living animals and are easily damaged even by gentle handling.

Avoid kicking up the sand. It spoils the visibility for you, as well as for other visitors, and damages corals and other reef organisms where it settles.

Do not spearfish. The Curaçao reefs are already depleted of medium- to large-size fish. Spearfishing, which gives reef fish no chance, will quickly rid the reefs of what is left.

Leave all corals and reef animals where they are. Corals are the "building blocks" of the reef and grow slowly. Even small pieces are already a number of years old. Lobsters and shells have become rare because too many people are taking them. Don't kill sea urchins to feed the fish. Sea urchins, too, have become scarce, due to disease, and are only just beginning to recover.

Divers, make sure you are properly weighted.

Boat owners, never anchor on corals; they are easily broken or damaged by anchors and you may break off corals several hundred years old. Tie up to a mooring buoy or anchor carefully in sand or rubble patches.

Remember: Take only photographs, leave only ripples.

For more information, contact Reef Care Curaçao (14 Kaminda Yakima, Curaçao, NA, 736.8120).

Getting Your Feet Wet in Curaçao

There's so much more to Curaçao's coast than just the beach. Snorkelers and scuba divers love the **Curaçao Underwater Park**, a premier snorkel and scuba environment that stretches along 12.5 miles of shore to the island's eastern tip. If boating and water sports are your game, here are a few organizations that can get you afloat:

Boating

Coral Cliff Diving Coral Cliff Resort and Beach Club, southwest of Weg naar Santa Krus, Santa Martabaai. 864.2822

Curaçao Yacht Club Spaansé Water. 767.4627

Sail Curaçao Spaansébaai. 767.6003

Seascape Dive & Watersports Curaçao Caribbean Hotel & Casino, John F. Kennedy Blvd (just south of Piscaderaweg). 462.5000, 800/44.UTELL

Top Watersports Lions Dive Hotel and Marina, Dr. Martin Luther King Blvd, Cornelisbaai. 461.7343

Snorkeling and Scuba Diving

Curaçao Diving Operators Association Curaçao Sea Aquarium, Dr. Martin Luther King Blvd, Cornelisbaai. 465.8991

Peter Hughes Divers Princess Beach Resort and Casino, 8 Dr. Martin Luther King Blvd (just west of Koraal Spechtweg). 465.8991

Seascape Dive & Watersports Curaçao Caribbean Hotel & Casino, John F. Kennedy Blvd (just south of Piscaderaweg). 462.5000, 800/44.UTELL

Underwater Curaçao Lions Dive Hotel and Marina, Dr. Martin Luther King Blvd, Cornelisbaai. 461.8100, 461.1644, 800/223.9815

Windsurfing

Sail Curaçao Spaansébaai. 767.6003

Seascape Dive & Watersports Curaçao Caribbean Hotel & Casino, John F. Kennedy Blvd (just south of Piscaderaweg). 462.5000, 800/44.UTELL

Top Watersports Lions Dive Hotel and Marina, Dr. Martin Luther King Blvd, Cornelisbaai. 461.7343

39 Avila Beach Hotel $$ This cheerful yellow hotel was originally built in 1780 as a British colonial governor's mansion, then used by his successors as a seaside getaway. Today the restored Dutch-style facade leads into a well-managed complex of guest quarters, meeting facilities, and public areas. Additions have doubled the capacity to 80 rooms and 18 apartments, all with air-conditioning, mini-bars, and terraces. Older units are an inexpensive choice for travelers on a budget, while the newer **La Belle Alliance** section offers modern deluxe accommodations that face the sea. Perks include a private beach, tennis court, outdoor bar, and relaxed fine dining at the open-air **Belle Terrace** restaurant. The **Bolívar Museum** is just next door, but the neighborhood is mostly residential. ♦ 130-34 Penstraat (east of Julianaplein). 461.4377, 800/448.8355; fax 461.1493

During her life span, a single conch lays approximately six million eggs, of which only three or four reach maturity. Because of this low rate of survival, and many years of steady fishing, the animal is in danger of extinction.

Princess Beach
RESORT & CASINO

40 Princess Beach Resort and Casino $$$$ Located directly in front of the island's prime diving and snorkeling spot, **Curaçao Underwater Park**, Curaçao's biggest resort boasts its own beach and water-sports cente two pools (one with a swim-up bar), two lighted tennis courts, a shopping arcade, a children's nursery and playground, three restaurants, a casino, and lively nightlife. The modern low-rise complex of 7 buildings offer 341 recently renovated rooms and suites wit private balconies or terraces. Request a "garden room" for the most reasonable rates ♦ 8 Dr. Martin Luther King Blvd (just west of Koraal Spechtweg). 736.7888, 800/992.2015 fax 461.4131

41 Lions Dive Hotel & Marina $ Scuba enthusiasts and Dutch business travelers frequent this pleasant property, just next to the **Curaçao Sea Aquarium** on Cornelisbaai.

They come for the easy access to the **Curaçao Underwater Park** and other premier dive sites, and the services of the **PADI** five-star **Underwater Curaçao,** the island's largest dive facility. Instruction, certification courses, equipment rentals, and boat dives are available. On shore, the complex offers the first-class **Ooms** health club and fitness center; 3 restaurants (including **Rumours,** see below); and 72 air-conditioned rooms with ocean views, private balconies, and tiny bathrooms. ♦ Dr. Martin Luther King Blvd, Cornelisbaai. 461.8100, 461.1644, 800/223.9815; fax 461.8200

Within the Lions Dive Hotel & Marina:

Rumours ★★$$ Salads, fresh catch of the day, and other casual eats are popular with the lively crowd at this open-air cafe. ♦ American ♦ Daily breakfast, lunch, and dinner. Reservations recommended. 461.7555

41 Curaçao Sea Aquarium More than 400 species of sea creatures who call the Caribbean home are on view at this aquarium, one of a very few in the world that raise marine life in replicas of the natural environment. A viewing platform overlooks the coral-encrusted 1906 wreck of the steamship *HMS Oranje Nassau,* which has settled just offshore at a depth of only 10 feet. For an underwater view, visitors can enter the permanently docked semisubmerged submarine at the facility. For those willing to get wet, the "Animal Encounter" is a must. Adventuresome visitors climb into wetsuits and strap dive tanks to their backs, then slip into a 12-foot-deep area (always accompanied by a diver-guide) to play with stingrays or feed lemon sharks through holes in a Plexiglas wall. The complex also offers a restaurant, an open-air bar, and access to the lovely Mambo Beach with water sports and changing facilities. ♦ Admission. Daily. Dr. Martin Luther King Blvd, Cornelisbaai. 461.6666

42 Fort Beekenberg Named for the Dutch engineer who designed the island's defense plan, this 1703 fort was besieged during the 18th century by pirates, as well as French and English forces. The well-preserved battle tower still guards the coast of Caracasbaai (Caracas Bay), now invaded primarily by cruise ships that dock at the wharf below. Long-range views are great, especially on Sunday afternoons when the seas are bright with sailboats and motorboats from the four yacht clubs at neighboring Spaansé Water (Spanish Water). ♦ Free. Daily. Caracasbaaiweg, Caracasbaai. No phone

 43 Strand van Santa Barbara (Santa Barbara Beach) White sand and good facilities (Sunfish and Windsurfer rentals, changing areas, rest rooms, snack bar) are the draws at this private beach on the southeastern end of the island. The drive here from Willemstad passes the colorful phosphate mountain called Tafelberg and the lovely **Landhuis Santa Barbara** (Santa Barbara Plantation House), built in 1662 and once one of the largest plantations on the island. ♦ Admission. Daily. Spaansébaai

Bests

Charla Nieveld
Curaçao Tourist Board Information Officer/1988 Carnival Queen

The **Curaçao Sea Aquarium's** "Animal Encounter" is something everyone should try. You feed sharks, you have stingrays swimming all over you.

The city on its own is really wonderful—the architecture, the shops. What I really like to do is sit at the **Bay Sight Terrace** restaurant at the **Otrobanda Hotel,** order a drink and watch the ships pass right in front of me. It's an impressive sight.

Carnival is one of the biggest festivities on the island. It brings people together. They dress up, forget their problems, and party. Everybody dances . . . it's beautiful to see. There are some parties that begin at 7PM and don't end until 7AM. One of my favorite parts is the tumba, the three-day musical competition to pick the best songs for Carnival and crown the tumba king. There are 10,000 to 15,000 people in the stadium, dancing until 3AM in the morning. Tourists and nontourists alike show up.

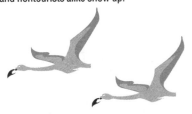

More than 400 flamingos make regular trips between Bonaire and Curaçao, where they reside at the salt flats near the Landhuis Jan Kok. Flamingos can fly for nine hours without taking a break.

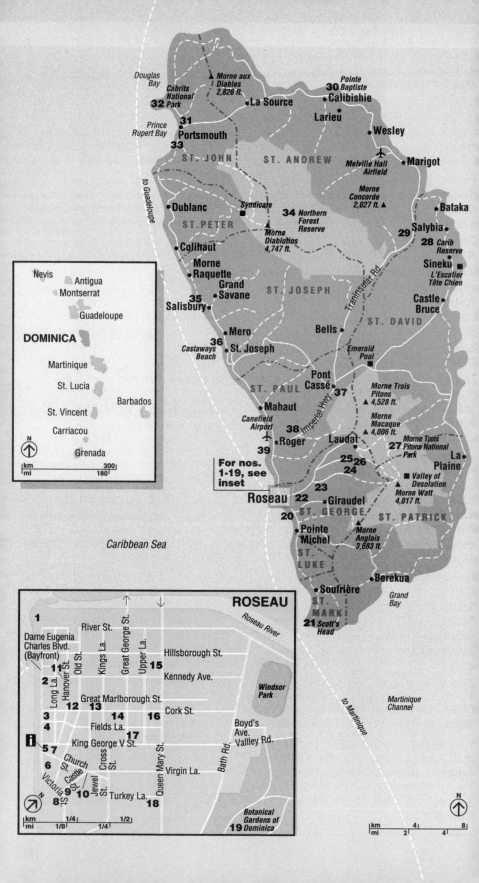

Douglas Bay

Morne aux Diables 2,826 ft. ▲

Pointe Baptiste
30 ●Calibishie

32 Cabrits National Park

●**La Source**

Larieu

31 ●Wesley

Prince Rupert Bay
●Portsmouth
33

ST. JOHN

ST. ANDREW

Melville Hall Airfield ✈

●Marigot

Morne Concorde 2,027 ft. ▲

●**Dublanc**

Syndicate ■

ST. PETER

34 Northern Forest Reserve

●**Bataka**

Salybia
29 ●
28 Carib Reserve

Morne Diablotins 4,747 ft. ▲

Sineku ■
L'Escalier Tête Chien

●**Colihaut**

Morne ●Raquette

Grand Savane

ST. JOSEPH

Castle Bruce

●**Salisbury** 35

ST. DAVID

●Mero

Bells ●

36
Castaways Beach
●St. Joseph

Emerald Pool

Pont Cassé

ST. PAUL **37**

Morne Trois Pitons 4,528 ft. ▲

●**Mahaut**

Canefield Airport

Morne Macaque 4,006 ft. ▲

38 ●Roger

Laudat ●

Morne Trois Pitons National Park
27
La Plaine

39

25 26
24

For nos. 1-19, see inset

23

■ Valley of Desolation
▲ Morne Watt 4,017 ft.

Roseau

22 ●Giraudel

20 ST. GEORGE

ST. PATRICK

●Pointe Michel

Morne Anglais 3,683 ft. ▲

Caribbean Sea

ST. LUKE

●Berekua

●Soufrière

ST. MARK

Grand Bay

21 Scott's Head

Inset (upper left):

Nevis
● Antigua
Montserrat
● Guadeloupe

DOMINICA

Martinique
St. Lucia
St. Vincent
Barbados
Carriacou
Grenada

N
km | 300
mi | 180

Inset (lower):

ROSEAU

1

Dame Eugenia Charles Blvd. (Bayfront)

River St.
Roseau River

Old St.
Kings La.
Great George St.
Upper La.

Hillsborough St.

11
15
Kennedy Ave.

2
Long La.
Hanover St.

Great Marlborough St.
Cork St.
Windsor Park

12 13
16

3
Fields La.

4
14
17

Boyd's Ave. Vallley Rd.
Bath Rd.

King George V St.

5 7
Cross St.
Queen Mary St.
Virgin La.

6
Church St.
Castle St.

8 9 10
Victoria St.
Jewel St.
Turkey La.
18

N
km | 1/4 | 1/2
mi | 1/8 | 1/4

Botanical Gardens of
19 Dominica

to Martinique

Martinique Channel

N
km | 4 | 8
mi | 2 | 4

to Guadeloupe

Dominica

The rugged heartland of the Commonwealth of Dominica (pronounced Dom-i-*nee*-ka) is the perfect place to step back in time to a more natural environment. A favorite with scientists and researchers, this is an ideal destination for bird watching, wilderness trekking, or scuba diving.

More functional than picturesque, the port capital of **Roseau** is vintage West Indian, without the Old World architectural influences so common in other Caribbean islands. Improvements to the historic **Bayfront** have added some eye appeal, but although most modern conveniences are available, this sleepy town is no place for those in search of fast nightlife or swank resorts.

To the north, **Morne Diablotins** commands this 290-square-mile island, rising 4,747 feet above sea level. Those lucky enough to reach the peak on a clear day are rewarded with spectacular views of Dominica and glimpses of nearby Guadeloupe and Martinique. Just be sure to bring rain gear—though coastal precipitation averages 75 to 80 inches per year, the mountainous areas are drenched by an annual 250 to 400 inches.

If trekking through the middle of a primordial rain forest seems like an appealing idea, the 17,000-acre **Morne Trois Pitons National Park** is a great destination. Reserve a room in one of the Edenlike mountain retreats, then head for waterfall-fed **Emerald Pool** or high-perched **Fresh Water Lake** (2,500 feet). Plan to spend at least 3 hours and be sure to hire an expert guide to see **Boiling Lake** (2,500 feet), where the pressure of escaping volcanic gases creates a huge plume of steam visible long before you see the bubbling water.

Though sandy beaches are few, swimmers can paddle through beautiful rivers, waterfalls, and hot mineral springs. Canoe trips into the verdant wilds of **Indian River** promise adventure on an Amazonian scale. At nearby **Syndicate**, bird-watchers may spot a rare jacquot or sisserou, Dominica's vanishing breeds of parrots.

Columbus named this peaceful isle for the day he first spotted it—Sunday, 3 November 1493. Europeans did not set up housekeeping here until French colonists arrived in 1632. Then, for more than a hundred years, England and France struggled for control before finally realizing that the true power lay with the fierce Carib Indians who had prevented any long-term settlement. With the 1748 Treaty of Aix-la-Chapelle, the two European powers pledged to leave the island to the locals. The agreement was short-lived though, and after several more switches, Dominica landed firmly in British hands.

Throughout these maneuvers, the Carib displayed no interest in socializing with the invaders. Plantation development was left largely to the British, who relied on the labor of slaves brought over from Africa. Slavery was abolished on Dominica in 1832. By 1903 (75 years before the island gained its independence within the British Commonwealth), England's control was strong enough to force the Carib to accept fixed boundaries on the **Carib Reserve**, about 3,700 acres on the northeast coast. It is now home to the friendly descendants of the pre-Columbian people who once ruled the entire territory. Here the roads are dotted with craft stands and natural attractions like the dramatic **L'Escalier Tête Chien** (Dog's Head Staircase), an 800-foot cascade of hardened lava jutting into the sea that—despite its name—actually looks like a snake.

Meanwhile, modern invaders who seek pristine marine environments won't be disappointed—scuba diving and snorkeling have been gaining a fast following here. The crystal-clear waters are lively with sea gorgonians, neon fish, coral forests, and giant tube sponges, and the spectacular ups and downs of Dominica's surface continue offshore, creating many unique dive sites with underwater gorges, slopes, and sheer walls.

Area code 767 unless otherwise noted.

Getting to the Island

Airlines

Interisland Carriers

Air Guadeloupe..................449.1060, 800/522.3394

American Eagle 445.7204, 800/433.7300

Cardinal Airlines 449.8922, 449.0600

LIAT (Leeward Island Air Transport) ....
....448.2421, 448.2422

Airports **Melville Hall Airfield** (445.7109), 29 miles from Roseau on the island's northeastern edge, is the takeoff and departure point for larger planes (46-seaters). The runway was carved out of a coconut plantation. Pilots make their approach over thick mountain jungle, and a nearby river nearly drowns out the sound of the propellers. The planes roll down the runway to stop just before reaching the sea. An expansion in the works calls for a new terminal building, a longer runway, and improved road access.

Smaller aircraft (up to 19 seats) land at **Canefield Airport** (449.1199), just 15 minutes from Roseau. Crosswinds can make for a dramatic touchdown between the mountains and the deep blue sea.

Ferries Rather rough trips aboard the high-speed catamaran *Caribbean Express* link Dominica with Guadeloupe and Martinique. For schedules and rates, contact **Whitchurch Travel Agency** (448.2181).

Getting Around the Island

Buses Set routes cover the entire island, and buses are an inexpensive, although undependable, way to get around. They don't run on any regular schedule or on Sunday. Buses can be hailed at stops marked along the road; be sure to ask the driver where he is headed—destinations are not marked on the buses.

Car Rental

Drivers must be at least 23 years old to rent a car.

Anslem's Car Rentals 448.2730

Avis....................................448.2481, 800/331.1212

Bonus Rentals..448.2650

Budget 449.2080, 800/527.0700

Island Car Rentals 448.3425, 448.0738

Sag Motors 449.1093

Tropical Jeep Rentals 448.4821

Valley Rent-a-Car 448.3233

Wide Range Car Rentals............................448.2198

Driving Stay on the left side of the road, British style, and be aware that many of the better arteries are only wide enough for one vehicle at a time. Thursday is banana day; banana trucks don't—and sometimes can't—stop for anything. You'll need a local driver's permit, which can be obtained at the **Department of Motor Vehicles** in Roseau (High St, between Bath Rd and Victoria St, 448.2222) or at either airport; you must present a valid driver's license. The cost of a permit is US$12 for 1 month, US$23 for 3 months.

Taxis

Didier's..448.3706

Linton's..448.2558

Mally's 448.3114

Nature Island Taxi and Tour......................448.3397

Tours For guided van, car, four-wheel-drive, hiking, boat, or scuba trips, contact **Anchorage Hotel & Dive Center** (448.2638, 800/223.6815), **Dive Dominica Tours** (448.2188, 800/468.4748), **Mally's Tours** (448.3114), **Nature Island Taxi and Tour** (448.3397), or **Paradise Tours** (448.5999).

In addition to standard tours, the following companies will also provide experienced guides for treks into the wilderness: **Antours** (448.6460); **Ken's Hinterland Adventure Tours** (448.4850), the only operator with full communications from any point on the island; and **Rainbow Rover** (448.8650). For wildlife tours or self-guiding maps and booklets, contact the **Division of Forestry** (Botanical Gardens of Dominica, Bath Rd and Queen Mary St, Roseau, 448.2401 ext 417; fax 448.5200).

FYI

Electricity The current is 220 to 240 volts/50 cycles, often with British three-square-pin outlets. North American appliances will need a converter.

Entry Requirements US and Canadian visitors must present a valid passport or other proof of citizenship (birth certificate, voter's registration card) and a photo ID, plus a return or onward ticket.

Language The official language is English. A local patois is spoken by many islanders.

Money The Eastern Caribbean dollar (EC$) is the official currency. US money is widely accepted, but buying power increases slightly if you make exchanges at a bank. Most are open Monday through Thursday from 8AM to 3PM and Friday from 8AM to 5PM. Credit cards are accepted at most hotels and restaurants, but some charge a fee of up to five percent.

Personal Safety Crime is rare, but don't leave valuables in an unlocked car. Exercise normal precautions.

Publications The *Dominica Chronicle* and *Tropical Star* are published weekly. The **Division of Forestry** (see "Tours," above) has a good selection of maps and guidebooks for sale.

Taxes A five-percent tax is added to hotel bills. There's also a three-percent sales tax.

Tipping Most hotels and some restaurants add a 10-percent service charge. Add more for special attention. There's no need to tip taxi drivers unless they perform a special service, such as unloading a lot of luggage.

Visitors' Information Office The **Division of Tourism of the National Development Corporation**'s main office (Valley Rd, northeast of Bath Rd, Roseau, 448.2351, 448.2045, 448.2186; fax 448.5840) is open Monday from 8AM to 1PM and from 2 to 5PM, Tuesday through Friday from 8AM to 1PM and from 2 to 4PM. The best place for tourists to stop, however, is the information office at the Bayfront (448.2045), which is located on the first floor of the building that houses the **Dominica Museum**. It's open Monday through Friday from 9AM to 1PM and 2 to 4PM, Saturday 9AM to 1PM. The tourist information desks at **Canefield Airport** (449.1242) are open from 6AM to 6PM seven days a week; the visitor's information booth at **Melville Hall** (445.7051) generally operates when flights are arriving.

Phone Book

Ambulance	448.2890
Directory Assistance	118
Diving Emergencies/Decompression Chambers/ Divers Alert Network	919/684.8111
Emergencies	999
Fire	448.2890
Hospital	448.2233, 448.2231
Police	448.2222
Post Office	448.2601

Roseau

Dominica's capital city is a jumble of older wooden or gray stone buildings graced with shutters and elaborate railings, mixed with no-nonsense newer structures of concrete block or stucco. Many are painted in vibrant, contrasting colors—not the light pastels common in other parts of the Caribbean.

1 Roseau Bayfront An extensive renovation project that started in late 1993 has given a face-lift to the original architecture that remains along Roseau's historic waterfront. An illuminated promenade, lined with trees and park benches, traces the sea wall, and a dock for cruise ships is in place. A Japanese-financed fishing complex with piers, a retail fish market, and a fish processing and handling facility have also been added. The waterfront street—still referred to by locals as "Bayfront"—was officially renamed Dame Eugenia Charles Boulevard in honor of the then–prime minister (1969-1995). ◆ Dame Eugenia Charles Blvd (between Church St and Laing La)

1 Open Market Mangoes, pawpaws, passion fruit, and carambola compete for attention with the colorful tropical blooms that abound here. Farmers leave their fields in the early hours on Friday to begin the trip to Roseau, where they spend the weekend selling their goods and buying supplies before they head home again on Sunday. Early morning is the best time to come to this market—it's when Dominicans meet to shop and gossip. ◆ F-Sa. Dame Eugenia Charles Blvd and Laing La

2 Dominica Pottery Shop Handpainted note cards and attractive pottery are the lure here. Note the pieces marked "prison pottery"; they were made by inmates under a prison work program. ◆ M-F; Sa until noon. No credit cards accepted. Kennedy Ave and Dame Eugenia Charles Blvd. No phone

3 Cartwheel Café ★$ Airy pastels set the calm tone at this comfortable waterfront eatery, where islanders and visitors congregate for inexpensive breakfasts, sandwiches, and hot lunches. ◆ Caribbean/American ◆ M-Sa breakfast and lunch. No credit cards accepted. Dame Eugenia Charles Blvd and John's La. 448.5353

4 Dominica Export/Import Agency Make arrangements a day or two ahead to stop here and pick up fresh Dominican grapefruit by the box to take home. The season runs roughly from August through March; be sure to ask the company to supply the necessary agricultural papers for clearing customs. ◆ Dame Eugenia Charles Blvd (between King George V St and John's La). 448.3494

5 Dominica Museum The city's old post office building has been beautifully restored and now houses the tourism office on the ground floor. The second floor is home to a small—but fine—museum that traces the island's history from pre-Columbian times to the present. There are artifacts left by indigenous people, art prints and engravings that show daily life in Dominica in the 1700s, and old photographs that depict sugarcane harvests and other traditions in the early 1900s. Note the reproduction of a room at a plantation home: The furniture is authentic—it belonged to a woman who inherited four of the most valuable estates on the island (two of which she visited only once in her life). ◆ Admission. M-F; Sa 9AM to noon. Dame Eugenia Charles Blvd and King George V St. 448.8923

When brewed in water, the bark of the *bois bandé* tree is believed to be a powerful aphrodisiac and enhancer of male sexual prowess. Although there's no scientific proof of the bark's effectiveness and it's against the law to damage the trees, some people go to great lengths to get the bark.

GARRAWAY HOTEL

6 Garraway Hotel $$ This red-gable high-rise, with wraparound balconies overlooking the re-created Roseau Bayfront area, has 31 tastefully decorated guest rooms, a restaurant, bar, terrace, and courtyard. Favored by business travelers, the hotel has a fully equipped conference room. Special facilities to accommodate people with physical disabilities are another feature. ♦ 1 Dame Eugenia Charles Blvd (at Victoria St). 449.8801, 800/223.6510; fax 449.8807

Within the Garraway Hotel:

Ashburry's The island's only duty-free shop is tucked into the hotel's lobby. Italian lingerie, French perfume, liquors, cigars (including Cuban stogies that cannot be brought into the US), and jewelry make up the bulk of the goods, although there are also good buys on leather and crystal. ♦ M-F; Sa until noon. Church St (between Old St and Dame Eugenia Charles Blvd). 448.2181

7 Old Market Plaza Most days this little covered structure, the original market from colonial days, is a quiet spot where locals escape the sun, get a cold drink, or window-shop at three handicraft kiosks. But the arrival of a cruise ship transforms the place into a bustling market where the goods run from alleged aphrodisiacs to T-shirts and straw hats. The city has constructed permanent craft stalls in the patio that once served as a slave-trading area. ♦ M-Sa. King George V St (between Old St and Dame Eugenia Charles Blvd). No phone

Within Old Market Plaza:

Manjé Domnik ★$ Drop by this laid-back snack bar with small tables for local fast food and fresh juices, including passion fruit and pineapple juice. Try the "stuffed bakes," a meat-filled pastry. This is the place to strike up a conversation with a Dominican. It's also a lively vantage point from which to watch the action at the crafts market. ♦ Snacks ♦ M-Sa breakfast and lunch. No credit cards accepted. No phone

8 Fort Young Hotel $$$ The original stone walls of a 1770 fort that overlooked the sea now front a charming complex of 50 rooms with hardwood decks, ceiling fans, air-conditioning, cable TV, a swimming pool, a bar (where folk-dancing shows are sometimes performed), and other amenities. Some split-level units have sitting areas, and all accommodations are charmingly fitted out with wooden blinds and pale tropical fabrics.

♦ Victoria St (east of Dame Eugenia Charles Blvd). 448.5000, 800/223.6815; fax 448.5006

Within the Fort Young Hotel:

Fort Young Restaurant ★★$$ The European and West Indian fare served in this elegant dining room includes stuffed crab backs, lobster, steak, and local "mountain chicken" (frog). Unlike in some other islands, the eating of this endangered species is considered acceptable during certain times of the year as the catch is controlled. ♦ Continental/West Indian ♦ Daily lunch and dinner. 448.5000

9 La Robe Creole ★★★$$ Blooms tumble over the window boxes of this colonial stone house, now an antiques-filled restaurant known for its Creole cuisine. Menu highlights include indigenous fish

and produce: Creole lobster, freshwater shrimp and crayfish, *lambi* (conch), land crab, pumpkin, and callaloo greens. Conservative diners can stick with hamburgers, salads, and the signature fruit punches. It's a popular lunch spot for local businesspeople. ♦ Creole ♦ M-Sa lunch and dinner. 3 Victoria St (at Castle St). 448.2896

10 Pearl's Cuisine ★★★$ At first glance, eight tables and a tiny bar tucked into an old stone mansion are all there is to this dinery. But then the food is served and it's a whole different story—this place is a real find. The Creole menu—recited not read—changes depending upon what is fresh that day. Service is friendly and the food is first-rate with savory spicing. Be sure to come hungry; portions are ample. ♦ Creole ♦ M-Sa lunch and dinner. 19 Castle St (at Church St). 448.8707

11 Blue Max Cafe & Deli ★★$ The only espresso bar on the island is a delightful little corner where locals, expatriates, and tourists come together for cappuccino and cake, a sandwich, a piece of pie, or even a bagel. Dominican coffee is a real treat, harvested from the same coffee family as Jamaica's famed Blue Mountain brew. Stop here for salad, fruit, or sandwich fixings from the deli counter before heading on a day's outing around the island. ♦ Cafe/Deli ♦ M-Sa. 16 Hanover St (at Kennedy Ave). 449.8907

12 Sutton Place Hotel $$ The proprietors built this inn onto their grandparents' stone-walled mansion to create a charming, family-run hostelry. One of the city's true delights, the hotel offers eight lovely rooms (including three suites), each decorated in a different color, with dark antique-style beds and furniture. Air-conditioning, cable TV, hair dryers, and balconies are just some of the other alluring features. The suites all have full kitchenettes. Typing and fax services are available. Creole cuisine is served in the dining room; a continental breakfast is included in the room rate. The former cellar is now a cozy bar. ♦ 25 Old St (between Cork St and Kennedy Ave). 449.8700; fax 448.3045

13 **Guiyave** ★★$$ Exotic fresh fruit juices and breezy island fare are served on the balcony of this old West Indian house, which is usually crowded with local business lunchers. Try the crayfish (when available), octopus, curried beef, or spicy baked *crapaud* (mountain chicken—frog). ♦ Creole ♦ M-Sa breakfast and lunch. Reservations recommended. 15 Cork St (at Kings La). 448.2930

14 **Cee Bee's** Check here for books about Dominica's past and present, including a Creole dictionary. This is also the best stop to pick up current American newsmagazines. ♦ M-Sa. 20 Cork St (between Kings La and Great George St). 448.2379

15 **Frontline Cooperative** This shop is dedicated to literature by and about African, Afro-Caribbean, and African-American peoples. It's a good source for historical books and local folklore. The eclectic inventory includes the complete works of famous Dominican writer Jean Rhys. T-shirts and music tapes are also sold here. ♦ M-Sa. 78 Queen Mary St (between Kennedy Ave and Hillsborough St). 448.8664

16 **World of Food** ★★★$ This restaurant is set in the patio of the home that belonged to Dominican novelist Jean Rhys in the 1930s. Today it is the province of Vena McDougal, a practiced Creole chef who also operates the 14-room **Vena's Guest House** on the premises. The moody old courtyard is a fine backdrop for callaloo soup, chicken or beef roti, curried goat, breadfruit puffs, and stuffed crab backs (in season). ♦ Creole ♦ Daily lunch and dinner. No credit cards accepted. 48 Cork St (at Queen Mary St). 448.3286

17 **The Orchard** ★★$$ Head to this wood-paneled, tropical greenery–filled restaurant for a lazy, cool meal of meat pies, rotis, sandwiches, burgers, and black pudding. Vegetarians will also find good pickings. ♦ Caribbean/American ♦ M-F lunch and dinner; Sa-Su dinner. King George V and Great George Sts. 448.3051

TROPICRAFTS

18 **Tropicrafts** Dominica's famous grass rugs are custom woven here and shipped to buyers the world over. Other handmade local crafts include authentic Carib basketry and other weavings, pottery, and dolls dressed in *robe douette*, the traditional national costume. ♦ M-Sa. Queen Mary St and Turkey La. 448.2747

19 **Botanical Gardens of Dominica** Forty rolling acres on the east side of Roseau were covered with sugarcane until 1890, when design and planting began for the gardens that today boast some 500 tropical specimens. Flamboyant trees, orchids, and national flower *bwa kwaib* (Carib wood) stand out among a collection of plants from all of the neighboring islands. In one area of the park, horticulturalists foster seedlings that are sold to plantation owners to diversify their crop base. The **Division of Forestry** (448.2401 ext 417; fax 448.5200), which is headquartered on the grounds, produces a good series of brochures, guidebooks, trail maps, and other materials on the island's natural attractions and wildlife. ♦ Free. Daily. Bath Rd and Queen Mary St. 448.2401 ext 3414

Elsewhere on Dominica

20 **Castle Comfort Lodge** $$ Guests soon feel completely at ease in this "family home" with 11 rooms on the waterfront. Derek and Ginette Perryman also run the on-site **Dive Dominica** (448.2188), a **NAUI** center whose tours lead guests through the virgin waters of the island's southern and western coasts. The inn also provides complimentary snorkeling gear. ♦ South of Roseau. 448.2188, 800/468.4748; fax 448.6088

Within Castle Comfort Lodge:

Castle Comfort Lodge Restaurant ★★★$$ Fresh seafood is the main ingredient on the Creole menu at this nautical spot that overlooks the sea and a tropical garden. ♦ Seafood/Creole ♦ Daily breakfast and dinner. Reservations required. 448.2188

20 **Anchorage Hotel & Dive Center** $$ Terraced accommodations hug a swimming pool with good views of the bay at this family-run operation. There are 32 pleasant rooms, each with 2 double beds and a private bath. Boaters set anchor or tie up at the hotel dock

to dine at the restaurant/bar, well known for fresh seafood and French Creole fare. The on-site **Anchorage Dive Center**, a **PADI** facility, provides full scuba services and water sports on the small, stony beach. The 41-foot custom dive boat also makes whale-watching trips. The hotel is home to Dominica's only squash court. ♦ South of Roseau. 448.2638, 800/223.6815; fax 448.5680

20 Evergreen Hotel $$ This easygoing family-operated hotel on the waterfront south of Roseau has a swimming pool and a restaurant that serves good Dominican fare. The 16 rooms are decorated with stone, brick, and native wood in an airy, modern style; the 2 guest rooms that face the sea are larger, while 4 streetside units have porches with mountain views. Guests may use the diving facilities at nearby **Castle Comfort Lodge.** ♦ South of Roseau. 448.3288; fax 448.6800

21 Scott's Head The top of this hill is an easy climb up a dirt-and-stone-covered road. Views are stunning, with the Atlantic on one side and the Caribbean on the other. Martinique is visible in the distance, and the lush mountains and valleys of Dominica stretch before you for miles. Although the sea has eaten most of it, what remains of Fort Cachacrou is a reminder of the military action between France and England in 1778 and 1805. On the road back to Roseau are Grand Soufrière Sulfur Springs (in the hills above Soufrière) and scenic Pointe Michel. ♦ South of Soufrière

22 Reigate Hall Hotel $$$ An 18th-century manor house was converted into this mountainside inn, trimmed with local stonework and fine hardwood. There are 18 handsomely furnished rooms (including 2 suites); suites have 4-poster beds and private Jacuzzis. There are terrific views from the lofty veranda, and tropical landscaping fringes the pool, tennis court, and patio bar (a popular watering hole). Other amenities include a sauna, gym, gameroom, and meeting room. ♦ Mountain Rd (off the road to Giraudel). 448.4031, 800/223.9815; fax 448.4034

Within Reigate Hall Hotel:

Reigate Hall Restaurant ★★★$$$ Local ingredients get a continental spin (mountain chicken in Champagne sauce, fresh-caught seafood au gratin) at this European-style dining room. Graceful service, candlelight, and a splashing waterwheel add plenty of romance. ♦ Continental ♦ Daily breakfast, lunch, and dinner. Reservations recommended. 448.4031

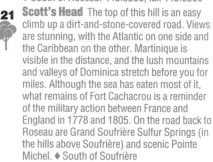

23 Chez Ophelia $$ Located near Trafalgar Falls, Wotten Waven Sulfur Springs, and Roseau River, the five duplex cottages of this family-run resort are ideally set in a verdant landscape. All have kitchen facilities; a small, on-site grocery stocks essentials. Meals are also available at the restaurant, which serves exotic fresh juices and Creole food. ♦ East of the road to Laudat. 448.3061; fax 448.3061

24 Wotten Waven Sulfur Springs Hot mud bubbles up, evidence that this volcanic isle is far from dormant. You'll also find clear thermal waters for natural mineral baths, although there are no facilities at the springs. ♦ Free. Daily. East of the road to Laudat

Papillote

25 Papillote Wilderness Retreat and Nature Sanctuary $$ One of the most intriguing inns on the island, its jungle setting is perfect for a Tarzan-and-Jane getaway, though children will also love the resident pets and birds, river bathing, and hot mineral pools. It's a friendly place, and owners Anne and Cuthbert Jean-Baptiste (he runs the restaurant; she's a marine biologist) are excellent guides to the local nature scene. The quarters consist of five rooms, one suite, and one two-bedroom cottage; accommodations are simple and comfort-able. The grounds, shrouded by thick vegetation and surrounded by herb gardens are crisscrossed with stone walls and hiking trails; a 10-minute walk leads to Trafalgar Falls. Be advised that this is a *rain* forest and downpours are common, but then so are wild orchids and other thirsty tropical blooms. Twice each year, a massage therapist trained in shiatsu, reflexology, and acupressure conducts three-week, wave-massage sessions in the hot mineral waters ♦ Closed in September. Trafalgar Falls Rd (east of the road to Laudat). 448.2287; fax 448.2285

Within Papillote Wilderness Retreat and Nature Sanctuary:

Papillote Wilderness Retreat Restaurant ★★★$$ Even if you can't manage a stay at this special lodge, plan a long lunch at its delightful, plant-filled thatch-roofed restaurant. Dine on *bookh* (tiny river shrimp) or crayfish with delicate homegrown salads, then stick around a while to go on an escorted hike to the waterfalls, swim in the mountain river, or dip into a hot mineral bath ♦ Creole/Continental ♦ M-Sa lunch and dinner; closed in September. Reservations required (make them well in advance). 448.2287

25 Trafalgar Falls Here, cold water tumbles over huge black rocks studded with ferns and orchids, and cascades into rocky natural swimming pools. (A second fall with hot water that filled a sister pool was also located here until the 1995 hurricanes interfered with its flow.) During the rainy season, another, smaller "baby falls" spills off to one side. Visitors can splash in the pools among the rocks, whcih are a short hike (about 15

*Trafalgar
Falls*

minutes) from the road. ♦ Trafalgar Falls Rd (east of the road to Laudat)

 26 Titou Gorge Soak in a hot sulfur spring, then take a refreshing plunge under a waterfall at this deep and narrow gorge. Be forwarned: The swim can be treacherous, so a guide is essential—especially when heavy rains make the falls flow heavily. ♦ Laudat

 27 Morne Trois Pitons National Park The 17,000-acre rain forest is a spectacular tangle of huge ferns and ancient trees intertwined with flowering vines and bright splashes of anthurium, bromeliads, and wild orchids. A network of marked trails does little to tame this splendid example of nature run amok, though experienced guides are available to lead visitors along the most slippery routes. The centerpiece is the majestic three-peaked mountain that gives the preserve its name; the highest point is 4,528 feet and a fair hike takes the intrepid almost to the summit. Rivers tumble down the slopes and thermal springs are heated by volcanoes that are still very much alive.

For great views of the east coast, take a four-wheel-drive vehicle to Fresh Water Lake (2,500 feet). Boeri Lake (3,000 feet) is another 45 minutes on foot. For guides, contact your hotel, the tourist office, the **Division of Forestry** (Botanical Gardens of Dominica, 448.2401 ext 417; fax 448.5200), or **Ken's Hinterland Adventure Tours** (62 Hillsborough St, Roseau, 448.4850). ♦ Free. Daily. Just east of Laudat

Within Morne Trois Pitons National Park:

 Valley of Desolation One of Dominica's most fascinating attractions, this area of sulfur springs is an eerie collection of boiling pools, gray bubbling mud, and streams streaked with color from the many minerals in the water.

 Boiling Lake Although it is only a six-mile haul, a half-day is needed to trek to this remote attraction—the rugged climb is treacherous even in the dry season. Only the most expert hikers should attempt the excursion, and an experienced guide is essential. A crater filled with bubbling gray water shrouded in thick vapor and heated by the volcano below makes up the "boiling lake"; measuring 210 feet across, it is the world's largest. Be sure to bring rain gear and a change of clothes.

 Emerald Pool Simply breathtaking, this lovely pool is filled by a waterfall and is surrounded by rocks overgrown with thick cascades of ferns and tropical blooms. Though deep in the forest, this natural paradise is an easy 10-minute hike from the road. ♦ The road to Castle Bruce (northeast of Pont Cassé)

On the Wild Side

Untamed Dominica is a primitive garden where rain forests and coastal flats are populated by an impressive collection of fauna, from freshwater crayfish to boa constrictors.

Although nearly 60 species of birds make Dominica their permanent home and more than 100 other varieties pass through, the two local branches of the parrot family get the most attention. The larger, bright-green sisserou is about 20 inches long, with a neck and breast of deep purple. The jacquot, also green, has more colorful plumage, with a red neck and occasional streaks of yellow. Both species are endangered. For the best chance to see them in the wild, head for **Syndicate** in the early morning or at dusk; contact the **Division of Forestry** (Botanical Gardens of Dominica, 448.2401 ext 417) for details.

In the mid-19th century, Caribbean whaling stations attracted whalers from around the world, many from France and most from Scotland. Now whale-watchers from around the globe come to observe the whales which still frequent these waters. Some species migrate here to mate and give birth. Other resident varieties are spotted year-round. The long list of recorded sightings includes singing humpbacks, sperm whales, orcas, and pilot whales.

Some of the action can be observed from shore, but for the best views join a boat tour—the peaceful giants may take an interest in watching you! The **Anchorage Dive Center** (south of Roseau, 488.2638, 800/223.6815) conducts whale-watching tours and, for the closest possible contact, exhilarating snorkeling opportunities. The unforgettable adventures also raise funds for the Dominica Conservation Association.

28 Carib Reserve The Caribbean is named for the people who now live in these six villages; it is the only Carib settlement left in these islands that the tribe once controlled. The reserve, created by the British at the turn of the century, occupies some 3,700 acres along Dominica's north and east coasts. The largest villages are Salybia, where the Catholic church altar is an Indian canoe; Bataka, site of the community school; and Sineku, home to L'Escalier Tête Chien, an 800-foot cascade of hardened lava jutting into the sea that looks like a snake (even though the French name literally translates to "Dog's Head Staircase").

Few full-blooded Carib are left, as women of other tribes and races have married into the community (non-Carib males are not accepted). People of pure Carib lineage have almond-shaped eyes, high cheekbones, and straight black hair. Although they formerly used two languages (Carib for males, Arawak for females), members now speak English and the French Creole patois of the island. They maintain a central chiefdom, as well as the independent nature that once gave them the fortitude to defend their homeland against the 18th-century's greatest military powers.

Modern visitors can expect a congenial, if shy, welcome. A paved road leads through swampland, valleys, and cliffs to the small communities where simple houses stand beside vegetable gardens and roadside stands sell handmade crafts and fresh produce. There is no charge to visit. The **Carib Territory Guesthouse** (445.7256) offers rustic overnight lodging and local food. ♦ Northeast coast

29 Floral Gardens $$ At the base of the **Northern Forest Reserve,** overlooking the **Carib Reserve,** this 18-room property is surrounded by tropical gardens and a small wildlife park that shelters native animals. It's a good hopping-off point for hikers and naturalists, with river bathing and challenging trails nearby. The management also offers "safari tours," guided treks through the **Northern Forest Reserve** to see animals in their natural environment. ♦ Traninsular Rd (between Bells and Carib Reserve). 445.7636; fax 445.7333

Within Floral Gardens:

Floral Gardens Restaurant $$ Locally grown fruits and vegetables, fresh crayfish, goat, and rabbit add plenty of color to the menu at this country restaurant on the edge of the **Carib Reserve.** ♦ Creole ♦ Daily lunch and dinner. 445.7636

Floral Gardens Gift Shop High-quality local crafts, many created by neighboring Carib Indians, include straw weavings, pottery, handmade coconut and wooden jewelry, foods, and skin-care products. ♦ 445.7636

From Florida, the West Indies islands stretch 1,200 miles to the southeast, then 500 miles west, then south along the north coast of Venezuela.

30 Pointe Baptiste The Atlantic coast can be rough, but this sheltered spot is a favorite of windsurfers. The honey-colored sand is shaded by coconut palms and sea grapes, but be forewarned—there are no public concessions or changing facilities. ♦ Just east of Calibishie

31 Portsmouth A cruise-ship berth debuted in Dominica's second "city" in 1991, and several hotels and restaurants have since set up shop along the gray sandy beach, but downtown Portsmouth is still little more than three streets that run parallel to Prince Rupert Bay. Here houses are painted in vibrant tropical pastels and adorned with little gardens, and neighborhood paths are trimmed in conch shells. The green at the back of town comes alive with cricket matches on Saturday afternoons. ♦ Northwest coast

At Portsmouth:

Indian River Boat rides travel up the winding, mangrove-lined river, a deep-green ribbon that has been compared to the Amazon and is now a tourist haunt. Make prior arrangements through the local tour-guide service on Boroughs Square, as hawkers on the jetty can be very aggressive. Insist on a rowboat to preserve the eerie muffled solitude. ♦ Fee. Daily.

32 Cabrits National Park A microcosm of the Caribbean, this 1,313-acre preserve encompasses coral reef, mountainous terrain, tropical forest, volcanic sand beaches, the ruins of old colonial structures, and Dominica's largest swamp. The peninsula is dominated by two hills covered in dry woodlands, one of few such regions in the West Indies. The park's marine area (1,053 acres) in Douglas Bay is graced with rock and coral formations set under cliffs—a fine destination for snorkelers. At the western tip of the park is the dramatic Prince Rupert's Bluff, also known as Cabrits Bluff (*cabrits* is Creole for goats). ♦ Admission. Daily. Northwest of Portsmouth

Within Cabrits National Park:

Fort Shirley Like others throughout the region, this 18th-century fort is a jumble of British and French construction. The scene of a famous mutiny in 1802, it was last used as a military post in 1854. Today some 50 structures survive, and a restoration project has added a small museum, snack bar, and gift shop. ♦ Free. M-F. No phone

33 Picard Beach Though crowded on public holidays, this long stretch of black volcanic sand dotted with palm trees and sea grapes is usually quite peaceful. Prince Rupert Bay is a good place for swimming and other water sports. There are no public concessions on the beach, but the nearby **Picard Beach Cottage Resort** and the **Coconut Beach Hotel** can provide refreshments, drinks, and water-sports equipment rentals. ♦ Just south of Glanvillia

On Picard Beach:

Coconut Beach Hotel $$ A good base for touring the wilds of the north, these accommodations are located on the waterfront near Portsmouth and Indian River. There are 5 cottages and 16 rooms, and safe anchorage for yachts, dock facilities, and water sports nearby. There's no pool, but the hotel is set on the milelong beach. ♦ 445.5393; fax 445.5693

Within Coconut Beach Hotel:

Coconut Beach Restaurant ★★$$$ Daily lunch specials, a bargain for day-trippers, offer hefty portions of Dominican standards. Alfresco dinners are served by candlelight. ♦ Caribbean ♦ Daily breakfast, lunch, and dinner. Reservations recommended. 445.5393

Picard Beach Cottage Resort $$ Conveniently located for exploring the northern region of the island, this property offers eight cottages. Each has a full kitchen and sleeps up to four people. There's also a restaurant, pool, and dive shop. Water-sports equipment is shared with the property next door. ♦ 445.5131, 800/223.6815; fax 445.5599

34 Northern Forest Reserve Some 22,000 acres in Dominica's mountainous north country have been protected since 1952. Environmentalists hope the reserve will eventually be established as **Morne Diablotin National Park,** the country's third. East of Dublanc

Within the Northern Forest Reserve:

Syndicate At the northwest corner of the forest reserve, 200 acres of an old banana plantation are set aside for two endangered Dominican parrots—the purple-breasted sisserou, and the jacquot, which is bright green with a red neck. The parrots nest here in old-growth trees at the lower elevations of the rain forest. Other colorful tenants include the red-legged thrush, pearly-eyed thrasher, and scaly-eyed thrasher. To catch a glimpse of the parrots, it's best to set out before daybreak; a guide is also recommended. If you must go it alone, contact the **Division of Forestry** (Botanical Gardens of Dominica, 448.2401 ext 417) for advice and detailed materials. ♦ Syndicate Rd

Morne Diablotins Dominica's tallest peak (4,747 feet) is usually draped in a fine mist. Thousands of years ago, lava flows from this ancient volcano created the northern coast, and today its rain forest–covered slopes are the source for several of the island's rivers. The challening climb to the summit (a guide is essential) crosses five vegetation zones, ranging from dry scrub to enchanting woodland. The last 2,000 feet are a stiff and slippery haul and there's only one established route, which begins at **Syndicate.** ♦ Southeast of Syndicate

35 Lauro Club $$$ These Swiss-owned cottages, eight in all, are cheerfully painted in bright tropical pastels with private sundecks that overlook the calm Caribbean waters of the island's leeward coast. The views are also fine from the swimming pool, which is set in a grassy hillside terrace. ♦ Salisbury. 449.6602, 800/742.4276; fax 449.6603

Within the Lauro Club:

Lauro Club Restaurant ★★★$$$ This airy dining room offers fresh conch and lobster and continental fare. Specialties include chicken with coconut, stewed codfish with local spices, grilled lobster and steak, and mountain chicken served in a garlic-and-tomato or white-wine sauce. There are open-air barbecues on Wednesday and Saturday nights. ♦ Creole/Seafood/Continental ♦ Daily breakfast, lunch, and dinner. Reservations recommended. 449.6602

The average annual rainfall of 300 inches on the summit of Morne Trois Pitons and 150 inches in the park's lower areas makes Dominica one of the Caribbean's lushest islands.

Some trees in Dominica's rain forest are believed to be over 300 years old.

The Carib Indians named this mountainous island *Waitikubuli,* which means "tall in her body."

36 Castaways Beach This milelong beach is lined with black volcanic sand and shaded by tall coconut palms. On the island's calm Caribbean coast, it's a great place to swim, snorkel, and windsurf. There are no public facilities, but **Castaways Beach Hotel** offers water sports, a dive center, a terrace restaurant, and a bar. ♦ Mero

On Castaways Beach:

Castaways Beach Hotel $ Feathery palms and tropical blooms shade a handsomely landscaped complex of 26 seaside rooms (5 with air-conditioning), set on a gray beach bordered by a low stone wall. The friendly management also offers tennis and the full-service **Dive Castaways** water-sports center (449.6244). ♦ 449.6244, 800/322.2223; fax 449.6246

Within the Castaways Beach Hotel:

Almond Tree Restaurant ★★$$$ Congenial service and fine sea views complement international cuisine and authentic Creole dishes at this terraced dining room. A brunch and evening beach barbecue on Sunday are welcome indulgences. ♦ Creole/Continental ♦ Daily breakfast, lunch, and dinner. 449.6244

37 Brother Matthew Luke Indian cotton is hand-painted with lovely rain-forest and tropical designs at this arts-and-crafts studio/gallery. ♦ Daily. Imperial Hwy (south of Pont Cassé). 449.1836

38 Springfield Plantation Guest House $$ Swim in a river-fed natural pool at this retreat high in the hills (1,200 feet) where nights are often cool enough for a fire. Lush virgin forest surrounds the Victorian-era plantation house and outbuildings, which have been converted into six guest rooms and three cottages. Accommodations are decorated with antiques (units **11** and **15** are the best), and the views are lovely. The entrance for **Morne Trois Pitons National Park** is two miles away and the management provides trail maps for hikers. ♦ Imperial Hwy (between Roger and Pont Cassé). 449.1401, 449.1224; fax 449.2160

Restaurants/Clubs: Red   Hotels: Blue
Shops/♥ Outdoors: Green   Sights/Culture: Black

Getting Your Feet Wet in Dominica

Mountainous Dominica is surrounded by underwater steep slopes and plunging gorges, similar to those on land, making these waters ideal for snorkeling and scuba diving. The boating is great, too, especially since whale sightings have become common offshore. Here are a few organizations that can help get you afloat:

Boating

Anchorage Dive Center Anchorage Hotel (south of Roseau). 448.2638, 800/223.6815

Castaways Beach Hotel Castaways Beach, Mero. 449.6244, 800/322.2223

Snorkeling and Scuba Diving

Anchorage Dive Center Anchorage Hotel (south of Roseau). 448.2638, 800/223.6815

Dive Castaways Castaways Beach Hotel, Castaways Beach, Mero. 449.6244, 800/322.2223

Dive Dominica Castle Comfort Lodge (south of Roseau). 448.2188, 800/468.4748

East Carib Dive Salisbury Beach, Salisbury. 449.6575

Sportfishing

Anchorage Dive Center Anchorage Hotel (south of Roseau). 448.2638, 800/223.6815

Castaways Beach Hotel Castaways Beach, Mero (see above)

Coconut Beach Hotel Picard Beach (just south of Glanvillia). 445.5393

Dominica Tours Roseau. 448.2638

39 Good Times Bar-b-que ★$ Pull up here for some stick-to-your-ribs basics—barbecued chicken, pork, steaks, fish, and lamb—all served with salad and french fries. Live music heats up the bar in this popular gathering spot. ◆ American ◆ W-Su dinner. Roger. 449.1660

39 Baroon Bijoux A wide range of imported and locally crafted jewelry features precious, semiprecious, and synthetic stones. There are shell and coral creations, too. ◆ M-F. Canefield Industrial Estate (just south of Roger). 449.2888

39 Candle Industries This plant produces a wide assortment of candles decorated with Dominican parrots and other colorful figures. Some examples are also sold in shops in Canefield. ◆ M-F. Canefield Industrial Estate (just south of Roger). 449.1006

Bests

Anne G.S. Baptiste

Innkeeper/Co-Owner/Nurturer of the Earth/Papillote Wilderness Retreat and Nature Sanctuary

The thrill of seeing the absolute greenness of Dominica from the air and knowing that on landing will be engulfed by it.

Snorkeling in the bubbling volcano "Champagne" Springs off the leeward coast.

Swimming through the cool, silent, and mysterious waters of **Titou Gorge.**

Walking on crust in the **Valley of Desolation** with the sounds of the earth's bubbling and hissing as it sends forth its gases and strangely colored waters.

Catching sight of a foraging agouti early in the morning, or a yellow-crowned night heron stalking land crabs in still forests.

Night sounds of the forest—frogs, geckos, bottle bugs, and night calling birds.

Gliding up the **Indian River** listening to parrots chattering over nature's bounty of fruits and seeds.

Shopping for fruits and vegetables at the magnificently abundant open-air market on Saturday morning.

The first woman to head a Caribbean government was Dame Mary Eugenia Charles, who served as Prime Minister of Dominica from 1969 to 1995, when she lost a re-election bid. Though known to some as "The Iron Lady of the Caribbean," to islanders she is affectionately called "Mamo." She was plunged into the international spotlight in 1983 when she successfully appealed to US President Ronald Reagan for an invasion of Grenada.

Dominican Republic

About 7.6 million Dominicans occupy the eastern two-thirds of **Hispaniola**, an island in the **Greater Antilles** that they share with Haiti. The country's many distinctive features include the Caribbean's highest peak (**Pico Duarte** at 10,417 feet), its longest beach (the white sands of **Costa del Coco—** Coconut Coast—stretch for 22 miles), and the greatest number of hotel rooms in the region (over 32,000). Visitors can expect uncrowded beaches and a mountainous interior, as well as busy cosmopolitan centers filled with Spanish Renaissance architecture, museums, and international restaurants.

Inhabited by the Arawak Indians before the arrival of Europeans, the Dominican Republic traces much of its recorded back to Christopher Columbus. The explorer landed here on his initial voyage in 1492; his brother Bartolomeo founded the capital city of **Santo Domingo** four years later; and his son Diego became governor in 1509. The first city in the New World, Santo Domingo boasts the oldest street, house, cathedral, fort, and university in the Western Hemisphere, as well as the ruins of its earliest hospital and monastery. The imposing **Alcázar de Colón** (Columbus Palace), built in 1509, was the center of the Spanish viceroyalty for 60 years.

The Spanish Empire's premier outpost in the Americas, Santo Domingo became the port from which all other expeditions embarked, launching Velázquez to Cuba, Juan Ponce de León to Puerto Rico, and Cortés to Mexico. But that expansive era ended when Britain's Sir Francis Drake burned the colony in 1586. Periods of French, Spanish, independent, and Haitian rule followed. The republic eventually achieved autonomy under the Trinitaria movement of Juan Pablo Duarte in 1844. Today more than 2.4 million people call Santo

THE BAHAMAS

Atlantic Ocean

Cuba

DOMINICAN
REPUBLIC

Haiti

HISPANIOLA

Jamaica

Puerto
Rico

Caribbean Sea

N

| km | 300 | 600 |
| mi | 180 | 360 |

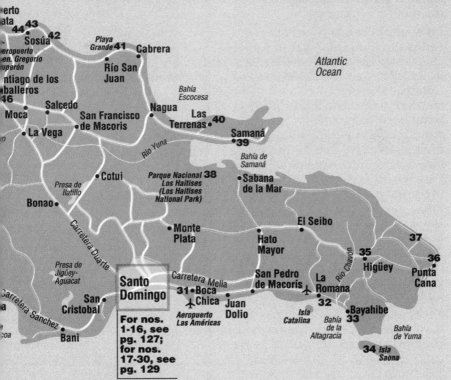

Puerto
Plata
44 43
Sosúa 42
Aeropuerto
Gen. Gregorio
Luperón
ntiago de los
Caballeros
46
Moca
La Vega

Salcedo

San Francisco
de Macoris

Río San
Juan

Playa
Grande 41 Cabrera

Nagua

Las
Terrenas 40

Samaná
39

Atlantic
Ocean

Bahía
Escocesa

Bahía de
Samaná

Presa de
Ilatillo

Cotui

Parque Nacional 38
Los Haitises
(Los Haitises
National Park)

Sabana
de la Mar

Bonao

Carretera Duarte

Monte
Plata

El Seibo

37

Río Yuna

Presa de
Jigüey-
Aguacat

Santo
Domingo

Carretera Mella

31 Boca
Chica

Aeropuerto
Las Américas

Juan
Dolio

Hato
Mayor

San Pedro
de Macorís

35

Higüey

36

Punta
Cana

La
Romana

Río Chavón

32

San
Cristobal

For nos.
1-16, see
pg. 127;
for nos.
17-30, see
pg. 129

Bani

Carretera Sanchez

Isla
Catalina

Bahía
de la
Altagracia

Bayahibe
33

Bahía
de Yuma

34 Isla
Saona

Caribbean
Sea

For nos.
1-16, see
pg. 127;
for nos.
17-30, see
pg. 129

N

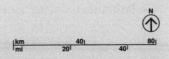

| km | 40 | 80 |
| mi | 20 | 40 |

Domingo home. Some of its modern attractions include a fine botanical garden, zoo, aquarium, and the **Plaza de la Cultura**, which incorporates the **Museo de Arte Moderno** and the **Teatro Nacional.**

A blend of Indian, Spanish, and African ingredients enlivens the regional cuisine, which includes such traditional dishes as *longaniza* (a spicy pork sausage), *pescado con coco* (fish in coconut sauce), stewed goat, and the ubiquitous rice and beans. Light it isn't, but you can always merengue the calories away or work them off on a shopping safari for hand-crafted masks, semiprecious amber, or fashions by island-born Oscar de la Renta. Visitors ca test their bargaining skills at the **Mercado Modelo**, where dozens of vendors sell brightly colored paintings, wooden carvings, and jewelry made from amber and the turquoise-like larimar, two stones indigenous to the island. Nightlife throbs at the mammoth **Guácara Taína**, a folklore center and disco set in a subterranean cave, and along the **Malecón**, a seaside avenue studded with cafes, clubs, and luxury hotels. Adventurers will find many opportuniti to venture off the beaten path. Divers can explore coral reefs or sunken ships landlubbers can enjoy tropical splendor in botanical gardens and national parks.

There are no beaches on the capital's rocky coastline, but the sands of **Boca Chica** and **Juan Dolio** lie just a few miles to the east. At **La Romana**, the villas and sporting facilities of the behemoth resort **Casa de Campo** sprawl over 7,000 acres; amenities include an international airport and an artists' colony in the form of a faux 16th-century village, complete with cobbleston and a 5,000-seat Greek amphitheater. Elsewhere on the island, you'll find resort complexes at the waterfront towns of **Puerto Plata**, **Sosúa**, **Cabarete**, **Barahona**, and **Punta Cana.** Guest houses and posh facilities have even infiltrated the isolated fishing village of **Samaná**, where some of the resident unlike most other citizens of this predominantly Spanish-speaking and Catholic nation, are Protestants whose primary language is English—a legacy of the thousands of slaves who fled from the US in the 1820s.

Santo Domingo's hotels and casinos suffered during the 31-year rule (1930-61 of Generalíssimo Rafael Leónidas Trujillo, whose dictatorship led to deservedl bad publicity that nearly strangled the tourism industry. But thanks to the country's natural beauty and often-favorable exchange rate for foreign currencies, tourism has bounced back strongly. Resorts—many all-inclusive— are scattered throughout the island, especially on the coastlines, and new hotels keep popping up. While the country still has its problems—at press tim electrical outages were almost a daily occurrence (most hotels and restaurants have their own generators)—many Europeans, Canadians, and Americans are discovering the many ways to enjoy the New World's oldest destination.

Area code 809 unless otherwise noted.

Getting to the Island

Airlines

Aeropostal	566.2334
Air Canada	547.2236, 800/776.3000
American	542.5151, 800/433.7300
Continental	562.6688, 800/231.0856
Copa	562.5824
	1/200.3134 (local toll-free number)
Iberia	686.9191, 800/772.464
Lufthansa	689.9625, 800/645.388
TWA	689.6073, 800/892.414
Varig	563.3434, 800/468.274

Interisland Carriers

ALM (Antillean Airlines)	682.3171, 800/327.723
American Eagle	542.5151, 800/433.730
Viasa	682.111
	1/200.1661 (local toll-free number

Airports **Aeropuerto Las Américas** (549.0450), the country's largest airport, is located 25 minutes east of Santo Domingo. The airport has money-exchange booths, duty-free shopping, and a tourist information booth that is open daily.

Aeropuerto General Gregorio Luperón (586.0219), a new international airport, is 15 minutes from Puerto Plata and is convenient to the resorts of the north coast.

Aeropuerto La Romana (556.5565), on the southeast coast, serves private jets and **American Eagle** flights from San Juan, Puerto Rico. It's about about an hour-and-a-half drive to Santo Domingo. **Aeropuerto Punta Cana** (686.8790), also on the east coast, serves **American Eagle** flights from San Juan, Puerto Rico. The airport is five to ten minutes from **Punta Cana** resorts and about a two-hour drive from Santo Domingo.

Aeropuerto Herrera (567.3900) in Santo Domingo, **Aeropuerto Cibao** (582.4894) in Santiago, **Aeropuerto María Montes** (524.7010) in Barahona, and **Aeropuerto Arroyo Barril** (566.5941) in Samaná handle small jets and commuter planes.

Getting Around the Island

Buses An efficient network covers the entire city of Santo Domingo, where buses are large though sometimes crowded, and fares are inexpensive. It's easy to make connections for other cities, but be sure to ask about the number of stops between points. For schedules and other information, contact the government-sponsored **Compañía Nacional** (565.6681), **Caribe Tours** (221.4422), or **Metro Tourist Services** (566.7126).

Car Rental

To rent a car, you must be 25 or older and present a credit card.

Avis	565.1818, 800/331.1084
Budget	567.0173, 800/626.4516
Hertz	221.5333, 800/654.3131
Nelly	549.0509, 544.1800, 800/526.6684

Driving You will not need a local permit; a driver's license from your home country is sufficient. Driving is on the right. In Santo Domingo, it's best to walk or take a taxi, especially in the **Ciudad Colonial** where parking is difficult. Otherwise, driving is fairly uncomplicated, though signs may be confusing and police sometimes stop motorists for dubious infractions. Dominicans are happy to offer directions.

Limousines

The Limousine Connection	540.5304

Taxis

Apolo	537.0000
El Conde	563.6131

Tours Many taxi drivers double as tour guides, but hire one who really knows the island and your language; ask at the hotel desk. English-speaking guides are available on some sight-seeing buses; among the best: **Ecoturista** (221.4104), **Emely Tours** (687.7114), **Metro Tours** (544.4580), **Omni Tours** (565.6591), and **Prieto Tours** (685.0102).

FYI

Electricity The current is 110 volts/60 cycles, the same as in the US and Canada.

Entry Requirements For US and Canadian citizens, a valid passport or other proof of citizenship (birth certificate, voter's registration card) plus a photo ID allows stays of up to 60 days. A return or onward ticket is required. Foreign visitors must purchase a Tourist Card ($10) upon entering the country.

Gambling More than 20 hotel casinos in Santo Domingo and coastal resort areas offer blackjack, craps, roulette, slot machines, poker, and baccarat.

Language Spanish is the official language, although most large hotels and resorts have English-speaking staff members. Visitors who don't speak Spanish may have trouble communicating outside of the major tourist areas, but Dominicans are friendly and willing to help bridge the gap.

Money The peso is the official currency. US dollars are not generally accepted, although most establishments accept traveler's checks and major credit cards. Foreign currency can be exchanged at **Banco de Reservas** booths, found in airports and large hotels, or at commercial banks. Banks are open Monday through Friday from 8:30AM to 3:30PM, and the **Banco de Reservas** booth at the airport is open when flights arrive.

Personal Safety Pickpockets are common, especially in urban areas (including Santo Domingo, Boca Chica, and Puerto Plata), and it's not safe to wander the streets of the capital after dark. Never get into an unmarked taxicab.

Publications The free weekly *Santo Domingo News* is distributed at hotels and shops; it primarily serves English-speaking residents, so coverage of tourist attractions is fairly light. Visitors might prefer *Bohío*, a free bilingual magazine. The guidebook *La Cotica: National Tourism Guide to the Dominican Republic* is free at tourist offices; there's a nominal charge at newsstands and shops. *Listín Diarío, El Caribe, El Siglo, Nuevo Diario, Hoy, El Nacional,* and *Ultima Hora* are the local Spanish dailies. Newsstands stock Puerto Rico's English-language *San Juan Star* and day-old newspapers from Miami and New York City.

Reservation Services and House Rentals

Remax	565.6262

Taxes An eight-percent sales tax is added to hotel and restaurant bills. There's a $10 departure tax.

Tipping Hotels and restaurants tack on a 10-percent service charge; room service carries an additional 5 percent charge and sometimes a nominal "energy charge." Add an extra 5 to 10 percent if the service is good, especially at restaurants not connected to hotels. Tip maids $1 or $2 per day, bellhops and porters 50¢ per bag (but never less than $1 total), and taxi drivers 10 to 15 percent of the fare.

Visitors' Information Offices The **Dominican Tourist Information Center** is located in Santo Domingo (Avs México and 30 de Marzo, 221.4660, 888/358.9594; fax 682.3806) and there's also an information center for the colonial area of the city on Parque Colón (686.3858). Other centers are located in Puerto Plata (Av Hermanas Mirabal, between Avs Circunvalación Norte and Luis Ginebra, 586.3806) and in **Santiago City Hall** (Av Juan Pablo Duarte, 582.5885). All of these offices are open Monday through Friday from 9AM to 5PM. The information counter at **Aeropuerto Las Américas** (542.0120) is open when flights arrive.

Phone Book

Ambulance	911
Directory Assistance	1411
Diving Emergencies/ Decompression Chambers	911
Emergencies	911
Fire	911
Hospitals	
La Romana	556.2555
Puerto Plata	586.2210
Santiago	583.4311
Santo Domingo (Centro Médico)	221.0171
Santo Domingo (Clinica Abreu)	688.4411
Police	911
Post Office	534.6218

The humble Dominican rice dish *locrio* is thought to have roots in Spanish paella. Today annatto seeds commonly replace saffron in some of the countless versions of this local mainstay.

In the rural areas of the Dominican Republic, Spanish has taken on some distinctive twists. For example, *un chin* means a little; *un chin-chin* means a tiny bit; and *rumba* means a whole lot.

The original name of the island of Hispaniola was *Haiti*, which among the Indians signified "high ground." The eastern part was called *Quisqueya*, "mother of the earth," while the western part was called *Babeque*, "land of many villages."

Ciudad Colonial de Santo Domingo (Santo Domingo's Colonial City)

The first permanent European settlement in the New World, **Santo Domingo** was founded on 4 August 1496 by Christopher Columbus's brother, Bartolomeo Columbus. The site of that original colony, this compact area bounded by **Río Ozama** (Ozama River) and **Palo Hincado** is packed with splendid Spanish Renaissance architecture and historic landmarks. You can hook up with a bilingual guide on the plaza in front of the **Catedral de Santa María la Menor.** The best way to see everything is on foot, so lace up your sensible shoes and step back in time.

1 Parque Independencia (Independence Park) A graceful introduction to the Ciudad Colonial, this large and pleasant square is crowned by the **Altar de la Patria** (Altar of the Nation), the tomb of national heroes Juan Pablo Duarte, Francisco del Rosario Sánchez, and Ramón Matías Mella. ♦ Palo Hincado (between Arzobispo Nouel and Las Mercedes)

At Parque Independencia:

Puerta del Conde (Conde Gate) Beneath these arches in 1844, the March for Independence ended with a proclamation declaring the country to be an autonomous republic. Today this 18th-century monument is the gateway to the Ciudad Colonial.

2 Calle El Conde This graceful pedestrian street leads into the old city's historic treasures. Before embarking on a tour of the many colonial sights, sip fresh fruit juice at one of the cafes or window-shop with the locals. A good place to start pricing souvenirs is **El Conde Gift Shop** (at Hostos, 682.5909). ♦ Between Las Damas and Palo Hincado

On El Conde:

Museo del Ambar (Amber Museum) The small museum is on the second floor, while the first floor is a shop selling good-quality amber and larimar jewelry. This place has no connection to the **Museo del Ambar** in Puerto Plata (see page 135). ♦ Daily. No. 107 (at Arzobispo Meriño). 221.1333

3 Parque Colón (Columbus Park) A larger-than-life-sized bronze statue of the famous explorer holds court here. Though Columbus actually landed on the island at La Isabela in 1492, this 19th-century statue is the sentimental starting point for a modern-day walking tour. ♦ El Conde (between Isabel La Católica and Arzobispo Meriño)

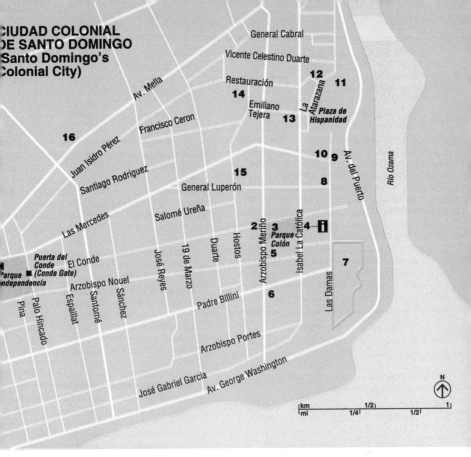

CIUDAD COLONIAL DE SANTO DOMINGO
(Santo Domingo's Colonial City)

4 Palacio de Borgella (Palace of Borgella) On the east side of the park, this structure was the seat of command for occupying Haitian rulers from 1822 to 1844. It's now a government office building with a small tourist information center (686.3858). ♦ Isabel La Católica (between Callejón de los Nichos and El Conde)

5 Catedral de Santa María la Menor (Cathedral of Santa María the Minor) The oldest cathedral in the Western Hemisphere, this Spanish Renaissance legacy was completed in the early 16th century. Within the gold coral limestone facade is an elaborately carved altar flanked by gilt Baroque paintings, gifts from Charles V of Spain. The 450-year-old nave was reputedly the resting place of Christopher Columbus until 1992, when that highly disputed dust (Spain also lays claim to his remains) was transplanted across town to the **Faro a Colón** (Columbus Lighthouse; see page 132). The cathedral still houses many other treasures, though, and a small tip buys a worthwhile half hour with one of the local guides. ♦ M-Sa. Arzobispo Meriño and Plazoleta de los Curas. 682.3848

6 Museo de la Familia Dominicana (Museum of the Dominican Family) Housed in the **Casa de Tostado**, this museum is a tribute to Victorian home life. Antique furnishings and memorabilia are on display throughout the 16th-century mansion, once the home of Francisco Tostado, a writer and university professor killed when Sir Francis Drake attacked the colony in 1586. Today the building is also known for an obscure architectural detail: "the only Gothic-geminated window remaining in a civil construction in the Americas." ♦ Admission. M-Sa. Padre Billini and Arzobispo Meriño. 689.5057

7 Calle Las Damas (Ladies' Street) The oldest street in the New World is a grand ramble graced with shade trees and majestic 16th-century landmarks. When Christopher Columbus's son Diego was viceroy, his wife María de Toledo would promenade here with the ladies of her court, hence the name.

7 Fortaleza Ozama (Ozama Fortress) The sinister **Torre del Homenaje** (Tower of Homage), former lookout post and death-row prison, soars above this medieval-style fort, begun in 1505. According to legend, Gonzalo Fernández de Oviedo penned his *General History of the Indies* here. And Diego Columbus made a dramatic entrance here when he assumed the title of New World Viceroy on 9 July 1509. ♦ Nominal admission. Daily. Las Damas (south of El Conde). 685.8472

8 Panteón Nacional (National Pantheon) Built as a Jesuit monastery in 1714, this building served as a tobacco warehouse and theater before it was restored in 1955 by order of Rafael Trujillo, who intended it as his burial site. Note the colossal bronze-and-onyx chandelier, presented by Spain's Franco, and the elaborate grilles—some say the carvings resemble swastikas. The ever-burning flame is in memory of the nation's first president/dictator, General Pedro Santana. Tour guides appreciate a nominal tip. ◆ Free. Daily. Las Damas and Plaza de María de Toledo. No phone

9 Capilla de los Remedios (Chapel of Our Lady of Remedies) Colonists attended Mass at this 16th-century church until the nearby **Catedral de Santa María la Menor** (see page 127) was completed. Today the interior is closed to visitors, who must be content with views of the Romanesque exterior. ◆ Las Damas (north of El Conde)

Next to Capilla de los Remedios:

Reloj de Sol (Sun Clock) The first sundial in the New World was commissioned by Governor Francisco Rubio y Penaranda in 1753. In the winter months, the clock runs about a half-hour late.

10 Museo de las Casas Reales (Museum of the Royal Houses) Handsome displays at this museum are spread throughout a complex of restored 16th-century colonial buildings, dedicated by King Juan Carlos of Spain in 1976. Models of the *Nina, Pinta,* and *Santa María* share space with an electronic map that traces Christopher Columbus's four voyages of discovery. Heraldic tapestries, coats of armor, antique coaches, Indian carvings, and other artifacts recall Santo Domingo's glorious past. Other exhibits include full-scale re-creations of a courtroom, pharmacy, and sugar mill. Visit the majestic offices of former dictator Rafael Trujillo, whose grandiose "throne rooms" are filled with royal portraits and crystal chandeliers. ◆ Admission. Tu-Su. Las Damas and Las Mercedes. 682.4202

11 Alcázar de Colón (Columbus's Palace) The first European castle in the Americas is still a magnificent sight. Here Diego Columbus, appointed Spanish viceroy in 1509, ruled the New World from 1510 to 1516. His viceregal palace at the foot of Las Damas was the main outpost of the Spanish viceroyalty for 60 years and greeted Cortés, Balboa, Ponce de León, and other explorer-conquerors. Today visitors tread the same halls to view the restored reception areas, dining room, bedrooms, kitchen, private chapel, and some of Diego's original furnishings. ◆ Admission. Daily. Plaza de la Hispanidad (east of La Atarazana). 687.5361

12 Las Atarazanas (The Dockyards) This bright white complex of restored 16th-century buildings houses a lively collection of boutiques and cafes. Sample local fare at **Fonda de la Atarazana** (687.6287) and shop for amber and larimar at **Ambar Tres** (688.0474). Some of these walls date from 1507; they formerly housed a colonial arsenal and Santo Domingo's original customs office. ◆ Hours vary. La Atarazana and Restauración

13 Casa del Cordón (House of the Cord) Above the door of the oldest surviving stone house in the New World (1503) is a cord carved in stone, the symbol of the Franciscan Order, which once owned the building. In the early 1500s, Diego Columbus and María de Toledo camped out here while their palace was under construction nearby. In 1586, ladies of the court gathered here to hand over their jewelry to Sir Francis Drake—his price to spare the smoldering remains of their colony. The building is open for self-guided tours and also hosts occasional art exhibits. ◆ Free. M-F. Emiliano Tejera and Isabel La Católica. 682.4333

14 Monasterio de San Francisco (San Francisco Monastery) Assaulted by hurricanes, earthquakes, Sir Francis Drake, and French artillery, the New World's oldest monastery (begun in 1512) still stands, albeit in ruins. Follow the old stone walkway from the street. The site is dramatically illuminated after dark. ◆ Free. M-Sa. Hostos (between Emiliano Tejera and Restauración). No phone

15 Hospital San Nicolás de Bari (San Nicolás de Bari Hospital) Wander among the tumbledown walls of the Western Hemisphere's first hospital, founded in 1503 by Governor Nicolás de Ovando. ◆ Free. Daily. Hostos (between General Luperón and Las Mercedes). No phone

16 Mercado Modelo (Model Market) The stalls of this marketplace are crammed with a colorful jumble of produce, spices, crafts, and furnishings. Here's the place to scout works by local artists, hand-carved wooden figures, and potent Dominican coffee. Bargaining is expected. If your Spanish is rusty, hire (for a small tip) one of the guides who hang out by the gate to act as your interpreter and haggle-mate. ◆ M-Sa. Av Mella (between Santomé and Del Monte y Tejada). No phone

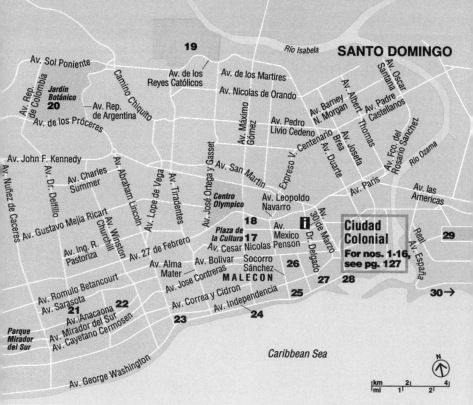

Santo Domingo

Map labels:
Av. Sol Poniente · Río Isabela · **SANTO DOMINGO** · Av. Rep. de Colombia · Jardín Botánico **20** · Camino Chiquito · Av. de los Reyes Católicos · Av. de los Martires · Av. Nicolas de Orando · Av. Oscar Santana · Av. Rep. de Argentina · Av. de los Próceres · Av. Máximo Gómez · Av. Pedro Livio Cedeno · Av. Barney N. Morgan · Av. Albert Thomas · Av. Padre Castellanos · Av. John F. Kennedy · Av. Charles Summer · Av. Abraham Lincoln · Av. Lope de Vega · Av. Tiradentes · Av. José Ortega y Gasset · Av. San Martin · Expreso V. Centenario · Av. Brea · Av. Joseta · Av. Fco. del Rosario Sánchez · Río Ozama · Av. Dr. Delfilio · Av. Nuñez de Caceres · Av. Gustavo Mejia Ricart · Av. Winston Churchill · Av. Ing. R. Pastoriza · Av. 27 de Febrero · Centro Olympico · Av. Leopoldo Navarro · Av. Duarte · Av. Paris · Av. las Americas · Plaza de la Cultura **17** · **18** · Av. Mexico · Av. 30 de Marzo · Dr. Delgado · **Ciudad Colonial** For nos. 1-16, see pg. 127 · **29** · Av. Cesar Nicolas Penson · Av. Romulo Betancourt · Av. Sarasota · **21** · Av. Anacaona **22** · Av. Mirador del Sur · Av. Cayetano Cermosen · Av. Alma Mater · Av. Bolivar · Av. Jose Contreras · Socorro Sánchez · **MALECON** · **26** · **27** · **28** · Real Av. España · **30→** · Parque Mirador del Sur · **23** · Av. Correa y Cidron · Av. Independencia · **24** · **25** · Av. George Washington · Caribbean Sea · km/mi · N

Modern Santo Domingo

Beyond the **Ciudad Colonial**, Santo Domingo has grown into a modern metropolis, populated by about 2.4 million citizens and sprawling over 144 square miles. In between residential sectors, the city offers top-rated cultural attractions, international restaurants, luxurious hotels, and lush gardens.

17 Plaza de la Cultura (Cultural Plaza) Here on the fountain-studded site of former dictator Rafael Trujillo's mansion, the grand **Biblioteca Nacional** (National Library) and **Teatro Nacional** (National Theater) share green lawns with a collection of Dominican museums. ♦ Av Máximo Gómez (between Avs Cesar Nicolas Penson and Pedro Henriquez Ureña)

Within Plaza de la Cultura:

Museo del Hombre Dominicano (Museum of the Dominican Man) Indian artifacts are a highlight of anthropological displays tracing Dominican peoples from pre-Columbian days to the present. ♦ Admission. Tu-Su. 687.3623

Museo de Arte Moderno (Museum of Modern Art) Works by 20th-century Dominican artists dominate the permanent collection here. ♦ Admission. Tu-Su. 685.2153

Museo Nacional de Historia y Geografía (National History and Geography Museum) The **1916-1961 Hall** showcases a collection of Rafael Trujillo memorabilia that includes many of El Benefactor's personal possessions. Other exhibits follow national development from the 1844 independence proclamation to modern times. ♦ Admission. Tu-Su. 688.6952

Museo Nacional de Historia Natural (National Natural History Museum) Don't miss the amber collection and the stuffed indigenous birds, among the other island treasures preserved here. ♦ Admission. Tu-Su. 689.0106

18 Gran Hotel Lina $$$ The 220 rooms in this hostelry are simple, but pleasant and immaculate, and the location is convenient to downtown attractions. There's also a swimming pool, an exercise room, business services, and a casino. ♦ Avs Máximo Gómez and 27 de Febrero. 563.5000, 800/942.2461; fax 686.5521

Within the Gran Hotel Lina:

Lina ★★★$$$
Seafood is a specialty at this modern international restaurant. Spanish dishes are well represented on the menu, which includes a stellar paella and *mero la zarzuela* (bass in a Pernod-spiked casserole). ♦ International/ Spanish ♦ Daily lunch and dinner. Reservations recommended; jacket requested. 563.5000

All About Amber

The color was fairly close, but amber wasn't the gold that drew Spanish conquistadors to the New World. It wasn't until 1949, after a geological survey of the country, that amber mining finally began on a large scale in the mountainous region of the **Northern Cordillera** (between **Santiago de los Caballeros** and **Puerto Plata**). The area is the site of the second-largest known amber deposit in the world.

Shortly after the find, a school was established to teach local crafters how to make the most of the abundant raw material, and today, amber jewelry, including the distinctive Dominican-style necklaces that feature gold wire wrapped around highly polished beads, is a favorite souvenir. In recent years there has been a resurgence of intererest in the resin, thanks to the film *Jurassic Park,* in which living dinosaurs are cloned from DNA extracted from fossils preserved in amber.

There are several beautiful varieties of amber. The finest transparent golden resin is called "The Amber of Santo Domingo." Red tones are attractive, but the rarest is "blue" amber (the bright reflected light on the surface creates a lustrous blue sheen). The most valuable pieces encase remarkably preserved insects and leaves that are 20 to 30 million years old. Such "inclusions" are found in about one of every 100 pieces.

Amber is rumored to bring good luck, but don't trust your fortune to street vendors who pass off plastic as amber. When rubbed, the real thing produces a hint of resinlike aroma, but some hustlers mask the telltale plastic smell with resin oils. For safe buys, stick with one of these established shops:

Ambar Tres La Atarazana, Ciudad Colonial de Santo Domingo. 688.0474

Harrison's Locations throughout the island. 586.3933

Museo del Ambar 61 Duarte (between Villanueva and Emilio Prudhomme), Puerto Plata. 586.2848

Museo del Ambar 107 El Conde (at Arzobispo Meriño), Ciudad Colonial de Santo Domingo. 221.1333

Rainbow 22 Duarte, Puerto Plata. 586.3005

19 Parque Zoológico Nacional (National Zoo) Animals roam freely in natural habitats surrounded by moats at this attractive 320-acre park on the Río Isabela (Isabela River). ♦ Admission. Tu-Su. Av del Zoológico (just north of Av de los Reyes Católicos). 562.3149

20 Jardín Botánico (Botanical Garden) Board a carriage, boat, or small train for a scenic ride through the biggest botanical gardens in Latin America. The Japanese garden is elegant, as are those created in English, Spanish, and other classic styles. Don't miss the great ravine and the floral clock. ♦ Admission. Tu-Su. Av de los Próceres (between Avs República de Argentina and República de Colombia). 565.2860

21 Guácara Taína This incredible dance club in a cave calls itself the only disco grotto in the world. The underground playground has 3 bars and 2 dance floors and holds more than 1,500 people. A folkloric show is staged on Tuesday and Thursday. ♦ Admission. Daily from 9PM. Parque Mirador del Sur, Av Mirador del Sur (between Avs Italia and Nuñez de Caceres). 530.2662

22 Mesón de la Cava ★★★$$$ Another underground wonder, this restaurant has a spectacular setting that in itself would be enough to attract enthusiastic crowds. But the steak and seafood dishes are very good, too, as are the folkloric shows. Merengue and disco music make this a popular hangout for locals. ♦ International ♦ Daily lunch and dinner. Reservations recommended. 1 Av Mirador del Sur (between Avs Jimenez Moya and Pedro Bobea). 533.2818, 533.4840, 532.2615

Malecón

Deluxe hotels and glitzy night spots crowd the palm-lined Caribbean coast at this urban resort area, which has been called "the world's largest open-air discotheque." A three-mile strip of waterfront, **Avenida George Washington,** is popular with tourists and locals who come here after dark for far-ranging views and drinks at sidewalk cafes.

23 Hotel Santo Domingo $$$ Dominican Oscar de la Renta designed the interiors of this stylish hotel, a favorite haunt of vacationing Latin American politicos. Adding to the appealing atmosphere are locally crafted furnishings and 14 acres of tropical landscape. Many of the 220 rooms face the ocean; ask about the **Premier Club** for special perks. Amenities include a pool, sundeck, sauna, three tennis courts, and three restaurants (including **El Alcázar,** see below).

After dark, **Las Palmas** piano bar attracts a stylish crowd. ◆ Avs Independencia and Abraham Lincoln. 221.1511, 800/877.3643; fax 535.4050

Within the Hotel Santo Domingo:

El Alcázar ★★★★$$$ Oscar de la Renta tented the walls and ceilings with bolts of billowing fabric, trimmed by a fantastic Moorish clutter of tiny mirrors and antique mother-of-pearl. Elegant continental cuisine is presented with dash at dinnertime; midday diners will find the lunch buffet to be a surprising bargain. ◆ Continental ◆ M-F lunch and dinner; Su lunch. Reservations recommended; jacket and tie requested for dinner. 221.1511

24 Vesuvio I ★★★$$$ The freshest ingredients make all the difference here, in everything from simple homemade cheeses to antipasto extravaganzas. Pasta and seafood are especially good, and the dessert tray is notoriously tempting. ◆ Italian ◆ Daily lunch and dinner. Reservations recommended Friday and Saturday. 521 Av George Washington (between Avs Máximo Gómez and Alma Mater). 221.1954

25 Ramada Renaissance Jaragua $$$$ A showy complex that sprawls over 14 acres on the Malecón, this high rollers' paradise offers a 20,000-square-foot casino (touted as the Caribbean's largest), an 800-seat tennis stadium, 4 lighted clay tennis courts, a European-style spa, the glitzy 1,600-seat **La Fiesta** theater (featuring twice-monthly shows), 4 restaurants (including the **Manhattan Grill** and **Figaro,** see below), a lounge, 300 guest rooms, and **Jubilee,** one of the city's most popular discos. The hotel recently added the **Renaissance Club** floor, featuring a business center and complimentary continental breakfast. ◆ 367 Av George Washington (between Av Pasteur and Socorro Sánchez). 221.2222, 800/228.9898; fax 686.0528

Within the Ramada Renaissance Jaragua:

Manhattan Grill ★★★$$$ Tourists can get a satisfying fix of North American comfort food here: Everything from New England chowder to gumbo is on the menu, and steak, lamb, and lobster are grilled in full view. Tables overlook the casino, and the service is remarkably attentive. ◆ American ◆ M-Sa dinner. Reservations recommended. 221.2222

Figaro ★★★$$$ An open kitchen is the backdrop for this trattoria, whose bill of fare ranges from eggplant parmigiana to tournedos Rossini. Virtuous diners can opt for spa cuisine (vegetable lasagna is hardly a sacrifice), then reward themselves with a creamy corn pudding for dessert. ◆ Italian ◆ Tu-Su dinner. Reservations recommended. 221.2222

25 Meliá Santo Domingo $$$ Formerly the **Sheraton Santo Domingo,** this hotel has long been popular with business travelers because of its convenient location, modern decor, efficient service, and health club with sauna and masseurs. Pleasure seekers will find a stellar disco, a nightclub, a casino, a pool, and two tennis courts. Most of the 260 guest rooms have sea views, and suites open onto private terraces. There are three restaurants on the premises. The Meliá chain, which recently purchased the property, has indicated that it will invest in renovations. ◆ 365 Av George Washington (between Av Pasteur and Socorro Sánchez). 221.6666, 800/336.3542; fax 687.8150

26 Reina de España ★★★$$$ The mixed seafood grill and the paella are popular with the crowds who flock to this celebrated restaurant. It continues to win local culinary awards for cross-cultural fare with a Spanish accent. ◆ Spanish ◆ Daily lunch and dinner. Reservations recommended Friday and Saturday. 103 Cervantes (south of Av Bolivar). 685.2588

27 V Centenario Inter-Continental $$$ This luxurious complex, right on the Malecón, was named in honor of the 500th anniversary of Christopher Columbus's landing here in 1492. Its attractions include a casino, a pool, two tennis courts, and the nation's first underground parking garage. The 201 deluxe rooms are accentuated by sweeping sea views, and guests can relax in 2 bars or feast on the Spanish or Dominican cuisine served in the 2 restaurants. ◆ 218 Av George Washington (at Presidente Vicini Burgos). 221.0000, 800.327.0200; fax 221.2020

28 Obelisco a Las Hermanas Mirabel (Obelisk to the Mirabel Sisters) Rafael Trujillo had this monument erected in his own honor, but the striking tower was re-dedicated in 1997 to the three Mirabel sisters, killed in 1960 by Trujillo supporters for their purported political agitation. The obelisk now bears the likenesses of the three women, painted in vibrant colors by artist Elsa Nuñez. The sisters—Patria, Minerva, and María Teresa—have only recently been recognized as national heroes. ◆ Av George Washington and Palo Hincado

The cotica is the Dominican Republic's native parrot. It is said that the bird not only repeats words but also takes on the personality of its owner.

29 Faro a Colón (Columbus Lighthouse)

This 7-story behemoth, meant to commemorate the 500th anniversary of Christopher Columbus's first voyage of discovery, debuted in 1992 amid a storm of protest over its cost (estimated between $70 and $250 million); the lack of sufficient power to fire the beacon (at press time it was being lit sporadically); and doubts about the whereabouts of Columbus's remains. Although Seville, Spain, also claims to be the explorer's final resting place, Columbus is supposedly entombed in the elaborate sarcophagus at the centerpoint of this cross-shaped building, which is nearly 700 feet long and 132 feet at its widest. The promised museums are little more than a collection of individual exhibits sponsored by various nations. The controversial energy-gobbling beacon is composed of 149 xenon lasers that beam upward to project the image of a giant cross on the clouds. ◆ Admission. Tu-Su. Parque Mirador del Este, Blvd el Faro and Av Estados Unidos. 592.5217

30 Acuario Nacional (National Aquarium)

At this verdant tropical park, giant turtles live in their natural surroundings and landlubbers can experience a close encounter with sharks (through glass). ◆ Admission. Tu-Su. Parque Litoral del Sur, Av España and Ata. 592.1509

30 Los Tres Ojos (The Three Eyes)

It's worth the 10-minute drive from downtown Santo Domingo to see these three subterranean lagoons (fresh, salt, and sulfur), which are fed by an underground river. Rock formations and luxuriant greenery set a cool and dramatic scene. Guides expect a nominal tip. ◆ Free. Tu-Su. Autopista Las Américas and Av Estados Unidos. No phone

Elsewhere in the Dominican Republic

31 Club Náutico Andrés

Rent a boat or join a deep-sea hunt for marlin, bonito, and other game fish at this club, set on the closest beach to Santo Domingo. ◆ Boca Chica. 523.4226, 685.4940

31 Treasure Divers

Explore underwater wrecks and caves or take an exciting night dive with the pros from this scuba shop at the **Don Juan Beach Resort.** ◆ Abraham Núñez (just west of Av Juan Bautista Vicini), Boca Chica. 523.5320

31 Coral Hamaca Beach Hotel

$$$ This fun-loving all-inclusive seaside resort lodges guests in 463 pleasantly decorated rooms. Expect ample water sports and energetic nightlife, including plenty of action at the resort's casino. Four restaurants offer plenty of dinnertime variety. ◆ Av Duarte (east of Av los Caracoles), Boca Chica. 523.4611, 800/945.0792; fax 526.6767

31 Neptuno's Club

★★★$$ One of the best kept secrets in Boca Chica, this open-air eatery overlooks the Caribbean and offers a great selection of fish. Come early, and you may see the owners, Rita and Claus Reprich, buying the ingredients for the evening's meal from local fishers. ◆ Seafood ◆ Tu-Su lunch and dinner. 12 Av Duarte (east of Av los Caracoles), Boca Chica. 523.4703

32 Casa de Campo

$$$$ Everything is first-class here, from the private airport to the posh rooms decorated by Oscar de la Renta. The 7,000-acre complex incorporates 3 polo fields (with attending coach), 2 famous Pete Dye–designed golf courses, 13 tennis courts, riding stables, shooting ranges, 14 pools, and deep-sea and river fishing (with guides and boats). There are 150 luxury villas staffed by maids, butlers, and baby-sitters, and 300 beautiful guest rooms. The resort also boasts 9 restaurants, 4 in a faux 16th-century Mediterranean village called **Altos de Chavón** (see below). Don't miss a sunset merengue at **La Caña,** a thatch pavilion with 360° views from the open dance floor. The disco crowd parties late into the night. Steer a golf cart to **Las Minitas,** a private palm-shaded beach with changing/shower facilities and a fun snack bar. ◆ Av Central (just east of La Romana). 523.3333, 800/877.3643; fax 523.8548

Within Casa de Campo:

Altos de Chavón It's hard to believe this "16th-century" village on the shores of the Río Chavón has been around for less than two decades. Italian set designer Roberto Copa created its cobblestone streets and rustic buildings as an artisans' colony and tourist attraction. Set around a Greek-style amphitheater are the picturesque **Iglesia Santo Stanislaus** (St. Stanislaus Church), a museum showcasing artifacts from the extinct Taíno tribe, artists' galleries and workshops, and four restaurants. ◆ Daily. 523.3333

Within Altos de Chavón:

Casa del Río ★★★$$$ Great views of river and valley are the highlights of this cliffside restaurant, where fresh fish and seafood dishes are served in a bucolic atmosphere. ♦ Seafood ♦ Daily dinner. Reservations required. 523.3333 ext 2345

La Piazzetta ★★★$$$ Romantic candlelight and violin music complement the showy wine list, pasta dishes, seafood, and carpaccio at this *ristorante*. ♦ Italian ♦ Daily dinner. Reservations required. 523.3333

33 Bayahibe Drive just 8 kilometers (5 miles) east along the coast from **Casa de Campo** to catch a fine open-air seafood meal at this charming fishing village, then walk off the calories at Playa del Rio San Juan (known to locals as Playa Niño), one of the prettiest beaches in the area. ♦ Bahía de la Altagracia

34 Isla Saona (Saona Island) Part of the **Parque Nacional del Este** (National Park of the East), this island boasts white-sand beaches and abundant marine life, including turtles and a variety of tropical fish. Many dive shops offer diving trips here, and boats can be hired from Bayahibe and La Romana. For information, call the **National Park Service** (221.5340) or **Ecoturista** (221.4104), which arranges day trips to the island. ♦ South of Bayahibe

35 Nuestra Señora de Altagracia Basílica (Basilica of Our Lady of Altagracia) The image of Our Lady of Altagracia has long been associated with a series of miracles. Her shrine, visited year-round by supplicants, is flooded with the faithful every 21 January, her feast day. The modern basilica is set in the workaday inland city of Higüey, originally settled in 1502 by Ponce de León and now capital of Altagracia province. ♦ Agustín Guerrero, Higüey. No phone

Punta Cana

36 Punta Cana Beach Resort $$$ Some 2,000 feet of shoreline are enlivened by 400 guest rooms, suites, and villas set in eclectic buildings that combine Victorian, Greek Revival, and island architectural elements. The decor is tropical, with lots of wicker and tile; all units have kitchenettes. Rates cover breakfast and dinner along with a full slate of activities—tennis, boat rides, diving, bicycling, folkloric shows, and theme parties. Guests may dine alfresco (at pig roasts and lobster barbecues) or in the **Mama Venezia Restaurant.** Also on the property are a marina, four tennis courts, and a large pool with swim-up bar. Nature trails meander through 150 acres and by 11 natural springs; there are also plans for an 18-hole golf course. ♦ Punta Cana. 688.0080, 800.972.2139; fax 687.8745

36 Club Med $$$ Located on the sparkling waters and pearl-white sands of the spectacular Costa del Coco (at 22 miles, the longest beach in the Caribbean), the local outpost of this chain offers a circus workshop (with "courses" in trapeze, tightrope, and clowning) in addition to tennis (on 7 courts), water sports, team games, nightly entertainment, and more. The resort was a pioneer in the all-inclusive movement; here a single tab buys everything except optional side trips and alcoholic drinks (complimentary beer and wine are served with meals). Guests are housed in a 600-bed village of 3-story bungalows facing the beach. The resort also offers a pool, three restaurants, and a disco. Children under five stay free, and all young guests are kept happily occupied at the well-regarded **Mini-Club.** ♦ Just north of Punta Cana. 567.5228, 567.5229, 800/CLUBMED; fax 565.2558

37 Bávaro Beach Resort $$$ This secluded complex along a pristine white-sand beach offers nearly 2,000 deluxe rooms in 5 separate hotels—the **Bávaro Beach** and **Bávaro Garden** hotels are right on the beach, the **Bávaro Casino Hotel** is near the casino, and the **Bávaro Golf** and sumptuous **Bávaro Palace** hotels are near the 18-hole golf course. Also part of the complex are 5 swimming pools, 9 tennis courts, 13 restaurants, 2 discos, and water-sports facilities galore. Rates include breakfast and dinner; the **Bávaro Palace** is all-inclusive. ♦ Playa Bávaro (northeast of the road to Punta Cana). 686.5797, 800/879.8687; fax 686.5859

37 Parque Manatí (Manatee Park) One of the newest attractions in the Dominican Republic, this $14-million zoo covers about 75 acres and features numerous tropical animals, birds, and fish as well as a recreated Taíno village. Shows star performing dolphins, sea lions, and horses. ♦ Admission. Daily. ♦ Playa Bávaro (northeast of the road to Punta Cana). 688.0702

The islands of the West Indies are formed by two main chains of mountains. One chain runs east-west and forms the islands of the Greater Antilles, and the other chain runs north-south and forms the Lesser Antilles.

In the past, forests covered most of the Caribbean islands, but many were destroyed during the plantation era, when sugar plantation owners cut down trees for firewood and to heat refining vats.

Restaurants/Clubs: Red **Hotels:** Blue
Shops/ Outdoors: Green **Sights/Culture:** Black

38 Parque Nacional Los Haitises (Los Haitises National Park) Strange rock formations, caves, and mangrove stands draw hikers to this breathtaking forest reserve. In the caves, look for Taíno drawings said to have been inscribed some 500 years ago. Boats that offer rides through the mangroves into the park can be found in Sabana de la Mar, just east of the park, or in Samaná, to the north across the Bahía de Samaná. **Ecoturista** (221.4104) offers park tours; call the **National Park Service** (221.5340) for additional information. ♦ Admission. Daily. Bahía de Samaná

39 Gran Bahía $$$ In winter, voyeurs can watch whales mating in the bay from the high reaches of this all-inclusive Victorian-style hotel on the Samaná Peninsula. What may well be the country's most intimate retreat offers 110 rooms and suites on a bluff with 2 tennis courts, a gym, 2 restaurants, 2 bars, and a 9-hole golf course. Other pleaasures include two sandy beaches, a private dock, and a fishing boat. ♦ Samaná. 538.3111, 800/424.5192; fax 538.2764

40 El Portillo Beach Resort $$ Even after becoming an all-inclusive resort, this picturesque inn has managed to maintain its charmingly rustic atmosphere. Set on a lovely beach, it has 171 rooms, 2 restaurants, 2 tennis courts, and facilities for sailing, windsurfing, and volleyball. Liquor and food are served throughout the day. ♦ Av Francia, Portillo (just northeast of Las Terrenas). 240.6100; fax 241.6104

41 Playa Grande This sweeping beach on the Dominican Republic's north coast was a secluded stretch of sand until hoteliers discovered its allure. Fortunately, there's still plenty of elbow room for day-trippers looking for a place to sun and relax. Here along the Costambar (Amber Coast), surrounding hills are rich with deposits of the semiprecious substance. ♦ Between Cabrera and Río San Juan

Residents of Santo Domingo flock to the Malecón after midnight on 31 December and stay until dawn. A glimpse of the New Year's first sunrise is thought to bring good luck during the year to come.

On Playa Grande:

Caribbean Village Playa Grande $$$ The first large hotel to be built on Playa Grande, this 300-room, all-inclusive property is operated by Allegro Resorts. Each guest room has air-conditioning, a garden or ocean vista, and a terrace or veranda. Activities include horseback riding, snorkeling, and tennis on three lighted courts. Scuba diving and deep-sea fishing can be arranged for an extra fee, and at press time an 18-hole, Robert Trent Jones Sr–designed golf course was scheduled to open. Other amenities include a pool, 3 restaurants, and **Kiddie Kraze,** a program that not only offers children's activities but allows the under-12 set to stay for free during the summer months. ♦ 582.1170, 800/858.2258; fax 582.6094

42 Playa Cabarete (Cabarete Beach) Said to be one of the 10 best windsurfing spots in the world, this beach draws a laid-back crowd from around the globe. International windsurfing competitions are held here in June. ♦ Cabarete

43 Playa Sosúa Locals will share their water skis (and expertise) for a price; vendors hawk everything from Haitian art to custom-made jewelry; and freelance *secretarios* (secretaries) offer to fetch beer and other necessities. Weary visitors may prefer to hide behind a palm tree and admire the pretty horseshoe-shaped beach in peace. In the 1930s and 1940s Jews fleeing Nazi persecution found asylum in the quaint village of Sosúa, and a strong Jewish community remains today. ♦ Sosúa

TROPIX
HOTEL

43 Tropix Hotel $ The lovely gardens and swimming pool are surrounded by a cozy complex of 10 rooms (4 suites and 6 doubles). Some have air-conditioning, some have fans, and all have small refrigerators. Guests can cook in a common kitchen and breakfast is served poolside, but there's no restaurant. ♦ No credit cards accepted. Sosúa. 571.2291

44 Jack Tar Village $$$ Singles, couples, and families are welcome at this all-inclusive resort, where guests enjoy golf, tennis (two courts), sailing, snorkeling, horseback riding, and lazing on the sands of Playa Dorada. Meals are served in the restaurant and at the poolside grill. Children receive special attention at the **Kids Klub,** and adults can enjoy the on-site casino, which is open to the public. The 240 rooms and suites are set in a beautifully tended landscape. ◆ Playa Dorada (just west of Sosúa). 320.3800, 800/999.9182; fax 320.4161

44 Playa Dorada Hotel $$$ This posh all-inclusive beach resort has it all: golf, a complete water-sports center, three lighted tennis courts, a pool with a swim-up bar, horseback riding, a casino, three restaurants, a disco, and nightly entertainment. The 351 deluxe guest rooms—decorated with a delightful blend of modern and Victorian furnishings—are graced by terraces and balconies. Request an ocean view. ◆ 102 Av 12 de Julio, Playa Dorada (just west of Sosúa). 320.3988, 800/545.8089; fax 320.1190

45 Museo del Ambar (Amber Museum) More a store than a museum, this old Victorian building sells an extensive collection of amber, larimar, and coral jewelry as well as ceramics and other locally crafted items. On the second floor is a small museum that traces the history of amber. This place has no connection to the **Museo del Ambar** in Santo Domingo (see page 126). ◆ Admission for museum. M-Sa. 61 Duarte (between Villanueva and Emilio Prudhomme), Puerto Plata. 586.2848

46 El Monumento de los Héroes de la Restauración (Monument to the Heroes of the Restoration) This imposing white marble landmark guards the entrance to the city of Santiago de los Caballeros. The 200-foot column, set on a 2-story base, was raised in the 1940s during the dictatorship of Rafael Trujillo. The interior features murals by Spanish painter Vela Zanetti and the observation balcony offers panoramic views. ◆ Free. Daily. Av Monumental (between Avs Salvador Estrella Sadhala and Francia), Santiago de los Caballeros. No phone

46 Museo del Tabaco (Tobacco Museum) The name tells the story of this small museum, which showcases those most sought-after national products—tobacco and cigars. ◆ Free. Daily. Plaza Duarte, Santiago de los Caballeros. No phone

47 Lago Enriquillo (Enriquillo Lake) Hordes of crocodiles (and an occasional iguana) populate this saltwater lake. Dominican law prohibits capture of the protected reptiles. **Prieto Tours** (685.0102) offers guided excursions. ◆ Southwestern interior. No phone

48 Riviera Beach Hotel $$$ The 108 rooms at this all-inclusive property offer either mountain or beach views. In addition to great vistas in an area known for ecological wonders, the hotel boasts a pool, a tennis court, snorkeling, a playground, a restaurant, and an excursion desk. ◆ 6 Av Enriquillo, Barahona. 524.5111; fax 524.5798

Getting Your Feet Wet in the Dominican Republic

The Dominican Republic offers boating opportunities and a variety of underwater activities. Here are a few outfits that can help get you afloat:

Boating

Casa de Campo Av Central (just east of La Romana). 523.3333, 800/877.3643

Club Med Just north of Punta Cana. 567.5228, 567.5229, 800/CLUBMED

Club Náutico Andrés Boca Chica. 685.4940, 523.4226

Metro Hotel and Marina Just west of Juan Dolio. 526.2811

Punta Cana Beach Resort Punta Cana. 688.0080, 800/972.2139

Snorkeling and Scuba Diving

Dominican Adventures Santo Domingo. 566.3483

Northern Coast Aquasports Sosúa. 571.1028

Treasure Divers Don Juan Beach Resort, Abraham Núñez (just west of Av Juan Bautista Vicini), Boca Chica. 523.5320

Sportfishing

Casa de Campo Av Central (just east of La Romana). 523.333, 800.877.3643

Club Náutico Andrés Boca Chica. 685.4940, 523.4226

Metro Hotel and Marina Just west of Juan Dolio. 526.2811

Virgin Islands
Anguilla St-Martin/St. Maarten
Barbuda
St. Kitts
Nevis Antigua

Guadeloupe

Dominica

Martinique

Caribbean Sea St. Lucia

St. Vincent Barbados

CARRIACOU

GRENADA

N

| km | | 300 |
| mi | | 180 |

CARRIACOU

Petit St. Vincent Island

Windward **32** *Petit Martinique*

Hillsborough Bay

Hillsborough **31**

Tyrrel Bay **Belmont** *Grand Bay*

Saline Island

Frigate Island

Large Island

N

| km | | 4 |
| mi | 2 | 4 |

Diamon Island

Rhonde Island *Le Tante*

Caille Island

London Bridge Island

Sauteurs Bay *Levera Island* *Green Island*

17 **18**

Duquesne Bay **Sauteurs** *Sandy Island*

19

St. Mark Bay **Union** *Grenada Bay*

Victoria *St. Patrick River* **River Sallee**

Lake Antoine

Caribbean Sea **Peggy's Whim** **Tivoli** **La Poterie**

16 *Little River* *Simon River*

Gouyave **Dunfermline**

Grand Roy Bay **Bylands** **Paradise**

Grand Roy *Great River* **20** **Grenville**

Concord *Grand Etang National Park* **Beauregard** *Grenville Bay*

Halifax Harbour **15** ▲ *Mt. Qua Qua 2,300 ft.* *Marquis Island*

14 *Grand Etang Lake* **Birch Grove**

13 *Concord Falls* **Marquis**

Willis *Main Interior Rd.* ▲ *Mt. Lebanon 2,347 ft.* **Munich**

▲ *Mt. Sinai 2,306 ft.* *St. Francis River*

Beaulieu **21**

Grand Mal Bay **Pomme Rose** *Great Bacolet Bay*

St. George's **29** **30** **St. David's** *Atlantic Ocean*

For nos. 1-12, see pg. 140

Grand Anse Bay *La Sagesse Estate*

Morne Rouge Bay **28** **Grand Anse** **Westerhall** **22**

27 **Calivigny** *La Sagesse Nature Center*

Point Salines International Airport *Westerhall Bay*

26 **25**

Point Salines **24** **23** *Hog Island* *Fort Jeudy*

Prickly Bay **Lance aux Epines** *Calivigny Island*

Glover Island

N

| km | | 4 | | 8 |
| mi | 2 | | 4 | |

Grenada

The scents of nutmeg, cloves, and cinnamon fill the air in this tropical paradise, hinting at the many aromatics cultivated and marketed here, and inspiring Grenada's nickname—"Isle of Spice."

Both black and white sands outline the deep-green interior of this volcanic charmer tucked away at the southern tip of the Windward Islands. Narrow mountain roads wind through lush foliage thick with bananas and calabash, past mahogany trees and giant bamboo alive with chattering monkeys. Rain forests that shelter secluded thermal springs and ancient petroglyphs are surrounded by farms carpeted in well-tended acres of cacao, breadfruit, plantains, and guava.

Though compact enough to tour in a day, Grenada (pronounced Gra-*nay*-da) is the largest of a 3-island nation that totals 133 square miles. Just off Grenada's north shore is tiny **Carriacou**, famous for the sturdy schooners that have been rigged and sailed by native boatbuilders for generations. East of Carriacou is **Petit Martinique**, whose beaches have seen few tourist footprints.

Colored by turquoise waters and distinctive tile roofs, capital **St. George's** hugs a perfect horseshoe of a harbor, flanked by the 18th-century battlements of **Fort George** and **Fort Frederick**. Cruise liners and commercial freighters from around the world deposit their passengers here along the **Carenage,** where they can lunch on mangoes and sip cool coconut milk as they shop for the freshest bay leaves and saffron to season the pots back home (and try to resist the strolling "fudge ladies").

Second city **Grenville** is known for such exotic seafood as barracuda and *lambi* (conch), and mauby, the energizing after-dinner drink that's made from tree bark. Every Saturday, housewives prowl through heaps of yams, callaloo greens, breads, and pastries in the market square, as vendors prepare steaming fish cakes, and weavers from the nearby village of **Marquis** fashion wild-pine strips into baskets and hats.

The spectacular **Grand Etang** district zigzags through **Grand Etang National Park**, splashed with waterfalls, rife with wild orchids, home to a large population of armadillos, and site of a lake set in the crater of an extinct volcano, while at **Great Bacolet Bay** the Atlantic surf batters miles of deserted beaches.

Christopher Columbus sighted Grenada on his third voyage in 1498, but the first known inhabitants were the Ciboney Indians. The peaceful Arawak followed, then the fierce Carib, who leapt to their deaths from the cliff at what is now called **Morne des Sauteurs** (Hill of the Jumpers), rather than submit to slavery at the hands of some French soldiers. France and England grappled for power throughout the 18th century, with the British assuming final control in 1783, but this is one Caribbean island with a recent history as colorful as its past.

Internal political struggles divided the population throughout the 1970s, when its declaration of independence from the United Kingdom resulted in a five-year dictatorship under Prime Minister Sir Eric Gairy, notorious for his obsession with black magic and UFOs. A 1979 coup led by Maurice Bishop and his New Jewel Movement brought close ties with Cuban President Fidel Castro. In October 1983, Bishop was assassinated by his more radical followers, a military junta took over the reins of government and, in response to the growing turmoil, US paratroopers poured out of the sky to begin their famous six-day invasion of Grenada at **Lance aux Epines** on the southwest coast. Grenada later rejoined the British Commonwealth, and today US tourists receive a warm welcome.

Since the invasion, US aid has contributed to the ever-improving island infrastructure—visitors are no longer hindered by primitive roads or an outdated phone system. In late 1997, a 10-year master plan for tourism development was unveiled, with great emphasis placed on expanding the eco-tourism market, wooing more cruise ships to the port, and adding hotel rooms—900 by the year 2000. Two large luxury hotels, including a branch of an international chain complete with an 18-hole championship golf course, are slated to break ground by the turn of the millenium. Other development projects in the works include a multimillion-dollar sports stadium, road repairs, and a new crafts market for tourists.

But for now, the island remains unhurried—the perfect place to spend a night on the town hoisting a few shots of grog, the local specialty that has been a legend among world travelers for centuries. Fittingly, the word "grog" originated here, an acronym for the "grand rum of Grenada."

Area code 473 unless otherwise noted.

Getting to the Island

Airlines

American Airlines 444.2222, 800/433.7300

BWIA International 440.3818, 800/327.7401

Interisland Carriers

Aerotuy 444.4732

Airlines of Carriacou 444.3549, 444.1475

BWIA International 440.3818

HelenAir ....444.2266, 444.4199 ext 290

LIAT (Leeward Islands Air Transport)........440.2796

Airport **Point Salines International Airport**

(444.4101), located at the island's southern tip about four miles from St. George's, services regular international and interisland flights.

Getting Around the Island

Buses Engines are rickety, seats are hard boards, and schedules are capricious, but the brightly colored old workhorses make great photographs. More modern minibuses travel between island points and charge according to the destination. Most buses depart from **Market Square** in St. George's; they can also be flagged on the road.

Car Rental

Barba's Auto Rentals 443.7454, 443.8167

Dollar Rent A Car..444.4786

McIntyre Bros 444.3944, 444.3945

Royston's...444.4316

Spice Isle/Avis Rentals 440.3936, 440.2624,

Driving Visitors must obtain a driving permit, available through most car-rental companies and at the fire station on the Carenage. Driving is on the left, British style.

Taxis and Water Taxis Taxi rates are fixed, but there are no meters, so settle on a price before you get in. Be aware of the after-dark surcharge. Taxi drivers don't expect tips unless they help with your baggage at the airport. Most cab drivers make good tour guides; hotels can arrange day-long jaunts that can be shared by several passengers. For more information contact the **National Taxi Association** (440.9621) or the **Progressive Airport Taxi Union** (**PATU;** 441.8213).

Water taxis make round-trips between **Grand Anse** and **Carenage Harbour** in St. George's and are cheaper than land taxis—but you might get your feet wet.

Tours To hook up with Grenadians who share similar jobs or interests, investigate **People-to-People.** The program is free; just pick up part of the tab for any excursion. Contact **New Trends Tours** (PO Box 438, St. George's, Grenada, West Indies, 444.1236; fax 444.4836) for more information. **New Trends** also offers flights to Union Island in the Grenadines with a return trip by schooner, and day trips to Isla de Margarita and Venezuela.

Other tour operators include:

Adventure Jeep Tour 444.JEEP

Arnold's Tours...........................440.0531, 440.221

Henry's Safari Tours, Ltd...........................444.531

K&J Tours..440.422

Mandoo Tours 440.1428

Trendy Tours...444.5757

World Wide Watersports...........................444.1339

FYI

Electricity Current is 220 volts/50 cycles. An adapter is advisable for small appliances.

Entry Requirements US and Canadian visitors must present a passport or other proof of citizenship (a birth certificate or voter's registration card) plus a photo ID, along with a return or onward ticket.

Language Grenada is a member of the British Commonwealth, and English is the official language.

oney Grenada's official currency is the Eastern
ribbean dollar (EC$). Shops do not offer discounts
r payment in US dollars. Banking hours are
onday through Thursday from 8AM to 2PM and
day from 8AM to 5PM.

ersonal Safety Most of the tourist facilities (and
and wealth) are concentrated on the southwest
rner of the island. Tourist areas are very safe, with
tle reported crime.

general, Grenadians are friendly and courteous,
d a majority favored the US–East Caribbean
tervention. People in the inland villages and in
latively poor settlements north and east of St.
eorge's are likely to be more guarded, however, and
rticularly resent being photographed without
rmission.

ublications Three island weeklies, *Grenada
oice, Grenada Today,* and the *Informer,* are good
urces for sports schedules and news of special
ents. For more vacation-oriented information, pick
 The Greeting Tourist Guide and *Discover Grenada*
agazine. Both are published annually and
stributed free at hotels and at the tourism office.

eservation Services and House Rentals
otel reservations:

renada Board of Tourism 440.2279

renada Hotel Association 444.1353;
....800/322.1753

ouse rentals:

llas of Grenada 444.1896

axes There's an eight-percent value added tax
AT) on food and beverages. A departure tax of
C$40 (US$16) is collected at the airport.

ipping Hotels add a 10-percent service charge
at takes care of bellhops, maids, waiters and
aitresses, and bartenders. If you visit another
otel's dining room, or an independent restaurant, tip
0 to 15 percent of the check. Taxi drivers don't
xpect tips unless they help with your baggage at the
rport.

isitors' Information Office The **Grenada Board
f Tourism** (Carenage, south of Tanteen Rd, St.
eorge's; 440.2279, 440.2001) is open Monday
rough Friday from 8AM to 4PM.

hone Book

mbulance 440.2051

irectory Assistance 411

iving Emergencies/
  Decompression Chambers 444.4800

mergencies 911

re...911

ospitals 434,
....440.2051

olice 911

ost Office 440.2526

St. George's

The colorful waterfront district of the **Carenage,** a
crescent-shaped area framed by pink, ocher, and
brick-red buildings that date from the 18th century, is
the center of activity in the capital. Fishing boats and
commercial schooners of all sizes and pedigrees
crowd this inner harbor—actually the crater of an
extinct volcano—where the weekly (Tuesday
afternoon) loading of produce bound for Trinidad is a
memorable feast for the eyes. Pedestrian walkways
are lined with shops and casual restaurants, and the
post office, public library, and tourist bureau are all
located here.

1 Rudolf's ★★$$ Stuffed crab backs and
homemade soursop ice cream are among the
fine local specialties here, but the diverse
menu also includes fish and chips, lamb
chops, and lobster prepared in a variety of
ways. The owners are Swiss, the food
international, and the pub British-style, with a
dark wooden bar. ♦ Caribbean/International
♦ M-Sa lunch and dinner. Reservations
required for dinner; no credit cards accepted.
Carenage and Young St. 440.2241

2 Nutmeg ★★$ Join the relaxed yachting
crowd for callaloo, lobster, or curried *lambi*
(conch) at St. George's most popular lunching
place, also a fine spot to enjoy a rum punch
overlooking the Carenage. ♦ Caribbean ♦ M-
Sa lunch and dinner; Su lunch when a cruise
ship is in town (call ahead) and dinner.
Carenage (between Young St and Rowleys
Alley). 440.2539

3 Best Little Liquor Store Stock up on the
"grand rum of Grenada" along with local
vodka and gin and imported wines and spirits.
♦ M-Sa. Carenage (between Hughes St and
Tryne Alley). 440.2198. Also at: Point Salines
International Airport. 440.3422

4 Grand Bazaar You'll find hand-painted
fancy and casual togs for both men and
women here, at comparatively low prices.
♦ M-Sa. Carenage (between Hughes St and
Tryne Alley). 440.3712

5 Frangipani In keeping with its flowery
name, this shop carries a profusion of vivid
watercolors and batiks by local artists, plus
wall hangings and breezy unisex clothing.
♦ M-Sa. Carenage (between Hughes St and
Tryne Alley). No phone

Bon Voyage

6 Bon Voyage Check these shelves for duty-
free crystal, china, watches, and jewelry. The
excellent stock includes Lalique, Waterford,
Daum, Orrefors, and other internationally
recognized names. ♦ M-Sa. Carenage (between
Tanteen Rd and Hughes St). 440.4217. Also at:
Point Salines International Airport. 444.4165

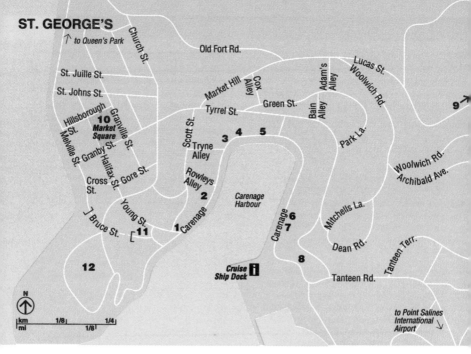

ST. GEORGE'S

↑ to Queen's Park

Church St.
Old Fort Rd.
St. Juille St.
St. Johns St.
Market Hill
Cox Alley
Lucas St.
Adam's Alley
Woolwich Rd.
Green St.
Tyrrel St.
Bain Alley
Hillsborough St.
Granville St.
10 *Market Square*
Melville St.
Granby St.
Halifax St.
Scott St.
Tryne Alley
3 4 5
Park La.
Woolwich Rd.
Archibald Ave.
Cross St.
Gore St.
Rowleys Alley
2
Carenage Harbour
Mitchells La.
Bruce St.
Young St.
11
1 Carenage
Carenage
6
7
Dean Rd.
Tanteen Terr.
8
12
Cruise Ship Dock
Tanteen Rd.
9↗

N

km 1/8 1/4
mi 1/8

to Point Salines International Airport ↙

7 **Gitten's Duty Free** Poke your nose inside for perfume and cosmetics by many of the famous names, including Calvin Klein, Christian Dior, Clinique, and Ralph Lauren. ◆ M-Sa. Carenage (between Tanteen Rd and Hughes St). 440.3174. Also at: Point Salines International Airport. 444.4101 ext 272

8 **Grenada Craft Center** Opened in mid-1996, the center provides a forum for 30 full-time artisans to demonstrate their crafts and sell their creations. Ceramics and fabric art are among their wares. ◆ Tanteen Rd (east of Carenage). 440.9512, 440.9514

9 **Government House** Now the residence of the queen's official representative, the governor-general, this Georgian landmark was built in the late 18th century, remodeled in 1802, and (some say) spoiled by the addition of an 1887 facade. Nevertheless, views of the town and harbor are great from the grounds here, and it's a prime destination for photographers. The building is not open to the public. ◆ Upper Lucas St (east of Old Fort Rd)

10 **Market Square** Stop by on Saturday mornings for a picturesque scene, as Grenadian women set up camp beneath umbrellas with their piles of mangoes, yams, pawpaws (papayas), bananas, exotic vegetables, and fresh spices. Meanwhile, vendors in the adjoining **Straw Mart** hawk brooms, baskets, and other woven goods. Take a look at, but don't buy, the tortoiseshell—it's illegal to import it into the US. Continue along the wave-splashed esplanade to see the fish and meat markets of the outer harbor. ◆ Free. Sa. Bounded by Halifax and Young Sts, and Granby and Hillsborough Sts. No phone

11 **Grenada National Museum** Set in the foundations of an old French army barracks and prison built in 1704, the small collection found here includes Josephine Bonaparte's marble bathtub, Indian artifacts, a rum still, and photos and news clippings about the US invasion in 1983. ◆ Nominal admission. M-S Young and Monkton Sts. 440.3725

12 **Fort George** Built by the French in 1705, Grenada's oldest fortress was originally called **Fort Royal**. Today the hilltop battlements serv as Grenada's police headquarters, and now th fort only fires its ancient cannons for official salutes. Recently restored areas are open to visitors, and signs relate the fort's history. On plaque in the central courtyard commemorate the bloody day when Maurice Bishop and his cabinet were executed. ◆ Free. Daily. Church St (south of Young St). No phone

Equal parts spectator sport and social event, cricket matches are held January through May on pitches (fields) that range from perfectly manicured Queen's Park to vacant lots. For times and locations, consult the tourist board, the sports section of the island daily, or the Sports Ministry (440.4999).

Elsewhere on Grenada

13 The Nature Hut ★★$ On the way to Concord Falls (see below) stop here for a typical Grenadian meal, a cold drink, or a swim. Hannah Lewis has transformed her hillside property into a lovely terraced garden leading to the freshwater pool below. Instead of crushed stones, she uses thousands of crushed nutmeg shells as groundcover. The "100-percent Grenadian" menu includes callaloo, pumpkin, and crayfish dishes. ♦ Grenadian ♦ Daily breakfast, lunch, and dinner. Between St. George's and Concord. 444.9119

14 Concord Falls Take a detour off the western coastal road to this spectacular hideaway, draped with lianas and giant elephant ears, where a 30-foot cascade tumbles into a turquoise pool. It's a very easy hike to the falls, which are a great picnic spot. Adventurers can trek 30 minutes farther inland—through spice plantations and tropical forest—for a brilliant view of the remote second fall. ♦ East of Halifax Harbour

15 Grand Etang National Park The most spectacular drive on the island winds past spice farms and cacao plantations, through banana groves and tropical thickets, high into the mountains to the glorious national preserve that crowns the summit. Here in this natural garden of flowers and hummingbirds, cascades and tumbling streams, well-marked hiking paths lead through the rain forest to the deep blue waters of Grand Etang Lake, cradled in an extinct volcanic crater. One of the more challenging trails climbs Mount Qua Qua to breathtaking vistas. Be on the lookout for native blue butterflies, mona monkeys, mongooses, and other exotic fauna. Stop by the **Grand Etang Visitors Center** for trail maps, videos, interpretive displays, snacks, and souvenirs. ♦ Admission. M-Sa. Main Interior Rd (between Beauregard and Beaulieu). 440.7425

16 Dougaldston Estate Grenada's famous spices are grown, sun-dried, and sorted here in the traditional manner. The fishing village of Gouyave, dotted with rustic tile-roofed houses, is also home to a nutmeg-processing plant, where tours lead over and under sacks of spices, past wooden cracking machinery, and around aromatic drying racks. ♦ Admission. M-Sa. Gouyave. 444.8213

17 Morne des Sauteurs (Hill of the Jumpers) The local lore about this spot, also called **Carib's Leap,** has it that in 1650 a delegation of 200 Frenchmen sailed over from Martinique and "bought" tribal land from the chief of the Carib Indians for a few trinkets. A series of battles followed this deal, until only about 40 Carib men remained. Rather than live as slaves to the French, the Carib men threw the tribe's women and children over these cliffs, then jumped to their own deaths on the jagged rocks below. Today **St. Patrick's Catholic Church** stands on the high bluff, and lovely palm-shaded Levera Beach (see below) lies to the east. ♦ Sauteurs

18 Levera Beach This long expanse of white sand is popular but ample enough that you can usually find a secluded spot for yourself. There are no facilities at the beach, so bring a picnic, along with water—and a friend if you plan to swim. A natural reef barrier restrains the Atlantic surf, but waves can still be a bit rough. ♦ East of Sauteurs

At Levera Beach:

Levera National Park and Bird Sanctuary Bird-watchers can roost in one of many lookouts, while grounded naturalists explore the marked trails that circumnavigate Levera Pond. ♦ Free. Daily. 442.1018

19 Morne Fendue ★★$$ If you're lucky, lunch will come with a story from Betty Mascoll, whose family has lived in this plantation great house for three generations. Don't miss her slow-simmered and savory pepper pot or homemade guava ice cream. Other specialties include callaloo greens, ginger chicken, and vegetables fresh from the kitchen garden. Most of the year, the grounds and interior rooms are splashed with extravagant poinsettias. The dining room is furnished with antiques and the walls are hung with island bric-a-brac and family memorabilia. This turn-of-the-century manor was built of hand-chiseled colored stones and mortared with lime and molasses. ♦ Caribbean ♦ M-F, Su lunch. Reservations required; no credit cards accepted. South of Sauteurs. 442.9330

20 Grenville Grenada's second city, on the eastern coast, is home to two markets. Grenadians crowd Market Square every Saturday to buy fruits, vegetables, and meats, as well as baskets and hats made in the village of Marquis, clothing, and other handicrafts. The small waterfront fish market near the docks offers the daily catch Monday through Saturday. The **Grenville Nutmeg Pool/ Grenville Curing Station** (Seaton Brown St, 442.7241) at the edge of town sells spices and spice baskets. Continue south to visit the village of Marquis, where expert Grenadian weavers create hats, baskets, and other goods with wild palm leaves. ♦ East coast

21 Great Bacolet Bay Miles of undeveloped beaches line this bay. Stretch out and enjoy the tranquillity of these uncrowded white sands, but be sure to bring a picnic lunch and water-sports equipment—there are no restaurants or dive shops in the vicinity. ♦ East coast

22 La Sagesse Nature Center Trails and guided nature walks crisscross this lush and lovely complex that is also home to a banana plantation and fine beach. ♦ Admission. Daily. South of La Sagesse Estate. No phone

Within La Sagesse Nature Center:

La Sagesse Nature Center Cottages and Restaurant $$ Ten comfortable rooms, located in the **Old Manor House** and a newly built cottage, feature high ceilings and screened-in verandas. This romantic hideaway is perfect for honeymooners who want to be very alone—and to fall asleep to the sound of the waves breaking just outside their room. The restaurant, open daily for breakfast, lunch, and dinner, serves delicious seafood and Grenadian fare that makes use of fresh local produce and spices. In short, it's a real gem. ♦ 444.6548

23 The Calabash Hotel $$$$ The ultimate in luxury, this hotel sends a maid to your room each morning to prepare breakfast while you sip coffee on a veranda right by the beach. The accommodations are divided among 12 buildings, set in 8 waterfront acres of tropical gardens. Eight of the 30 suites have private plunge pools; 22 have private Jacuzzis; all have pantries. Other pluses on the premises: a tennis court, water sports, a large swimming pool, billiards tables, a beach bar, and **Cecily's,** one of Grenada's best restaurants (see below). For a thrill request the pool suite, **Number 7.** Make reservations well in advance. ♦ Lance aux Epines. 444.4334, 800/528.5835; fax 444.5050

In addition to Carriacou and Petit Martinique, Grenada has several small island dependencies, including Ile de Ronde, Green Bird, Conference, and Kick-em-Jenny (the intriguing name probably evolved from *caye qui gêne,* meaning "troublesome shoal.") Most are so tiny that they're important only as landmarks for cruising yachters. All other Grenadine islands are administered by St. Vincent.

Within the Calabash:

Cecily's ★★★★$$$ A landscaped terrace decked with colorful blooms is the setting for authentic Grenadian cuisine with a modern spin. Chef Graham Newbold, private chef to Prince Charles and Princess Diana for four years, has won awards for his fresh takes on seafood and native fruits and vegetables. The coco shrimp in semisweet guava sauce, chicken pau-pau (with papaya), and flying-fish salad are all excellent. ♦ Seafood/Caribbean ♦ Daily dinner. Reservations required. 444.4334

23 Horse Shoe Beach $$ Turn in for the night in a hand-carved four-poster bed in one of 18 Mediterranean cottage suites, or choose one of 6 modern suites. All have patios, air-conditioning, TV sets, and telephones. The beautifully landscaped grounds incorporate a scenic restaurant, small beach, and pool; other perks include water sports, table tennis billiards, and croquet. ♦ Lance aux Epines. 444.4410, 800/223.9815; fax 444.4844

23 Coral Cove $$ The 18 guest rooms and suites with kitchenettes here offer full maid and laundry service. While the actual cove is shallow, it's fine for some water sports, and the white-sand beach is pretty. Other amenities include a swimming pool and tennis court, but there's no on-site restaurant. The management will arrange car rentals and fishing charters. ♦ Lance aux Epines. 444.4422, 800/322.1753; fax 444.4718

Secret Harbour Resort

23 Secret Harbour Resort $$$$ For swank atmosphere and peaceful nights, stay at this oasis—a luxurious maze of brick arches and terraces crowned with warm tile roofs. The 20 units are lavished with sunken tubs, stained glass, and hand-carved four-poster beds. Guests enjoy a swimming pool, tennis court, sandy beach, and 50-slip marina administered by **The Moorings** (444.4548; fax 444.2790), with sailboats available for charter. Dine in the **Mariners** restaurant, which is intriguingly decorated with local art, comfortable chaise longues, a giant painted chess set, and other antiques. ♦ Lance aux Epines. 444.4548, 800/437.7880; fax 444.4819

23 Twelve Degrees North $$ The term "housekeeping vacation" may seem to be an oxymoron, but the setup here is painless enough. Maids are on duty from 8AM to 3PM to clean, cook, and do laundry for 8 1- and 2-bedroom cottages. They'll even prep dinner (most convenient, as the property has no restaurant). Meanwhile, homemakers on holiday can laze on the beach or by the swimming pool, play tennis (one court), go boating (on a Sunfish or Boston Whaler), shuttle over to a nearby private island, or just hang out by the thatch-roofed beachside bar/barbecue. No children under 15 are allowed. ♦ Lance aux Epines. 444.4580, 800/322.1753; fax 444.4580

23 Boatyard ★$$ Crowds spill through the doors for twilight Happy Hour, when this bar/restaurant in the **Spice Island Marina** is packed with a congenial mob of locals and visitors. Fish and chips, burgers, and the like are served at lunch, while freshly caught seafood is featured in the evenings. ♦ Seafood ♦ Tu-Su lunch and dinner. Spice Island Marina, Lance aux Epines. 444.4662

23 The Red Crab ★★$$$ Stylish fare and informal surroundings make for a relaxing meal at this easygoing spot. Unwind over fresh seafood and Grenadian specialties. ♦ Seafood/Caribbean ♦ M-Sa lunch and dinner. Reservations recommended. Lance aux Epines. 444.4424

24 True Blue Inn $$ Overlooking picturesque True Blue Bay, this comfortable and secluded inn features whitewashed cottages and apartments (10 units in all) outfitted with bamboo furnishings, air-conditioning, cable TV, and direct-line telephones. There's no beach, but you can dive off the dock and swim in the bay, and a free shuttle transports guests to Grand Anse Beach, just a five-minute walk away. **Indigo's Restaurant** serves local specialties for breakfast, lunch, and dinner daily, and the **SCUBA Express** dive center, also on the premises, offers full diving and snorkeling facilities. ♦ True Blue Bay. 444.2000; fax 444.1247

25 LaSource $$$$ From the folks who created **LeSport** on St. Lucia comes Grenada's first all-inclusive resort. Set on 40 acres, it offers 100 rooms and suites, 2 beautiful beaches, and a free-form pool complete with waterfall. The guest rooms, trimmed with marble and vibrant Grenadian fabrics, have telephones and seaside balconies, but no TV sets. The tab covers all meals and snacks at the two restaurants, land and water sports (including scuba diving), spa services, tips, and airport transfers. ♦ Pink Gin Beach (between Hardy and Grand Bays). 444.2556, 800/544.2883; fax 444.2561

26 Rex Grenadian $$$ A waterfall gushes into the swimming pool, and tropical gardens adjoin a three-acre lake at Grenada's largest hotel. The 212 rooms, many with views of St. George's across the bay, are decorated in pastel colors, with West Indies/tropical flair.

Other amenities include two beaches, water sports, two tennis courts, a fitness center, a scuba center, eight restaurants and bars, and a terrace cafe. ♦ Point Salines. 444.3333, 305/471.6170; fax 444.1111

27 Canboulay ★★★$$$ Don't pass up a chance to sink your teeth into *moko jumbies* (huge skewered shrimp), *parang poulet* (orange-ginger chicken), or red snapper steamed in banana leaves at this stellar hillside restaurant with sweeping views of Grand Anse Beach and St. George's cityscape. While you're waiting for the main event, snack on breadfruit with pickled cucumber, or coconut buns stuffed with salt fish *souse* (a salad of salted cod, tomatoes, onions, and spices). ♦ Caribbean ♦ M-Sa lunch and dinner. Reservations required for dinner. Morne Rouge (southwest of Grand Anse). 444.4401

28 Grand Anse Beach The most famous of Grenada's 45 beaches is a 2-mile curve of pure white sand. These sheltered Caribbean waters have a gentle surf that's perfect for a wide variety of water sports, and equipment is available right on the beach. Nonguests can pay a small fee to use chaises and changing facilities at area hotels. ♦ Grand Anse

At Grand Anse Beach:

Blue Horizons $$ Grand Anse is just 300 yards away, the landscape is well tended, and the price is right at this pleasant property. There are 32 cottage suites, a pool, a whirlpool, a playground, and access to beach and water sports at the nearby **Spice Island Beach Resort** (see page 144). All units are equipped with kitchenettes, air-conditioning, telephones, clock radios, and other comforts. Private cooks are available by request. Children under 12 can room with their parents for free. ♦ 444.4316, 800/742.4276; fax 444.2815

Within Blue Horizons:

La Belle Creole ★★★$$$ Sample the Hopkins family's creative Caribbean cookery in this balcony dining room, one of Grenada's finest restaurants. The dishes always feature local produce, herbs, and spices. Consider the christophene vichyssoise, Grenadian caviar (sea urchin roe), or the salads and bisques made of lobster, conch, and shrimp. The Sunday afternoon barbecue, held during the winter, features live entertainment and should not be missed. The five-course prix-fixe gourmet meal is also an exceptional experience. ♦ West Indian/Continental ♦ Daily lunch and dinner. Reservations required. 444.4316

Getting Your Feet Wet in Grenada

Whether you come to Grenada for the sun or the beach, you shouldn't limit yourself to dry land. Here are a few outfits that can get you afloat:

Boating

Go Vacations Prickly Bay. 444.4924, 444.4342

Grenada Yacht Services St. George's. 440.2508, 440.2883

The Moorings Secret Harbour Resort, Lance aux Epines. 444.4548

Rhum Runner (glass-bottom boat) St. George's. 440.4FUN

Spice Island Marine Services Lance aux Epines. 444.4257

Snorkeling and Scuba Diving

Dive Grenada Grenada Renaissance Resort, Grand Anse Beach, Grand Anse. 444.1092, 444.5875

Grand Anse Aquatics Coyaba Beach Resort, Grand Anse Beach, Grand Anse. 444.4219 ext 144

Grenada Yacht Services St. George's. 440.2508, 440.2883

SCUBA Express True Blue Inn, True Blue Bay. 444.2133

SCUBA World Rex Grenadian, Point Salines and Secret Harbour Resort, Lance aux Epines. 444.3333, ext. 584 for both locations

Sportfishing

Captain Peters Spice Island Marina, Lance aux Epines. 440.1349

Evans Chartering Service Spice Island Beach Resort, Grand Anse Beach, Grand Anse. 444.4422, 444.4217

Sanvics Grenada Renaissance Resort, Grand Anse Beach, Grand Anse. 444.4371, 800/228.9898

Tropix Professional Sport Fishing Grenada Yacht Services, Lagoon and Ballast Ground Rds, St. George's. 440.4961, 444.1422

 Grenada Golf Club A two-way view of the Atlantic Ocean and the Caribbean Sea adds some character to this otherwise undistinguished nine-hole course, which is open to visitors. There's a snack bar, and club rental, instruction, and caddy service are available.
♦ Greens fee. Daily. 444.4128

Grenada Renaissance Resort $$$ Grenada's second-largest resort boasts 20 acres of palm-shaded beachfront, 2 tennis courts, a swimming pool, all water sports (including scuba diving), a bar, and shops. Each of the 186 rooms has a private patio or balcony, air-conditioning, a telephone with voice mail, and satellite TV. **The Terrace** offers meals alfresco or in an air-conditioned dining room.
♦ 444.4371, 800/228.9898; fax 444.4800

The cassava plant that grows throughout the Caribbean is used in many island recipes. When ground up, the juice of the cassava's fleshy, edible rootstock becomes *cassareep,* a preservative and spice used in a traditional West Indian dish called "pepper pot." Because *cassareep* is among the ingredients, the spicy stew can cook for years without spoiling. In fact, the pepper pot served at Grenada's Plantation House Morne Fendue has been cooking steadily since the early 1980s.

Spice Island Beach Resort $$$ Known simply as "Spice" to Grenadians, this efficient and well-appointed hotel is especially popular with honeymooners. The stylish modern suites front 1,600 feet of white-sand beach, all 56 units have whirlpool baths, and 13 open onto private pools and gardens. Four **Royal Suites** are outfitted with additional upgraded amenities; each has a marble bath, sauna, exercise bike, CD player, and TV set. The tennis court is floodlit for night play. There's one restaurant on the premises, barbecues are held each Friday, and a gourmet "Grenadian Creole" buffet takes place one night a week. Guests also get to enjoy live music four nights a week. Ask about the reasonable summer package rates. ♦ 444.4423, 800/742,4276; fax 444.4807

The Flamboyant Hotel

The Flamboyant Hotel $$ The view's the thing at this hillside hotel that overlooks gorgeous Grand Anse Beach, the harbor, and St. George's. The 41 air-conditioned units—studios, 1- and 2-bedroom suites, and cottages—share a swimming pool. Most units have full kitchens, but you'll also find a good restaurant and bar on the premises. Be aware, though, that they're down a steep hillside from the rooms and getting to and from them is quite a hike. ♦ 444.4247, 800/223.9815; fax 444.1234

28 Le Sucrier Locals and visitors dance the night away at this old sugar mill that has been converted into a nightclub and snack bar. ♦ W-Sa. Grand Anse roundabout. 444.1068

29 Fort Frederick Stop here for commanding views of St. George's and the harbors. The structure, begun by the French in 1779 and completed by the British in 1783, is undergoing ongoing renovation. Informative signs posted throughout the fort explain its history. ♦ Free. Daily. Richmond Hill. No phone

30 Bay Gardens Only the most determined bird-watchers will spot the elusive pripri birds, but their song brightens this six-acre tropical eden. Tour guides point out native fruits and spices among the thick foliage, as well as the fine-feathered residents. Winding paths are covered in nutmeg shells and the nearby **Tower House** (open by appointment) is filled with island relics and antiques. It's an other-worldly experience, well worth the 20-minute drive to the suburb of St. Paul. ♦ Admission. Daily. St. Paul. 443.7403

31 Carriacou A dependency of Grenada and the largest of the Grenadines, this island's natural harbors and white-sand beaches are a powerful draw for yachters, who especially favor lovely Tyrrel Bay. In tiny Windward on the east coast, the beachfront is littered with the sturdy skeletons of boats in progress. Villagers of Scottish descent still build wooden trade schooners by hand—the McLarens, MacLaurences, McQuilkins, MacFarlands, and Comptons are known throughout the Caribbean as masters of the craft. Inland, the 13 square miles of rolling hills are dotted with ruins of old stone great houses and windmills, reminders of early European planters (cotton and peanuts have since replaced sugar as the main local products). Today capital Hillsborough is home to 580 of the island's 7,000 residents. The main street traces the beach, and the pier is a lively scene when "engine boats" arrive with produce (Monday) or mail (Saturday).

Accommodations here are limited. If you want to stay on the island, eight large, pleasant rooms are available at the **Caribbee Inn** (443.7380; fax 443.8142). Another good choice is **Silver Beach** (443.7337, 800/742.7165; fax 443.7165), with 18 units ranging from fully equipped apartments with kitchenettes to rooms with private patios. ♦ 16 miles northeast of Grenada

On Carriacou:

Carriacou Historical Museum This tiny museum is filled with Indian pottery, African masks, and artifacts from European colonization. But the big draw is the work of prolific self-taught folk artist Canute Caliste, whose colorful paintings with their entertaining (and sometimes misspelled) captions are well known in the region. ♦ Admission. M-Sa. Patterson St, Hillsborough. 443.8288.

Carriacou Islander This glass-bottom catamaran affords visitors the perfect way to explore Carriacou and its nearby desert islands, Sandy Isle and Jack-A-Dan. Coral and sea life are visible through the boats' glass bottom as the vessel slips over reefs, then docks at isolated beaches. (Snorkeling gear is provided if you want to explore on your own.) Full-day outings include a savory buffet lunch complete with rum punch. Half-day excursions are also available. ♦ 443.8182

32 Petit Martinique Home to an assortment of able-bodied seamen, this tiny island sits 2 miles east of Carriacou. Today the 600 or so French descendants who populate the 3-square-mile island remain very protective of their privacy, and though generally pleasant, they offer few accommodations for visitors. ♦ 2 miles east of Carriacou

Bests

Gina-Lee Johnson
Chef/Manager/Owner, Canboulay

The breathtaking views from most hillside locations overlooking **St. George's** or **Grand Anse Bay**.

The vibrant colors and bustling activity of Market Day on any Saturday in the St. George's **Market Square**.

A smile and a chat with most Grenadians. They are full of humorous and friendly conversation.

A day on **Sandy Isle,** off **Carriacou**. It is a picture-perfect little island surrounded by a white-sand beach, the token coconut trees, lots of sea grapes, and terrific snorkeling in azure-blue waters.

Driving through the nutmeg and spice plantations, where the aroma is so amazing you want to bottle it.

Driving up to **Grand Etang Lake** through the rain forest. The view, the foliage, and the air are what dreams of a Caribbean island are made of.

Inset map

Puerto Rico

Virgin Islands

Anguilla

St-Martin/ St. Maarten

Barbuda

St. Kitts
Nevis
Montserrat

Antigua

Caribbean Sea

GUADELOUPE

Dominica

Martinique

St. Lucia

N

km 300
mi 180

Main map

Ilet à Kahouanne

N2

Grand Anse
31

Deshaies

D18

Ste-Rose

Monplaisir

32

Grande Rivière á Goyaves

33 **Lamentin**

Ilet à Fajou

Vieux-Bourg

Grand Cul-de-Sac Marin

L'Aéroport International de Guadeloupe Pôle-Caraïbes

Le Abyme

Baie-Mahault

N1

Ans Bertran

N

Port-Louis

Pointe-Noire

D17

Pointe-à-Pitre

For nos. 1-11, see pg. 151

D23

Versailles

27 **26**

Ba

Le Go

Mahaut

Parc Zoologique et Botanique

Rte. de la Traversée

Tabanon **28**

D1

Petit-Bourg

Malendure

Ilet Pigeon

30

D15

▲ ▲
Les Deux Mamelles

Cascade aux Ecrevisses

29
Parc National

34 **Cabout**

Petit Cul-de-Sac Marin

to Iles des Saintes; Roseau, Dominica; Fort-de-France, Martinique

Bouillante

N2

Goyave

BASSE-TERRE

35 **Ste-Marie**

Caribbean Sea

Marigot

Vieux-Habitants

Matouba

42 ▲ **36** *Les Chutes du Carbet*

La Soufrière 4,813 ft.

Capesterre-Belle-Eau

Allée Dumanoir

41
St-Claude

D11

D4

Baillif

Basse-Terre

N3

40
39

Gourbeyre

N1

D7 **38**

St-Sauveur
Bananier

Trois-Rivières **37**

Vieux-Fort

D6 *Grand Anse*

to Iles des Saintes

N

km 4 8
mi 2 4

Guadeloupe

14 *Pointe de la Grande Vigie*

15 *Porte d'Enfer*

D122

D120

•Campêche

GRANDE-TERRE

les Mangles

Gros Cap

D120

N6

13•Richeval

D123

Morne-à-l'Eau

12•

N5 Bellevue•**17**

16

18 Le Moule

Plage de l'Autre Bord

Château-Gaillard

D114

N5

Douville

Châteaubrun

Ste-Marthe

22

20

21

St-François

Pointe Tarare ■

to La Désirade

19

Pointe des Châteaux

23

•Ste-Anne

24

N4

Atlantic Ocean

to Iles des Saintes

to Grand-Bourg, Marie-Galante

to Grand-Bourg, Marie-Galante

km 20
mi 10

N

GUADELOUPE

•Pointe-à-Pitre

St-François•

La Désirade

Iles de la Petite Terre

Basse-Terre

Trois-Rivières•

MARIE-GALANTE

Grand-Bourg•

TERRE-DE-HAUT, ILES DES SAINTES For nos. 43-52, see pg. 159

For nos. 53-62, see pg. 161

MARIE-GALANTE

Guadeloupe

The French tricolor flies over one of the Caribbean's culinary capitals (Guadeloupe is home to more than 200 restaurants) where diners can dig into grand European classics or pull up a chair on the cook's own front porch for peppery stewed conch and *crabes farcis* (stuffed crabs). One of the island's biggest events is the Fête des Cuisinières, which each August honors Guadeloupe's celebrated women chefs, who parade in local costumes swinging baskets of indigenous eats—a hearty appetizer for the music, pageantry, and five-hour feast to come.

Like its famous Creole cuisine, Guadeloupe is a mélange of French, African, and West Indian cultures, spiced by later East Indian settlers who contributed among other things, the ubiquitous madras.

What looks like a butterfly from the sky is really two islands, totaling 582 square miles, connected by two drawbridges that span the narrow saltwater strait called **Rivière Salée**. The craggy western wing, known as **Basse-Terre** (not to be confused with the country's capital which shares its name), is crowned by wisps of sulfurous vapor at the summit of **La Soufrière** (4,813 feet). Here the majestic **Parc National** dedicates more than 74,000 acres to rain forests, botanical gardens, and waterfall-fed swimming ponds. Those who prefer undersea spectacles head offshore to **Ilet Pigeon** (Pigeon Island), named among the world's 10 best dive sites by Jacques Cousteau.

Most hotels and tourist facilities are concentrated on Guadeloupe's eastern wing of **Grande-Terre,** a chalky flatland fringed with well-sheltered beaches and coral cliffs. Schooners and cargo ships crowd the main port of **Pointe-à-Pitre**, where amusements range from the **Musée St-John Perse** to raffish waterfront saloons. Open markets are good places to loiter around the madras-scarved vendors; you might hear a tale from Guadeloupe's vivid past that begins with a solemn *"tim-tim,"* the Creole patois for "once upon a time. . . ."

White sands and wild nightlife have long established nearby **Le Gosier** as "Guadeloupe's Riviera," but bustling **St-François** is gaining fast. In the modern university town of **Bas du Fort**, boîtes blare the frenetic dance tunes known as zouk, though those looking for a more traditional evening can still dance the beguine or find a comfortable seat in a jazz club.

Grande-Terre's formidable Atlantic coastline is marked in the east by the castlelike rocks that loom above the surf at **Pointe des Châteaux**, with the nearby nudist beach **Pointe Tarare**, and by the north's jagged **Porte d'Enfer** (Gate of Hell) and the stark white bluffs of **Pointe de la Grande Vigie**.

Christopher Columbus first hit these shores in 1493, wresting the isle from the Carib Indians for Spain. The Carib regained control in 1604 and held the island until 1635, when French volunteers settled here under orders from Cardinal Richelieu. When the 1789 French Declaration of the Rights of Man abolished the slave labor that supported their cane fields, enraged Guadeloupeans presented their island to the enemy British. France responded in 1794 with a gift of her own: the very latest in guillotines, imported from Paris and mounted in the public square of **Basse-Terre** and Pointe-à-Pitre. Some 4,000 local heads rolled before the bloody road show moved on.

Today Guadeloupe is represented in the French Parliament as a department and *région* of France, incorporating five dependencies that include the offshore archipelago of **Iles des Saintes, Marie-Galante**, and **La Désirade**, as well as satellite islands St-Martin and St-Barthélemy, some 140 miles to the northwest.

Some English is spoken at most major resorts, but brush up on your *vocabulaire* for remote villages and outer islands, and pack a good phrase book for a stay at any one of the charming family-run inns from the association Relais Créoles. After all, you won't want to miss any stories that begin *"tim-tim. . . ."*

To call from the US, dial 011 (the international access code), 590 (the country code), and the 6-digit local number. On Guadeloupe, dial only the 6-digit number unless otherwise indicated.

Getting to the Island

Airlines
Air Canada...........................836241, 514/393.3333
American Airlines 836262, 800/433.7300

Interisland Carriers
Air Caraïbes...821225
Air Guadeloupe..915344
Air Martinique 515151
LIAT (Leeward Islands Air Transport)...........821226

Airports **L'Aéroport International de Guadeloupe Pôle-Caraïbes** (937399), five kilometers (three miles) from Pointe-à-Pitre, is Guadeloupe's new international airport.

Aérodrome de Terre-de-Haut is in Les Saintes (995123), and **Aérodrome les Basses** is Marie-Galante's airport (979025). Both service small planes only.

Ferries Ferries operated by **L'Express des Iles** (831245) make several trips a week to and from Dominica, Martinique, and St. Lucia, as well as daily expeditions to Iles des Saintes and Marie-Galante. In winter, service extends to the islands of St-Martin, St. Barts, Antigua, St. Kitts, and St. Vincent. **Brudey Frères** (900448) run ferries among Pointe-à-Pitre, Basse-Terre, Trois-Rivières, Les Saintes, and Marie-Galante. There is also ferry service from St-François to Les Saintes, Marie-Galante, and La Désirade.

Getting Around the Island

Bicycles and Motorbikes
Archipel Rent Service, Les Saintes 995263
Easy Rent, St-François 887627
Espace VTT, Marie-Galante 887991
Karucyclo, Pointe-a-Pitre 822139
MM, St-François 885912

Buses Grab a phrase book and hop on one of the colorful jitneys that travel throughout Grande-Terre and Basse-Terre. Small, late-model vans depart from two stations in downtown Pointe-à-Pitre: the **Gare Routière de Bergevin** (Blvds de l'Amitié des Peuples de la Caraïbe and Chanzy) for Basse-Terre destinations; the **Gare Routière Dubouchage** (Rue Dubouchage, between Rues Raspail and Duplessis) for Grande-Terre hotels and resorts. They leave every 10 to 30 minutes (generally when they are full), depending on the importance of the route.

Car Rental
On Guadeloupe:
Avis......................................211354, 800/331.1212
Azur Auto 895561
Budget 902637, 800/527.0700
Europcar 825051

EuropRent...914216
Hertz 211346, 800/654.3131
Thrifty 915566

On Marie-Galante:
Caneval Station Shell....................................979776

Driving The tourist office in Pointe-à-Pitre (see "Visitors' Information Offices," on page 150) provides maps and a booklet of good driving tours. Grande-Terre roads are fine and the going is easy. Basse-Terre's mountain routes—with their steep ascents, descents, and switchbacks—are definitely not for the nervous. Cars with automatic transmission are in short supply. Only people who own businesses are allowed to have cars on Les Saintes, where most visitors travel by motorbike. A valid US or Canadian driver's license will suffice for up to 20 days.

Taxis
Basse-Terre and Pointe-à-Pitre 207474,
....836394
Les Saintes...995061
Marie-Galante...........................978197, 977297

Tours Among the best and most personalized are guided groups organized by **Georges Marie-Gabrielle** (839417). Otherwise, your concierge or hotel travel desk will have current details and rates on available tours and can make arrangements that include pickup at your hotel. Taxis can be hired by the hour and small groups can share the fare.

FYI

Electricity The current is 220/50 cycles. Some large hotels have adapters, but it's best to bring your own.

Entry Requirements US and Canadian visitors must present a valid passport or proof of citizenship (voter registration card, birth certificate) and a photo ID, plus a return or onward ticket. Visas are required for stays longer than three months.

Gambling The island's two casinos are at **Casino de la Marina** (Ave de l'Europe, St-François, 884131), and **Casino Caraïbe Club** (just west of Rte D119, Le Gosier, 841833) on the grounds of the **Arawak Hotel**. Both are open by admission daily for roulette, blackjack, and baccarat from 9PM to 3AM (4AM on Friday and Saturday). Slot machines (admission free) are available starting at noon in St-François, from 10AM in Gosier. The minimum age is 18 and proofs of age and identity—with photo—are required.

Language The official language is French, and many people speak Creole. Some service personnel in major tourist areas speak English, but if your *français* is rusty, better pack a good phrase book.

Money The official currency is the French franc, but many shops will accept US dollars. Some tourist-oriented Pointe-à-Pitre shops offer a discount to customers who pay with US traveler's checks or a major credit card. Like most Guadeloupean businesses, banks are closed for lunch between noon and 2:30PM, as well as Saturday and Sunday.

Personal Safety Although crime is not really a problem here, exercise normal precautions. Don't leave valuables unguarded on the beach or in an unlocked car. There have been reports of motorcycle-riding purse snatchers.

Publications The official visitor booklet, *Bonjour à Guadeloupe,* is published periodically in both French and English and is available free at the tourist office, airport, and most hotels. For details on six excellent driving tours, pick up a free copy of *Guadeloupe Excursions* at the tourist office in Pointe-à-Pitre. *Ti Gourmet,* a guide to Guadeloupe restaurants that features color photographs and sample menus, is available at major hotels and restaurants. The French-language daily *France-Antilles* is well written and carries entertainment ads that are easily understood, even by those who don't speak French. Parisian papers and the English-language *International Herald Tribune* usually hit local newsstands the day after publication.

Reservation Services and House Rentals
Association des Villas et Meublés de Tourisme de la Région Guadeloupe, Pointe-à-Pitre 820262

Les Gîtes de France Guadeloupe

Pointe-à-Pitre.................................912844

Les Saintes...................................995224

Marie-Galante.............................974051

Taxes There's a nominal hotel tax, which varies depending on the type and location of the hotel.

Telephone *Télécartes* (phone cards) are needed to make calls from a pay phone; they can be purchased at the post office or at other places signposted "Telecarte en Vente Ici." There are no coin-operated phones on the island.

Tipping French law requires a 15-percent service charge on all restaurant and bar bills. Tip room maids about $1 or $2 a day; porters about 85¢ per bag. Most taxi drivers own their own cars and do not expect tips.

Visitors' Information Offices
The **Office Départemental du Tourisme de la Guadeloupe** near the waterfront in Pointe-à-Pitre (5 Pl de la Banque, between Rues Bébian and de Provence; 820930) supplies maps, information, and advice. The office is open Monday through Friday from 8AM to 5PM and on Saturday from 8AM to noon. The staff will also answer phone queries in English. There is also a tourist office in Basse-Terre at the **Maison du Port** (Cours Nolivos, 812483), which is open Monday through Friday from 8AM to noon and from 2 to 5:30PM, and in St-François (Av de l'Europe, 884874), which is open Monday, Tuesday, Thursday, and Friday from 8AM to noon and from 2 to 5:30PM, Wednesday from 8Am to 12:30PM, and Saturday from 8AM to noon.

> The drawbridge over the Rivière Salée—Pont de la Gabarre—opens every day at 4AM to let boats go through to the Atlantic.

Restaurants/Clubs: Red   **Hotels:** Blue
Shops/ Outdoors: Green   **Sights/Culture:** Black

Phone Book

Pointe-à-Pitre

This is **Grande-Terre**'s port and Guadeloupe's main city—busy, but compact enough to explore in half a day. Mornings are the best time to ramble the narrow streets and tree-shaded squares, when the outdoor markets and waterfront stands are crowded with bustling islanders and vendors wearing their famous madras turbans. For maximum charm, stick to the **Old Town** near the harbor, where the main shopping area is bounded by **Rue Achille-René-Boisneuf**, running east and west, the harbor, and **Rues de Nozières** and **Frébault** (both of which run south and north). Most stores are closed at midday for a couple of hours, on Saturday afternoon, and on Sunday.

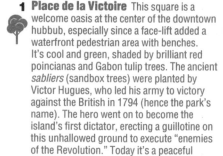

1 Place de la Victoire This square is a welcome oasis at the center of the downtown hubbub, especially since a face-lift added a waterfront pedestrian area with benches. It's cool and green, shaded by brilliant red poincianas and Gabon tulip trees. The ancient *sabliers* (sandbox trees) were planted by Victor Hugues, who led his army to victory against the British in 1794 (hence the park's name). The hero went on to become the island's first dictator, erecting a guillotine on this unhallowed ground to execute "enemies of the Revolution." Today it's a peaceful scene, surrounded by old colonial houses.
◆ Bounded by Rues Cdt.-Mortenol and Bébian, and Rues Duplessis and Alexandre-Isaac

2 La Darse Pointe-à-Pitre's active harbor is filled with visiting yachts, cruise ships, and other craft. This is the place to catch interisland ferries to Marie-Galante and Les Saintes, or to cruise the daily market for local crafts and foodstuffs.

3 Centre Saint-John Perse Named for the celebrated local poet and Nobel laureate, this $20-million harborfront complex houses the headquarters of Guadeloupe's Port Authority,

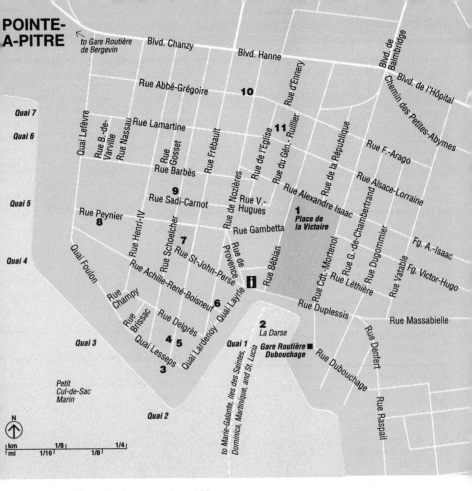

POINTE-A-PITRE

to Gare Routière de Bergevin

Blvd. Chanzy

Blvd. Hanne

Blvd. de Bainbridge

Rue Abbé-Grégoire

10

Rue d'Ennery

Blvd. de l'Hôpital

Chemin des Petites-Abymes

Quai 7

Quai 6

Quai Lefèvre

Rue B.-de-Varville

Rue Nassau

Rue Lamartine

Rue Frébault

Rue Gosset

Rue Barbès

Rue de l'Eglise

11

Rue du Gén.-Ruillier

Rue de la République

Rue F.-Arago

Rue Alsace-Lorraine

Quai 5

Rue Sadi-Carnot

9

Rue de Nozières

Rue V.-Hugues

Rue Alexandre Isaac

Rue Peynier

8

Rue Henri-IV

Rue Schoelcher

Rue St-John-Perse

7

Rue Gambetta

1
Place de
la Victoire

Rue Cdt.-Mortenol

Rue G.-de-Chambertrand

Rue Dugommier

Rue Vatable

Fg. A.-Isaac

Quai 4

Quai Foulon

Rue Achille-René-Boisneuf

Rue de Provence

Rue Bébian

Rue Léthière

Fg. Victor-Hugo

Rue Champy

Quai Layrle

6

Rue Duplessis

Rue Massabielle

Rue Brissac

Rue Delgrès

4 **5**

Quai Lesseps

3

Quai Lardenoy

Quai 3

Quai 1

2
La Darse

Gare Routière ■
Dubouchage

Rue Dubouchage

Rue Denfert

Rue Raspail

to Marie-Galante, Iles des Saintes, Dominica, Martinique, and St. Lucia

Petit
Cul-de-Sac
Marin

Quai 2

N

km
mi   1/16   1/8   1/8   1/4

---

as well as a bank, hotel, restaurants, and 80 stores (look here for duty-free bargains on local rum, French perfume, and Champagne). ♦ Quai Lesseps (between Quai Lardenoy and Rue Brissac)

Within the Centre Saint-John Perse:

St-John Anchorage Hotel $ Guests enjoy great views of the harbor and bay from 44 comfortably appointed waterfront units (some with private terraces) furnished in locally crafted mahogany. The hotel has no dining room, but there are several restaurants within the **Centre**. ♦ 825157; fax 825261

4 Phoenicia Good prices on French perfumes and other imported cosmetics are the draw at this well-known shop. There's even an extra discount for customers who pay with US traveler's checks. ♦ M-Sa. 8 Rue Frébault (between Quai Lesseps and Rue Delgrès). 835036. Also at: 121 Rue Frébault, 822575; Grande Escale, Le Gosier, 908556

5 Rosébleu Check inside for the island's largest selection of cosmetics and fashion accessories. ♦ M-F; Sa morning. 5 Rue Frébault (between Quai Lesseps and Rue Delgrès). 829344

6 Musée St-John Perse Winner of the 1960 Nobel Prize for Literature, the celebrated local writer was born Alexis Léger in Guadeloupe in 1887, moved to France after the earthquake in 1897, and took the pseudonym St-John Perse in 1925 when he became a poet. The late 19th-century colonial mansion houses a collection of his works, objets d'art, and photographs. A plaque at 54 Rue René-Boisneuf marks his birthplace. ♦ Admission. M-F; Sa morning. 9 Rue de Nozières (at Rue Achille-René-Boisneuf). 900192

7 Marché Couvert (Covered Market) This open-air food market rings with chatter and laughter, especially in the early morning, when local housewives come to do their day's shopping. The haggling over prices is a show in itself. ♦ Daily until midday. Bounded by Rues Frébault and Schoelcher, and Rues St-John-Perse and Peynier

8 Musée Schoelcher The memorabilia on display here were bequeathed to Guadeloupe by French abolitionist Victor Schoelcher, who helped end slavery on Guadeloupe and Martinique. ◆ Admission. M-Tu, Th-F; Sa morning; closed midday. 24 Rue Peynier (between Rue Henri-IV and Quai Lefèvre). 820804

9 **Floral Antilles** This florist carries several varieties of the island's beautiful flowers. They'll even expertly pack your purchases so you can bring them home. ◆ M-F; Sa morning. 50 Rue Schoelcher (at Rue Sadi-Carnot). 829765

10 **Grain D'Or** Fashionable gold jewelry is the attraction at this outpost of the Parisian shop. ◆ M-F; Sa morning. 84 Rue de Nozières (at Rue Abbé-Grégoire). 821173

11 **Cathédrale de St-Pierre et St-Paul** This tenacious church, dubbed "the Iron Cathedral," has bolted iron ribs designed to protect it from hurricanes and earthquakes. The design is effective, and the lovely yellow-and-white facade opens onto a peaceful square. ◆ Pl de l'Eglise (between Rues du Général-Ruillier and de l'Eglise)

Elsewhere on Grande-Terre

12 **Le Cimetière de Morne-à-l'Eau (Morne-à-l'Eau Cemetery)** Most of the above-ground crypts at this amphitheater-shaped cemetery are faced with tile—primarily black-and-white mosaic designs, but there are also some floral patterns and pastels. It is always ablaze with thousands of candles on the first night in November, when villagers decorate the tombs of the deceased to celebrate All Saints' Day. The grounds are packed tight but, as they say, there's always room for one more. ◆ Daily. Rte N5 and Blvd Nelson Mandela, Morne-à-l'Eau

13 **La Piquante Creole** Savory local spices, hot sauces, curries, and pickled delicacies line the shelves in this delightful factory outlet. ◆ M-F; Sa morning. Rte N6, Richeval. 246595

14 **Pointe de la Grande Vigie (Great View Point)** On a clear day you can see 35 miles—all the way to Antigua—from the northernmost point of Guadeloupe. Just beyond the plains of Campêche, these stark white limestone cliffs rise dramatically from the Atlantic. ◆ North of Rte D122

15 **Porte d'Enfer (Gate of Hell)** The "gateposts" are two cliffs battered by the crashing Atlantic surf—one of the most spectacular sights along the jagged northern coast. From here, the panorama takes in the seven points along the coastline known as *Sept Merveilles* (Seven Wonders). Nearby is Trou Madame Coco, a grotto named for the legendary Madame Coco, who supposedly walked into the sea carrying a parasol and was never seen again. ◆ Rte D122 (northeast of Anse-Bertrand)

16 **Musée Edgar Clerc** Named for the celebrated historian and archaeologist, this museum overlooking the sea houses Clerc's personal collection of Arawak and Carib Indian artifacts, as well as other ancient objects. One of the loveliest pieces is a pre-Arawak necklace of amethyst, crystal, and jade. The museum was Clerc's lifelong dream and he was to be its curator but, sadly, he died two years before it opened. Nearby lies the old sugar port of Le Moule, the former capital of Guadeloupe. ◆ Admission. M-Tu, Th-Su; W morning. Parc de la Rosette, Rte N5 (just east of Rte D123). 235757

17 **Distillerie Bellevue** One of Guadeloupe's greatest exports is *rhum agricole,* a pure rum fermented directly from the juice of sugarcane. Locals swear you can drink as much as you like without suffering a hangover. As elsewhere in the Caribbean, sugar production was the raison d'être for colonial Guadeloupe in the 17th and 18th centuries. Today only two cane distilleries remain on the island, but the production of rum continues. Here you can observe the process up to bottling, and even get a *dégustation* (tasting) of its Rhum Damoiseau in the shop. ◆ Free. M-Sa. Rue Bellevue-Damoiseau, Bellevue. 235555

18 **Tropical Club** $$ A good value on the beautiful crescent beach at Le Moule, each of the 96 terraced apartments (with kitchenettes and sea-view balconies) can accommodate up to 4 guests. Set within a coconut grove, the complex offers a pool, windsurfing, scuba diving, a restaurant, a snack bar, and a lively lobby bar. Golf is nearby. ◆ Plage de l'Autre Bord (just north of Rte N5). 939797, 800/322.2223; fax 939700

19 **Pointe des Châteaux** This startling castlelike rock formation, reminiscent of Land's End in San Francisco and Finisterre in Spain, stands guard on the peninsula where

the Atlantic and Caribbean meet. Views are spectacular from the crest of a well-marked nature trail that rambles through native woodland. The surf-pounded promontory, crowned by an old rugged cross that has survived for over a century, lies just a few hundred feet from protected coves that are perfect for swimming and picnics. On the north side is Pointe Tarare, a nude beach. ◆ Rte D118 (east of St-François)

20 Golf International de St-François Considered one of the best in the eastern Caribbean, this Robert Trent Jones Sr.–designed 18-holer tests golfers' mettle with water holes and windswept greens. At 6,755 yards and par 71, it's definitely a challenge. ◆ Greens fees. Daily. St-François. 884187

21 Méridien St-François $$$$ This 265-room beachfront resort offers water sports, 4 tennis courts, a swimming pool, and 3 restaurants. Golf and a marina are nearby, and it's a short walk to the village of St-François. For a real thrill, try your wings here in a rented ULM, a low-power seaplane you can fly yourself. ◆ Just east of St-François. 885100, 800/543.4300; fax 884071

La Cocoteraie

21 La Cocoteraie $$$$ This lovely property is set on a private beach with water sports, offering guests a secluded location that is still convenient for forays into the busy resort center of St-François. The 52 deluxe suites are fitted out with luxurious octagonal bathtubs, scenic balconies, mini-bars, safes, TV sets, and direct-dial telephones. The colonial decor is softened by pastels; the restaurant and bar overlook the swimming pool. ◆ St-François. 887981, 800/543.4300; fax 887833

21 Hamak $$$$ Each of the 54 very private bungalows at Jean-François Rozan's elegant retreat has a patio and terrace. The property features gorgeous tropical gardens and a private artificial beach that offers a full range of water sports. The seaside restaurant serves a good buffet breakfast, and other eateries and nightlife are within walking distance. ◆ St-François. 885999, 800/633.7411; fax 884192

21 Les Artisans Caraïbes Come here to shop for stylish local handicrafts—everything from chess sets to vibrant toy buses. ◆ M-Sa; closed midday. Little Gallery, Ave de l'Europe, St-François. 886938

21 L'Ile au Trésor A colorful inventory of island-made madras sportswear for adults and children is sold here; there are lots of souvenirs, too. ◆ M-Sa. Ave de l'Europe, St-François. 884827

Creole Primer

Famous for the French/Spanish/African cuisine that is stirred up by island cooks throughout the West Indies, Guadeloupe could rightfully be called the Creole capital of the Caribbean. Spicy soups, curries, fish stews, and court bouillons make good use of fresh seafood and native vegetables—especially peppers and tomatoes. If the going gets hot, you can always cool the fire with a good French wine or rum punch. Better yet, end the meal with a tropical ice cream flavored with *goyave* (guava), *papaye* (papaya), or *mangue* (mango).

Here are a few terms to help you navigate the menu.

accras	hot, puffed, cod fritters
assaisonnement	marinade of lime, garlic, hot peppers, and other seasonings
belangre	eggplant
blaff	fish poached with peppers and herbs
boudin	blood sausage
chadec	a grapefruitlike fruit
chatrou	octopus
christophine	chayote
colombo	a curried stew of pork, kid, lamb, or chicken
crabes farcis	stuffed crabs
féroce	avocado spiced "ferociously" with different peppers
fruit à pain	breadfruit
gombo	okra
igname	yam
lambi	conch
langouste	lobster
ouassous	river shrimp (a local crayfish)
oursin	sea urchin
piment	hot pepper
ti-nain	unripened green banana, eaten as a vegetable
vivaneau	red snapper

22 Plantation Ste-Marthe $$$ Set in the hills above St-François, yet close to the **Golf International de St-François** (see above) and some of Guadeloupe's greatest beaches, this elegant resort is designed to resemble a sprawling manor house. On a former sugar plantation, the 15-acre resort boasts the largest pool on the island, 4 lighted tennis courts, a health club, horseback riding, its own 9-hole golf course, and water sports. The 120 guest rooms are graced with wrought-iron balconies with beautiful views of the surrounding countryside. French fabrics and mahogany furniture add colonial polish to accommodations that also offer cable TV, hair dryers, and other modern perks. ♦ Ste-Marthe (just north of St-François). 931111, 800/223.9815; fax 887247

Within Plantation Ste-Marthe:

Vallée d'Or ★★★$$ Contemporary versions of classic French fare are complemented with imported wines and cheeses in this sophisticated dining room. Appetizers include *fondant de tomate et des filets de canard fumé* (tomato mousse with slices of smoked duck) and *baluchons de saumon à la tombée d'oignons* (raw marinated salmon with a creamy onion sauce). These can be followed by *châteaubriand aux échalottes confites* (steak in shallot sauce), *nage de vivaneau à la Bergamote* (a creamy stew of boiled red snapper), *medaillons de veau au pamplemousse et au miel* (veal with grapefruit and honey sauce), or *pot au feu de canard aux légumes pays* (duck stew with local vegetables). Then top off the meal with *croustillant de bananes au miel* (bananas and honey in a thin pancake) or *mousse aux trois chocolats* (three-chocolate mousse—dark, milk, and white). For an extra-special treat, go for the *rêve d'enfant* (child's dream)—an assortment of homemade pastries. ♦ French ♦ Daily lunch and dinnner. 884358

23 Ste-Anne Guadeloupe's most picturesque village is an old sugar town graced with a pretty church and a renovated *Hôtel de Ville* (Town Hall) in pastel tones. The town square, Place Schoelcher, is named for French abolitionist Victor Schoelcher, whose statue on the plaza was erected by islanders to commemorate the end of slavery in 1848. ♦ South coast

24 Caravelle Club Méditerranée $$$ A favorite with couples and thirtysomething singles, this link in the pioneering all-inclusive chain is set on a spectacular milelong beach that fringes a protected cove, with an area set aside for bathing au naturel. One tab covers lodging (324 rooms available), meals with unlimited wine in two restaurants, sports (windsurfing is particularly fine here), and entertainment. Facilities include a fitness center and six lighted tennis courts. This Clu Med is heavily marketed in Paris, so be prepared for many activities (especially in summer) conducted *en français*. ♦ Rte N4 (just west of Ste-Anne). 854950, 800/CLUBMED; fax 854970

25 Centre d'Art Haïtien The vibrant inventor showcases hand-crafted textiles, wall hangings, painted metal cutouts, and paintings by Haitian artists. ♦ M-Sa. Rte de Gosier, Le Gosier. 840484

25 Bananier ★★$$ Traditional Creole cuisin gets a nouvelle spin (clam ravioli with julienned vegetables, for instance) under the direction of the former chef of the **Auberge d la Vieille Tour** dining room (see below). The wine list is extensive. ♦ Creole ♦ Tu-Su lunch and dinner. Rte de Gosier, Le Gosier. 843485

25 Restaurant Pizzeria Napoli ★★$ The casual setting is just right for excellent housemade pasta, fresh salads, and imaginative pizza (for a finishing touch, drizzle some hot pepper–flavored olive oil on top), for those looking for a respite from *cuisine Créole*. ♦ Italian/Pizza ♦ Daily dinner until 1AM. Rte de Gosier, Le Gosier. 843485

25 Auberge de la Vieille Tour $$$$ The grande dame of Gosier hotels, now owned b the Sofitel chain, is loaded with French colonial atmosphere, from the 1835 sugar mill tower out front to the network of steep stone steps that keeps guests on their toes. If you crave a little more exercise, head for the lighted tennis court, volleyball court, or swimming pool. Ocean views are fine from balconies of the 180 guest rooms. There are two restaurants, the casual poolside **Ajoupa** and the **Auberge de la Vieille Tour** (see below), and two bars. ♦ Rt de Gosier, Le Gosier. 842323, 800/322.222: fax 843343

Within the Auberge de la Vieille Tour:

Auberge de la Vieille Tour ★★★$$$ Nouvelle creations range from red snapper with mango butter to prawns with cabbage at this longtime local favorite. The wine list is impressive, and the kitchen makes good use of the freshest local seafood in a variety of

innovative entrées. ♦ Creole/French ♦ Daily
breakfast, lunch, and dinner. 842323

25 Callinago Beach $$ Named for a Carib
military hero, this beachfront property offers
60 guest rooms, a French/Creole restaurant, a
poolside cafe, and one of the island's best
water-sports centers. Rates include buffet
breakfast. ♦ Just west of Rte D119, Le Gosier.
842525, 800/223.6510; fax 842490

25 Callinago Village $ Guests have full use
of the facilities at the adjacent sister operation
Callinago Beach (see above). This pleasant
beachfront enclave is an economical choice
for families, with kitchen facilities in the 69
studios, 32 duplexes, and 3 apartments (the
latter accommodate up to 6 guests each). A
small supermarket is located on the premises.
♦ Just west of Rte D119, Le Gosier. 842525,
800/223.6510; fax 842490

25 Arawak $$$ The **Casino Caraïbe Club,** a big
pool, and ample guest services are among the
attractions at this beachfront complex, known
for its wide range of sports. The 8-story hotel
offers 150 neat rooms and 6 penthouse suites,
as well as a French/Creole restaurant and
popular terrace bar. ♦ West of Rte D119, Le
Gosier. 842424, 800/223.6510; fax 843845

25 Hôtel le Clipper $$ Guadeloupe's newest
resort hotel looms large and impressive in the
heart of the Gosier beachfront. The striking
building was designed to resemble a large
boat, and the 89 rooms and 3 suites are air-
conditioned and boast terraces and large
picture windows with sea views. Other pluses:
a large pool, a Creole restaurant, a bar, a
conference room, two tennis courts, and, of
course, the beach. ♦ West of Rte D119, Le
Gosier. 840175; fax 843815

**25 Résidence Canella
Beach** $$$ These 150
beachfront units
(studios, junior suites,
and duplex suites) are
housed in 3-story,
pastel-colored buildings
perched on a small
beach. Savvy general
director Jean-Pierre Reuff caters to
Americans, who especially appreciate the
beachfront location and the many English-
speaking staff members. Amenities include
kitchenettes, a balcony or terrace, water
sports, and a swimming pool. ♦ West of Rte
D119, Le Gosier. 904400, 800/223.9815,
800/322.2223; fax 904444

Within the Résidence Canella Beach:

La Véranda ★★★$$$ The menu may be
short on choices, but the Creole and French
fare is long on flavor. The freshest local
seafood gets the royal treatment: smoked
marlin, grouper with ginger *en papillotte,*
and fillet of red snapper with cucumbers.
There's also a good selection of omelettes,
sandwiches, salads, and other light meals,
plus a generous wine list. ♦ Creole/French
♦ Daily lunch and dinner. 904400

26 Fort Fleur d'Epée Climb to the top of this
18th-century stronghold for a panorama that
sweeps across the islands of Marie-Galante
and Iles des Saintes to the mountains of Basse-
Terre and the island of Dominica. The fortress
(and its dungeons) saw quite a bit of action
when France and England struggled over the
island in 1794. There is a small historical
museum. ♦ Free. Daily. Bas du Fort. 909461

27 Fleur d'Epée Novotel $$$ The namesake
fort guards the hill above this Y-shaped
beachfront hotel, set in lovely tropical
gardens. Guests in the 190 rooms (most with
balconies) enjoy a pool, four tennis courts, a
wide variety of sports, and two international
restaurants offering Creole and international
fare. ♦ Bas du Fort. 904000, 800/221.4542;
fax 909907

27 Marissol $$$ Near the marina, this friendly
195-room beachfront complex has its own
spa/fitness center, water sports, 2
restaurants, 2 tennis courts, a disco, and
weekly folkloric shows. ♦ Bas du Fort.
908444, 800/221.4542; fax 908332

27 Rosini ★★$$ Diners are warmly welcomed
at the Rosini family's charming *ristorante,*
where classic Italian fare is the real thing—
from antipasto to homestyle desserts. The
mixed housemade pasta salutes the colors of
the Old Country (red, white, and green), while
local river shrimp *fra diavolo* (in a spicy
sauce) is a traditional treatment of New World
ingredients. ♦ Italian ♦ Daily lunch and dinner.
Bas du Fort. 908781

27 A La Recherche du Passé View the
nautical paraphernalia, antique books, and
assorted bibelots offered for sale here. ♦ M-F;
Sa morning. La Marina, Bas du Fort. 908415

27 Aquarium de la Guadeloupe About 1,000
fish, sharks, and crustaceans reside in this
2,640-square-foot exhibition center, making it
a great place to watch the citizens of the sea
without getting wet. There's a gift shop.
♦ Admission. Daily 9AM-7PM. 2 Pl Créole, La
Marina, Bas du Fort. 909238; fax 907929

Base-Terre

28 Auberge de la Distillerie $$ Guest quarters are named for flowers (and identified by the painted blooms) at this tile-roofed country inn surrounded by fields of sugarcane and pineapple. The 15 rooms and 6 cottages are simple, but comfortably furnished; continental breakfast is included in the rates. Sharing the tranquil grounds are a small garden pool, an informal cafe, a Creole/international restaurant, and a congenial bar. ♦ Rte de Versailles, Tabanon. 942591, 800/322.2223; fax 941191

29 Parc National Arguably the best natural park in the Caribbean, this gorgeous preserve covers one-fifth of Guadeloupe's total land area. Nearly 170 miles of well-marked trails ramble through a lush tropical landscape graced by deep green rain forests, waterfalls, mountain pools, and fumaroles (steam holes). A popular 42-mile hiking path cuts through the park from one side to the other; picnic areas and overnight refuges are found at intervals along the way. The park's official mascot is Titi the raccoon, but hikers are likely to come across a wide range of wildlife—and hundreds of different trees and flowers—that thrive within 74,000 acres where hunting and fishing are forbidden. The park service has information and a map of trail paths (808606). For guided hikes contact **Organisation des Guides de Montagne** (Maison Forestière, Matouba, 991873). ♦ Interior

Parc National

Within the Parc National:

Route de la Traversée (Transcoastal Highway) Get ready for plenty of breathtaking views on this well-maintained road that passes through the **Parc National** route from Basse-Terre to Pointe-à-Pitre. The climb starts just north of Pigeon at Mahaut and continues 7 kilometers (4 miles) east, passing the twin peaks dubbed Les Deux Mamelles (The Two Breasts). The park is rich with forests, lakes, and waterfalls. Along the way, you'll be treated to a panorama that takes in the hills, valleys, and coasts of Basse-Terre and the bays called Grand and Petit Cul-de-Sac Marin. ♦ Between Rtes N1 and N2

Cascade aux Ecrevisses (Crayfish Falls) A short and well-marked trail leads to this sparkling little waterfall that cascades into the Rivière Corossol. Bring along a bathing suit so you can dive in and swim with the crayfish. But be forewarned, those little guys can really pinch.

LE PARC
ZOOLOGIQUE ET
BOTANIQUE

Parc Zoologique et Botanique (Zoological and Botanical Park) Stroll along the paths here to get a good look at the native trees, ferns, raccoons, mongooses, iguanas, and crab-eater birds. Cool off afterward in the on-site restaurant. ♦ Admission. Daily. 988352

30 Malendure This tiny village is best known as the hopping-off point for the celebrated Réserve Cousteau and Ilet Pigeon (Pigeon Island), surrounded by busy waters that Jacques Cousteau once declared to be one of the world's 10 best areas for scuba diving and snorkeling. Complete rental outfits are available, but all components are French, so US divers may need to bring along familiar gear. Most local instructors and guides are certified under the French **CMAS,** rather than **PADI** or **NAUI.** For diving excursions to Ilet Pigeon, contact **Aux Aquanautes Antillais** (988730), **Les Heures Saines** (988663), or **Plaisir Plongée Caraïbes** (988243), which face the island from the beach at Malendure. Landlubbers can still enjoy the undersea view aboard one of the glass-bottom boats operated by **Nautilus Club** (988908), also headquartered on the beach. ♦ West coast

At Malendure:

Chez LouLouse ★$ This rustic charmer is usually filled with hungry divers returning from Ilet Pigeon—and spontaneous bursts of song are not uncommon. Specialties on the well-priced menu include fish and chicken dishes and a variety of salads. ♦ Creole/

Seafood ◆ Daily lunch and dinner. No credit cards accepted. 987034

31 Grande Anse This palm-shaded beach is one of the loveliest—and one of the widest—on Guadeloupe. The secluded stretch of beige sand is a fine place for picnics or swimming in the Caribbean waters. ◆ Northwest coast

On Grand Anse:

Le Karacoli ★★$$ Dine alfresco with friendly and attentive service at this family-run eatery, headed up by lovely Lucienne Salcède. The outstanding *colombos* (island curries) and *coquilles Karacoli* (scallops with Creole spices) are served indoors or on a shaded beachside terrace. ◆ French/Creole ◆ Daily lunch. 284117

32 Musée du Rhum In the 1950s, there were 14 sugarcane factories on the island, but only two remain today. The story of how this industry changed the island nation is captured at this museum near the northern point of Basse-Terre. Multilingual exhibits and a short video in English trace three centuries of sugarcane and rum production, explaining how the harvest takes place and how the liquor is distilled. At the end of the tour, located in a building next to a working sugarcane factory, visitors can taste a variety of rums and cane liquors, ranging from dark aged rum to clear *rhum agricole*. ◆ Admission. M-Sa. Southwest of Monplaisir. 287004

33 Ravine Chaud Tapping into hot mineral water from a volcanic spring, this well-equipped spa surrounded by lush gardens offers two tepid swimming pools, a children's mineral pool, and a solarium. Lucette Corder claims to listen to your muscles as she massages away aches and pains. There is also a long list of other treatments, including facials, manicures, saunas, aromatherapy, water massages, and seaweed wraps. A terrace bar and restaurant overlook the tranquil countryside where spa food and Creole and international dishes are served. The friendly director speaks a fair amount of English. ◆ Fee. Spa: daily; restaurant: Tu-Sa lunch and dinner. Lamentin. 257592

34 Domaine de Valombreuse Parc Floral (Valombreuse Floral Park) Hundreds of varieties of tropical plants and flowers, including orchids and torch gingers and the butterflies that favor them, splash this private park with color. Set within the 6 tranquil acres is an aviary filled with 500 brilliant tropical birds. Flowers and plants are also for sale. ◆ Admission. Daily. Cabout. 955050

Within the Domaine de Valombreuse Parc Floral:

Au Pipirite ★★$$ This dining room seems secluded in a lush tropical forest, the perfect place to lose yourself in *tarte ouassous* (river shrimp tart), *fricassée de lambis* (conch stew), and other island fare. ◆ Creole ◆ Daily lunch. 955050

35 Ste-Marie This town's New World history dates back to 1493, when Columbus stepped ashore here on his second voyage to the Caribbean. Today the great explorer is immortalized in the town square. After the eradication of slavery in 1848, East Indians were brought to Guadeloupe to work on the plantations; their descendants now make up the majority of the local population. To the south of town lies Allée Dumanoir; the giant palm trees that flank this picturesque road were originally planted by Pinel Dumanoir (who is also remembered for another unlikely contribution—his French dramatization of *Uncle Tom's Cabin*). ◆ Southeast coast

36 Les Chutes du Carbet (Carbet Waterfalls) From the sea, Columbus's crew took this trio of waterfalls to be "avalanches of white stones." The 2 highest falls tumble over 300 feet; the lowest falls is still impressive at a height of 60 to 70 feet. To get here, follow the road inland from the coastal village of St-Sauveur, past the round mountain lake called Grand Etang, climbing **La Soufrière** to a cleared lookout near the three cascades. From the road, it's a 25-minute walk to the pool at the foot of the lowest cascade. ◆ Rte D4 (northwest of St-Sauveur)

37 Parc Archéologique des Roches Gravées (Archaeological Park of Rock Engravings) The pre-Columbian Arawak petroglyphs of animal and human figures are believed to date from around AD 300. You'll also see a collection of native plants and trees that the Indians introduced to European settlers, including cocoa, cassava, and calabash. The bearded fig tree gets its French name, *maudit* (cursed), from its countless and tenacious roots. ◆ Admission. Daily. Bord de Mer (just south of Trois-Rivières). 929188

Le Jardin Malanga

38 Le Jardin Malanga $$$ Set in the middle of a 15-acre banana plantation, this establishment consists of a wood-shingled colonial house, built in 1927, with 2 guest rooms, plus 3 cottages that can accommodate up to 6 people each. The rooms are all equipped with air-conditioning, TVs and VCRs, mini-bars, telephones, and hair dryers. The property also offers a restaurant, a swimming pool, and a terrace with a bar and a panoramic view of Les Saintes. It's a 12-minute drive to the beach at Grande Anse and a 10-minute drive to the Carbet Waterfalls. ♦ L'Hermitage, Rte N1 (just east of Rte D8). 904646, 800/322.2223; fax 904699

39 Manioukani This "thalassotherapy" center at the foot of the Basse-Terre mountains offers a wide range of spa treatments, many of which involve the seawater here, which is believed to have especially therapeutic qualities. ♦ Fee. M-Sa. Marina de Rivière-Sens, Rte D6 (just southeast of Rte N1). 990202; fax 816523

40 Basse-Terre Guadeloupe's capital is a tenacious little city that has endured British and French invasions, hurricanes, and volcanic eruptions. The last major upheaval was in 1976, when La Soufrière went off and residents were evacuated for six months. The narrow streets and palm-filled parks are nestled between the sea and the green volcanic slopes. Local sights include a colorful outdoor market and the 17th-century **Cathédrale de Notre Dame de Guadeloupe.** For majestic reminders of the island's colonial past, view the three imposing buildings known as the **Préfecture, Conseil Général,** and **Palais de Justice.** ♦ Southwest coast

In Basse-Terre:

Fort Delgrès Formerly called **Fort St-Charles,** it was renamed in 1990 to honor Louis Delgrès, whose death in 1802 made him an early hero in the abolition movement. The historic bastion has safeguarded the city of Basse-Terre since it was founded in 1643. The Rivière Galion, which starts at La Soufrière, runs under the fortifications to the sea. ♦ Free. Daily. Rue Amédée-Tiengard. 813748

41 Hôtel St-Georges $$ This small, modern hotel in the charming town of St-Claude in the foothills of La Soufrère has 40 comfortable rooms, each with air-conditioning, a TV set, and a telephone, as well as a terrific view of the city of Basse-Terre and the surrounding Caribbean. Amenities include a pool, snack bar, and fine restaurant, as well as a fitness center, billiards room, and squash court. ♦ Rue Gratien-Parize, St-Claude. 801010; fax 803050

Most of the fish on Guadeloupe come from Les Saintes.

42 La Soufrière This dormant volcano is a light sleeper, a grumbling heap of steamy fumaroles and gurgling mud cauldrons that has given Guadeloupeans more than a few nightmares. You can drive to the foot of the 4,813-foot-high crater and pull into the Savane-à-Mulets parking lot to feel the heat rising from underground lava. Take in the spectacular panorama that stretches across Basse-Terre and the sea, all the way to Iles des Saintes and Dominica. If that's not enough, hike one of four marked trails to look over the edge into a five-acre center of bubbling lava and eerie rock formations. Hiring a guide is strongly recommended; some of the area is dense with vegetation and is often shrouded in mist. The round-trip trek can take from one to three hours, depending on the trail you choose—and your endurance. You can pick up a *Guide to the Natural Park* from the tourist office, which grades the trails by difficulty. For guides, contact **Club des Montagnards** (PO Box 1085, Pointe-à-Pitre, 942911). ♦ D11 (northeast of St-Claude)

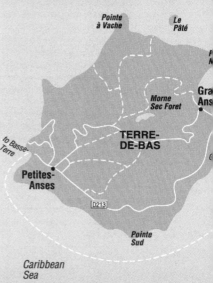

Terre-de-Haut, Iles des Saintes

With about 1,500 inhabitants and no cars (except for those owned by the island's businesspeople), Terre-de-Haut is perfect for a daylong getaway trip, or better yet, a relaxing vacation from the "mainland," just 7 miles away by plane or catamaran. Part of the Iles des Saintes archipelago, Terre-de-Haut is its main island, and the only one with hotels. (Only hostelries of 20 rooms or fewer are permitted.) There are a number of ways to get around: foot, bicycle, scooter, or *taxi de l'île* (minibus). Whichever way you choose to see the sights, you won't have far to travel—Terre-de-Haut is small, just three miles long and one mile wide. Fishing is the main industry here, and brightly colored boats line the island's shores. If you're lucky, you'll be able to find a *salako* to take home; it's a big round straw hat covered with white cloth that fisherfolk wear and is unique to these islands. Don't leave without trying a *tourment d'amour*, a coconut tart available at restaurants and from vendors on the pier.

43 Le Bourg One of the Caribbean's prettiest towns has a quaint, tiny main square, rows of small, uniquely painted houses, and flowers everywhere. The ferries dock here, and the port has shops, cafes, and scooter and bicycle rental places. As you enter the harbor, be sure to look to your left at the house that looks like a ship's bow (it is the home of the island's only doctor). Just north of town is **Kaz An Nou** (Rte de Pompierre, 995229), a crafts gallery, which specializes in miniatures. ◆ West coast

In Le Bourg:

Nilce's Bar ★★$$ In an old building at the boat pier, this spot offers an authentic bistro setting and evening entertainment. Nilce, a Brazilian singer married to an islander, performs most nights. Salads, sandwiches, and other light fare is served at lunch; seafood and Creole specialties are offered at dinner. ◆ Creole ◆ Daily lunch and dinner. 995680

44 Auberge les Petits Saints aux Anacardiers $$ On a small hill above the island's main town, this hostelry (formerly the mayor's house) makes visitors feel as though they are guests in a private home. There are 10 rooms in the main house as well as a

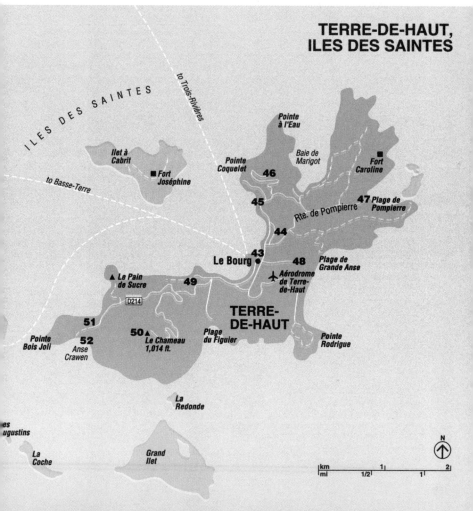

TERRE-DE-HAUT, ILES DES SAINTES

separate bungalow; all are decorated with antiques but offer modern amenities such as mini-bars. The grounds are filled with fruit and nut trees and include a pretty garden and a beautiful pool. There's also a sauna and a boat used for excursions. The excellent restaurant features French and Creole fare and great views of the harbor. ◆ La Savanne. 995099, 800/322.2223; fax 995451

45 Kanaoa $ Request a view of the cove at this bayfront inn, which offers all water sports, a pleasant terrace restaurant, and a snack bar. Guests are lodged in 18 rooms and 2 bungalows; rates include breakfast. ◆ Anse Mire. 995136; 800/755.9313; fax 995504

46 Fort Napoléon There has never been a single shot fired at this bastion built to protect the island from British invaders. Completed in 1867, it was abandoned some 40 years later, and nature took over. In 1973, a group of *Saintois* volunteers cleaned the fort, and today it is a museum of military history and modern art. Its *jardin exotique* (tropical garden) is filled with cacti and succulents from all over the world. The view of the bay of Terre-de-Haut is particularly pleasing. ◆ Admission. Daily until noon. North of Anse Mire. 995358

47 Plage de Pompierre One of the island's loveliest beaches is on a horseshoe-shaped bay—its crystal-clear, tranquil water makes it an ideal place to swim, and the palm trees provide the perfect spot for a picnic. ◆ Rte de Pompierre (northeast of Le Bourg)

48 Le Cimetière de Grande Anse (Grand Anse Cemetery) Right next to the airport (its very short runway has a mountain-pass approach) is the island's cemetery. The white tombs, hand-carved crucifixes, and conch shell–framed grave sites pay homage to the island's Breton ancestors and to sailors who vanished at sea. The shells were used to ornament the graves because cement was too expensive. ◆ Daily. Just east of Le Bourg

49 Centre Nautique des Saintes ★★$$ Stop here for the best grilled fish on the island, but begin with *salade pirate* (smoked tuna and swordfish with potatoes). There are also a few guest rooms, and scuba-diving excursions can be arranged. ◆ M, W-Su lunch and dinner. Plage de la Colline. 995425

50 Tour Modèle (Model Tower) This mountaintop watchtower on Le Chameau was once part of the island's fortifications. Today it offers spectacular vistas of the natural reserve below, Le Pain de Sucre (Sugarloaf Hill), the bay, Marie-Galante, and Dominica. ◆ Free. Daily. Le Chameau. No phone

Hotel Bois Joli
Iles des Saintes GUADELOUPE

51 Hotel Bois Joli $$ From the hilltop at this scenic complex, which offers two lovely beaches, water sports, and boat trips, the views are *superbe*. Guests are lodged in 10 beach cottages and 21 small, neat rooms (13 air-conditioned) with private baths or showers. The restaurant serves good Creole fare, especially seafood. Bus and boat shuttles make regular trips into town. ◆ Anse à Cointe. 995038, 800/322.2223; fax 995505

52 Anse Crawen Although there's a sign in town that says *"Le Nudisme est interdit dans Les Saintes"* ("Nudity is forbidden in Les Saintes"), sunbathing at this isolated, white-sand beach is au naturel. ◆ Southwest coast

Marie-Galante

First inhabited by the Arawak and Carib Indians, then "discovered" by Christopher Columbus in 1493 (he named the island after one of his ships, *Maria Graciosa*), Marie-Galante passed among French, English, and Dutch hands until it officially became French in 1816. Spanish sailors nicknamed Marie-Galante "El Sombrero" because of its shape—the island is round and flat, except for **La Grande Barre**, a plateau that divides the island in two. Sugar and rum are the main industries, and the island is still dotted with scores of windmills, and with oxen who pull sugarcane to the distilleries. Not as well developed from a tourist's point of view as most of its sister islands in the French West Indies, Marie-Galante possesses a pastoral allure unmatched in the Guadeloupe archipelago. Not only does it have some of the best and most pristine beaches in the Caribbean, but it offers a bit of sight-seeing as well.

53 Grand-Bourg Although it's the largest of the three main towns in Marie-Galante and the administrative and commercial center of the island, it still feels like a sleepy village. Ferries from Guadeloupe dock here, and it's the best place to rent cars and bicycles. Because Marie-Galante is fairly flat, two-wheelers are an excellent way to see the almost 60-square-mile island. ◆ Southwest coast

Within Grand-Bourg:

Immeuble Le Maistre One of the few supermarkets on the island, it has everything from dried, salted cod to shampoo. ◆ M-Sa. Rue Jeanne-d'Arc. 977702

Auberge de L'Arbre à Pain $ There are seven simply furnished rooms with private baths at this clean hotel in the heart of town. Its restaurant serves good Creole dishes. ◆ Rue Jeanne-d'Arc. 977369

MARIE-GALANTE

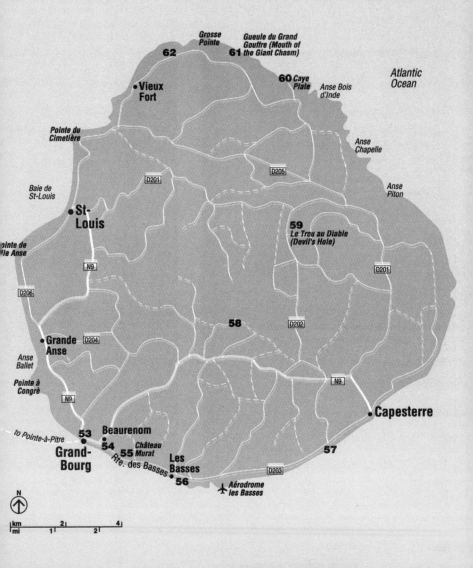

Atlantic Ocean

Grosse Pointe

Gueule du Grand Gouffre (Mouth of the Giant Chasm)

62

61

60 Caye Plate

Anse Bois d'Inde

Vieux Fort

Pointe du Cimetière

Anse Chapelle

D205

Baie de St-Louis

Anse Piton

D201

St-Louis

Pointe de l'Ile Anse

59
Le Trou au Diable (Devil's Hole)

N9

D201

D206

58

D202

Grande Anse

D204

Anse Ballet

N9

Pointe à Congrè

N9

Capesterre

to Pointe-à-Pitre

53

Beaurenom

54

Château Murat

55

57

Grand-Bourg

Rte. des Basses

Les Basses

56

D203

Aérodrome les Basses

N

km
mi
1   2
2   4

Getting Your Feet Wet in Guadeloupe

There's so much more to Guadeloupe than just the beach. Jacques Cousteau named the waters around **Ilet Pigeon** (Pigeon Island) among the world's 10 best diving areas. The undersea world is especially lively off the western and southern coasts of **Basse-Terre**. Most hotels rent snorkeling and windsurfing equipment, as well as Sunfish and other small craft. Here are some other organizations that can help get you afloat:

Boating

ATM Yachts La Marina, Bas du Fort. 909202, 800/634.8822

Massif Marine Antilles Pointe-à-Pitre. 908280

The Moorings Pointe-à-Pitre. 908181, 800/535.7289

Snorkeling and Scuba Diving

Aqua Fari Plongée Callinago Beach (just west of Rte D119), Le Gosier. 842525, 800/223.6510

Caraïbes Plongée Résidence Canella Beach Hotel (west of Rte D119), Le Gosier. 904400

Centre Nautique des Saintes Plage de la Colline, Terre-de-Haut. 995425

Les Heures Saines Le Rocher de Malendure, Ilet Pigeon, Basse-Terre. 988663

Plaisir Plongée Caraïbes Malendure, Basse-Terre. 988243

Sportfishing

Caraïbe Pêche La Marina, Bas du Fort. 909751

Fishing Club Antilles Rte de Birloton, Bouillante, Basse-Terre. 907010

Le Rocher de Malendure Ilet Pigeon, Basse-Terre. 987084

Windsurfing

Union des Centres de Plein Air (UCPA) St-François. 886480

Le Moana Pizzeria ★$ When you are ready to take a break from such local dishes as *boudin créole* (blood sausage), try the delicious pizza served here. ♦ Pizza ♦ M-W, F-Su dinner. Rue du Presbytère. 978597

54 Restaurant Côté Plage ★★★$ Excellent Creole fare is the highlight at this eatery located across from the beach. Specialties on the menu include *crabes farcis* (stuffed crab), *tarte poisson* (fish pie), and *lambi fricassée* (conch stew). ♦ Creole ♦ Daily lunch. Rte des Basses, Beaurenom. 977625

55 Château Murat This splendid restored manor house was built in the 1830s for Dominique Murat, a coffee plantation owner, by the architect **Mademoiselle Murat** (no relation) who had studied at the Ecole des Beaux Arts in Paris. The lovely grounds include remnants of the property's sugar mill, including a windmill in fairly decent shape, and a beautiful herb garden. If you're lucky, you'll catch the gardener, who can tell you about the traditional medicinal plants and their continued use today to cure a variety of ailments. ♦ Free. Daily. North of Rte des Basses. 974141

56 Thiéry Villas $$ Owned by Dominique Thiéry of the **Distillerie Bielle** (see below), a studio and villa provide comfortable accommodations right on the water. Each can be rented separately or together, making it an ideal arrangement for families. The villa has a washing machine, dryer, pinball machine, lovely deck, and hammock. ♦ Rte des Basses. 979362

57 Petite Anse (Little Bay) True beach buffs favor this long golden strand for picnicking, sunning—or doing nothing at all. There are no facilities, though there are a few Creole eateries here. ♦ Rte D203 (east of Aérodrome les Basses)

About 1.2 million bottles of Champagne are drunk annually in Guadeloupe.

Guadeloupe has the highest standard of living in the Caribbean.

Coral is made by tubular-shaped animals called polyps, which are about the size of a pencil eraser and are topped by a ring of tentacles that are similar in appearance to the polyp's relative, the sea anemone.

If you want to try your luck in the Caribbean, the countries with the greatest number of casinos are Aruba, the Dominican Republic, Puerto Rico, and St. Maarten.

58 Distillerie Bielle One of the few remaining rum distilleries on Marie-Galante, this factory produces about 45,000 bottles a year of the *rhum agricole*. It's quite a sight to watch how the liquor is processed, from the extraction of juice from sugarcane up to fermentation. Posters in English, French, and German detail all the steps. The pungent aroma in the air is also a heady experience. There's a tasting bar and a small shop that sells the pottery of a local ceramist. ♦ Free. Daily. Northeast of Grand-Bourg). 979362

59 Le Trou au Diable (Devil's Hole) Hike down from the road to this striking geological site, a grotto filled with stalactites. You'll need a guide to go into the grotto itself; contact **L'Association pour la Promotion Touristique de Marie-Galante**

(978197) for a referral. ♦ Rte D202 (just south of Rte D201)

60 Caye Plate Pull off the road, walk down some stairs, and you'll be treated to a great view of the northern coastline, as well as of the green-and-blue surf hitting the cliffs. ♦ North of Rte D205

61 Gueule du Grand Gouffre (Mouth of the Giant Chasm) The roar of the Atlantic Ocean rises from the whirling waters in the bottom of this abyss. The churning tide crashes against the cliffs, and the wind is strong enough to knock you over—so be sure to hold onto your hat! There are lots of small deserted beaches between here and Caye Plate. Just pull over by the side of the road and walk down to the water. ♦ North of Rte D205

62 Au Village du Ménard $$ There are seven bungalows (one with air-conditioning, the others cooled naturally by the refreshing trade winds) at this lovely property in the north. Each has a full kitchen, bar, and television, and can sleep up to four people. There is also a swimming pool, and the owners talk of adding a tennis court. It even has its own windmill, but no restaurant. ♦ Northeast of Vieux Fort. 970945

Bests

Myron Clement
President, The Clement-Petrocik Company

Pointe-à-Pitre:

La Fête des Cuisinières—This once-a-year "Cooks' Festival," with some 150 costumed women cooks having their culinary specialties blessed at the cathedral, then parading them through town to an afternoon of dining and dancing, is worth the trip. On a Saturday near mid-August.

Marché Couvert—Outdoor marketplace in the heart of bustling Pointe-à-Pitre with picturesque vendors and wide variety of produce. Ask before taking photos.

Aquarium—For family fun, visit the aquarium, just outside Pointe-à-Pitre. This aquarium ranks number four in all of France.

Elsewhere on Grande-Terre:

St-François

Pointe des Châteaux—It's the French West Indies' *Finistère*—Land's End—nothing Caribbean about it; huge rocks rising from the sea with the ocean crashing against them. And the offshore island of **La Désirade** in the background.

Hamak—Guadeloupe is not noted for deluxe hotels, but this is a beautifully landscaped exception. It was here that the 1979 summit meeting with Presidents Carter and Giscard d'Estaing took place. Just across from the fine **Golf International de St-François,** too.

Basse-Terre:

Parc National—A 74,000-acre natural park, with the 4,813-ft. bubbling **Soufrière** volcano, lush tropical forest, waterfalls, and pre-Columbian rocks, is a "must" for eco-tourists.

Ilet Pigeon (Pigeon Island)

"One of 10 best dive sites in the world!" not say I, but said celebrated underwater authority, Jacques Cousteau. Dominique Deramé's **Les Heures Saines** for dives, Franck Nouy's **Le Rocher de Malendure** to stay.

Karacoli—A beachside Creole restaurant in **Deshaies,** run by genial proprietress, Lucienne Salcède. Have a drink, take a dip, enjoy a delicious meal.

Terre-de-Haut, Iles des Saintes:

Charming offshore island (1 hour by boat, 10 minutes by air) with fine food, good accommodations. It's what St. Barts was more than 15 years ago.

Marie-Galante:

Another offshore island—unspoiled; it's what Terre-de-Haut was like more than 10 years ago.

Central Paris, with two million residents, has the same area as Marie-Galante, with a population of 12,000.

Marie-Galante is known as "L'Ile aux 100 Moulins" (the Island of 100 Windmills). All of the windmills on the isle have names.

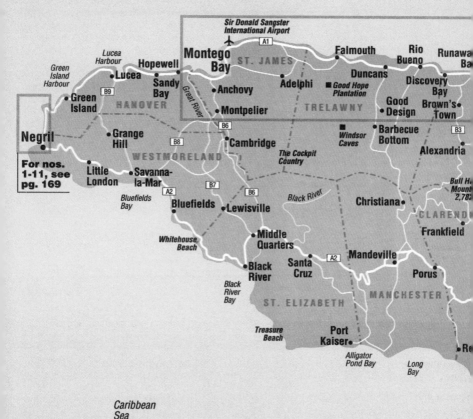

Sir Donald Sangster
International Airport

✈ A1

**Montego
Bay**

ST. JAMES

● **Falmouth**

**Rio
Bueno**

**Runawa
Ba**

Green
Island
Harbour

Lucea
Harbour

● **Lucea**

● **Hopewell**

● **Sandy
Bay**

B9

● **Anchovy**

● **Adelphi**

■ *Good Hope
Plantation*

● **Duncans**

**Discovery
Bay**

HANOVER

● **Green
Island**

● **Montpelier**

TRELAWNY

**Good
Design**

**Brown's
Town**

Great River

● **Grange
Hill**

B8

● **Cambridge**

■ *Windsor
Caves*

● **Barbecue
Bottom**

B3

Negril

WESTMORELAND

*The Cockpit
Country*

Alexandria

For nos.
1-11, see
pg. 169

● **Little
London**

● **Savanna-
la-Mar**

B7

B6

Black River

● **Christiana**

CLAREND

*Bull Ha
Mount
2,78*

*Bluefields
Bay*

A2

● **Bluefields**

● **Lewisville**

● **Frankfield**

*Whitehouse
Beach*

● **Middle
Quarters**

● **Santa
Cruz**

● **Mandeville**

A2

● **Porus**

● **Black
River**

*Black
River
Bay*

ST. ELIZABETH

MANCHESTER

*Treasure
Beach*

● **Port
Kaiser**

● **Re**

*Alligator
Pond Bay*

*Long
Bay*

*Caribbean
Sea*

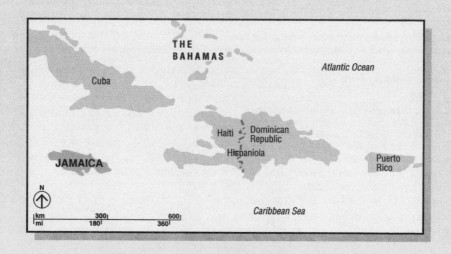

**THE
BAHAMAS**

Atlantic Ocean

Cuba

Haiti ● **Dominican
Republic**

JAMAICA

Hispaniola

Puerto
Rico

N

| km | 300 | 600 |
| mi | 180 | 360 |

Caribbean Sea

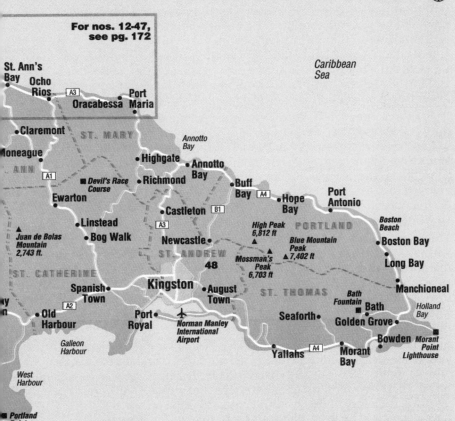

For nos. 12-47, see pg. 172

Jamaica

Xaymaca (the land of wood and water) was the name given to this island by the gentle Arawak who first inhabited it. Here rivers rush down the central mountains, forming waterfalls and tributaries and feeding the rain forest that turns the countryside green. Tropical flowers add vivid splashes of red, purple, yellow, and pink to the landscape, and a blazing sun shimmering off miles of white-sand beaches and surrounding sea completes the dramatic picture.

Jamaica is the third-largest Caribbean island, and the people who live here are (for the most part) proud, opinionated, and fond of laughter. You'll meet outgoing islanders at every turn—from the street vendors who are among the most persistent on earth, to the hotel waiter who introduces himself and shakes your hand, to the bartender who smiles and insists, "No mon, you don't want no scotch and soda. You try a Red Stripe. It's Jamaican beer, mon, the best in the world." Some tourists are taken aback by this gregariousness; others find it fun, interesting, and a memorable part of their island experience. If you feel hassled, just say so. Most likely, you'll be met with a smile and the response, "No problem, mon" (the words are virtually Jamaica's national slogan). Remember, tourism is the number one industry here; Jamaicans want you to enjoy your stay and think well of their country.

Jamaica has three major tourist areas. **Montego Bay** (or "Mobay" as the locals call it) is the island's second-largest city (**Kingston** is number one) and the premier tourist destination. It's the site of a number of grand 17th- and 18th-century plantation homes called great houses and several championship golf courses. Mobay is also the starting point for some of the most popular island tours, making it ideal for those who want great beaches, sight-seeing, shops, and lots of nightlife without the complications of taking a minibus to the resort towns of **Ocho Rios** or **Negril.**

Ocho Rios is the island's fastest-growing resort area, with an active cruise port, duty-free shopping centers, and a number of straw and crafts markets. Some of Jamaica's deluxe resorts can be found along Ocho Rios's dramatic coastline. Horseback riding, golf, and sight-seeing excursions are popular daytime activities, as the beaches here tend to be small and water sports are best enjoyed in the mornings, when the sea is calm. An hour-and-a-half drive east on the northern coastal road will take you to **Port Antonio**, an out-of-the-way resort town where relaxing is a time-honored art.

True beach and water-sports lovers should consider Negril, an adult haven with a "kick off your shoes, anything goes" attitude. It's far from the madding crowd, with seven miles of spectacular beach and a sunset that sets the clouds afire with color. By law, no building in Negril is higher than the town's tallest palm tree. There are few modern distractions and not much sight-seeing, which seems to suit the hippies and yuppies who flock here just fine.

As you choose among these destinations, keep in mind that Jamaica is the king of all-inclusive resorts. All-inclusive on this island means just that: upscale rooms, all meals and snacks, alcoholic beverages, water and land sports, nightly entertainment, taxes, tips, and airport transportation for one set price. It's a way of vacationing that is catching on throughout the Caribbean, but Jamaica still does it best.

If you want to see museums and art galleries, take one of the daylong tours to Kingston offered in all the resort areas. The seat of government and a business hub, Kingston is off the tourist track, although in recent years there has been an effort to spruce up its cultural attractions in hopes of luring visitors. There are also some spectacularly lovely inns in the **Blue Mountains** (home of the world-famous coffee) above the city. However, Jamaica's most populated metropolis suffers crime and poverty rates that are much higher than in the tourist areas, handicapping it in the battle for a piece of the tourism pie. Kingston is also the center of political unrest, whenever it occurs—Jamaicans are zealous about their politics.

Rastafarianism is a religion that commands a large following throughout the island. Known for their flowing dreadlocks and sacramental use of marijuana, "Rastas" revere the late Emperor Haile Selassie of Ethiopia. Many are fine artists, and Rastafarians helped popularize reggae, the distinctive national music that is celebrated every summer (usually in July or August) at Reggae Sunsplash, one of the world's premier music festivals.

Whether you're dancing to the rhythm of a reggae band or hiking through a rain forest, the best way to enjoy yourself on the island is to relax and adopt the Jamaicans' unofficial motto: "Don't worry, be happy." Then learn the word *irie* (pronounced *eye-ree*), which means "everything's okay"—and believe it.

area code 876 unless otherwise noted.

Getting to the Island

Airlines

Air Canada.........................924.8211, 800/776.3000

Air Jamaica 952.4300, 800/523.5585

American Airlines......................................952.5950,
......................952.5951, 952.5952, 800/433.7300

Continental.......................952.4460, 800/231.0856

Northwest 952.2803, 800/225.2525

Interisland Carriers

Air Jamaica Express 952.5401, 952.5403

ALM (Antillean Airlines).....926.1762, 800/327.7230

BWIA (British West Indies Airways) International.....
....929.3770, 800/327.7401

Cayman Airlines 926.1762, 800/422.9626

Airports Sir Donald Sangster International Airport (952.3801) should be your choice, unless you're going to Port Antonio. By flying nonstop into this recently upgraded airport in Montego Bay, you won't waste precious beach time sitting on the tarmac in Kingston. **Norman Manley International Airport** (924.8361) is about 20 minutes from downtown Kingston.

Getting Around the Island

Buses A bus ride is an experience many tourists prefer to skip. Jamaican buses are old, uncomfortable, and crowded—with people, luggage, crates of vegetables, and (sometimes) boxes of squawking chickens. There are no local buses for travel within Montego Bay, but buses to Ocho Rios and Kingston leave from Mobay's **Harbour Street Station,** and buses from Montego Bay to Negril depart from the **Creek Street Station** (just east of St. James St). Schedules and information are available at the stations.

Car Rental

In Kingston:

Avis 924.8013, 926.1560, 800/331.1212

Budget 923.8762, 800/626.4516

Island Car...926.8861

National..............................924.8344, 800/328.4567

In Montego Bay:

Avis..952.4543, 800/331.1212

National..............................952.2769, 800/328.4567

United 952.3077

In Negril:

Vernon's Car Rental 957.4354

In Ocho Rios:

Caribbean...974.2123

National..............................974.2266, 800/328.4567

Sunshine...974.2980

In Port Antonio:

Eastern Car Rental 993.3624

Driving Renting a car is a good way to get around if you can handle the rules of the road, including driving on the left, British style. Jamaicans like to get where they are going quickly; they drive fast and will pass you at every opportunity. Driving at night between towns is not a good idea. If the car breaks down, you may well be stuck until morning. Or you may be deluged with well-meaning locals who swear they can fix anything mechanical. The roads are generally good, but they're filled with sharp curves and potholes, and wandering cows, goats, and chickens have the right of way. *Do not* rent a moped or scooter unless you are interested in checking out the island's medical facilities.

Intraisland Flights Air Jamaica Express (952.5401, 952.5403) is the island's main air taxi, with daily flights among four of Jamaica's major towns (Kingston, Montego Bay, Negril, and Port Antonio). The planes range from a small, single-engine puddle jumper to an 18-passenger aircraft; if you're easily unnerved, ask which type of plane is flying before you reserve—or stick to ground transportation.

Taxis Cabs are everything from modern, air-conditioned minibuses to beat-up old station wagons. If airport transfers are not included in your hotel package and you're not going far, take a **Jamaica Union of Travelers Association (JUTA)** cab. The fixed-rate sheet isn't strictly adhered to, so be sure to agree on the fare before getting into the cab. Plan on spending up to US$15 to get from **Sangster International Airport** to the hotels in Montego Bay; trips from the airport to Kingston cost about $20. It will cost about $90 for a taxi ride to Ocho Rios or Negril from Montego Bay, or to Port Antonio from Kingston. For more information, call **JUTA** (952.0813) in Montego Bay.

If you're headed away from Montego Bay, and not in a rush, you can save money by purchasing a seat on a minibus (about US$16) from the **Tourwise** desk (974.2323) just outside **Sangster International Airport**'s luggage area. The only drawback is that the bus won't leave until it's at least half full.

Jamaican cabbies are friendly, patient, and often informative tour guides. Most can be hired for a half-day, with rates running about US$25 an hour.

A number of restaurants in Montego Bay offer free pickup and drop-off cab service; call ahead.

Tours Jamaica's great diversity of landscapes lends itself to an incredible variety of tours. You can raft along a river, ride horseback into the hills, travel by train into the interior, hike the Blue Mountains, take a jitney through a working plantation, or climb a waterfall (see **Dunn's River Falls** on page 179). For a bird's-eye view of the island, contact **Helitours Jamaica Ltd** (974.2265 in Ocho Rios; 929.8150 in Kingston).

Sight-seeing, city, and shopping tours can be arranged through **Blue Danube Tours** (952.0886 in

Montego Bay, 974.2031 in Ocho Rios); **Holiday Service** (974.2948 in Ocho Rios); **Jamaica Tours** (952.2887 in Montego Bay, 974.1673 in Ocho Rios); **JUTA** (993.2684 in Port Antonio); **Tourmarks** (929.5078 in Kingston); and **Tourwise Ltd** (957.4223 in Negril, 952.4943 in Montego Bay).

Special-interest tours that focus on Jamaica's diverse culture, folk art, gardens, plantation houses, and exotic birds are offered by the **Country Style Community Tours** (Mandeville, 962.3725) and **Touring Society of Jamaica** (Strawberry Hill, 944.8400). **South Coast Safaris** (Black River, 965.2513) features photographic safaris, guided boat tours up the **Black River,** and fishing expeditions. **Sense Adventures** (Strawberry Hill, 927.2097) offers individually designed nature tours.

FYI

Electricity The standard current is 110 volts/50 cycles, although the current at some hotels is 220 volts. Where necessary, hotels supply adapters.

Entry Requirements All visitors must present a valid passport or other proof of citizenship (voter's registration card or a birth certificate) plus a laminated photo ID card.

Language The official language is English.

Money The official currency is the Jamaican dollar, but US currency is accepted everywhere. In fact, many stores, restaurants, and cab drivers quote prices in US dollars. Banks are open Monday through Thursday from 9AM to 2PM and Friday from 9AM to noon and 2:30 to 5PM. Some banks are also open Saturday mornings.

Personal Safety Theft is the biggest crime challenge in the tourist areas. In an effort to curb this problem, the government has beefed up its police foot patrols. Always use the same precautions you would at home: Don't wander down dark streets at night and don't leave personal belongings unattended on the beach or packages in open view on the front seat of your car, even if the car is locked. Use the safe deposit box provided at your hotel to store your valuables.

Beware of the young men who insist you need a guide to walk with you around town. They expect a tip. If you feel harassed, remind them you are a tourist and they are giving you a bad impression of their country. This line almost always works, because Jamaicans know how important tourism is to their economy.

Kingston, like most large cities, has a high crime rate. It's best to stay with the crowds while you're walking around. That said, don't miss the nightlife in New Kingston, the city's developing nightlife district, with its many clubs and restaurants. Use the same precautions you would in big cities in the United States like New York or Washington DC and you'll be fine.

Ganja (marijuana) is grown on the island and you're likely to be asked if you want to buy some. Smoking marijuana on the street and in public places is illegal but Jamaican police tend not to target tourists for this kind of arrest, especially in Negril. But expect to be arrested if Jamaican authorities catch you importing or exporting even the smallest amount. Also note: Smoking *ganja* and/or drinking while driving isn't treated lightly, and random traffic stops are not unheard of.

Publications The local newspapers are the *Daily Gleaner,* the *Jamaica Herald,* and the *Star,* all published daily, and the biweekly *Western Mirror.* The day's edition of *The New York Times* is usually available at the hotel newsstands by afternoon.

Free tourist publications include the twice-weekly *Visitor,* the biweekly *Vacationer,* the *Daily Gleaner's* semiannual tourist guide, and the annual pocket magazine, *Jamaica Vacation Guide.* All are available through the tourist office and are distributed at major hotels.

Reservation Services and House Rentals

Fly-Drive Jamaica...............................800/423.4095

Jamaica Alternative Tourism, Camping & Hiking
    Association (JATCHA)...........................927.2097

Jamaica Association of Villas and Apartments (JAVA)
    ....312/883.3485, 800/221.8830, 800/VILLAS6;
    ....fax 312/883.5140

Villas and Apartments Abroad 212/759.1025,
    ....800/433.3020

Taxes A "general consumption tax" of 6.5 percent to 12.5 percent is levied on hotels; often it's already included in the room rate.

Tipping Most hotels and restaurants add a service charge of 10 percent; otherwise, tip waiters 10 to 15 percent and chambermaids US$1 or US$2 per day. Give porters and bellhops 50¢ per bag (but never less than US$1 total) and cab drivers 10 percent of the fare.

Visitors' Information Offices

The main office of the **Jamaica Tourist Board** is at Kingston's **Tourism Centre** (2 St. Lucia Ave, 929.9200, 929.9213; fax 929.9375).

Regional offices are located in Montego Bay (Kent Ave and Sunset Blvd, 952.4425, 952.4428; fax 952.3587); Ocho Rios (Ocean Village Shopping Centre, Main St, off A3, 974.2570, 974.2583; fax 974.2559); Port Antonio (City Centre, Harbour and West Sts, 993.3051, 993.2589; fax 993.2117); Black River (1 High St, 965.2076); and Negril (Adrija Plaza, just south of the traffic circle, 957.4243, 957.4489). All offices are open Monday through Friday from 8:30AM to 4:30PM; the regional offices are also open Saturday from 9AM to 1PM.

The free "Meet the People" program is the best way to experience the real Jamaica. If you're interested in meeting locals as you travel around the island, contact **Hyacinth Ford,** the program founder, at the tourist board in Montego Bay (see above) at least three days in advance.

Negril

On Jamaica's western tip, the resort area of Negril extends from **Negril Lighthouse** in **Westmoreland** to **Bloody Bay** in **Hanover.** Here the white-sand beach, among the world's greatest, stretches for seven miles. Accommodations range from all-inclusive resorts to simple inns, but no building is taller than the palm trees.

1 West End Road Narrow, winding, and part dirt in places, this road is lined with cottages, small hotels, restaurants, and shacks selling T-shirts, straw hats, wooden sculptures, and Rasta berets. Several chicken stands sell jerk-seasoned chicken and pork. It's safe to eat, but watch the hot sauce— even locals refer to it as "hellfire." ♦ Between the Negril Lighthouse and the traffic circle

On West End Road:

Rick's Cafe ★★$$ Drinks and music flow freely at one of Negril's most famous eating spots. The time to see and be seen is about an hour before sunset, when visitors pay homage to the setting ball of fire in a manner that's part pagan, part absurd, and all fun. Young people flaunt their immortality by over-imbibing and jumping from the cliffs into the sea more than a hundred feet below. After the show is over, be sure to try some of the fresh fish and lobster dishes. On Sunday there's a good brunch; a highlight is the Eggs Benedict Caribe, with lobster instead of the usual Canadian bacon. ♦ West Indian/Seafood ♦ M-Sa lunch and dinner; Su brunch, lunch, and dinner. Reservations recommended for dinner. 3 miles south of the traffic circle. 957.4335

Rockhouse $$ One of Negril's oldest hotels, this property has been given a completely new lease on life by new owners, who have expanded it and overseen a major renovation. The result is a moderately priced,

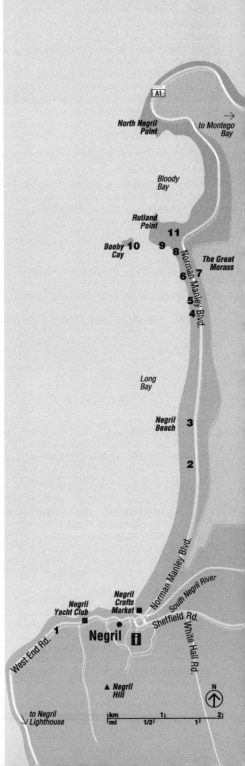

NEGRIL

rustic but stylish hideaway that features stylish architecture, bright colors, and locally crafted furniture. The 28 rooms are set in 12 thatch-roofed octagonal cottages constructed of stone and wood and set amidst tropical foliage on a cliff overlooking the sea. Simple, but comfortable, they offer great views, wraparound terraces, outdoor showers, four-poster beds, ceiling fans, and mini-bars. The property has no beach, but ladders and stairs carved into the rock provide access to the aptly named Pristine Cove and there's also a new, cliffside freshwater pool. A new restaurant/bar with multilevel decks and porches and a Caribbean/continental menu, a pool bar, a shop, and water sports facilities round out the list of amenities. No children under 12 are allowed. ♦ 2.5 miles south of the traffic circle. 957.4373, 212/807.0868 in New York; fax 212/807.0868 in New York

The Hungry Lion ★★★$$ Stop at this casual outdoor restaurant on the cliffs for excellent vegetarian shepherd's pie and steamed kingfish. The juice bar serves delicious natural fruit juices, including such exotic combinations as watermelon/pineapple/papaya—with or without rum. ♦ Caribbean/Seafood ♦ Daily dinner. Reservations recommended. 2 miles south of the traffic circle. 957.4486

2 Charela Inn $$ For those who want to pay as they go, this is a good and reasonably priced alternative to the better-known all-inclusive hotels. Quiet and peaceful, the 49-room property is on the beach and serves excellent French and West Indian fare indoors or around a circular pool set in a garden. Guests enjoy a complimentary sunset cruise. There's also a small gym and a water sports complex for sailing, kayaking, and windsurfing. The family-style hospitality is another plus. ♦ Norman Manley Blvd. 957.4277, 800/423.4095; fax 957.4414

2 Silver Sand ★★★$$ Enjoy great sea views at this indoor/outdoor cafe with a menu that ranges from bacon and eggs to French cuisine to Jamaican fare, with a little of everything in between. If you're feeling adventurous in the morning, try callaloo, green plantains, and salt fish. Lunch specialties include lobster, curried goat, and oxtail. Dinner has a Jamaican/continental/Chinese twist—a Chinese chef ruled the kitchen some years back, and the menu still reflects his influence. The lo mein with oyster sauce and the curried oxtail are two fine examples. ♦ Caribbean/Seafood/Chinese

♦ Daily breakfast, lunch, and dinner. Norman Manley Blvd. 957.4207

FOOTE PRINTS ON THE SANDS HOTEL

3 Foote Prints On The Sands Hotel $$ This 30-room family-owned property was one of the first small hotels in Negril. Popular with German tourists, it has comfortable air-conditioned rooms with TV sets and telephones, a bar/restaurant, and a beach water-sports area. Kids under 12 stay free. ♦ Norman Manley Blvd. 957.4300; fax 957.4301

Within Foote Prints On The Sands Hotel:

Robinson Crusoe's ★★$$$ Try the lobster thermidor at this stylish and relaxed place known for great seafood. Drop in on Tuesday for the Jamaican buffet or Friday for the beach barbecue; both feature live entertainment. ♦ Caribbean/Seafood ♦ Daily breakfast, lunch, and dinner. 957.4300

4 Swept Away $$$ This impressive all-inclusive couples-only oasis is geared toward fitness-and-health enthusiasts. The big draw here is a 10-acre sports complex, with 10 tennis courts (clay, hard, and stadium), air-conditioned squash and racquetball courts, a state-of-the-art gym, a basketball court, and an outdoor running track. Free, half-hour individual lessons in all the sports are offered daily by resident pros. A water-sports shack on the beach offers snorkeling, sailing, and windsurfing equipment and instruction. There's also scuba diving (two tank dives are included in the rate), a pool, and a spa.

The property is divided by Negril's main road, with the sports complex on one side and accommodations and the main body of the resort on the beach side. The 134 veranda suites are tastefully minimalist in decor, with screened, wood-louvered walls, king-sized beds, terra-cotta tiles, and showers big enough for two. The enormous verandas double as sitting, breakfast, and sunning rooms. There are neither TV sets nor radios, but a television room is available for those who need a fix.

Both restaurants, as well as the beachside veggie-bar, feature health-oriented cuisine, with an emphasis on homemade pasta, fresh seafood, poultry, and Jamaican dishes. Four bars serve liquor, others pour fresh carrot and fruit juices. There is live entertainment nightly ♦ Norman Manley Blvd. 957.4061, 800/545.7937; fax 957.4060

5 Beaches Negril $$$ Owned by the folks who brought you the Sandals properties, this is a variation on the Sandals theme—an all-inclusive resort catering to families and singles as well as couples. An Italianate marble entranceway and lobby hint at the upscale decor that awaits in the 225 guest rooms and suites. There are plenty of pluses for those traveling with kids. The 2-bedroom beachfront junior suites are ideal for families, and the **Kids Camp** program is super, with activities to keep everyone from newborns to 16-year-olds entertained. There are also special early-evening kids' meals and a video games center (a real hot spot among the younger set). After-hours baby-sitting is available at a nominal charge. Adults can keep themselves amused at the resort's two pools, fitness center, complete water-sports facility, five restaurants, four bars, and disco. ◆ Norman Manley Blvd. 957.9270, 800/BEACHES; fax 957.9269

6 Poinciana Beach Hotel $$$ The 130 rooms, suites, studios, and villas at this elegant all-inclusive resort are airy and tropical, with tile floors and local art. A program for children ages 3 to 12 offers supervised activities at the **Kiddie's Play House** and playground, while parents lounge at the two pools, get massaged at the spa, play tennis on a lighted court, enjoy water sports, or work out in the gym, open around-the-clock. There are three restaurants, including the **Captain's Table** with an international and West Indian menu and buffets five days a week. **The Upper Deck** offers late-night snacks. ◆ Norman Manley Blvd. 957.5100, 957.5256, 800/468.6728; fax 957.5229, 305/749.6794

7 Anancy Mini-golf, rides, a culture center, and a nature trail attract crowds to this family amusement park. Jamaican Garfield Munroe built this attraction just across the road from his **Poinciana Beach Hotel** (see above). "Anancy" is the name of a mystical, mischievous spider from Jamaican folk tales. ◆ Admission. Daily. Norman Manley Blvd. 957.4100, 800/468.6728; fax 957.4229

8 Sandals Negril Beach Resort $$$ Still the most romantic all-inclusive property in Negril, this couples-only resort is set amidst lush foliage on 1,800 feet of luscious private beach shaded by palm trees under which hammocks swing.

The 215 rooms are spacious and decorated in soothing tropical colors; the bi-level suites are the most spectacular. Jacuzzis (just right for two) are located on the beach, surrounded by high hedges. Reggae and jazz fill the air in the public areas (piped through speakers that look like rocks) as the setting sun turns the sky aflame with color. Casual dress is the byword here.

There are four restaurants, including one that serves light, low-calorie cuisine. Sing-alongs around the piano bar follow the nightly cabaret shows, but the real emphasis here is on water sports. Waterskiing, snorkeling, scuba diving, sailing, and windsurfing are included in the package, as are glass-bottom boat tours and the use of Hobie Cats and aquatrikes built for two. Other facilities include four tennis courts, three pools (one is used for scuba training), a health club, a spa, and a special croquet lawn. Organized exercise classes are part of the daily schedule of activities. There's also an offshore island for clothing-optional sunbathing. Guests have full exchange privileges at all other Sandals resorts in Jamaica. ◆ Norman Manley Blvd. 957.5216, 800/726.3257; fax 957.5338

9 Hedonism II $$$ This haven on a private stretch of sand on Long Bay's five-mile beach is true to its name. The 280-room resort is Jamaica's answer to Club Med, but better executed. Almost anything goes at this free and easy, upscale sleepaway camp for adults only. Meals are mostly buffet style, and the action continues around the clock. The beach is divided into nude and prude, with each section equipped with its own bar. The disco hops 'til the wee hours—it closes only when the last person calls it a night. Almost all land and water sports (except golf and horseback riding) are included; there's even a circus workshop. ◆ Rutland Point, Long Bay. 957.5200, 800/869.SUPER; fax 957.5289

10 Booby Cay Take a kayak or motor launch over to this small offshore island popular with snorkelers and nude sunbathers. Several higglers (the local name for vendors) have set up shop beneath the thatch-roofed huts. There are no food stands, however; most visitors bring picnic lunches. Butterflies dance and flit over the verdant foliage, and bathers disperse to find their own private patch of sand. Several scenes from *Twenty Thousand Leagues Under the Sea* were filmed here. ◆ Southwest of Rutland Point

Local wood carvers are a common sight along Jamaica's roadsides and at island craft markets. Buyers should examine works carefully for balance and materials. If green wood was used, the carving will split, and worms can be detected by minute holes.

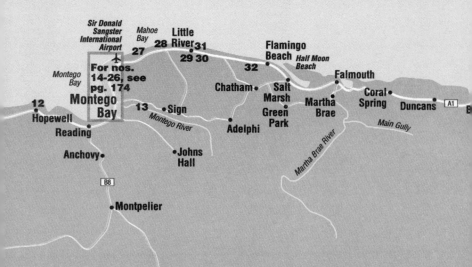

Caribbean Sea

Sir Donald Sangster International Airport
Mahoe Bay
Little River
27 28 29 30 31
Montego Bay
For nos. 14-26, see pg. 174
Montego Bay
12 Hopewell
Reading
Anchovy
13 Sign
Montego River
Johns Hall
Adelphi
Chatham
32
Salt Marsh
Green Park
Flamingo Beach
Half Moon Beach
Martha Brae
Falmouth
Coral Spring
Duncans
A1
Main Gully
Martha Brae River
B8
Montpelier

GRAND LIDO

11 Grand Lido $$$$ Here is the only hotel on Bloody Bay, which is lined by a two-mile unspoiled crescent of sand backed by an impressive strand of palm and sea-grape trees. (Try to ignore the bay's unpleasant name, which dates from the long-ago days when whalers butchered their catch in these waters.)

A branch of the SuperClubs chain, the resort is geared toward professionals age 30 and up seeking a stress-free escape, with a 1-price-covers-all policy and an emphasis on pampering. Accommodations are in 200 bi-level junior suites in 2-story Mexican-style buildings stretched along the beach. Each has a terrace or patio and a sunlit living room area with a TV and CD player. Guests have their choice of one king-size or two double beds (make the request in advance). A large yacht, formerly owned by Prince Rainier of Monaco, sits at anchor in the bay. It is available for sunset cruises and weddings (marriage ceremonies are free for guests).

The crowd is international, and everything at this 200-suite resort is top-shelf, from the liquor to the white-gloved waiters at the gourmet restaurant. Smart casual dress is the norm, although men are required to wear jackets at **Piacere,** one of the three restaurants. The kitchen never closes, and

room service is available around the clock (late nights are standard here). Other amenities include two pools, five Jacuzzis, four tennis courts, a complete water-sports facility, a state-of-the-art fitness center, a plush video theater, a beauty salon, a disco, and nine well-placed bars. There's a private clothing-optional beach, but it's in an area where the sea can be choppy.

The only drawback is that some units are rather close to the water-treatment plant across the road and, depending on the direction of the wind, the smell can be decidedly downscale. On the plus side, the service is good and, since the property is spread out, there is never a feeling of being part of a crowd. No guests under age 16 are allowed. ♦ Rutland Point, Bloody Bay. 957.4013, 957.5010, 800/859.7873; fax 957.4317

Montego Bay and Environs

Jamaica's second-largest city, and the capital of **St. James Parish,** Montego Bay is home to over 30,000 people. It's been a vacation resort since the turn of the century; visitors originally came here to bathe in the "medicinal" waters at **Doctor's Cave.** Today Mobay boasts the island's biggest concentration of hotels and restaurants, four championship golf courses, numerous tennis courts, and other tourist attractions.

12 Round Hill $$$$ This chic resort has attracted a crowd of socialites, movie stars, and jet-setters since it opened in 1953. Ralph Lauren (owner of two of the property's villas)

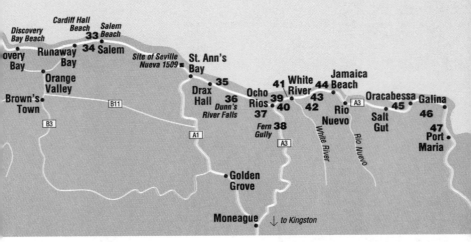

designed some of the fabrics used in the decor. Surrounded by a pineapple and coconut plantation, the elegant complex encompasses the 36 rooms (decorated with mahogany antiques) in **Pineapple House** and 26 privately owned villas, each containing 2 to 4 suites with separate entrances and living areas. Guests enjoy a large seaside swimming pool (22 of the villas have their own pools), a private beach, water sports facilities, a health spa, 5 tennis courts, and golf privileges at nearby courses. There are three restaurants and a bar on the premises. ♦ Hopewell. 956.7050, 800/972.2159; fax 956.7505

13 Julia's ★★★$$$ Splurge at this romantic enclave high in the hills overlooking the bay. The excellent Italian fare, continental ambience, and spectacular view from the terrace make for a three-way winner. Prix-fixe six-course dinners share the menu with such à la carte favorites as homemade pasta, chicken cacciatore, and red snapper *française*, prepared in lemon butter with a light tomato sauce. The lasagna alla Julia, made with homemade pasta, spicy meat sauce, and several cheeses, is mouthwatering. The restaurant offers diners free transportation to and from their hotels; take them up on it, as this place can be tricky to find. ♦ Italian ♦ Daily lunch and dinner. Reservations required for dinner. East of Rte A1. 952.1772

14 Appleton Express This popular all-inclusive, daylong bus tour through Jamaica's heartland used to be a train ride, but with Jamaican rails no longer in operation, motor coaches have been put into use. Historical trivia can be heard over a loudspeaker as the bus moves up into the hills, and free rum drinks are poured throughout the ride. Don't miss the stop in Catadupa, where children will greet you, their arms laden with wooden birds and straw place mats. The adults follow with bolts of brightly patterned cotton and polyester and samples of clothing that can be sewn to your measurements by the time the bus returns late in the afternoon. Bring along a dress or shirt you like, pick out some cloth, and let the skilled seamstresses and tailors duplicate it.

A few drinks later, the bus stops at **Ipswich Caves,** where there's an awe-inspiring limestone "cathedral" complete with formations that look like monks at prayer. Hawkers line the path leading to the caves, a good place to bargain. Lunch (a generous helping of curried goat, barbecued chicken, callaloo, jerk pork, and peas and rice) is served in the rum-tasting lounge of the **Appleton Sugar Factory and Distillery.** A tour of the facility, where rum and sugar have been produced since 1749, follows. The famous Appleton Rums are sold here, although the airport's duty-free liquor store may have better prices. Pickups can be arranged from any hotel in Negril, Montego Bay, and Ocho Rios. ♦ Fee. Daily. Reservations required (make them well in advance). Railway La (west of Catherine La). 979.9387, 963.2210

Restaurants/Clubs: Red   Hotels: Blue
Shops/♥ Outdoors: Green   **Sights/Culture:** Black

173

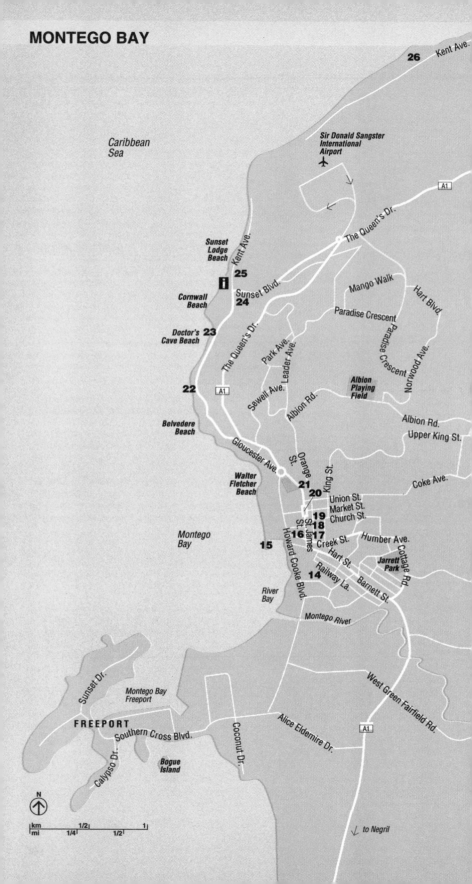

15 Pier 1 ★★$$ Popular with businesspeople, tourists, and yachting folk, this casual waterfront restaurant is a good place to sip a tropical drink. Choice dishes include snapper broiled in lemon butter with a white wine sauce, spicy chicken, and stewed beef and pork. Lunch is served on the outside deck, dinner is upstairs overlooking the marina. Late Friday nights, this is the hottest spot in town, with dancing and music on the pier deck until dawn. A superb brunch is the lure on Sunday. Free transportation is arranged for diners. ♦ Seafood/West Indian ♦ M-Sa lunch and dinner; Su brunch and dinner. Reservations recommended for dinner. West of Howard Cooke Blvd. 952.2452

16 Craft and Straw Market Rows of narrow stalls overflow with straw baskets, place mats, hats, and coasters as well as T-shirts, swimsuit cover-ups, children's clothing, wooden carvings, dolls, and shell jewelry. The market bustles with shoppers and hagglers. The hawkers are crafty; they view the bargaining process as a game and are unlikely to sell you an item below the price they have in mind. Be firm—if you mean "no," say so. ♦ Daily. Harbour and Creek Sts. No phone

17 St. James Parish Church Built in 1775 to resemble a Greek cross, this Anglican edifice was badly damaged by an earthquake in 1957. It has since been restored and is one of Jamaica's most impressive places of worship. The interior is open to the public only on Sunday, but the exterior architecture is of interest. ♦ Su. Payne St (between Creek and Church Sts). 952.2775

18 Town House ★★$$$ This 1765 landmark has been home to an island governor's mistress and a synagogue. Queen Victoria slept here when she toured Jamaica. Today it's a very popular restaurant, where specialties include red snapper *en papillote* (baked in parchment paper), stuffed lobster, and excellent lobster appetizers. In fair weather, ask to sit outside. ♦ Continental/West Indian ♦ Daily lunch and dinner. Reservations recommended. 16 Church St (between Payne and Orange Sts). 952.2660

19 Gallery of West Indian Art Load up on unique gifts at this small gallery. Owner Liz Delisser has collected the island's best hand-carved, hand-painted art. Cedar animals painted in bright colors and whimsical patterns greet shoppers. Purple-whiskered lions share space with red polka-dotted parrots. The walls mimic this carnival of color with canvases from top Jamaican and Haitian artists. The prices are reasonable. ♦ M-Sa. 1 Orange St (at Church St). 952.4547

20 Sam Sharpe Square Slave and part-time preacher Sam "Daddy" Sharpe is credited with starting the slave uprising known as the Christmas Rebellion of 1831. Sharpe's last words before he was hanged were "I would rather die on yonder gallows than live as a slave." The revolution, albeit short-lived and bloody, started a chain of events that ended seven years later with the abolition of slavery in Jamaica. In the northeast corner of the square is a tableau of five bronze statues showing Sharpe preaching to a group of followers. Formerly called **The Parade**, the square serves as a popular meeting spot. ♦ St. James and Fort Sts

On Sam Sharpe Square:

The Cage Constructed in 1806, this building once held runaway slaves. Today it is a ticket office for local music, theater, and other cultural events, and the bars have been replaced by windows.

21 Jenny's Citimart Here's the spot to stock up on flavorful sauces and condiments to season your food back home. Try the Pickapepper, Hot Pepper, Scott's Jerk, or Gray's Spicy sauces. Also look for marmalades, Blue Mountain coffee, pimento liquor (used for marinating meat), and Busha Browne's spicy love-apple sauce. ♦ M-Sa. CitiCenter Shopping Centre, Fort St (just north of North St). 952.3313

22 Pelican Grill ★★$$ This restaurant is one of Mobay's most popular spots. Businessfolk crowd in around noon; tourists and locals arrive for dinner. Jamaican favorites like curried goat and escovitched fish (flavored, then sautéed with vegetables and sauce) share the menu with such American staples as cheeseburgers and milk shakes. The adjacent **Pelican Cascade Room** is a bit more expensive, but the seafood and plush atmosphere are well worth it. ♦ West Indian/American ♦ Pelican Grill: Daily breakfast, lunch, and dinner. Pelican Cascade Room: Daily dinner. Reservations recommended for the Pelican Cascade Room. Gloucester Ave (between Rte A1 and Kent Ave). 952.3171

Marguerites
Seafood by the Sea

22 Marguerites ★★★$$$ The hills across the bay from this lovely eatery twinkle with lights, while the water laps at the terrace, where dining is beneath the fronds of an almond tree and a canopy of Caribbean stars. A sophisticated menu features the best smoked marlin appetizer in town, a tangy shellfish seviche, deep-fried Caribbean lobster, and "Tijuana Shrimp" (in a tequila cream sauce over pasta). A trio of musicians performs after 8PM. Free transportation to and from most hotels is provided for guests.

♦ Caribbean ♦ Daily dinner. Reservations recommended. Gloucester Ave (between Rte A1 and Kent Ave). 952.4777, 979.3197

Caribbean Bar and Grill

22 Margueritaville ★★$ Burgers, pizza, and fajitas, along with specialty cocktails, are the standard fare at this raucously popular spot. Entertainment is provided by a large-screen TV, a 110-foot water slide, and (on Sunday) a reggae band. ♦ International ♦ Daily lunch and dinner. Gloucester Ave (between Rte A1 and Kent Ave). 952.4777, 979.3197. Also at: Norman Manley Blvd, Negril. 957.4467

23 Doctor's Cave Beach Mobay's most famous stretch of sand was once owned by Dr. Alexander McCatty, who helped promote the curative powers of seawater. He donated the beach to the town as a bathing club in 1906. It's now open to the public and popular with local families as well as tourists from the hotels across the street. The crystal-clear sea is both pleasant and placid. There are changing rooms, a snack bar, and a beach bar. The popularity of this spot prompted local tourism officials to develop the adjacent 300-yard Cornwall Beach. ♦ Admission. Daily. Gloucester Ave (between Rte A1 and Kent Ave)

24 Pork Pit ★$ Easy on the wallet, this shaded outdoor restaurant is a good place to try a typical Jamaican lunch—you'll vie for space with local office workers and tourists. Munch on spicy jerk pork or jerk chicken with sweet potatoes and rolls, and wash it all down with a Red Stripe beer. ♦ Jamaican ♦ Daily lunch and dinner. No credit cards accepted. Gloucester and Kent Aves. 952.1046

25 Sandals Inn $$ This all-inclusive, couples-only resort is tailored for twosomes on a somewhat restricted budget who like the intimacy of a small hotel and don't mind the lack of a private beach on site. The motel-like main building has a comfortable, tropical ambience; it offers 52 rooms (some with terraces), 2 restaurants, room service, 2 bars, and a small fitness center. The grounds are compact, but there is a pool, a tennis court, and a volleyball court. There's a small public beach across the road, and Doctor's Cave Beach is a short walk away. Guests can take the complimentary shuttle over to nearby **Sandals Montego Bay** and **Sandals Royal Jamaican,** where they can enjoy the private beaches, use the water-sports facilities (including scuba diving, windsurfing, and water skiing), and eat and drink at the

restaurants and bars at no additional charge. The only distinction between the premium a deluxe rooms is the view—ask for a room above the first floor. ♦ Kent Ave (north of Sunset Blvd). 952.4140, 800/726.3257; fax 952.6913

26 Sandals Montego Bay $$$ The original Sandals couples-only, all-inclusive resort, this place is in need of a bit of a face-lift. Nonetheless, the 243-room resort continues to attract a young and active crowd. The rooms offer mahogany four-poster beds, air conditioning, ceiling fans, and hair dryers. Also on the premises are three restaurants (Jamaican, Italian, and Asian), a disco, a late-night piano bar (where everyone gets to sing along), a swim-up pool bar, and a first-rate fitness club that's open around the clock. Water sports are emphasized here, and the beach is the largest private stretch of sand in Montego Bay. There's also nightly entertainment followed by dancing. (Escapis can retreat to one of several secluded hammocks built for two.) Another drawback the resort's proximity to the airport—those with sensitive ears, beware. ♦ Kent Ave (wes of Rte A1). 952.5510, 800/726.3257; fax 952.0816

Between Montego Bay and Ocho Rios

27 Sandals Royal Jamaican $$$ A European atmosphere and an international crowd distinguish this all-inclusive, 190-roo resort. It's more laid-back than **Sandals Montego Bay** and geared to couples seeking an elegant, sporty getaway. The genteel setting is lavish, with well-tended gardens, a generous crescent of beach, and peacocks that stroll onto your terrace. The nicest, mos sumptuous accommodations are the 55 honeymoon beachfront and royal suites.

Meals are sumptuous feasts. There are two restaurants, one serving grilled food and the other featuring Indonesian cuisine. Buffets a held twice weekly, with dining available unde the stars by the pool or on the beach. Guests can get a workout at the fitness center or on the walking/fitness trail, and then relax in on of the five Jacuzzis or four swimming pools (two with swim-up bars). A private island wi a swimming pool offers clothing-optional sunbathing and swimming. Golf at the nearb **Ironshore Golf and Country Club** or the **Half Moon Golf, Tennis and Beach Club** is also included in the rate. ♦ Rte A1, Mahoe Bay. 953.2231, 953.2788, 956.5673, 800/726.3257

28 Holiday Inn Sunspree $$$ This 520-roo hotel is the worldwide chain's first all-inclusive resort. It's especially popular with families, singles, and corporate-incentive or convention groups who want a lot to do. The nonstop program of activities ranges from limbo contests to crab races. The children's program keeps kids of all ages happy while their parents relax on the beach. Other features include four lighted tennis courts, nightly entertainment, a lagoon-style pool, a fitness center, and a complete water-sports center. Three restaurants offer a range of dining options, and there's a shopping complex just across the street. ♦ Rte A1 (between Little River and Mahoe Bay). 953.2485, 953.2486, 800/352.0731; fax 953.2840

29 Half Moon Golf, Tennis and Beach Club
$$$$ Peace and quiet reign, and classic elegance awaits guests at this sprawling country club–like resort with 418 units. A getaway for royalty, politicians, and celebrities, it offers several types of ultra-luxurious accommodations, including spacious beachfront royal suites, one-bedroom villas complete with a cook, and five-to seven-bedroom villas that are staffed with a cook and a butler and feature wide terraces, enormous bathrooms, kitchens with stocked refrigerators, and a tasteful mixture of Old World and modern decor. The resort has 3 restaurants (including the excellent **Sugar Mill**), a beautiful beach, 2 main pools, 17 semiprivate pools shared among the villas, 4 squash courts, a spa and sauna, a

comprehensive water-sports center, and 13 tennis courts (7 lighted). Of special note is the 18-hole Robert Trent Jones Sr. championship golf course and clubhouse. Evenings are dressy here, especially in winter. ♦ Rte A1, Little River. 953.2615, 800/237.3237; fax 953.2731

30 Rose Hall Reputedly haunted by its husband-murdering mistress, this restored great house on sprawling grounds looks out to the Caribbean Sea. According to the tale, John Rose Palmer inherited the mansion and in 1820 brought his wife, Anne, here to live. Anne purportedly dabbled in black magic, poisoned her husband, tortured and bedded her slaves, and became feared as the White Witch of Rose Hall. At the age of 29, she was strangled to death, supposedly by a slave lover, and it is said her ghost still haunts the house. After your visit, sip a Witch's Brew in **Annie's Pub** (formerly the dungeons). ♦ Admission. Daily. South of Rte A1, Little River. 953.2323

31 Wyndham Rose Hall Beach Club $$$ This gorgeous property is a splashy complex of 489 rooms and 36 suites that offers an 18-hole championship golf course, 13 tennis courts (9 lighted) and a resident pro, water sports, 3 linked swimming pools, and a gameroom with slot machines. All-inclusive packages are available, and diners may choose among five restaurants. There's late-night dancing at the **Junkanoo** disco. ♦ Rte A1, Little River. 953.2650, 800/WYNDHAM; fax 953.2617

Rose Hall

River Rafting

Thanks to the imagination of actor Errol Flynn, who lived in **Port Antonio,** river rafting has become a popular pastime on Jamaica. Flynn saw the sleek bamboo rafts carrying produce downriver and envisioned both a fun sport and a romantic excursion. Some say Flynn took two raft trips a day, each with a different woman.

Today, visitors can float down Jamaica's rivers on 26-foot rafts that are built for two and are steered and poled like a gondola by a skilled "captain." The rafts drift toward the sea, passing cars backed into the river for washing, cavorting children, and hawkers selling fresh coconut juice. Passengers can swim from the raft, eat a picnic lunch, be regaled by the captain's tales, or just hold hands and enjoy the scenery.

The best and longest rafting excursions are on the **Rio Grande.** The two-and-a-half-hour trip run by **Rafting on the Rio Grande** (993.2778) begins at **Rafter's Rest** in **St. Margaret's Bay,** 15 minutes west of Port Antonio. Near **Montego Bay, Rafter's Village** (952.0889) offers a one-hour trip aboard the *Martha Brae.* **Mountain Valley Rafting** (952.0527) runs a one-hour tour of the **Great River,** south of Montego Bay, which wends its way through the mountainous interior, ending at a recreation area where there are hammocks and complimentary donkey rides for kids. **Mountain Valley** also offers a torch-lit night rafting excursion called "An Evening on the Great River"; the trip ends at a re-created Arawak Indian village where participants are served dinner and drinks while being entertained by fire-eaters and a steel band.

32 Greenwood Great House and Antique Museum Sugar baron Sir Richard Barrett, a cousin of the English poet Elizabeth Barrett Browning, built this plantation house in 1790. Among the antiques now displayed here are an inlaid rosewood piano and a mantrap used for catching runaway slaves. The museum's collection also includes the Barrett family's library, with books that date back to 1697.
♦ Admission. Daily. Rte A1 (between Flamingo Beach and Little River). 953.1077

33 Breezes Golf and Beach Resort Runaway Bay $$$ Formerly **Jamaica Jamaica,** this all-inclusive SuperClubs resort prides itself on offering guests an immersion into all things Jamaican. The emphasis is on sports, entertainment, and social interaction—which may explain why the resort attracts so many single guests. The 234 rooms and 4 suites are comfortable, with TV sets, CD players, and coffeemakers. The beach is wide and inviting—heaven for sports enthusiasts. One section is designated for nude sunbathing. The resort's **Golf Academy** is an intensive program with professional instruction, video presentations, swing analysis, lectures, daily play at the nearby 72-par **SuperClubs Golf Club**, and practice at the on-site putting and driving ranges. Tennis buffs receive equal attention, with one-on-one instruction, video analysis, and four lighted courts. Activities are wide-ranging, including relaxing horse-and-buggy jaunts, scuba diving, and trampoline and trapeze clinics. Meals emphasize Jamaican cuisine. Children under 16 are not allowed. ♦ Rte A1, Cardiff Hall Beach. 973.2436, 973.2437, 973.2438, 800/GO.SUPER; fax 973.2352

34 FDR Resort $$ Also known as "Franklin D. Resort," this upscale all-inclusive property is one of the top places on the island for families. Suite accommodations range from one to three bedrooms, all with a master bedroom, kitchen, and living room with a sofa bed. Included in the package are the services of a maid who arrives at 9AM, leaves at 4:30PM, and acts as a nanny, cook, housekeeper, and kitchen stocker. For a slight charge, she'll baby-sit in the evenings.

The daily program for children and teens runs the gamut from arts and crafts to volleyball and donkey rides. There's even a petting zoo, a playground, and a mini-club with video games. The Mediterranean villa–style hotel also offers two restaurants and a beach grill, several bars, a lighted tennis court, a pool, a fitness center, a piano bar, and a discotheque. There's no beach, but it's only a short walk to the public sands across the street.

Rates include maid service, all meals, airport transfers, a glass-bottom boat tour, a shopping trip to nearby Ocho Rios, land and water sports (including scuba diving), and nightly entertainment. Children under 16 stay free in their parents' suite. ♦ Rte A1 (between Salem and Runaway Bay). 973.3067, 800/654.1337; fax 973.3071

Ocho Rios and Environs

A former banana port, Ocho Rios (Eight Rivers) is still lush with fruit trees and tropical gardens. Located at the center of Jamaica's long northern coast, the area is known for its waterfalls, working plantations, beaches, and elegant small resorts. It's also the favored jumping-off point for excursions to such natural attractions as **Dunn's River Falls** and **Fern Gully.**

35 Sandals Dunn's River $$$ The ritziest Sandals resort has an Italian Renaissance decor, with an open-air lobby that flows onto a piazza shaded by almond trees. The 256 rooms are elegantly decorated and offer mini-bars and other extras. A highlight is the ultramodern spa/fitness center, open to sea

breezes, with massage rooms, saunas and steam rooms for two, and a Roman-style hot tub and cold plunge pool. Although the resort is on the beach, guests tend to loll around the two pools, especially the huge, free-form main pool with a swim-up bar and waterfall. There are four restaurants (Asian, continental, Jamaican, and Italian) and five bars. Like other Sandals resorts, this property is for couples only, and the all-inclusive rate covers meals, drinks, sports, and activities, with a tour of Dunn's River Falls thrown in for good measure. ♦ Rte A3, Drax Hall. 972.1610, 800/726.3257; fax 972.1611

36 Dunn's River Falls These famous falls are featured in virtually all the Jamaican ads and brochures. They're a must-see attraction, for where else can you literally climb up a 600-foot-high waterfall and return with photographs to prove it? This get-wet experience (there's no escaping the water) calls for old sneakers or scuba boots. Guides lead groups of people safely up the falls. Almost any guide is glad to hang your camera around his or her neck, take your picture under the falls, and show you the placid pools and sliding rapids. Just be sure to give your guide a US dollar or two, per person, as a tip. ♦ Admission. Daily. Rte A3 (between Ocho Rios and Drax Hall). 974.2857

37 Shaw Park Botanical Gardens Tranquillity—and usually not many tourists—can be found in these tropical gardens, located on a ridge in the hills overlooking Ocho Rios Bay. Roam past a tumbling waterfall, whispering streams, giant banyan trees, and ponds covered with water lilies to reach gardens filled with flamboyant chenille plants, bougainvillea trees, and hibiscus. Exotic flowers such as the bird of paradise and torch ginger also color the 25-acre grounds. ♦ Admission. Daily. Milford Rd (south of Rte A3), Ocho Rios. 974.2723

Within Shaw Park Botanical Gardens:

Coyaba River Garden and Museum *Coyaba* means "paradise" in Arawak. This verdant showcase is filled with pre-Columbian artifacts, as well as unique displays tracing island history from Spanish colonization, through pirates and plantations, to Bob Marley and Marcus Garvey. ♦ Admission. Daily. 974.6235

THE ENCHANTED

37 The Enchanted Garden $$$ Years ago Jamaica's then–prime minister, Edward Seaga, developed the grounds of his family estate as a 20-acre botanical paradise filled with orchids, ferns, palm trees, and 14 waterfalls, and opened it to the public. Now the estate has been turned into this all-inclusive hillside retreat that attracts both singles and couples (children under 16 are not allowed). The 113 suites are modern oases of comfort; 40 even boast private plunge pools. A fully equipped spa offers massages, facials, manicures, pedicures, and other beauty and health treatments. There are two tennis courts and two pools on the grounds, and horseback riding can be arranged for an additional fee. Hidden gardens, private hammocks overlooking gurgling falls, and an aviary filled with tropical birds help this hotel live up to its name.

Five restaurants serve specialties ranging from Italian to French to Lebanese to Thai, and the **Seaquarium,** a combination gameroom, bar, and breakfast room, serves drinks and spa cuisine against a backdrop of 15 fish-filled tanks.

The one-price-covers-all policy includes meals, wine, bar drinks, nightly entertainment, tennis, greens fees (and transportation to the golf course), taxes, tips, and airport transfers. You can even get married in the garden for free. ◆ Eden Bower Rd (south of Rte A3), Ocho Rios. 974.1400, 800/554.2008, 800/847.2535; fax 974.5823

37 Evita's ★★★★$$ Northern Italian cuisine is accompanied by a spectacular view from the terrace of this authentic 1860 gingerbread house nestled on the hillside overlooking Ocho Rios Bay. Good service, consistent quality, and fine fare—both creative dishes and traditional favorites—make this place a winner. Try the fettuccine Carib-Alfredo (with seafood in a light white wine and cream sauce), *rigatoni ai frutti di mare* (pasta with seafood in a light red sauce), the Rastafarian lasagna (made with ackee and callaloo), or the snapper stuffed with crabmeat. Children under 12 eat for half price. Eva, for whom the restaurant is named, is from Venice and can converse with diners in English, Italian, French, German, and Spanish. Her gracious hospitality makes dining here truly special. ◆ Italian/Seafood ◆ Daily lunch and dinner. Reservations recommended for dinner. Mantalent Inn, Eden Bower Rd (south of Rte A3), Ocho Rios. 974.2333

38 Fern Gully Nature has turned this old stretch of riverbed into a tunnel, with a roof made from the interlocking leaves and branches of tall trees and 600 types of ferns. The riverbed is

now part of the road leading from Ocho Rios to Kingston, so if you're driving to the capital, your car will be immersed in a cool green world for three miles. ◆ Rte A3 (south of Ocho Rios)

39 Jamaica Grande, A Renaissance Resort $$$ This all-inclusive property geared toward families is Jamaica's largest, with 720 rooms and suites. It also has the most extensive convention and meeting facilities on the island. Here you'll find a water-sports center, four lighted tennis courts, a pool complex with a waterfall and swim-through grottoes, a health club, five restaurants (including the **Cafe Jamaique** bistro and **Mallards Court** buffet), eight nightclubs and bars (including **Jamaican Me Crazy,** see below), nightly entertainment, and several shops. A supervised program for kids and a full schedule of activities for adults keep everyone busy and happy. ◆ Main St (off Rte A3), Ocho Rios. 974.5378, 800/HOTELS-7; fax 974.5378, 974.2289

Within the Jamaica Grande:

Jamaican Me Crazy Both locals and tourists can be found on this club's high-energy, jungle-motif dance floor. Everyone boogies, and you don't need a partner to show off your moves. There's a steep cover charge ($30 at press time) for those not staying at the resort, but it includes unlimited beverages. ◆ Cover for nonguests. M-Sa. 974.5378

39 Double V Jerk Pork Centre ★★$ Step around the side of this friendly roadside diner to see how the seasoned meat is cooked on racks of allspice wood. The portions are hefty, easy on the wallet, and come with roasted yams and a sweet roll. Without a doubt, this place serves some of the best jerk pork and jerk chicken in Ocho Rios. ◆ Jamaican ◆ Daily 24 hours. 109 Main St (off Rte A3), Ocho Rios. 974.2084

39 Hibiscus Lodge $$ An oasis of simplicity, this relaxed oceanfront hotel offers 26 basic fan-cooled rooms (only 9 have air-conditioning), a pool, a tennis court, and a congenial open-air bar. A private beach and a golf course are nearby. ◆ Rte A3 (just east of Ocho Rios). 974.2676, 800/JAMAICA; fax 974.1874

Within the Hibiscus Lodge:

The Almond Tree ★★$$ This patio restaurant on the gingerbread-trimmed back veranda of the **Hibiscus Lodge** attracts locals and visitors alike with great views and outstanding food. There's fine West Indian fare, including tasty pepper pot and pumpkin soup, along with continental-style dishes such as "lobster Almond Tree" (in a white wine and cream sauce). Don't miss the fresh fish sautéed with onions and island fruit.
♦ Caribbean ♦ Daily lunch and dinner. Reservations recommended. 974.2813

39 Sandals Ocho Rios Resort and Golf Club $$$ Babbling brooks and manicured gardens interlace the grounds of this 237-room, all-inclusive, couples-only resort, where white-washed buildings are linked by lighted and landscaped walkways and hammocks are strung between the palm trees. Music flows over the massive courtyard from ground speakers, and somehow the whole resort seems in tune with the romantic and serene orchestration. There are four restaurants, offering Southwestern, Italian, and Caribbean cuisine, plus a beach grill and a seaside bar that transforms into **Jamie's** disco after dark. A differend show is staged each evening, and there are several theme parties, including Pirates and Wenches Night, when guests are encouraged to wear fun costumes. Three freshwater pools complement the beach; guests can also avail themselves of a fitness center, two whirlpools, two tennis courts, and a roster of water sports. An 18-hole golf course is an added attraction, with greens fees included in the rate. Every couple also receives a complimentary tour of nearby Dunn's River Falls. Honeymoon rooms on the concierge level include a stocked in-room bar and other upgraded amenities. ♦ Rte A3 (between White River and Ocho Rios). 974.5691, 800/SANDALS; fax 974.2544, 974.5700

40 Ciboney Spa and Beach Resort $$$$ Nestled in the hills overlooking the sea, the 289 rooms and villas of this ambitious all-inclusive resort provide a blend of privacy and pampering in a luxurious atmosphere. Guests, particularly those staying in the villas, are treated like visiting royalty. Even the standard rooms have such upscale amenities as stocked refrigerators, while each villa has an attendant who will unpack bags, iron clothes, prepare and serve breakfast, stock the bar and refrigerator, and even have cold drinks and a fruit platter waiting after your afternoon set of tennis. The modern villas feature spacious bathrooms, living rooms with remote-control TVs and VCRs (movies can be borrowed at the concierge desk), private balconies or patios, and private swimming pools.

Open-air jitneys transport guests to their villas, the **Great House** (where all the action is), and the beach. Also on the grounds are two pools with swim-up bars, a well-maintained running track, and an ultramodern, Grecian-style spa and health club (all guests receive a complimentary session that includes Swedish massage, foot reflexology, a back and neck rub, a manicure, and a pedicure). Tennis aficionados will find six lighted courts, plus free daily clinics, while golfers can play at a nearby course (greens fees and transportation are included). There are four excellent restaurants on the premises as well as six bars and a nightclub. ♦ Rte A3 (between White River and Ocho Rios). 974.1027, 974.5600, 800/777.7800; fax 974.5838

41 Shaw Park Hotel $$ Beyond the fast pace and loud crowds of other resorts is this peaceful, 118-room beachfront retreat, where guests enjoy on-site water sports, 2 tennis courts, a swimming pool, a restaurant, and a disco called **Silks.** ♦ North of Rte A3, White River. 974.2552, 974.2554, 800/223.6510; fax 974.5042

42 Prospect Plantation See how Jamaica's crops are grown and learn how they affect the economy at this working plantation established in the 18th century by a Scotsman, Sir Harold Mitchell. Visitors get a close-up view of the banana, sugarcane, pineapple, and coffee fields from the seat of a tractor-drawn trailer, while a tour guide regales them with interesting anecdotes. For example: Some of the trees here were planted by the likes of Sir Winston Churchill and Henry Kissinger. Guests who are comfortable in the saddle can tour the plantation on horseback. There are three different guided trails to explore on 1.5-hour rides. ♦ Admission; children under 12 free. Daily; call an hour ahead to hire horses. South of Rte A3 (between Jamaica Beach and White River). 974.2058

43 Harmony Hall A gingerbread-trimmed Victorian mansion–turned–art gallery features the work of some of Jamaica's top artists and artisans. Look for the famous Annabella boxes made out of wood; well-crafted bamboo furniture; hand-embroidered cushions; brightly painted ceramics; and jewelry made from shells, leather, and beads. Watercolors, drawings, and oil paintings cover the walls, while shelves of Jamaican herbs, spices, and marmalades sit near the cash register. Thanks to liberal customs laws, you can buy all the Jamaican art you want without having to pay a duty tax. ♦ Daily. Rte A3 (between Jamaica Beach and White River). 975.4222

Within Harmony Hall:

Harmony Hall Cafe ★★$ Dine alfresco beneath a white lattice overhang in a garden-alcove setting. The Jamaican lunch special (a delicious sampler of red snapper escovitch, ackee and codfish, rice and peas, and assorted vegetables) is filling, well made, and reasonably priced. Other good bets are curried shrimp and Appleton Rum cake. Free transportation is provided to and from area hotels. ◆ West Indian/Seafood ◆ Tu-Sa lunch and dinner; open Su by previous arrangement only. Reservations recommended for dinner. 975.4785

COUPLES

44 Couples $$$ The original all-inclusive, couples-only resort allows no singles or children. Pluses include a private island for nude sunbathing, an ultramodern fitness facility, and four restaurants (all seat two or three couples at the same table to encourage socializing). This 212-room resort is ideal for young, sporty couples who want around-the-clock activity. You can ride horses, sail, scuba dive, play golf (greens fees and transportation are included), play racquetball or squash, or participate in activities ranging from hat weaving to beach volleyball.

The fast pace continues at night, with a different show each evening, followed by dancing and then singing around the piano bar. Couples can get married here for free. ◆ Tower Isle (just north of Rte A3, between Jamaica Beach and White River). 975.4271, 975.4272, 975.4273, 975.4274, 975.4275, 800/859.7873; fax 974.4439

Within Couples:

Mingles Shops This charming boutique offers beachwear for men and women, fine French perfume, crystal, gold jewelry, crafts, and more. ◆ Daily. 974.5524. Also at: Breezes Runaway Bay, Rte A1, Cardiff Hall Beach. 973.2570; Jamaica Grande, Main St (off Rte A3), Ocho Rios. 974.2200 ext 454

Elsewhere on Jamaica

45 Boscobel Beach $$$ Another all-inclusive SuperClubs resort, this one has 209 rooms and is geared for families traveling with children. Most of the property is childproof, with sturdy furniture. There's an extensive, supervised program for infants and young children, and another for preteens and teens. Sports, computer games, picnics, donkey rides, movies, arts and crafts, and a separate disco keep the kids happily entertained.

Getting Your Feet Wet in Jamaica

Everyone who comes to Jamaica should take advantage of the beautiful blue waters. Most hotels and resorts offer water sports and beachfront boat and equipment rentals and can set up fishing charters. The **Jamaican Board of Tourism** requires all licensed diving operators to have first aid supplies as well as oxygen on board, and to subscribe to a 24-hour medical service. Here are some organizations that can get you afloat:

Boating

Montego Bay Yacht Club Sea Wind Hotel, Sunset Dr, Montego Bay. 979.8038

Morgan's Harbour Marina Morgan's Harbour Beach Hotel, Port Royal. 967.8030, 800/44.UTELL

Royal Jamaica Yacht Club Off Norman Manley Hwy (between Harbour View and Port Royal). 924.8685, 924.8686

Snorkeling and Scuba Diving

Aqua Action Port Antonio. 993.3318

Buccaneer Scuba Club Port Royal. 967.8061

Club Caribbean Runaway Bay. 973.3507

Fantasea Divers Sans Souci Lido, Rte A3, White River. 975.4504

Jamaica Rose Divers Walter Fletcher Beach, Montego Bay. 979.0104

Negril Scuba Centre Negril Beach Club, Norman Manley Blvd, Negril. 957.4425

Poseidon Nemrod Divers Ltd. Chalet Caribe, Rte A1, Reading. 952.3624, 952.6088

Seaworld Wyndham Rose Hall, Rte A1, Little River. 953.2180

Sundivers Ambiance Jamaica, Rte A1, Runaway Bay. 973.2346

Village Resorts Hedonism II Rutland Point, Long Bay, Negril. 952.4200

Adults enjoy scuba diving, golf, tennis, the beach, and an activities program designed just for them. There are three restaurants, two pools, a fitness center, several bars, and a piano lounge. Two children under the age of 14 stay free in their parents' room. ♦ Rte A3 (between Oracabessa and Salt Gut). 974.3330, 800/859.7873; fax 975.7370

46 **Firefly** Writer Noel Coward's restored former home sits atop a hill 1,000 feet above Blue Harbour, commanding a spectacular view of the mountains and sea. The location is said to be the lookout spot favored by Sir Henry Morgan, the pirate who later become governor of Jamaica. Coward wrote his only novel, *Pomp and Circumstance,* here. He entertained often, and his guest list reads like a *Who's Who* of Hollywood: Errol Flynn came, as did Laurence Olivier, Vivien Leigh, Mary Martin, Katharine Hepburn, and David Niven. Coward is buried on the grounds just above the view he loved. ♦ Admission. Daily. Off Rte A3, Galina. 997.7201

47 **Blue Harbour** $$$ Some of Noel Coward's original furnishings grace these 3 villas, with room for up to 15 guests. Stop here and join the eminent ranks of one-time visitors Sir Winston Churchill, Marlene Dietrich, Katharine Hepburn, and Alec Guinness. (This was Coward's retreat before the increasing crowds of celebrities, socialites, and dignitaries made him flee to neighboring **Firefly,** above.) Gardens and walkways meander past saltwater pools, and the staff cook stirs up fine Jamaican meals. There's no air-conditioning, but ceiling fans maintain that old Caribbean atmosphere. ♦ Port Maria. 994.2262

48 **Strawberry Hill** $$$$ A snaking road leads 3,100 feet up into the Blue Mountains, but the tortuous drive is worth the trouble—at the end of the trip lies a breathtaking view of Kingston and one of the most talked-about inns in the country. Intimate luxury is the key at this plantation-style complex opened by millionaire Island Records mogul Chris Blackwell. (Blackwell's own home is nestled inside a botanical garden at the top of the hill.) Sitting on the site of a 17th-century great house that was whisked away by a hurricane, a dozen white gingerbread villas house 18 studio and 1- to 3-bedroom apartments. All are bursting with plants and decorated with four-poster beds draped in mosquito netting and topped by down comforters. Ceiling fans (the mountain breezes make air-conditioning unnecessary) and wraparound verandas complete the picture at this intimate retreat. Some units have kitchens and phones; fax machines, TV sets, and CD players are available upon request. Spa services include massage and aromatherapy. A shuttle provides

transportation to and from the airport in Kingston (about a 30-minute drive), and helicopter service is also available. ♦ Rte B1, Irish Town. 944.8400, 800/OUTPOST; fax 944.8408

Within Strawberry Hill:

Strawberry Hill ★★★★$$$$ A panoramic view of Kingston draws diners to the open-air patio of this mountain restaurant. Chef Peter Birkwiser puts a distinctive signature on his West Indian dishes, serving such tantalizing creations as curried squash soup, jerked lamb with guava and roasted garlic, and grilled fish in spicy mango marinade. There's an extensive wine list. Afternoon tea is served on Friday and Saturday; Sunday brunch is offered against a backdrop of live music. ♦ West Indian ♦ M-Th breakfast, lunch, and dinner; F-Sa breakfast, lunch, afternoon tea, and dinner; Su brunch and dinner. Reservations recommended. 944.8400

Eva Myers

Owner, Evita's Restaurant, Ocho Rios

What I love most about Jamaica is that people here are warm, and always ready to laugh.

A favorite spot is **Frenchman's Cove** in **Port Antonio.** The hotel is closed, but the beach is wonderful. A clear river runs into this seaside bay; immerse yourself in this river and you'll feel as if you've stepped into a glass of bubbling Champagne.

Soaking up the serene greenness of the **Coyaba River Garden,** a nature sanctuary near Ocho Rios.

Climbing up **Dunn's River Falls.** It's touristy, but must be experienced at least once.

Visiting **Firefly,** Noel Coward's hilltop house, the original room with a view. It's wonderful to rent the house for a special event, especially under the light of a full moon.

Reggae music, which originated in Jamaica, combines elements of calypso, soul, and rock 'n' roll. The name reggae is derived from *rege-rege,* Jamaican English for ragged clothing.

Before the arrival of Christopher Columbus in 1492, most of the Caribbean was inhabited by three groups of people: the Ciboney or Guanahuatebey, the Arawak or Taino, and the Caribs.

Among the foods crops that originated in the Caribbean are peanuts, cashews, potatoes, tomatoes, pineapples, and pumpkins.

Restaurants/Clubs: Red   Hotels: Blue
Shops/♥ Outdoors: Green   Sights/Culture: Black

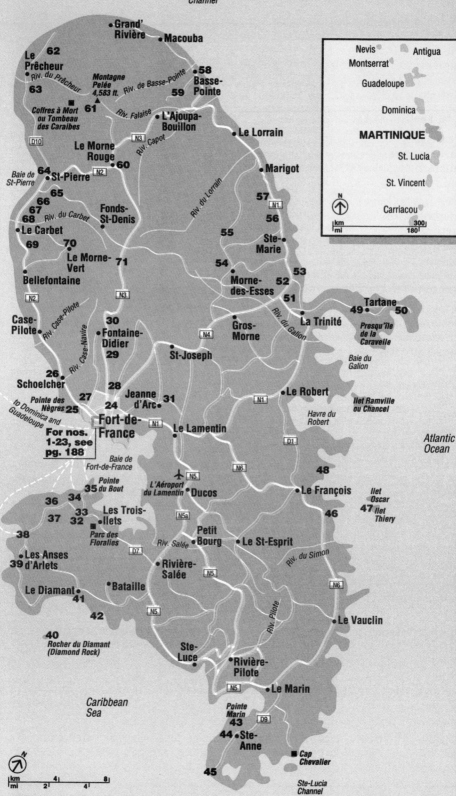

Martinique

To the Carib Indians, Martinique was *Madinina* (Isle of Flowers), and today mountain roads are still splashed with bougainvillea, hibiscus, frangipani, wild orchids, and the island's signature bloom, the anthurium. Ferns grow as tall as trees in the rain forests, and poinsettias brighten city sidewalks.

The heart of the arc formed by the Windward Islands in the Lesser Antilles is home to about 384,000 people and countless tropical gardens. But, like its sister island Guadeloupe, Martinique is a full-fledged French *région* with a distinctly Gallic accent. Locals grumble *en français* as their Renaults and *bicyclettes* whiz past gendarmes directing traffic on **Rue Victor-Hugo** and **Rue de la Liberté** in the capital, **Fort-de-France**. Baccarat crystal and Hermès silks are (relative) bargains, and perfume prices are among the lowest in the world. Gastronomes can choose from over 150 restaurants, many with fine wine cellars, before they shuffle off to bed at a sophisticated resort or one of the family-run inns known as Relais Créoles.

Evenings belong to bistros, boîtes, and the beguine (a popular dance resembling the rhumba). Night music slides from the steamy West Indian rhythms of zouk to the coolest jazz, while **Les Grands Ballets de la Martinique, Pom' Cannelle**, and **Les Balisiers** draw crowds with their dashing folk extravaganzas. As for gambling, there are two casinos: the **Casino de la Batelière Plazza** and the casino in the **Hôtel Méridien Trois-Ilets** at the resort area of **Pointe du Bout**.

Across the bay, Fort-de-France hugs the harbor, stepping upward against a mountainous green backdrop—an unforgettable introduction for visitors who arrive by sea. Some 100,000 residents tread these narrow streets, where town houses trimmed with lacy balconies are crowded by cafes and boutiques and public squares are dotted with flower beds and open-air markets.

St-Pierre, on the northwest coast, had a reputation as the "Paris of the West Indies" but that ended on 8 May 1902, when **Montagne Pelée** erupted, wiping out the town and 30,000 citizens in three minutes flat—and abruptly changing its nickname to "the New World Pompeii." The volcano is now dormant, and visitors can learn about it from English-speaking guides at the well-organized **Musée Volcanologique**.

A scenic drive from Fort-de-France to St-Pierre takes less than an hour, but it's worth it to pause and admire the quaint fishing villages along the route. **Le Carbet**, where artist Paul Gauguin lived and painted in 1887, merits a longer stop. It is the site of the **Centre d'Art Musée Gauguin** (Gauguin Museum), and the **Vallée des Papillons** (Valley of the Butterflies), which shelters over 1,500 brilliant specimens that flutter among the ruins of the island's earliest 17th-century settlement.

Martinique prospered thanks to sugar and rum production until the late 19th century, and the landscape is dotted with elegant manors, processing factories, windmills, and cane fields.

On the mountainous northwestern half of the island, beyond the avocado groves and pineapple farms, **La Trace** is a dazzling route through the rain forest. At **Gorges de la Falaise**, mini-canyons frame the **Rivière Falaise**, which cascades into a waterfall. In the southeast, the region around **Ste-Anne** is known for great beaches, especially **Grand Anse des Salines** and **Cap Chevalier.**

Spend mornings on this island exploring the museums and shopping for bargains, afternoons soaking up the sunshine and engaging in water sports, and evenings dining on gourmet fare and enjoying the ballet. Just be sure to stop and smell the *fleurs*.

To call from the US, dial 011 (international access code), 596 (country code), and the 6-digit local number. On Martinique, dial only the 6-digit local number unless otherwise indicated.

Getting to the Island

Airlines

Air France	553300
American Airlines	421919, 800/433.7300

Interisland Carriers

Air Guadeloupe	421671
Air Martinique	510809
LIAT (Leeward Island Air Transport)	422111, 800/253.5011

Airport L'Aéroport du Lamentin (421600) is a $100-million facility just inland of the harbor's eastern edge, about 20 minutes from Fort-de-France and 30 minutes from Pointe du Bout. This airport serves both international and interisland carriers.

Ferries and Interisland Cruises Express des Iles (631211), also called **Caribbean Express,** provides regular ferry service between Martinique, Dominica, and Guadeloupe. **Brudey Frères** (700850) runs ferries between Martinique and Guadeloupe. **Madinina** (630646), **Somatour** (730553), and **L'Impératrice** (718228) travel between points on Martinique.

Getting Around the Island

Bicycles and Motorbikes

Basalt	550184
Central du Cycle	502854
Funny	633305
Moppett	715161
Parc Régional de la Martinique Bike Trail Information	644259
VT Tilt	660101

Buses Buses are plentiful, but do not follow a fixed timetable and sometimes wait to leave until the bus has filled up. Bus stops are marked, and drivers will not stop for dropoffs or pickups between them. Public buses stop running at 6PM. Another form of local transportation is the *taxis collectifs (TCs)*, minivans whose rates vary depending on the distance traveled. Most *TCs* depart from Pointe Simon on the waterfront in Fort-de-France, and operate from early morning until around 6PM. To use the buses confidently, you should speak some French or know exactly where you want to go.

Car Rental

Avis	701160, 421692, 800/331.1212
Budget	421688, 636900, 800/527.0700
Europcar	733313
Hertz	606464, 421690, 800/654.3131
Pop's Car	781446
Thrifty	660959
Tropicar	633741, 582681

Driving Your driver's license is good in Martinique for up to 20 days; for longer stays, obtain an international driving permit from the **American Automobile Association (AAA)** before you leave (you don't have to be a member). The island is crisscrossed by a well-maintained network of paved roads, some of which are steep and winding. The tourist office has brochures detailing six self-guided driving tours that take a half to a full day to cover.

Ferries **Somatour** (730553) links the Fort-de-France waterfront (opposite Place de la Savane) with the marina in Pointe du Bout from early morning until midnight. **Madinina Vedette** (630646) connects Fort-de-France with the beach resorts of **Anse Mitan, Anse à l'Ane,** and **Grande Anse d'Arlet** from early morning until late afternoon.

Taxis

Radio Taxi	636362

Tours Local operators provide half- and full-day tours of the island along five key routes that offer historical sites, scenery, and (usually) a sample of good Creole cooking. The standard trips travel north to St-Pierre or **Leyritz Plantation** or both; east to the Atlantic coast; southeast to the village of Ste-Anne and the beach at **Des Salines,** or to **La Pagerie** and **Le Diamant** with its white-sand beach and landmark rock. Among the best operators are **Madinina Tours** (706525) and **S.T.T. Voyage** (716812, 733200), both in Fort-de-France, and **Caribtours** in Le Lamentin (509352).

FYI

Electricity The current is 220 volts/50 cycles. You'll need an adapter.

Entry Requirements US and Canadian visitors must present a valid passport or proof of citizenship, plus a picture ID (such as a driver's license, a valid passport, or a passport expired less than five years), and a return or onward ticket. A visa is required for visits of over three months.

Gambling Martinique has two casinos, **Casino de la Batelière Plazza** in the **Hôtel La Batelière** (see page 190) and the casino at the **Hôtel Méridien Trois-Ilets** (see page 192). Both offer roulette, blackjack, and slots nightly from 9PM to 3AM. The legal gambling age is 18 and all players must present a valid photo ID.

Language The official language is French, but most people also speak Creole. Although many service people in major tourist areas speak English, it's a good idea to carry a phrase book when exploring in the countryside.

Money Martinique's official currency is the French franc. Several stores offer a 20-percent discount when shoppers use traveler's checks or credit cards (but not cash) to pay for purchases. Francs are best for restaurant meals, taxi fares, and other day-to-day expenses. Banks are generally open Monday through Friday from 7:30AM to noon and 2:30 to 4:30PM.

Personal Safety Crime is not widespread, but follow normal precautions, especially in metropolitan Fort-de-France and the resort area of Pointe du Bout.

Publications Free tourist publications (available at hotels, restaurants, and the tourist office) include the English-language *Choubouloute* and *Ti Gourmet,* a guide to Martinique restaurants featuring photographs and sample menus. The French-language daily *France-Antilles* is well written and carries entertainment ads easily understood even by those who don't speak French. Parisian papers and the English-language *International Herald Tribune* usually hit newsstands the day after publication.

Taxes A value added tax (VAT) of 9.5 percent is added to most purchases. The nominal hotel tax varies depending on the type and location of the hotel.

Telephone *Télécartes* (phone cards) are needed to make calls from pay phones; they can be purchased at the post office or at other places signposted "Télécarte en Vente Ici." AT&T calling cards can be used to call the US.

Tipping A 15-percent service charge is usually added to restaurant and bar bills. If you tip extra in a restaurant or nightclub, leave cash—credit card gratuities go directly to the establishment, not to the individual server. Give bellhops and porters about five or six francs per bag. Most cab drivers own their cars and do not expect tips.

Visitors' Information Offices The waterfront tourist office (Blvd Alfassa, between Rues de la Liberté and Schoelcher, Fort-de-France, 637960; fax 736693) is open Monday through Friday from 8AM to 4 PM and 2 to 5 PM and Saturday from 8AM to noon, as is the office in Ste-Marie (Rue de l'Eglise, 691383; fax 690305). The Les Trois-Ilets branch (Pl Gabriel-Hayot, 684763) is open Monday through Friday from 8AM to 4:30PM, Saturday from 8:30AM to 2:30PM, and Sunday from 9AM to noon. The airport information desk (512855) is open daily from 9AM to 5PM; it's closed Saturday afternoon in the off-season.

Phone Book

Fort-de-France and Environs

Martinique's capital is a picturesque port town with narrow balconied streets that are busy by day, peaceful at night. It's a great place to explore on foot, beginning at the waterfront **Place de la Savane,** a centrally located park within easy rambling distance of tourist attractions, restaurants, shops, and blocks of historic buildings trimmed with lacy ironwork and tropical courtyards. Deep-green mountains are the backdrop for the docks and the yacht-filled anchorage of **Baie des Flamands** (Flamingo Bay).

1 **Cruise Terminal** Just east of **Fort Saint-Louis** are docking facilities and quay-side duty-free shops that are an easy stroll from the center of town. ♦ East of Blvd Chevalier-de-Ste-Marthe

2 **Fort Saint-Louis** From its rocky perch jutting out into the Baie des Flamands, this stronghold has stood guard over the harbor since 1640. The thick stone walls, studded with 26 guns and protected by a moat, still house a French naval base. ♦ Tu-Sa 9AM-3PM. Blvds Chevalier-de-Ste-Marthe and Alfassa. 637207 ext 109

3 **Place de la Savane** Facing the harbor, this square boasts beautiful gardens filled with benches and walkways and is surrounded by hotels, restaurants, museums, shops, a crafts market, and food vendors. The once-beautiful *Impératrice Joséphine* statue, dedicated in 1859, was beheaded in 1991 by vandals (some say because Napoleon's empress championed the slave system that cursed the Martiniquais's ancestors). The neighboring statue of *Pierre Belain d'Esnambuc* hasn't lost its head; this French nobleman claimed the island for the mother country in 1635. On the edge of the park nearest the water, craftspeople daily set up sales tables displaying straw hats, T-shirts, bright beach wraps, and other souvenirs. ♦ Bounded by Blvd Chevalier-de-Ste-Marthe and Rue de la Liberté, and Blvd Alfassa and Ave des Caraïbes

4 **Le Vieux Milan** ★$ Try this cheerful *ristorante* for anything from a simple pizza to showy dishes such as tagliatelle with salmon, carpaccio, and gnocchi with gorgonzola. Finish with the ultrarich tiramisù. ♦ Italian ♦ M-F lunch and dinner; Sa dinner. Reservations recommended. 60 Ave des Caraïbes (at Rue Redoute-de-Matouba). 603531

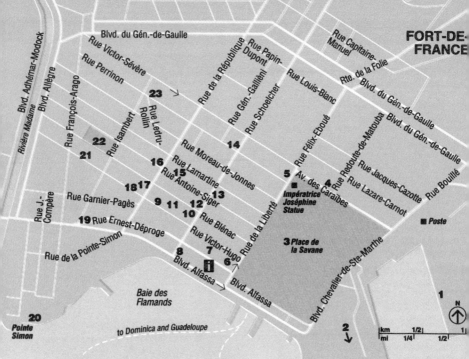

5 La Bibliothèque Schoelcher (Schoelcher Library) Martinique's architectural showpiece is a Romanesque-Byzantine jewelbox that was originally built for the Paris Exposition of 1889, then dismantled, shipped, and reassembled on the island with every mosaic in place. The library is named for local hero Victor Schoelcher, the French abolitionist who helped end slavery here in 1848. (His statue stands in front of the **Palais de Justice**). ♦ Free. M-F; Sa morning. Rue de la Liberté (between Rues Perrinon and Victor-Sévère). 702667

Schoelcher Library

6 Roger Albert The best-known store in Martinique, this longtime shoppers' mecca stocks Parisian perfumes, Baccarat and Lalique crystal, Limoges china, watches, sportswear, and other chic imports. Those who pay with credit cards or traveler's check receive a 20-percent tax rebate on the spot. ♦ M-F; Sa morning. 7 Rue Victor-Hugo (between Rues de la Liberté and Schoelcher 714444. Also at: Hôtel Méridien Trois-Ilets, Pointe du Bout. 660000

7 Albert Venutolo Check here for good pri on jewelry and crystal. A 20-percent tax reb is given if you pay with US-dollar traveler's checks or a credit card. ♦ M-F; Sa morning. 13 Rue Victor-Hugo (between Rues de la Liberté and Schoelcher). 725744. Also at: 1 Rue Antoine-Siger (between Rues de la Liberté and Schoelcher). 714334; Centre Commercial, Cluny. 735013; Rue Ernest-André, Le Lamentin. 511158

7 Carambole Quality souvenirs include handicrafts by local and regional artisans, jewelry, books on Martinique, and swimwea ♦ M-F; Sa morning. 17 Rue Victor-Hugo (between Rues de la Liberté and Schoelcher 734651. Also at: 20 Rue Ernest-Déproge (at Rue de la République). 639363

8 West Indies Bar & Restaurant ★$$ Across the mall from the tourist office, this informal cafe/restaurant serves light meals— and great drinks. Try the *assiette créole* (a sampler of typical Creole dishes), the lamb *colombo* (with eggplant, chayote, and curry) or the coconut chicken. ♦ Creole/French ♦ M Sa lunch and dinner. Rues Ernest-Déproge and Schoelcher. 636377

9 Salines Shop Small catwalks crisscross an indoor lagoon—fun for rummaging through stylish women's swimwear, hand-embroidered dresses, batik fashions, and lively kids' clothes. ♦ M-F; Sa morning. 66 Rue Victor-Hugo (between Rues Schoelcher and de la République). 702828

10 Le Second Souffle ★$ The menu here is vegetarian and includes hot dishes simmered in coconut milk or curried Creole-style, tropical fruit juices, elaborate salads, homemade tofu, breads, and housemade fruit desserts. The setting is bright and airy and overlooks the cathedral square. ♦ Vegetarian ♦ M-F lunch and dinner. No credit cards accepted. 27 Rue Blénac (between Rues Schoelcher and de la République). 634411

11 Othello This men's shop offers European-cut suits, jackets, slacks, shirts, and ties at good prices. ♦ M-F; Sa morning. 43 Rue Blénac (between Rues Schoelcher and de la République). 635659. Also at: 37 Rue St-Germain (between Rues Schoelcher and de la République). 713838

12 Cathédrale de St-Louis Though the earliest chapel dates back to 1671, this tenacious Catholic church has been rebuilt seven times following various disasters ranging from earthquakes to cyclones. The sturdy iron building that stands today, built in the late 1800s, is known for its 200-foot steeple, decorated transepts, and magnificent organ. ♦ Rue Schoelcher (between Rues Blénac and Antoine-Siger). No phone

13 Merlande While the inventory is smaller here than at well-known **Roger Albert**'s (see page 188), so are the crowds. This shop delivers good prices on imported fragrances and cosmetics, handbags, sunglasses, hats, and other accessories. Purchases made with US traveler's checks or major credit cards are further discounted. ♦ M-F; Sa morning. Rues Schoelcher and Antoine-Siger. 718950

MⓄUNIA

14 Boutique Mounia Check inside for the latest women's fashions from Paris as well as owner Mounia's own designs. (Mounia was the first model from Martinique to grace a Paris runway.) ♦ M-F; Sa morning. 26 Rue Perrinon (between Rues Schoelcher and Général-Gallièni). 737727

15 Hit Parade The wide-ranging selection of CDs, tapes, and records found here is big on beguines, zouk, mazurkas, and folk songs. ♦ M-Sa. 55 Rue Lamartine (between Rues Schoelcher and de la République). 700151

16 Cadet-Daniel This well-established shop has been around since the mid-19th century. Look for bargains on 18-karat gold and silver chains, Baccarat and Lalique crystal, and Limoges china. There's also Creole jewelry, including the traditional *collier chou* (necklace) and *chaîne forçat* (bracelet), as well as brooches and earrings. ♦ M-F; Sa morning. 72 Rue Antoine-Siger (at Rue de la République). 602657

17 Boutique Michel Montignac Pack a picnic or stock up on edible French souvenirs from an irresistible inventory of fresh foie gras, pastries, chocolates, breads, preserves, flavored vinegars, teas, fruit juices, sparkling wines, and health products. ♦ M-F; Sa morning. 77 Rue Blénac (between Rues de la République and Isambert). 702169

18 Forum Africain Exotic African imports include batik clothing and fabrics, fine leather, woodwork, jewelry, paintings, and handmade accessories. ♦ M-F; Sa morning. 100 Rue Victor-Hugo (between Rues de la République and Isambert). 602012

19 La Vieille Chaumière ★★$$$ This second-floor dining room offers Creole fare with continental flair and an English-speaking staff. Specialties include gratin of crayfish in sea urchin butter and veal escallop with fresh crab. ♦ Creole/Continental ♦ M-Sa lunch and dinner. Reservations required. 98 Rue Ernest-Deproge (at Rue Isambert). 637060

20 Pointe Simon Cruise Terminal This docking facility allows cruise-ship passengers to disembark in the heart of Fort-de-France. ♦ South of Rue de la Pointe-Simon

21 Marie-Sainte ★★$ Delightful and decidedly inexpensive, this casual eatery serves Creole specialties for breakfast and lunch. Try the *coq fricassée* (chicken fricassee), cod fritters, or the crayfish in a wine and vegetable sauce. Expect a line at lunchtime. ♦ Creole ♦ Tu-Sa breakfast and lunch; closed holidays. Reservations required. 160 Rue Victor-Hugo (between Rues Isambert and François-Arago). 700030

22 Le Grand Marché (Central Market) Open stalls in a graceful cast-iron structure offer colorful island produce, plants, spices, condiments, soaps, and straw goods. ♦ M-Sa. Bounded by Rues Isambert and Suchet, and Rues Blénac and Antoine-Siger. No phone

Carnival in the French West Indies continues right through the first day of Lent, providing revelers with an extra day of merrymaking.

L'UNIVERS

23 L'Univers The Chevignon-style *parisien* fashions found here are a big hit with young men and women, as are the tropical shirts, fine shoes, and accessories. ♦ M-F; Sa morning. 90 Rue Perrinon (between Rues de la République and Isambert). 638884

24 La Mouïna ★★★$$$ Presidents George Bush and François Mitterrand dined at this lovely old colonial villa in 1991, a politic choice as the name in local parlance means "house of reunion." Book a table on the terrace for hillside views across Fort-de-France and outstanding regional fare such as *bonito en papillote* (fish with butter and herbs), *crabes farcis* (stuffed crabs), and avocado sherbet. ♦ French/Creole ♦ M-F lunch and dinner. Reservations required. 127 Rte de la Redoute/N4 (north of Blvd du Général-de-Gaulle). 793457

25 Squash Hotel $$ Overlooking the harbor just outside Fort-de-France, this 108-room property is named for its three squash courts, but active vacationers will also find a fitness center, Jacuzzi, and small outdoor pool. The house restaurant and bar, **La Bistrot de la Marne**, serves high-quality brasserie-type fare. ♦ 3 Blvd de la Marne (just west of Blvd Attuly). 630001, 800/823.2002; fax 630074

25 Le Mareyeur ★$$$ You feel like you've entered a garden when you walk into this restaurant with big windows, plants, and brightly hued flowered fabrics. If you can't decide what to order, request the *assiette* for generous tastes of several house specialties. The menu features *lambi* (conch), *blaff de poisson* (spiced steamed fish), shark in coconut milk, and other exotic seafood. ♦ Seafood/Creole ♦ M-F lunch and dinner; Sa dinner. Reservations recommended. 183 Blvd Pointe des Nègres (south of Blvd de la Marne). 617470

26 Hôtel La Batelière $$$ One of Martinique's top resorts, this modern white stucco hotel offers 197 spacious rooms with air-conditioning, balconies, and fine views of the Caribbean. The property is set in illuminated tropical gardens with its own pretty beach, full water sports, a pier, sundeck, six lighted tennis courts, and a fitness center. Three restaurants include a seaside cafe/bar; **Le Queen's** is a popular disco. The **Casino de la Batelière Plazza** (617323) is also on the premises. ♦ Rte N2, Schoelcher. 614949, 800/888.4747; fax 616229

27 La Belle Epoque ★★★$$$ Lavish turn-of-the-century decor and haute cuisine suit the romantic name of this suburban restaurant with a long-held reputation for fine fare. ♦ Continental ♦ Tu-F lunch and dinner; Sa dinner; Su lunch. Reservations recommended. 97 Rte de Didier, Didier. 644119

A Little Night Music

Flashy folklore shows are staged by **Les Grands Ballets de la Martinique, Pom' Cannelle,** and **Les Balisiers.** These lively troupes of talented young dancers, singers, and musicians make regular rounds of the cruise ships and big hotels. Their tales of plantation days are choreographed with colorful valses, beguines, and mazurkas. Weekly performances usually take place at the **Hôtel Bakoua-Sofitel** (Pointe du Bout, 660202), **Carayou-Novotel** (Pointe du Bout, 660404), **Diamant-Novotel** (Pointe du Marigot, Le Diamant, 764242), **Hôtel La Batelière** (Rte N2, Schoelcher, 614949) and **Hôtel Méridien Trois-Ilets** (Pointe du Bout, 660000).

Many small hotels present live entertainment once or twice each week. Otherwise, resort discos blare until the wee hours. The **Hôtel Méridien Trois-Ilets's La Baraka** (660000 ext 2147) is small, dark, and loud. **La Paillote** at the **Carayou-Novotel** (660404) has great bay views and live bands. From ballet to limbo shows, **Hôtel Bakoua-Sofitel**

(660202) schedules different entertainment nearly every night. The very popular **Le Queen's** at **Hôtel La Batelière** (614949) is a beachfront watering hole that rings with updated beguines, Latin rhythms, and the frenetic West Indian dance music known as zouk.

If you want to venture beyond the resort areas, you can meet the locals at any of the following music clubs in and around Fort-de-France:

Manikou Nights & St. James Club Rue Piétonne, Jambette, Fort-de-France. No phone

Le Manoir Rte des Religieuses (north of Pl Stalingrad). 702823

Le Monte Carlo 20 Blvd Allègre (between Rues Garnier-Pagès and Victor-Hugo). 631555

Le New Hippo 24 Blvd Allègre (between Rues Garnier-Pagès and Victor-Hugo). 602022

Palace Club D14, Palmiste (north of Jeanne d'Arc). 505638

Le Zenith 18 Blvd Allègre (between Rues Garnier-Pagès and Victor-Hugo). 603559

28 La Fontane ★★★$$$ An elegant private home is the serene setting for a collection of creative French and Creole dishes. Specialties include lamb with mushrooms in mango sauce, sea urchin omelettes, and crepes with conch stuffing. ◆ French/Creole ◆ Tu-Sa lunch and dinner. Reservations required. Rte N3 (Km 4). 642870

29 Sacré Coeur de Balata (Sacred Heart of Balata) Like Sacré-Coeur atop Montmartre in Paris, Martinique's version of the famed basilica commands fine views from the hills above Fort-de-France. Drive up on Sunday to see local families dressed for Mass. ◆ Rte N3, Balata-Tourtet

30 Jardin de Balata (Balata Gardens) This hillside botanical park is ablaze with more than 1,000 types of tropical plants and flowers, including hibiscus, orchids, anthuriums, and flaming red torch lilies. ◆ Admission. Daily. Rte N3 (north of Balata-Tourtet). 644873

31 Martinique Cottages $ Just 15 minutes from both Fort-de-France and Le Lamentin, 8 small hillside bungalows, fringed by a blooming landscape, are equipped with kitchenettes, private verandas, and telephones. Other perks include a pool, Jacuzzi, and one of the island's finest restaurants (see below). ◆ Jeanne d'Arc. 501608; fax 502683

Within Martinique Cottages:

La Plantation ★★★$$$ This celebrated dining room has won awards for creative treatments of seafood, beef, lamb, and fowl. Don't miss the stellar seafood ratatouille. The colonial villa that houses the restaurant is surrounded by a beautiful garden filled with palm trees and red and orange lilies. ◆ French/Creole ◆ M-F lunch and dinner; Sa dinner. Reservations required. 501608

Pointe du Bout and Les Trois-llets

Across the bay from Fort-de-France, the busy resort area of Pointe du Bout is home to some of the island's best hotels and beaches, along with a variety of restaurants, bars, cafes, shops, and a bustling marina. Just south is Les Trois-llets, the birthplace of Empress Josephine. It's now home to noted pottery makers whose work is sold from traditional Creole houses.

32 La Pagerie Napoleon's Empress Josephine was born here, and the ruins still evoke a fine West Indian sugar plantation, with its crumbled great house, tall chimney, and extensive grounds. The former plantation kitchen is now a cottage museum that traces the early years of the famous islander. Treasures include paintings, her childhood bed, a white net stocking (monogrammed and mended), and other bits of clothing. Be sure to see the passionate love letter from Napoleon (translated into English). Some

southbound tours stop here and follow with a beach outing and lunch at the popular resort area of **Le Diamant** (see below). Otherwise, it's an easy moped ride from Pointe du Bout or a fun stop on the way to the golf course at Les Trois-llets. ◆ Admission. Tu-Su. Rte D38 (south of Rte D7). 683834

32 Le Black Horse Ranch Explore the coast and countryside on guided horseback excursions from this riding stable near **La Pagerie**. Make arrangements early as outings are limited to groups of six. ◆ Fee. M-Tu, Th-F. Rtes D38 and D7. 683780

33 Golf de l'Impératrice Joséphine Two kilometers (1 mile) from Pointe du Bout and 32 kilometers (20 miles) from Fort-de-France, this sporty Robert Trent Jones Sr. course (18 holes, 6,640 yards, par 71) adjoins the grounds of **La Pagerie**. Amenities include an English-speaking pro, a good pro shop, and **Le Country** bar/restaurant. Clubs, carts, and caddies are available for hire. ◆ Greens fees. Daily. Rtes D38 and D7. 683281

34 Eden Beach $$ Newly renovated, this beachside hotel at Anse Mitan offers 28 rooms, 2 suites, and 9 bungalows smartly done up in West Indian decor. The terrace restaurant, **Le Sucrier,** offers French and Creole fare and views across the bay to Fort-de-France. The hotel bar, **Le Colibri,** is a popular rendezvous spot every evening starting at 6PM. There's no pool, but water-sports facilities are available on the beach. ◆ Anse Mitan. 660119; fax 660466

34 Bambou $$ This easygoing beachfront hotel houses guests in 60 rustic tile-roofed chalets (136 rooms total). Simple but comfortable, all accommodations are air-conditioned, and the poolside terrace restaurant with spectacular bay views serves French and Creole cuisine. A host of water sports round out the amenities. ◆ Anse Mitan. 660139; fax 660505

34 Rivage $$ Nineteen studios (with kitchenettes and air-conditioning) share a pool, barbecue pit, and bar at this friendly beach hotel with a cordial English-speaking staff. ◆ Anse Mitan. 660053; fax 660656

34 La Villa Créole ★★$$ A lamplit open-air deck, surrounded by a luscious garden filled with tropical plants and fountains, creates a beautiful veranda-like setting. Dine on *blaff* (here you get a choice of what goes into this thick seafood stew—even sea urchins), court bouillon (meat or fish boiled with vegetables), conch tart, or redfish terrine at Guy Dawson's romantic garden restaurant. There's dancing to live music every evening. ♦ Creole/Seafood ♦ M dinner; Tu-Sa lunch and dinner. Reservations recommended. Anse Mitan. 660553; fax 660856

35 La Karacoli $ Set on a hillside right over the water, this congenial family-operated inn has a small beach, swimming pool, and solarium. Accommodations include 18 modern rooms and 8 1-bedroom apartments, each with a terrace, kitchen facilities, and a telephone. Air-conditioning is available, but seldom necessary, thanks to ocean breezes. Breakfast is provided for an extra charge. ♦ Pointe du Bout. 660267; fax 660241

35 La Pagerie $$ An easy walk to area beaches and restaurants, this do-it-yourself hotel complex is also convenient to the Fort-de-France ferry, **Golf de l'Impératrice Joséphine** (see above), several restaurants, and a small supermarket. There are a pool and a lobby bar on the premises, and guests may use the health clubs, sports facilities, and other amenities of some neighboring deluxe hotels. Balconied studios (64 with kitchenettes, 28 with refrigerators) are decorated simply, with tile floors and modern furnishings. ♦ Pointe du Bout. 660530, 800/221.4542; fax 660099

35 Marina Pointe du Bout Charter companies operating on the premises include **Agi Cat Club** (660301), **Caraïbes Evasion** (660285), **Star Voyage** (660072), and **Tropic Yachting** (660385). Hourlong undersea tours in semi-submersible **Aquascopes** are offered several times daily (683609). For scuba and snorkeling trips, contact the dive boat **Planète Bleue** (660879). ♦ Daily. Pointe du Bout

Within Marina Pointe du Bout:

Bougainvillea, which grows on Martinque in magenta, red, mauve, pink, coral, orange, and white, was named for Louis de Bougainville, who brought the plant to the island from Brazil in 1768

Drinks at Martinique discos, especially those with scotch and whiskey, are expensive (starting around $8 a shot with taxes and service charge). Rum drinks and the local Lorraine beer are better buys.

La Marine ★$ Join the boating crowd for brick-oven pizza, roasted chicken, or Creole fare on the lively dockside patio; or imbibe a tall *planteur* (planter's punch—a rum and fruit-juice drink) in the adjoining bar. ♦ American/Creole ♦ Daily lunch and dinner. Reservations recommended. 660232

35 Carayou-Novotel $$$ With its casual family atmosphere in the midst of a glitzy resort area, this pleasant beachfront property (part of a European chain) offers 201 guest rooms, three restaurants, a bar, a disco, a pool, two tennis courts, archery, golf practice areas, and water-sports equipment. Scuba, fishing, and boat trips can be arranged; waterskiing, golf, and horseback riding are nearby. ♦ Pointe du Bout. 660404, 800/221.4542, 800/322.2223; fax 660057

35 Hôtel Méridien Trois-Ilets $$$$ Though one of a chain of hotels (owned by Forte), this swank complex has plenty of style. The 295 modern rooms are small but pleasant, with balconies and great Caribbean views. The indoor/outdoor lobby features a **Roger Albert** boutique. At **La Case Créole**, waitresses in traditional costume serve excellent regional cuisine. On the beach, near the restaurant, is the **Cocoteraie Bar.** Water sports include scuba and deep-sea fishing, the pool is large and attractive, and there are two tennis courts, a disco, and a casino (see below). ♦ Pointe du Bout. 660000, 800/543.4300; fax 660074

Within the Hôtel Méridien Trois-Ilets:

Hôtel Méridien Trois-Ilets Casino One of only two casinos on the island, this one glitters (though the dress code is casual and men needn't wear jackets or ties). Try your luck at roulette and blackjack, or play the slot machines in a separate salon (no admission fee). The legal gambling age is 18, and a valid photo ID is required to enter. ♦ Admission. Daily 9PM-3AM. 660000

Méridien Plongée This establishment offers scuba excursions for all levels of diving experience. Certification courses available. ♦ Fees. 660000, 660075

35 Hôtel Bakoua-Sofitel $$$$ This posh beachfront property, set in hillside gardens, is one of Martinique's most glamorous resorts. A full program of water sports is supplemented by a big swimming pool, two tennis courts, a squash court, and a workout room; riding stables and a golf course are nearby. For lazy times, there's a small library, a gameroom, two good restaurants, and two bars (one floats in the lagoon). Public areas are decorated in soft Caribbean colors and native woods; the 139 air-conditioned guest rooms have patios or balconies. ♦ Pointe du Bout. 660202, 800/322.2223; fax 660041

36 Frantour-Trois Ilets $$ Attractive peach buildings line the beach at this friendly hotel, which offers 77 rooms on palm-shaded grounds with a beautiful swimming pool, a fine restaurant, a beach bar, and an especially gracious staff. Children will enjoy the playground—it has an antique carousel and a shallow pool. Rates include breakfast. ♦ Anse à l'Ane. 683167; fax 683765

36 Le Panoramic $$ Aptly named, this hilltop property is just a short walk from the beach. Each of the 36 spacious rooms has a balcony and kitchenette and can accommodate up to 4 people. Some face the water; others overlook Fort-de-France. There is a swimming pool on the grounds. There's no restaurant, but continental breakfast is included in the rate. ♦ Anse à l'Ane. 683434; fax 500195

37 Ranch de Galochat (Ranch-Jack) Climb aboard here for horseback rides along mountain trails, cane and banana fields, and secluded coves. ♦ Fee. M-Tu, Th-Su. Call ahead to make arrangements. East of Rte D7. 686397

es Anses d'Arlets

he white-sand beach of this picturesque village is cattered with brightly painted *gommiers* (fishing oats), nets spread out to dry in the sun, and local nildren swimming from the public pier. Of particular ote are the pretty steepled church, old-fashioned andstand, and **Rue du Président-Kennedy.**

38 Ti Sable ★★$$ A Creole-style house graced by verandas and a canopied terrace is a relaxed setting for a traditional island menu of seafood, grilled meats, and curries. ♦ Seafood/Creole ♦ Daily lunch and dinner in season; M-F lunch, Sa-Su dinner off-season. Reservations recommended. Grande Anse d'Arlet. 686244

39 Le Flamboyant des Iles ★★$$$ A *gastronomique* treatment of local produce yields such exotica as grilled octopus, shrimp fritters, conch fricassee, fish *colombo* (curry), and flambéed bananas. This romantic restaurant gets its name from the magnificent trees that shade the grounds, but views of the jagged crescent coastline are equally spectacular. Ask for a table on the candlelit deck. ♦ Creole/Seafood ♦ M, W-Sa lunch and dinner; Su buffet brunch. Reservations recommended. 686775

Le Diamant

This rapidly expanding resort community is accessible either by the coastal road from **Les Anses d'Arlets** or by expressway from the airport or **Fort-de-France**. Here "residence hotels" offer travelers homey accommodations at modest rates.

40 Rocher du Diamant (Diamond Rock) The only rock ever commandeered as a ship by the British navy was designated a sloop-of-war for 18 months between 1804 and 1805. Looming 600 feet above the Caribbean, the *HMS Diamond Rock* had an English "crew" and was bombarded by the French, who held Martinique. According to legend, the French sent over some liquor then retook the rock while the Brits were under the spell of the demon rum. ♦ Southeast of Pointe du Diamant

41 Marine Hotel $$ On a hillside perch, all 149 rooms at this property have kitchenettes and balconies with great views of Rocher du Diamant and the sea. Amenities include a bar, a restaurant, a pretty pool with a water slide, two floodlit tennis courts, and a boat pier. ♦ 764600, 800/221.4542; fax 762599

41 Diamant les Bains $$ Right in town, this long-established, laid-back beachfront hotel offers a flower-rimmed swimming pool and a terrace restaurant that specializes in Creole  cuisine. The 24 air-conditioned units include a few beach cottages with fine views of Rocher du Diamant. ♦ Closed in September. 764014; 800/823.2002; fax 762700

41 Plein Sud $$ Across the road from Le Diamant beach, this property has 53 apartments of various sizes, all with kitchenettes. In addition to the pool, shops, and market, a sort of concierge service is provided by a couple who arrange everything from sports to tours. There's no restaurant on the premises, but guests may dine at the hotel across the street. ♦ 762606; fax 762607

41 La Cavale Guided horseback treks take in the coast and surrounding hills. ♦ Fee. Daily. Call ahead to make arrangements. 762294

41 Relais Caraïbes $$ The 15 bungalows at this complex are trim and comfortable, with sea views from a hillside perch and lush landscaping for privacy. Rooms are air-conditioned, with modern baths and direct-dial phones. Other perks are a swimming pool, a small dining room with music and dancing, and access to the beach at the nearby **Diamant-Novotel.** ♦ 764465, 800/223.9815; fax 762120

42 Diamant-Novotel $$$$ Set on a dramatic peninsula where lush seaside gardens are banked by white-sand beaches, this casual resort is popular with honeymooners. It offers 181 air-conditioned rooms with small balconies, 2 fine restaurants, 2 bars, 2 tennis courts, a gift shop, and a long roster of water sports. A footbridge straddles the large and showy swimming pool, and there is a separate shallow pool for children. Horseback riding and sailing trips can be arranged. Many staffers speak English. ♦ Pointe du Marigot. 764242, 800/221.4542, 800/322.2223; fax 762287

Ste-Anne

One of Martinique's prettiest villages enchants visitors with its tree-shaded town square, old church, picturesque streets lined with French West Indian houses, and white-sand beaches.

Club Med

43 Les Boucaniers Club Méditerranée (Buccaneers' Creek Club Med) $$ This lively link in the all-inclusive chain features 308 basic (but air-conditioned) rooms scattered along the beach and gardens. Active types will appreciate the water sports, seven tennis courts, aerobics, basketball, and other exercise. Lazier times can be had in the attractive dining room, theater, bar, marina cafe, late-night restaurant, and disco. One weekly tab covers all, but if it's luxury you're after, you may want to go elsewhere. ♦ Pointe Marin. 767272, 800/CLUBMED; fax 767202

43 Le Touloulou ★★$ This beach shack is a great place to find grilled *lambi* and *poulet* (chicken), as well as *colombo* dishes. Island posters and steel-band music (Wednesday and Friday nights) suit the casual atmosphere. ♦ Seafood/Creole ♦ Daily lunch and dinner in high season; call in advance during off-season. Pointe Marin. 767327

44 Hameau de Beauregard $$ At this residence hotel with a restaurant on the edge of town, 90 apartments (with kitchenettes) surround a large pool and pretty aquatic gardens. Salines beach is a 10-minute walk away, and the helpful concierge will set up sports, tours, and other activities. ♦ 767575; fax 769713

More than 40 varieties of bananas grow in Martinique.

44 Domaine l'Anse Caritan $$ Newly renovated, this lively and busy hotel offers 144 rooms with ocean views, kitchenettes, and air-conditioning; a tiny beach; a pool; water sports; and a restaurant. ♦ 767412, 800/322.2223; fax 767259

44 La Dunette $ Dive into village life at this beachside hostelry in the heart of Ste-Anne, with 18 air-conditioned rooms (most with sea views and terraces), a good restaurant, and a bar. ♦ 767390; fax 767605

44 Poï et Virginie ★$$ Bamboo, ceiling fans, and flowery drinks add island atmosphere to this seaside eatery. Lobster and crab salad are the stars of the menu, which also features good seafood platters, curries, and steaks. ♦ Seafood/Creole ♦ Tu lunch; W-Su lunch and dinner. 767222

44 Manoir de Beauregard $$ One of Martinique's most beloved hotels, damaged by a fire five years ago, has been restored and refurbished in its original manor house style. Still the domain of the St. Cyr family, it has 11 rooms and 2 restaurants, including a spacious dining room featuring Creole cuisine. ♦ 767340; fax 769324

44 Aquascope Zemis Hourlong cruises on a semisubmersible craft with big glass windows push off from the public pier several times daily. ♦ Fee. Daily. 748741

45 Grande Anse des Salines One of Martinique's greatest beaches, these white sands are favored by locals. This undeveloped spot is ideal for swimming, but there's not much in the way of water sports. Palm trees supply some shade. Expect crowds on weekends. ♦ Rte D9 (south of Ste-Anne)

Elsewhere in Martinique

46 Frégate Bleue $$$ This inn is set in a tranquil colonial house with simple Mediterranean decor. Each of the seven guest rooms has a kitchenette, telephone, TV, air-conditioner, and a fan. There's also a swimming pool. The dining room serves only breakfast. ♦ Rte N6 (east of Le François). 545466; fax 547848

47 Les Ilets de l'Impératrice $$$$ If you really want to get away from it all, book your own private island from the same folks who operate the tony **Habitation Lagrange** (see page 195). Each of the two islets has a beach and boat dock, as well as a rustic Creole-style guest house, complete with maid, cook, and boatman. The house on Ilet Oscar has five bedrooms with private baths, while the property on Ilet Thiery has six bedrooms, each with private toilet and sink (showers are shared). Rates include airport transportation, all meals, drinks, water sports, and use of a motorboat. ♦ East of Baie du François

477540; or contact Habitation Lagrange 536060, 800/633.7411; fax 535058

48 Plein Soleil $$$ Newly opened, this hostelry offers 12 lovely rooms in Creole-style hillside bungalows with views of the sea. Bring plenty of reading material, as tranquillity is the hotel's main amenity. All units are equipped with kitchenettes, and the services of a cook can be arranged. The property also offers a beach, a pool, a dining room (for guests only), and a bar. ♦ Pointe Thalémont (east of Rte D1). 655377; fax 655813

49 Baie du Galion Hotel $$ Contemporary in style, this 145-room hotel offers panoramic views of the sea surrounding Caravelle Peninsula from its guest quarters and from its large dining room. There's also a great pool and a tennis court. ♦ Tartane. 586530, 800/223.9815; fax 582576

49 Le Madras ★$$$ The pace really picks up on weekends during the summer months, when Martiniquais flock to hear lively local bands at this beachfront hangout in a fishing village. The seafood is a good choice, though the medaillon of beef with goat cheese is a succulent alternative. ♦ Continental/Seafood ♦ Daily lunch and dinner. Tartane. 583395

50 Château Dubuc Set on the very tip of the Atlantic peninsula, these ruins have a history as dramatic as their setting. They were once the ancestral home of a fascinating local family. Louis-François Dubuc helped forestall the spread of the French Revolution to Martinique. Aimée Dubuc de Rivery was captured by pirates, sold into slavery, and eventually given as a present to the Sultan of Constantinople, who made her Sultana Validé. The ruins are now part of the nature preserve of Presqu'île de la Caravelle (Caravelle Peninsula), one segment of the huge *réserve naturelle* that also includes the northern mountains and highlands south to Les Salines. Hiking the surrounding nature trails requires some stamina, but no special skills. ♦ Free. Daily. Rte D2 (east of Tartane). For more information, contact the **Syndicat d'Initiative**: 582681

51 Le Brin d'Amour ★$$$ A garden manor surrounded by flowers provides a graceful setting for this formal dining room. The menu features local seafood, along with an array of French, Italian, East Indian, and Creole dishes. ♦ International ♦ M-Sa lunch and dinner; Su lunch. Reservations recommended. Brin d'Amour (just west of La Trinité). 585345

St aubin hotel

52 St-Aubin $$ This French colonial *maison de campagne* (country house) is an impressive gingerbread confection, although the 15 air-conditioned guest rooms are far from elegant, with ordinary furnishings and neither telephones nor TV sets. The gardens and pool are beautiful, and solitude reigns at this peaceful retreat set in sugarcane country above the Atlantic. There's a first-rate dining room (for hotel guests only), and it's a short drive to the crystal-clear waters of Grand Anse des Salines, Le Diamant, Ste-Anne, and Les Anses d'Arlets. ♦ Rte N1 (just north of Rte D25b). 693477, 800/223.9815; fax 694114

53 Primerêve $$ Surrounded by gorgeous hillside gardens, this hotel is ideal for families. There are 25 single and double rooms and 86 suites (that sleep up to 4), all set in cottages with sea views. Water sports are offered on a secluded beach; other perks include a large pool, two lighted tennis courts, a restaurant, a bar, and a beachside snack stand. ♦ Anse Azerot. 694040, 800/322.2223; fax 690937

54 Le Colibri ★★$$$ Guests at Mme. Palladino's home are treated to spectacular hillside views and attentive service. Her kitchen turns out wonderful sea urchin tart, roasted suckling pig, stuffed pigeon, and crab callaloo. ♦ Seafood/Creole ♦ Daily lunch and dinner. Closed September. Reservations required. Morne-des-Esses. 699195

54 Wickerwork Art Centre This fiber-weaving workshop at Morne-des-Esses is known throughout the island for its basketry. All styles and sizes are available at the stands here. ♦ Tu-Su. Morne-des-Esses. 698374

55 Ella In a tiny village near Ste-Marie, this gourmet food store stocks a unique assortment of homemade jams, purees, preserves, and liqueurs as well as island-grown spices. ♦ M-F; Sa morning. Bézaudin. No phone

56 Centre Culturel du Fond St-Jacques

Dominican fathers established a community here in 1658. It is now a cultural center featuring a chapel (rebuilt in 1769) and the semi-restored outbuildings of an old sugar plantation. The cavernous room used for drying sugar, still stands under an arched ceiling. The **Musée Père Labat** commemorates the famous member of the local Dominicans, who lived here from 1693 to 1705 and penned his *Voyages to the American Islands*, perhaps the first Caribbean guidebook. ♦ Admission. M-Sa. Just west of Rte N1. 691012

57 Habitation Lagrange $$$$ The ultimate in luxury is accorded visitors to this 18th-century guest house set on the grounds of a former sugar plantation and rum distillery. Rooms—there are 17 in the main house and 3 cottages—are filled with antiques and boast four-poster beds as well as modern amenities (TVs, VCRs, and mini-bars). The dining room and bar are both very good. There's a lighted tennis court and a good beach is about 20 minutes away; the management will also arrange guided hikes, sailboat excursions, and other activities. The last half-mile of road leading to the hotel is very bumpy. ♦ Off Rte N1 (5 km/3 miles southeast of Marigot). 536060, 800/633.7411; fax 535058

Getting Your Feet Wet in Martinique

Martinique offers plenty of fun in the sun. Most hotels and resorts offer water sports and beachfront boat and equipment rentals. Here are some other outfits that can get you afloat:

Boating

Bambou Yachting Port de Plaisance du Marin, Le Marin. 747805

Catana Antilles Le Marin. 748887

Locaboate Marina Pointe du Bout, Pointe du Bout. 660757

Moorings Le Marin. 747539

Star Voyage Marina Pointe du Bout, Pointe du Bout. 660072

Tropical Yacht Service Le Marin. 749222

Snorkeling and Scuba Diving

Bleue Marine Marine Hotel, Le Diamant. 764600, 800/221.4542

Club de Plongée Hôtel La Batelière, Rte N2, Schoelcher. 614949, 800/888.4747

Diamant-Novotel's Sub Diamond Rock Club Pointe du Marigot, Le Diamant. 762580

Dive Boat Planète Bleue Marina Pointe du Bout, Pointe du Bout. 660879

Méridien Plongée Hôtel Méridien Trois-Ilets, Pointe du Bout. 660000

Okeanos Club Le Diamant. 762176

Plongée Caritan Anse Caritan Hotel, Ste-Anne. 768131

Tropicasub Rte D10 (just north of St-Pierre). 783803

Sportfishing

Blue Marine Evasions Marine Hotel, Le Diamant. 764600, 800/221.4542

Caribtours Le Lamentin. 509352

Yves Pélisson Le Diamant. 762420

58 **Chez Mally Edjam** ★★$ A celebrated Martiniquais cook (and her French-born assistant) serve seafood and Creole meals in her modest home at the island's northernmost tip. Diners drive from all over the island to reach this landmark eatery. ♦ Seafood/Creole ♦ Daily breakfast and lunch; dinner only by request; closed mid-July to mid-August. Reservations required for dinner. Basse-Pointe. 785118

59 **Hôtel Plantation de Leyritz** $$ This lovely old island inn is set in a restored 18th-century manor with trim lawns and tropical gardens, surrounded by a working plantation that grows bananas and pineapples. Sixty-seven guest rooms are scattered throughout restored outbuildings, with modern baths, air conditioning, and traditional local furnishings. Amenities include a restaurant, tennis court, and a swimming pool. Nonguests may tour the antiques-filled main house and gardens, which are open daily (admission charge). A doll museum showcases miniatures of celebrated women, each made of plant materials. This is the final destination of some day tours, a swim-and-lunch stop on others. The nearest beaches are a 30-minute drive away, but the hotel provides transportation for guests. ♦ Rte D21 (south of Rte N1). 785392, 800/755.9313; fax 789244

60 **L'Auberge de la Montagne Pelée** $ Although located at the foot of a mountain, this peaceful hotel restaurant, with its spectacular view, seems to be at the mountain's peak. On clear days you can dine in sight of both the Pacific and Atlantic oceans. Fish is the specialty, but start with the callaloo soup. ♦ Seafood/Creole ♦ Daily lunch. Le Morne Rouge. 523209; fax 732075

61 **Montagne Pelée** This famous volcano is a challenge for serious hikers, but be aware that trails may be overgrown (hiding deep holes), and cloud cover often obscures views from the summit. If you'd still like to give it a try, a guide is essential. To reserve an experienced leader for the climb, contact the **Parc Naturel Régional** (644259). Count on spending four to six hours for the round trip. Less strenuous, but still spectacular, treks through the nearby **Gorges de la Falaise** or the rain forest between Grand' Rivière and Le Prêcheur offer adventures at various levels of difficulty. For offbeat hiking tours that include bus departure, lunch, and guides, contact **Caribtours** (509352). Otherwise, you can drive part way up a bumpy and unreliable road from the town of Morne Rouge to an elevation of around 2,700 feet (the volcano's peak is 4,583 feet). ♦ Daily. Northwest of Le Morne Rouge

62 **Habitation Céron (Céron Plantation)** Set aside a full day for an excursion to this faithfully restored 1670 estate, which encompasses a main house (private residence

of the owner), a sugar refinery (now a restaurant), and a huge garden; there are also well-preserved ruins of various outbuildings. Visitors have free run of the grounds and nearby forest and are welcome to take a dip in the estate's river. This is a stop on some day tours to the island's northwest coast that also include trips to the beach and boating. ♦ Admission. Daily. Anse Céron. 529453; fax 515232

63 La Belle Créole ★$$ An authentic Creole menu featuring shark pâté, fried sea urchins, crab soufflé, and chicken stewed in coconut milk makes this a good lunch stop. The decor is simple, but the terrace looks out over the sea. ♦ Creole ♦ Daily lunch and dinner. Reservations recommended for dinner. Le Prêcheur. 529623; fax 529713

64 St-Pierre One of the world's best-known ghost towns was created when Montagne Pelée erupted in 1902, eradicating both town and townspeople in three minutes flat. All that remains are the ruins of the theater and cathedral and rubble that was once homes, walls, and the subterranean prison cell that held the disaster's lone survivor. ♦ Northwest coast

Within St-Pierre:

Musée Volcanologique Fused coins, a charred sewing machine, photos, a partially melted bottle that still contains perfume, and a clock that stopped at the exact moment of eruption are among the displays at this museum that traces the tragic disaster that killed 30,000 people. ♦ Admission. Daily. Rue Victor-Hugo (south of Rte D10). 781541

65 Le Fromager ★★$$ A good spot for seafood or *z'habitant* (large freshwater crayfish), this dining room has panoramic views of St-Pierre and the Caribbean from the slopes above town. ♦ Seafood/French ♦ M, Th-F, Su lunch; Tu-W, Sa lunch and dinner. Reservations recommended. Rte D1 (just east of St-Pierre). 781907

66 Vallée des Papillons (Valley of the Butterflies) There are more than 1,500 species to be seen throughout the gardens and conservatory at this lovely attraction, which has been cultivated to provide each variety with its own feeding plant. It is set in a deep ravine amongst the 17th-century ruins of **Habitation Anse Latouche,** one of Martinique's earliest plantations, which was destroyed by the volcanic eruption of Montagne Pelée in 1902. The best time to observe the butterflies is from 10AM to 3PM. A small tearoom/ice-cream parlor is on the grounds. ♦ Admission. Daily. Rte N2 (just south of St-Pierre). 781919

67 La Datcha ★★$$ Funky decor and the friendliest ambience imaginable make this seaside spot a favorite. Other highlights include delicious fresh lobster (the only thing on the menu) and equally delicious tropical drinks. Things are especially lively on Saturday nights, when a local band plays music for dancing. ♦ Lobster ♦ Tu-Sa dinner. Rte N2 (north of Le Carbet). 780445

67 Centre d'Art Musée Paul-Gauguin (Gauguin Museum) The nearby beach of Anse Turin has changed little since it appeared in Gauguin's painting, *Bord de Mer*. The artist and his friend Charles Laval lived on Martinique in 1887. This small museum traces his visit through documents, letters, and reproductions of his work. ♦ Admission. Daily. Rte N2 (north of Le Carbet). 782266

68 Le Marouba $$ This property, one of the few recommended hotels on the rugged northwest coast, has 124 air-conditioned rooms decorated in Creole style. Perks include a spacious beach with water sports, a tennis court, and a continental/Creole restaurant that features theme-night specials. ♦ Le Carbet. 780021; fax 780565

69 Jardin Zoologique Amazona (Amazona Zoological Garden) More than 60 animal species from the Caribbean, Amazon Basin, and Africa are exhibited at this recently renovated facility. ♦ Admission. Daily. Le Coin, Le Carbet. 780064

70 Bel Air Village $$ Explore the nearby rain forest or laze on Anse Turin at Le Carbet, which is just 1 mile from this small property set in the green hills of Morne Vert. Four studios and 12 1-bedroom apartments with kitchenettes are decorated in Creole style. There's a swimming pool on the premises, but no restaurant. ♦ Le Morne-Vert. 555294; fax 555297

71 La Trace This serpentine road runs from Fort-de-France to lofty Morne Rouge with great views all the way. It's a dazzling route along the mountainous half of the island, through rain forest and cane fields, banana plantations and avocado groves. ♦ Rte N3 (between Fort-de-France and Le Morne Rouge)

Rodolphe Desire
President, Martinique Tourist Office

Tour des Yoles Rondes An eight-day yawling contest in July, when approximately 20 boats set off in a tremendous show of color.

Carnival Five days of celebration. Groups on foot and floats fill the street of the town, to the sound of wild music.

Cuisine Martinique is proud of its cuisine which, like the island, is exotic, varied, and colorful. Before sitting down to a meal, you must not refuse the "Ti-Punch," given as an aperitif (4/5 white rum, 1/5 syrup, and a zest of lime).

Atlantic
Ocean

Isabela • 113
Camuy • Hatillo Arecibo
Aguadilla • 2 22 22 (under constr.
112 Bosque Estatal 129 10 2 Mar
de Guajataca 635 625 140 149
115 119 Hato
Rincón • San 81 82 Viejo
80 2 Sebastián • 111 Parque de 83 Bosque Estatal 146
las Cavernas de Río Abajo
109 del Río Camuy 111 140
108 83 111
Utuado 141
78 79 106 120 140 144 533
Mayagüez • 105 128 129 10 140 144
102 135 Reserva
77 100 105 Forestal
Cabo 2 Reserva 105 128 Adjuntas 143 Toro Negro 143
Rojo • 102 76 Forestal CORDILLERA CENTRAL
Maricao 68
San Bosque 503 505 139
75 Germán Estatal 67
101 de Susua 10 14
74 •Corozo 301 Yauco • 52 149
72•71 116 66
73 Parguera Guánica Bosque Estatal 2 Ponce
70 69 de Guánica

Caja de
Muertos
Caribbean
Sea

N
km
mi 10 20 20 40

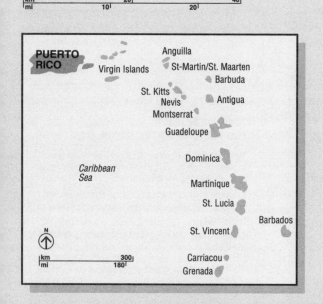

PUERTO
RICO
Anguilla
Virgin Islands St-Martin/St. Maarten
Barbuda
St. Kitts
Nevis Antigua
Montserrat
Guadeloupe

Dominica
Caribbean
Sea Martinique
St. Lucia
Barbados
St. Vincent

N
km 300
mi 180 Carriacou
Grenada

For nos. 1-55
see pg. 204

84 85
Dorado   88   San Juan
22   86
Bayamón   87   Canóvanas   58   59
2   20   56   Río   Luquillo 61
165   Grande   191   62
                                                              to Culebra
Naranjito   174   1   60 Fajardo
                              185   El Yunque ▲
167   3,494 ft.   Ceiba
152   156   156   El Toro ▲ 57
Comerío   30   3,524 ft.   3
156   173   172   Caguas 31   Naguabo
              172   Juncos
162   171   52   30   924   Pasaje de
          Cidra   Vieques   Mosquito
14 Aibonito Cayey 181 Humacao   Buena   63
                  Cerro de   Vista   Vieques
Coamo   1   Santa ▲ 182   906
              15 Reserva   3   64
Las   Forestal
Flores   Carite   Yabucoa
          179
          184
      Guayama   Patillas
ta Salinas 3   Arroyo
el

Puerto Rico

Although Puerto Rico (its name means rich harbor in Spanish) is best known for its casinos and glitzy hotels, modern-day explorers who venture beyond the resorts to discover the island's wealth of historical and natural treasures will also have a truly rich experience.

Located at the eastern end of the Greater Antilles, Puerto Rico measures roughly 100 miles east to west and 35 miles south to north. The **Cordillera Central** mountain range dominates the middle of the island, with peaks soaring more than 4,000 feet above sea level. Miles of pristine beaches trace the coastline, facing the **Atlantic Ocean** to the north and the **Caribbean Sea** to the south. Mountain towns grow coffee and some tobacco, while the low-lying areas support the rum, textile, and sugar industries.

The island was deeded to the **United States** after the Spanish-American War in 1898, and Puerto Ricans were granted American citizenship in 1917. Until 1946, island governors were federally appointed. In 1948 Puerto Rico had its first popularly elected governor, Luis Muñoz Marín, and in 1952 the island adopted its current commonwealth status. Muñoz Marín's innovative Operation Bootstrap program brought industrialization to his homeland—and one of the highest standards of living in Latin America. His Popular Democratic Party, or PDP, remains a major political force in island politics, and Muñoz Marín is revered as a national hero.

While the island's political status has long been a topic of debate between those who want to remain a commonwealth and those who want independence, another alternative—statehood—has been gaining support over the last decade. In the most recent status plebescite in 1993, statehood narrowly lost to commonwealth status; independence received less than five percent of the vote.

More than a third of the island's 3.6 million residents live in the greater San Juan area. The capital city is really composed of two cities. **Old San Juan**, a 45-square-block area, is steeped in more than four centuries of Spanish history and architecture, whereas metropolitan San Juan is a growing amalgam of old and new sections, including **Puerta de Tierra, Miramar, Santurce, Condado, Hato Rey,** and **Río Piedras. Isla Verde**, San Juan's most popular beach area, lies just east of the city proper.

Founded in 1521, Old San Juan boasts 16th- and 17th-century Spanish colonial landmarks that still pulse with activity in their present-day incarnations as museums, art galleries, boutiques, stylish restaurants, and sidewalk cafes. Among the sights is **Casa Blanca** (White House), built in 1523 to house the colony's first governor, Ponce de León. Island leaders ever since have resided at **La Fortaleza**; built in 1540, it is the New World's longest continuously occupied executive mansion. Here also are the mighty waterfront battlements of **El Morro**, which were fortified from 1540 to 1586 to fend off foreign advances, including those by Britain's Sir Francis Drake in 1595. Stately **Catedral de San Juan** was one of the earliest churches in the Western Hemisphere. And the **Museo de Pablo Casals** honors the famous cellist who spent the last 20 years of his life here.

For more than a quarter of a century, tourism has helped shape the development of Puerto Rico. The San Juan area—mainly the Condado and Isla Verde strips of beaches, hotels, and casinos—is the most popular destination, and Old San Juan draws millions of visitors yearly. But visitors who limit their rambles to San Juan and nearby beaches will miss the island's other attractions. Travelers who roam beyond the city limits can stay in the picturesque Paradores Puertorriqueños, moderately priced government-sponsored country inns in the mountains or by the sea, to soak up an even wider array of Puerto Rico's natural and cultural riches.

There's 28,000-acre **El Yunque**, in the eastern part of the island, the only tropical rain forest under the aegis of the US Forest Service, and glorious bioluminescent bays lie off the southwest coast and near the island of **Vieques,** off the eastern coast. Second city **Ponce** is home to the Caribbean's largest art museum, noted for its late Renaissance and Baroque works; the collection includes more than 800 paintings and 400 sculptures. **San Germán**, the island's second-oldest settlement, was founded by the Spanish more than 400 years ago in the southwestern corner of the island, in the hills at the foot of the Cordillera Central mountain range. The streets that run through the center of town are lined with white colonial buildings and town houses from the era of prosperous coffee traders. An underground river flows through **Parque de las Cavernas del Río Camuy** (Río Camuy Cave Park) in the western interior. And the **Arecibo Observatory**, on the island's north coast, boasts the world's biggest radar-radio telescope, equal in size to 13 football fields.

With its extraordinary variety of attractions, Puerto Rico is drawing an increasing number of visitors, who are finding that it lives up to its nickname—"the island of enchantment."

Area code 787 unless otherwise noted.

Getting to the Island

Airlines

American Airlines	800/433.7300
British Airways	800/247.9297
Canadian Airlines International	800/426.7000
Carnival Air	800/824.7386
Delta	800/221.1212
Iberia	800/772.4642
Lacsa Airlines	800/225.2272
Mexicana Airlines	800/531.7921
Midway	800/446.4392
Northwest	800/447.4747
Pan Am	800/359.7262
Trans World Airlines	800/892.4141
United	800/241.6522
US Air	800/428.4322

Interisland Carriers

Air St. Thomas	800/522.3084
American Eagle	800/433.7300
BWIA International Airways	800/538.2942
Flamenco	723.8110
Hill Aviation and Helicopters	723.3385
LIAT (Leeward Islands Air Transport)	791.3838; 800/468.0482
Vieques Air Link	722.3736

Airports **Luis Muñoz Marín International Airport** (791.8110), located on the eastern outskirts of **San Juan,** is the island's primary airport, servicing all major airlines. It's also a Caribbean hub, with flights to numerous other islands. When departing, it's best to arrive at least two hours before your flight; check-in is often snarled by the large number of cruise-ship passengers who travel through this airport. **Isla Grande Airport** (725.5700) is located on **Isla Grande,** a strip of land jutting out into **San Juan Bay** west of Miramar. It was once part of a US Navy base. Today it's used for general aircraft and privately owned planes, although a few small commuter airlines make their headquarters here. The 5,000-footlong runway and air-traffic control tower accommodate large aircraft, but no jets.

Getting Around the Island

Bicycles

The Bike Stop	764.4987
Condado Cycles	722.6288

Buses Buses run on regular routes in the greater San Juan area. Terminals in **Old San Juan** are at **Plaza Colón** and at the **Covadonga** parking garage on **Marina.** Elsewhere, bus stops are marked by yellow posts or metal signs that read "*Parada*" or "*Parada de Guaguas.*" For information, call 250.6064 or 763.4141.

Also watch for *públicos,* public vehicles that run on regular daytime schedules to all island towns. The cars and vans are designated by a "P" or "PD" on the license plate and depart from public squares.

Car Rental

Avis	791.2500, 800/331.1084
Budget	791.3685, 800/626.4516
Dollar	791.5500, 800/800.4000
Hertz	791.0840, 800/654.3131

Driving US driver's licenses are valid, and speed limits are given in miles, though road signs give distances in kilometers. Puerto Ricans are not shy about blowing their horns. Be sure to honk when approaching blind curves to warn approaching cars to keep right. For the best views, travel the **Ruta Panorámica,** a scenic road that meanders across the island.

Ferries Ferries leave daily every half hour from 6AM to 9PM from Old San Juan to Hato Rey and **Cataño;** each trip takes 10 to 15 minutes. Ferries depart from **Playa de Fajardo** to Vieques and **Culebra** daily; both trips take about 90 minutes. The government has announced plans to introduce faster ferries but the launch date was uncertain at press time. For ferry information call 863.0852.

Limousines

Airport Limousine Service	791.4745
Bracero Limousines	253.5466, 740.0444
Carey Limousine	724.6281
Cordero Limousine Services	786.9114

Taxis

Major Taxi Cabs	723.2460
Rochdale Taxi Cabs	721.1900

Tours A full range of bus tours is offered by **Gray Line SightSeeing** (727.8080), **Rico Suntours** (722.2080, 722.6090), and **United Tour Guides** (725.7605).

Trolleys After a few hours of walking along the cobblestone streets of **Old San Juan,** climb aboard one of the five trolleys that run through the historic city to give your feet a rest and your eyes a treat—all for free.

The open-air buses resemble San Francisco cable cars, except they run on rubber tires, sans rails. The drivers provide colorful anecdotes as they point out the 16th-century landmarks. Passengers can hop aboard the cars at any trolley stop, or at the **Covadonga** and **La Puntilla** parking lots near the pier area. Trolleys operate daily from about 6:30AM to 6:30PM.

The word *motel* in Puerto Rico usually means a place that caters to illicit lovers.

FYI

Electricity The current is 110 volts/60 cycles, the same as in the US and Canada.

Entry Requirements Since Puerto Rico is a commonwealth of the US, no passports are needed for US citizens, but airlines require a photo ID. Canadians must present a valid passport or other proof of citizenship (birth certificate, voter's registration card) plus a photo ID.

Gambling Gambling has been legal in Puerto Rico since 1948, and most of the gaming takes place in the hotels of San Juan, **Dorado,** and **Mayagüez.** Casinos are generally open from noon until at least 4AM. Only those 18 years or older may enter. For more information, see "The Rules of the Game" on page 219.

Language Spanish and English are both official languages here. English is taught from kindergarten through high school and many residents speak it fluently, especially in San Juan.

Money The US dollar is the official currency and credit cards are widely accepted.

Personal Safety The countryside is safer than San Juan, but it's always wise to exercise caution and be aware of your surroundings. Avoid back streets, public housing projects, and isolated areas.

Publications The English-language daily *San Juan Star* commands a substantial readership, while the Spanish-language *El Nuevo Día* and *El Vocero* are the two most popular dailies. *Caribbean Business,* an English-language weekly, is widely read within the business community. *Qué Pasa* is a fact-filled, English-language tourist guide published quarterly by the **Compañía de Turismo de Puerto Rico** (Puerto Rico Tourism Company); at press time it was to be replaced with a new, as-yet-to-be-named guide.

Reservation Services and House Rentals

Caribbean Hotel Association.....................725.9139

Compañía de Turismo de Puerto Rico ....
....800/223.6530

Paradores Puertorriqueños 800/443.0266

RE/MAX 268.1241, 800/876.3629

Taxes The hotel tax is 9 percent; 11 percent at hotels with casinos. The airport departure tax is included in the price of your airline ticket.

Tipping Service charges are sometimes included in hotel bills, but gratuities are usually not added to restaurant bills; 15 percent is the usual tip.

Visitors' Information Offices The two main visitors' offices of the **Compañía de Turismo de Puerto Rico** are at the **Luis Muñoz Marín International Airport** in San Juan (791.1014, 791.2551; fax 791.8033) and **La Casita Information Center** near **Pier One** in Old San Juan (722.1709, fax 722.5208). The airport office is open daily from 9AM to 10PM; the Pier One office is open from 9AM to 8PM Monday through Wednesday and Saturday and Sunday; from 9AM to 5:30PM Thursday and Friday.

Branches (open Monday through Friday from 9AM to 4 or 4:30PM) are located in the city halls of most major towns.

Phone Book

Ambulance 343.2550, 911

Directory Assistance 411

Diving Emergencies/
   Decompression Chambers 343.2550

Emergencies 911

Fire..343.2330

Hospitals

   Ashford Memorial Community Hospital, Condado
   ....721.2160

   Carolina Health Center, Carolina 257.2700

   Children's Hospital Guaynabo 783.2226

   Hato Rey Community Hospital................754.0909

   Metropolitan Hospital, Río Piedras 793.6200

   San Juan Health Center, Santurce 725.0202

   San Pablo Hospital, Bayamón.................740.4747

   Teachers' Hospital, Hato Rey.................758.8383

Police...343.2020

Post Office 767.2890

Old San Juan

The historic heart of the capital city beats within Old San Juan. History envelops the massive limestone and sandstone **Muralla** that belts the old city. **La Fortaleza,** the home of the governor, was originally built in 1540 to protect against marauders (a purpose it failed to fulfill). The venerable **Puerta de San Juan** (San Juan Gate), north of **La Fortaleza,** still stands as a passageway through the **Muralla.** From its narrow cobblestone streets, Spanish architecture, and ancient churches to its artsy shops, galleries, and harbor views, Old San Juan is a living museum.

  1 Paseo de la Princesa (Princess Promenade) A stroll down this tree-lined boulevard is a step back in time, though the 19th-century-style walkway was created in 1992. It traces the old **Muralla** and passes the former prison, **La Princesa.** A fountain graces one end of the promenade. ♦ Between San Justo and Puerta de San Juan

  On Paseo de la Princesa:

  La Princesa Built as a prison in 1837, this building is now home to the administrative offices of the **Compañía de Turismo de Puerto Rico.** Be sure to see the changing art exhibits and the three restored jail cells. ♦ Free. M-F. 721.2400

  2 Muralla (City Wall) The Spanish began to erect this fortification in 1630 to protect San Juan from pirates and European invaders. The 40-foot-high wall, made of limestone, mortar, and sandstone, varies in thickness from 20 feet at the base to 12 feet at the top.

3 La Fortaleza (The Fortress) The home of the governor of Puerto Rico was occupied by the British and Dutch during the 16th and 17th centuries. Erected in 1540 and renovated in 1846, the building is the oldest executive mansion in continuous use in the Western Hemisphere. ◆ Free. M-F. Tours in English every hour on the hour, in Spanish every hour on the half-hour. Recinto Oeste and Fortaleza. 721.7000 ext 2211

4 Puerta de San Juan (San Juan Gate) One of the sights in the Old City guaranteed to draw oohs and aahs is this gate, where a pedestrian walkway ducks down and through the massive **Muralla.** Painted bright pink in 1992, this was one of six heavy wooden doors that for centuries were closed at sundown to cut off access to the city. ◆ Caleta San Juan and Recinto Oeste

5 Fuerte San Felipe del Morro (El Morro Fort) In its heyday more than 300 years ago, this fort, with 16-foot-thick walls rising 140 feet above the sea, protected the city. Today it is protected by the National Park Service. **El Morro** (*morro* means "headland") overlooks the Atlantic, providing a great view. The cannons, sentry boxes, and tunnels date back to the 16th century. The vast field that spreads behind it, once used as a small golf course, is traversed by all kinds of people out for a walk. Just below ground is a system of tunnels constructed in the 1500s to connect this fortress with the **Fuerte San Cristóbal** (see page 208).

Attacks on San Juan were commonplace during the 16th and 17th centuries, the most famous antagonist being English navigator Sir Francis Drake. **El Morro** and **San Cristóbal** were instrumental in keeping the island under the Spanish flag. **El Morro** was last under siege in 1898, when the Americans pounded it with shells during the Spanish-American War. Orientation and slide programs are available in Spanish and English. ◆ Admission. Daily. Del Morro (northwest of Norzagaray). 729.6960

6 La Perla (The Pearl) On a slope between Norzagaray and the sea, just outside the northern **Muralla,** are the homes of some of San Juan's poorest people. The shacklike houses, most topped with red or green roofs and TV antennas, are so closely grouped that you often can reach through the window of one house to touch the house next door. The anthropological study *La Vida,* written by Oscar Lewis in the late 1960s, portrays the degrading conditions in this slum. With the growth of the island's drug culture in the 1970s, this area became known for its "shooting galleries," where addicts inject heroin and other drugs, and it remains quite dangerous because of drug-related murders. Although La Perla should be avoided, it can be seen from Norzagaray. ◆ San Juan Blvd (north of Norzagaray)

Fuerte San Felipe del Morro

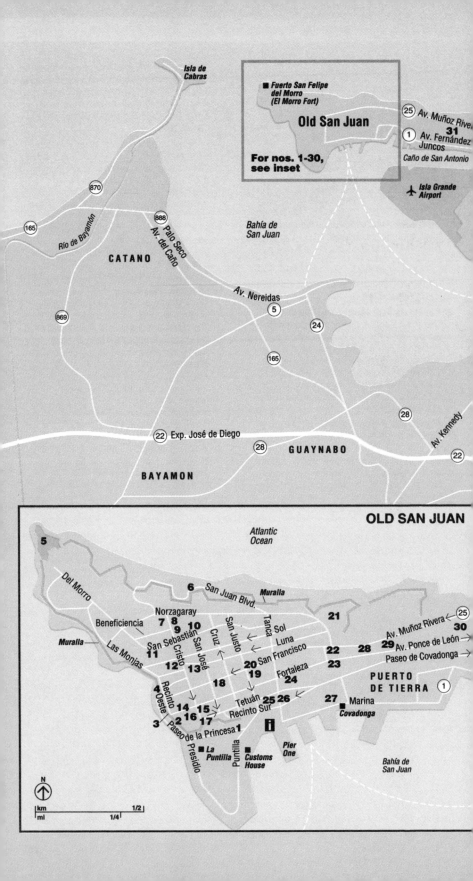

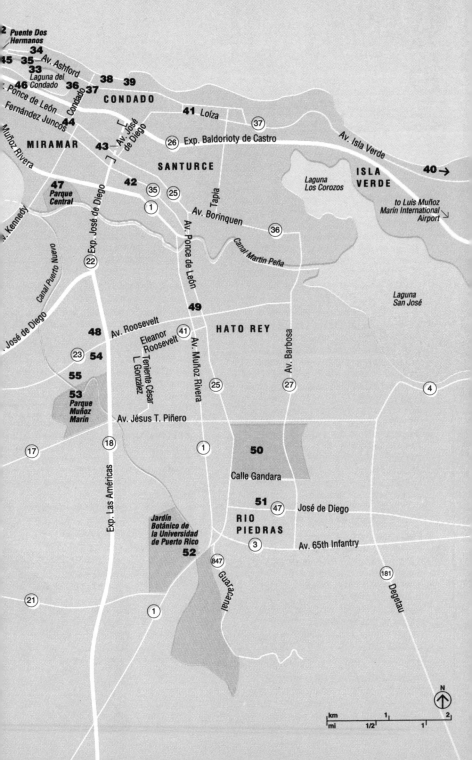

SAN JUAN

Atlantic
Ocean

2 Puente Dos
Hermanos
34
45 35 Av. Ashford
33
Laguna del
46 Condado
Ponce de León 36 37 38 39
Fernández Juncos
44 CONDADO
41 Loíza
Muñoz Rivera
43 26 Exp. Baldorioty de Castro
MIRAMAR
SANTURCE
47 Parque Central
42 35 25
1
Av. Borinquen
Tapia
22
Av. Ponce de León
Canal Puerto Nuevo
49
José de Diego
48 Av. Roosevelt 41 HATO REY
Eleanor Roosevelt
23 54
Teniente César
L. Gonzalez
55
53 Parque Muñoz Marín
Av. Jésus T. Piñero
17 18
1
50
Calle Gandara
51 47 José de Diego
Jardín Botánico de la Universidad de Puerto Rico
52 RIO PIEDRAS
3 Av. 65th Infantry
847
Guaṣacanal
21 1

Av. Isla Verde

37

ISLA VERDE
40 →

Laguna Los Corozos
to Luis Muñoz Marín International Airport

36

Canal Martín Peña

Laguna San José

Av. Barbosa

27
25
4

181

Degetau

Exp. Las Américas

N

km   1   2
mi   1/2   1

Plaza del Quinto Centenario

7 Plaza del Quinto Centenario This plaza in the Old City is graced by a fountain with a hundred streams set on several levels, meant to symbolize the past five centuries. The centerpiece—a 40-foot modern sculpture of black granite studded with bits of ceramic—has received some negative reviews, but sculptor Jaime Suárez says it represents the earth and clay of America. ♦ Bounded by Cristo, Norzagaray, and Beneficiencia

8 Convento de los Domínicos (Dominican Convent) This versatile building, built in 1523, was a convent until 1838. In its early years it also served as a shelter for women and children during attacks by Carib Indians. Between 1898 and 1966 it housed the Antilles command for the US Army. Today the galleries are used for art exhibits and conferences and the interior plaza is the site of concerts. Near the plaza entrance, the **Institute of Puerto Rican Culture** maintains a book, music, and arts and crafts store that carries literature pertaining to Puerto Rico, sheet music of works by Puerto Rican composers, and the work of island artists and artisans. ♦ Free. Convent: Daily. Store: M-Sa. 98 Norzagaray (between Cruz and Cristo). Store 721.6866

9 Plaza San José The statue of Juan Ponce de León that stands in this popular plaza was made from a cannon captured during the British attack on San Juan in 1797. It had been believed that the blue stones used in the streets were originally ballast from Spanish galleons, but studies have identified them as *adoquines* (paving stones) cast by 19th-century European iron foundries. ♦ San Sebastián and Cristo

On Plaza San José:

Iglesia de San José (Church of St. Joseph) The Ponce de León coat of arms hangs to the right of the altar in this church, the second-oldest in the Western Hemisphere (construction began in 1532). This was the Ponce de León family's church, and the body of the explorer Juan Ponce de León rested here until it was moved to the **Catedral de San Juan** (see page 207) in 1913. Vaulted ceilings supported by coral-rock walls and Romanesque arches are the highlights of the ancient Dominican chapel. ♦ 725.7501

Museo de Pablo Casals One of Puerto Rico's truly great musical sons has been immortalized in a museum next to the **Iglesia de San José.** The two-story building displays memorabilia of the cellist-conductor Don Pablo Casals, who was born in Spain but settled in his mother's birthplace, Puerto Rico late in his life. The master's well-worn cellos are displayed along with manuscripts, photographs, recordings, and videotapes. ♦ Admission. Tu-Sa. 723.9185

10 Casa de los Contrafuertes (House of Buttresses) Historians believe this to be the oldest private residence in San Juan, dating back to the early 18th century. It now houses the **Museo de Farmacia** (Pharmacy Museum) a replica of a 19th-century drugstore, complete with old bottles, scales, and historical documents. ♦ Free. W-Su. San Sebastián (between Cruz and Cristo). 724.5477

11 Casa Blanca (White House) Home to the family of Juan Ponce de León during the 16th and 17th centuries, this building (pictured at right) now houses the **Museo Juan Ponce de León,** which illustrates domestic life of that period. Ponce de León never actually lived

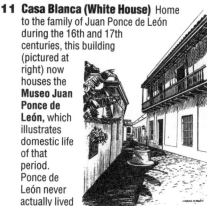

here; he died in Cuba while the house was being built. In 1779 the family sold it to the Spanish government, which in turn lost it to US forces in 1898. It is the oldest continuously inhabited residence in the hemisphere. Of special note are the lush gardens and fountains. ♦ House: Admission. Gardens: Free. House: Tu-Sa. Gardens: Daily. 1 San Sebastián (at Del Morro). 724.4102

HOTEL EL CONVENTO

12 El Convento Hotel $$$$ This 17th-century Dominican convent in the heart of the Old City is now a charming hotel with 59 rooms. New owners recently added a casino, a plunge pool, and a Jacuzzi, and refurbished the rooms, which are equipped with TV sets, VCRs, refrigerators, and ironing boards. Continental breakfast is included in the rate. ♦ 100 Cristo (at Caleta Las Monjas). 723.9020, 800/525.4800; fax 721.2877

Within El Convento Hotel:

Picoteo ★★★$$$ Rapidly becoming *the* place in Old San Juan, this European-style tapas bar offers a wide selection of finger food to be eaten indoors or on the patio. ♦ Tapas ♦ Tu-F, Su noon to midnight; Sa 6PM-midnight. 723.9020

12 Step Streets Inspiration for many artists, two weathered *escalinatas* (step streets) climb the Old City. One is behind **El Convento Hotel,** between Caleta de San Juan (San Juan Cove) and Caleta de Las Monjas (Nun's Cove), and the other is between Caleta de Las Monjas and Sol.

13 Catedral de San Juan The remains of Spanish explorer Juan Ponce de León are entombed in marble here. The original cathedral, built of wood and thatch, was knocked down by strong winds and reconstructed in 1540. The cathedral standing here today was built in the 19th century. ♦ 153 Cristo (between San Francisco and Luna). 722.0861

13 Calle Cristo One of the most interesting streets in the Old City runs north-south, with a few small museums, shops, and novel eating places along the way. The restaurant **Chef Marisoll** (No. 202, 725.7454), hidden away in an interior patio surrounded by shops, serves international cuisine. The **Spicy Caribbee** shop (No. 154, 724.4690) sells Caribbean spices and perfumes and colorful souvenirs. ♦ Between Tetuán and Norzagaray

14 Calle Fortaleza A variety of shops and restaurants line this street. Among the

eateries are **Butterfly People** (No. 15, 723.2432), serving sandwiches and light lunch items, and the new **Café Tabuc** (No. 262, 725.6785), where cigar lovers can choose their favorite brand from a humidor covering one wall and stay for drinks and/or coffee. Jewelry stores dominate the busy street, but galleries and souvenir shops are also plentiful. **Puerto Rican Art and Crafts** (No. 204, 725.5596) is considered by many to be the best crafts store in Puerto Rico. **Albanese** (No. 311, 722.1261) deals in first-rate professional culinary equipment; the store carries a wide range of items, from Italian coffeemakers to Puerto Rican orange peelers. ♦ Between Plaza Colón and Recinto Oeste

15 La Casa del Libro (Book House) Located in a restored 18th-century house, this small museum reveres its rare editions. The unique library of 4,000 volumes contains master-pieces of bookmaking, some of which go back centuries. Special exhibitions are held periodically. ♦ Free. Tu-Sa. 255 Cristo (between Tetuán and Fortaleza). 723.0354

Take Me Out to the Ball Game

Some of baseball's all-time great players have graced Puerto Rico's ball fields: Roberto Clemente, Johnny Bench, Gary Carter, Wally Joyner, Mike Schmidt, Reggie Jackson, and Orlando Cepeda, among others. And while fans must await the spring season in the States, Puerto Ricans get an early start on the grand old game. The six professional clubs in the island's **Winter League** throw the first pitch in November and wrap up the season at the end of January. The champion goes on to the **Caribbean Series,** to compete against top-winning teams from the Dominican Republic, Mexico, and Venezuela.

Whether you're rooting for the **San Juan Senators,** the **Santurce Crabbers,** the **Arecibo Wolves,** the **Caguas Criollos,** the **Mayagüez Indians,** or the **Ponce Lions,** you can usually find a seat at their games in the San Juan and Ponce ballparks, although the play-offs always draw large crowds. Best of all, tickets are inexpensive—about $5, depending on the seating area.

16 Parque de las Palomas (Pigeon Park)
This vest-pocket park is located at the top of the **Muralla**, overlooking La Puntilla, a flat area of residential homes and parking. It commands a magnificent view of the harbor and a wide perspective of the island. Enjoy a rest from the rush on a tree-shaded bench.
♦ Cristo (between Tetuán and Fortaleza)

17 La Capilla del Cristo (Christ Chapel)
Legend has it that a young man on horseback jumped over the **Muralla** and fell from his mount on this site during a traditional race in honor of St. John the Baptist. The young man died as a result of the fall, and—the story goes—the chapel was erected here in 1753 in memory of the rider and to prevent further accidents. Its ornate altar was made from medals and metal donated by local worshipers. ♦ Tu. Cristo and Tetuán

18 Plaza de Armas This square was named for the drills carried out here by the city's early inhabitants in preparation for attack. It later became a social gathering place. First built in the 16th century, the plaza has gone through several transformations—the kiosks and fountain are more recent additions. The recently renovated **Alcaldía** (City Hall), which faces the plaza, hosts changing art exhibits on the ground floor. ♦ Free. M-F. San Francisco (between Cruz and San José). 724.7171

19 La Mallorquina ★★★$$$ Popular with locals and visitors alike, this elegant restaurant in an old Spanish building was established in 1848. On the menu are traditional Puerto Rican and Spanish specialties, including *asopao de pollo* (chicken and rice stew), *arroz con pollo* (chicken and rice), seafood dishes, and flan. ♦ Puerto Rican/Spanish ♦ M-Sa lunch and dinner. 207 San Justo (between Fortaleza and San Francisco). 722.3261

20 Calle San Francisco Shoe stores, clothing boutiques, garish souvenir emporiums, glittering jewelry shops, and restaurants line this colorful street. Stop at **La Bombonera** (No. 259, 722.0658) for a sandwich or pastries. A Franciscan church stands serenely above the crowds. ♦ Between O'Donnell and Recinto Oeste

When Portuguese pirate José Almeida was put to death for his deeds, his boatswain and two of his crew traveled to a deserted islet off Puerto Rico looking for the "treasure" that Almeida had regularly visited. After unearthing a large box covered with copper planks they fought among themselves. When the one surviving crewman finally opened the lid he discovered the body of Almeida's bride, who had been killed right after their marriage. Today this spot of land is called Caja de Muertos, or Coffin Island.

21 Fuerte San Cristóbal (Fort San Cristóbal) It is said that some nights the spirit of a lone sentry walks his post at this fortress. This strategic masterpiece was built in the 18th century when **El Morro** needed reinforcement at its eastern flank. The 27-acre fort is made up of 5 bastions that reach as high as 150 feet above the sea. An orientation film is shown in English and Spanish.
♦ Admission. Daily. Norzagaray (between Av Muñoz Rivera and San Juan Blvd). 729.6960

22 Plaza Colón A stately, towering statue of Christopher Columbus greets all who enter the Old City at this plaza on its eastern side. Columbus landed on the western side of Puerto Rico in 1493 during his second trip to the New World. Although he was never actually in San Juan, in 1848 a statue of Columbus and the record of his voyages was erected here, replacing the original statue of Juan Ponce de León, the city's founder.

The plaza usually bustles during the day. Bus passengers queue up at the stop, and visitors and residents check out the surrounding shops before wending their way through the historic area. ♦ O'Donnell and San Francisco

23 Teatro Tapia Drama, dance, music, and poetry are part of Puerto Rico's soul, and many local performers have appeared on this stage. The oldest proscenium theater in the Western Hemisphere, the playhouse first lifted its curtain in 1832 as the **Municipal Theater**. The building was renovated in 1878, renamed in 1937 for Alejandro Tapia, Puerto Rico's first playwright, and renovated again in 1949, 1976, and 1995. While its boards have been trod by international performers over the years, it takes a back seat to the modern **Centro de Bellas Artes Luis A. Ferré** in Santurce (see page 214). ♦ Av Ponce de León and O'Donnell. 722.0407

24 Parrot Club ★★★$$$ This new eatery offering "Nuevo Latino" cuisine has taken Old San Juan by storm. The tangerine-colored, palm-lined restaurant is now one of the trendiest dining spots in town. Menu highlights include Caribbean crab cakes, seared pork loin with white rice and vegetables in sweet cumin sauce, and flank steak with sweet plantains. There are martini nights, cigar nights, and jazz nights—call ahead to check on the schedule of special events. ◆ Nuevo Latino ◆ Tu-Su dinner. 363 Fortaleza (between O'Donnell and Tanca). 725.7370

25 Hard Rock Cafe ★★$$ Part museum, part bar/restaurant, this link in the international chain offers rock 'n' roll memorabilia and an all-American menu. Bands occasionally add to the lively atmosphere. ◆ American ◆ Daily lunch and dinner. 253 Recinto Sur (between Tanca and San Justo). 724.7625

26 Yukiyu Sushi Bar and Restaurant ★★★$$$ This fine Japanese restaurant is known for its artistic and delicious sushi and sashimi. Other dishes include stuffed calamari, salmon with miso sauce, and chicken-breast teriyaki. Indulge in any or all of these specialties at the sushi bar or in the modern dining room accented in black. ◆ Japanese ◆ M-F lunch and dinner; Sa dinner. 311 Recinto Sur (at Tanca). 721.0653

27 Wyndham Old San Juan Hotel & Casino $$$$ This glitzy new hotel in Old San Juan has 200 rooms, 40 suites, a restaurant, 2 bars, a rooftop pool, a fitness center, and a 10,000-square-foot casino that's always hopping. At press time, a bevy of retail stores was scheduled to open in **Isla Bonita,** a renovated building connected to the hotel by a sky bridge. ◆ 101 Brumbaugh (at Marina). 721.5100, 800/WYNDHAM; fax 721.1111

Puerta de Tierra

The eastern part of the peninsula that holds **Old San Juan** connects the old city with newer sections of the capital. Colonial buildings still dot the landscape, but there's also an amalgam of newer homes and office buildings.

28 Biblioteca Carnegie (Carnegie Library) Endowed by Andrew Carnegie in the early 20th century, this library features a circulating collection of books for public use as well as a periodicals room. ◆ Daily. 7 Av Ponce de León (east of Plaza Colón). 722.4739

29 Ateneo Puertorriqueño A private society funds this library, small museum, and theater, where plays are presented by Spanish- and English-speaking acting troupes. Courses for would-be dramatists also are given here. ◆ Free. M-F. Av Ponce de León (east of Plaza Colón). 722.4839

30 El Capitolio (Capitol Building) Puerto Rico's bicameral legislature gets down to business in this magnificent white-domed structure, built in the 1920s. Be sure to see the Puerto Rican constitution on display in the rotunda. ◆ Free. M-F. Av Ponce de León (east of Plaza Colón). 721.6040 ext 2458

31 Archivo General y Biblioteca General de Puerto Rico (Archives and General Library) Built in 1877 as a hospital, this was the last of the great buildings constructed by the Spaniards. It has since been used as a prison, cigar factory, and rum plant, and currently

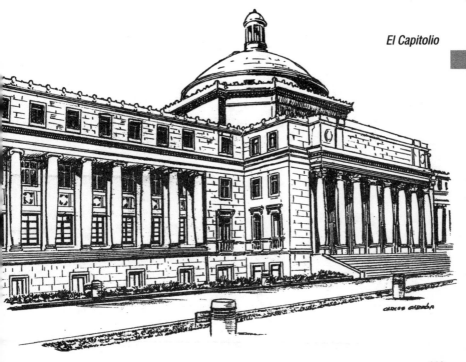

El Capitolio

What the Natives Nibble

Traditional Puerto Rican cuisine has been influenced by the food of ancient Taíno Indians; Spanish and African fare; and more recently by Cuban, Dominican, Argentine, Mexican, and US dishes.

Tubers, rice, beans, and plantains are the staples of most native dishes, even though rice and beans are not grown on the island. The exception is *gandules,* a lentil-like bean that grows in the hills and is usually prepared for celebrations.

Yautia, a starchy root, is a primary ingredient of many dishes, although the *papa* (potato) has made deep inroads in recent years, especially at the growing number of fast-food restaurants.

Plantains appear frequently, and in many guises. The ripe version resembles a large banana and is usually fried or baked and served as a side dish. A simple cooked dish of ripe, sweet plantains is called *amarillos;* unripe green plantains that have been sliced, pounded into flat cakes, and deep-fried are called *tostones* (they taste something like potatoes); and mashed plantains mixed with garlic and pork rinds are known as *mofongo.*

Bacalaítos (codfish fritters) and *alcapurrias* (yautia and banana fritters filled with beef or crabmeat) are favorite snack foods.

Arroz con pollo (rice and chicken) is probably the most commonly eaten main dish, followed by *asopao,* a rice stew with seafood, chicken, or meat.

Pasteles, a holiday favorite, are plantains and yautia that have been seasoned, wrapped in banana leaves, and boiled.

houses historical documents and books. ♦ Fr M-F. 500 Av Ponce de León (between San Agustin and Paseo de Covadonga). 722.2113

32 Caribe Hilton $$$ Since it was built in 19 as part of Operation Bootstrap, a governmen program to encourage industry, this hotel ha been dear to islanders' hearts. Puerto Rico's showplace hotel grew right along with the island's burgeoning economy. It's not unusu to spot heads of state, superstar performers, and great athletes in the lobby. Although the 668-room luxury hotel has undergone major changes over the years, it still enjoys a stron local following and an international reputatio It boasts a lovely crescent of beach, a nightclub, two pools, a health club, and fine facilities for tennis, racquetball, and more. Remnants of the 18th-century Spanish fort S **Gerónimo** stand behind the hotel. ♦ Rosales (east of Av Muñoz Rivera). 721.0303, 800/445.8667, 800/447.7323; fax 724.6992

Within the Caribe Hilton:

El Batey ★★★$$$ This is one of the be seafood restaurants on the island. The light, airy dining room has large windows that loo out onto the ocean, and there are nautical touches throughout—model ships on side tables and buoys on the wall. The lavish, expensive shellfish buffet (more than $40 pe person) leaves little to be desired. You can also order from the menu, which offers suc dishes as seviche; pasta with scallops; fresh swordfish, marlin, and snapper cooked in a variety of ways; and red snapper in Creole sauce. ♦ Seafood ♦ Daily dinner. 721.0303

Peacock Paradise ★★$$ As its name implies, this restaurant's decor is colorful. Specialties from various regions of China ar featured, including seafood in Szechuan sau with mixed vegetables, stir-fried beef with vegetables, and stir-fried chicken with bamboo shoots. ♦ Chinese ♦ Daily lunch an dinner. 721.0303

Rotisserie Il Giardino ★★★$$$ The fine fare served here ranges from homemad pasta to seafood to rack of lamb and veal. Try the mussels in white wine sauce or the smoked salmon. Lush tropical vegetation ca be seen from the dining room's large window (*giardino* means "garden" in Italian). ♦ Northe Italian/Continental ♦ M-F lunch and dinner; Sa-Su dinner. 721.0303

33 Laguna del Condado Puente Dos Hermanos (Two Brothers Bridge) spans a portion of this lagoon where Puerta de Tierra meets Condado. Fishers drop their lines ove the side of the bridge, while the teenage cro congregates here on weekends. Sailboats ar kayaks (jet skis are outlawed here) keep the inlet's azure waters churning at the end of th bridge. A small beach borders the **Condado Plaza Hotel.** ♦ Southeast of Puente Dos Hermanos

Condado, San Juan

The narrow peninsula between **San Juan Island** and **Santurce** long flourished as the exclusive playground for Puerto Rico's well-heeled society. The blue lagoon and two miles of immaculate beaches attracted the carriage set in the early part of the 19th century. When Cornelius Vanderbilt built the **Vanderbilt Condado Beach Hotel** in 1919, visitors came from around the world, setting the groundwork for a construction boom 30 years later.

In the 1950s and 1960s, row upon row of condos took root in the Condado, thanks in part to the **Department of Tourism**'s convincing pitch: Build it, and the tourists will come. As promised, vacationers arrived in droves via prop airplanes and cruise liners.

The tourist explosion mushroomed in the 1970s, bringing all sorts of business establishments, notably the fast-food restaurants, snack stands, and pizza parlors that now give the section its honky-tonk appearance. A concerned citizenry has tried to hold the garishness to a minimum, but "progress" marches on. This area is now competing heavily with **Isla Verde** as the "in" spot for San Juan tourists.

34 Avenida Ashford This main drag is named after Dr. Bailey Ashford, a pioneer in tropical medicine. It begins at Puente Dos Hermanos and hugs the ocean until it reaches Calle Krug, almost two miles away. The avenue runs two ways, except for a stretch of one-way traffic between the **Ashford Medical Center** at Avenida Washington and **El Centro** convention center. Once richly landscaped with palm trees, the avenue is now chock-full of hotels, restaurants, and boutiques, causing traffic to come to a near-stop on weekend evenings, when Ashford is at its liveliest. One of the few remnants of the past is Dr. Ashford's home at the corner of Avenida Cervantes; at press time it was expected to become a tourist information center.
♦ Between Krug and Puente Dos Hermanos

34 Condado Plaza Hotel and Casino $$$
A clear Plexiglas-enclosed bridge connects the two buildings of this hotel that spreads out on both sides of Avenida Ashford. Before the bridge was built, tightrope walker Karl Wallenda fell to his death while attempting to cross the avenue on a wire stretched from building to building six floors up. The great aerialist did not take the heavy breezes into account. In addition to 566 rooms, 6 restaurants (including **Tony Roma's**, see below), 3 pools, a fitness center, and a disco, the property has one of the largest casinos on the island. Those looking for superior service should stay on the **Plaza Club** floor, which provides an on-floor concierge desk, a private lounge, and complimentary breakfast and snacks. ♦ 999 Av Ashford (between Av Magdalena and Puente Dos Hermanos). 721.1000, 800/468.8588; fax 721.4613

Within the Condado Plaza Hotel and Casino:

Tony Roma's ★★$$$ This is *the* place in town for ribs, ranging from baby backs to the restaurant's own patented Carolina Honeys. ♦ Steak house ♦ Daily lunch and dinner. 722.0322

35 Ajili-Mojili ★★★$$$ Formerly located elsewhere in the Condado, this restaurant now has newer, larger digs. The place still has a lived-in look, however—the dining room walls are painted to look like old bricks and the rocking chairs scattered throughout add a comfy touch. The *criollo* menu includes local favorites such as *arroz con pollo* (rice and chicken) and filet mignon sautéed in onions. ♦ Puerto Rican ♦ M-F lunch and dinner; Sa dinner. 1052 Av Ashford (between Av Magdalena and Puente Dos Hermanos). 725.9195

36 Ramiro's ★★★★$$$ Owner/chef Jesús Ramiro offers highly unusual haute cuisine with a Spanish accent and the most imaginative presentation on the island. Star dishes include sweet red pepper stuffed with salmon and, for dessert, sliced caramelized mango on a bed of strawberry sauce. With a large wine loft, wood details, and elegant ambience, this is a restaurant to remember. ♦ Continental ♦ Tu-F, Su lunch and dinner; Sa dinner. Reservations recommended. 1106 Av Magdalena (between Condado and Av Ashford). 721.9049

37 Diamond Palace $$ Formerly the **Dutch Inn,** this local favorite has been spruced up by new owners, who also expanded the casino to 9,000 square feet. The 144-room hotel is one block from the beach and features a pool and 2 restaurants (see below). ♦ 55 Condado (at Av Ashford). 721.0810, 800/468.2014; fax 725.7895

Within the Diamond Palace:

Green House ★★$ A favorite for late-night and early-morning snacks, this casual spot stays open into the wee hours. The menu includes juicy hamburgers, omelettes, and cold plates as well as daily specials. ♦ American ♦ Daily lunch and dinner until 4:30AM. 725.4036

Spanish and English are both official languages of Puerto Rico.

Restaurants/Clubs: Red   **Hotels:** Blue

Shops/♥ Outdoors: Green   **Sights/Culture:** Black

Putters Prefer Puerto Rico

This island was destined to be a golfer's mecca, thanks to its rolling foothills and warm year-round climate. There are numerous scenic championship courses on Puerto Rico, most located at the larger resorts on the northern shore and many designed by prominent names in business.

With 2 18-hole courses apiece, each designed by Robert Trent Jones Sr, the **Hyatt Dorado Beach Hotel** and **Hyatt Regency Cerromar Beach Hotel** (both at 796.1234, 800/233.1234) near **Dorado** offer a top-of-the-line golf complex. The popular S-shaped, 540-yard 13th hole on the **Dorado**'s **East Course** and the L-shaped, par-5 14th hole on the **West Course** will challenge even the most accomplished pro. As you tee off the **West Course**'s eighth hole, take careful aim: Juan "Chi Chi" Rodriguez lives just off the fairway, and you wouldn't want to break any of the great golf pro's windows.

Greens fees start low and go as high as $80; also factor in rental of a golf cart, which is mandatory at practically every course on the island. The lower-priced **Dorado del Mar Country Club** (796.2030), just east of the **Hyatt** resorts, features some of the longest holes on the island, but was closed for refurbishment at press time (call for current information).

East of **Luis Muñoz Marin International Airport,** there's **Bahía Beach Plantation** (256.5600) and **Berwind Country Club** (876.3056), each with an 18-hole course, and 2 18-hole courses at the new **Westin Rio Mar Beach Resort and Country Club** (880.6000, 800/4.RIOMAR), including the **Ocean** course, designed by Tom and George Fazio, and the **River** course (with a spectacular mountain backdrop), designed by Greg Norman. There's also a challenging course at **Wyndham Palmas del Mar** (east of Rte 906, Buena Vista, 852.6000, 800/999.3426). Gary Player lined this 6,660-yard layout with palm trees and mangroves. A small river cuts through the fairway on the 18th hole. At press time, a second 18-hole course, this one designed by Rees Jones, was slated to open at **Palmas del Mar.** The **Punta Borinquen** (890.2987) course in **Aguadilla** offers 18 holes that are ideally suited for beginners. Near **Fajardo, El Conquistador** (Playa Las Croabas, 863.1000, 800/468.5228) allows only resort guests on its 18-hole, par-72 championship course.

Martino ★★★$$ Chef/owner Martin Acosta serves excellent Italian fare in an inviting roof garden with a view of the Condado. Try the hot seafood antipasto and veal- and spinach-stuffed gnocchi in pesto sauce. ◆ Italian ◆ Daily dinner. 722.5256

38 San Juan Marriott $$$ Located on the site of the former **Dupont Plaza Hotel,** which was destroyed by a fire in 1986, this hotel barely resembles its predecessor. It's more upscale, more modern, and offers more amenities. There are 525 rooms (including 15 suites), most with views of the ocean and all with balconies and mini-bars. Four executive floors offer extra amenities and services, including a private lounge where complimentary breakfast is served and drinks are available (though not for free). There are also 2 restaurants (including the **Tuscany Restaurant,** see below), 2 pools, 2 lighted tennis courts, a health club, and the 11,000-square-foot **Stellaris Casino.** ◆ 1309 Av Ashford (between Av Cervantes and Condado). 722.7000, 800/223/6388; fax 722.7045

Within the San Juan Marriott:

Tuscany Restaurant ★★★★$$$ You might think you are in Italy when you enter this elegant restaurant decorated in warm sand and brick tones. A wood-burning oven turns out good pizza. Or try one of the pasta dishes—linguine with crab meat in tomato sauce or ravioli with cheese and spinach in a white asparagus cream sauce are good choices. Meat specialties include veal in a pink pepper sauce and roasted rack of lamb. ◆ Italian ◆ Daily dinner. 722.7000

38 El Canario $ This modest 25-room inn offers the comforts of home at a reasonable price in the heart of the tourist district. The rooms have cable TV, air-conditioning, and telephones, and it's just a short walk to the beach. Rates include breakfast. ◆ 1317 Av Ashford (between Av Cervantes and Condado). 722.3861, 800/533.2649; fax 722.0391

39 Ambassador Plaza $$ A busy, noisy casino on the ground floor welcomes visitors to this garish but inviting Radisson property, one of the Condado's most popular hotels. There are 146 rooms and 87 suites, and guests can enjoy the rooftop pool, sports bar, lounge, and 2 restaurants (see below). ◆ 136? Av Ashford (between Av Washington and Huicy). 721.7300, 800/468.8512; fax 723.6151

Within the Ambassador Plaza:

Larry Sweeney's Original Scotch and Sirloin ★★★$$$ Popular local chef Larry Sweeney has finally reopened his **Scotch and Sirloin** restaurant in this new location (the original closed in 1989, thanks to Hurricane Hugo). In addition to great steaks, the menu offers a smattering of local dishes including rice and beans and *tostones,* and deep-fried green plantains. There's also rack of lamb and seafood. ♦ Steak house ♦ M-F, Su lunch and dinner; Sa dinner. 721.7300

La Scala ★★$$ Such delights as linguine in clam sauce, veal Marsala, and halibut sautéed in lime juice and white wine are offered at this Italian eatery. ♦ Italian ♦ Daily dinner. 721.7300

sla Verde

is beachfront area has boomed since the early 80s, attracting a number of upscale hotels and ops. The pristine stretch of sand that fronts many the hotels is probably the best beach in the etropolitan San Juan area. It attracts lots of locals, pecially on holidays and weekends. The scene ays lively into the night, when the casinos and staurants become the main attractions.

40 San Juan Grand Beach Resort & Casino $$$ Formerly the **Sands Hotel,** this 420-room hotel has a casino and a pool with a swim-up bar. There's also a new $1-million spa with exercise equipment and a full menu of health and beauty treatments—massage, facials, saunas, and the like. ♦ Av Isla Verde (west of Rte 187). 791.6100, 800/443.2090; fax 791.8525

Within the San Juan Grand Beach Resort & Casino:

Ruth's Chris Steak House ★★★$$$ Part of the popular US chain, this eatery serves mouth-watering steaks along with Maine lobster, other seafood, and veal. Enjoy it all in a dining space that has the feel of an old Caribbean plantation house—it's decorated in dark blue tones, and palm plants abound. ♦ American ♦ Daily dinner. 253.1717

40 El San Juan Hotel $$$ This hotel's international atmosphere and marbled, wood-paneled lobby hark back to turn-of-the-century Europe. The large bar in the center of the lobby is generally crowded,and tables are spread about the grand room, made even grander by the presence of a harpist. Located near the **Muñoz Marín Airport,** the 392-room resort hotel offers beach and water-sports facilities, a health club, a huge glitzy casino, six restaurants (including **Aquarella** and **Back Street Hong Kong,** below), and a cigar bar with humidors that guests can rent. The property is in the midst a $72-million long-term renovation project, which includes the construction of 56 luxury oceanfront suites with private terraces and Jacuzzis. The new units were scheduled to be completed at press time. ♦ Av Isla Verde (west of Rte 187). 791.1000, 800/468.2818; fax 253.0178

Within the El San Juan Hotel:

Aquarella ★★★★$$$$ Chef Douglas Rodriquez, a forerunner in the "Nuevo Latina" craze, recently opened this sleek new restaurant, which is getting rave reviews among locals. The modern decor is punctuated with ocean-themed paintings and glass sculptures of sea creatures, but the food is king here. Among the innovative creations on the menu are Venezuelan corn pancakes topped with lobster and shrimp and served with black bean purée, grilled chayote, and a green tomato and cilantro sauce. ♦ Nuevo Latino ♦ Daily dinner. 792.1000

Back Street Hong Kong ★★★$$$ This is one of the most imaginatively designed restaurants on the island. The entrance is a replica of a street in Hong Kong, originally displayed at the 1964 World's Fair in New York. A huge aquarium lights up the dining room, which is constructed of fine woods that call to mind China before the revolution. Mandarin, Szechuan, and Hunan dishes are served, with or without MSG. ♦ Chinese ♦ M-Sa dinner; Su lunch and dinner. 791.1224

40 Ritz-Carlton San Juan $$$$ Scheduled to open at press time, this luxury resort is on eight acres of beachfront property on the outskirts of Isla Verde. The 419 rooms will have TV sets, refrigerators, mini-bars, and marble bathrooms. Guests will also enjoy a spa/fitness center, a 7,200-square-foot swimming pool, 2 lighted tennis courts, 3 restaurants, 2 lounges, a bar, and an 18,000-square-foot casino with entertainment. ♦ Rte 187 (Km 1.5). 253.1700, 800/241.3333; fax 253.0700

Santurce, San Juan

This is the real San Juan, where people go about their daily lives in just about every conceivable occupation. Santurce is made up of myriad pastel-colored, small frame houses, and scores of high-rise condominiums. Unfortunately, one of the fastest-growing enterprises is the multimillion-dollar grillwork business. The iron bars were once used as ornamentation, especially in Spanish-style architecture, but now they're primarily in demand for security reasons.

41 Calle Loíza This colorful and busy street teems with locals who come here to catch the *público* to outlying areas or do their shopping. Visit **Bell, Book and Candle** (728.5000) at the corner of Loíza and Avenida José de Diego for a huge selection of books in English and Spanish. ♦ Between Avs Isla Verde and José de Diego

42 La Casona ★★★$$$ Garlic soup, rack of lamb, vanilla flan, and other traditional dishes are served amid the Santurce foliage in this old Spanish mansion. Enjoy your meal either on the outdoor terrace or in one of several formal dining rooms. ♦ Spanish ♦ M-F lunch and dinner; Sa dinner. 609 San Jorge (at Av Fernández Juncos). 727.2717

43 Centro de Bellas Artes Luis A. Ferré (Luis A. Ferre Performing Arts Center) The big show in town is usually staged at this complex built in the 1970s and named for one of the island's former governors. There are dramas, symphonies, operas, and films, but the center is probably best known for the Pablo Casals Festival held here every June. ♦ Avs Ponce de León and José de Diego. 724.7474, 725.7334

44 Egipto Formerly **Peggy Sue,** this club is decorated, of course, in an Egyptian theme. Dance the night away to disco, Latin jazz, or rock 'n' roll. (The place doesn't close until the crowd thins out.) ♦ W 8PM-closing; Th-F, Su 5PM-closing; Sa 9PM-closing. 1 Roberto H. Todd (at Av Ponce de León). 725.4664

Miramar, Hato Rey, and Río Piedras, San Juan

Generally off the tourist track, these areas provide a glimpse of the capital city's diversity. Miramar, one of San Juan's most upscale neighborhoods, is filled with gracious homes and garden patios. Hato Rey, site of San Juan's banking district, is lined with skyscrapers and office buildings. Río Piedras, meanwhile, is the home of the **University of Puerto Rico,** which draws students from around the island, as well as a popular market, which attracts shoppers looking for the best deals.

45 Club Náutico de San Juan Some of the classiest yachts drop anchor in this marina in Miramar, one of the most fashionable neighborhoods on the island. Deep-sea fishing trips may be arranged through Mike Benítez (723.2292), who owns a fleet of fishing and pleasure boats. ♦ Av Fernández Juncos (just north of Puente Esteves), Miramar. 722.0177

46 Augusto's ★★★$$$$ Always on the lists of best local dining spots (and most recently named the best gourmet restaurant in San Juan by *San Juan* magazine), this elegant place offers 250 wines to complement its changing menu. The lobster, ravioli, and

venison dishes are favorites, as is the delicious chocolate souffle. ♦ International ♦ Tu-F lunch and dinner; Sa dinner. Excelsior Hotel, 801 Av Ponce de León (at Cuevillas), Miramar. 725.7700

47 Parque Central (Central Park) Built for the 1979 Pan American Games, this park has top-notch facilities. It attracts joggers and walkers by the hundreds, and has baseball fields and tennis courts. ♦ Av Kennedy and Expreso Muñoz Rivera, Hato Rey. 722.1646

48 Plaza Las Américas This three-level shopping center is the largest in the West Indies, with more than 190 stores. **J.C. Penney** and **Sears** are the large "anchor" stores here, and between them is a multitude of smaller shops stocked with everything from jeans to TV sets. "Plaza," as it's called by locals, has an air-conditioning system that keeps the building comfortable even when temperatures reach the 90s outside. The center also features a floor of fast-food restaurants, where throngs of shoppers queue up at **Taco Bell, Gyros,** and **Pampas BBQ,** among others. ♦ Daily. Expreso Las Américas and Av Roosevelt, Hato Rey. 753.3333

49 Metropol Restaurant ★★$ Busy most of the day, this no-nonsense restaurant is located in Puerto Rico's Golden Mile business center. Patrons stream from the corporate offices and banks that line Avenidas Ponce de León and Muñoz Rivera to feast on some of the island's tastiest black bean soup, smoked stuffed chicken, rice and beans, and sangria. ♦ Cuban ♦ Daily lunch and dinner. 124 Av Roosevelt (at Av Ponce de León), Hato Rey. 751.4022. Also at: Rte 187 (east of Rte 26), Isla Verde. 791.4046; 105 Av José de Diego (between Expreso Baldorioty de Castro and Loíza), Santurce. 268.7116

50 Universidad de Puerto Rico Packed into this campus's single square mile are classroom buildings, student and faculty living quarters, a museum that generally offers a worthwhile special exhibit in addition to its regular collection, and an extensive library with a Puerto Rican room that is invaluable to students of island history and customs. The university's clock tower is a well-known landmark. ♦ Av Ponce de León (between Gandara and Av Jésus T. Piñero), Río Piedras. 764.0000

51 Mercado de Río Piedras (Río Piedras Market) The local market near the **Universidad de Puerto Rico** harks back to the good old days, when food shopping meant going from the tomato stall to the spice dealer to the butcher. There's always an abundance of mangoes, passion fruit, limes, yams, onions, garlic, poultry, meat, clothing, toys, auto parts, radios—and people, people, people. The indoor market will never pass a hygiene test, but the merchandise is usually good order and the best buys in town are found here. ◆ M-Sa. José de Diego (between Avs Barbosa and Ponce de León), Río Piedras. No phone

52 Jardín Botánico de la Universidad de Puerto Rico (University of Puerto Rico Botanical Gardens) The 35 acres of gardens emphasize local plants such as orchids, succulents, and night bloomers. This fragrant spot has become a popular place to say "I do," with about 40 weddings scheduled here each year. ◆ Daily. Rte 1 (just south of Av 65th Infantry), Río Piedras. 763.4408

53 Parque Muñoz Marín (Muñoz Marín Park) This 144-acre green space is a haven for families on weekends and school groups during the week. A cable car runs right through the center of the park and crosses a small canal. The gazebos host picnickers, and the paths for walking, jogging, and bicycling get plenty of traffic. Kids keep busy racing toy boats on the lake and enjoying a futuristic playground. ◆ Parking fee. Tu-Su. Av Jésus T. Piñero and Expreso Las Américas, Hato Rey. 763.0568

54 Estadio Hiram Bithorn (Hiram Bithorn Stadium) **Winter League** baseball teams play in this ballpark from November through January (see "Take Me Out to the Ball Game" on page 207). The stadium is also used for a multitude of other activities, from car races to religious meetings. It was named for Hiram "Hi" Bithorn, a Puerto Rican major leaguer who pitched for the **Chicago Cubs** in the 1940s. ◆ Av Roosevelt and Expreso Las Américas, Hato Rey. 765.5000

55 Coliseo Roberto Clemente (Roberto Clemente Coliseum) Basketball games, boxing and wrestling matches, rock concerts, trade shows, circuses, and college graduations are all held at the coliseum, named after Puerto Rico's superstar baseball player who was killed in an airplane crash in 1972 while attempting to bring food and medicine to victims of an earthquake in Nicaragua. ◆ Av Roosevelt (between Expreso Las Américas and Andalucia), Hato Rey. 781.2258

Eastern Puerto Rico

56 El Comandante Pari-mutuel horse racing is held five days a week at this modern track in Canóvanas. Agencies around the island offer off-track betting. There's a glass-enclosed restaurant overlooking the track, with TV sets scattered around the room to monitor the action. ◆ Admission. M, W-F, Su. Rte 3 (Km 15.3), Canóvanas. 724.6060

57 El Yunque This 28,000-acre rain forest is considered the crown jewel of the island, with dozens of trails leading through 4 types of forest. Just 20 miles east of San Juan, the

area is home to more than 200 tree species native to the area, wild orchids, and tree snails as wide as a small child's forearm. The tranquillity is punctuated by the call of Puerto Rico's national mascot—the tiny tree frog called *coquí*. Also a bird sanctuary, the forest is home to the rare Puerto Rican parrot, the *Amazona vittata*. El Yunque and El Toro mountains peak at 3,494 feet and 3,524 feet, respectively. Expect brief showers on your hike—more than a hundred billion gallons of rain fall here every year—but shelters dot the trails. From the observation tower (where the air is thin at more than 3,000 feet above sea level) listen to the sounds of silence within the low-lying clouds. **El Portal**, a new educational center, has interactive exhibits designed to teach children about the rain forest and the creatures that live in it. It also features a 10-minute film on the rain forest and provides information on 12 hiking trails here. ◆ Forest: Free. El Portal: Fee. Daily. Rte 191 (Km 11.6). 888.1810, 766.5335

W E S T I N
Rio Mar Beach

58 Westin Rio Mar Beach Resort & Country Club $$$$ This 600-room oceanfront hotel spans 481 acres and features 2 18-hole golf courses carved out of a lush mangrove forest. The resort also offers a spa and fitness center, a dive shop, 13 tennis courts, and 2 pools; horseback riding can be arranged. In addition there are 10 restaurants and lounges and a 5,000-square-foot casino. Each guest room features a balcony or terrace—guests enjoy views of the ocean, the golf courses, or **El Junque** rain forest. Business services are available. ◆ Rte 968 (north of Rte 3), Palmer. 880.6000, 800/4.RIOMAR; fax 888.6600

The Symphony Orchestra of Puerto Rico was founded in 1959 by cellist Pablo Casals, who brought the annual Casals Festival to the Puerto Rico Conservatory of Music that same year. Since then, the concert series has consistently attracted world-class performers and is the centerpiece of the local cultural calendar.

Stop numbers are often used in place of addresses on Avenidas Ponce de León and Fernández Juncos. This practice dates back to when a trolley traveled along these avenues.

59 Playa de Luquillo (Luquillo Beach) Bask in the sun on this world-renowned tropical beach surrounded by coconut palms, just 20 miles east of San Juan. Snack bars and small restaurants specialize in seafood fritters, and a wide assortment of alcoholic beverages are sold at this very popular stop for day-trippers. The town of Luquillo has become home to many "snowbirds" (people who live here during the winter months, when it's cold in the US); this formerly low-key area is now dotted with high-rise condominiums. ♦ Nominal fees for parking and use of shower facilities. Daily; facilities closed Monday from September through May. Rte 193 (off Rte 3), Luquillo

Cave Country

Spelunking opportunities abound in Puerto Rico, which is the home of the famous **Cavernas del Río Camuy** (Camuy Caves), a series of limestone caves 200 feet below ground that are part of the undeveloped **Río Camuy** cave network. (The Camuy is the third-largest underground river in the world.) Guides lead tours of the caves and their amazing stalactites and stalagmites, first in a rubber-tire trolley and then on foot. The government-controlled site is on **Route 129**, southwest of **Arecibo**.

For the very adventurous, there are dozens of caves in the Río Camuy system that have been explored by only a handful of people over the years. One is **Los Angeles**, which is located south of the Camuy caves on **Route 111**. A steep, slippery path leads down the 500-foot-deep sinkhole to the mouth of the cave. Falls are not uncommon, so be careful.

A guide is strongly recommended for the exploration of a major cave system (some solo spelunkers have never returned). **Aventura Tierra Adentro** (Río Piedras, San Juan, 766.0470) and **Encantos Ecotours** (Guaynabo, 272.005, 800/272.7241) offer spelunking tours. If you insist on going on your own, follow the river into the bowels of the cave. And be sure to bring a good map, a flashlight, a helmet, a backpack with a change of clothes (in case you get wet), food, water, rope, and a life jacket (for managing the underground river at various points).

60 Las Pailas Kids and adults have slipped down the rocks of this natural water slide for years. Getting here means parking your car a the road, then descending a winding trail to the falls. ♦ Rte 983 (south of Rte 991), Saba

EL CONQUISTADOR

61 El Conquistador $$$$ Overlooking the Atlantic Ocean and the Caribbean Sea from a 300-foot cliff, this behemoth 918-room reso offers guests their choice of "environments," including a golf village, a marina/sports complex, and the main hotel, with its 6 pools lounge, and piano bar/library. Guests also enjoy a private 100-acre island, an 18-hole g course, 7 tennis courts, and 18 restaurants, cafes, and bars (including **Cassave** and **Otello's,** below). The doors opened in 1962, and the guest register has been autographed by Omar Sharif, Maureen O'Sullivan, and Jac Palance, among others. Though hard times closed the place in 1980, it was revamped and resurrected in 1993—bigger and better than ever. At press time, the resort was constructing a 22,000-square-foot spa, whic will offer facials, massage, and nutrition/ dietary counseling. ♦ Playa Las Croabas. 863.1000, 800/468.5228; fax 253.0178

Within El Conquistador:

Cassave ★★★★$$$$ Innovative cuisin of the Caribbean sets this restaurant, one of the newest at the resort, apart from the rest. Award-winning chef Jeremie Cruz fuses flavors from all over the West Indies and has developed cassava bread—made of yuca flour and cheese—and other unique specialties. Try the Caribbean seafood grill and *mofongo* (mashed plantains mixed with garlic and pork rinds). ♦ Caribbean ♦ Daily dinner. 863.1000

Otello's ★★★$$$ This *ristorante* serves such Northern Italian fare as homemade gnocchi with ham, mushrooms, and peas in a pink cream sauce; homemade veal-stuffed ravioli; and pasta with fresh seafood. Come here for a romantic evening amid the Renaissance sculptures. ♦ Northern Italian ♦ Daily dinner. 863.1000

61 Reserva Natural de Las Cabezas de Sar Juan (Las Cabezas de San Juan Nature Reserve) Explore forests, mangroves, lagoons, cliffs, and coral reefs at this 316-ac nature reserve. Don't miss **El Faro,** a 19th-century lighthouse with a small maritime exhibit—the view from this landmark is spectacular. ♦ Admission. F-Su. Reservation required for reserve. North of Rte 987, Playa

Las Croabas. Weekdays 722.5882, weekends 865.2560

62 Puerto del Rey All sorts of boats (and pilots, too) may be chartered from one of Puerto Rico's largest marinas for day trips to nearby islands. ♦ Daily. East of Fajardo. 860.1000

63 Vieques Pronounced Be-*a*-kess, the name means "little island" in the Taíno language. A 90-minute ferry ride (863.0852) from Fajardo leads to a wealth of near-deserted beaches with spectacular snorkeling and scuba diving. The bioluminescent Bahía de Mosquito (Mosquito Bay) is considered one of the best of its kind in the world. ♦ 15 miles southeast of Playa de Fajardo

On Vieques:

Casa del Francés $ If it's peace you seek, check into this turn-of-the-century plantation manor featuring 18 basic rooms with ceiling fans and private bathrooms. It's a 15-minute walk from the beach (lovely Playa Sombé), and 10 minutes from the waterfront restaurants and bars of the village of Esperanza. ♦ Rte 996 (just north of Esperanza). 741.3751; fax 741.2330

Inn on the Blue Horizon $$$ Local legend has it that a bishop built this lovely villa on the site of a pineapple plantation, importing wood and tiles from Italy. Unfortunately, he became ill and moved to Mexico City without ever living here. The villa stood empty for more than a decade, falling prey to the elements. Several years ago, new owners lovingly restored the property, creating an antiques-filled, charming inn set on rolling landscaped grounds. The nine guest rooms (three in the main house and six in separate cottages) boast dark wood, fine artwork, and a vista of the Caribbean. A lovely pool shares the view. Also on the premises are a good restaurant (**Café Blu,** see below) and the **Blu Bar,** a large octagonal pavilion with a round, lapis-blue cement bar and tiled tables where tropical drinks and food are served. At press time three more cottages were planned. ♦ Closed in September. Rte 996, Esperanza. 741.3318; fax 741.0522

Within the Inn on the Blue Horizon:

Café Blu ★★★$$$ Enjoy a meal either indoors in the antiques-filled manor dining room or alfresco on the veranda overlooking the pool. Chef Michael Glatz offers a selection of dishes with an Asian touch, such as beef tenderloin with "garlic candy" sauce. Sushi is

featured one night a week, and baby back ribs are flown in weekly from Montana. ♦ Continental/Asian ♦ Daily breakfast for guests only; dinner M, Th-Su dinner (open to the public). 741.3318

WYNDHAM PALMAS DEL MAR
RESORT & VILLAS

64 Wyndham Palmas del Mar $$$ This 2,700-acre resort includes a former coconut plantation, a pristine beach, a marina, 21 tennis courts, and 2 18-hole championship golf courses (one scheduled to open as this book went to press). Guests can stay in one of two hotels, the **Palmas Inn** or the **Candelero Hotel** (see below), or in one of the villas next to the marina (there are 400 in all, but only about 150 are available for rent). Other features include a children's program, teen activities, miniature golf, horseback riding, nature trails, water sports, deep-sea fishing, a fitness center, and a casino. Guests can choose from among 10 restaurants and 4 bars. ♦ East of Rte 906, Buena Vista. 852.6000, 800/999.3426; fax 852.6330

Within Wyndham Palmas del Mar:

Palmas Inn $$$ This intimate, family-run hideaway has 23 junior suites and a swimming pool exclusively for inn guests. ♦ 852.6000

Candelero Hotel $$$ Ample guest quarters with cathedral ceilings and king-size beds are offered at this 102-room hotel, which includes a restaurant and a conference center. ♦ 852.6000

Ponce and Southern Puerto Rico

Puerto Rico's second-largest city is often called the "Pearl of the South." The pace in this sleepy southern town (whose name is pronounced *Pont*-say) is slower than in **San Juan.** Ponceños are proud of their brilliant white town square, **Plaza Las Delicias.** The legendary red-and-black wood firehouse, the signature landmark of Ponce, faces the plaza.

65 Parador Baños de Coamo $ During the 1940s and 1950s this was the "in" spot to stay when traveling beyond San Juan. FDR and Frank Lloyd Wright are said to have "taken the waters" of the thermal springs here. Now slightly frayed at the edges, the 46-room parador, about 35 kilometers (21 miles) east of Ponce, still has charm, and is a favorite getaway for those seeking peace and quiet. In addition to the thermal springs there is a freshwater pool and delicious Puerto Rican meals are served in a separate building once used as a ballroom. ♦ Rte 546 (west of Las Flores). 825.2186, 800/443.2239; fax 825.4739

66 Parque de Bombas (Firehouse) Built in 1883 as an exhibition booth for agricultural fairs, this wacky red-and-black-striped structure subsequently became a firehouse. Today it is a museum of firefighting memorabilia. ♦ Free. Daily. Plaza Las Delicias, Ponce. 842.4252

66 Museo d'Arte de Ponce This charming town's claim to fame is its art museum, designed by **Edward Durell Stone.** Former Governor Luís Ferré's gift to the people, the museum has earned a fine reputation for its impressive collection of Renaissance, Baroque, and local art. The most celebrated work here (it appears on museum posters and in ads) is Lord Frederick Leighton's *Flaming June,* a large 19th-century painting of a young woman asleep on a sofa. ♦ Admission. Daily. Av Las Américas (between Av Hostos and Molina), Ponce. 848.0511

67 Parque Ceremonial Tibes (Tibes Indian Ceremonial Center) The grounds of this ancient cemetery and religious center include seven courts built by pre-Columbian tribes, presumably for some kind of ball games. The Amerindian site was discovered in 1974; since then, an Arawak village of thatch huts has been re-created. Archaeologists have also uncovered two dancing grounds. ♦ Admission. W-Su. Rte 503 (Km 2.7). 840.2255

68 Hacienda Buena Vista This restored coffee and corn farm from the 19th century contains a farmhouse, slave quarters, coffee mills, and agricultural machinery. Watch the original machinery pulp, ferment, rinse, dry, and husk the coffee beans. An intricate network of waterways drives the operation. ♦ Admission. F-Su; groups W-Th. Reservations required. Rte 10 (Km 16.8). Weekdays 722.5882, weekends 848.7020

Southwestern Puerto Rico: Ponce to Mayagüez

69 Bahía de la Ballena The tropical splendor of this bay is complete, with mangroves, swaying palm trees, and a small, white-sand public beach. ♦ Rte 333 (south of Guánica).

70 Mary Lee's by the Sea $$ Eight whimsical, furnished houses and apartments look out on the water here. The units are all colorfully decorated and feature fully equipped kitchens—quite useful as there is no restaurant on the premises. A boat takes guests around the bay or out to nearby Gilligan's Island, which you just might have to yourself on a slow day (but never on the weekend). ♦ Rte 333 (south of Guánica). 821.3600; fax 821.3600

70 San Jacinto Restaurant and Boats This rickety establishment is a restaurant, bar, and boat-rental concession. Pick up some sodas and snacks to go and take a ride around the bay on a colorful launch. You can also arrange to be deposited on Gilligan's Island (just offshore) and picked up at an appointed time for about $3 per passenger. ♦ Daily. Rte 333 (south of Guánica). 821.4941

71 Bahía Fosforescente The quiet fishing town of Parguera is famous for this bay, where millions of dinoflagellates (microscopic, luminescent, ocean-dwelling organisms) light up when the water is disturbed. There are two *paradores* and a bevy of seafood restaurants nearby. ♦ Rte 324 (east of Parguera)

72 Parador Villa Parguera $ Simple, clean accommodations and wholesome local fare characterize this inn. There are 61 rooms, a

Hacienda Buena Vista

swimming pool, and a dining room that serves fresh seafood. The proximity to Bahía Fosforescente makes this place popular with fisherfolk. ♦ Rte 304, Parguera. 899.3975, 800/443.0266; fax 899.6040

73 El Faro (The Lighthouse) A dramatic landmark, the lighthouse is sealed (its beacon is operated by a flip of a switch in the nearby Department of Natural Resources building), but its grounds offer majestic views of the rugged coast. A crescent-shaped beach inhabited by pelicans spreads out below. ♦ South of Rte 301

74 Playa El Combate (El Combate Beach) A variety of boats bob about on the calm water off this large beach, a hangout for young people—many on motorcycles. The long wooden pier draws lots of fishing enthusiasts. ♦ West of Corozo

75 Playa Boquerón (Boquerón Beach) Islanders consider this white-sand paradise the best that Puerto Rico has to offer. The government provides spartan, inexpensive accommodations that must be reserved in advance; contact the **Department of Recreation and Sports** (722.1551, 724.2500). Seafood lovers will find plenty of small restaurants and snack stands to choose from nearby; vendors on the street even shuck oysters and clams while you wait. ♦ South of Rte 101

75 Playa Buyé (Buyé Beach) Families crowd this jewel of a beach on weekends and holidays. There are changing facilities, rest rooms, and food stands. ♦ Rte 101 (west of Rte 100)

76 Iglesia Porta Coeli (Porta Coeli Church) Built in 1606 on San Germán's main plaza by Dominican friars, this recently renovated church now serves as a museum of religious art, featuring mostly Mexican works and 18th- and 19th-century wood statuary. It also hosts temporary exhibits and occasional lectures. *Porta Coeli* is Latin, meaning "Heaven's Gate." ♦ Admission. Tu-Su. San Germán. 892.5845

77 Joyuda More than 20 small seafood restaurants are crammed into this beach area. Broiled red snapper, Caribbean lobster, shrimp, and grouper dominate the menus. ♦ Rte 102 (west of Rte 100)

Mayagüez

Puerto Rico's third-largest city (pronounced Ma-ya-gwehss) was rebuilt after a devastating earthquake in 1917. The main industry of this bustling port city is tuna canning, and Mayagüez's best-known landmark is the **Universidad de Puerto Rico Recinto Mayagüez.** Also of interest are the city's Victorian and Baroque buildings. A statue of Christopher Columbus stands in the town plaza to greet all visitors.

78 Universidad de Puerto Rico Recinto Mayagüez Agricultural and engineering courses are offered here. The university's botanical gardens feature thousands of plants and trees and are used for research. ♦ Gardens: Free. M-F. Av Paris and Post. 831.3435

79 Mayagüez Zoo Puerto Rico's only zoo— sprawling over 90 acres—offers the usual big cats, reptiles, monkeys, and elephants. There's also an aviary with a large group of hawks. At press time a $14-million renovation was underway. The project includes the creation of some "natural habitats," areas where animals will live without cages. The zoo remains open during the refurbishment. ♦ Admission. W-Su. Rte 108 (north of Av Paris). 834.8110

Elsewhere in Western Puerto Rico

80 Horned Dorset Primavera $$$$ This small Mediterranean-style hotel on the rocky west coast has a reputation for sophisticated elegance. It caters to those who seek privacy and luxury. The 31 suites are furnished with fine antiques, four-poster beds, and rattan furniture; 4 suites have their own small pools. Also available is a private villa with a pool and terrace. Surfers are drawn here by Rincón's giant ocean waves, and many other visitors are lured by the possibility of seeing humpback whales frolicking near the shores between December and March. No children under 12 are allowed. ♦ Rte 429 (west of Rte 115). 823.4030, 823.4050, 800/633.1857; fax 823.5580

The Rules of the Game

Puerto Rico's gambling houses feature elegant, almost Monte Carlo–like settings, with pit bosses and croupiers in formal attire. The dress code for gamblers, however, has changed over the years. Where black-tie attire used to be required, shirts and trousers are now acceptable—but swimsuits are still banned.

Casino gambling has been legal in Puerto Rico for almost 50 years, and government inspectors make sure the action goes according to the rules. Each casino provides a book on the rules and methods of play. Most of the gambling takes place in the hotels in **San Juan, Dorado,** and **Mayagüez.**

Recently, the government revised the casino code to allow alcoholic beverages to be served in casinos on the island. The doors generally open at noon, and the house stays busy until at least four in the morning.

Within the Horned Dorset Primavera:

Horned Dorset Primavera Restaurant
★★★★$$$ The resort's candlelit dining room, with its black-and-white marble floor and antique-style furniture, is a top candidate for the most romantic spot on the island. Choose either a six-course prix-fixe dinner or from the à la carte menu. Lobster à l'orange is one of the restaurant's most well-known dishes. The wine list is extensive.
♦ Continental ♦ Daily dinner. 823.4030

81 **Parque de las Cavernas del Río Camuy (Río Camuy Caves Park)** After an orientation in the theater here, visitors board a tram that winds down a sinkhole to the mouth of the cave, part of one of the most massive cave networks in the Western Hemisphere. From there a footpath leads into the 170-foot-high cave, where the views extend all the way to the underground portion of the Río Camuy (see "Cave Country" on page 216). **Cueva Clara** is filled with dramatic stalactites and stalagmites. The park has a cafeteria and a gift shop. ♦ Admission. Tu-Su. Rte 4456 (south of Rte 129). 898.3100

82 **Arecibo Observatory** This is where Cornell University scientists operate the world's largest radio telescope, a 20-acre dish constructed within a large sinkhole. The observatory is known for discovering pulsars and quasars and in the early 1990s was involved in a project to search for extraterrestrial life. A new visitors'/education center introduces guests to the basics of astronomy and atmospheric science and also offers breathtaking views of the surrounding karst hills. ♦ Admission. W-F noon-4PM; Sa-Su and holidays 9AM-4PM. Rte 625 (south of Rte 635). 878.2612

Among other legacies, the Arawak Indians contributed several words to the English language, including hammock, tobacco, potato, hurricane, maize, barbecue, cannibal, and canoe.

The namesake for Booby Island, Booby Hill, Booby Hole, Old Booby, and other such sites scattered throughout the Caribbean is the common brown pelican.

83 **Parque Ceremonial Indígena (Caguana Indigenous Ceremonial Park)** South of Arecibo are Taíno grounds that contain 10 playing courts. It is believed that more than 800 years ago the inhabitants here played a ball game similar to soccer. A small museum displays artifacts traced to the Taíno. ♦ Free. W-Su. Rte 111 (Km 12.3). 894.7325

84 **Hyatt Regency Cerromar Beach Hotel** $$$$ This 504-room giant near the **Hyatt Dorado Beach Hotel** (a free shuttle runs continuously between the 2 properties) has 4 restaurants, 3 bars, a casino, 14 tennis courts, a health club, and a small beach. Two programs, one for children 3 to 12 and another for teens 13 to 15, keep youngsters happily occupied. The 1,700-foot freshwater **River Pool** has a current just like a real river. The resort shares 4 18-hole golf courses with the **Hyatt Dorado Beach.** ♦ Rte 693 (east of Rte 690). 796.1234, 800/233.1234; fax 796.4647

85 **Hyatt Dorado Beach Hotel** $$$$ The land was originally a grapefruit and coconut plantation owned by Clara Livingston, Puerto Rico's first female pilot. When fruit prices declined in the 1950s, she sold the 1,600 acres to Laurance Rockefeller, and he built the world-famous 298-room hotel, complete with 4 restaurants, 2 pools, a Jacuzzi, 7 tennis courts, bicycle paths, walking trails, a casino, a ballroom, and a convention center. The beautiful beach is great for snorkeling. Together, this property and the **Hyatt Regency Cerromar Beach Hotel** (see above) offer golfers four championship courses. Juan "Chi Chi" Rodríguez, the former director of golf here, plays the fairways year-round. ♦ North of Rte 693. 796.1234, 800/223.1234; fax 796.4647

Within the Hyatt Dorado Beach Hotel:

Su Casa ★★★$$$ One of the island's most charming restaurants is located in an old plantation house furnished in Spanish-style antiques. Kings and presidents have dined at this illustrious spot where some of the porticoed rooms on the veranda overlook La Sardinera Bay. While the hotel refers to the

Restaurants/Clubs: Red   Hotels: Blue
Shops/♥ Outdoors: Green   **Sights/Culture:** Black

Getting Your Feet Wet in Puerto Rico

Everyone who comes to Puerto Rico should take advantage of its beautiful blue waters. Most hotels and resorts offer water sports and beachfront boat and equipment rentals. Some other organizations that can get you afloat are:

Boating

Caribe Aquatic Adventures Radisson Normandie, Av Muñoz Rivera (between Av Ponce de León and San Agustin), Puerto de Tierra, San Juan. 724.1882

Club Náutico International Powerboat Rentals Puerto del Rey (east of Fajardo). 860.2400

Marina de Salinas Salinas. 752.8484

Marina Puerto del Rey Puerto del Rey (east of Fajardo). 860.1000

Puerto Chico Fajardo. 863.0834

Riviera Yacht Charters Marina de Palmas, Wyndham Palmas del Mar (east of Rte 906), Buena Vista. 852.6000

San Juan Bay Marina Bahía de San Juan, San Juan. 721.8062

Villa Marina Yacht Harbor Northeast of Fajardo. 863.5131, 728.2450

Snorkeling and Scuba Diving

Caribe Aquatic Adventures Radisson Normandie, Av Muñoz Rivera (between Av Ponce de León and San Agustin), Puerto de Tierra, San Juan. 724.1882

Coral Head Divers Wyndham Palmas del Mar (east of Rte 906), Buena Vista. 850.7208, 800/635.4529

Sea Ventures Fajardo. 863.3483, 800/739.DIVE

Spread Eagle Villa Marina (northeast of Fajardo). 863.1905

Sportfishing

Captain Mike Benítez Club Náutico de San Juan, Av Fernández Juncos (just north of Puente Esteves), Miramar, San Juan. 723.2292

José Castillo ESJ Towers, Isla Verde, San Juan. 791.6195 days, 726.5752 evenings

Karolett Fishing Charters Marina de Palmas, Wyndham Palmas del Mar (east of Rte 906), Buena Vista. 850.6000

Maragata Charters Marina de Palmas, Wyndham Palmas del Mar (east of Rte 906), Buena Vista. 850.7548

Surfing

West Coast Surf Rincón. 823.3935

food as "gourmet Spanish," new chef Alfredo Ayala's menu includes many "Nuevo Latino" dishes, including a pan-fried snapper fillet with cucumber and melon chutney, swordfish with a coconut and corn cream sauce, and beef fillet with fried yucca. Strolling musicians and candlelight add to the romantic ambience. ◆ Spanish/Nuevo Latino ◆ Daily dinner. 796.1234

86 Parque de Las Ciencias Luis A. Ferré (Luis A. Ferre Science Park) This small park aims to expose children to science. US rockets loom next to the **Museo de Geografía y Ciencia Física** (Museum of Geography and Physical Sciences), while Taíno artifacts are showcased within the **Museo de Arqueología** (Museum of Archaeology). Antique cars are the draw at the **Museo de Transportación** (Museum of Transportation), and a display of mounted animals and a small zoo are set next to a lake with paddleboats. ◆ Admission. W-Su. Rte 167 (between Main Oeste and Expreso José de Diego), Bayamón. 740.6868

87 Parque Central de Bayamón (Central Park of Bayamón) The grounds here are highlighted by a 19th-century schoolhouse and a working sugarcane train from the 1930s. ◆ Free. Daily. Rtes 2 and 174, Bayamón. 798.8191

88 Bacardi Rum Distillery Located just across the bay from Old San Juan, this factory distills as many as 100,000 gallons of rum in a day. Guided tours are given and complimentary rum drinks are served. From Old San Juan, take the ferry (863.0852) and then a *público* or bus. ◆ Free. M-Sa. Av Nereidas (just east of Av del Cano), Cataño. 788.1500

Bests

Robert Becker
Assistant Managing Editor, *San Juan Star*

My favorite part of Puerto Rico is its spectacular mountain zone, a wondrous place of breathtaking vistas and rural folk stubbornly clinging to a slower more pleasurable way of life as it used to be lived.

Spotted throughout the island's twisting, turning mountain roads are *lechoneras*, outdoor restaurants that, on weekends, become the gathering place for Puerto Rico's families. This is how you relax in Puerto Rico. Whole pigs and chickens roast slowly over charcoal fires, while groups play the island's traditional folkloric music.

Pile your plate up with roast pig seasoned with salt, pepper, and oregano, or with half a roast chicken, a heaping mound of rice with pigeon peas, and a couple of slices of sweet, braised ripe plantain. Wash it all down with an ice-cold local beer. Now that's weekends in Puerto Rico.

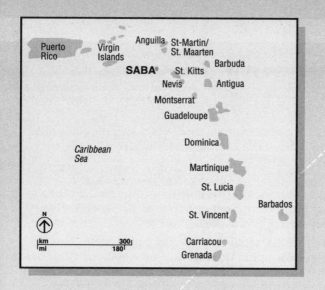

Puerto Rico

Virgin Islands

Anguilla

St-Martin/ St. Maarten

SABA

St. Kitts

Barbuda

Nevis

Antigua

Montserrat

Guadeloupe

Dominica

Martinique

St. Lucia

St. Vincent

Barbados

Carriacou

Grenada

Caribbean Sea

N

| km | 300 |
| mi | 180 |

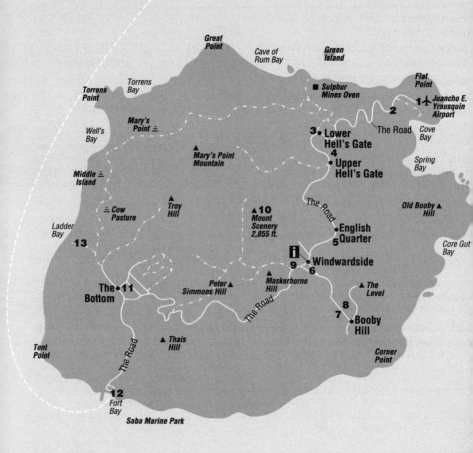

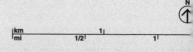
to Philipsburg, St. Maarten

Great Point

Cave of Rum Bay

Green Island

Flat Point

Torrens Point

Torrens Bay

■ Sulphur Mines Oven

1 ✈ Juancho E. Yrausquin Airport

2

Mary's Point ≃

The Road

Cove Bay

Well's Bay

3 ● Lower Hell's Gate

Mary's Point Mountain

4 ● Upper Hell's Gate

Spring Bay

Middle ≃ Island

Old Booby Hill ▲

≃ Cow Pasture

Troy Hill ▲

▲**10** Mount Scenery 2,855 ft.

The Road

Core Gut Bay

Ladder Bay

13

● English Quarter

5

ℹ

9 ● Windwardside

6

The Bottom ● **11**

Peter ▲ Simmons Hill

Maskerhorne Hill ▲

▲ The Level

8

Thais Hill ▲

The Road

7 ● Booby Hill

Tent Point

Corner Point

12

Fort Bay

Saba Marine Park

Caribbean Sea

| km | 1 |
| mi | 1/2 | 1 |

N

Saba

Although the diving is great on Saba (pronounced *Say*-bah), the island doesn't offer the sandy beaches that you would expect on a typical tropical isle. The tip of an extinct volcanic range that juts some 3,000 feet above the Caribbean, Saba's rocky coastline is no place to build sand castles. Instead, centuries of tough construction conditions have produced clusters of doll-size houses that cling to the hillsides, connected by a unique network of rough-hewn stone stairwells.

Donkeys and sensible shoes were the dominant modes of transportation until the island's only major thoroughfare was completed in the early 1950s. Switchbacks and sudden plunges mark the hairy 10-kilometer (6-mile) drive, but the route is simply named and easy to find: just ask for directions to **The Road.**

Air travelers make a dramatic entrance at **Flat Point,** heading straight for a mountainside, with a sharp last-second twist onto one of the world's shortest runways: just 1,312 feet between opposite cliffs.

From sea level, hikers can climb 800 stone steps to the capital town, **The Bottom;** almost everything else is uphill from there. The strenuous 30-minute huff up **The Ladder** rewards climbers with fine perspectives of the coastal bluffs and engenders great sympathy for early settlers who made the trek lugging all their worldly goods. Another of the island's famous "stairwell hikes" scales 1,064 steps to the crest of **Mount Scenery** (2,855 feet), a 3-hour round-trip that rewards the stouthearted with views of Windward Island neighbors St. Eustatius and St. Maarten. Those who prefer to vacation at a more stately pace can join monthly croquet matches on the grounds of the **Harry L. Johnson Memorial Museum,** a restored sea captain's home in **Windwardside.** Just remember to wear your whites and keep your cool.

Saba Marine Park, where visibility exceeds 125 feet and sites vary from towering walls to shallow reefs and elkhorn coral forests, offers divers virtually virgin depths to explore. A spectacular underwater mountain charted by the *M/V Caribbean Explorer* in 1992 brings the park's total to four, but locals still speak of several other sea mounts yet to be discovered.

Saba was sighted by Christopher Columbus on his second voyage in 1493; it changed hands 12 times before the Dutch assumed control in 1816. Today the island is the 5-square-mile home of some 1,200 self-governing citizens of the Netherlands Antilles. Their primary language is English, however—a holdover from the original colonists, who were Shetland Islanders.

Because of its isolation and severe topography, many of Saba's other historic milestones are quite recent: The first car (a Jeep carried ashore by 50 men) arrived in 1947, the first supermarket in 1963, and the first cruise ship in 1966.

A fiber-optic phone system improved intraisland connections in 1989, and the eastern Caribbean's only recompression chamber enhanced the local scuba scene in 1990. Since then, a few hotels have opened, including the **Cottage Club** and **Willard's of Saba.** In 1995 the government put a moratorium on building new hotels in order to fend off speculation and overdevelopment. Meanwhile, nightlife is pretty limited: Friday and Saturday dances at **Guido's** and friendly bar crowds at **Captain's Quarters** and **Scout's Place** pretty much cover it.

Days are great for divers, bird-watchers, naturalists, and hammock lovers. Watercolorists love the villages of picturesque Dutch gingerbread houses (by tradition they are all painted white with red-tile roofs and green shutters), set incongruously in the sheer tropical landscape that inspired Saba's nickname, "the big green gumdrop." Art lovers can check out the galleries of Windwardside while shoppers can track down the intricately drawn threadwork known as Saba lace and the piquant 151-proof rum liqueur, Saba Spice. And then there's the most tempting option—doing nothing at all.

To call from the US, dial 011 (international access code), 5994 (country code), and the 5-digit local number. On Saba, dial only the 5-digit local number unless otherwise indicated.

Getting to the Island

Airline

Interisland Carrier

WINAIR (Windward Island Airways).....5995/54237, ...5995/54230 on St. Maarten

Airport **Juancho E. Yrausquin Airport** (62222) is the destination for **WINAIR**'s short takeoff and landing (STOL) craft that make the 15-minute hop from St. Maarten's **Juliana Airport** to Flat Point five times daily. Services here are basic and there are no porters, so travel lightly.

Ferries The catamaran, *The Edge* (63347), carries day-trippers from St. Maarten every Wednesday, Friday, and Sunday, departing St. Maarten at 9AM and leaving Saba at 3:45PM. The ride takes about an hour and a quarter each way. A newer ferry, *Voyager I* (5995/2409), leaves St. Maarten on Monday and Wednesday through Sunday at 8:30AM, returning from Saba's **Fort Bay** at 4PM.

Getting Around the Island

Car Rental

Johnson's Rent-A-Car 62269

Mike's Car Rental 63259

Scout's Place ....62205; fax 62388

Driving A clean and well-tended fleet of 16 rental cars is distributed among the three agencies listed above, but considering the dramatic topography of the island, it might be best to hitch a ride.

Hitchhiking Here's the traditional mode of transportation, a safe and friendly alternative to driving yourself and a good way to meet the island's residents. There are a couple of standard pickup spots: in The Bottom, sit on the wall across from the **Anglican Church**; at Fort Bay, sit on the wall across from **Saba Deep**. Otherwise, just stick out your thumb and someone is sure to pull over.

Taxis Saba's 13 taxis are all independently owned. Call 160 for pickup.

Tours All taxi drivers offer a two-hour island tour that makes the rounds of villages and major sights. Just ask.

FYI

Electricity The current is 110 volts/60 cycles, the same as in the US and Canada.

Entry Requirements US and Canadian visitors must present a valid passport or other proof of citizenship (birth certificate, voter's registration card) plus a photo ID and a return or onward ticket. Saba is a free port.

Language Sabans greet each other as they pass with a brisk "Howzzit? Howzzit?" The official language is Dutch, plastered on all public signs, but everyone here speaks English, a legacy of the original Scottish-English-Irish settlers.

Money Although the official currency is the Netherlands Antilles florin (NAf, also known as a guilder), US dollars are widely accepted, as are Visa and MasterCard. Banks are open Monday through Friday from 8:30AM to noon.

Personal Safety Saba is practically crime free.

Publications *The Guardian* and *The Daily Herald* are dailies delivered from St. Maarten; each features stories from the Saba bureau. The island's own *Saba Herald* is published monthly.

Reservation Services and House Rentals Several private owners rent houses and apartments. For a list of available properties, contact the **Saba Tourist Bureau** (see "Visitors' Information Office," below).

Taxes There's an eight-percent tax on hotel bills. The airport tax is $2 for those flying to Saba or St. Maarten, $10 for other flights.

Tipping First check restaurant, bar, and hotel bills for the standard 10- to 15-percent service charge; otherwise, that's the correct amount to tip. Give cab drivers $1 or $2.

Visitors' Information Office The **Saba Tourist Bureau** (Lambert Hassell Building, Windwardside, 62231, 62322; fax 62350) is open Monday through Friday from 8AM to noon and from 1 to 5PM.

Phone Book

Ambulance 63288, 63289

Directory Assistance 63211

Diving Emergencies/
   Decompression Chamber...........................63295

Emergencies 63237

Fire...62222

Hospital..63288, 63289

Police..63237

Post Offices..
   The Bottom..63217
   Windwardside 62221

Steep and rocky Saba has never needed battlements to protect itself. In the past, islanders rolled boulders down on the heads of invaders who tried to climb up from the shoreline.

Before The Road was completed, everything that landed on Saba had to be heaved up the 800 steps between sea level and The Bottom. It took 12 men to carry a Steinway grand piano, four men and a sedan chair to hoist a visiting bishop.

1 Juancho E. Yrausquin Airport Don't despair as you approach one of the world's shortest runways—1,312 feet bracketed by facing cliffs. The precision touchdown is a thrill—almost like landing on an aircraft carrier—but more than 160,000 passengers have screeched to a halt here since **WINAIR** began regular service from St. Maarten in 1963. The airport claims one of the only flat sites on this bumpy island, 130 feet above sea level on the northeast coast. Even so, the 1959 construction project was a feat of engineering, led by aviation pioneer Rémy de Haenen, former mayor of St-Barthélemy (home to another infamous airstrip that's nearly twice the length of this one). There's a snack bar. ◆ Flat Point. 62222

2 The Road People who fear flying are often told that the most dangerous part of the trip is the drive into town from the airport. Climb aboard here for heart-stopping supporting evidence—10 kilometers (6 miles) of switchbacks, deep plunges, and hairpin curves that scale the steep side of the island, wind through the interior towns, then descend to Fort Bay on the opposite coast. "The road that couldn't be built" was a 20-year project for determined Sabans, who laid the concrete marvel by hand after local designer Josephus Lambert Hassell completed a correspondence course in engineering. Be sure to notice the charming, quaint villages of Lower Hell's Gate, Upper Hell's Gate, and English Quarter. ◆ Between Juancho E. Yrausquin Airport and Fort Bay

3 The Gate House $$ Set in the hilltop seclusion of Lower Hell's Gate, this gingerbread hostelry is one of Saba's newest lodging options. It has six rooms, two with kitchens, and a wraparound balcony with stunning views of St. Barts, St. Maarten, and Statia. The **Gate House Cafe**'s dinner menu features Saban seafood and vegetarian specialties. ◆ Lower Hell's Gate. 62416; fax 62550

4 Community Center Here's a good place to buy Saba lace, the elaborate Spanish-style embroidery created by local artisans since the 1870s. Look for well-crafted table and bed linens, clothing, and accessories. The prices are high, but with proper care (hand laundering is de rigueur), these souvenirs of a slower world should last a lifetime. ◆ Daily mornings. Upper Hell's Gate. 62300

5 Cottage Club $$$ This neat cluster of gingerbread cottages offers 10 spacious accommodations with private balconies, fully equipped kitchens, TV sets, telephones, ceiling fans, and sea breezes. The lobby of the main building—built in authentic Saban stone-and-wood style with the mandatory red-tiled roof—is decorated with antiques, including Italian Renaissance chairs. There's no restaurant, but there is a swimming pool and at press time a Jacuzzi was on the drawing board. Children under 12 stay free in their parents' room. ◆ English Quarter. 62486; fax 62476

6 Windwardside Saba's second city—well, village—is home to most of its guest rooms, tourist shops, and restaurants. It commands "the top of The Road," just east of the thoroughfare's midpoint at an elevation of 1,804 feet.

In Windwardside:

Harry L. Johnson Memorial Museum Sign the guest book and you'll be in swank company (an unexpected visit from Jacqueline Kennedy Onassis added that prized autograph on 28 March 1978). The exhibits are always evolving at this tiny restored house, also known as the **Saba Museum,** which was formerly home to a Dutch sea captain. There's old Saban lacework, hand-carved furnishings, pre-Columbian artifacts, a rock oven, an antique organ, and other local memorabilia. In the adjoining meadow a bust of Simón Bolívar honors the freedom fighter who visited the island in 1816 to enlist support for his South American campaigns. Croquet games are held on the museum grounds the first Sunday of the month. ◆ Admission. M-F. No phone

Lambert Hassell Building This place houses the **Saba Tourist Bureau** as well as a number of shops and galleries, including the **Breadfruit Gallery** (62509), featuring works by local artists, and **Saba Tropical Arts** (62373), with myriad other island products. ◆ M-F

Jobean Designs Jo Bean's colorful glass jewelry is displayed and sold here. ◆ M-Sa. 62490

Guido's Pizzeria ★$ Equal parts recreation hall and pizzeria, this friendly hangout is best known for the open-invitation town dances at its **Mountain High Club,** which attract big turnouts on Friday and Saturday nights. Expect reasonable burgers and Italian food, big-screen TV, loud music, and good darts. ◆ Italian/American ◆ Daily dinner. 62230

Juliana's $$ For quiet and functional accommodations, check out this Old World charmer offering nine double rooms with private balconies and small refrigerators. A one-bedroom apartment and two two-bedroom cottages are each equipped with a full kitchen and patio. The tidy frame buildings, painted white, share great sea views, mountain landscape, a restaurant (see below), and a swimming pool. ♦ 62269, 800/223.9815; fax 62389

Within Juliana's:

Tropics Cafe ★$ This poolside cafe overlooking the Caribbean serves a full breakfast and burgers and sandwiches for lunch. At dinnertime the menu goes more upscale, offering fresh fish and lobster dishes and salads of greens grown on the premises. ♦ American ♦ M breakfast and lunch; Tu-Sa breakfast, lunch, and dinner; Su breakfast. 62269

Captain's Quarters $$$ The early 19th-century home of Saba sea captain Henry Hassell (whose image can be seen in an old photo hanging near the front door) is the setting for this charming hotel. The 14 rooms are big, airy, and cooled by sea breezes rather than air-conditioning. Many are furnished with four-poster beds and antiques and all feature long-range views of the sea, TV sets, and mini-bars. (There are no telephones in the rooms, but cell phones are available.) The terrace and swimming pool are perched a scenic 1,500 feet above the Caribbean, and greenery trims the graceful West Indian–style buildings. The hotel has a fine restaurant and one of the most congenial bars in town (both were closed at press time but were slated to reopen soon). Rates include full breakfast. ♦ 62201, 800/446.3010; fax 62377

Saba Chinese Family Restaurant ★$ The atmosphere is campy and the ambitious menu offers more than 100 Cantonese and Indonesian dishes as well as steak. Crowds fill the bar to watch satellite TV, especially on Saturday and Sunday. ♦ Chinese ♦ Daily lunch and dinner. 62268

The 151-proof rum liqueur known as Saba Spice, marketed through local shops, is made by local women in their homes. No two bottles are the same, as each cottage distiller uses her own secret recipe.

The dreaded pirate Henry Morgan died not by enemy sword or walking the plank, but from being "much given to drinking and sitting up late."

Scout's Place $$ Formerly owned (and still frequented) by Scout Thirkield, this very popular guest house and restaurant (see below) are now run by Thirkield's former cook, Dianna Medero, and barman, Harold Levenstone. Stop here for "Bed 'n' Board, Cheap 'n' Cheerful." Four basic doubles share a small pool and sweeping views with 10 newer rooms with four-poster beds. All units have balconies and cable TV, but don't look for air-conditioning or telephones. The best way to enjoy this place is to join the jovial regulars over a cold beer. Rates include breakfast. ♦ 62205; fax 62388

Within Scout's Place:

Scout's Place Restaurant ★★$$ Linger for after-dinner cards and kibitzing at Saba's most popular eatery, where the menu ranges from Caribbean fish dishes to American entrées to stewed goat and mutton. The open-air dining room has fine views; ask to be seated outdoors on the terrace at sunset. ♦ Caribbean/American ♦ Daily breakfast, lunch, and dinner. Reservations recommended. 62205

Brigadoon ★★$$ An open-air patio lends a casual air to the eclectic menu at this dining spot. Saba-born owner Greg Johnson no longer personally runs the kitchen, but the menu still features his signature fresh fish dishes (try the mahimahi with a mustard and citrus sauce), steaks, and homemade desserts. ♦ Caribbean/Continental ♦ Daily dinner. 62380

7 Willard's of Saba $$$ Watch the sunset from an outdoor spa 1,700 feet above the sea at this cozy resort. Most of the seven bungalow rooms open onto balconies or patios, and the views are outstanding. There are no TV sets or telephones to disturb the peace (although they are available on request), and air-conditioning is provided by sea breezes and ceiling fans. A heated swimming pool, a tennis court, and a restaurant (see below) are also on the premises. ♦ Booby Hill. 62498; fax 62482

Within Willard's of Saba:

Willard's of Saba Restaurant ★★$$$ Hotel manager and chef Corazon de Johnson whips up delicious Asian and Caribbean dishes, including chicken Szechuan and broiled lobster. Caribbean artwork brightens the walls. ♦ Asian/Caribbean ♦ Daily breakfast, lunch, and dinner. Reservations recommended. 62498

8 El Momo Cottages $ A bit of a hike up Booby Hill, this new hotel with gingerbread architectural details is bargain-priced but reliable. The five rooms with private porches are set among lush greenery. Other perks include maid service, a pool, and great sunset views. There's no restaurant, but breakfast is available. ♦ Booby Hill. 62265; fax 62265

9 Saba Trail Shop At the bottom of the steps up Mount Scenery, this shop sells hand-crafted souvenirs, maps, and guidebooks, rents walking sticks to hikers, and takes reservations for guided rain-forest hikes. The shop is operated by the Saba Conservation Foundation, and all proceeds benefit the foundation. ♦ Northwest of Windwardside. 62630

10 Mount Scenery Just beyond Windwardside, a "stairwell hike" up 1,064 rough-hewn steps leads through a rain forest lush with giant "elephant ears," wild orchids, and tree ferns to the summit of this mountain, 2,855 feet above the sea. The spectacular vistas of the Caribbean and neighboring islands more than compensate for the uphill climb. Allow three hours for the round-trip.

11 The Bottom The name of Saba's capital must have puzzled early visitors who had to climb 800 stone steps up from the shore. Actually, it's an Anglicized version of *botte,* Dutch for bowl—the town is set in a gently sloping plateau surrounded by volcanic domes. The local council changed the name to **Leverock Town** in the 19th century to honor former leader Moses Leverock, but the new title didn't take. Today it's a picture-perfect village, an Old World community of steep gabled roofs and trim gardens. Stroll by the peach-and-white governor's house with its small park, then peruse the charming watercolors at **Heleen's Art Gallery** (63348).

In The Bottom:

Saba Artisans Foundation Silk-screened clothing and household accessories are splashed with palm fronds, flowers, or patterns drawn from the famous Saba lace. Also appealing are the hand-printed cotton items created by Saban artists. The colorful stock includes leatherwork and dolls from Curaçao. ♦ Daily. 63260

Cranston's Antique Inn $ Once the official government guest house, this 130-year-plus hotel with typical island architecture has 7 guest rooms with 4-poster beds. Over the past few years the rooms have become rather run-down, but are currently undergoing renovation. To feel like royalty, request room **No. 1,** where Dutch Queen Juliana once stayed. ♦ 63203

12 Fort Bay Both visitors and supplies land at this 250-foot pier. It's literally the end of The Road and the site of the island's only power plant and gas station. Locals like to swim here (down some steps), and scuba types will find two dive shops. ♦ Southwest coast. 63294

At Fort Bay:

Saba Marine Park (SMP) This carefully tended preserve encircles the island, protecting the seabed and all waters to a depth of 200 feet. Fishing and anchoring are completely prohibited throughout five recreational diving zones, where the virgin reefs and towering sea mounts are explored by fewer than 1,000 visitors per year. Beginners can rent a waterproof laminated map for a fun self-guided tour of the **Edward S. Arnold Snorkel Trail** at Torrens Point. For guidebooks, maps, and more information, stop by the tourist office or the preserve's information office, which also schedules free slide shows. For information on boat and equipment rentals, see "Getting Your Feet Wet in Saba," below ♦ 63295

In Two Deep ★★$ This casual breakfast and lunch spot overlooks the ocean and offers a recently revamped lunch menu in which the traditional chili, baked Buffalo wings, and homemade soups have been joined by jalapeño poppers with salsa and grilled snapper sandwiches. Come on Sunday for the popular brunch—it's the only day that the restaurant's much-talked-about eggs Benedict are served. ♦ American ♦ M-Sa breakfast and lunch; Su brunch. 63438; fax 63347

13 The Ladder Here's the notorious 800-step stairwell that used to be the only route from the dock to town. Hikers who whine at midpoint should note that some of their predecessors once made it to the top carrying a grand piano. ♦ Between The Bottom and Ladder Bay

Getting Your Feet Wet in Saba

Saba is building a worldwide reputation as one of the best diving destinations in the Caribbean. Sportfishing is also good in these waters. Here are a few organizations that can get you afloat:

Snorkeling and Scuba Diving

Caribbean Explorer 800/322.3577 (weeklong live-aboard trips)

Go Diving 5610 Rowland Rd, Suite 100, Minnetonka, MN 55343, 800/328.5285

Saba Deep Dive Shop Fort Bay. 63347, 717/346.6382

Saba Reef Divers Windwardside. 62541

Sea Saba Windwardside. 62246

Sportfishing

Arrindell Hassell Windwardside. 62473

Greg's Fishing Charters Windwardside. 62510

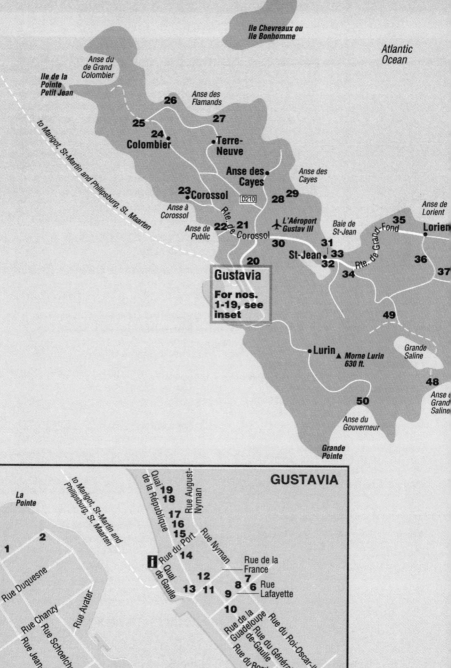

Atlantic Ocean

Ile Chevreaux ou Ile Bonhomme

Anse du de Grand Colombier

Ile de la Pointe Petit Jean

to Marigot, St-Martin and Phillipsburg, St. Maarten

26 Anse des Flamands

27

25

24 Colombier

Terre-Neuve

Anse des Cayes

Anse des Cayes

23 Corossol

Anse à Corossol

D210

28 **29**

Rte. de Corossol

Anse de Public

22 **21**

L'Aéroport Gustav III

Baie de St-Jean

Anse de Lorient

35

Lorien

30 St-Jean

31

33

32

34

Rte. de Grand-Fond

36

37

20

Gustavia

For nos. 1-19, see inset

49

Grande Saline

Lurin

Morne Lurin 630 ft.

48

Anse Grand Saline

50

Anse du Gouverneur

Grande Pointe

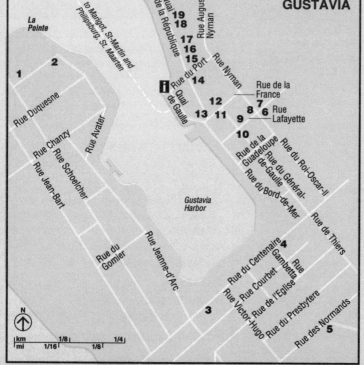

GUSTAVIA

La Pointe

1

2

Rue Duquesne

Rue Chanzy

Rue Schoelcher

Rue Jean-Bart

to Marigot, St-Martin and Phillipsburg, St. Maarten

Rue Avater

Quai de la République

Rue August-Nyman

19
18

17
16
15

Rue Nyman

Rue du Port

14

i

Quai de Gaulle

Rue de la France

12

13 **11**

8 **7**

9 **6** Rue Lafayette

10

Rue de la Guadeloupe

Rue du Général-de-Gaulle

Rue du Bord-de-Mer

Rue du Roi-Oscar-II

Rue de Thiers

Gustavia Harbor

Rue du Gomier

Rue Jeanne-d'Arc

3

Rue du Centenaire

Rue Courbet

Rue Victor-Hugo

Gambetta

Rue de l'Eglise

4

Rue du Presbytere

Rue des Normands

5

N

km
mi
1/16
1/8
1/8
1/4

Pointe
Lorient

Ile
Tortue

ot 39

Anse de
Marigot
40 **41** Anse du
Grand
D209   **43** Cul de **45**
Sac
44
42
**Grand
Cul de Sac**
46 •**Petit Cul
de Sac**

▲ Morne
du Vitet
922 ft. •**Toiny**
Grand **47**
• **Fond**
Anse
D211 Toiny

Anse de
Grand Fond

km
mi 1/2 1 1 2

N

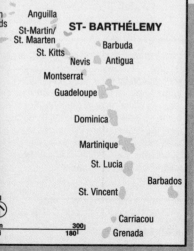

Anguilla
St-Martin/   **ST- BARTHÉLEMY**
St. Maarten
St. Kitts   Barbuda
Nevis Antigua
Montserrat
Guadeloupe

Dominica

Martinique
St. Lucia
Barbados
St. Vincent

Carriacou
300
180 Grenada

St-Barthélemy

A favored nesting spot for royals, rock stars, and Rothschilds, St-Barthélemy (pronounced San Bar-*tay*-le-mee) has a Mediterranean-village atmosphere that recalls the Côte d'Azur in its heyday. And though pricey, room and board are the best that money can buy in this eight-square-mile playground of immaculate beaches, elegant villas, and mountain farms ringed by low stone fences. Here haute privacy and ultracasual chic reign supreme. If you want to keep pace with the idle rich, dress down and consume inconspicuously.

You won't find movie theaters (better to go stargazing), big discos (town dances on weekends can be fun), or high-rise hotels (the largest, swank **Guanahani,** has only 76 rooms). There are no casinos, but you can get in on a hot game of dominoes with the sailors and young locals who hang out at **Bar de l'Oubli** and **Le Sélect.**

First sighted by Christopher Columbus in 1493 and named for his brother Bartolomeo, "St. Barts" is now home to 6,500 French citizens, most descended from the Breton, Norman, and Poitevin colonists who settled here in the 17th century. In the postcard villages of **Corossol** and **Colombier,** a few blue-eyed older women still wear starched white bonnets, go barefoot, and weave the fine baskets, hats, and other straw goods that have been a local specialty for over 200 years.

French pirates once swarmed these shores, loaded down with booty from their raids on Spanish galleons. Legend has it that the dreaded buccaneer Monbars the Exterminator kept his headquarters here, along with a major stash that some believe is still concealed in the coves of **Anse du Gouverneur** beach or beneath the sands of **Grande Saline.**

The only Caribbean island with Swedish bloodlines, St-Barthélemy was traded in 1784 to King Gustav III, who declared the harbor a free port—a lucrative status that it still retains. France reacquired the property in 1878, b a few Viking footprints remain: a capital town called **Gustavia,** some sharp-edged Nordic architecture, a cemetery, and street names posted in both Swedish and French.

Today St. Barts is a dependency of Guadeloupe, an overseas department and *région* of France that lies 125 miles to the southeast. Islanders participate in French elections, but have their own mayor and town constable, as well as a security force with 6 police officers and 13 gendarmes.

In true Gallic tradition, more than 60 restaurants crowd this tiny resort islar many staffed by seasoned chefs from Europe and the US. Diehard burger addicts can even get a quick fix at **Cheeseburger in Paradise,** named in honor of sometime-resident Jimmy Buffet. Many hotels and restaurants clos for several months during the off-season (roughly July through October). It' best to call ahead before booking your flight.

Water-sports enthusiasts will find no time to be bored. The island often hosts trans-Atlantic regattas, and there is no shortage of scuba, windsurfing, and charter outfits. Each January, the **St. Barts Music Festival** imports international artists for two weeks of classical and jazz programs at Gustavia 18th-century Anglican church and the nearby hamlet of **Lorient.**

Those in search of quieter pursuits can hire one of the canopied buggies known as mini-mokes or gurgels and easily explore the entire island on one tank of gas. The **Route de Grand-Fond** passes the beautiful beaches of **Baie St-Jean, Anse de Lorient, Anse de Marigot, Anse du Grand Cul de Sac,** an **Anse du Petit Cul de Sac.** The mountain landscape and tile-roofed houses a **Vitet** evoke a miniature Normandy. Surfers love the big waves at Lorient, an local families flock to the sands of Marigot. Grand Cul de Sac is lively with seaside cafes and water-sports concessions.

There are no official nude beaches (cavorting *au naturel* is strictly for *les enfants*), but monokinis are a common sight and, although nude bathing is not sanctioned, it is sometimes practiced at **Anse de Grande Saline.** Shy visitors can pick up something a bit more modest at dozens of quaint little shops sporting such legendary names as **Hermès, Gucci, Stéphane & Bernard.** Just don't expect any bargains.

To call from the US, dial 011 (international access code), 590 (country code), and the 6-digit local number. On St. Barts, dial only the 6-digit local number unless otherwise indicated.

Getting to the Island

Airlines

Interisland Carriers

Air Guadeloupe	276190
Air St-Barthélemy	277190
Air St. Thomas	277176
WINAIR (Windward Island Airways)	
in St. Barts	276101,
in St. Maarten	5995/54230
in the US	800/634.4907

Airport L'Aéroport Gustav III (Rte D209, between Baie de St-Jean and Rte D210, 276541) caters to light aircraft making interisland flights.

Ferries and Interisland Cruises Several boats ferry passengers between St-Martin/St. Maarten an Gustavia Harbor on St. Barts. **Voyager** (277724) leaves from Marigot on St-Martin's French side; others, such as **White Octopus** (5995/23170 in St. Maarten) leave from Philipsburg on the Dutch side where there is a departure tax. Private charters are available through **Marine Service** (Gustavia, 277034), **Sibarth** (Gustavia, 276238), or **WIMCO** (**West Indies Management Company, 800/932.3222**).

Getting Around the Island

Bicycles and Motorbikes

Denis Dufau's Rent Some Fun	27705
St-Barth Motobike	27678

Car Rental

Avis	277143, 800/331.108

Budget 276630, 800/527.0700

Charles Gréaux..276190

Europcar 277333

Hertz 277114, 800/654.3131

Mathieu Aubin Car Rental.............................277303

Soleil Caraïbe 276718, 276506

Driving A valid driver's license is all that's required to drive on the island. You'll need to reserve a car far in advance during peak season. Stick-shift minimokes and four-wheel-drive vehicles are best for this hilly terrain. Good scenic drives are Route de Grand-Fond and **Route de Corossol.**

Taxis

J-Claude Blanchard 273680

Line Bernier...276971

Mathilde Laplace 276059

Taxi Stand 276631

Tours Operators offering island tours include **Bruno Béal** (276005), **Céline Gréaux** (276598), **Emile Gréaux** (276601), and **Robert Magras** (276312).

FYI

Electricity The current is 220 volts/60 cycles; French plug adapters and converters are necessary for North American appliances. Many hotels provide hair dryers.

Entry Requirements US and Canadian travelers must present a valid passport or other proof of citizenship (birth certificate, voter's registration card) plus a photo ID, along with a return or onward ticket. Visas are required for stays longer than three months.

Language French is the official language and, though many islanders speak English, a phrase book and patience will come in handy. Some of the older women of Corossol still speak an obscure Norman dialect.

Money The official currency is the French franc. Stores and restaurants freely accept US dollars and traveler's checks (but offer no discount for them); Canadian currency is not as readily taken. Banks in Gustavia are open Monday through Friday from 8AM to noon and 2 to 3:30 or 4PM. Most other businesses also close midday for lunch. Credit cards are not honored everywhere, so be sure to ask before checking into your hotel or ordering at a restaurant.

Personal Safety Crime is rare, but don't leave valuables in an unlocked car or unguarded on the beach.

Publications Seasonal periodicals include *Tropical St-Barth* and the *Guide Saint Barth,* both published by the local hotel association. They are available in book stores, souvenir shops, and hotels. *Bonjour St-Barth!,* a bilingual guidebook published periodically, offers practical information, good illustrations, maps, and local lore. All three publications are in French and English. Georges Bourdin's *History of St. Barthélemy* is a more scholarly work published by Porter Henry. The latter two are usually available at **Le Colibri** (Quai de la République, Gustavia, 276092).

Reservation Services and House Rentals

CMI 278088

Ici & Là Saint Barth 277878, 800/504.9923

Immo-Antilles 279045

New Agency 278114

Sibarth Real Estate 276238

WIMCO (West Indies Management Company) ....
.................................401/849.8012, 800/932.3222

Also see "Making Yourself at Home on St. Barts" on page 236.

Taxes At press time there were no sales, hotel, or restaurant taxes.

Telephones *Télécartes* (phone cards) are needed to make calls from pay phones; they can be purchased at the post office and at *tabacs.* There are no coin-operated telephones on the island.

Tipping A 10- to 15-percent service charge is added to hotel bills and restaurant checks, and is adequate except in cases of extra-special service. If no service charge has been added, leave 15 percent of the check. Taxi drivers, most of whom own their cars, don't expect a tip.

Visitors' Information Office The tourist information bureau (Quai de Gaulle, between Rues de la France and du Port, Gustavia, 278727; fax 277447) is open Monday through Friday from 8:30AM to 12:30PM and 2 to 5PM, and Saturday from 9AM to noon.

Phone Book

Ambulance 18, 276231

Directory Assistance 12

Diving Emergencies/
   Decompression Chambers 18

Emergencies 18

Fire 18, 276231

Hospital...276035

Police 17, 276666

Post Office 276200

There is one restaurant for every 110 people on St. Barts.

Female sea turtles lay their eggs at Anse des Flamands and Anse à Corossol from April through August. Leave the turtles and the eggs alone—it is a crime to disturb them.

Gustavia

The harbor in this pretty, quaint capital city is so tiny that cruise ships have to anchor offshore. However, the port is often crowded with the yachts of the rich and famous, who love lounging around in the town's bars and restaurants. After a lazy day in the sun, join the crowds at the **Carl Gustaf, Le Sélect,** or **Bar de l'Oubli** for refreshment and conversation. Or pass the time shopping at the numerous chic boutiques filled with duty-free French fashions and jewelry.

1 Musée Municipal de Saint-Barthélemy
This tiny museum has antique photos, old maps, and centuries-old documents that guide visitors through the history of the island. A section also details the island's flora and fauna. It is housed in **Le Wall House,** a restored colonial stone building with a hazy past—the only thing definitely known is that it survived a disastrous fire in 1852. ♦ Admission. M afternoon; Tu-F; Sa morning. Rue Schoelcher (north of Rue Avater). 278907

2 Wall House Restaurant ★★★$$$
Named for its historic neighbor farther along the street, Jean-Pierre DeLage's lovely restaurant is a culinary bright spot. Try the grilled snapper in basil butter or grilled giant prawns spiked with whiskey. ♦ Continental ♦ M-F, Su lunch and dinner; Sa dinner. Rue Avater (between Rues Duquesne and Schoelcher). 277183

3 Au Port ★★★$$$ For years regulars have flocked to this dining spot, one of the oldest restaurants on the island. Signature starters such as conch sausage with avocado and sweet potato salad with Antillean stuffed crab are always dependable. Specialities of the house include an outstanding *filet de boeuf* (beef fillet) and sole with Champagne sauce. For a West Indian–style meal, try the *colombo* of lamb, a curry-style stew with roasted bananas. ♦ French/Creole ♦ Daily dinner Sept-Apr; M-Sa dinner May-Aug. Reservations recommended. Rue du Centenaire (between Rues Victor-Hugo and Jeanne-d'Arc). 276236

4 Le Sapotillier ★★★$$$ Try for a table under the namesake sapotilla tree, though the

inside dining room is a homey retreat. This restaurant is known for its exotic treatments of sea bass and huge shrimp; other flashy entrées include steamed stingray with horseradish sauce and pasta, duck with hazelnuts, and gratin of spinach and sweet potato. Wind up with a white-and-black chocolate mousse or tiramisù. ♦ French ♦ Daily dinner Sept-Apr, Sept-Dec; M-Sa dinner May-Aug; closed several weeks in ear May and late October. Reservations recommended. Rues du Centenaire and Gambetta. 276028

5 Carl Gustaf $$$$ Famous for its wonderfu views, this hostelry has 14 red-roofed cottage that climb a hillside draped in bougainvillea and tall stands of ginger. Inside are lofty gues rooms with ceiling fans and white marble floors, extravagant baths, kitchens, stereos, fax machines, and other welcome comforts. Breakfast is served on your own garden terrace, complete with a small pool, overlooking the harbor-front of Gustavia and the shores of St. Maarten beyond. Named for the current King of Sweden, this aristocratic property features a fitness center, a swimmin pool, and an elegant poolside restaurant and piano bar. ♦ Rue des Normands (southwest o the road to Lurin). 278283, 800/948.7823, 800/5GUSTAF, 800/322.2223; fax 278237

Within the Carl Gustaf:

Carl Gustaf ★★★★$$$$ Excellent haut cuisine stands up to towering views that sweep across the night lights of Gustavia and the surrounding hills. Chef Patrick Gateau's creations range from a pairing of filet mignon with apples and shallot cream sauce to class foie gras. Desserts are truly sumptuous, and soft music from the piano bar adds an elegan note. ♦ French ♦ Daily lunch and dinner. Reservations required. 278283

6 Vietnam ★★$$$ Thai, Vietnamese, and Indian fare are commingled at this restaurant decorated with Asian artwork. Try such exotica as curried fish with coconut milk, chicken sautéed with citronella, and spicy shrimp stuffed with diced vegetables. Conservative diners will also find the usual fried wontons, sweet-and-sour pork, and other Cantonese mainstays. ♦ Asian ♦ M-Sa lunch and dinner; Su dinner. Rues du Roi-Oscar-II and Lafayette. 278137

7 Le 'Ti Marché Crafters at Gustavia's outdoor market sell island-made wares ranging from straw goods to handwoven white linens. Don't miss the quayside stand with **Belou's "P"** products, an intoxicating inventory of home-brewed body oils and shampoos, rum punches and *digestifs* (liqueurs), all infused with local herbs and spices by transplanted Parisians Franck and Helene Garcia. ♦ Tu.-Th. Rues du Roi-Oscar-II and Lafayette

8 La Rôtisserie Stop here to pack a picnic of French sausages, roast chicken, pâtés, salads, fine wines, and other deli goods. And don't pass up the fresh pastries. ♦ Daily. Rues du Roi-Oscar-II and Lafayette. 276313. Also at: Rue St-Jean, St-Jean. 277346

9 Sophie Laurent With or without imprinted logo, men's and women's casuals from this boutique are among the newer status-wear. ♦ M-Sa. Rues du Général-de-Gaulle and Lafayette. 276757

10 Pipiri Palace ★★★$$ Formerly **Inès' Ghetto** (which for many years was **Eddy's Ghetto**) this favorite haunt is now under the management of Pierrot and Régine, who are hardly new to the spot, having worked at the restaurant for about 10 years. They're keeping both the ambience and cuisine that made the place such a big success for so long. The culinary focus remains on simple but substantial Creole and West Indian dishes as well as delicious barbecues. ♦ Caribbean ♦ Daily dinner. No credit cards accepted. Rue du Général-de-Gaulle (between Rues de la Guadeloupe and Lafayette). 278933

11 Le Sélect Sailors, deck hands, and young locals gather here day and night for beer, dominoes, and the latest gossip. The outdoor grill, **Cheeseburger in Paradise,** is named in honor of singer and sometime-island-resident Jimmy Buffett. It's not uncommon for other famous visitors to drift in, but this is one bar crowd that doesn't impress easily. ♦ M-Sa 10:30AM-1AM. Rues du Général-de-Gaulle and de la France. 278687

12 Bar de l'Oubli Step right across the street to the island's other primary watering hole. This open-air hangout for drinks and snacks is popular with the same crowd as **Le Sélect.** ♦ Daily 7:45AM-10PM. Rues de la République and de la France. 277006

13 Loulou's Marine Well known among the yachting crowd, this store is the place to stock up before fishing, snorkeling, boating, or other outdoor enterprises. *Tout le monde* sails into this famous chandlery for sporting gear, marine equipment, and men's and women's nautical clothes. Check the bulletin board for the latest yachting news. ♦ M-F; Sa mornings. Rue de la République and Quai de Gaulle. 276274

14 Stéphane & Bernard Be prepared for sticker shock at this exclusive boutique featuring women's fashion collections by an international stable of designers. ♦ M-F; Sa mornings. Rue de la République (between Rues de la France and du Port). 276569. Also at: Centre Commercial La Savane, Rte D209 (between Baie de St-Jean and Rte D210). 276913

15 Carré d'Or This two-level complex has a smorgasbord of shops, ranging from perfumeries to clothing stores to home decorating boutiques. It's a quiet place to stop, and a nice alternative when the main streets are crowded. ♦ Daily. Quai de la République and Rue du Port. No phone

Within Carré d'Or:

Free Mousse This two-shop store offers a wide selection of French perfumes, soaps, and housemade scents, as well as linens, rugs, and African-inspired home decorations (including wood carvings and tapestries). ♦ M-Sa. Level one. 277504

16 Manuel Canovas If you have to ask, you probably can't afford the high-fashion bath and table linens, coordinated china/linen breakfast services, beach towels, totes, luggage, bathing suits, and designer fabrics at this exclusive shop. ♦ M-Sa. Quai de la République (north of Rue du Port). 278278

17 Hermès Dress for noblesse at the local outpost of the posh purveyor that supplies Queen Elizabeth with those regal head scarves. You'll also find handbags, linen, jewelry, and other accessories at prices that will make your blood run blue. ♦ M-Sa. Quai de la République (north of Rue du Port). 276615

18 Sunset $ Ask for one of the three guest rooms that overlook the harbor at this pretty, old eight-room hotel. Basic accommodations are pleasantly furnished, with air-conditioning, mini-bars, and private baths. There's also a restaurant and bar. ♦ Quai de la République (north of Rue du Port). 277721; fax 278159

19 Le Repaire ★$$ This cafe on Gustavia's harbor front, a whitewashed charmer cooled by ceiling fans, has canned reggae playing in the background. Sit outside by the fish pond for a light meal of pastries, sandwiches, exotic salads, or fresh seafood. ♦ Continental ♦ Daily breakfast, lunch, and dinner. Quai de la République (north of Rue du Port). 277248

20 Donna Del Sol Long a fixture on Main Street in South Hampton, the Caribbean branch of this shop presents Donna's one-of-a-kind collection of jewelry. ♦ M-F; Sa mornings. Rue August-Nyman (north of Rue du Port). 279053

The St. Barts airport lies in an area called La Tourmente—so named, no doubt, for the emotion first-timers feel when they contemplate its short runway.

Elsewhere on St-Barthélemy

21 Route de Corossol Drive along this picturesque road to see the beauty of the northwestern part of the island. ♦ Between Rte D210 and Corossol

On Route de Corossol:

Les Grands Vins de France Stop in for a tasting with wine importer Jean Patrick Gay and assistant Stéphane Dantec. Gay's company offers over 400 different vintages at below-retail prices in this showroom adjoining his home. ♦ M-Sa; mornings only in summer. 277744; fax 277744

22 Maya's ★★★$$ Join the crowd on the waterfront terrace for authentic Creole *accras de giraumon* (squash fritters) or *salade de patate douce au beurre de cari* (curried sweet potato salad). Martiniquan chef Maya changes her menu daily but features the freshest grilled fish and lobster, curries, and excellent chicken dishes as well as tropical sorbets and other housemade desserts (don't miss the dense chocolate cake). ♦ Creole ♦ M-Sa dinner; closed June–mid-July, September–mid-October. Reservations recommended. Anse de Public. 277361

23 Corossol Descendants of the earliest French settlers who arrived over 300 years ago still live in the "straw village" of Corossol. You'll find old women making and selling fine straw baskets, hats, and similar items here, a few of them barefoot and sporting traditional white Breton bonnets. (Be sure to ask before photographing, as many don't like to have their pictures taken.) Don't miss **Marion Vinot**'s tiny one-room gallery (call before visiting as hours vary, 277897), located among the straw stands. Her paintings portray fashionable Parisian-type women. Colorful fishing boats line the beach at the end of the road. ♦ Anse à Corossol

24 François Plantation $$$ A twisting road leads high into the hills to this elegant retreat, where pastel tin-roofed cottages open onto terraces with glorious sea views. Owner

François Beret, also a skilled chef and gardener, has created a tame jungle of palms and palmettos, sun-washed terra-cotta walkways, and bougainvillea-draped loggias. The 12 guest rooms are spacious and subdued, decked out with Provençal fabrics, and boasting four-poster beds and other colonial-style antique reproductions. More comforts include baths filled with keystone coral and marble, air-conditioning, ceiling fans, refrigerator/bars, wall safes, telephones and TV with US and French programs. The pool is carved into a slope at the very top of the property, where swimmers can drink in the panorama of the deeper blue waters and offshore islands below. A full breakfast is laid out in the garden dining room or (for a small extra charge) on cottage terraces. ♦ Colombier. 277882, 800/932.3222; fax 276126

Within the François Plantation:

La Route des Epices ★★★$$$$ A discreetly posted sign advises diners that the house "Coutancie" beef comes from pampered stock that "drinks three litres of beer daily and twice daily are rubbed down vigorously." Guests are coddled from the entryway, an arbor of cascading blooms, through dessert, a sumptuous collection of pastries and dense *chocolats*. The fare is French—with a twist. Typical offerings include smoked crayfish, tabbouleh with chives and spicy bread, and ravioli in a truffle sauce. ♦ French ♦ Daily dinner. Reservations required Dec-Apr; reservations recommended May-Nov. 277882

25 Le P'tit Morne $$ Perched high above Colombier on this "little hill," this hostelry has dazzling views, and the Atlantic breezes suit the cool and easygoing atmosphere. The 14 studio apartments are pleasantly furnished and equipped with air-conditioning (seldom necessary) and full kitchens. A snack bar by the swimming pool serves breakfast and lunch. ♦ Colombier. 276264; fax 278463

26 Auberge de la Petite Anse $$ Simple accommodations are dressed up with plenty of natural beauty at these peaceful hillside bungalows set in a secluded corner of Petite Anse. Sixteen spotless air-conditioned rooms are divided among eight houses with balconies overlooking the sea. A path leads down to the beach. There's no restaurant. ♦ Petite Anse. 276489; fax 278309

27 Anse des Flamands Though it lacks sufficient shade, this wide strand is one of the island's most beautiful beaches and home to a handful of small independent hotels. The long stretch of glittering white sand is dotted with a few lantana palms. ♦ North of Terre-Neuve

On Anse des Flamands:

Isle de France $$$$ The gleaming white veranda of this plantation-style great house welcomes guests to one of the island's most prestigious hotels. Here 30 units—bungalows, suites, and studios—are finished with French finesse-marble floors, fine linens, clouds of mosquito netting, and roomy terraces with spectacular sea views. Furnishings are a mix of European antiques and regional handicrafts, while marble baths offer both showers and sunken tubs (some with whirlpools). The property also features a small fitness center, a tennis court, and the island's only squash court. The fine **Case de L'Isle** restaurant and open-air bar overlook one of two freshwater pools. ♦ 276181, 800/628.8929; fax 278683

28 Hôtel Yuana $$ The sea views from this perch are amazing. Breezy blue-and-peach wicker, white ceramic tile, and tropical fabrics adorn 12 hilltop studios furnished with kitchenettes, TV sets, telephones, and air-conditioning. There's a grocery store within walking distance and a swimming pool on the grounds. Deep-sea fishing excursions can be arranged. ♦ Anse des Cayes. 278084, 800/932.3222; fax 277845

28 New Born ★★★$$ Follow the sign with the nursing baby to this Creole eatery. Easily the best on the island, this simple dining room is set in a private home within casting distance of the shoreline, where fresh seafood is hooked and netted for wood-fire–grilled fish and lobster (choose your own from the basket) or smoked shark. Lamb kabobs are another specialty, and blood pudding tastes better than it sounds. ♦ Creole ♦ M-Sa dinner. Anse des Cayes. 276707

29 Hôtel Manapany Cottages $$$$ Billed as "a tiny refuge from the world for the very worldly," one of the island's best-known cottage colonies has 46 rooms in gingerbread cottages scattered along the beach and terraced hillside. The best accommodations are in balconied bungalows and the beachfront "club suites," which feature large marble baths, full kitchens, bars, and open-air living/dining areas. The other red-roofed units house small double rooms or adjoining suites (bedrooms, kitchenettes, and large living room/dining terraces) that may be rented together. There's a swimming pool, lighted tennis court, closed-circuit TV, Jacuzzi, water sports, and a good bar. ♦ Anse des Cayes. 276655, 800/847.4249; fax 277528

Within Hôtel Manapany Cottages:

Ouanalao ★★★$$$ Sea views, flowers, and candlelight set a romantic mood for *classique* and nouvelle French fare that ranges from escargot turnovers to smoked salmon with dilled whipped cream. Exotic fruits are hardly a sacrifice for dessert, but it would be a shame to pass up the elegant housemade pastries. Tropical drinks from the adjoining bar are garnished with fresh blooms. ♦ French/Continental ♦ M-Sa dinner; Su brunch and dinner mid-Sept–mid-Apr. Reservations required. 276655, 800/847.4249; fax 278714

30 Thalassa The name means "sea" in Greek, a suitably romantic image for an exotic stock of women's swimwear and lingerie. ♦ M-Sa. Centre Commercial La Savane, Rte D209 (between Baie de St-Jean and Rte D210). 276911

31 Baie de St-Jean One of the island's liveliest beaches sprawls across two narrow golden crescents (divided by Eden Rock) that trace the bay. Here you'll find plenty of water-sports centers, trendy seaside cafes, and lots of company. Nudity is forbidden, but microscopic monokinis test the very limit of the law. ♦ St-Jean

31 Hôtel Emeraude Plage $$$ The sandy palm-shaded grounds and tropical garden of this property are shared by 25 bungalows, 3 suites, and a villa (with 2 bedrooms, 2 baths, and great bay views). Accommodations are basic but pleasant, with air-conditioning, kitchenettes, showers, and porches. There's no restaurant, but it's an easy walk to area restaurants and shops. Guests receive a discount at nearby water-sports concessions. Though located on a main thoroughfare, this well-managed property is set back from the street noise, and it attracts a congenial family crowd. ♦ Rte D209, St-Jean. 276478, 800/932.3222; fax 278308

31 Hôtel Tom Beach $$$ With a heavenly locale on the Baie de St-Jean, this hotel has 12 rooms set in peach-colored gingerbread cottages with red roofs. Each unit has a private terrace (two are on the beach), air-conditioning, a wet bar, and ceiling fans. Other extras include 24-hour room service, a small pool, nearby water sports, a luncheon terrace that packs in guests daily, and the island's only underground garage. ♦ Rte D209, St-Jean. 275313, 800/322.2223

32 Cup's ★★$$ Named in honor of the America's Cup Race by the sailing enthusiasts (two brothers) who own it, this restaurant and bar features nautical decor and a menu that includes a range of seafood dishes (mahimahi in lobster sauce, red snapper in pastry, lobster stew) as well as roasted duck, lamb cutlets, and prime rib. You can take a swim in the pool between courses, and there's live music nightly. ♦ French ♦ Daily dinner; closed June through September. Rte D209, St-Jean. 277092

Making Yourself at Home on St. Barts

One of the most affordable ways to enjoy St. Barts is from the comfort of your own private villa, beach house, or apartment, all of which can be rented by the week or month. From mid-April to mid-December, a couple can stay in a one-bedroom house with kitchen, living room, maid service, and other comforts for as low as $700 per week. In the high season, weekly rates for a very luxurious four-bedroom villa with a pool can go as high as $5,000—still a great value on this very pricey isle where hotel rooms can cost upwards of $600 per night. Spring, summer, and fall rentals on many properties drop 25 to 40 percent in price.

If you don't want to spend your vacation cooking—and who does?—stop by a rotisserie or *boulangerie* (bakery) to pick up a chicken, tabbouleh, quiche, or pizza . . . and dine reasonably well for a fraction of what the tab would be at a trendy restaurant. Cooks are also generally available for $15 an hour.

Brook and Roger Lacour's well-established **Sibarth Real Estate** (Rue Général-de-Gaulle, Gustavia, 276238; fax 276052) lists over 200 properties; **WIMCO (West Indies Management Company;** PO Box 1461, Newport, RI 02840, 401/849.8012, 800/932.3222) is their US representative. Another good contact is **Ici & Là Saint Barth** (Quai de la République, Gustavia, 277878, 800/504.9923; fax 277828).

If you prefer the amenities of a hotel with the seclusion of a villa, three local resorts offer suites with (small) private swimming pools: **Carl Gustaf, Guanahani,** and **Le Toiny.** Just be prepared to pay through the *nez.*

---

33 Hôtel Filao Beach $$ A well-sheltered beach is the setting for this very comfortable place. The service is good, and sea views are spectacular from most of the 30 rooms, each with private deck, sitting area, refrigerator, direct-dial telephone, radio, and bath with built-in hair dryer. There are on-site water sports and boat rentals. ♦ Rte D209, St-Jean. 276484, 800/755.9313; fax 276224

Within the Hôtel Filao Beach:

Filao Beach Restaurant ★★★$$$ This poolside cafe is popular with locals as well as hotel guests for fresh seafood, omelettes, salads, stuffed land crabs, and other hearty lunches. Lobster turns up often, grilled with Creole sauce, or featured in specials (try the duck-and-lobster medaillons with honey and pineapple butter). ♦ Continental/Creole ♦ Daily breakfast and lunch. Reservations recommended. 276484

33 Eden Rock $$$$ The island's first hotel was built in the mid-1950s by Remy de Haenen, who (in 1947) was also the first pilot to land on the island; he remained here and

served as mayor for many years. Now owned by British expats David and Jane Mathews, this picturesque 11-room inn is perched on a quartzite rock between two white beaches. The restored air-conditioned cottages are tropically dressed with red roofs, terra-cotta floors, antiques, and mosquito-netted beds. Most have terraces with fabulous views. Two new eateries, **The Beach** and **The Sandbar,** are at ground level; upstairs is the sumptuous new dining room, **The Rock** (reservations recommended), done up in chic antique trappings. ♦ North of Rte D209, St-Jean. 277294, 800/932.3232, 800/322.2223; fax 278837

34 Villa Créole This shopping center is lined with "suburban" branches of Gustavia's finest boutiques. Stores here tend to stay open later (usually until 8PM) than those in the capital, but keep in mind that many close for several hours at lunchtime, according to French custom. ♦ Hours vary. Rue St-Jean, St-Jean

34 Vincent Adam ★★★$$ For 10 years Gilles Malfroid's relaxed terrace in the hills above St-Jean Carénage has been filled to capacity with happy diners—both locals and visitors. The innovative French menu changes weekly, and the superb, expertly prepared dishes, served at reasonable prices, are the reason for the restaurant's *succès fou.* ♦ French ♦ Daily dinner. South of Rte D209, St-Jean. 279322

34 Hôtel Tropical $$ Accommodations surround a dense little jungle of a garden at this friendly hillside gingerbread complex. Twenty rooms, furnished with twin beds and refrigerators, open onto terraces or balconies (nine have views of Baie de St-Jean). Guests congregate in a common area to read, listen to music, do yoga and stretching exercises, or watch videos in French and English. Other comforts include a terrace where breakfast and lunch are served, a snack bar, an antiques-filled bar, and a small pool. Water sports are available on the beach, just 50 yards away. ♦ Just south of Rte D209, St-Jean. 276487, 800/223.9815, 800/322.2223; fax 278174

34 Village St-Jean $$$ Visiting "villagers" may choose among terraced rooms, deluxe cottages with kitchens, one- and two-bedroom villas, and a deluxe Jacuzzi suite. All 25 units are white stucco, trimmed in native red stone, and simply furnished with ceiling fans, air-conditioning, and tile baths. Enjoy the sweeping vistas from the poolside spa. Ask about your room's view and proximity to the road when you book. Lively Baie de St-

Jean is a five-minute walk away, and the property also has a library/listening room, commissary, and an Italian restaurant (see below). Incidentally, the cottage kitchens must be up to task—Craig Claiborne put this place on the map. ♦ South of Rte D209, St-Jean. 276139, 800/322.2223; fax 277796

Within the Village St-Jean:

Le Patio ★★$$ One of the finest Italian restaurants on St. Barts, this warm and woody spot offers incredible views of Baie de St-Jean as well as first-rate fare. Diners choose from a variety of pasta preparations, a daily fish special, and such traditional dishes as *saltimbocca alla Romana* (veal with prosciutto and sage) and *scaloppina alla Milanese* (veal cutlet with tomatoes and basil). ♦ Italian ♦ Daily breakfast, lunch, and dinner. 277067

35 La Banane $$$ The namesake trees shade nine cottages (five are air-conditioned) with simple white-wood exteriors and striking interiors. **No. 1** is filled with live plants and trees, the tub and shower within swinging distance of the four-poster bed. A very private terrace is concealed in **No. 4.** All are graced with antiques, ceiling fans, Haitian art, TVs, VCRs, and plenty of character. The little community surrounds two freshwater pools—one a romantic grotto with a waterfall and lush foliage that assures privacy. Breakfast is included in the rate. It's a three-minute walk to the beach. ♦ Rte de Grand-Fond (between Lorient and St-Jean). 276825, 800/932.3222; fax 276844

36 Le Manoir St-Barth $$$ A 17th-century Norman country house is the pastoral centerpiece of this small "artists' colony" created by **Jeanne Audy Rowland,** architect, designer, museum curator, and author, who later sold the property to new owners. Guests are lodged in five villas, which range from one to three bedrooms. Grounds are graced by mango and papaya trees and a waterfall that tumbles into a pond filled with tropical fish and aquatic plants. Hammocks and heaps of cushions set an easygoing mood. The beach is a short walk away. There's no restaurant. ♦ Just south of Lorient. 277927; fax 276575

36 La Ligne de St-Barth Beauty lotions and suntan oils made from island plants and other natural sources are produced by Birgit and Hervé, Brin, whose ancestors settled on St. Barts hundreds of years ago. Their boutique and laboratory is well worth a visit. ♦ M-F; Sa 9AM-12:30PM. Just south of Lorient. 278263; fax 277093

36 La Normandie $$ Blend into village life at this friendly little inn within walking distance of the beach, town church, and other local gathering spots. Eight tidy rooms share a bar/restaurant and a garden with a small pool. ♦ No credit cards accepted. Just south of Lorient. 276166; fax 279883

37 Les Islets Fleuris $$ Secluded and serene, the mountaintop setting of this hostelry offers magnificent views and a lofty landscape. Six large studios and one suite are cooled by ceiling fans and surrounded by a lovely garden with a swimming pool. ♦ South of Lorient. 276422; fax 276872

38 Hotel Christopher Sofitel Coralia $$$ Atlantic waves pound the coast below this dramatic terraced hotel that steps up the hillside at Pointe Milou. There are 41 large rooms furnished in colonial style, with Mexican tile and polished mahogany. Each unit has a private balcony and sitting area. Baths have luxurious tubs, separate showers, and other plush comforts (some open onto garden patios). Tropical landscaping winds throughout a complex that also houses a French restaurant with one of the most creative chefs on the island, a complete fitness center, and a spectacular sea-view swimming pool (at 4,000 square feet, the biggest on St. Barts). It's a five-minute drive to the beaches of Lorient and Marigot. Ask about special health and fitness and couples packages. ♦ North of Marigot. 276363, 800/221.4542, 800/932.3222, 800/322.2223; fax 279292

39 La Cave de St-Barthélemy Temperature-controlled "cellars" house an impressive stash of France's great vintages. ♦ M-F; Sa-Su morning. Rue Marigot, Marigot. 276321. Also at: La Cave du Port Franc, Quai de la République, Gustavia. 276527

40 Marigot Bay Club $$ Fine sea views can be had from this picturesque and popular little hotel that clings to the hill across the road from Anse de Marigot beach. Six simple one-bedroom studios have steep roofs, exposed beams, kitchenettes, air-conditioning, and sunny terraces. ♦ North of Rte de Grand-Fond. 277545; fax 279004

Within the Marigot Bay Club:

Marigot Bay Club Restaurant ★★★ $$$ Chef Florant Demangeon fishes daily to stock his kitchen for the famous fresh-grilled seafood topped with aioli, fennel, or Creole sauce (ask for some of each). Across the street from the accommodations, this beachfront bistro is well known among outdoorsy diners who swim or snorkel between courses of *christophine farcie* (chayote stuffed with lobster), *accras* (codfish and lobster fritters), and imported filet mignon. The rum-spiked *petit punch* is notorious. ♦ Seafood/Continental ♦ Tu-Sa lunch and dinner. 277545

41 Guanahani $$$$ This beachfront gingerbread complex fronting two beaches is the largest resort on St. Barts, with 76 West Indian–style rooms, 2 freshwater pools, a fitness center, a Jacuzzi, 2 lighted tennis courts, and full water-sports facilities. Guests are lodged in lofty deluxe rooms and one- and two-bedroom suites (many with tiny private pools); all accommodations have sea view decks, air-conditioning, ceiling fans, and TVs. Most offer kitchen facilities, and rooms may be combined into customized "clusters" for families or other groups. Airport transfers are included. ◆ Anse du Grand Cul de Sac. 276660, 800/223.6800; fax 277070

Within Guanahani:

Le Bartoloméo ★★★$$$$ Chef Phillipe Masseglia blends southern French and Italian cooking styles for such dishes as goose liver pâté or lobster on spinach covered with a seafood sauce. The haute cuisine, colonial decor, and attentive service are enhanced by music from a pianist in the adjoining bar/ salon. ◆ French ◆ M-Tu, Th-Su dinner. Reservations recommended. 276660

L'Indigo ★★$$$ This poolside cafe is a casual spot for sandwiches or a light three-course lunch. Midday Gallic specials might be rack of lamb with java beans, duck confit, or a fish tart with leeks and tomatoes. The service is very professional, and there is an air of relaxed sophistication. ◆ Cafe ◆ Daily breakfast, lunch, and dinner. 276660

42 Hostellerie des Trois Forces $$ A "New Age inn" is set in the "Alps of St. Barts" near Morne du Vitet. Here French owner/chef Hubert Delamotte, a serious astrologer, has named each of his eight mountainside bungalows for a sign of the zodiac. The cedar-sided gingerbread cottages have private terraces and hammocks. Early-morning yoga classes are one of the highlights here, and the pool has a swim-up bar. ◆ Grand Cul de Sac. 276125; fax 278138

Within the Hostellerie des Trois Forces:

Restaurant de l'Hostellerie des Trois Forces ★★★$$$ Potatoes are roasted in the wood-burning fireplace, which also grills meat to a turn, at this charming dining spot. Other specialties include lobster flamed with Cognac and cream, fish mousse with hollandaise sauce, a variety of vegetarian dishes, and lovely desserts. The well-scrubbed French country decor recalls the owner's native Brittany. He's also known for powerful rum concoctions and astrological forecasts (clients around the world depend on his charts). ◆ French ◆ M-Sa lunch and dinner; Su dinner. Reservations recommended. 276125

43 El Sereno Beach Hotel $$$ Surrounded by a sandy tropical landscape, this hotel has 18 rooms with a garden view and 14 deluxe bea suites. Each unit includes a small refrigerato telephone, wall safe, and TV set hooked into closed-circuit video system. Nine villas on th road above the hotel are brightly furnished ir white tile and rattan, each with a roomy living area, kitchen facilities, and a terrace. A narro bit of beach offers windsurfing and other wat sports, and the very attractive swimming po is flanked by a fully equipped fitness center. ◆ Anse du Grand Cul de Sac. 276480, 800/223.9815, 800/322.2223; fax 277547

Within El Sereno Beach Hotel:

West Indies Café ★★★$$$$ A roman spot, this modern open-air restaurant over-looking the sea serves casual breakfasts and lunches and elegant dinners. Try the mussel ravioli with saffron or veal kidneys with a bas and beer sauce. Late-night cabaret shows staged Tuesday through Saturday are naugh but nice. ◆ French ◆ Daily breakfast, lunch, a dinner. Reservations recommended. 276480

44 Club Lafayette ★★★$$$$ You might spot a few famous faces among the fashion conscious clientele who crowd this local institution, a very stylish "beach club" wher you can have a swim in the small pool befor casual feast of barbecued lobster, breast of duck, or grilled fish with hot-pepper sauce. Finish with a rich chocolate mousse or fres fruit sorbet. A tall rum-laced *planteur* is the intoxicant of choice. ◆ French/Caribbean ◆ Daily lunch Nov-Apr. Reservations requir Anse du Grand Cul de Sac. 276251

45 St-Barth's Beach Hôtel $$$ A favorite tour groups, this peaceful older complex offers a thin stretch of beach, water sports o a sheltered lagoon, tennis, and a saltwater pool. The 36 rooms are pleasantly furnished with vaulted ceilings, terra-cotta floors, and balconies. Eight two-bedroom beachfront villas—a good choice for families—offer lar living rooms, oceanview terraces, TVs, VCR and other small luxuries. ◆ Anse du Grand C de Sac. 276070, 800/223.9815; fax 277557

45 Le Rivage ★★$$ If the adventurer in yo craves blood sausage or Tahitian raw fish, t this seaside restaurant that just happens to one of the most popular spots on St. Barts. Tamer fare such as pasta, rabbit pâté, currie lamb, flame-broiled steaks, lobster, and Creole crab is also available. ◆ Caribbean ◆ Daily lunch and dinner. Reservations strongly recommended, especially for lunch Anse du Grand Cul de Sac. 278242

Getting Your Feet Wet in St-Barthélemy

Don't just stop at the beach; keep going and head into the crystalline waters that surround St. Barts. At most beaches near hotels, water-sports concessions offer Sunfish and small boats for a nominal hourly fee. Several of the beachside hotels have equipment for hire. Game fish are plentiful but be aware that fish caught in tropical waters can be toxic, so be sure to get an expert opinion before consuming your catch. Here are a few outfits that can help get you afloat:

Boating

Marine Service Boat Rental and Diving Center Gustavia. 277034

Nautica Gustavia. 275650

St-Barth Ship Service Gustavia. 277738

Snorkeling and Scuba Diving

Marine Service Boat Rental and Diving Center Gustavia. 277034

Ocean Must Marina Gustavia. 276225

St-Barth Plongée Gustavia. 275444

Sportfishing

Fabriano Gustavia. 270173

Marine Service Boat Rental and Diving Center Gustavia. 277034

Ocean Must Marina Gustavia. 276225

Windsurfing

Ouanalao Gustavia. 278127

St-Barth Wind School Baie de St-Jean, St-Jean. 277122

Wind Wave Power Anse du Grand Cul de Sac. 276273

46 Chez Pompi ★★$$ Pompi, aka Louis Ledec, runs a bulldozer or creates exuberant paintings when he's not busy at his Creole restaurant. A celebrated *artiste naïf,* he lines the walls with his works. The food is simple and plentiful, and includes such specialties as blood sausage and curried chicken. ◆ Creole ◆ M-Sa lunch. Reservations required. East of Rte de Grand-Fond, Petit Cul de Sac. 277567

LE TOINY

47 Le Toiny $$$$ One of the island's premier resorts, this Relais & Châteaux property is set on a secluded hill, where 12 luxurious cottages with private gardens and swimming pools are surrounded by picket fences. Interiors are graced with four-poster beds, hardwood floors, sunken tubs, and fine linens. A complimentary breakfast is served on the bungalows' terraces overlooking the surrounding mountains, pastureland, and sea. Another hillside pool is shared by all guests. Service is of the highest order, as are the tabs. ◆ Rte de Grand-Fond, Toiny. 278888, 800/932.3222; fax 278930

Within Le Toiny:

Le Gaiac ★★★★$$$$ Crashing ocean waves set a dramatic tone at this starlit dining room, while an open-air setting beside the hillside pool adds a tranquil note of romance. Extravagant presentations set off such splashy masterpieces as ravioli of scallops poached with wild morels, roast monkfish with apricots, and fillet of beef with coffee-and-pepper sauce. ◆ French ◆ Daily lunch and dinner. Reservations recommended. 278888

48 Anse de Grande Saline Although nudity is officially illegal, naked sunbathing is quite common here, and those in suits stick out. This crescent of white sand is nestled against the surrounding hills. Here the surf is bold, and a couple of nearby rocky islands nose out of the clear blue-green sea. You'll have to park at the salt ponds and walk down a quarter-mile path. Be sure to bring everything you need and plenty to drink, as civilization is far from this pristine shore. Legend has it that the notorious pirate Monbars the Exterminator buried his treasure here. ◆ South coast

49 Le Tamarin ★★★$$$ Lots to do while you wait for a table at this hangout for the rich and *branché* (hip): work on your archery skills, doze in a hammock, or talk to the resident parrot (but don't touch him—he bites). Exit the bumpy road to Anse de Grande Saline for a delicious meal of seviche with lime and coconut, grilled snapper with Creole sauce, honey-and-prune chicken, or steak tartare. For dessert splurge on *tarte tatin* (apple pie) or *gâteau au chocolat* (chocolate cake). Tables are set along the porch and on the grass, where you can have drinks under the namesake tamarind tree, which has been guarding the lovely landscape for centuries. ◆ French/Creole ◆ Daily lunch and dinner Nov-Apr; Tu-Su lunch May-Oct. Reservations recommended. Just northwest of Grande Saline. 277212

50 Anse du Gouverneur Smaller and much more subdued than Grande Saline, this natural beach hideaway is secluded behind Morne Lurin. Dunes and sea grapes further shield the chestnut-colored strand, though you can park right alongside. Again, it's BYO everything—even shade. No shelter here, so sunscreen is a must. ◆ Southeast of Lurin

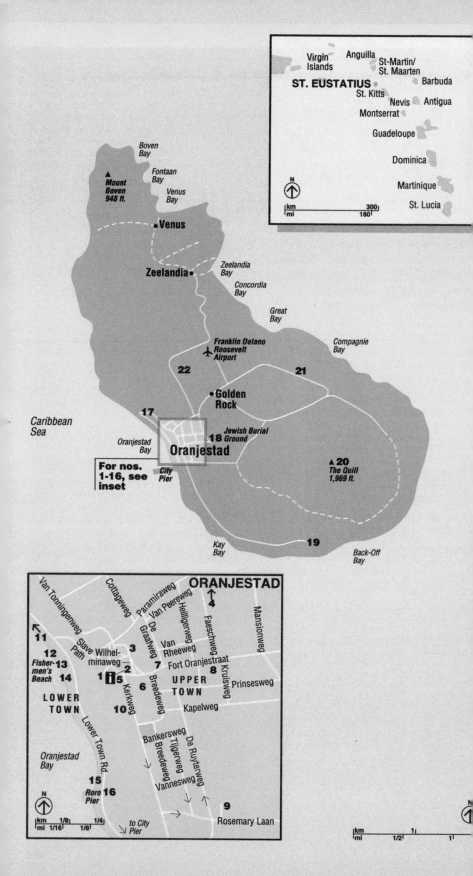

Boven
Bay

Fontaan
Bay

▲
Mount
Boven
948 ft.

Venus
Bay

●Venus

Zeelandia
Bay

Zeelandia ●

Concordia
Bay

Great
Bay

Compagnie
Bay

Franklin Delano
Roosevelt
Airport

22   21

●Golden
Rock

17

Caribbean
Sea

Oranjestad
Bay

18 Jewish Burial
Ground

Oranjestad

For nos.
1-16, see
inset

City
Pier

▲ 20
The Quill
1,969 ft.

19

Kay
Bay

Back-Off
Bay

ST. EUSTATIUS

Virgin
Islands

Anguilla

St-Martin/
St. Maarten

Barbuda

St. Kitts

Nevis   Antigua

Montserrat

Guadeloupe

Dominica

Martinique

St. Lucia

N

|km   300|
|mi   180|

ORANJESTAD

Van Tonningenweg

Cottageweg

Paramiraweg

Van Peereweg

De Graafweg

Heiligerweg

Faeschweg

Mansionweg

4

11

Slave
Path

12

Wilhel-
minaweg

3

Van
Rheeweg

Fisher-13
men's
Beach 14

2

1   5

7

Fort Oranjestraat

8

Kruisweg

Prinsesweg

UPPER
TOWN

6

Kerkweg

Breedeweg

LOWER
TOWN

10

Kapelweg

Oranjestad
Bay

Lower Town Rd.

Bankersweg

Tijgerweg

Breedeweg

De Ruyterweg

Vannesweg

15

Roro 16
Pier

9

to City
Pier

Rosemary Laan

N

|km   1/8   1/4|
|mi 1/16 1/8|

|km   1|
|mi   1/2   1|

N

St. Eustatius

If sophisticated restaurants and gaudy discos are not your idea of a good time, if you consider golf resorts and swim-up bars offenses against nature, if you have no need to track down duty-free bargains or browse through chic boutiques or haggle with street vendors, have we got an island for you.

Welcome to St. Eustatius ("Statia" for short), a low-pressure world of neat cottage gardens and hearty food, where there are no traffic lights, donkeys graze on the main street, and chickens have to be shooed off the airstrip. A casual island with no dress code to speak of, Statia is a place to get far away from it all and spend your days staring out to sea.

True, there are a few museums, colonial forts, restored houses, and a couple of moody old graveyards—fine for atmosphere, but nothing to tax even the most casual sightseer. Many of the island's historical landmarks sit undisturbed in their natural state, so you won't be limited by tour guides and velvet ropes (or walls and roofs, for that matter). Here ruins are just that, sketchy outlines for amateur sleuths to explore.

Some of the more interesting rubble lies just beneath **Oranjestad**, the island's capital, in a 200-year-old "sunken city"—a scattering of submerged warehouses, taverns, a cannon, and assorted antique litter reclaimed by **Oranjestad Bay**. The waters are also the final resting place of more than 250 shipwrecks, several of which are at depths accessible to novice snorkelers. The part of Oranjestad that is still dry land is divided into **Upper Town** and **Lower Town,** each area comprising just a few square blocks.

While today's Statia enjoys an overabundance of peace and quiet, this eight-square-mile retreat harbors a noisy history—and special ties with the US. Back in the 17th and 18th centuries, Dutch St. Eustatius was known as "The Golden Rock," a prosperous international port that served thousands of ships and, for a time, was the only connection between Europe and the North American colonies. Postmaster Benjamin Franklin routed mail via the island, while supplies and ammunition flowed north from the docks of Oranjestad (at a healthy markup) to George Washington's rebel forces.

Statia was the first foreign government to officially recognize the fledgling United States of America. On 16 November 1776, **Fort Oranje** fired an 11-gun salute to a US brig, the *Andrew Doria,* which was flying the red-and-white flag of the Continental Congress. That set off a chain of events that eventually destroyed the richest port in the Caribbean. In 1781, British Admiral George Rodney seized Statia in retaliation for the island's goodwill gesture, confiscated all salable goods, and trapped 150 ships in the harbor. What followed was a fate common to many Caribbean islands. It was passed back and forth among Great Britain, France, and the Netherlands for decades.

Unlike other isles, however, Statia never developed the strong, slavery-based plantation system that could have picked up the slack when its merchant economy collapsed. From a high point of 7,830 in the glory days of 1790, St. Eustatius's population has declined to around 2,100 today, and tourism has replaced commerce as the top industry.

The main attraction here is plenty of nothing, but those looking for things to do will find lovely hiking trails, a dormant volcano—**The Quill**—with a rain forest in its crater, more than 40 pristine dive sites, and uncrowded beaches lined with black sand.

Though support of the colonial agitators helped lead to The Golden Rock's downfall, St. Eustatius still bills itself as "America's Childhood Friend" and greets US travelers with a warm welcome.

To call from the US, dial 011 (the international access code), 599 (the country code), 3 (the city code), and the 5-digit local number. On St. Eustatius, dial only the 5-digit local number unless otherwise indicated.

Getting to the Island

Airline

Interisland Carrier

WINAIR (Windward Island Airways).........................
  on Statia.......................................82362 or 82381
  on St. Maarten 5995/54210

Airport **Franklin Delano Roosevelt Airport** (82620) services STOL (short takeoff and landing) **WINAIR** craft from St. Maarten, St. Kitts, and Nevis, as well as charter flights from St. Croix and St. Thomas. In 1993, the runway was extended, air-conditioning was added to the terminal, and international security checks were put in place. The airport is about a five-minute drive from Oranjestad.

Getting Around the Island

Car Rental

Avis...82421, 800/331.1084

Brown's Car Rental...82266

Lopes Car Rental..82291

Rainbow Car Rental...82811

Walter's Car Rental...82320

Driving You must have a valid driver's license and be 21 or older to drive here. Driving is on the right side of the road, as in the US. Most roads are two-laned and paved, except near The Quill where they are narrower and winding.

Motorbikes

Lopes Car Rental..82291

Taxis

Blondell...82406

Charles Jack..82275

Helen Richardson..82378

Tours A two-hour taxi tour (with taped commentary by the historical foundation, available in several languages) takes in Upper and Lower Towns, plus a ride along the coastal road to **Fort de Windt.** Contact Josser Daniel (82358). Ellis Lopes, the director of the **St. Eustatius Historical Museum** (82288), occasionally leads tours. All taxi services (see above) offer private and group tours.

FYI

Electricity The current is 110 volts/60 cycles, the same as in the US and Canada.

Entry Requirements US and Canadian citizens must present a passport or other proof of citizenship (birth certificate, voter's registration card) plus a photo ID along with a return or onward ticket.

Language Dutch is the official language, used on most signs, but everybody speaks English.

Money The official currency is the Netherlands Antilles florin (NAf or guilder), but US dollars can be used island-wide. Major credit cards have become much more widely accepted than in years past, but it's still a good idea to ask. **Barclay's Bank** (Wilhelminaweg, Upper Town Oranjestad, 82392) is open Monday through Thursday from 8:30AM to 3:30PM and on Friday from 8:30AM to 12:30PM and again from 2 until 4:30 PM. **Windward Islands Bank** (Fort Oranjestraat, Upper Town Oranjestad, 82846, 82848) is open Monday through Thursday from 8A to noon, and Friday from 8AM to noon and 2 to 4:30PM.

Personal Safety No problem here, but exercise normal precautions. Avoid leaving belongings unguarded on the beaches.

Publications The English-language *Chronicle, Herald,* and *Guardian,* all dailies published on St. Maarten, arrive late each morning. Tourist-oriented *St. Maarten Holiday* features very limited coverage of events and attractions on Statia. Ypie Attema's *St. Eustatius, A Short History* is a great reference book, available through the tourist office (see "Visitor's Information Offices," below), the **St. Eustatius Historical Museum** (see page 243), and **Mazinga Gift Shop** (see page 244).

Reservation Services and House Rentals The tourist office publishes a list of guest houses.

Taxes Hotels tack on an additional seven-percent government tax. The departure tax is US$10 for those returning to the US, US$5 to continue to another Netherlands Antilles destination.

Tipping A 15-percent service charge is added to restaurant, bar, and hotel bills, which covers tips for waiters, bartenders, and maids. There are no bellhops or porters, so travel light. Tip taxi drivers US$1 or US$2.

Visitors' Information Offices The **St. Eustatius Tourist Office** is in the **Government Guesthouse** at Fort Oranje in Upper Town Oranjestad (82213; fax 82433). It's open Monday through Thursday from 8AM to noon and 1 to 5PM; Friday from 8AM to noon and 1 to 4:30PM. The **St. Eustatius Historical Museum** (see page 243) is another good place to get information. At press time, a visitors' center for divers was under construction near City Pier.

Phone Book

Ambulance 82211, 8237

Directory Assistance 82320

Diving Emergencies/
  Decompression Chambers 8221

Emergencies 82333

Fire...82366

Hospital..82211, 8237

Police..82331

Post Office 8220

Upper Town

An ongoing $20-million project has restored many of the landmarks in Upper Town Oranjestad.

1 Fort Oranje The cannon volley by which the "sovereignty of the United States of America was first formally acknowledged by a foreign government" was fired from this 1636 fort on 16 November 1776. That act of defiance helped provoke a war with the British that eventually broke "the Golden Rock," but Statia's return salute to the US ship *Andrew Doria* remains a source of local pride (and some contention, as St. Croix claims its Fort Frederik saluted the ship weeks earlier). At any rate, an official commemorative plaque was presented to the fort by President Franklin D. Roosevelt, and annual reenactments of the big boom punctuate a festive holiday celebrated all over the island. Thanks to Upper Town's extensive restoration project—started at the fort in 1976 in honor of the US bicentennial—the cliffside battlements are now in good condition. Views of Oranjestad Bay are great here. ♦ Free. Daily. Fort Oranjestraat and Emmaweg. No phone

2 Ocean View Terrace ★★★$$ Chef Percy Arnaud, formerly of **The Grill House,** has taken over this spot in the courtyard of **Government Guesthouse** (home of the tourist office) to purvey his fine international cuisine. Menu highlights include succulent steaks, baby-back ribs, and grilled lobster. If Arnaud's Louisiana pudding, a delicious bread pudding with a lime sauce, is on the dessert menu, be sure to leave room. ♦ International ♦ M-Tu, Th-Su breakfast, lunch, and dinner. Fort Oranjestraat (between Wilhelminaweg and Emmaweg). 82733

3 St. Eustatius Historical Museum Located in the meticulously restored **Simon Doncker House**—formerly the home of a successful Statian merchant and used as the British headquarters when Admiral George Rodney's forces occupied the island in 1781—this museum traces the island's history, from pre-Columbian days through its Golden Period. Check out the letter written in 1775 by a visiting journalist who described Lower Town as both disgusting (because everyone smoked so much) and cosmopolitan (due to all the different stores and visitors from around the world). Booklets, postcards, and other souvenirs are for sale. ♦ Nominal admission. M-F; Sa-Su 9AM-noon. Wilhelminaweg (between Fort Oranjestraat and Paramiraweg). 82288

4 Peace and Love on the Bonk Percy Arnaud of the **Ocean View Terrace** (see above) recently opened this good-time nightclub, which jumps to disco and the occasional live band on weekends. A kitchen serving light meals with a Statian flavor is open until late. ♦ Daily 3PM-1:30AM (or later on weekends). 42 Paramiraweg (between Weg naar Jeems and Faeschweg). 82195

5 Town House This dilapidated structure is a fine, if neglected, example of classic Statian stone-and-wood construction. It can be viewed from the street only and is not open to the public. ♦ Fort Oranjestraat and Kerkweg

6 Honen Dalim Look just behind the **Town House** to see the ruins of the second-oldest synagogue in the Western Hemisphere (after Mikve Israel on Curaçao), which dates from 1739. Yellow-brick walls, stone arches, and a

Fort Oranje

staircase leading to the women's gallery still stand. The name means "the one who is charitable to the poor." ◆ Synagogped (between Breedeweg and Fort Oranjestraat)

7 Sonny's Place ★★$ Pull up a chair and mingle with the locals at this casual bar/restaurant, one of the island's most popular hangouts. Sandwiches and local food are featured here, and you can even get Trinidadian roti. On most nights, Happy Hour lasts until midnight. ◆ West Indian ◆ M, W-Sa 9AM-midnight; Tu, Su 9AM-7PM. Fort Oranjestraat (between De Graafweg and Wilhelminaweg). 82609

7 Mazinga Gift Shop Stop here for the local soursop schnapps known as Mazinga Mist, as well as for books, cigarettes, liquor, magazines, toiletries, T-shirts, and a few Dutch imports. ◆ M-Sa. Fort Oranjestraat and De Graafweg. 82245

8 Grill House ★$ What used to be the premier continental restaurant on the island has joined an increasing crowd of Cantonese eateries. The atmosphere is casual and the menu is pretty standard, although there are some good dishes featuring fresh local fish and lobster. ◆ Chinese ◆ Daily lunch and dinner; hours are not completely predictable, so call ahead. Fort Oranjestraat (between Kruisweg and Logeweg). 82915

9 Tennis Court The single concrete court at the **Community Center** on **Madam Estate** is basic, but it's open to the public and lighted after dark. Players must supply their own equipment. ◆ Fee. Daily. Rosemary Laan (east of De Ruyterweg). 82249

10 Dutch Reformed Church Although the stone tower and choir loft were restored for a 1980 state visit by the Netherlands' Queen Beatrix, this stately 1755 church now lies in partial ruins. The churchyard is worth a ramble; look for the 1775 marker of Jan de Windt, complete with skull and crossbones. Nearby are the remains of an old sisal factory and sugar mill, and the site is on the coastal road that leads to tiny **Fort de Windt**. Contact the tourist office to arrange for a guided tour of the area. ◆ Kerkweg (between Wilhelminapark and Fort Oranjestraat).

Lower Town

In the 18th century this was the commercial center of Statia, but now the great warehouses of Lower Town are just ruins at the base of **Fort Oranje**. From **Upper Town,** walk or drive down the cobblestone **Slave Path** to wander around the rubble or watch the fishermen in their brightly colored skiffs. Today donkeys graze along the main street of what was once the richest port in the Caribbean, while much of the original settlement lies beneath the bay—a ghostly cityscape for snorkeling sightseers.

11 Ruins Once a center of international trade and a flourishing harbor, Statia's former port area is now nothing but ruins. Wander among the crumbling warehouses and

imagine the bustling trade community that once did business here, dealing in sugar, wine, cotton, and slaves. Corruption and laziness among Statia's merchants, along w the departure of the Dutch West Indies Company, led to the decline of Statia's economy and its port. No one repaired the seawall when storms destroyed it, and the eventually returned, leaving parts of the tov underwater. ◆ Lower Town Rd and Slave Pa

11 Smoke Alley Beach Here's the jumping-point for snorkelers who want to paddle ove the ruins of the 17th-century town that lies just below Oranjestad's harbor. Black sands fringe the coast of Lower Town, with cocon trees for shade. Water-sports equipment is available at **Dive Statia** (see below), and nearby hotels offer casual outdoor dining. ◆ Lower Town Rd and Slave Path

12 Dive Statia St. Eustatius is bounded by 5 square miles of reef, more than 40 dive site and 250 shipwrecks (of which 31 have beer identified). This shop in the **Old Customs House** offers scuba-diving equipment renta and sales, **PADI** instruction, underwater camera rentals, computer diving capability, and a 26-foot power catamaran. Owners Rinda and Rudy Hees also rent snorkel equipment so non-divers can explore the many spectacular sights, including the submerged ruins in surrounding shallow waters. Ask about combo packages with the neighboring island of Saba. ◆ Daily. Lower Town Rd (just south of Slave Path). 82435, 405/843.3040 in the US; fax 82539

13 Old Gin House and Mooshay Bay Publick House $$$ At press time, this popular local hangout set in an 18th-centu warehouse had been sold to a group of investors and was closed for renovation. It hard to predict what that will mean for a place whose popularity was based on an atmosphere of worn elegance and raggedy charm. The new owners plan to modernize the facilities (adding air-conditioning and TV sets in the 20 rooms, for example), but promise that everything else—including th classic pub, with walls made of bricks from cotton gin originally used on the premises will be more or less the same. The reopenir date had not yet been set at press time; ca for information. ◆ Lower Town Rd (south Slave Path). 82309

14 Golden Era Hotel $$ Some balconies overlook Oranjestad Bay, while others face concrete walls at this comfortable hotel near the beach. The 20 harbor-front rooms are basic but neat, with private baths, air-conditioning, TV sets, and telephones. There's a swimming pool and a restaurant/bar serving good West Indian fare at moderate prices. Continental breakfast is included in the rate. ♦ Lower Town Rd (south of Slave Path). 82345; fax 82445

Within Golden Era Hotel:

Scubaqua Statia's newest dive shop, under Swiss management, offers **PADI** instruction (up to assistant instructor level) as well as day and night dives. ♦ Daily. 82160

15 Golden Rock Dive Center This dive shop offers **PADI** instruction as well as day and night dives. The owners will also take clients deep-sea fishing, either for a full or half day; gear and bait are provided. ♦ Daily. Lower Town Rd (south of Slave Path). 82964, 800/311.6658

16 Blue Bead ★★★$$ This restaurant offers everything: delicious food, great atmosphere, terrace dining, and an ocean view. The menu includes a range of dishes—West Indian, American, Continental, Indonesian—as well as daily specials. Saturday is barbecue night, when steak, ribs, and chicken are grilled to perfection. ♦ International ♦ Daily lunch and dinner. Reservations recommended for groups of six or more; no credit cards accepted. Lower Town Rd (south of Slave Path). 82873

Elsewhere on the Island

17 Kings Well $$ Romantically situated on a cliff overlooking the sea at the north end of Lower Town, the grounds of this hotel are a prime habitat for the island's rare *iguana delicatissima* species, which the owner will be delighted to show you. There are eight spacious fan-cooled rooms, two with kitchenettes and all with terraces, TV sets, VCRs, and refrigerators. Still in the planning stages are a Swiss-style health center, a Jacuzzi, and a pool. The on-site restaurant serves German and continental food. ♦ Lower Town Rd (north of Slave Path), Oranjestad. 82538; fax 82496

18 Jewish Burial Ground On the outskirts of Oranjestad are some 20 grave markers, dating from 1742 to 1825, inscribed in Hebrew, Portuguese, Dutch, and English. This carefully tended little cemetery adjoins what may have once been a *mikvah* (Jewish ritual bath), though some disputants claim the ruin was actually part of an old rum distillery. ♦ Prinsesweg (just east of Oranjestad)

19 Fort de Windt The ruins of this fort—built in the late 19th century and one of the few remaining in Statia—have been restored. The site offers beautiful views all the way to St. Kitts. ♦ Free. Daily. Weg naar White Wall (south of Upper Town Oranjestad). No phone

20 The Quill Getting up the slopes of this dormant volcano used to be a major huff, but a new, easier trail has been cut by the **St. Eustatius National Parks (STENAPA) Foundation.** The old trail is still open for those who prefer to do it the hard way (there are several nice rest stops). However you get up, the views are ample reward for your exertions. A lush rain forest fills the crater at the 1,969-foot summit. It's possible to hire a guide (contact the tourist office a day in advance), but even beginners should be able to handle the half-day climb without assistance. The tourist office has maps for 12 nature trails that range from the taxing **Crater Track** descending into the volcano to the breezy **White Bird Track** that visits nesting grounds along Oranjestad Beach beneath Powder Hill. STENAPA is also restoring the **Track Around the Mountain,** which leads hikers from town around the Quill to the future site of the **Miriam C. Schmitt Botanical Garden.** The garden, under construction at press time, will be devoted to the preservation of Statia's nearly extinct Statia morning glory and will also feature indigenous epidendrum, oncidium, and brassavolla orchids; no opening date has been announced. ♦ Free. Daily. Southeast interior

21 Domestic Museum of the Berkel Family This picturesque collection of farm tools, household artifacts, and personal memorabilia (including "Ma's Bible" and "Pa's Parting Works") traces one island family through the 19th and 20th centuries. ♦ Free; donations requested. Daily. Lynch Plantation, Kortelsweg. 82338

22 Talk of the Town $$ This is a good choice for both food and lodging. The 17 modern rooms and 3 kitchenette-equipped efficiency units are well fitted out with locally hand-crafted furnishings, air-conditioning, cable TV, and telephones. The nine newest rooms are divided among four Caribbean-style cottages clustered around a pool. Buffet breakfast is included in the rate. ♦ L.E. Saddlerweg (just west of Franklin Delano Roosevelt Airport). 82236; fax 82640

Within Talk of the Town:

Talk of the Town Bar & Restaurant ★★★$$ One of the island's most popular restaurants offers fresh seafood, chicken, and steak. Specials vary and occasionally include curried goat or other Statian delicacies. ♦ Caribbean ♦ Daily breakfast, lunch, and dinner. 82236

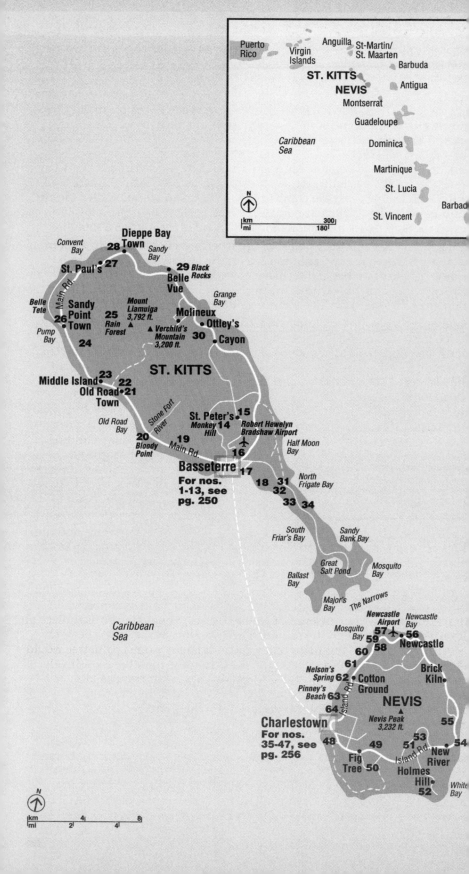

Puerto Rico

Virgin Islands

Anguilla

St-Martin/ St. Maarten

Barbuda

ST. KITTS

Antigua

NEVIS

Montserrat

Guadeloupe

Caribbean Sea

Dominica

Martinique

St. Lucia

Barbad

St. Vincent

N

km
mi
300
180

Convent Bay

Dieppe Bay Town

28

Sandy Bay

27

St. Paul's

29 *Black Rocks*

Belle Vue

Belle Tete

26

Sandy Point Town

25

Mount Liamuiga
3,792 ft.

Rain Forest

Grange Bay

Molineux

Ottley's

Pump Bay

24

▲ Verchild's Mountain
3,200 ft.

30

Cayon

ST. KITTS

23

Middle Island

22

Old Road Town

21

St. Peter's

15

Stone Fort River

Monkey Hill

14

Old Road Bay

20

19

Bloody Point

Main Rd.

16

Robert Hewelyn
Bradshaw Airport

Half Moon Bay

Basseterre

For nos. 1-13, see pg. 250

17

18

31

32

North Frigate Bay

33

34

South Friar's Bay

Sandy Bank Bay

Ballast Bay

Great Salt Pond

Mosquito Bay

Major's Bay

The Narrows

Caribbean Sea

Newcastle Airport

57

Newcastle Bay

Mosquito Bay

59

56

58

Newcastle

60

61

Brick Kiln

Nelson's Spring

62

Cotton Ground

Pinney's Beach

63

NEVIS

64

Nevis Peak
3,232 ft.

55

Charlestown

For nos. 35-47, see pg. 256

48

49

53

51

54

New River

Fig Tree

50

Holmes Hill

52

White Bay

N

km
mi
2
4
4
8

St. Kitts and Nevis

Monkeys outnumber people on St. Kitts and Nevis (pronounced *Nee*-vis), where the 46,100 residents of the sister islands share stomping grounds with a simian population that tops 125,000 at any given time.

Clearly, nature is held in high esteem here—by law, no buildings may be taller than the palm trees—and the two islands offer a wealth of opportunities to enjoy it. Divers are just beginning to scout what could be the largest concentration of unexplored wrecks in the Caribbean: An estimated 400 ships sank in these waters between 1493 and 1825, yet scarcely a dozen sites have been identified so far. Eco-tourists tromp through cane fields into St. Kitts's rain forest, a tangle of huge buttress trees, hanging vines, deep red poinciana, and exotic birds. Daring types can climb inside the dormant volcano called **Mount Liamuiga**, the islands' highest point (3,792 feet), whose prehistoric lava flows created the jagged rock formations and black sand of the northern shoreline.

Golden sand lines St. Kitts's southern tip, where beachcombers can walk from the Atlantic Ocean to the Caribbean Sea on the **Frigate Bay Peninsula.** Nevis's vast pink beaches and secluded coves are virtually deserted, and thermal springs still flow within the ruins of the 18th-century **Bath Hotel,** where the crème de la Caribbean once gathered to take the waters.

Separated by a two-mile channel, St. Kitts and Nevis are shaped, respectively, like a cricket bat and a ball. The description reflects a local obsession with cricket that is just one of many holdovers from centuries of British rule. The first English settlement, the mother colony for all of the later West Indian outposts, was established here in 1623 by Sir Thomas Warner. (Prior to the arrival of the Europeans the island was inhabited by Carib Indians.) The imposing fortress that crowns 700-foot-high **Brimstone Hill** on St. Kitts was built in the 17th century, when England and France were pummeling each other for control of this 68-square-mile patch of land and the surrounding isles of Montserrat, Saba, St-Barthélemy, St. Eustatius, and St-Martin/St. Maarten. A self-governing nation since 1983, St. Kitts and Nevis may undergo another change in government in the near future. As this book went to press, a referendum was planned in which Nevisians will vote whether or not to secede from St. Kitts.

St. Kitts's **Basseterre** is a slow-paced town filled with friendly people and trim colonial architecture. The main hub, known as **The Circus,** is a far cry from London's Piccadilly, but its duty-free shops are stocked with European imports and the world-famous Caribelle batik, manufactured locally at **Romney Manor.** Nevis's **Charlestown,** with its one main street and handful of side streets, may not be as picturesque as Basseterre, but its simple attractions include the **Museum of Nevis History**, housed in the birthplace of Alexander Hamilton, and the ruins of a 17th-century synagogue. Locals say it's usually so quiet in this town that a coconut falling from a palm tree would make the front page—although on the weekends, the nightlife is positively lively. The biggest news to hit Nevis in centuries was Princess Diana's vacation at **Montpelier Plantation Inn** in 1993. The island, known internationally by philatelists for its colorful stamps, issued the first commemorative stamp in honor of the princess after her death.

Many travelers prefer to stay at the islands' picturesque old guest houses, plantation manors, and converted sugar mills. However, recent inroads into the wilds of St. Kitts's **Southeast Peninsula** have attracted several modern resorts to the rugged slopes of **Sir Timothy's Hill,** and cruise-ship arrivals have almost tripled since 1990. **Port Zante,** a cruise port in Basseterre designed to accommodate up to 3 ships and 150,000 passengers, opened in

1997; the construction of restaurants, a hotel, and boutiques at the new port was in the works as this book went to press. In addition, St. Kitts's **Robert Hewelyn Bradshaw Airport** recently added a new $22-million terminal building. If the Ministry of Tourism's efforts to boost the number of island visitors continues on track, monkeys could soon be the minority party here.

Area code 869 unless otherwise noted.

Getting to the Islands

Airlines

Interisland Carriers

Air St. Kitts Nevis 465.8571

American Eagle 465.8490, 800/433.7300

Carib Aviation...465.3055

LIAT (Leeward Islands Air Transport).......465.8200, 800/468.0482

WINAIR (Windward Island Airways)..........468.0482

Airports **Robert Hewelyn Bradshaw Airport** (465.8472) is a mile from Basseterre, St. Kitts. Interisland flights depart from and land at this airport. **Newcastle Airport** (469.9343) is just west of Newcastle, Nevis. Interisland flights to and from St. Kitts, Antigua, and St-Martin/St. Maarten take off and land here, as do charters to and from St. Thomas.

Getting Around the Islands

Bicycles and Motorbikes

Meadville, Charlestown, Nevis...................469.5235

Pringle Enterprises, Basseterre, St. Kitts ...465.1456

Buses Bus service is available on both St. Kitts and Nevis, but there are no set schedules, and taxis are much more convenient for visitors.

Car Rental

On St. Kitts:

Avis 465.6507, 800/331.1212

Caine's 465.2366

Delisle Walwyn & Co 465.8449

Island Car Rental.......................................465.3000

Sunshine...465.8651

TDC...465.2991

On Nevis:

Avis 469.1240, 800/331.1212

Strikers 469.2654

TDC...469.1005

Driving Driving is on the left, British style. On St. Kitts, local driver's licenses are available at the fire station in Basseterre; on Nevis you can get them at the police station in Charlestown. You must present a valid license from home; the fee is US$12.

Ferries The government-operated ferry runs between Basseterre on St. Kitts and Charlestown on Nevis, making one or two trips every day except Thursday and Sunday. The 45-minute crossing is usually calm and pleasant. Schedules are published in the *Traveller Tourist Guide*, distributed free by the tourism office; call the **St. Kitts Tourist Board** (465.4040) for information. (Don't be surprised if an unscheduled crossing to St. Kitts is announced when there's an important soccer game in Basseterre—the ferry's captain is an avid sports fan.)

Taxis

St. Kitts Taxi Association 465.4253, 465.7818

Nevis Taxi Association..............469.1483, 469.9790

Tours Taxis on both islands offer guided tours. To join an organized group, contact **Kantours** (465.2098) or **Tropical Tours** (465.4039, 465.4167). On St. Kitts, **Greg's Safaris** (465.4121, 465.5209) and **Kriss Tours** (465.4121) offer hiking and walking tours of the rain forest. On Nevis, **Top to Bottom Tours** (469.9080) offers hikes and walks for all ages.

FYI

Electricity The current is generally 220 volts, though a number of hotels are now wired for 110 volts (the same as in the US and Canada). Call ahead or bring a converter.

Entry Requirements US and Canadian visitors must present a valid passport or other proof of citizenship (birth certificate, voter's registration card) and a picture ID, plus a return or onward ticket.

Gambling The casino in the **Jack Tar Village Royal St. Kitts Hotel** is open nightly. The minimum legal age for gambling is 18.

Language English is the official language.

Money The official currency is the Eastern Caribbean dollar (EC$), though US and Canadian bills are widely accepted. Most banks are open Monday through Thursday from 8AM to 3PM, and Friday from 8AM to 5PM.

Personal Safety Although crime is rare, take normal precautions and don't leave valuables unguarded on the beach.

Publications On St. Kitts, the weekly *Democrat* is published every Saturday, and the *Labor Spokesman* is published Wednesday and Saturday. *The Chronicle, The Herald,* and *The Guardian* are dailies from St. Maarten. *The Observer* is published weekly and distributed on both Nevis and St. Kitts. US papers are not generally available, but some hotels distribute faxed summaries from major US and British papers. A tourist map of hotels and points of interest on St. Kitts and Nevis is available free at the tourist office and sells for about US$1 at shops. The urist board also distributes the free *Traveller ourist Guide*. The *Walking and Riding Guide of Nevis* is available free from the tourist board or for S$1 at the **Museum of Nevis History** (see page 57).

Reservation Services and House Rentals

ualie Realty 469.9403

Taxes There is a seven-percent tax on hotel and estaurant bills. Visitors pay an EC$27 (US$10) eparture tax.

Tipping Hotels add a 10-percent service charge, which covers tips for the entire staff. If you're dining ut and no service charge is included, tip 10 to 15 ercent. Cab drivers should also get a 10 to 15 ercent tip.

Visitors' Information Offices The **St. Kitts ourist Board** is in Basseterre (Pelican Shopping Mall, Bay Rd, between Adam and Fort Sts, 465.4040, 65.2620; fax 465.8794). It's open Monday and uesday from 8AM to 4:30PM; Wednesday through riday from 8AM to 4PM, Saturday from 8AM to 2:30PM, and whenever a cruise ship is in port. here's also a desk at **Robert Hewelyn Bradshaw Airport** (465.8970), which is open daily from 8:30AM o 5:30PM. The **Nevis Tourist Office** is in the former Cotton Ginnery in Charlestown (D.R. Walwyn Plaza

and Market St, 469.1042; fax 469.1066). It's open Monday and Tuesday from 8AM to 4:30PM; Wednesday through Friday from 8AM to 4PM, and Saturday from 8AM to 12:30PM.

Phone Book

On St. Kitts:

Ambulance	911
Directory Assistance	411
Emergencies	911
Fire	333
Hospital	465.2551
Police	911, 707
Post Office	465.2521

On Nevis:

Ambulance	911
Directory Assistance	411
Emergencies	911
Fire	333
Hospital	469.5473
Police	911, 707
Post Office	469.5221

St. Kitts

1 The Circus This traditional English-style roundabout was created in 1867, when most of Basseterre was rebuilt following a disastrous fire. The bright green **Berkeley Memorial Clock** is a tribute to Thomas Berkeley, former president of the General Legislative Council. The cast-iron monument is a charming bit of Victoriana, an elaborate little tower with four clock faces, coats of arms, and a small fountain at its base. St. Kitts's answer to Big Ben is the customary meeting spot for islanders. ♦ At Bank St, Liverpool Row, and Fort St, Basseterre

On The Circus:

Ballahoo Restaurant ★$ Set in an old stone building with a tin roof and a red British phone box outside, the comfy second-floor dining room is known for fresh local seafood and West Indian cuisine—try the conch in garlic butter. Sit on the balcony to catch the sea breezes and watch the action around The Circus. ♦ Caribbean/Continental ♦ M-Sa breakfast, lunch, and dinner. 465.4197

Palms Arcade This pleasant arcade houses a collection of stores that includes **Scruples Boutique and Gift Shop** (women's fashions; 465.1664); **The Linen Chest & Boutique Hand Picked** (fine linens, beachwear, and accessories; 465.7037); and the **Orchid Boutique** (menswear; 465.1981). ♦ M-Sa

Within Palms Arcade:

PalmCrafts Here are plenty of tropical treats, including Island to Island resortwear designed by Canadian John Warden and made on St. Kitts. (His designs are also available at **Lemonaid** in the **Golden Lemon Inn & Villas**; see page 254). Also in stock are Sunny Caribbee spices and teas, as well as jewelry set with larimar, sea opal, coral, and amber. ♦ M-Sa. 465.2599

2 StoneWalls ★★$$ British journalist Garry Steckles and his Kittitian wife, Wendy, inaugurated this perfect pub in 1993, serving up ice-cold beer and good food at reasonable prices in an open courtyard. The menu often includes a curry dish, pork with ginger and garlic, roast lamb with mint sauce, Yorkshire pudding, marlin with dill butter, and

Jamaican-style jerk chicken. Desserts range from chocolate cake to mango ice cream. West Indian music adds to the charm. ♦ West Indian/International ♦ M-Sa dinner Jan-May, Nov-Dec; M-F dinner June-Oct. Princes St (between Fort and Church Sts), Basseterre. 465.5248

3 A Slice of the Lemon St. Kitts's largest inventory of duty-free fragrances for women and men shares space with jewelry, Portmeirion china, and Sunny Caribbee spices and teas. ♦ M-Sa. Fort St (between Princes and Central Sts), Basseterre. 465.2889

3 Wall's Deluxe Record and Book Shop Caribbean and international recordings feature calypso, reggae, and steel-band music. Also look for regional books, works by West Indian authors, maps, stationery, and cards. ♦ M-Sa. Fort St (between Princes and Central Sts), Basseterre. 465.2159

4 TDC Mall Among the fine shops here are **Splash** (465.9640), which carries bright tropical clothing, batik items, swimwear, and wood carvings, and the **Brown Sugar Boutique** (466.4664), set in a 150-year-old rum cellar, which sells fashions by local designer Judith Rawlins. ♦ M-Sa. Fort St (between Bank and Central Sts), Basseterre

5 St. George's Anglican Church Christened **Notre Dame** by the French in 1670, the original church was burned to the ground in 1706 by the British, who rebuilt it four years later and named it for the patron saint of England. It was destroyed three more times (two fires and an earthquake), and the present building dates from 1869. The graves in the churchyard go back to the early 18th centur♦ ♦ Cayon St (between Victoria Rd and Colleg♦ St), Basseterre. 465.2167

6 Independence Square Built in 1790 for slave auctions and council meetings, this public square was named on 19 September 1983 to celebrate independence from Great Britain for the two-island federation of St. Kitts and Nevis. Today it is a popular gatheri♦ spot for both locals and visitors, surrounded by carefully preserved colonial architecture. ♦ Bounded by Independence Sqs E, W, S, an♦ N, Basseterre

7 Spencer Cameron Gallery Here Rose Cameron Smith re-creates colorful scenes o♦ Kittitian life in paintings and prints. Her well-known Carnival clowns and masqueraders have been featured on the island's postage stamps. Smith's original designs are also sil♦ screened onto fabrics and clothing, greeting cards, posters, and other wares. The walls o♦ this colonial building are hung with works by♦ more than 20 other artists as well as prints, maps, and reproductions. Custom framing is available. ♦ M-Sa or by appointment. Independence Sq N, Basseterre. 465.1617

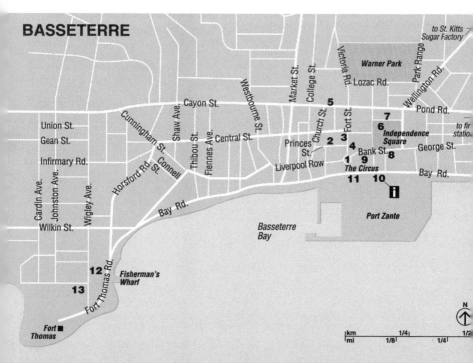

8 Mango's Garden Bar & Bistro ★★$ The garden behind the Georgian House has been transformed into an oasis of classical music, jazz, and intimate conversation. Enjoy a tasty burger or salad in the adjacent **Rain Forest Garden,** but be forewarned: The 12-foot-high sprinklers turn on every 20 minutes and envelop the place in mist, keeping the foliage lush and adding to the tropical ambience. ♦ West Indian/Continental ♦ M-Sa 11AM-11PM. Independence Sq S, Basseterre. 465.4049

9 Bayembi Cafe ★$ The best place in town to get a latte, this coffeehouse attracts locals and visitors with its funky flare. The crowds spill onto the sidewalk after dark, with conversation mixing with a soundtrack of reggae and calypso tunes. Toasted sandwiches and snacks are served, along with pastries. Once inside, look up—you'll see coconuts painted to resemble fish, original watercolors on silk, and other local art, all sold at bargain prices. ♦ Coffeehouse ♦ M-Sa 7AM-11PM. Bank St (between Independence Square W and The Circus). 466.5280

10 Pelican Mall Stop at this harborside center for duty-free shopping. Standouts include **Island Style** (465.7488) for locally made baskets, coconut-tree products, and clothing; **Linen & Gold** (465.9766) for international linens and jewelry; **Smoke n' Booze** (465.2631), with the island's largest selection of duty-free liquors and tobacco products; and **Little Switzerland** (465.9858) for duty-free jewelry, watches, china, and flatware. ♦ Daily. Bay Rd (between Adam and Fort Sts), Basseterre. No phone

10 St. Kitts Philatelic Bureau The fascinating stamps of St. Kitts and Nevis are prized among collectors, who rank the colorful issues among the best in the Caribbean, surpassed only by those of the British Virgin Islands. ♦ M-Sa. Bay Rd (between Adam and Fort Sts), Basseterre. 465.2521

11 Treasury Building This black-and-white building (not open to the public) is an example of West Indian architecture at its best. ♦ Bay Rd and Fort St, Basseterre

Ocean Terrace Inn

12 Ocean Terrace Inn $$ Known to locals as the **OTI,** one of St. Kitts's best resorts stands on a hilltop at the far western edge of Basseterre Harbour. Views are great from the breezy terraced rooms that are decorated in bright West Indian style with white-tiled floors. All 72 units have air-conditioning and TV sets; the 3 VIP suites offer wraparound views and upgraded amenities. Elaborately landscaped grounds feature a waterfall grotto, three pools, three restaurants, two swim-up bars, and shops. A free shuttle makes trips to the casino, **St. Kitts Golf Course,** and **Turtle Beach Bar & Grill** (see page 256) on lovely Turtle Bay on the island's Southeast Peninsula, which offers a full range of water sports. ♦ Wigley Ave (between Fort Thomas Rd and Wilkin St), Basseterre. 465.2754, 800/524.0512; fax 465.1057

Within Ocean Terrace Inn:

Ocean Terrace Inn Restaurant ★★$$ Ask for a table on the protected balcony or the open-air patio overlooking Basseterre Bay. The menu changes daily, reflecting seasonal ingredients. A guitarist plays background music nightly, and there's also a fashion show every Wednesday. Steel bands perform on Fridays during the high season. ♦ Caribbean/Continental ♦ Daily breakfast, lunch, and dinner. Reservations required for dinner for nonguests. 465.2754

Fisherman's Wharf ★★★$$ Conch chowder is the specialty here, though grilled seafood, steaks, chicken, and ribs attract a congenial group to picnic tables at the water's edge. A steel band generally performs on Friday, and there's also live music some Saturday nights. ♦ Seafood/Caribbean ♦ Daily lunch and dinner. Reservations recommended Friday. 465.2754

Fort Thomas Hotel

13 Fort Thomas Hotel $ This budget modern hotel, just a few minutes' walk from Basseterre and set on the grounds of an original fort, is one of the best deals on the island—and it's getting better. The owners have launched an ambitious expansion program, with plans to eventually increase the number of units from 64 to 260, all available on a time-share basis. The 64 existing rooms have air-conditioning, pink-and-green tropical decor, private balconies, TV sets, and telephones. The **Lemon Grass Restaurant** is known for its seafood and Caribbean cuisine. There's also a pizza and ice-cream parlor, a terrace bar, and an Olympic-size pool with great views of the sea and nearby Nevis. A free shuttle makes the rounds to the nearby beach, golf course, and tennis courts. ♦ Just west of Wigley Ave, Basseterre. 465.2695, 800/851.7818; fax 465.7518

Although St. Kitts and Nevis are one nation, each issues its own stamps—all widely admired by philatelists worldwide.

14 Monkey Hill Named for the sister islands' black-faced monkeys (their numbers now exceed 125,000), this 1,159-foot knoll is home to some of the shy creatures—you may even spot a few. It's an easy climb, and even if you don't see a monkey, you'll be amply rewarded by fine views from the summit. Be sure to notice the overgrown ruins of **The Glen,** a former plantation great house. ♦ Just west of St. Peter's

15 The White House
$$$ At the foot of Monkey Hill, a restored great house (circa 1758) is now an inn furnished with antiques and imported fabrics. The restaurant (see below) and the drawing room are in the great house, and the eight guest rooms are set in the old

carriage house, the stable, and three new stone cottages. The three acres of manicured grounds offer a pool, grass tennis court, and croquet lawn. The rates include breakfast (served on a garden terrace), afternoon tea, and dinner. A courtesy shuttle makes the rounds to several area beaches. ♦ St. Peter's. 465.8162, 800/223.1108; fax 465.8275

Within The White House:

White House Restaurant ★★★$$$
Guests are served in the great house's original dining room or on a garden terrace. The atmosphere is decidedly elegant. Lunch and a multicourse, set-menu dinner feature island produce. The prix-fixe dinner might include such savories as rack of lamb with a roasted garlic and horseradish sauce, sea bass with white butter and parsley sauce, and mushroom-and-escargot pancakes. This is also a fine destination for a civilized afternoon tea. ♦ International ♦ Daily lunch, afternoon tea, and dinner. Reservations required; jackets requested. 465.8162

16 St. Kitts Sugar Factory For centuries, the sugar of St. Kitts has been rated among the best in the world. This factory on the outskirts of Basseterre also produces the sugarcane liqueur called CSR (Cane Spirit Rothschild), developed by Baron Edmond de Rothschild. The best time to tour the factory is during cane-grinding season (February to July), when visitors can observe the transformation of raw cane into bulk sugar. ♦ Free. Tours by appointment. Sugar Factory Rd (north of Taylor's Rd). 465.8173

16 Carib Beer Brewery This plant turns out the most popular beer in the Caribbean. You'll be treated to a cold one after the tour. ♦ Free. Tours by appointment only. Sugar Factory Rd (north of Taylor's Rd). 465.2309

17 Lighthouse Gourmet Restaurant ★★$
Here diners are treated to sophisticated cuisine, good service, and a stunning view of Basseterre. Specialties include conch and lobster with horseradish mayonnaise, onions and peppers; warm shrimp salad with passion-fruit dressing; and carpaccio with green peppercorn dressing, diced onion, tomatoes, and parmesan cheese.
♦ Continental ♦ Daily dinner. Reservations recommended. Just east of Basseterre. 465.0739

18 Bird Rock Beach Hotel $$ Perched on a elevated bluff overlooking a sheltered cove and crescent-shaped beach, 38 units offer private sea-view terraces, air-conditioning, and cable TV. Studios and suites have fully equipped kitchens. Other perks include two restaurants, a tennis court, a pool with swim up bar, and an on-site dive operation (see below). ♦ Southeast of Basseterre. 465.8914 800/621.1270; fax 465.1675

18 St. Kitts Scuba Ltd. This dive operation offers **PADI** and **NAUI** instruction as well as day and night dives and supervised snorkelin outings. Dive packages are available. ♦ Daily. Southeast of Basseterre. 465.8914

19 Fairview Inn $ Situated in a great house built for a French officer in 1701, what were 30 basic rooms are gradually being refurbished and freshened with bright colors and rattan furnishings. The property also offers a pool, a fine restaurant (see below), and the **Banana Patch Bar & Grill,** which serves up live music on the weekends (inn owner Adrian Lam is also a musician and his band, Toucan, performs here regularly). A fre shuttle takes guests to Frigate Bay Beach. ♦ Just north of Main Rd, Boyd's. 465.2472; fax 465.1056

Within Fairview Inn:

Fairview Restaurant ★★★$$ The inn's restaurant serves some of the best local cuisine on the island. The menu changes daily, but might include West Indian beef stew, pink bean soup, curried beef roti, and baked turkey with Creole stuffing. Desserts are always a tropical delight: Try the rum-and raisin ice cream, banana pudding with brandy sauce, or papaya pie. ♦ Caribbean ♦ Daily breakfast, lunch, and dinner. Reservations recommended for lunch and dinner. 465.247

20 Bloody Point A fearsome battle took place here in 1626 when, according to some accounts, the Carib Indians mustered a force of 3,000 to drive British and French settlers from the island. The Europeans learned of the plan and attacked first. When the dust cleare more than 2,000 Carib lay dead in this canyo and ravine. ♦ Main Rd, Challengers

21 Old Road Town The first permanent British settlement in the West Indies was establishe here in 1623 by Sir Thomas Warner, his family, and 14 followers. The farming community served as the island capital until 1727, when the center of government was moved to Basseterre. ♦ Main Rd (3 miles northwest of Challengers)

22 Wingfield Petroglyphs Boulders at the edge of what is now known as **Wingfield Estate** were etched with ancient symbols and human figures by the Carib. At the beginning of the island's recorded history, this land was the province of Chief Tegreman, the Carib tribal leader who befriended Sir Thomas Warner when he arrived with a band of British colonists in 1623. ♦ Wingfield Estate, Wingfield Rd (north of Old Road Town)

22 Romney Manor/Caribelle Batik A few minute's drive beyond the Wingfield Petroglyphs on Wingfield Road leads to a 17th-century plantation great house, reconstructed in 1995 after a fire destroyed everything but the foundation. It's now the stately home of **Caribelle Batik**, a fabric and clothing workshop surrounded by 5 acres of tropical gardens with terraces, a croquet lawn, a bell tower, and a 350-year-old *saman* (rain tree). Visitors can watch artisans using the ancient Indonesian technique of batik to create the hand-dyed and hand-painted Sea Island cotton fabrics, clothing, and wall hangings that are sold throughout the Caribbean. There's a large selection of items for sale, and custom designs are available. ♦ M-F. Wingfield Estate, Wingfield Rd (just north of Old Road Town). 465.6253

23 St. Thomas Church Stop by the churchyard to see the 1648 tomb (engraved in Old English) of Sir Thomas Warner, who headed the first European settlement on the island. ♦ Just north of Main Rd, Middle Island. 465.6311

24 Brimstone Hill Fortress One of the most spectacular historic sights in the Caribbean (pictured at right), the "Gibraltar of the West Indies" commands views of six islands (Nevis, Montserrat, Saba, St. Eustatius, St-Martin/St. Maarten, and St. Barts) from the summit of Brimstone Hill. Set 700 feet above the Caribbean, this massive fortress, built by slaves, took 105 years to complete. Volcanic stone walls up to 12 feet thick link an impressive series of bastions. Today visitors may view the remnants of the practical works (the hospital, storerooms, cookhouses, asylum, cemetery, and freshwater cistern system) as well as the military facilities (the parade, barracks, officers' quarters, and mess). The restored **Prince of Wales Bastion** now houses a visitors' center, a small museum, and a souvenir shop. Last used as a fort in 1851, it has been a national park since 1965. The surrounding slopes are great for a panoramic picnic; you can purchase food and drinks at a small snack bar in the complex. ♦ Admission. Daily. Main Rd (between Middle Island and Sandy Point Town). 465.2609, 465.6211

24 J's Place ★$$ Views are great from the upstairs gallery of this West Indian restaurant below **Brimstone Hill Fortress.** Menu options include lobster salad and goat water (goat stew with celery, thyme, onions, pepper, cloves, and garlic). ♦ Caribbean/Seafood ♦ Daily lunch and dinner. Reservations recommended; no credit cards accepted. Main Rd (between Middle Island and Sandy Point Town). 465.6264

25 Rain Forest Dense tropical forest covers 35 percent of St. Kitts, running along the upper slopes of the rugged mountain range that is the island's central spine. The crown of the Northwest Range, the dormant volcano Mount Liamuiga (aka Mount Misery), is the island's highest point at 3,792 feet. Several outfitters offer hiking tours (including a climb into the volcano's crater) as well as guided walks among the tropical blooms for less hardy souls. Local hotels can books tours, or call **Greg's Safaris** (465.4121, 465.5209) or **Kriss Tours** (465.4121), with knowledgeable

Brimstone Hill Fortress

Vandell "Kriss" Berry at the helm. There are no biting insects, poisonous plants, or snakes in this rain forest. ♦ Northwest interior

Within the Rain Forest:

 Dos D'Anse Pond The hike to this crater lake atop Verchild's Mountain (3,200 feet) is a spectacular one-and-a-half-hour tromp through virgin tropical forest aflame with bright red poinciana trees. There are no trail maps, however, so an experienced guide is recommended; contact **Greg's Safaris** (see above) to arrange for half- or full-day trips.

26 Sandy Point Town Though the first permanent British settlement was established at Old Road Town, the settlers originally landed at this spot in 1623. Later the village was headquarters for the Dutch, who ran a prosperous tobacco-trading operation here. Today the area is carpeted in fields of sugarcane, which has been a major island crop since the 17th century. ♦ Main Rd

27 Rawlins Plantation $$$ Set on a 17th-century sugar plantation, this owner-operated resort sprawls over 12 hillside acres. The original foundations of the great house have been converted into the main building and dining room (see below); the old boiling houses now surround a cool courtyard vibrant with colorful blooms and tropical birds. The 10 guest rooms are set in cottages and outbuildings; a special suite, complete with sitting room and modern bath, is in the old mill. All the units have stone walls and ceiling fans and are furnished with British antiques. There's also a spring-fed swimming pool and a grass tennis court. Rates include breakfast, dinner, afternoon tea, and laundry service. ♦ Closed mid-August–mid-October. Plantation Rd (south of Main Rd). 465.6221, 800/346.5358; fax 465.4954

Within Rawlins Plantation:

Rawlins Plantation Restaurant ★★★★$$$ An unforgettable culinary experience awaits at this country inn with its fine views from the foothills above Dieppe Bay. Claire Rawson, who runs the inn with her husband Paul, cooks a delicious West Indian buffet for lunch; it might include meatballs in ginger sauce, chicken curry, and roasted sweet potatoes. Dinners are a four-course, prix-fixe meal with a set menu that blends French cooking techniques with West Indian flavors. Many of the ingredients are grown on the plantation. ♦ French/Caribbean ♦ Daily lunch and dinner; closed mid-August–mid-October. Reservations for dinner required by noon. 465.6221

28 Dieppe Bay This north coast beach, with its volcanic sands in shades of gray and black, and shores lined with colorful fishing boats, a fine destination for a swim and picnic. At one end is a palm-fringed point where the Atlantic and Caribbean meet. The adjoining **Gibbons Pasture Estate,** formerly both a sugar mill and a fort, is now nothing but ruins—virtually all that remains are two cannons that were discovered on the reef below. ♦ Dieppe Bay Town

On Dieppe Bay:

Golden Lemon Inn & Villas $$$ Owner Arthur Leaman, former decorating editor for *House & Garden,* created this inn "for the discriminating few who like to do nothing, in grand style." There are 32 exquisitely furnished guest rooms, including 15 seaside villas. All have canopy beds with mosquito nets and ceiling fans. Rates include breakfast. The property is rich with elegant galleries, spectacular artwork, and spacious gardens and courtyards; there's also a tennis court, a freshwater pool, a small black-sand beach, and **Lemonaid** (465.7260), an exclusive boutique. No children under age 16 are allowed. ♦ 465.7260, 800/633.7411; fax 465.4019

Within Golden Lemon Inn & Villas:

Golden Lemon Restaurant ★★★$$$ Lunch and drinks are served in the tropical poolside garden or the elegant dining hall filled with antiques from around the world. At dinner, an innovative menu that changes nightly blends West Indian and continental cuisine in such dishes as grilled lamb with West Indian chili butter. Vegetarian dishes are also available. The service is particularly gracious and the Sunday buffet brunch is extremely popular. ♦ Caribbean/Continental ♦ Daily breakfast, lunch, and dinner. Reservations required for dinner. 465.7260

29 Black Rocks These dramatic coastal cliffs were created in the 15th century by molten lava from Mount Liamuiga. Now dormant, the nearby volcanic peak is the island's highest point (3,792 feet). The path to the base of the cliffs is very dangerous and the waves are rough, so it's best to admire this spot from on high. ♦ Main Rd (just east of Belle Vue)

OTTLEY'S
PLANTATION INN

30 Ottley's Plantation Inn $$$ An 18th-century sugar plantation has been meticulously restored in English colonial style. Set on 35 rolling acres at the foot of the Southeast Range, the veranda-circled great house and stone cottages share lofty views; there's also an outstanding restaurant (see below) and a gorgeous spring-fed swimming pool. Hikers can walk right into the rain forest. Public rooms are lined in native stone, and the 15 guest rooms are decorated in crisp West Indian style. The inn offers shuttle service to beach, golf, tennis, and shopping. This extraordinary property is frequently listed among the best in the region; *New York Magazine* named it "the most majestic guest house in the Caribbean." Meal plans are available. ◆ Southwest of Ottley's. 465.7234, 800/772.3039; fax 465.4760

Within Ottley's Plantation Inn:

Royal Palm Restaurant ★★★★$$$
Chef Pamela Yahn is building a worldwide reputation with her "New Island" cuisine, featuring such dishes as Creole pumpkin soup, fresh mango-and-tomato salad, grilled sea scallops with Kittitian salsa, and roasted rack of lamb with chutney and ginger crisps. The Sunday Champagne brunch is a weekly ritual. ◆ Caribbean/International ◆ Daily breakfast, lunch, and dinner. Reservations required for dinner and brunch, recommended for lunch. 465.7234

31 Frigate Bay Peninsula If St. Kitts is shaped like a cricket bat, this is the handle. The long, skinny stretch that connects the main region of the island with the remote Southeast Peninsula is the site of several modern hotel and condominium projects. Here you can walk from the Atlantic Ocean to the Caribbean Sea: The dramatic windward beach at North Frigate Bay is battered by the Atlantic surf, while the calmer leeward waters of the Caribbean splash the golden sands of Frigate Bay.

31 Jack Tar Village Royal St. Kitts Hotel
$$$ Like the other links in the Jack Tar chain, this modern golf resort charges one price that includes all meals and drinks, golf, water sports, tennis, horseback riding, nightly entertainment, and tips. An 18-hole golf course and casino keep the action lively, and there are beaches on both the Atlantic (closer) and the Caribbean (reached by free shuttle service). Nonguests may use all facilities with a $50 day pass. All 242 air-conditioned rooms have private balconies or patios. ◆ North Frigate Bay. 465.8651, 800/858.2258; fax 465.1031

Within the Jack Tar Village Royal St. Kitts Hotel:

 St. Kitts Golf Course This par-72 layout is the only 18-hole golf course on St. Kitts. Golfers must negotiate 7 lakes on these 160 acres. Lessons and carts are available, but there are no caddies. ◆ Greens fees for those not staying at the hotel. Daily. 465.8339; fax 465.4463

31 Sun 'n Sand Beach Resort $$ At this family-friendly complex, 13 cottages and 32 studios are scattered over 5 acres on North Frigate Bay. A recent $3-million renovation included the creation of 26 deluxe rooms with kitchenettes, high ceilings, and air-conditioning. Also on the premises are a swimming pool, a baby pool, two tennis courts, a restaurant/bar, a small conference center, a grocery store, and a gift shop. Several restaurants are nearby. ◆ North Frigate Bay. 465.8037, 800/468.3750; fax 465.6745

31 Island Paradise Beach Village $$ This condominium development on an Atlantic beach provides 35 1-bedroom, 19 2-bedroom, and 8 3-bedroom apartments with full kitchens. It also has a freshwater pool, a restaurant, a small grocery store, barbecue grills, and laundry facilities. ◆ No credit cards accepted. North Frigate Bay. 465.8035, 800/828.2956; fax 465.8236

32 Frigate Bay Resort $$ You'll enjoy views of both the Caribbean and Atlantic from the grounds of this attractive complex. Each of the 64 units is furnished in West Indian style with archways and tiled floors; they are also equipped with air-conditioning, ceiling fans, a private terrace, a TV, and a telephone. Suites have kitchens and breakfast bars. The low-rise, Mediterranean buildings hug an Olympic-size pool (with a swim-up bar) that adjoins **The Garden Room** restaurant (see below). It's a five-minute walk to the beach. Golf greens fees are included in the rate, and scuba, honeymoon, and meal packages are available. ◆ Frigate Bay. 465.8935, 465.8936, 800/468.3750; fax 465.7050

Within Frigate Bay Resort:

Garden Room ★★$$ Sit on an open-air terrace overlooking a swimming pool or indoors in the split-level dining area of this congenial restaurant. The menu features steaks, chicken, seafood, and vegetarian dishes, as well as a daily chef's special. Try the lobster or the mahimahi in banana, thyme, and lime sauce. ◆ Caribbean/Continental ◆ Daily breakfast, lunch, and dinner. Reservations recommended for dinner. 465.8935

Restaurants/Clubs: Red   **Hotels:** Blue
Shops/ Outdoors: Green   **Sights/Culture:** Black

33 Coconut Beach Club $$ This attractive, modern complex is located on a swath of sand at the foot of Sir Timothy's Hill. Now managed by the Fairweather hotel group, it has 31 air-conditioned units, each with 1 or 2 bedrooms, a patio or balcony, and a full kitchen. Also on the premises are a pool, a water-sports center, a gameroom, and the **Banana Tree Restaurant,** where seafood is cooked on an open grill. Golf packages are available. ♦ Frigate Bay. 465.8597, 800/345.0271; fax 466.7085, 800/345.0271.

34 Southeast Peninsula Until the 1989 debut of Dr. Kennedy Simmonds Highway, the wilds of St. Kitts's Southeast Peninsula were accessible only by boat or a grueling hike over Sir Timothy Hill. Today the six-mile road leads from Frigate Bay past secluded coves, pastures of tall guinea grass, and nine pristine beaches (beautiful Cockleshell Bay and Banana Bay are best for swimming). The pink Great Salt Pond (which gets its color from millions of tiny krill shrimp) is the main source of salt for residents of St. Kitts and Nevis. The protected wilderness area is populated by black-faced vervet monkeys, white-tailed deer, and tropical birds (the best time to sight them is early in the morning). Though camping is permitted, there are no facilities. At press time there were rumors that a major all-inclusive resort company and a large international hotel chain were planning to build in this area. ♦ Southeast of Frigate Bay Peninsula

On Southeast Peninsula:

TURTLE BEACH
Bar & Grill

Turtle Beach Bar & Grill ★★$$ This casual oceanside spot offers rib-sticking local cuisine and plenty of water sports, including snorkeling, ocean kayaking, windsurfing, scuba instruction, and deep-sea fishing. Even if you don't eat here, you're welcome to use the beach and the sports facilities (there's a fee for each activity). **Turtle Tours** (469.9094) offers kayaking tours and rentals, with pick-ups at hotels around the island. For a small fee, a boat will shuttle passengers across the bay to Nevis, just a 10-minute ride. Bikes are also for rent. A steel band draws crowds to the Sunday brunch buffet. For a truly quiet hideaway, rent the new self-catering 1-bedroom apartment atop the bar—perfect

for honeymooners who don't mind being truly alone after the place closes up tight at 10 or 11PM. ♦ Caribbean ♦ M-Sa lunch and early dinner; Su brunch and early dinner. Turtle Bay. 469.9086

Sandy Bank Beach This is a powdery oasis—secluded, private, and truly magical. One enterprising local, who goes by the name Gong, rents chairs and umbrellas and sells cold drinks. He's usually here seven days a week, from 8AM to 6PM. ♦ Sandy Bank Bay

---

Nevis

With a mere 3,000 citizens (1,200 in the capital, **Charlestown**), Nevis has a lifestyle far different from that of larger Caribbean islands. You might say Nevisians spend much of their time waiting for their ship to come in—meat, vegetables, and even tourists come to this peaceful isle by ferry.

Like several other British islands, Nevis is divided into parishes: **St. Thomas Lowland, St. James Windward, St. Paul Charlestown, St. George Gingerland,** and **St. John Fig Tree.** Massed rows of palm trees form a coconut forest on the island's west side, while single palms bend in the breeze along the windward eastern coast. The black-sand beaches in the northwest rank high as sightseeing attractions, but many tourists prefer the white-sand beaches to the north and west for swimming.

35 Market Place Stroll past the colorful displays of fruit and vegetables. The scene is especially lively when locals do their shopping on Tuesday, Thursday, and Saturday mornings. ♦ M-Sa 6AM-5PM. Market St (west of D.R. Walwyn Plaza), Charlestown. No phone

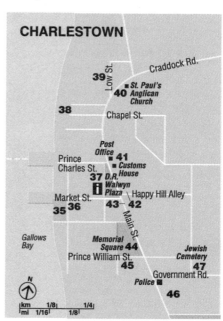

CHARLESTOWN

36 Nevis Philatelic Bureau The colorful stamps of St. Kitts and Nevis make charming and inexpensive souvenirs. Look for issues featuring crabs, shells, insects, fish, butterflies, and other national—and natural—treasures. ♦ M-F. Market St (west of D.R. Walwyn Plaza), Charlestown. 469.5535

37 Nevis Handicraft Cooperative Society Ltd. In a stone building next to the tourist office, island crafts and inexpensive handmade souvenirs are sold, including a wide selection of locally made condiments, such as guava and soursop jellies, banana and mango chutneys, coconut oil, and hot sauces. ♦ M-Sa. No credit cards accepted. D.R. Walwyn Plaza (between Market and Prince Charles Sts), Charlestown. 469.1746

38 Unella's Waterfront Bar & Restaurant
★$$ The easy atmosphere of a former private house complements a West Indian and continental menu that features pasta, fresh seafood, curried lamb, island spareribs, conch dishes, tropical drinks, and exotic fruit juices. ♦ Caribbean ♦ M-Sa breakfast, lunch, and dinner; Su dinner. Just west of Main St, Charlestown. 469.5574

39 Museum of Nevis History American statesman Alexander Hamilton was born here in 1755, the illegitimate son of Scotsman James Hamilton and Nevisian Rachel Fawcett (the family left the island in 1760). The original 1680 house was destroyed by a hurricane around 1840, but a replica is now a museum dedicated to Hamilton and local lore. Exhibits feature papers authored by Hamilton, island artifacts, old photos, and antique furniture. The gift shop sells useful maps and guides, including the *Walking and Riding Guide of Nevis*. ♦ Admission. M-Sa. Low St (just north of Main St), Charlestown. 469.5786

40 Gallery of Nevis Art Stop in to view works by local artists. ♦ M-Sa 10AM-3PM and by appointment. Main St (north of Chapel St), Charlestown. 469.1381

41 Knick Knacks Local art lines the walls, and the eclectic inventory also includes spices, jams, jellies, souvenirs, and shell jewelry, as well as cotton sportswear for men and women. ♦ M-Sa. Just east of Main St, Charlestown. 469.5784

42 Main Street Grocery Shop for a picnic or pick out regional foods for tasty souvenirs. Try Nevis Hot Pepper Sauce made by owner Eulalie B. Williams, or CSR (Cane Spirit Rothschild), the sugarcane liqueur manufactured at **St. Kitts Sugar Factory** (see page 252). ♦ M-Sa; closed midday. Main St (between Happy Hill Alley and Chapel St), Charlestown. 469.5226

43 Eddy's Restaurant & Bar ★★$$
On a balcony overlooking Main Street, this Charlestown eatery proffers specialty cocktails (Eddy's Dream is a winner), an incredible ginger-pumpkin soup, and the best bread pudding in town. ♦ Caribbean ♦ M-W, F-Sa lunch and dinner. Main St (between Government Rd and Happy Hill Alley), Charlestown. 469.5958

44 Memorial Square A cordoned-off area honors the men who served in both World Wars. ♦ Main and Prince William Sts, Charlestown

45 Courthouse and Public Library This impressive coral-stone building with a box-shaped clock tower faces Memorial Square. It was rebuilt in 1873, after a fire destroyed the original structure and many of the valuable books and records that were stored there. ♦ M-Sa. Prince William St (just west of Main St), Charlestown. 469.5521 ext 2055

46 Synagogue/Mikvah Identified in 1993 by David Robinson, curator of the Nevis Historical and Conservation Society, as the remains of either an ancient synagogue or its *mikvah* (a ceremonial bathhouse), this one-story building behind Nevis's government headquarters may date back to the early 1650s, which would make it one of the oldest synagogues in the Western Hemisphere. Still extant are splendid stone columns, a barrel-vaulted ceiling, and a stone-walled path known as "Jews' Walk" that leads to the old Jewish cemetery. ♦ Free. By appointment. Main St (between Grove Park Cricket Ground and Government Rd), Charlestown. 469.5786

47 Jewish Cemetery Here lies all that remains of the Jewish community that once made up a quarter of the island's population. Sephardic Jews found asylum on Nevis after being exiled from Brazil in the 17th century. The 19 gravestones (engraved in English, Hebrew, and Portuguese) date from 1658 to 1758. ♦ Government Rd (east of Main St), Charlestown

48 Bath Hotel and Spring House Now in ruins, this once-grand hotel was built by John Huggins in 1778 at the then-exorbitant cost of £40,000. The posh bathhouses, which still stand on a fault over a hot spring, attracted the rich and rheumatic with thermal mineral baths and spa services. A major social spot for wealthy West Indian planters, the 50-room hotel, with its celebrated ballroom and dining room, was also frequented by members of the British gentry and European nobility. After abolition toppled the plantation system, the property fell into disrepair and was finally abandoned in 1870. It reopened briefly in the early 20th century, then was badly shaken by an earthquake in 1950. The impressive landmark has been acquired by the Nevis Island Government, which at press time was planning to restore the building for public use. The **Spring House** is closed, but the warm sulfur waters still flow in the stream behind it. ♦ Bath. No phone

257

49 Horatio Nelson Museum This museum houses one of the largest collections of Lord Nelson memorabilia in the Western Hemisphere. ♦ Admission. M-Sa. Island Rd (between Beach Road and Fig Tree). 469.4221 ext 2117

49 Hermitage Plantation $$$ Set on acres of lawns and tropical gardens in the hilly countryside, a 250-plus-year-old great house is the centerpiece of this lovely inn. There are 15 guest rooms, set in West Indian–style cottages and a former carriage house, all with large balconies or porches and carefully selected antiques; many have small kitchens. Also on the premises are a restaurant (see below), a swimming pool with a sea view, riding stables, and a tennis court. ♦ North of Island Rd. 469.3477, 800.742.4276; fax 469.2481

Within Hermitage Plantation:

Hermitage Plantation Restaurant ★★ $$$ Fine Caribbean cuisine is served in the beautiful gardens or antiques-filled dining room. The menu varies nightly depending on the ingredients available—and on the diners' tastes. The staff asks what you like when you make your reservation, and will tailor the dishes to your preferences. ♦ West Indian/American ♦ Daily breakfast, lunch, and dinner. Reservations required. 469.3477

50 Montpelier Estate The two gateposts at the entrance are all that remains of this onetime great house, the scene of the wedding of "Horatio Nelson, Esquire, Captain of His Majesty's Ship, the *Boreas,* to Frances Herbert Nisbet, Widow," on 11 March 1787. The grounds are still lovely, and the original 1794 sugar mill has been restored and is now part of the **Montpelier Plantation Inn and Beach Club** (see below). ♦ Free. Daily. South of Island Rd

Within Montpelier Estate:

Montpelier Plantation Inn and Beach Club $$$$ The prettiest of the old estate inns, this elegant retreat was bombarded with international attention when Princess Diana vacationed here in 1993. Despite the fanfare, the owner, James Gaskill, maintains a quiet and comfortable English house party atmosphere that attracts a lofty clientele to his family home. Guests are lodged in 16 rooms and a suite set in cottages, sans TV. The two main buildings contain the great room and bar, library/cards room, drawing room, the main dining room, and a sunny breakfast room. Walkways wind through formal tropic gardens, and the huge tiled swimming pool surrounded by murals and has mountain views. There's also a tennis court, and transportation is provided to a private three-acre area of Pinney's Beach. Rates include breakfast. No children under 8 are allowed. ♦ Closed mid-August–October. 469.3462, 800/223.9832; fax 469.2932

Within Montpelier Plantation Inn:

Montpelier Plantation Inn Restaurant ★★$$$ Head chef Neal Savage from Great Britain, assisted by two chefs from Europe and three from Nevis, whips up imaginative international cuisine at this lovely plantation inn. Dinner menus change nightly, but if they're offered, try the roasted rack of lamb with shallot and rosemary sauce or the grille lobster with garlic and chive butter. Other entrées make good use of fresh seafood and estate-raised pigs, lambs, chickens, and produce. Dinner is served in the main dining room (actually an open-air candle-lit terrace lunch is served on the mill's terrace and courtyard; and breakfast is in a brightly decorated breakfast room. ♦ International ♦ Daily breakfast, lunch, and dinner. Reservations required. 469.3462

51 Old Manor Estate & Hotel $$ This restored 1690 sugar plantation has great views of the Caribbean Sea and nearby islan from its 800-foot perch. The cut-stone main house and outbuildings of the original estate have been converted into 13 spacious guest rooms and suites with four-poster beds, hig ceilings, hardwood floors, and huge breezy windows. The swimming pool, edged with c stone and tropical landscaping, is set in the plantation's former cistern. Meal plans are available; the restaurant (see below) is one o the best on the island. ♦ Just north of Island Rd, Market Shop. 469.3445, 800/892.7093; fax 469.3388

Within Old Manor Estate & Hotel:

The Cooperage ★★★$$$ The Friday night steak-and-lobster cookout, accompani by a buffet of island vegetables and salads, is special treat, but meals are always imaginativ from green-pepper soup to fresh tropical sorbets. ♦ West Indian/ Continental ♦ Daily breakfast, lunch, and dinner. Reservations recommended. 469.3445

52 Indian Castle Racetrack Horse races are held eight times a year, including New Year's Day, Easter Monday, Labour Day (the first Monday in May), August Monday (the first Monday in August), Independence Day (19 September), and Boxing Day (26 December). Other dates are announced as they are scheduled; for details, contact Richard Lupinacci at **Hermitage Plantation** (469.347 ♦ Admission. South of Holmes Hill

53 Golden Rock Plantation Inn $$ This estate derives its name from the golden hue given off by the nearby mountains at sunset. The evening scenery is fantastic, and monkeys live wild on the grounds, which are graced with 12 stone plantation buildings that date from 1800. Visitors lodge in 16 pleasant guest rooms scattered among cottages and an old stone sugar mill. Distinctive four-poster beds are made of bamboo grown on the property. Amenities include a tennis court, a swimming pool, nature trails, and free shuttle service to Charlestown and to beaches on both leeward and windward coasts. Nonguests are welcome to enjoy the nature trails and stroll the grounds. Have a drink at the bar and say hello to Lulu the Amazon parrot. Both MAP (Modified American Plan, including breakfast and dinner) and EP (European Plan, without meals) rates are available. ◆ Between Island Rd and Stonyhill. 469.3346, 800/8223.9815; fax 469.2113

Within Golden Rock Plantation Inn:

Golden Rock Restaurant ★★$$$ Lunch is served in a tropical garden with great views across the hills of Gingerland to the Caribbean Sea. Fresh lobster is a specialty. Saturday nights bring a West Indian buffet and local music by the Honey Bees String Band. ◆ West Indian ◆ Daily breakfast, lunch, and dinner. Reservations required for dinner. 469.3346

54 New River Estate The last operating sugar mill on Nevis shut down in 1956, but you can still explore its ruins. Like other stone mills on the Leeward Islands, the mill here was was originally turned by cattle, donkeys, or horses, then converted to steam power in the late 19th century. ◆ Island Rd (north of New River)

55 Eden Brown Estate Rumored to be haunted, this gray ruin is all that survives of an estate built and furnished in grand style for a rich planter's daughter. It was left to crumble after her fiancé was killed by his best man in a drunken duel on the eve of the wedding. ◆ Island Rd (just south of Mannings)

56 Nisbet Plantation Beach Club $$$$ This luxurious inn fronts a half-mile beach on the grounds of a 1778 plantation. A long alley of coconut palms stretches from the sea to the antiques-filled great house, where guests meet in the cordial lounge, dining room (see below), and bar. Accommodations are in 38 cottages with pretty bedrooms and small screened-in sitting areas; rates include breakfast and dinner. Other amenities include a tennis court and lawn croquet. Breakfast and lunch are served in a casual poolside cafe (see below); nonguests are welcome to stop for lunch and a swim. The property is owned by David Dodwell, who also owns **The Reefs** in Southampton, Bermuda. ◆ North of Island Rd (between Camps and Newcastle). 469.9325, 410/628.1718, 800/742.6008; fax 469.9864

Within the Nisbet Plantation Beach Club:

Coconuts ★$$ This poolside cafe on the beach is the scene of Thursday-night barbecues featuring 10 different varieties of fresh fish grilled to perfection. On Sunday nights a string band performs. ◆ West Indian/American ◆ Daily breakfast, lunch, and dinner. Reservations required. 469.9325 ext 417

The Great House ★★★$$$ Dinner is served in the plantation house dining room—a five-course table d'hôte menu that showcases local ingredients prepared in continental style by German chef Klaus Ryborz. Nevisian Lloyd William, who plays flute and saxophone, entertains nightly in season. Afternoon tea is also served here. ◆ Continental ◆ M-W, F-Su dinner. Reservations required. 469.9325 ext 404

56 Newcastle One of the island's main fishing fleets operates out of this tumbledown old village near the airport. Mornings are best for buying lobster, conch, and fish fresh off the boat for a do-it-yourself beach barbecue. ◆ North coast

In Newcastle:

THE MOUNT NEVIS HOTEL AND BEACH CLUB
NEVIS, WEST INDIES

Mount Nevis Hotel and Beach Club $$$ This modern hotel is dressed up with whitewashed buildings, colonial archways, and sprawling verandas. The 16 deluxe rooms and 16 suites (which sleep up to 4 people) have air-conditioning, TV sets, VCRs, and private balconies with views of St. Kitts; kitchen units are available. There's a restaurant and freshwater pool on the property, and a free shuttle transports guests to the beach, where there's another restaurant and a water-sports facility offering windsurfing, waterskiing, and fishing trips. Diving can be arranged, and there are hiking trails next to the property. Continental breakfast is included in the rate; meal plans are available. ◆ 469.9373, 800/75.NEVIS; fax 469.9375

Getting Your Feet Wet in St. Kitts and Nevis

St. Kitts and Nevis offer a variety of underwater activities, as well as boating. The following organizations can help get you afloat:

Boating

Kenneth's Dive Centre Basseterre, St. Kitts. 465.2670, 465.7043

Leeward Island Charters Basseterre, St. Kitts. 465.7474

Newcastle Bay Marina Watersports Centre Newcastle, Nevis. 469.9395

Tropical Tours Basseterre, St. Kitts. 465.4039, 465.4167

Snorkeling and Scuba Diving

Kenneth's Dive Centre Basseterre, St. Kitts. 465.2670, 465.7043

Pro Diver Turtle Bay, Southeast Peninsula, St. Kitts. 465.3223

Scuba Safaris Oualie Beach Hotel, Island Rd, Oualie Bay, Nevis. 469.9518

St. Kitts Scuba Bird Rock Beach Hotel, southeast of Basseterre, St. Kitts 465.1189

Sportfishing

Captain Ken Newcastle Bay Marina Watersports Centre, Newcastle, Nevis. 469.9395

Kenneth's Dive Centre Basseterre, St. Kitts. 465.2670, 465.7043

Tropical Tours Basseterre, St. Kitts. 465.4039, 465.4167

Windsurfing

Mr. X Watersports Frigate Bay, St. Kitts. 465.0673

Newcastle Bay Marina Watersports Centre Newcastle, Nevis. 469.9395

Roy Gumbs Watersports Frigate Bay, St. Kitts. 465.8050

Windsurfing Nevis Oualie Beach Hotel, Island Rd, Oualie Bay, Nevis. 469.9682, 469.9735

The poinciana tree was named for Count de Poinci, a botanist and 17th-century governor of St. Kitts.

Newcastle Pottery Before scouting the gift items and cookware, watch the potters at work here. The clay is fired over burning coconut shells. ♦ M-Sa. 469.9746

57 Yamseed Inn $$ Guests wake up to fresh homemade breads, Nevis fruits, cereal, and eggs at this charming bed-and-breakfast. There are four spacious bedrooms, each with a bath and separate entrance, set on a peaceful beach with grand views of St. Kitts. It's a gem of a hideaway. ♦ Island Rd (west of Newcastle Airport). 469.9361

58 Cottle Church (St. Mark's Chapel of Ease) Gentle Thomas Cottle, once president of Nevis and owner of the 980-acre **Round Hill Estate**, built this Anglican church in 1824 so his family and servants could attend services together. Because it was against the law for slaves to congregate, the chapel was never consecrated, and it fell into disuse. A 1974 earthquake destroyed the remains, but visitors can still wander among the ruins. Large boulders in the road are a hazard to navigation, so plan on walking a mile to the site from Island Road. ♦ South of Island Rd

58 Round Hill Climb to the top—1,014 feet—for a panorama that takes in St. Kitts and Booby Island, named after the brown pelican that is the national bird of Nevis. The relatively easy hike takes about 1.5 hours round-trip. ♦ Southeast of Island Rd

59 Oualie Beach Hotel $$ Named after the old Carib word for Nevis (Oualie, meaning beautiful water), this charming hotel was originally a small beach bar. Owner John Yearwood's property—in the Yearwood family since an early ancestor came to the West Indies as a soldier in the late 1600s—now has 22 rooms in gingerbread cottages on the beach, each with ceiling fans, a telephone, a refrigerator, a mini-bar, and cable TV. Some of the rooms have air-conditioning, and the honeymoon suites have canopy beds. Sports facilities include **Scuba Safaris** (469.9518), a complete **NAUI** and **PADI** dive center (ask about special dive packages), and **Windsurfing Nevis** (469.9682, 469.9735), the island's first windsurfing school, which also offers mountain bike tours and rentals. Snorkeling, sailing, and deep-sea fishing are also available. ♦ Island Rd, Oualie Bay. 469.9735, 800/682.5431; fax 469.9176

Within Oualie Beach Hotel:

Oualie Beach Restaurant ★★★$$ The beachfront restaurant's chef, Patrick Fobert, formerly with the Four Seasons resort, offers international and West Indian cuisine and a special kid's menu. Some of his creations include potato-and-leek soup, marinated lamb chop salad with ginger and guava vinaigrette, stir-fried ginger pork, and grilled swordfish. On Saturdays, there's a Nevisian string band and a Carnival masquerade troupe that dances to traditional songs. ◆ Caribbean/International ◆ Daily breakfast, lunch, and dinner. Reservations recommended for dinner. 469.9735

59 Miss June's ★★★$$$ You will attend a dinner party like no other at this gingerbread-style dining spot. Hosted by June Mestier, the extraordinary experience starts with hors d'oeuvres and cocktails (try the house rum punch). Guests then move into a formal dining room where a 5-course meal, which includes more than 20 different Caribbean, Asian, and international dishes, is served. The evening is topped off with wine, liqueurs, coffee, and brandy. The fixed price includes everything, and the bar doesn't close until the last guest is ready to leave. ◆ International ◆ Dinner served three nights a week; call for schedule. Reservations required. Island Rd, Jones Bay. 469.5330

60 The Inn at Cade's Bay $$ This sparkling new hotel features 16-beachfront bungalows that sleep from 2 to 4 people. There's a pool, and on the beach is **Tequila Sheila's**, a seaside bar that serves tasty local fare (try the jerk chicken with guava ketchup) along with breakfast and lunch for inn guests. It's the place the locals go on Saturday night for a good time; Happy Hour is also lively. ◆ Island Rd, Cades Bay. 469.8139

61 Fort Ashby These ruined battlements overlook what is believed to be the site of the settlement of Jamestown, which was swallowed whole by an earthquake and tidal wave around 1680. There's not much left of the fort, either, though it was once used to guard Horatio Nelson's ships during provisioning stops. ◆ Island Rd (between Cotton Ground and Cades Bay)

62 Nelson's Spring At this lagoon in the village of Cotton Ground, Horatio Nelson replenished his ships with fresh water before sailing north to fight in the American Revolution. ◆ Island Rd, Cotton Ground

63 Pinney's Beach Although hurricanes and tropical storms regularly strip this beach—one of the most famous in the Caribbean—of sand, dredging operations are vigilant and ongoing, with all efforts made to maintain the nearly six-mile golden stretch. Reef-protected waters are great for snorkeling and swimming. ◆ West of Island Rd (between Charlestown and Cotton Ground)

63 Sunshine's Literally a shack on the beach, this take-out place serves drinks and fresh-caught fish to **Four Seasons** guests and others looking for a "local" experience. There's no bathroom or running water. ◆ Daily. Pinney's Beach. No phone

63 Beachcomber Bar & Grill ★$ Located right on Pinney's Beach, this friendly bar and restaurant serves tasty snacks like tuna fritters, terrific burgers, and grilled local fish.

Vegan dishes are also on the menu. It's a great place to watch the sunset, and don't leave without checking on the boutique inside—the stuff is terrific. ◆ Caribbean/American ◆ Daily lunch and dinner. Pinney's Beach. 469.1192

FOUR SEASONS RESORT ESTATES

63 Four Seasons $$$$ A member of the swank chain, the island's most luxurious—and expensive—resort offers 196 rooms in 12 "cottages" that overlook either the golf course or gorgeous Pinney's Beach. The centerpiece is a plantation-style great house with restaurants, bars, and a library. A marble staircase leads to the pool pavilion, beach, and dock. Guest rooms are lush with tropical decor and have huge marble bathrooms, air-conditioning, and private patios or screened balconies. A supervised activities program keeps kids busy. Other perks include a health club and fitness center, a spa, 10 tennis courts, 24-hour room service, and a gracious staff. Golf packages, with unlimited use of the course (see below), are available. Two top-notch gift shops offer beautiful handicrafts and the best selection of newspapers and magazines on the island. ◆ Pinney's Beach. 469.1111, 800/332.3442; fax 469.1040

Within Four Seasons:

Four Seasons Golf Course The first course to be built on Nevis is a dramatic 18-hole masterpiece designed by Robert Trent Jones Jr. It begins at sea level, slopes toward 3,232-foot Mount Nevis, and ends up on the beach. The 15th hole, with a ravine and 600-yard drop to the green, is the most challenging. The views are smashing, the fairways uncrowded, and staffers patrol the course with refreshments. ◆ Fee. Daily. 469.1111, 800/332.3442

64 Pinney's Beach Hotel $ This comfortable property is set on the famed golden sands of Pinney's Beach, a seven-minute walk from Charlestown. The 36 air-conditioned rooms are large and come with TV sets and ocean-view patios. A dining room, pool, and tennis court are on the premises, and the management will arrange fishing, sailing, and horseback riding. ◆ Pinney's Rd (west of Island Rd). 469.5207, 800/742.4276; fax 469.1088

64 Sea Spawn Guest House $ These 18 simple and inexpensive rooms are in a central location, convenient for shopping and walking tours of Charlestown. The dining room serves breakfast, lunch, and dinner to guests and others who reserve in advance. There's no pool, but the beach is close by. ◆ Old Hospital Rd (between Main St and Pinney's Rd), Charlestown. 469.5239

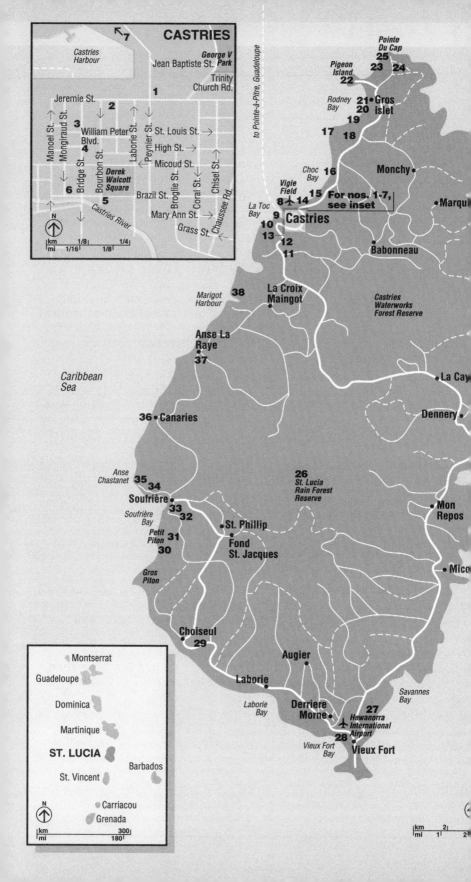

CASTRIES

Castries Harbour

↖ 7

George V Park

Jean Baptiste St.

Trinity Church Rd.

Jeremie St.

↓ 2

1

↓

Manoel St. →

Mongiraud St.

3

William Peter Blvd.

St. Louis St. →

High St. →

Micoud St.

4

Bridge St.

Bourbon St.

Laborie St.

Peynier St.

Derek Walcott Square

Broglie St.

Coral St.

Chisel St. →

Chaussee Rd.

6

5

Brazil St.

Mary Ann St. →

Grass St.

Castries River

N

↑

| km | | 1/8 | 1/4 |
| mi | 1/16 | 1/8 | |

to Pointe-à-Pitre, Guadeloupe

Pointe Du Cap

25

23 24

Pigeon Island

22

Rodney Bay

21 • Gros Islet

20

19

17

18

• Monchy

Choc Bay

16

Vigie Field

15

8 ✈ 14

For nos. 1-7, see inset

• Marqui

La Toc Bay

9

Castries

10

13

12

• Babonneau

11

Marigot Harbour

38

La Croix Maingot

Castries Waterworks Forest Reserve

Anse La Raye

37

Caribbean Sea

• La Cay

36 • Canaries

Dennery •

26
St. Lucia Rain Forest Reserve

Anse Chastanet

35 34

Soufrière •

33

32

31

30

St. Phillip

Fond St. Jacques

Petit Piton

Gros Piton

• Mon Repos

• Mico

Choiseul

29

Augier •

Laborie

Laborie Bay

Derriere Morne •

27
✈ Hewanorra International Airport

Savannes Bay

28

Vieux Fort Bay

Vieux Fort

Montserrat

Guadeloupe

Dominica

Martinique

ST. LUCIA

Barbados

St. Vincent

N

↑

Carriacou

Grenada

| km | | 300 |
| mi | | 180 |

| km | 2 |
| mi | 1 | 2 |

St. Lucia

With its landscape of extraordinary beauty, the avocado-shaped island of St. Lucia is a nature-lover's paradise. Here the twin peaks of the **Pitons** soar a half-mile out of the sea, serving as magnificent gateposts for the 19,000-acre **St. Lucia Rain Forest Reserve.** Lush with giant ferns, wild orchids, and towering stands of bamboo, the reserve is a favorite of bird-watchers, who haunt its paths searching for the rare indigenous parrots called jacquots and other exotic residents.

At the "world's only drive-through volcano," **Mount Soufrière,** motorists and hikers follow a road through the eerie rock formations of an ancient crater, where yellow-brown sludge plops and simmers, reeking of brimstone and spewing clouds of steam 50 feet overhead. Nearby, **Diamond Falls** tumbles in six stages through sulfur springs that color the cascades with splashes of yellow, green, and purple. The thermal springs also feed adjacent mineral ponds that bubble among the ruins of 18th-century baths (commissioned by King Louis XVI of France) where visitors still congregate to take the waters.

The virginal cove near **La Croix Maingot,** a secluded natural harbor and former hideout for pirate ships, is one of the most beautiful in the Caribbean. At the coastal villages of **Anse La Raye** and **Canaries,** locals still fish from dugout canoes. After bringing in the day's haul, the men stretch their nets along the shoreline while the women scrub the family wash against the rocks and spread it out to dry in the sun. **Reduit Beach** is lively with windsurfers and day sailors. Divers head for **Anse Chastanet,** where coral reefs are populated by sponges, lobsters, and moray eels.

Morning markets are the main attractions in the island's modern capital, **Castries,** which lost most of its historic architecture to fires in 1948 and 1951. The battlements atop **Morne Fortune** command sweeping views, while **Fort Charlotte** is a jumble of Gallic stone and English brick construction, a legacy of the high turnover of occupying forces. For a glimpse of true West Indian style, prowl the old French stronghold of **Soufrière,** where gingerbread buildings are trimmed with lacy balconies.

On St. Lucia, even everyday meals are celebrated with a tall glass of rum-piked tropical fruit juice over crushed ice. Mangoes, papayas, and pineapples also turn up on dinner plates, along with grilled flying fish, curries, and pepper pot, a highly seasoned stew. Local ingredients are open to inspection at historic plantations, where tours visit fields of bananas, coffee, nutmeg, cacao and other cash crops.

Located midway between French Martinique and British St. Vincent, St. Lucia was passed back and forth between France and Great Britain 14 times as the 2 countries traded deeds to the Caribbean. The island finally became British in 1814, but centuries of land flips shuffled plenty of *français* into the local culture and patois.

A self-governing state since 1967, St. Lucia was granted total sovereignty and full-fledged membership in the British Commonwealth in 1979. Since then, the stable and prosperous agricultural economy has been boosted by careful development of light industry and tourism.

Still, the Caribbean of simple ways and comfortable accommodations lives on in the quiet towns and uncrowded beaches that line one of the most spectacular coastlines in the islands. Although many visitors are content to doze in the sun, there's plenty to do here: take a horseback ride along the beach, catch up on your reading (local poet and playwright Derek Walcott won the 1992 Nobel Prize for Literature), shop for the island's famous hand-printed fabrics, sample the callaloo soup, or step back in time by strolling through a historic plantation.

Area code 758 unless otherwise noted.

Getting to the Island

Airlines

American Airlines 454.6777, 800/433.7300

BWIA (British West Indies Airlines) 452.3950

Interisland Carriers

Air Martinique 452.2463

American Eagle 452.1820, 800/433.7300

Eagle Air...452.1900

LIAT (Leeward Island Air Transport) 452.3051

St. Lucia Helicopters, Ltd 453.6850

Airports **Hewanorra International Airport** (Vieux Fort, 454.6249, 454.6259) services international long-distance flights. (Only **American Airlines** and **BWIA** offer direct flights from the US, departing from both New York City and Miami.) The airport's location at the island's southern tip—more than an hour's drive from the capital town of Castries—is inconvenient for the more heavily trafficked tourist areas. **Vigie Field** (Peninsular Rd, between Castries–Gros Islet Hwy and Clarke Ave, 452.1156) is smaller and older, but within reach of the northern resorts. It's about a mile from Castries. Most interisland flights and some **American Eagle** flights land here.

Getting Around the Island

Buses Minibuses and jitneys offer cheap (and crowded) transportation between Castries, Soufrière, **Cap Estate,** and **Vieux Fort.** You can flag them down on the road or pick one up at a bus stop. Be sure to ask the driver about the destination—they're often not clearly marked.

Car Rental

Avis 452.2700, 452.2202, 800/331.1212

Budget 452.0233, 800/527.0700

Courtesy...450.8142

CTL Rent-A-Car 452.0732

Hertz 451.7351, 800/654.3131

National...........................450.8721, 800/328.4567

Driving Stay on the left, British style, and watch for potholes. An international or St. Lucia driver's license is required. Those with international licenses must have them validated for use on the island; the traffic department and most car-rental agencies will do so at no charge. If you don't have an international license, a St. Lucia license can be obtained at the airport or through most car-rental agencies on the island for about US$14; you must present a valid US, Canadian, or UK driver's license.

Taxis

Taxi Association 454.6316

Tours Options include half- or full-day island tours, day trips to surrounding isles, land and sea excursions, rain forest walks, and guided shopping. For details, contact **Barnard's Travel** (452.2214, 452.2215) or **Sunlink Tours/St. Lucia Representative Service** (452.8232). A complete list of other tour operators is available from the tourist office (see "Visitors' Information Office," below).

FYI

Electricity The current is 220 to 230 volts/50 cycles. Most hotels have special outlets for electric shavers, but converters are needed for hair dryers and other small appliances.

Entry Requirements US and Canadian visitors must present a valid passport or other proof of citizenship (birth certificate, voter's registration card) and a picture ID, plus a return or onward ticket.

Language English is the official language, but a French-Creole patois is also spoken by some islanders.

Money St. Lucia uses the Eastern Caribbean dollar (EC$). US and Canadian dollars are accepted by stores, restaurants, and hotels, as are traveler's checks and most major credit cards. Banks are generally open Monday through Thursday from 8AM to 3PM, Friday from 8AM to 5PM. The **Barclay's Bank** branch near **Rodney Bay Marina** at **Gros Islet** is open Saturday mornings.

Personal Safety Use normal precautions: Don't pick up hitchhikers, leave valuables unguarded, wear expensive jewelry, or wander in deserted areas. The possession or sale of drugs means big trouble here; don't risk it.

Publications The four local weeklies are the *Crusader, One Caribbean, Star,* and *Voice of St. Lucia.* Pick up the monthly *Tropical Traveller* for tourist-oriented listings. The regional *Caribbean Week* is published in Barbados. *The New York Times* usually hits the stands two days late.

Reservation Services and House Rentals The tourist offices at **Hewanorra International Airport** (454.6644) and **Vigie Field** (452.2595) can arrange accommodations. They are staffed Monday through Friday at flight arrival times.

Taxes An eight-percent tax is added to hotel bills.

Tipping A 10-percent service charge is included in hotel bills; it covers room maids and other staff. Restaurants add a 10-percent service charge to the check, which covers the waiter's tip. Cab drivers expect about 10 percent of the fare. Airport porters depend on tips for a substantial portion of their income; tip US$1 per bag.

Visitors' Information Office The main tourist office of the **St. Lucia Tourist Board** (Pointe Seraphine, west of John Compton Hwy, Castries, 453.0053, 452.4094; fax 453.1121) is open Monday through Friday from 8AM to 4:30PM. The **Jeremie Street** branch (452.5978) is open Monday through Friday from 8AM to 5PM and Saturday from 9AM to noon. Other branches are located at **Vigie Field** (Peninsular Rd, between Castries–Gros Islet Hwy a

Clarke Ave, 452.2595), **Hewanorra International Airport** (454.6644), and on **Bay Street** in Soufrière (459.7419). The airport offices are staffed weekdays when flights arrive; the Bay Street branch is open Monday through Friday from 8AM to 9PM.

Phone Book

Ambulance	999
Directory Assistance	411
Diving Emergencies/ Decompression Chambers	100
Emergencies	999
Fire	999
Hospitals	
St. Jude's Hospital, Vieux Fort	454.6041
Victoria Hospital, Castries	452.2421
Police	999
Post Office	452.2611

Castries

St. Lucia's capital will come as a surprise to visitors who expect colonial charm. Several fires in the mid-20th century wiped out most of the original buildings, and their modern replacements reflect the bland utilitarian style of the times. Nonetheless, there are still a few patches of local color, especially at the open market, where farmers and householders meet to barter and catch up on the news. And the natural setting is beautiful, with the **Caribbean** in the foreground and the slopes of **Morne Fortune** providing a dramatic backdrop.

1 Open Market The air is scented with cinnamon, nutmeg, and bay leaves at this picturesque place. A rainbow of fresh island fruits, vegetables, spices, and herbs shares space with pottery, straw goods, and other handicrafts. The biggest market day is Saturday, when there are the most stalls and shoppers. ♦ Daily. Jeremie and Peynier Sts

2 Noah's Arkade Touristy, but fun, this shop stocks steel drums, straw goods, wood carvings, and other West Indian crafts. ♦ M-F, Sa morning. Jeremie St (between Laborie and Cadet Sts). 452.2523. Also at: Pointe Seraphine (west of John Compton Hwy). 452.7488; Hewanorra International Airport, Vieux Fort. 454.5288

3 St. Lucia Philatelic Bureau Because St. Lucia's population is so small, the island's colorful postage stamps are released in extremely limited issues. The stamps, sold at this bureau in the **General Post Office**, are especially valued by collectors and also make fun souvenirs. ♦ M-Sa. Bridge St (between Micoud and Jeremie Sts). 452.3774

4 J.Q. Charles, Ltd. Castries's big department store is worth a look. ♦ M-F, Sa morning. Bridge St (between Micoud St and William Peter Blvd). 452.2721

5 Rain ★★$$$ A marvelous Victorian mansion is the spot for Creole specialties. Try the spicy land crab served in its own shell or red snapper simmered in a tomato, onion, and butter sauce. There's a dinner buffet on Wednesday and Friday nights. ♦ Caribbean ♦ Daily lunch and dinner. Reservations recommended. Brazil and Bourbon Sts. 452.1515

6 Artsibits Gallery Paintings, pottery, and wood carvings are among the works by local artists for sale here. ♦ M-F, Sa morning. Brazil and Mongiraud Sts. 452.7865

7 Pointe Seraphine The more than 30 stores in this shopping center sell china, porcelain, crystal, local crafts, cosmetics, liquor, and other duty-free goods. Adjacent to the cruise-ship terminal, the complex also houses a tourist information center, car-rental agencies, a taxi stand, and other conveniences. ♦ M-Sa; Su when a cruise ship is in port. West of John Compton Hwy

Elsewhere on St. Lucia

8 Jimmie's ★★$$ The bar is a popular watering hole, and the restaurant has great views of the harbor, with a Creole menu that features fresh fish, lobster, octopus, and *lambi* (conch). ♦ Caribbean ♦ M-Sa lunch and dinner; Su dinner; closed early July–early August. Reservations recommended. Vigie Cove Marina (west of Peninsular Rd). 452.5142

9 Bagshaws The dramatic setting atop a sea-pounded cliff is worth the trip in itself. The studio/shop here creates and sells internationally known tropical fabrics, splashed with flowers and wildlife, which are crafted into everything from evening wear to tea cozies. Visitors are welcome to watch the silk-screening process, as printmakers apply one color to the fabric at a time, working at 104-foot-long tables. Some elaborate designs require as many as 12 separate screenings. The final effect is brilliant, but not *too* flashy—as conservative as fabrics printed with jungle birds and exotic blooms can be. ♦ M-Sa. La Toc Bay. 452.2139. Also at: Pointe Seraphine (west of John Compton Hwy), Castries. 452.7570

10 Sandals St. Lucia $$ This beachfront property is part of the Sandals chain of all-inclusive, couples-only resorts. Surrounded by tropical gardens, the complex features 272 luxurious rooms and suites (the latter with four-poster beds and satellite TV; some also have private pools) and 3 dining rooms featuring Asian, Caribbean, and Italian fare. Sports facilities include three pools (one with a swim-up bar), a nine-hole golf course, five lighted tennis courts, and a health club. ♦ La Toc Bay. 452.3081, 800/SANDALS; fax 452.1012

11 Fort Charlotte This 18th-century fortress guards Castries from the summit of Morne Fortune. At the height of the colonial wars, it was traded back and forth between French and British forces more than a dozen times—a history reflected in its eclectic array of architectural styles. French stone buildings stand beside British brick; several construction projects were begun by one faction and finished by the other. The view is more harmonious—a fine panorama stretches from the Pitons in the south to Pigeon Island in the north. ♦ Free. Daily. Morne and Henry Dulieu Rds. No phone

12 Caribelle Batik Visitors can observe the 60 crafters practicing the 2,000-year-old Indonesian art of batik in this workshop, which is both a sight-seeing attraction (the house is believed by many islanders to be haunted) and a boutique. Hand-printed cotton fabrics, wall hangings, and clothing are created and sold on site. The operation is set in **Howelton House,** a carefully restored Victorian building with fine views of Castries Harbour from high on Morne Fortune. ♦ M-F; Sa morning. Old Victoria Rd (off Morne Rd). 452.3785, 452.3786; fax 453.0287

12 Bon Appétit ★★$$$ This lofty perch atop Morne Fortune offers panoramic views of Castries, Pigeon Island, and Martinique. Simple and charming, the restaurant also serves a good feast. Favorite entrées include crayfish, veal *escallop,* and rib steaks. ♦ Caribbean/American ♦ M-F lunch and dinner; Sa-Su dinner. Reservations recommended. Red Tape La (between Victoria and Morne Rds). 452.2757

12 Green Parrot ★★★$$$ Chef Harry is a native of St. Lucia, but he trained at **Claridge's** in London, which explains his creative Anglicized versions of local dishes. The mixed grill and steaks will please beef-eaters, while soups and Creole cassoulets make good use of island produce. The setting on Morne Fortune promises great views across Castries to the sea, but the in-house show can be just as spectacular. The entertainment every Monday and Wednesday ranges from fire-eaters to limbo dancers; Friday is reserved for jazz. Monday is Ladies' Night, when any *femme* with a flower in her hair (escorted by a man in jacket and tie) is treated to a free dinner. Fixed-price dinners are offered on Saturday. ♦ Continental/Caribbean ♦ Daily lunch and dinner. Reservations recommended; jacket and tie required Monday and strongly recommended at all other times. Red Tape La (between Victoria and Morne Rds). 452.3167

13 San Antoine ★★★$$$ This landmark restaurant is set in a 100-year-old building that was restored after a fire in 1970. Guests enjoy sweeping views of the Castries harbor and an elegant menu that includes honey roast rack of lamb and breast of chicken in puff pastry with spinach. There's a tempting dessert trolley, too. ♦ Continental/Caribbean ♦ M-F lunch and dinner; Sa dinner. Reservations recommended. Morne Rd (between Victoria and Government House Rds). 452.4660

14 Rendezvous $$ No singles or children are allowed at this getaway for couples (a "couple" is defined as "any two mutually interested people"). A single tab covers meals and drinks, all sports (including scuba diving), two-day excursions, nightly entertainment, and even cigarettes. The 100 rooms are set in either waterfront cottages or the main hotel in a lavish tropical landscape on palm-shaded Malabar Beach. There is a pool with a swim-up bar and two dining rooms, and guests have access to the **St. Lucia Racquet Club.** ♦ Off Peninsular Rd. 452.4211, 800/544.2883; fax 452.7419

Sandals

15 Sandals Halcyon $$$ The second property in the Sandals chain on the island, this all-inclusive couples-only resort has three pools, two tennis courts, and full water-sports facilities. The 170 rooms are set in cabanas with private patios that overlook the beach or well-tended gardens. Meals are served either in **Mario's**, an international restaurant featuring Italian fare, or in a casual cafe on the wharf, where the disco has live entertainment on Monday, Wednesday, and Friday nights. There are also three bars, and guests can use the nine-hole golf course at the **Sandals St. Lucia** property (see above). ♦ Castries–Gros Islet Hwy, Choc Bay. 453.0222, 800/SANDALS fax 451.8435

16 Wyndham Morgan Bay $$$ Set on a nearly 22-acre nature preserve, this 238-room beachfront resort is decorated with floral pastels and wicker furniture. The all-inclusive rate covers meals at either of 2 restaurants, drinks (except Champagne), 25 different sporting opportunities, 2 sight-seeing trips, and airport transfers. ◆ Castries–Gros Islet Hwy, Choc Bay. 450.2511, 800/WYNDHAM; fax 450.1050

17 Windjammer Landing Villa Beach Resort $$$$ This property's 227 villas pepper a wooded hillside above a small but lovely beach. Each of the Mediterranean-style villas has a fully equipped kitchenette, living room, and balcony; all except the one-bedroom units have their own plunge pools as well. One two-bedroom villa and one four-bedroom unit have their own full-size pools and full-time staff. For an additional charge, a cook provides meals. Two bars, five eateries, a fitness center, shops (including a grocery store), water sports, two lighted tennis courts, and a kids' program are on the premises; golf and horseback riding can be arranged. ◆ Off Castries–Gros Islet Hwy (between Choc Bay and Gros Islet). 452.0913, 800/743.9609; fax 452.0907

Within Windjammer Landing Villa Beach Resort:

Papa Don's ★★★$$$ This casual hillside eatery offers super Italian fare served alfresco. Try the grilled vegetable lasagna or a pizza pulled from a wood-fire oven. ◆ Italian ◆ Daily lunch and dinner. 452.0913

18 Orange Grove Hotel $ The price is right, and views of Reduit Bay are spectacular at this trim complex of 54 rooms and 8 air-conditioned cottages—each with a living room, kitchenette, and 1 or 2 bedrooms. There's also a pool and a free daily shuttle to Reduit Beach. The restaurant serves local fare. ◆ Off Castries–Gros Islet Hwy (between Choc Bay and Gros Islet). 452.8089; fax 452.7584

19 Capone's ★★$$$ Jazzy 1920s decor trims this tropical speakeasy, which features southern Italian cuisine along with seafood, pizza, and steaks. There's also an ice-cream parlor for dessert. ◆ Italian/American ◆ Daily dinner. Reservations recommended. Rodney Bay. 452.0284

19 Snooty Agouti ★★$$ Surf the Internet while you sip a hot espresso, fork into home-style fare (fried chicken, meaty burgers) or feast on gooey desserts at this tranquil open-air eatery with a computer terminal for patrons' use. Local art, Cuban cigars, and fresh local juices are also for sale here. ◆ Caribbean/International ◆ Daily breakfast, lunch, and dinner. Rodney Bay. 452.0321

19 Mortar & Pestle ★★$$$ The Caribbean views are great from this waterfront spot, where an international menu features an especially wide variety of regional specialties. Try the Jamaican salt fish, Guyana pepper pot,

Grenadian stuffed jack fish, or Bajan flying fish. ◆ International/Caribbean ◆ Daily lunch and dinner. Reservations required (call well in advance). Rodney Bay. 452.8756

19 The Lime ★★$ Both islanders and visitors like this simple eatery, where inexpensive fare runs the gamut from seafood lasagna to chargrilled steaks and chops. Prices are particularly reasonable at lunch, when the menu offers roti, sandwiches, and steak-and-kidney pie. The West Indian atmosphere is pleasant, with eight tables inside and another five outdoors. There is live music and dancing in the evening at the neighboring **Late Lime Night Club;** diners are admitted free. ◆ Caribbean/International ◆ M, W-Su lunch and dinner; closed the first three weeks of September. Rodney Bay. 452.0761

19 Bread Basket Stop in to pick up freshly baked bread, pastries, or light snacks to munch on while you're driving around and seeing the sights. ◆ Daily. No credit cards accepted. Rodney Bay. 452.0647

20 Reduit Beach This white-sand beach attracts a lively crowd, drawn by the wide range of activities available through the **Rex St. Lucian Hotel,** the island's premier sports center (see below). Palm trees shade one end of the milelong strand. ◆ Rodney Bay

On Reduit Beach:

Rex St. Lucian Hotel $$ All water sports (except diving) are included in the room rates here, and the on-site disco, **Splash,** is a popular gathering spot, with limbo dancing and steel bands. The 120 guest rooms, all with balconies and terraces, are set in pastel buildings on beautiful Reduit Beach. Other facilities include a pool, two tennis courts, and two restaurants—the casual **Quarterdeck Cafe** and the more formal **Oriental Restaurant** (see below). ◆ 452.8351, 800/223.9868; fax 452.8331

Within the Rex St. Lucian Hotel:

Oriental Restaurant ★★$$$ Authentic specialties from China, Japan, India, and Thailand are prepared by Chef Adil Sherwaini in this pastel-hued, subtly lit, elegant dining room. Try the lemon-marinated swordfish kabobs over carrot and coriander pilaf or spicy Hunan beef with scallions and sweet red peppers. There is live music some evenings. ◆ Asian ◆ Daily breakfast, lunch, and dinner. Reservations recommended for dinner. 452.8351 ext 403

Restaurants/Clubs: Red   **Hotels:** Blue
Shops/ ♥ Outdoors: Green   **Sights/Culture:** Black

Scuba St. Lucia This full-service **PADI** facility offers snorkeling and scuba equipment, instruction, and reef and wreck trips. ♦ 452.8009. Also at: Anse Chastanet Hotel, Anse Chastanet. 459.7000; fax 459.7700

Royal St. Lucian $$$$ Situated on one of the finest beaches on the island, this all-suite luxury resort on Reduit Beach offers complete water sports facilities, four interconnecting swimming pools, two restaurants—including **L'Epicure**, with its popular Monday night Caribbean buffet—and nightly entertainment. Piped-in music (light classical in reception areas, soft Caribbean on the beach and around the pool) contributes to an already soothing atmosphere. One of the 98 unattached suites has a small private pool; all face the beach or the pool. ♦ 452.9999, 800/255.5859; fax 452.9639

20 Charthouse ★★$$$ The open-air dining room overlooks the yacht harbor and is appropriately "yachty," with lots of wood paneling, nautical charts, and greenery. Steak and lobster are the specialties here, but the menu also offers spicy West Indian soups, fresh fish, and barbecued ribs. ♦ American/Caribbean ♦ M-Sa dinner. Reservations required. Rodney Bay Lagoon. 452.8115

20 Harmony Marina Suites $ Children are welcome at this family-operated complex of 30 2-bedroom apartments, each with a separate living area, kitchen, and spacious balcony; 8 deluxe suites all have hot tubs and sundecks. Guests may choose accommodations with one or two bathrooms and optional air-conditioning. A pool and restaurant are on the premises. ♦ Rodney Bay Lagoon. 452.0336; fax 452.8677

21 Gros Islet Everyone is welcome at this village's Friday night "jump-up," a block party with steel bands, reggae, and dancing in the street. The event starts rocking after 10PM and draws a good crowd of both locals and visitors. ♦ Rodney Bay

THE GREAT HOUSE
RESTAURANT ST. LUCIA

22 Pigeon Island A scenic causeway links this island to Gros Islet. Drive across to visit the ruins of **Rodney Fort,** a designated historic site. In 1839 British admiral George Rodney sailed from here with his fleet to intercept the French in the Dominica Passage near the Iles des Saintes, Guadeloupe. The result was the Battle of the Saints, which secured Britain's dominance on the seas. Rodney's penchant for breeding pigeons gave the island its name. You can explore on your own or join a guided tour. Afterwards, order a drink or light meal at **Jambe de Bois** (450.8167), a casual restaurant serving good Creole lunches. The nearby **Pigeon Island Interpretation Centre** traces local history. It's open Monday through Saturday and there's a nominal admission charge. In the archways below the center is **Captain's Cellar** (450.8167), a pub owned by local jazz musician Luther François and his wife, Dahlia. There are live jazz performances here on Friday and Saturday. Also nearby is the open-air **Derek Walcott Theatre** (450.0211), built on the original foundations of the historic Cap Estate house. It features a lineup of dramatic, musical, and dance performances. The adjoining **Great House Restaurant** (450.0450) offers dinners featuring French cuisine and Sunday brunch; afternoon tea is also served on days on which there are theater performances. ♦ Northwest coast

23 Club St. Lucia $ There are great views of the curving bay from this all-inclusive resort with 372 guest bungalows. Pluses include three free-form pools, water sports (all except scuba diving are included in the rate), seven lighted tennis courts, a squash court, a gym, children's program, and two restaurants. Guests also may use the **St. Lucia Racquet Club.** ♦ Cap Estate. 450.0551, 800/223.9815 fax 450.0281

23 St. Lucia Golf & Country Club Formerly known as the **Cap Estate Golf Club,** this par-36, 9-hole golf course sits on a lovely spot on the northern tip of the island on what was once a plantation. Clubs, pull carts, and caddies are available for hire. (The island's other course, at **Sandals St. Lucia,** is also open to visitors; see page 266.) ♦ Greens fees.Daily.Cap Estate. 450.8523

24 Trim Stables Riders of all levels of expertise can find a suitable mount here. Horse-and-buggy jaunts and beach picnic excursions are also available. Fees include transportation from your hotel. ♦ Northeast of Cap Estate. 452.8273

25 LeSport $$$ This 102-room, all-inclusive resort on Anse de Cap, at the northernmost tip of the island, has an impressive lineup of activities ranging from scuba diving to fencing. In addition there's healthy dining on *"cuisine légère"* (light cooking) and an invigorating program of thalassotherapy—seawater massages, jet baths, and other water-related spa treatments. Guests can also rent a 3-bedroom hilltop plantation house with its own pool and 13 acres of gardens, just a 5-minute drive from the resort. ◆ Anse de Cap. 450.8551, 800/544.2883; fax 450.0368

26 St. Lucia Rain Forest Reserve About 13 percent of the woodlands on St. Lucia—a total of 19,000 acres—is rain forest. A good way to see some of it is on a nature walk through either the **Edmond Forest Reserve** or the **Quilesse Forest Reserve,** which make up the southernmost half of the rain forest. Both reserves are home to many plant species, such as tree ferns, bromeliads, and wild orchids, and a wide variety of birds including the endangered jacquot (or St. Lucia parrot), illustrated below—and both offer numerous well-cut trails. Two good choices are the seven-mile **Des Catier Trail,** with an entrance near the east-coast town of Micoud, and the five-mile **Barre de L'Isle Trail.** The **St. Lucia Forestry Department** (452.2231) arranges excursions geared to participants' fitness levels. Exploring the rain forest without a guide is not recommended.

27 Club Aquarius $$ Sprawled across 95 acres at the southern tip of the island, this link in the international Club Med chain of all-inclusive resorts offers 256 air-conditioned rooms with sea views from the balconies. Guests enjoy tennis (eight lighted courts), horseback riding, diving, volleyball, soccer, archery, basketball, softball, aerobic workouts, and other sports. Also available are a pool, a mini-pool for children, and 2 large sailboats that accommodate up to 24. Children are well tended at the "Mini-Club," and grownup kids can join the circus school. There's also a restaurant and a nightclub. ◆ Northeast of Vieux Fort. 454.9855, 800/CLUBMED; fax 454.6017

28 Chak ★$$ Sample Creole cooking or stick with more familiar continental fare at this eatery. Two bars and a large courtyard often offer live musical entertainment. ◆ Caribbean/Continental ◆ Daily breakfast, lunch, and dinner. Vieux Fort. 454.6260

29 Choiseul Arts and Crafts Straw weavings, baskets, pottery, and woodwork stand out in a collection of local handicrafts. ◆ M-Sa. La Fargue. 459.3226

30 Jalousie Plantation $$$$ Suites and cottages with private plunge pools climb the hillside above a beautiful secluded cove lined with gray sand. More than 325 acres graced with tropical gardens and palm-shaded lawns are cradled between the twin peaks of the Pitons. Renovated in 1997, the 114-room property offers a rate that includes meals,

drinks, sports facilities, and cigarettes. Among the amenities on the premises are four good restaurants, a fully equipped spa, horseback riding, four tennis courts, a pool, and water sports. ◆ South of Soufrière. 459.7666; fax 459.7667

30 Bang Between the Pitons ★★$$ This outdoor waterfront restaurant is, as the name implies, right between the Piton peaks. (You can get here by boat or by driving through the **Jalousie Plantation** resort; see above.) Eating areas are arranged around a central courtyard and the specialties of the house are roasted lamb, sun-dried jerk chicken, and jerk fish with salad. ◆ Creole ◆ Daily lunch and dinner. Reservations recommended. South of Soufrière. 459.7864

31 Ladera $$$$ This 19-room hideaway has received international raves for its stellar dining room and grand setting. The splendid West Indian–style villas (with two or three bedrooms) open onto views of the towering green Pitons set against the blue Caribbean Sea. One entire wall folds back to take full advantage of the dramatic scenery (though the beds are draped in clouds of mosquito netting, guests with a low tolerance for insects may want to keep their walls closed). Some units have Jacuzzis and private plunge pools fed by a mini-waterfall, and there is a free-form pool for all guests' use. The restaurant, **Dasheene,** serves local treats with a continental flair; try the smoked kingfish wrapped in crepes. One drawback: To reach the beach, guests are shuttled down to Soufrière, where they hop a boat to Anse Chastanet. ◆ South of Soufrière. 450.8551, 800/544.2883; fax 450.0368

Jacquot Parrot

Plantation Tours

Today many Caribbean islands have little more than a few windmills and crumbling ruins to recall the days when sugar was king, but several plantations still operate on St. Lucia, and a number allow visitors to see the mammoth working estates in action.

Until the turn of the century, **Marquis Plantation** in the northeast was a major sugarcane producer; today it is St. Lucia's biggest banana estate. A tour of the estate starts with a break for cool local fruit juices, after which visitors are guided through the copra shed, the old cacao-drying area, and the sugar factory. Depending on the season, they may also view workers packing bananas for export to Britain, or fertilizing the fruit on the 150 acres under cultivation. The next part of the tour is a motorboat trip

down the **Marquis River** through mangrove forests to the Atlantic coast. Afterwards, guests return to the main house for a Creole lunch, served on the veranda. For information on **Marquis Plantation** tours, contact **Sunlink Tours** (452.8232, 800/SUNLINK) or your hotel's tour desk.

There are also guided excursions to other plantations where nutmeg, sugarcane, coffee, citrus fruits, and other island products are grown. Contact **M&C Tours** (452.2811) or **Cook's & Co.** (452.2211).

32 The Still ★★★$$ An old rum distillery next to a mahogany forest is now one of the island's finest West Indian restaurants. The Creole lunch buffet is a tasty bargain, and the dinner menu also features authentic local fare; many of the ingredients are provided by the owners' plantation. ◆ Caribbean/Continental ◆ Daily lunch and diner. Reservations advised for dinner. South of Soufrière. 459.7224

32 Mount Soufrière The "world's only drive-through volcano" is an eerie moonscape of sulfurous steam and gurgling yellow-gray mud. Hikers and motorists can travel right into the crater and walk among rock formations that are millions of years old. Nearby natural hot springs are a smelly treatment for tired bones. ◆ South of Soufrière

32 Diamond Mineral Baths Originally built in 1785 by order of Louis XVI as a therapeutic retreat for French soldiers stationed in the West Indies, these thermal baths were rebuilt after World War II and are now privately owned. Guests are welcome to take the waters or walk through the botanical garden surrounding the baths. ◆ Admission. Daily. South of Soufrière. 452.4759

33 Soufrière Visitors who are disappointed by the workaday architecture of Castries will like the colonial style in St. Lucia's "second city." The old French capital is filled with buildings trimmed with lacy balconies and plenty of gingerbread. From this rustic village, fishing families still go to sea in narrow dugout canoes and cast homemade nets into the surf Beyond the tangle of jungle foliage and thick forest stand the majestic Pitons, rising abruptly from the Caribbean to half-mile twin peaks. ◆ Southwest coast

34 Hummingbird ★★★$$$ The lovely gardens at this dining spot are filled with the restaurant's namesakes. The eatery is part of the **Hummingbird Beach Resort** (with 10 basic and somewhat run-down-looking guest rooms and a cottage), and guests are welcome to cool off in the resort's swimming pool. Afterward, settle in for a long lunch with great views of the Pitons. The menu features both French and West Indian specialties—don't miss the crayfish in lime or garlic butter ◆ International ◆ Daily breakfast, lunch, and dinner. Reservations recommended. Between Soufrière and Anse Chastanet. 459.7232

35 Anse Chastanet Hotel $$$$ This enclave of octagonal cottages, in the verdant hills overlooking the Caribbean, is one of the island's best treasures. Views sweep over the Pitons, across the valley, and out to sea. The 36 hillside units, though wonderfully secluded for reading and dozing, are a steep 125 steps from the beach below. (Watersports enthusiasts should request one of the 12 beachside units.) The gray sands also feature a snack bar, chaises, Sunfish, and a **PADI** dive center. Some of the island's best dive sites are right off Anse Chastanet, where coral reefs lie just 10 to 20 feet below the surface. Other attractions include three restaurants and four tennis courts. ♦ Anse Chastanet. 459.7000, 800/223.1108; fax 459.7700, 914/763.5362

36 Canaries On this unspoiled beach where one of the island's rivers meets the sea, women from Canaries village come to do their laundry, scrubbing the family wash against the rocks. ♦ West coast

37 Anse La Raye Fishermen still go to sea from here in the same type of canoes used by Carib warriors 400 years ago. After a day's work, they return and spread out their nets and clean their catch along the shore. ♦ West coast

38 Marigot Harbour Yachters around the world know of this spectacular anchorage, where most of the palm-lined shore remains in its natural state; it's one of the most beautiful coves in the Caribbean. ♦ West coast

At Marigot Harbour:

The Moorings Marigot Bay Resort $$ With several outposts in sailing centers around the globe, **The Moorings** is one of the world's premier yacht charter operations. Boaters can come ashore at this property for a rest, or hire a craft for adventures at sea. Set against the scenic and secluded bay, the **Moorings Vacation Club** complex features 16 1-bedroom cottages. The nearby **Inn on the Bay** offers four two-bedroom suites, while **The Great House** is an elegant three-bedroom villa with the only swimming pool in the area. Two restaurants, several boutiques and bars, a wide range of water sports, a **PADI** dive center, a beautiful swimming beach, and yacht berths keep landlubbers and seafarers busy. ♦ 451.4357, 800/334.2435; fax 451.4353

Within The Moorings Marigot Bay Resort:

Doolittle's ★$$ Jump on a ferry that looks like Tom Sawyer's river raft to reach this open-air waterfront eatery located on the north side of the bay. Fresh seafood, salads made from local fruits and vegetables, burgers, sandwiches, and colorful tropical drinks are served. ♦ Caribbean/American ♦ Daily breakfast, lunch, and dinner. 451.4974

Getting Your Feet Wet in St. Lucia

With so many water sports available on St. Lucia, it would be a shame to spend all your time lolling on a beach. Most hotels have Sunfish and Windsurfers for loan or rent, and diving is part of the deal for guests at most all-inclusive resorts. Here are a few other outfits that can get you afloat:

Boating

Destination St. Lucia Rodney Bay. 452.8531

The Moorings Marigot Harbour. 451.4357, 800/334.2435

Sunsail Rodney Bay. 452.8648, 800/327.2276

Snorkeling and Scuba Diving

Buddies Scuba Vigie Marina (west of Peninsular Rd), Castries. 452.5288

Dolphin Divers Rodney Bay. 452.9485

The Moorings Scuba Centre Marigot Harbour. 451.4357, 800/334.2435

Scuba St. Lucia Anse Chastanet Hotel, Anse Chastanet. 459.7000; Rex St. Lucian Hotel, Reduit Beach, Rodney Bay. 452.8351

Windjammer Landing Off Castries–Gros Islet Hwy (between Choc Bay and Gros Islet). 452.0913

Sportfishing

Captain Mike Lunir Park, Castries. 452.7044

Mako Watersports Rodney Bay. 452.0412

Windsurfing

Island Windsurfing Limited Vieux Fort. 454.7400

Rex St. Lucian Hotel Reduit Beach, Rodney Bay. 452.8351

Bests

Leonard Germain
Shuttle Driver, Windjammer Landing

Go out and take a tour of the place.

Visit the rain forest and our national parks. The parks are very beautiful places and shouldn't be missed.

Go sailing.

Head to the beach—any beach. All our beaches are nice. Just see as much as you can.

Try our local dishes: plantains, roti, yams, our fish. And don't forget the beer.

Get involved with the local people. We love to talk to visitors. Ask us questions. Come to our Friday night street party—the "jump up" in **Gros Islet.** Come after 10PM. Or come to our discos on weekends and learn our island dances.

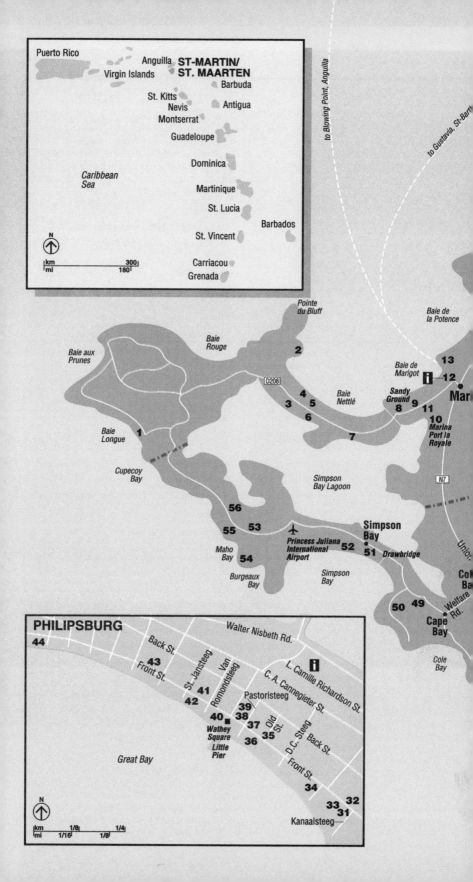

Puerto Rico

Anguilla

Virgin Islands

**ST-MARTIN/
ST. MAARTEN**

Barbuda

St. Kitts
Nevis
Montserrat

Antigua

Guadeloupe

Dominica

*Caribbean
Sea*

Martinique

St. Lucia

Barbados

St. Vincent

Carriacou
Grenada

N

| km | 300 |
| mi | 180 |

to Blowing Point, Anguilla

to Gustavia, St-Barth

*Pointe
du Bluff*

*Baie de
la Potence*

*Baie
Rouge*

2

*Baie aux
Prunes*

13

*Baie de
Marigot*

12

4

*Baie
Nettlé*

*Sandy
Ground*

9

3 5

8 9 11

Mar

6

10

*Marina
Port la
Royale*

7

*Baie
Longue*

1

N7

*Cupecoy
Bay*

*Simpson
Bay Lagoon*

56

53

**Simpson
Bay**

55

Uni

50

54

*Maho
Bay*

✈

*Princess Juliana
International
Airport*

52

51 *Drawbridge*

Co

Ba

*Burgeaux
Bay*

*Simpson
Bay*

50 49

*Welfare
Rd.*

**Cape
Bay**

*Cole
Bay*

PHILIPSBURG

Walter Nisbeth Rd.

44

Back St.

43

Front St.

St. Jansteeg

Van

L. Camille Richardson St.

41

Romondsteeg

C. A. Cannegieter St.

42

Pastoristeeg

40

39

38

37

35

Old St.

D.C. Steeg

Back St.

*Wathey
Square
Little
Pier*

36

34

Great Bay

Front St.

34

33 32
31

N

Kanaalsteeg

| km | 1/8 | 1/4 |
| mi | 1/16 | 1/8 |

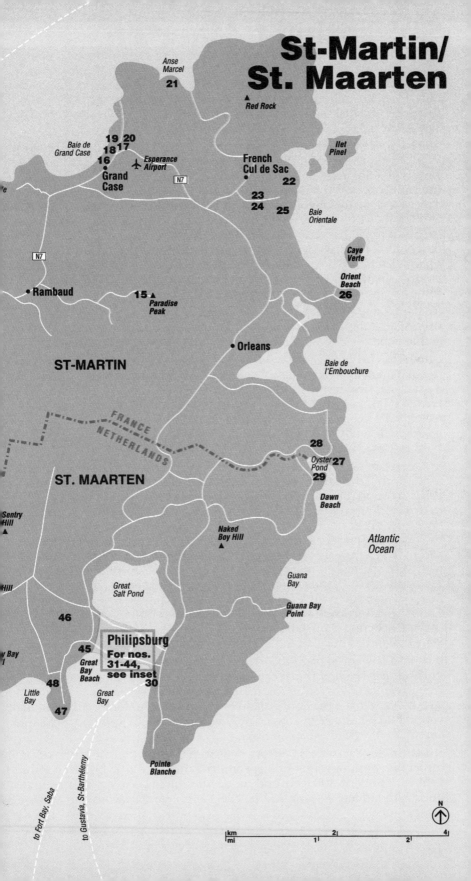

St-Martin/St. Maarten

According to popular legend, St-Martin/St. Maarten's boundaries were established in a walking contest around the island's perimeter in 1648. Setting off in opposite directions, a Frenchman paced off 21 square miles, and a less speedy Dutchman covered only 16 square miles. Today it's the smallest land mass in the world shared by two governments, though residents and tourists alike travel freely from one side to the other.

The island's unusual political arrangement dates back to the Eighty Years' War between Spain and the Dutch Republic. As the war drew to an end in early 1648, Spain surrendered the island to the Dutch. However, before the Dutch arrived to take possession, the French laid claim to the island. After a few skirmishes, an agreement between the two nations—signed on 23 March 1648—cut St-Martin/St. Maarten roughly in half. Though the island changed hands at least 16 times after that, the people here have peacefully coexisted since the final settlement was reached in 1816. Thanks to its two governments, the island is considered part of three island groups: the Dutch Leewards, the Netherlands Antilles, and the French West Indies.

No national border is easier to cross than the one that separates St-Martin from St. Maarten. There are no customs inspectors and no frontier guards; just a small roadside obelisk commemorating the 1648 apportionment.

Differences between the two sides exist, however. Dutch St. Maarten, with a population of approximately 35,000, has bustled for years with cruise-ship passengers, large resorts, and gambling casinos. By contrast, St-Martin (the French side), with slightly fewer residents, began its expansion only fairly recently. Its sleepy fishing villages are just awakening to the activity of stylish bistros and trendy boutiques—the mood remains easygoing and decidedly West Indian.

Just as the French and Dutch governments here have worked independently for centuries, the cultures of both sides have remained distinct. The southern (Dutch) region is brightened by pastel gingerbread houses covered with fretwork and surrounded by flowers. The fine restaurants, bistros, and boutiques of the northern (French) end are laced with charming wrought-iron balconies. Despite the European influences, this island is still very much a part of the Caribbean: bright aqua waters surround lush green mountains, with a new panorama around every corner. Even on a whirlwind tour, you'll get a taste of the island's three cultures: Dine one day on bouillabaisse and Burgundy, another on hearty pea soup and Dutch beer, and a third day on Caribbean lobster and rum punch. Shopping expeditions will reap delft china and Limoges porcelain, gouda and camembert cheese, Dutch chocolate, French brandy, and West Indian guavaberry liqueur.

If you really want to paint the island red, spend the day shopping in **Philipsburg**, the tiny Dutch capital; drive nine miles to dine in **Marigot**, the French capital; then return to the Dutch side for an evening of gambling. In fact, it's easy to see the entire island by car in less than four hours (although you should set aside a full day). The "big" towns of Philipsburg and Marigot are small enough to explore on foot.

St-Martin/St. Maarten also offers a wide variety of natural attractions. Salt flats carpet the south side, mountains dominate the north (the highest is **Paradis Peak**, just under 1,400 feet), and gentle hills roll in between. The perimeter is lined with hidden coves and 37 powdery white-sand beaches—an average of one per mile.

It's those beaches (with a full range of water sports) and outstanding shopping bargains (no taxes on imported goods) that still draw nearly a million visitors to the island each year. The effects of Hurricane Luis in 1995 are a thing of the past; near-continual construction has added new hotels and shops, restoring the island to pre-hurricane conditions. However, two major resorts (**Port de Plaisance** and **Mullet Bay**), which originally closed due to hurricane damage, had not yet reopened at press time. For updated information, contact the tourist office.

If you're eager to combine great beaches with shop-dine-and-gamble-till-you-drop fun and excitement, St-Martin/St. Maarten may be the place for you.

To call St-Martin from the US, dial 011 (international access code), 590 (country code), and the 6-digit local number. To call St. Maarten from the US, dial 011 (international access code), 5995 (country code), and the 5-digit local number. To call the French side from the Dutch side, dial 00 and the 6-digit local number; to call the Dutch side from the French side, dial 005995 and the 5-digit local number.

Getting to the Island

Airlines

American Airlines	52040, 800/433.7300
BWIA (British West Indies Airways) International	54234, 800/538.2942
Continental Airlines	53444, 800/231.0856, 800/634.5555
US Airways International	52545, 800/622.1015

Interisland Carriers

Note: Confirm and reconfirm all reservations.

Air Aruba	54230
Air Guadeloupe	54212, 875374
Air Martinique	54212
Air St-Barthélemy	53651, 877346
Air St-Martin	54212, 871036
ALM (Antillean Airways)	54240, 800/327.7230
LIAT (Leeward Island Air Transport)	54203, 55428, 800/468.0482
WINAIR (Windward Island Airways)	54237, 54230, 800/634.4907

Airports **Princess Juliana International Airport** (54211) in St. Maarten services both international and interisland flights. It is 10 kilometers (6 miles) from Marigot and 7 kilometers (4 miles) from Philipsburg. **Esperance Airport** (875303) in St-Martin is used for island hopping. The airport is 7 kilometers (4 miles) from Marigot, 16 kilometers (10 miles) from Philipsburg.

Ferries and Interisland Cruises Ferries and high-speed catamarans connect St-Martin/St. Maarten with Anguilla, Saba, St-Barthélemy, St. Eustatius, and St. Kitts. For more information, contact **Bobby's Marina** (22366, 24096) or the **Great Bay Marina** (22167) in Philipsburg, or **Marine Time** (872028) in Marigot.

Getting Around the Island

Bicycles and Motorbikes

Moto Caraïbes (French side)	872591
Bike Power Cycle (French side)	871374
Moped Cruising (Dutch side)	22330
Tri-Sport Rent-a-Bike (Dutch side)	54384

Buses Buses run from 6AM to midnight throughout the island, connecting Philipsburg, Marigot, and **Grand Case.** They can be flagged down anywhere.

Car Rental

In St-Martin (French side):

Avis	875060
Dan's	872191
Hertz	877301, 800/654.3001
Sandy G	878825

In St. Maarten (Dutch side):

Avis	52847, 55300, 800/331.1212
Budget	54030, 800/472.3325
Hertz	54541, 54314, 800/654.3001
Risdon	54239

Driving Drive on the right side of the road, as in the US. Although posted speed limits are few and far between, 80 kilometers (50 miles) per hour is considered the maximum speed. US and Canadian driver's licenses are valid.

Stay alert: Caribbean drivers are very friendly and may stop suddenly in the middle of the road to give directions or strike up a conversation.

Taxis

St-Martin	875654, 877579
St. Maarten	22359, 54317

Tours Taxis (see above) may be hired by the hour for island tours. Bus tours, designed primarily for cruise-ship passengers, are conducted by **St. Maarten Sightseeing Tours** (52646) and **Calypso Tours** (23514). Also in St. Maarten, **Bobby's Marina** (22366) and **Great Bay Marina** (22167) offer coastal cruises, picnics on offshore islands, and day sails to the neighboring islands of Anguilla, Saba, St-Barthélemy, St. Eustatius, and St. Kitts. In St-Martin, several local companies offer similar cruises; ask at any hotel desk.

FYI

Electricity In St. Maarten the current in most hotels is 110/60 cycles, the same as in the US and Canada. In St-Martin, the current is 220/50 cycles, so US and Canadian appliances will need French plug adapters and converters. In either case, it's a good idea to check with individual hotels.

Entry Requirements US and Canadian visitors to St-Martin must present a valid passport or other proof of citizenship (a birth certificate or voter registration card) plus a picture ID. Visitors to St. Maarten need a valid passport and a return or onward ticket.

Gambling Eight casinos are located on the Dutch side of the island: **Casino Royale** at the **Maho Beach Hotel** (see page 286); **Rouge & Noir Casino** (near the **Seaview Hotel,** Front St, between Apotheek and Afloopsteeg, Philipsburg, 22952); **Golden Casino** at the **Great Bay Beach Hotel** (see page 284); **Atlantis** at Cupecoy Beach (54600); the **Divi Little Bay Beach Resort Casino** (see page 285); the **Pelican Resort and Casino** (see page 285); the **Coliseum Casino** in Philipsburg (see page 284); the **Lightning Casino** near the airport (69 Welfare Rd, Cole Bay, 43290), with betting on televised sports events; and **Slots World** (Front St, Philipsburg, 32721).

Language English is spoken everywhere, but the official languages are French in St-Martin and Dutch in St. Maarten.

Money Although the US dollar is accepted everywhere, the florin is the legal tender on the Dutch side and the franc the legal currency in French territory. Banks in St-Martin are open Monday through Friday from 8:30AM to 1:30PM, but close on holidays. Bank hours in St. Maarten are Monday through Thursday from 8:30AM to 3:30PM and Friday from 8:30AM to 5PM; at the airport, daily 8:30AM to 5:30PM. ATMs are plentiful.

Personal Safety There are pockets of poverty and crime on St-Martin/St. Maarten. Stay away from deserted areas or anyplace that makes you feel uncomfortable. The highways on the Dutch side are busier and better lit than those on the French side, where it is wise to avoid the lonely roads. Know where you're going at all times and be alert to your surroundings. Don't hesitate to ask if you're unsure what areas are safe to visit; the staff at hotel information desks will steer you in the right direction. Although drug dealers aren't as open or aggressive on St-Martin/St. Maarten as, for example, on Jamaica, avoid them—local authorities are not friendly to tourists who abuse their laws.

Publications For news and local information on the Dutch side, choose from three dailies: *The Chronicle, The Daily Herald,* and *The Guardian.* Also check out the tourist-oriented *St. Maarten Events* (published annually), *Focus* and *What to Do* (both published twice yearly), and the biannual *St. Maarten Nights,* a guide to after-dark fun and games. On the French side, *St-Martin's Week* is an English-language weekly. There's also *Reflets,* published annually by the **St-Martin Tourist Office,** and *Ti Gourmet,* a yearly restaurant guide.

Discover St. Martin, another magazine for visitors, comes out once a year and covers both sides of the island.

Reservation Services and House Rentals

In St-Martin (French side):

Carimo 875758

Immobilier St-Martin Caraïbes 875521

WIMCO (West Indies Management Company) ......
....800/932.3222

In St. Maarten (Dutch side):

St-Martin Rentals 54330

Taxes A five-percent tax is added to all hotel bills on the Dutch side. French-side hotels add a *taxe de séjour* of up to $3 per person per day. Expect to pay a US$20 departure tax from **Princess Juliana International Airport** in St. Maarten. A 15-franc departure tax is included in the airfare when you depart from **Esperance Airport** in St-Martin.

Tipping Most hotels and restaurants on St-Martin/St. Maarten automatically add a 10- to 15-percent service charge to your bill. If in doubt, ask. Tip taxi drivers US50¢ or US$1, more for tours.

Visitors' Information Offices The **St-Martin Tourist Office** is near the taxi stand at the harbor in Marigot (875721; fax 875643). It is open Monday through Friday from 8:30AM to 1PM and from 2:30 to 5:30PM and Saturday mornings.

The **St. Maarten Tourist Bureau** (23 Walter Nisbeth Rd, between Vogessteeg and D.A. Peterson St, Philipsburg, 22337; fax 24734) is open Monday through Friday, 8AM to noon and 1 to 5PM. There's also a tourist information center on **Wathey Square** at the cruise-ship tender dock (22337); it's open Monday through Friday from 8AM to noon and from 1 to 5PM.

Phone Book

In St-Martin (French side):

Ambulance 15, 878625

Directory Assistance 12

Fire..18, 875008

Hospital..295757

Police 17, 875010

Post Office 875317

In St. Maarten (Dutch side):

Ambulance..22111

Directory Assistance 22211

Emergencies 22222

Fire...22222

Hospital..31111

Police 22222

Post Office 54200

St-Martin

St-Martin's main draw is its tranquillity. You won't find glitzy casinos or hot night spots. There are no caves to explore or waterfalls to ponder. What draws visitors here year after year is the region's relaxed atmosphere and miles of beautiful white-sand beaches. There's definitely a French air to this half of the island; it's evident in the language of the locals, the croissants served at breakfast, the cafes and chic boutiques of the capital, **Marigot,** and the beautiful *plages* (beaches) where some beachcombers sun themselves *au naturel.* Away from where most cruise ships drop anchor, St-Martin is lower-key and much more relaxing than its Dutch counterpart.

1 La Samanna $$$$ This superposh resort with an air of exclusivity and Moorish charm has long had a reputation as a luxury hideaway. Owned and managed by Orient-Express Hotels it has 80 air-conditioned rooms with refrigerators, sinks, and counters; wicker, bamboo, and mahogany furnishings; telephones; a private terrace or patio; and gorgeous sea views. A full breakfast and airport transportation are complimentary. There are water sports, three tennis courts, a freshwater pool (with a poolside grill), daily aerobics classes, and state-of-the-art fitness equipment. Rather pricey for what's actually offered, the resort draws many repeat visitors. ◆ Closed September through October. West of Rte D208, Baie Longue. 875122, 800/322.2223, 212/575.7030; fax 878786

Within La Samanna:

La Samanna Restaurant ★★★$$$$ Food, wine, and romance receive equal attention in a formal dining room with an elegant arched terrace overlooking Baie Longue (Long Bay). Ask to be seated under the thatch roof at the breezy outer reaches and prepare yourself for a treat. The freshest local ingredients are used in the preparation of the French fare. The specials of the day might be grilled rock lobster served with curry butter and a warm plantain salad or roasted rack of lamb with baby vegetables and a truffle ragout of white beans. A bit of caviar should help pass the time until your entrée arrives. ◆ Continental ◆ Daily breakfast, lunch, and dinner; closed September and October. Reservations recommended. 876400

2 La Belle Créole $$$$ This resort was closed at press time, but plans were in the works for its reopening. ◆ North of Rte D208. 905/803.8898

3 Domaine de l'Anse Marigot $$ Tropical gardens surround 96 rooms, including 38 attractive 1-bedroom suites. There are two swimming pools, two Jacuzzis, a bar, and a good restaurant that serves French and local fare. ◆ Rte D208, Simpson Bay Lagoon. 879201, 800/322.2223; fax 879213

4 Nettlé Bay Beach Club $$ This beachside resort includes **The Villas,** a visitors' complex of 220 standard hotel rooms and suites set in 2-story buildings arranged around the property's 5 pools. The set-up is especially convenient for families and groups. There are also three tennis courts and two French restaurants on the premises. ◆ Just north of Rte D208, Baie Nettlé. 876868, reservations 876805, 800/999.3543; fax 872151

5 Royal Beach Hotel $ This simple, airy hotel is located right on the beach. Each of the 113 rooms has a terrace; some are equipped with kitchenettes. There are a number of shops and a restaurant on the premises. ◆ Just north of Rte D208, Baie Nettlé. 878989; fax 878989

6 Le Flamboyant $$ Situated on 1,200 feet of beach, this resort offers an all-inclusive option, with meals, drinks, entertainment, water sports, and sight-seeing excursions covered by the price. It has 271 elegant rooms and 1- and 2-bedroom suites, each with air-conditioning, a TV set, and a telephone. The pleasant tropical decor is right on target, with two open-air bars, two freshwater pools, a Jacuzzi, and a complete water-sports center. ◆ Rte D208, Simpson Bay Lagoon. 876000, 800/221.5333; fax 879957

7 Laguna Beach Hotel $ This small, 46-room hotel offers the traditional resort amenities (air-conditioning, telephones, and TVs), plus such extras as hair dryers, videos, and private safe-deposit boxes. Water sports, three tennis courts, a swimming pool, shops, two bars, and a restaurant are also on the grounds. ◆ Rte D208, Simpson Bay Lagoon. 879175, 800/223.9815; fax 878165

8 Le Jardin Créole ★★$$ Isabelle and Alain Volpei, natives of France, ran restaurants in Paris, Marseilles, and other French West Indies isles before settling on St-Martin. Gracious hospitality and high-quality food are the hallmarks of their dining room. The menu changes seasonally, but conch stew, curry stew with fresh lobster, and fried crayfish flavored with basil are popular entrées. ◆ Creole/Seafood ◆ Daily lunch and dinner. Reservations recommended. 60 Eagle Rd, Sandy Ground. 879956

9 Beach Plaza $$ This hotel (under the same management as **Laguna Beach**) offers 138 small but brightly decorated rooms and 6 suites with large balconies and living rooms. Amenities include a restaurant, a bar, a pool, and game and meeting rooms. Breakfast is included in the room rate. It's a short walk to Marina Port la Royale. ♦ Rte D208, Marigot. 878700, 800/423.4433; fax 871887

10 Marina Port la Royale The port offers some of Marigot's finest boutiques, boat rentals, and excellent restaurants in a postcard-perfect setting. The marina has 46 berths. ♦ Daily. Just south of Rue de Président-Kennedy, Marigot. 872043

Within the Marina Port la Royale:

Hotel Marina Royale $$ Huge oceangoing sailboats in the harbor add to this property's pleasing ambience. Each of the 60 studios and suites has a private terrace or patio. There's no restaurant at the hotel, but several are nearby. ♦ 875246; fax 879288

Jean Dupont ★★$$$ Bearing its owner's name, this restaurant has become one of the "in" places at the port. Crabmeat pâté is a house specialty, and the off-the-water breezes are refreshing. The portions are huge. ♦ French ♦ Daily lunch and dinner; closed Sunday lunch April through November. Reservations required. 877113

Le Café de Paris ★$$$ This terraced restaurant offers a view of the water and *très bonne* cuisine. Offerings range from pizza and hamburgers to lobster and fresh fish. The gazpacho with basil and the salad niçoise are both notable. ♦ French ♦ M-Sa lunch and dinner; Su dinner. 872043

Gingerbread Gallery Haitian art and handicrafts are gracefully displayed at this shop. ♦ Daily. 877321

Dalila This boutique carries women's and men's casual clothing with a Caribbean flair, as well as hand-painted Indonesian sarongs. Brightly painted wood carvings are among the many souvenirs also found here. ♦ M-Sa. 872206. Also at: Old St (between Front and Back Sts), Philipsburg. 24623

Paris 7 Art gallery owner Christine Pelletier features local artists' work depicting typical Caribbean themes. A variety of media is represented, from delicate watercolors to vivid oils. ♦ M-Sa. 878503, 876600

According to a centuries-old tradition known as "The Queen's Walk," St. Maarten's shoreline is the property of the Dutch crown. As a result, all beaches are free to everyone.

Restaurants/Clubs: Red   **Hotels:** Blue
Shops/♥ **Outdoors:** Green   **Sights/Culture:** Black

Brasserie de la Gare ★$ This is a great spot for people watching while enjoying an informal meal or a quick snack. The menu offers French entrées as well as grilled fare, pizza, and ice cream. The harbor is always humming with activity. ♦ French ♦ Daily lunc and dinner. 872064

Le Cigare Santo Domingan cigars, painstakingly made with age-old techniques, are sold here. ♦ Daily. 875851

On the Trail of the Arawaks The island's history from 1500 BC through the 20th century is traced in this tiny museum in the marina parking lot. Although photos and drawings are the main media, there are also some archaeological finds on display. ♦ Admission. M-Sa. 292284

11 Cafe Terrasse de Mastedana ★★$ Th sidewalk cafe and bakery is named for Oliver and Nicole Drouin's four children: Mark, Steve, Dany, and Nancy. The family moved to St-Martin from Montreal in the early 1980s. After years of working first for an internation bottling company and then for a Canadian ad agency, Oliver responded to a newspaper ad for a "Caribbean Bakery"; four months later h was running it. Steve is the baker now, turnin out delightfully light croissants and brioche o the outer perimeter of **Marina Port La Royal** The lunch menu includes pizza and pasta, bowing to France with a great quiche Lorrain ♦ French/Italian ♦ Daily breakfast, lunch, anc early dinner. Rue d'Anguille (between Rues Charles-de-Gaulle and de la Liberté), Marigo No phone

11 Le Poisson D'Or ★$$$ Chef Sylvain Boulais has the golden touch with fish and seafood. Try the chilled cream of cucumber and crabmeat soup, red snapper in puff past with red wine sauce, or the smoked lobster i a salmon, egg, and dill sauce. ♦ Seafood ♦ Daily lunch and dinner; closed September mid-October. Rue d'Anguille (between Rues Charles-de-Gaulle and de la Liberté), Marigo 877245

Island Fare

The island's gastronomic center is on the French side, *naturellement,* where the capital, **Marigot,** a former fishing village, is now home to more than 50 restaurants. Many are staffed by Gallic expats whose family-run bistros and cafes offer visitors a culinary tour of the *régions* of France. Here you may breakfast on Parisian-style pastries and croissants, lunch on hearty Alsatian sausages, and order the classic foods and wines of Burgundy for dinner.

The little French town of **Grand Case** may have the largest concentration of restaurants in the Caribbean. More than 20 crowd the main street—an international roundup that offers menus from a half-dozen different cultures. Diners have a tough choice. Will it be *parisien* or *créole* French, *classique* or *nouvelle?* Or how about Italian? Swiss? Chinese? Vietnamese? The signs are all tempting, but so are aromas from the *lolos,* inexpensive stands near the beach that vend down-home West Indian barbecue.

Meanwhile, restaurants and hotels in St. Maarten offer the Indonesian treat known as rijsttafel ("rice table"), a

buffet of many dishes, flavored with exotic spices and fresh tropical fruits. The traditional Indonesian meal, now common throughout Holland and the Netherlands Antilles, was brought back from the East Indies by Dutch colonists.

For yet another type of island repast, dine offshore aboard the *Lady Mary* (53892), a yacht charter that offers romantic starlight dinner cruises Tuesday through Saturday departing from the **Remax Dock** (Airport Rd, Simpson Bay) at 5 and 7PM. Calypso music complements a multicourse meal of coconut chicken with sauces, red snapper in creole sauce, and other Caribbean fare. Reservations are recommended; call 53892.

11 Gucci The typical array of the Italian designer's leather goods, watches, and clothing is sold here. The selection is good, with prices far below those in the US. ◆ Daily. Rue Charles-de-Gaulle, Marigot. 878424. Also at: 83 Front St (between Afloopsteeg and Loodssteeg), Philipsburg. 23537

11 Beauty and Scents Select from an excellent range of French cosmetics and fragrances at prices to match. Lancôme, Clarins, Yves Saint Laurent, Dior, and Chanel are all carried here. ◆ Daily. Rue Charles-de-Gaulle, Marigot. 875877

11 Primavera Choose from a potpourri of outstanding glass, crystal, and porcelain objets d'art for yourself or the folks back home. ◆ Daily. Rue Charles-de-Gaulle, Marigot. 877420

12 Mini Club ★★$$ Chef Claude Plessis's menu, with its combination of French flair and Creole spice, has made this eatery a longtime favorite. The spacious restaurant on an upper-level terrace feels like a treehouse built in the coconut palms. ◆ French/Creole ◆ M-Sa lunch and dinner; Su dinner. Reservations recommended, especially for the Wednesday and Saturday dinner buffets. Blvd de France and Rue de la Liberté, Marigot. 875069

Le Bar de la Mer

12 Le Bar de la Mer ★★$$ This authentic French brasserie overlooking the harbor has pastel-hued walls and a bar set with colorful tiles, creating a cozy setting for a leisurely drink or a light snack. The emphasis, of course, is on seafood, but pizza is also available. ◆ French ◆ Daily breakfast, lunch, and dinner. Blvd de France, Marigot. 878179

12 L'Arhawak ★$ A sidewalk cafe, it serves inexpensive local dishes as well as international fare. There's live music and dancing Wednesday through Saturday nights. ◆ International ◆ Daily breakfast, lunch, dinner, and late-night meals (until 2AM). Blvd de France, Marigot. 879967

12 Oro de Sol Gift items sold here include fragrances, jewelry, Pratesi linens, and watches by Ebel, Piaget, Patek Phillipe, and Cartier. ◆ M-Sa. Blvd de France, Marigot.

875651. Also at: Rue de la République, Marigot, 878098; Front St, Philipsburg, 871666

12 Messalina ★★$$$ With all the French restaurants in town, a trattoria is a most welcome change. Created by Roger Petit of **Le Poisson d'Or** and **La Vie en Rose** (see page 278 and below), the menu includes lasagna Messalina made with lobster, and grilled swordfish stuffed with mozzarella. But the food—as good as it is—runs second to the harbor views. ◆ Italian ◆ M-Sa lunch and dinner, Su dinner mid-December through March and May through August; M, W-Sa lunch and dinner, Su dinner April, September, and mid-November to mid-December; closed October to mid-November. Blvd de France and Rue de la République, Marigot. 878039

La Vie en Rose

12 La Vie en Rose ★★★$$$$ Many consider this the premier French restaurant on the island. One specialty is smoked salmon with salmon roe and tomatoes; another is the apple tart with crème anglaise. The earlier you eat the better chance you have of getting a much-desired balcony table. ◆ French ◆ M-Sa lunch and dinner; Su dinner. Reservations required. Blvd de France and Rue de la République, Marigot. 875442

13 Fort St-Louis Climb to the top of the hill for an outstanding panoramic view of Marigot, Marigot Harbor, and (on a clear day) Anguilla. The fort was built in 1786 and has since been restored; the 20-minute trek up is well worth the effort. ◆ Free. Daily. Rue de l'Hôpital, Marigot. No phone

14 Baie de Friars (Friar's Bay) This lovely, intimate beach and cove are popular with the fins-and-masks crowd. A small shack has basic gear for rent, but it's best to bring your own since this place is closed more often than it's open. ◆ Northwest of Rte N7

15 Paradise Peak St-Martin's highest peak, at just under 1,400 feet, is considered by photographers to be the best spot from which to shoot the French and Dutch capitals and nearby islands. ◆ East of Rambaud

16 Fish Pot Restaurant ★★★$$$ Fine food is served on charming gray-and-apricot china at tables overlooking Grand Case Bay. The creamy lobster bisque is excellent, as is the fresh lobster prepared with a ginger-and-lemon sauce. Fresh vegetables and scalloped potatoes accompany each meal. The restaurant isn't air-conditioned, but there's always a breeze; try to get a terrace table. ◆ French/Seafood ◆ Daily dinner Oct-Apr; M-Sa dinner May-Aug; closed September. Reservations required. Grand Case. 875088

16 Le Tastevin ★★$$$ The pretty decor of this restaurant is complemented by fine service. Specials here include lobster bisque, smoked salmon with grilled vegetables, and seared tuna steak with pepper sauce. The name is the French word for the wine taster's cup, so the excellent wine list should come as no surprise. ◆ French ◆ Daily lunch and dinner. Reservations recommended. Grand Case. 875545

16 Hévéa ★★$$$ The charming country French decor is enhanced by elegant personalized service at the intimate dining room of the eight-room **Hotel Hévéa,** operated by Jean-Philippe and Annick Grace. Specialties of the house include homemade foie gras, scallops with mussels and shrimp, and Maine lobster for two. There's also a Creole menu offering such dishes as stuffed crab, marinated conch salad, conch fricassee and Caribbean fish stew. ◆ French ◆ Daily dinner Dec–mid-Apr; Tu-Su dinner mid-Apr–Nov; closed September. Reservations required. Grand Case. 875685

16 Chez Martine ★★$$$ The charming terrace eatery of this eight-room guest house on the bay side of restaurant row specializes in Lyonnaise cuisine. The menu, which changes seasonally, may include frogs' legs i Champagne sauce and lobster tail in puff pastry. ◆ French ◆ Daily lunch and dinner. Grand Case. 875159

17 Rainbow ★★$$$ Fleur Raad and David Hendrich's casual and classy beachside bistro is perennially popular. Their menu features grilled meat and fish, as well as crispy roasted duck and sautéed sweet-breads. ◆ International ◆ Daily dinner Oct-Apr; M-Sa dinner May-Sept. Reservations recommended. 176 Blvd de Grand-Case, Grand Case. 875580

18 Flamboyant Beach Villas $ The beautifu royal poinciana trees that lend their name to the property are ablaze in summer. The property sits on Grand Case Beach and has nine modest villas with one or two bedrooms apiece. Three units are air-conditioned, though none has a TV or telephone. There's no restaurant. ◆ Grand Case. 875098; fax 878104

18 Sebastiano ★$$$ Here's an island of Northern Italian cuisine in a sea of French cooking. The bill of fare is varied, but the pasta with seafood dishes are good choices. ♦ Italian/Seafood ♦ Daily dinner Oct-Mar; M-Sa dinner Apr-Aug; closed September. Reservations recommended. Grand Case. 875886

19 Grand Case Beach Club $$ Located on the ocean just outside the village of Grand Case, the club offers a wonderful view of nearby Anguilla. Seventy-two studios and one- and two-bedroom units are available, complemented by a full water-sports program, a tennis court, and a restaurant. Continental breakfast is included in the rate. ♦ North of Rte N7. 875187, 800/447.7462, 212/223.2848; fax 875993

19 Le Petit $$$ A tiny, nine-room charmer is right on the beach near the entrance to Grand Case village. Under the same ownership as **L'Esplanade** (see below), it offers rooms with private beach terraces, kitchenettes, TV sets, telephones, air-conditioning, and marble baths. There's no restaurant and no pool, but guests may swim at **L'Esplanade.** North of Rte N7. 870919, 800/633.7411; fax 290965

20 L'Esplanade $$$

Minutes from Grand Case and a 5-minute downhill walk from the beach, this lovely hotel has 23 suites with bougainvillea cascading from terraces, which offer great views of the famous Grand Case sunsets. A small but pretty pool is on the premises. There's no restaurant, but more than 20 are in the nearby village. ♦ North of Rte N7. 870655, 800/633.7411; fax 872915

21 Le Méridien $$$$ The 1,600-foot white sand beach of this pricey, traditional resort would be right at home in a Gauguin painting. The 150-acre property also boasts a 100-slip marina, 4 restaurants, 3 freshwater pools, and charming gingerbread architecture. The 251 West Indian–style rooms and suites in the 8 2- and 3-story buildings of the resort's original **L'Habitation** section have terraces, mini-refrigerators, air-conditioning, TV sets, and telephones. Lively Caribbean pastels brighten the luxurious **Le Domaine** wing, which is geared toward couples and those seeking privacy. It has 125 rooms and 20 suites with air-conditioning, TV sets, telephones, and large, round bathtubs. The nearby **Le Privilège** sports complex and a program for kids ages 4 to 10 keep guests young and old happy. Many have been coming here for years. ♦ Anse Marcel (northwest of French Cul de Sac). 876700, 800/543.4300; fax 873038

22 Little Key $$$ A new and upscale beachfront property, this 94-room hotel has an open-air restaurant, bars, and 4 pools—1 large and 3 small. Another plus: a fabulous location opposite Ilet Pinel, where guests can enjoy water sports and daytime meals alfresco (the hotel provides ferry service to the islet). ♦ Just east of French Cul de Sac. 874919, 800/322.2223; fax 874923

23 Orient Bay Hotel $ The 31 air-conditioned studios and apartments of this property are set on a hillside amid lush foliage. TV sets may be rented. Other features include two pools and a restaurant. ♦ Between Rte N7 and French Cul de Sac. 873110, 800/223.5695; fax 873766

24 Les Jardins de Chevrise $$ The traditional Caribbean architecture is attractive and the ambience serene at this apartment hotel with 29 studios and duplexes overlooking Orient Bay. Rooms are air-conditioned, but have no TVs or telephones. A pool and restaurant are on the property and the beach is a five-minute walk away. ♦ Between Rte N7 and French Cul de Sac. 873779, 800/223.5695; fax 873803

25 Hôtel Mont Vernon $$ The hotel boasts 370 rooms and suites, most with outstanding views of the ocean. Amenities include a pool, water sports, two tennis courts, and three eateries. ♦ Baie Orientale. 876200, 800/223.6510; fax 873727

26 Orient Beach Naturists as well as swimsuit-clad sun worshippers enjoy one of St-Martin's finest beaches, more than a mile long and made even wider by Hurricane Luis. The sand, as white as confectioner's sugar, and the amazingly turquoise water are part of the attraction. There are T-shirt and souvenir shops and refreshment stands. ♦ Baie Orientale

On Orient Beach:

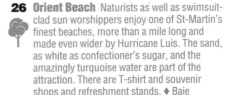

Club Orient Naturist Hotel $$$
Completely rebuilt after Hurricane Luis, this is the island's premier clothing-optional resort. The 136 units all have kitchens, front porches with picnic tables, back porches with outdoor showers, and ceiling fans; some are air-conditioned. On-site amenities include a beach bar/restaurant, a market, water sports, tennis, volleyball, and a health club offering Swedish or shiatsu massage. ♦ 873385, 800/452.9016; fax 873376, 914/733.5298

Kon Tiki ★★$ An outdoor beachfront restaurant, this spot does a nice job with snacks, salads, and light meals like grilled chicken. China and silverware are an elegant touch—even though the people at the next table may have left their clothes at home. ♦ American ♦ M-Sa breakfast, lunch, and early dinner. 874327 .

27 **Sol 'Ambience** $ A small Creole-style hostelry, this serene spot has eight air-conditioned rooms with terraces and kitchens. There's a pool on the premises and the beach is a five-minute drive away. There's no on-site restaurant. ♦ Oyster Pond. 873810; fax 873223

27 **La Caravelle** $$ Run by the genial Mireille Bernard, this hotel on Oyster Pond features superb views of the sea and of **Captain Oliver's** marina (see below). Most of the 11 rattan-furnished rooms offer air-conditioning, kitchenettes, and terraces, but none have telephones. An apartment that sleeps six people is also available. The property has two pools, but no dining room; restaurants, bars, a beach, and shops are within walking distance. Children are welcome at this convivial, family-friendly place. ♦ Oyster Pond. 873949; fax 873949

27 **Captain Oliver's Hotel Resort** $$ This luxurious gingerbread-style complex is named for proprietor Oliver Lange, who owned a restaurant in Paris before opening the hotel here in 1983. Guests are housed in 50 pink bungalows linked by boardwalks and overlooking the bay. Decorated in white rattan, each unit has a kitchenette, marble bath, terrace, and satellite TV; many have ocean views. The eponymous restaurant specializes in seafood and there's also a pool bar and a snack bar. Breakfast is included in the rate. The property has no beach, but guests can take taxi boats to sandy stretches nearby. A pool, tennis court, and marina complete the picture. ♦ Oyster Pond. 874026; fax 874084

28 **Le Mississippi** $$ A hillside retreat, this hotel has 13 1- and 2-bedroom suites with French country charm. Each suite boasts an ocean view as well as a Jacuzzi, full kitchen, TV set, mini-bar, and hair dryer. Other highlights include a pool with a deck and Jacuzzi, and a restaurant that serves Creole dishes at dinner; continental breakfast is included in the rate. The beach is within walking distance and a golf course is nearby. ♦ Oyster Pond. 873381; fax 873152

There are more than 20 art galleries in St-Martin.

Coral reefs have "cleaning stations" where fish line up to be scoured of parasites by smaller fish and shrimp.

Restaurants/Clubs: Red **Hotels:** Blue
Shops/♥ Outdoors: Green **Sights/Culture:** Black

28 **Blue Beach Hotel** $ Nineteen rooms and bungalows sit on a hill above Oyster Pond; each is equipped with a kitchenette, air-conditioning, a TV set, and a terrace. There's also a pool and a restaurant/bar serving fine fare. The beach is about a five-minute drive away. ♦ Oyster Pond. 873344; fax 874213

St. Maarten

This is the busier side of the island, particularly when the cruise ships are in and thousands of visitors crave the Dutch capital, **Philipsburg,** to search for perfect gifts or test Lady Luck at the numerous casinos. This small city has just three main streets—**Front Street, Back Street,** and **Walter Nisbeth Road,** also known as **Pondfill Road**—and the traffic sometimes becomes so snarled that it seems that no one is going anywhere. So when you've had your fill of island-style city life, head for one of St. Maarten's many resorts. They're big and plush, with all the comforts you wish you had at home.

29 **Oyster Bay Beach Resort** $$$ Hills on one side and lagoon and sea on the other make this a delightfully isolated spot. The posh resort offers elegant accommodations-20 rooms and 20 suites with terraces—overlooking the water or a pleasant garden. Guests can cool off in the lagoon, at lovely Dawn Beach nearby, or in a saltwater pool. Scuba diving, snorkeling, and horseback riding can be arranged. ♦ Oyster Pond. 3604 800/231.8331; fax 36695.

Within the Oyster Bay Beach Resort:

Oyster Bay Restaurant ★★★$$$ Lunch in the peaceful courtyard or feast by candlelight in the fine dining room—the beautiful surroundings only accentuate your gustatory experience here. Among the tasty appetizers are minted cold cucumber soup and fresh asparagus in puff pastry; favorite entrées include a medaillon of lobster with truffles, tomato, and basil. Desserts are scrumptious too; try the banana, chocolate, or raspberry soufflé. ♦ International ♦ Daily breakfast, lunch, and dinner. Reservations recommended. 36040

30 **Great Bay Marina** It's a large marina full of fishermen in their big boats and vendors offering boat rentals. Many rental packages include lunch, wine, and use of an underwater camera and snorkel equipment. ♦ Daily. Juancho Irausquín Rd (south of Front St), Philipsburg. 22167

Adjacent to Great Bay Marina:

Chesterfields ★★$$ Popular with boaters, this restaurant's decor is nautical. Shrimp salad—made with shrimp that may have been swimming only a few hours earlier—is a specialty. If you're tired of seafood, this is a good place to order a cheeseburger. ♦ Seafood/American ♦ Daily breakfast, lunch, and dinner. Reservations required. 23484

30 Bobby's Marina From here you can rent a boat to go sailing to the nearby island of St. Barts, where you can snorkel and picnic for half a day. ♦ Daily. Juancho Irausquín Rd (south of Front St), Philipsburg. 22366

Within Bobby's Marina:

Dockside Management Stop here and book a ferry ride to St. Barts on the *White Octopus* or the *Voyager 1.* The trip takes around 90 minutes. The well-informed managers here can also provide information on a variety of day trips, sunset sails, and sea excursions that depart from either St-Martin or St. Maarten. ♦ Daily. 24096

31 Simart'n Museum This small museum highlights the island's forts, military history, and artifacts, as well as the cultures of the Arawak and Carib Indians. There's a small gift shop. ♦ Admission. M-Sa. 7 Front St (at Kanaalsteeg), Philipsburg. 24917

32 Guavaberry Choose from dozens of spiced and flavored rums (try the coconut variety) or the traditional rum-based guavaberry liqueur (most visitors take home at least one bottle) in this shop. There's also a collection of island-made fragrances for men and women, with names like Carnival Jump-Up, Carib Lime, and Reggae Rose. ♦ Daily. 10 Front St (between Emmaplein and Secretarissteeg), Philipsburg. 22965

33 Pasanggrahan Royal Inn $ Set in what was once a governor's beach residence, this is St. Maarten's oldest inn. The colonial-style main building dates from 1905. The property offers 30 air-conditioned rooms (no telephones or TV sets), a white-sand beach, and the **Ocean View Bar and Restaurant.** The Front Street shops are just outside the door. The name, *pasanggrahan*, is Indonesian for "guest house." ♦ 15 Front St (between Kanaalsteeg and Loodgietersteeg), Philipsburg. 23588, 800/223.9815; fax 22885

34 American West India Company Everything in this boutique located in an old West Indian home comes from the Caribbean. Be sure to check out the larimar jewelry from the Dominican Republic and the hot spices that are grown everywhere from Belize to Trinidad. ♦ M-Sa. 17 Front St (at Loodgietersteeg), Philipsburg. 25230

Guavaberry is an island folk liqueur that has been produced in private homes in St. Maarten for at least 200 years. When mature, the rum-based drink has a distinctive woody, fruity, bittersweet flavor. Guavaberries (no relation to the guava fruit) are found high in the green hills of St. Maarten; they ripen only around Christmastime, making guavaberry a traditional holiday drink that is also popular at weddings and other joyful occasions. It is available through local liquor stores, grocers, gift shops, and delis.

The Caribbean Sea may be rich in coral and colorful fish, but it's poor in nutrients, which is why the water is pale rather than dark blue.

Philipsburg Shopping

	SCHOOLSTEEG
	L'Escargot *French restaurant*
LOODSSTEEG	**HOTELSTEEG**
Gucci *leather goods*	**La Romana** *jewelry*
AFLOOPSTEEG	**ST. JANSTEEG**
Rouge Et Noir *casino*	
Le Bec Fin *French restaurant*	
	Coliseum Casino
APOTHEEK	**VAN ROMONDSTEEG**
Ric's Place *American/Mexican restaurant*	**H. Stern** *jewelry*
	WILHELMINASTRAAT
WATHEY SQUARE	**HENDRIKSTRAAT**
Horizon View Hotel	**Little Switzerland** *jewelry, crystal*
	Boolchand's *electronics, jewelry*
KERKSTEEG	**PASTORISTEEG**
Holland House Beach Hotel	**Shipwreck Gift Shop** *souvenirs*
	Colombian Jewelers *jewelry*
	OLD STREET
Polo/Ralph Lauren *clothing*	**Grill & Ribs Co.** *Caribbean/American restaurant*
Lipstick *cosmetics, perfumes*	**D.C. STEEG**
American West India Company *Caribbean crafts, spices*	
LOODGIETERSTEEG	**SECRETARISSTEEG**
Pasanggrahan Royal Inn *hotel, restaurant*	**Guavaberry** *liquors, perfume*
Simart'n Museum	
KANAALSTEEG	
	EMMAPLEIN

FRONT STREET

35 Old Street Two blocks east of the old courthouse, this thoroughfare was designed to resemble a street in Old Amsterdam. Its brightly colored buildings house a variety of fine boutiques and restaurants. ♦ Between Front and Back Sts, Philipsburg

At Old Street:

Grill & Ribs Co. ★$ Serving baby-back ribs, grilled chicken, and johnnycake (a fried biscuit of sorts), this down-home eatery mixes local fare with US favorites. ♦ Caribbean/American ♦ Daily lunch and dinner. 100 Front St. 30276

36 Holland House Beach Hotel $$ Smack in the middle of the shopping/casino district, this property also boasts a pretty beach. Each of the 54 air-conditioned rooms has a TV, telephone, kitchenette, balcony, and view. ♦ 35 Front St (between Rinksteeg and Kerksteeg), Philipsburg. 22572, 800/223.9815, 212/476.9444; fax 24673

37 Shipwreck Gift Shop This place is a treasure trove of Caribbean merchandise. Batik items, baskets, books, hammocks, handmade jewelry, wood carvings, woven mats, and rugs are among the booty. Most visitors walk away with something. Look for the big gorilla outside. ♦ Daily. 34 Front St (at Pastoristeeg), Philipsburg. 22962

38 Little Switzerland The Caribbean's best-known purveyor of jewelry, watches, crystal, and china has shelves of goodies by Lladrò, Aynsley, Baccarat, Lalique, Waterford, Audemars-Piguet, Vacheron & Constantin, and Girard-Perregaux. ♦ M-Sa. 42 Front St (between Pastoristeeg and Hendrikstraat), Philipsburg. 23530

39 Kangaroo Court Caffé
★★$ Here's a real find: an eatery serving outstanding veggie sandwiches, light meals, home-baked goods, and designer coffees at reasonable prices. The Caribbean-colorful historic building and decor are as inviting as the food, and there's even a peaceful outdoor courtyard. It's just behind the courthouse and cruise ship dock—look for the giant coffee cup on the roof. ♦ American/West Indian ♦ M-Sa breakfast, lunch, and early dinner. No credit cards accepted. 6 Hendrikstraat (between Front and Back Sts), Philipsburg. 24278

The land area of the West Indies islands is approximately 91,000 square miles.

Christopher Columbus made four voyages to the Caribbean between 1492 and 1502.

40 Ric's Place ★★$ For those who miss the USA, this place serves up burgers, Philly cheesesteaks, and sports on a big-screen TV. ♦ American/Mexican ♦ Daily breakfast, lunch, and early dinner. 69 Front St (between Wathey Sq and Apotheek). 26050

41 Coliseum Casino The setting is Roman, but there are no gladiators or lions in sight—just 6 blackjack tables, more than 300 slot and video poker machines, and 2 roulette wheels. ♦ Daily until 4AM. Front St and Van Romondsteeg, Philipsburg. 32101

42 Le Bec Fin ★★$$$ This is a long-established spot for elegant dining: Queen Beatrix of the Netherlands has supped here, as has actor Omar Sharif, and the restaurant was featured on TV's "Lifestyles of the Rich and Famous." The menu features such classic French dishes as onion soup, lobster bisque, marinated rack of lamb, and steak au poivre. The 18th-century courtyard adds to the charm. ♦ French ♦ Daily breakfast, lunch, and dinner mid-Dec–mid-Apr. Reservations recommended; minimum age 18. 119 Front St (between Apotheek and Afloopsteeg), Philipsburg. 22976

42 Rouge Et Noir There's plenty of action here, thanks to 132 slot machines, 4 roulette wheels, 2 blackjack tables, and a baccarat table. ♦ Daily until 4AM. Minimum age 18. Front St and Afloopsteeg, Philipsburg. 22952

EST. 1972

43 L'Escargot ★★$$$ Look for a 250-year-old gingerbread Antillean house adorned with an orange mural to find this *café très francais*, a favorite since 1970. The atmosphere is refined, thanks to soft music and lighting; the snail dishes and crisp duck in pineapple and banana sauce are among the menu highlights. ♦ French ♦ Daily lunch and dinner. Reservations required. 84 Front St (between Hotelsteeg and Schoolsteeg), Philipsburg. 22483

44 The Wayang Doll
★★$$$ Dine on authentic Indonesian fare, originally brought to the island by Dutch settlers. Try the rijsttafel ("rice table"), an Indonesian meal that

includes more than a dozen dishes.
♦ Indonesian ♦ M-Sa dinner. Reservations recommended. 167 Front St (at Visserssteeg), Philipsburg. 22687

45 Great Bay Beach Hotel $$ The convenient location, on milelong Great Bay Beach and close to Philipsburg's shops and port, is a great asset. Refurbished in 1996, the 285-room hotel has 2 swimming pools, a tennis court, and 2 restaurants. Every room boasts a marble bath, air-conditioning, a direct-dial telephone, and a TV set. The **Golden Casino** features live entertainment nightly; there's also a nightclub and a disco that rocks until 6AM. ♦ Just west of Philipsburg. 22446, 800/223.6510, 212/969.9220 in New York City; fax 23859

46 Fort William The English began building this fort, then called Fort Trigge, on the western edge of Philipsburg in 1801. The Dutch renamed it Fort William in 1816. Both countries had financial problems, so they built the walls without cement; consequently, the battlements quickly fell to ruin. The drive to the fort is treacherous, so plan to walk; the hour-long hike to the top of the hill is not too strenuous. Start out in the early morning or late afternoon from the dirt road just opposite the **Great Bay Beach Hotel**. It's easy to keep your bearings—just look for the television transmitter tower. Not much is left of the fort, but the views of the entire island and area are outstanding. ♦ Free. Daily. Just west of Philipsburg. No phone

47 Fort Amsterdam Established at Great Bay Harbour in 1631, this fortress protected the first Dutch port in the Caribbean. Two years later Spain captured the fort, making it the country's most important bastion east of Puerto Rico. Spain demolished much of the structure before leaving it to the Dutch in 1648. ♦ Free. Daily. Southwest of Philipsburg. No phone

48 Divi Little Bay Beach Resort $$ Totally renovated after Hurricane Luis, this property's 163 appealing units sprawl along a peninsula. Each room is air-conditioned and has a TV set and a private patio or balcony. On-site facilities include two pools, three tennis courts, the **Papagayo** restaurant, and a casino. ♦ Little Bay. 22333; fax 23911

49 Plaza del Lago Shopping Center This 30-store open-air shopping center has a strong Spanish theme, with whitewashed walls and a terra-cotta tiled roof. Stop at **Nativa** (42748) for a wide selection of crafts from around the world, **Delft Blue** (43052) for—what else?—delft earthenware, and **Island Time** (42039) for the latest fashions. Beautiful tile murals depict life in a typical Spanish fishing village. ♦ M-Sa. West of Cape Bay. 42799

Within the Plaza del Lago Shopping Center:

Saratoga ★$$ Chefs John and Daniel Jackson, graduates of the Culinary Institute of America, showcase local seafood with an innovative menu. The menu changes daily, but might include grilled kingfish with spicy cherry tomato salsa or batter-dipped softshell crabs with parmesan and herbs. ♦ American ♦ M-Sa dinner. 42421

50 Pelican Resort and Casino $$$ Short on nature, but long on views and amenities, this resort offers 343 rooms and suites that sprawl up and down a hillside just 7 minutes from the airport. Comfortable air-conditioned rooms have safe-deposit boxes and refrigerators. A mini-market makes light meal preparation convenient. **L'Aqualine Health Spa Massages** offers state-of-the-art beauty and health care. Other amenities include a Las Vegas–style casino, three restaurants, six tennis courts (three lighted), six pools, three beaches, and a wide range of water sports. Guests can book sails on 2 60-foot catamarans that sail to Anguilla and St. Barts from the resort's own docks. ♦ West of Cape Bay. 42503; fax 42133

Within the Pelican Resort and Casino:

Crocodile Express Cafe ★$$ Meals are served in a traditional great house with a balcony overlooking the resort's vast grounds (but not the sea). ♦ American ♦ Daily breakfast, lunch, and dinner. 42503

51 The Horny Toad Guest House $$ At one time this lovely little spot was the home of the island's governor; it's now a homey, friendly mom-and-pop inn. Each of the eight roomy apartments has a balcony or terrace overlooking Simpson Bay Beach. There's no restaurant on site, but dining spots and casinos are nearby, and it's less than five minutes to the airport. ♦ No credit cards accepted; no children under seven. Simpson Bay. 54323, 800/417.9361 ext. 3013; fax 53316

Getting Your Feet Wet in St-Martin/St. Maarten

Water sports abound in St-Martin/St. Maarten, and most hotels can provide you with the necessary equipment. Other outfits that can set you afloat:

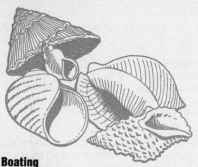

Boating

In St-Martin:

Dynasty Yachts Just south of Rue de Président—Kennedy, Marigot. 878521

The Moorings Oyster Pond. 873255

Stardust Marine Port Lonvilliers, Le Méridien, Anse Marcel (northwest of French Cul de Sac). 874030

In St. Maarten:

Bobby's Marina Juancho Irausquín Rd (south of Front St), Philipsburg. 22366

Great Bay Marina Juancho Irausquín Rd (south of Front St), Philipsburg. 22167

Mullet Bay Marina Mullet Bay. 52801 ext 337, 54363

Snorkeling and Scuba Diving

In St-Martin:

Blue Ocean Laguna Beach Hotel, Rte D208, Simpson Bay Lagoon. 878973

Lou Couture's Scuba Club Baie Nettlé. 871661

Scuba Sun Caraïbe Le Méridien, Anse Marcel (northwest of French Cul de Sac). 876790, 873613

In St. Maarten:

Divi Little Bay Watersports Divi Little Bay Beach Resort, Little Bay. 22333, 22334

Ocean Explorers Simpson Bay. 44357

Watersports Great Bay Beach Hotel (just west of Philipsburg). 22446, 800/223.6510, 212/969.9220 in New York City

Sportfishing

In St-Martin:

Sailfish Caraïbes Port Lonvilliers, Le Méridien, Anse Marcel (northwest of French Cul de Sac). 875971

In St. Maarten:

Bobby's Marina Juancho Irausquín Rd (south of Front St), Philipsburg. 22366

Great Bay Marina Juancho Irausquín Rd (south of Front St), Philipsburg. 22167

Windsurfing

In St-Martin:

Orient Watersports Baie Orientale. 874034

In St. Maarten:

Pelican Watersports and Excursions Pelican Resort and Casino (west of Cape Bay). 42503, 800/626.9637

52 Mary's Boon Beach Plantation $$$ A dozen efficiency apartments near the airport exude true island charm. Each air-conditioned unit is furnished with four-poster beds and antiques and has a kitchenette, a patio overlooking Simpson Bay, a TV set, and a telephone. There's also a small pool and a restaurant (see below). ♦ No credit cards accepted; no children under 16. Simpson Bay. 54235; fax 53403

Within Mary's Boon Beach Plantation:

Mary's Boon Restaurant ★★$$ The food makes up for the occasional noise from the airport runway at this popular eatery, which attracts CEOs and loyal "Boonies" alike. There's only one seating (at 8PM) and the menu is set nightly; call ahead to find out what's cooking. ♦ French/American ♦ Daily dinner. Reservations required. 54235

53 La Plage at Royal Islander Club $$$ The 120 attractively decorated 1- and 2-bedroom time-share apartments at this beachfront property share an Olympic-size swimming pool. Each unit is air-conditioned and has a full kitchen and TV set; the property is close to several restaurants. ♦ Maho Bay. 52388; fax 52595

54 **Millenium Beach Resort** $$$ Opened in late 1997, this luxury time-share resort features 118 peach-colored suites and bungalows lining Burgeaux Bay just behind the airport. The two-bedroom, two-bath units are decorated in rattan, mahogany, and marble, and have full kitchens. Other pluses: three pools, a Jacuzzi, two tennis courts, a fitness center, a casino, a theater, a restaurant, and full conference facilities. The appealingly landscaped grounds are accented with terra-cotta urns and pottery. ◆ Burgeaux Bay. 54000, 800/616.1154; fax 54001

55 **Maho Beach Hotel and Casino** $$$ This hotel boasts 600 rooms and seemingly as many activities along a half-mile stretch of white sand. There are 4 tennis courts, a spa, 2 pools, water sports galore, badminton, volleyball, and a shopping arcade, along with 12 restaurants (see below) and 2 bars. Guest rooms feature European furniture and Italian-tile floors. **Casino Royale,** with 15 blackjack tables, 8 roulette wheels, 250 slot machines, and 3 craps tables, is just across from the hotel. ◆ Maho Bay. 52115, 52116, 800/223.0757; fax 53180

At the Maho Beach Hotel and Casino:

Ristorante Roma ★★$$ Substantial, traditional food is nicely prepared at this Italian dining spot. There's the usual selection of pasta and veal dishes, with equal attention given to local seafood. The attractive decor and gracious personnel are important pluses. ◆ Italian ◆ Daily dinner. 42025

Cheri's Café ★$$ Enjoy live entertainment along with burgers, omelettes, salads, and pasta dishes at this popular open-air spot. ◆ American ◆ Daily lunch and dinner. 53361

56 **Mullet Bay Golf Course** While the **Mullet Bay Resort and Casino** was closed indefinitely at press time, this 18-hole championship layout was still open to the public—and the only game in town. In fact, guests at the posh **Cap Juluca** on nearby Anguilla arrive by boat to enjoy this venerable course, so reserve ahead. ◆ Greens fee. Daily. Mullet Bay. 52801

The West Indies is a crescent-shaped group of islands more than 2,000 miles long. They separate the Gulf of Mexico and the Caribbean Sea on the west and south from the Atlantic Ocean on the east and south.

Saba's jail has two cells and a rooftop deck, so inmates can sun during the day.

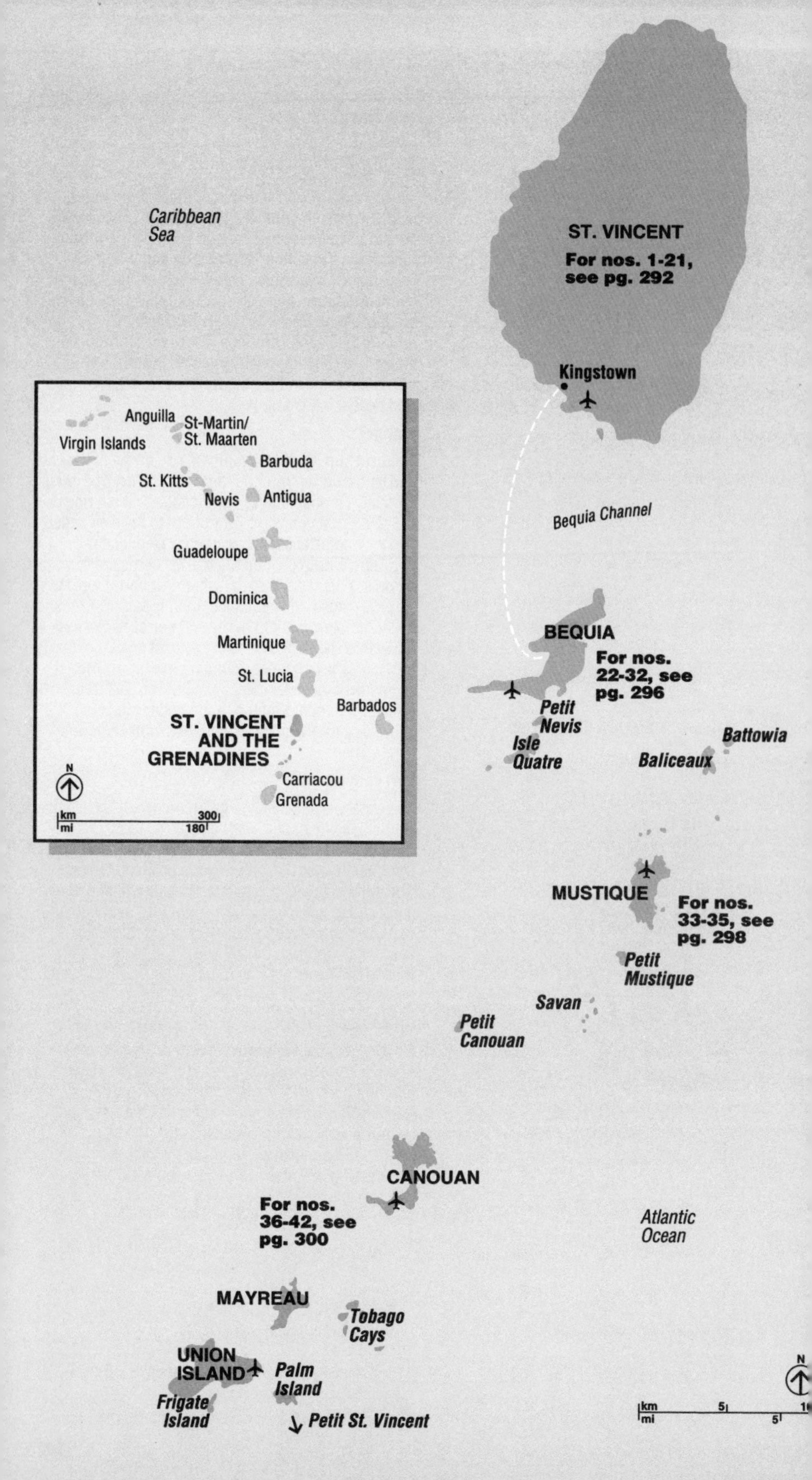

Caribbean
Sea

ST. VINCENT

**For nos. 1-21,
see pg. 292**

Kingstown ✈

Bequia *Channel*

Anguilla St-Martin/
           St. Maarten
Virgin Islands
        St. Kitts   Barbuda
          Nevis   Antigua
      Guadeloupe

        Dominica

        Martinique
          St. Lucia
                      Barbados
**ST. VINCENT
AND THE
GRENADINES**

N

|km   300|
|mi   180|

Carriacou
Grenada

BEQUIA

**For nos.
22-32, see
pg. 296**

*Petit
Nevis*
*Isle
Quatre*   *Battowia*
              Baliceaux

MUSTIQUE

**For nos.
33-35, see
pg. 298**

*Petit
Mustique*

                Savan
*Petit
Canouan*

CANOUAN

**For nos.
36-42, see
pg. 300**

*Atlantic
Ocean*

MAYREAU

              *Tobago
              Cays*

**UNION
ISLAND** ✈ *Palm
            Island*
*Frigate
Island*
        ↓ *Petit St. Vincent*

N

|km   5|
|mi   5| 10

St. Vincent and the Grenadines

If you've always wanted to learn to sail or scuba dive, "SVG" is the perfect place to begin. Cruising experts and inexperienced day-trippers alike love the 32 islands that make up this tropical archipelago. Beginning at Bequia in the north, the Grenadines are sprinkled like stepping stones for 40 miles to the southwest, so you can head for new shores every day and still make landfall with plenty of daylight to spare. The entire chain is known for warm, crystalline aqua waters, beautiful beaches, quiet coves, and pristine, uncrowded (except by fish) reefs, ideal for snorkeling and scuba diving.

St. Vincent is the largest (150 square miles) of these islands and the main port of entry for the Grenadines. The island is supplied by international freighters that load and unload on the docks of **Kingstown;** its mountainous interior is carpeted with fields of bananas, breadfruit, coconut palms, and arrowroot, now used as a coating for computer paper.

The nearby island of **Bequia** (pronounced *Beck*-wee) is a picturesque beauty— a favorite haunt of the yachting crowd, and home to a small community of whalers who hunt with the same small boats and harpoons their ancestors used in the 18th century. **Mustique** is a chic retreat and a wintering spot for Princess Margaret, Mick Jagger, David Bowie, and other celebrities. **Union Island, Canouan** (pronounced *Can*-no-wan), and **Mayreau** (pronounced *My*-row) are known for prime beaches and dive/snorkel sites. Guests on **Young Island, Palm Island**, and **Petit St. Vincent** are masters of all they survey— each island is a single private resort hideaway.

Some Grenadines are still accessible only by sea, but others have landing strips; that, plus regular ferry service, makes it easy for nonsailing divers, nature lovers, and other vacationers to reach places where they can while away slow days in tranquillity.

St. Vincent was probably first discovered by the Ciboney Indians, who paddled over in small boats from South America long before King Tut ruled Egypt. Arawak and Carib tribes followed, and Europeans came still later. Both the French and the English had many serious clashes with the Carib. In 1797 the last group of pure-blooded Carib moved to the wilds of the north, putting a volcano between themselves and the British; today their descendants continue to live near **Sandy Bay**. A larger contingent of black Carib (the offspring of Africans and Indians) was forced to surrender and was shipped off to Central America.

After decades as a British colony and British Associated State, St. Vincent and the Grenadines became an independent state within the British Commonwealth on 27 October 1979.

Today, tourist accommodations on these islands tend toward two extremes: either simple cold-water guest houses or luxurious private-isle resorts and sumptuous Mustique vacation mansions (available for rent when owners are not in residence). Resort facilities vary as well; some offer various water sports and evening entertainment, while others barely manage to produce morning coffee. Air-conditioning is uncommon, except at deluxe properties, and this is a fine place to escape telephones and television.

Thanks to the easygoing residents and ever-changing temporary population of sailors and divers, the atmosphere on these islands is decidedly casual. Here even crowned heads run about in bare feet, enjoying that ever-rarer treat: the Caribbean as it used to be.

Area code 809 unless otherwise noted.

Getting to the Island

Airlines

Interisland Carriers

Air Martinique
   on St. Vincent...458.4528
   on Union Island.....................................458.8326
   on Canouan...458.8888

Airlines of Carriacou.................................444.3549

American Eagle 458.4380

LIAT (Leeward Islands Air Transport).......457.1821,
....457.2000, 800/253.5011

Mustique Airways.............458.4380, 800/526.4789,
....800/223.0599

SVG Air 456.5610

Airports **E.T. Joshua Airport** (458.4960) on St. Vincent, a mile from **Kingstown,** is the island chain's main airport, but it can hardly be described as major; it's little more than an airstrip for small planes going to and from Barbados, Martinique, and St. Lucia. **J.F. Mitchell Airport** (458.3948) on **Bequia** and the airports on **Mustique** (458.4621), **Union Island** (458.8754), and **Canouan** (458.8049) have tiny airstrips for commercial and private prop planes.

Getting Around the Islands

Bicycles and Motorbikes

Lighthouse Tours, Bequia 458.3084

Mustique Co. Ltd ....458.4621 on Mustique,
....457.1531 on St. Vincent

Sailor's Cycle, St. Vincent.........457.1712, 457.1274

Buses Minivans leave **Market Square** in Kingstown, St. Vincent, and travel the main roads; just stick out your hand and they'll stop. (Make sure the van is headed where you want to go; there are several different routes.) They're inexpensive, efficient, and fun, but be prepared to listen to loud music.

Car Rental

The Cotton House, Mustique 456.4777

David's Auto Clinic, St. Vincent 456.4026,
....456.1116

Kim's Rentals, St. Vincent 456.1884

Mustique Co. Ltd ....458.4621 on Mustique,
....457.1531 on St. Vincent

Sunset View Rental, Bequia.......................457.3558

Star Garage, St. Vincent 456.1743

Driving For visitors with valid US licenses, temporary driver's licenses (US$15) are available in St. Vincent at **E.T. Joshua Airport** or in Kingstown at the police station on **Bay Street** or the **Licensing Authority** on **Halifax Street.** Driving is on the left, and the mountainous roads can narrow, curvy, pock-marked, and/or badly paved. Drive cautiously.

Ferries An alternative to flying is taking a boat between islands. The *M/V Barracuda* (no phone), also known as the mail boat, runs twice a week down the Grenadine chain from St. Vincent to Union Island and back; there's also service Monday through Saturday between St. Vincent and Bequia. The ferries *Admiral I* and *Admiral II* (458.3348) connect St. Vincent and Bequia Monday through Saturday, as does the no-frills island schooner *Sand Island* (458.3472). The *Bequia Express* also connects St. Vincent and Bequia three times a day on Monday, Wednesday, and Friday. Check with the **St. Vincent Department of Tourism** (457.1502, 800/729.1726 in the US) for all boat schedules.

Taxis

Sam's Taxi, Bequia 458.3686

Taxi Drivers Association, St. Vincent.........457.1807

Tours Touring St. Vincent by public van can be a true island experience, complete with blasting reggae music. Catch one in Market Square in Kingstown, or stick your hand out when you see one coming down the road, and it will stop. Minibus or taxi tours are also available on St. Vincent through **Barefoot Holidays** (456.9334), **Fantasea Tours** (457.4477), **Global Travel** (456.1601), **Grenadine Tours** (458.4818), and the **Taxi Drivers Association** (457.1807). On Bequia, tours are available through **Sam's Taxi Tours** (458.3686). If you're interested in boating tours, **Dive St. Vincent** (Young Island Dock, Villa, St. Vincent, 457.4714) makes speedboat trips along the west coast to the **Falls of Baleine** and **Wallilabou.** For a quieter ride, the **Sea Breeze** guest house (Arnos Vale, St. Vincent, 458.4969) sponsors a sailing trip to the **Falls of Baleine** on a 36-foot sloop that leaves from **Indian Bay.**

FYI

Electricity With the exception of Petit St. Vincent and a few hotels that have both 110- and 220-volt outlets, the current is generally 220 volts/60 cycles. Bring converters and adapters for US appliances.

Entry Requirements US and Canadian visitors must present a valid passport or proof of citizenship (a birth certificate or voter's registration card) and picture ID, plus a return or onward ticket.

Gambling The one formal gaming room on St. Vincent in no way resembles Las Vegas. The small, basement-level casino at the **Emerald Valley Resort & Casino** (see page 294) offers blackjack, craps, roulette, and slot machines. It's open every day except Tuesday from 9PM to 3AM. The minimum age is 18, and an admission fee is charged.

Language The official language is English, often spoken in local patois.

Money The Eastern Caribbean dollar (EC$) is the official currency; US dollars and traveler's checks are widely accepted, but taxis and market vendors prefer EC$. Banks are open Monday through Thursday from 8AM to 1PM, and Friday from 8AM to 1PM and from

3PM to 5PM. **Barclay's Bank** (Halifax St, Kingstown, 456.1706) is open Friday from 8AM to 5PM.

Personal Safety St. Vincent and the Grenadines are generally safe islands, but use common sense, especially at night. Don't walk in areas of St. Vincent and Bequia that make you uncomfortable. Never take anything to the beach that you don't absolutely need.

Publications There are six weekly newspapers published in St. Vincent and the Grenadines. The *Vincentian, Searchlight, Unity,* and *News* appear on Friday. The *Crusader* comes out on Wednesday and, on Bequia, the *Herald* is published on Tuesday. *Discover St. Vincent* and *Escape* are colorful and informative magazines for visitors, available free of charge in shops, hotels, and at all tourism offices.

Reservation Services and House Rentals

Bequia Villa Rentals ....458.3383; fax 458.3417

Mustique Company, Ltd
  on Mustique 458.4621
  on St. Vincent..457.1531
  in the US ....800/557.4255; fax 456.4565

Taxes A seven-percent tax is added to hotel bills. There's also a departure tax of US$8 (EC$20).

Tipping Most hotels add a service charge of 10 to 15 percent to bills. Restaurants usually add 10 percent to the check as well; if not, a 10-percent tip is generally the rule. Tip taxi drivers 10 percent of the fare.

Visitors' Information Offices The **St. Vincent Department of Tourism** office in Kingstown (Lower Bay St, 457.1502) is open Monday through Friday from 8AM to noon and from 1 to 4:30PM. A branch at **E.T. Joshua Airport** (458.4685) in **Arnos Vale** is open daily during the same hours. The **Bequia Tourist Information Office** (458.3286), on the waterfront in **Port Elizabeth,** is open Monday through Friday from 9AM to 12:30PM and from 1:30 to 4PM, Saturday from 9AM to noon. The **Union Island Tourist Office** (458.8350) at the airstrip in Clifton is open daily from 8AM to noon and from 1 to 4PM.

Phone Book

Ambulance 999, 456.1185

Directory Assistance 118

Diving Emergencies/
  Decompression Chambers 999

Emergencies 999

Fire...999

Hospital...456.1185

Police 999, 457.1211

Post Office 456.1111

There have been five documented eruptions of La Soufrière in the past 300 years—the most recent in 1979. A 24-hour watch is maintained by the La Soufrière Monitoring

St. Vincent

Sometimes called the "mainland" of the Grenadines, this lush 133-square-mile volcanic island yields an abundance of produce and spices. Its steep mountain ridges and valleys are dominated by the 4,049-foot active volcano known as **La Soufrière.** The island's windward side is rugged with cliffs and rocky shores, while the Caribbean coast is lined with both black- and gold-sand beaches. Capital **Kingstown,** home to around 25,000 residents, is a busy port trafficked by island schooners and transatlantic freighters. Saturday mornings are especially lively, when farmers and householders meet in the marketplace to haggle over colorful heaps of tropical fruit and fish.

1 Visions Perhaps the most unusual shop on St. Vincent, this women's clothing boutique features only locally made garments. Designer/owner Dawn Bacchus-Thomas specializes in bright cottons and flowing fabrics; her most distinctive offerings are hand-painted dresses. The striking items are well worth the somewhat lofty prices. ♦ M-F; Sa mornings. Granby and James Sts, Kingstown. 457.1308

2 Made in de Shade Casual clothes and beachwear for women and men are displayed against a vibrant backdrop of local art and harbor views. ♦ M-Sa. Heron Hotel, Upper Bay St and South River Rd, Kingstown. 457.2364. Also at: The Gingerbread Complex, Port Elizabeth, Bequia. 458.3001

3 Noah's Arkade Local and regional crafts include Haitian wood carvings, basketry by the Carib Indians of Dominica, clothing from Trinidad, and dolls in various national dress. Sterling silver and black-coral jewelry by Josette Norris is inspired by St. Vincent's pre-Columbian petroglyphs. ♦ M-Sa. Upper Bay St and South River Rd, Kingstown. 457.1513. Also at: Hotel Frangipani, Port Elizabeth, Bequia. 458.3424

4 Cobblestone Inn $ What was an 1814 sugar warehouse is now a historic harborfront inn with 19 simple rooms—a popular stop for business travelers. Gray cobblestone arches, walkways, and staircases are trimmed in deep green. The third-floor **Roof Top Restaurant,** which serves breakfast and light lunches, has a lively cocktail bar with a panoramic view. ♦ Upper Bay St (between South River Rd and Egmont St), Kingstown. 456.1937; fax 456.1938

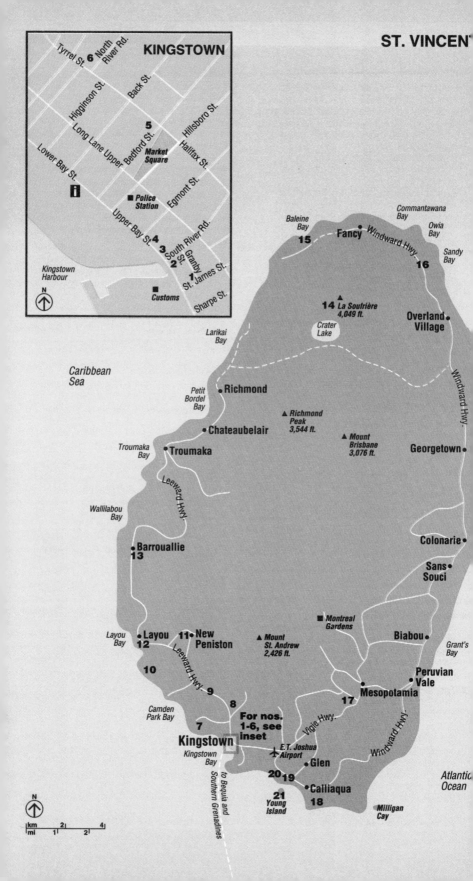

KINGSTOWN

Tyrrel St.
North River Rd.
Higginson St.
Back St.
Long Lane Upper
Bedford St.
Hillsboro St.
Market Square
Halifax St.
Lower Bay St.
Egmont St.
Police Station
Upper Bay St.
South River Rd.
Granby St.
St. James St.
Sharpe St.
Customs

6
5
4
3
2
1

Kingstown Harbour

N

Caribbean Sea

Commantawana Bay
Owia Bay
Baleine Bay
Fancy
Windward Hwy
Sandy Bay
15
16

La Soufrière
4,049 ft.
14
Crater Lake
Overland Village

Larikai Bay

Petit Bordel Bay
Richmond
Richmond Peak
3,544 ft.
Mount Brisbane
3,076 ft.
Georgetown

Chateaubelair

Troumaka Bay
Troumaka

Windward Hwy

Leeward Hwy.

Wallilabou Bay

Barrouallie
13
Colonarie

Sans Souci

Montreal Gardens

Biabou

Layou Bay
Layou
New Peniston
Mount St. Andrew
2,426 ft.
Grant's Bay
12
11
10

Peruvian Vale
Leeward Hwy.
9
8
Mesopotamia
17

Camden Park Bay
7
For nos. 1-6, see inset
Vigie Hwy.
Windward Hwy.

Kingstown
Kingstown Bay

E.T. Joshua Airport
Glen

20
19
Calliaqua
18

21
Young Island

to Bequia and Southern Grenadines

Milligan Cay

Atlantic Ocean

N

km 2 4
mi 1 2

4 Basil's Bar and Restaurant ★★$$ The much ballyhooed **Basil's Beach Bar** is the most famous public house on Mustique, and flamboyant owner Basil Charles is also at the helm of this spinoff operation, a cool stone-and-brick tavern with a big mahogany bar on the ground floor of the building that houses the **Cobblestone Inn** (above). Like the Mustique original, this place is known for fresh seafood (especially grilled lobster and red snapper), but you'll also find good burgers, salads, and omelettes. Reasonably priced lunch buffets, served Monday through Friday, and Friday-night Chinese buffets are very popular. ♦ Seafood/Continental ♦ M-Sa lunch and dinner. Reservations recommended. Upper Bay St (between South River Rd and Egmont St), Kingstown. 457.2713

4 Stechers Jewellers Great buys on fine silver jewelry, crystal, and English bone china can be found at this shop. Bring your airline ticket or cruise-ship pass for extra duty-free discounts. ♦ M-Sa. Cobblestone Arcade, Upper Bay St (between South River Rd and Egmont St), Kingstown. 457.1142

5 Aggie's Bar & Restaurant ★$ Soccer banners decorate this bright upstairs cafe, a lively place to try conch, lobster (in season), whelks (snails), souse, breadfruit, and other local specialties. A lunch buffet is served on Friday. ♦ West Indian ♦ M-Sa breakfast, lunch, and dinner; Su dinner. Grenville and Bedford Sts, Kingstown. 456.2110

6 St. Mary's Catholic Church Built in 1823 and redesigned in the 1930s by a Flemish monk, this dark structure of volcanic-sand brick is a conglomeration of Romanesque, Gothic, and Moorish styles. ♦ Tyrrel St and North River Rd, Kingstown

7 Fort Charlotte A dramatic setting on a promontory 636 feet above the sea affords great views of St. Vincent and the Grenadines. Built in 1806 to defend the island against French invasion (though the only casualty recorded here was an officer attacked by one of his own men), the fort was named for the wife of Britain's King George III. The battlements once supported more than 600 troops and 34 guns (3 of the original cannons remain); today the former living quarters house a museum with a series of murals

tracing black Carib history. ♦ Free. Daily. Just west of Kingstown. 456.1165

8 St. Vincent Botanical Gardens The infamous Captain William Bligh was headed here with his cargo of Tahitian breadfruit trees when a mutiny on the HMS Bounty scuttled his mission. His second voyage was successful, however, and a descendant of one of the original trees now thrives on the grounds. The oldest botanical gardens in the Western Hemisphere, founded in 1765, sprawl over 20 acres and showcase an impressive collection of tropical plants. Rare Vincentian parrots are housed in a small aviary. ♦ Small per-hour fee for guided tours. Daily. Leeward Hwy, Kingstown. 457.1003

Within St. Vincent Botanical Gardens:

St. Vincent National Museum The small collection here includes pre-Columbian artifacts and displays tracing the island's earliest known settlers, the Ciboney, who arrived circa 4000 BC. ♦ Admission. W, Sa. 457.1003, 456.1787

9 Leeward Highway The Caribbean coastal highway leads north from Kingstown to the town of Richmond over a hilly landscape with spectacular views. **Wallilabou Beach** is a fine spot for a swim and picnic along the way. Richmond, at the end of the highway, is one starting point for hikers who want to follow the western trail up the live volcano known as **La Soufrière**. ♦ Caribbean coast

10 Petit Byahaut $$$ If you're itching for a strong dose of nature, consider this basic-but-beautiful retreat. Accessible only by boat, it's set on a horseshoe-shaped bay in a secluded 50-acre private valley hidden by jungled peaks and ridges. Perfect for an escape from modern civilization, seven scattered room-size tents with decks offer fine sea views and plenty of privacy. Shielded by thick tropical vegetation, each of the wooden decks has a roofed and netted sleeping area, queen-size bed, table and chairs, solar-powered lamps, and hammock. Fresh water is pumped to each site for showers. The higher-priced sites have full private toilet facilities; others have outdoor flush toilets. Simple, tasty, mainly vegetarian fare is served on an open-air patio beside the 500-foot black-sand beach. The water-sports center is well equipped, offering snorkeling and scuba gear, sailboats, and kayaks; excellent walk-in dive sites are just offshore. The rate includes everything but beverages, scuba diving, and optional island tours. ♦ Caribbean coast (between Anse Cayenne and Buccament Bay). 457.7008; fax 457.7008

Touring the Tobago Cays

Over a thousand Marine Conservation Areas have been established around the globe, and 10 are scattered throughout the Grenadines. The Tobago Cays (pronounced *keys*) site is among the most famous in the world.

The five uninhabited islets off **Mayreau** lie within 2 miles of **Horseshoe Reef,** a huge 40-to-60-foot wall populated by an undersea rainbow of coral, brilliant sponges, and fish in a stunning variety of neon hues. For an even deeper plunge, **Sail Rock** dips down 80 feet, with remarkable underwater visibility that extends to 120 feet.

Smallest and southernmost, the island of **Petit Tobac** boasts what many believe to be the cays' best beach on its eastern side. Gorgeous white sands also line the south shores of both **Petit Rameau** and **Baradal.** To catch some shade, head for the northern coast of **Petit Bateau.**

These cays offer true Robinson Crusoe getaways (BYO *everything*) but you'll find plenty of magnificent picnic sites and beautiful sheltered waters for an overnight float. If you don't have access to a private boat, several companies offer group day sails. Contact **Grenadine Tours** (458.4818) on **St. Vincent** or **Wind & Sea Ltd.** at the **Anchorage Yacht Club** (458.8647, 458.8678; fax 458.8569) on **Union Island.**

11 Emerald Valley Resort & Casino $$
Rooms overlook a river and five acres of floodlit tropical gardens at this pretty stone property. Each of the 12 units, quartered in 6 cottages, has a kitchenette and balcony. A small casino (the only one on St. Vincent) offers craps, roulette, blackjack, and video slot machines. Other perks include two freshwater pools (one adjoining the airy restaurant/bar), two tennis courts, horseback riding, and horseshoes. Marked nature trails meander through the surrounding hills (one leads to a parrot lookout in the rain forest), and a courtesy van makes regular trips into town. ♦ Just west of New Peniston. 456.7824, 456.1523; fax 456.2622

12 Layou This village has a Carib petroglyph that dates back 13 centuries—just ask any villager to point the way to "the picture rock," a short walk away. ♦ Leeward Hwy

13 Barrouallie The fishermen of this village (pronounced *Bare*-a-lee), still hunt whales from little wooden boats, just as island residents have since the 18th century. (The average catch for the entire island chain is less than one per year.) The tourist board points out that environmental groups app two kills per year, as these old-time whale are more of an endangered species than t sea creatures they hunt. ♦ Leeward Hwy

14 La Soufrière Hikers love this 4,049-foot volcanic mountain near the north coast of t island. From Richmond, it's a strenuous three-hour climb to the crater lake. Be forewarned: After the 2-hour, 26-mile drive from Kingstown to Richmond, the trek can extremely tiring and the view is often hidde by clouds. The hike is somewhat easier approached from the windward side of the island. Starting at Bamboo Range, an area bamboo trees, the trail goes from a lowlan forest through a tropical rain forest to the crater of the still-active volcano (which last erupted in 1979). Either way, a guide is necessary; your hotel or the tourist bureau can arrange for one. ♦ Northern interior

15 Falls of Baleine Swim in a huge rocky p beneath a 60-foot waterfall at this popular attraction, which is virtually unapproachab by land. Boats make the day trip out of Kingstown or Villa Beach, usually a packag deal that includes stopovers for a beach lu and snorkeling. Contact **Baleine Tours** (457.4089) or **Dive St. Vincent** (457.4714) ♦ Baleine Bay

16 Windward Highway The town of Fancy marks the northern end of the route that traces St. Vincent's eastern shore. Though four-wheel-drive vehicle is not necessary t enjoy the surf-pounded Atlantic coast, it's good idea to have one at the northern tip o the island, site of one of the largest cocon plantations in the world. As it heads south road passes the lush fields of bananas, coconut palms, and arrowroot that domin the landscape between Georgetown and Peruvian Vale. Next come the beaches of Calliaqua, Indian Bay, and Villa. The road e at the airport. ♦ Atlantic coast

17 Marriaqua Valley Also known as the Mesopotamia Valley, or simply "Mespo," S Vincent's bread basket spreads out on bot sides of scenic Vigie Highway for a bucolic journey past terraced farms, forests, rivers and boys on donkeys. Just north of Mespo signs point to the secondary road for **Montreal Gardens** (458.5452), a tropical retreat warmed by natural mineral springs filled with fruit trees and exotic blooms lik anthuriums. ♦ Vigie Hwy (between Peruvi Vale and E.T. Joshua Airport)

18 Lagoon Marina & Hotel $$ This mode complex of native stone and wood offers 1 balconied rooms that overlook a full-servic marina with docking facilities. Land-side attractions include a waterfront restaurant bar, a small two-tiered freshwater pool, an beach with water sports. Ask about land/sea packages for yacht charters or short day trips to nearby islands. ♦ South of Calliaqua. 458.4308, 800/74.CHARMS; fax 457.4308

19 Lime Restaurant & Pub ★$ On the mainland just across from Young Island, this congenial English-style pub is a fun spot for chilled mugs of "draught," gourmet pizzas, fresh grilled seafood, local specialties, and espresso (it's the only espresso bar on St. Vincent). Visitors no longer need to negotiate a ledge over the beach to get here; there's now a landlubber's entrance. Tables that once sat in a garden are now on a patio, greatly reducing the mosquito problem after sunset. There's a separate dining area on a wooden deck adjacent to the patio. ♦ International ♦ Daily lunch and dinner. Villa Beach. 458.4227

19 The Umbrella Beach Hotel $ A stay here is a comfy way to save some cash. Surrounded by green lawn and hibiscus are nine simply furnished kitchenette apartments with patios bordering a garden or the beach. ♦ Villa Beach. 458.4651; fax 457.4930

French Restaurant

19 French Restaurant ★★$$ A white picket fence trims the street side of this Gallic charmer next to (and owned by the same folks as) **The Umbrella Beach Hotel.** Tables are set on a gleaming gingerbread-bedecked terrace that overlooks the beach. Make your choice at the live lobster pool, or try one of the menu's French/West Indian alliances like seafood cassoulet or red snapper in gratinéed basil sauce. The lunch menu features quiches, salads, and other light fare. ♦ French/ Caribbean ♦ Daily breakfast, lunch, and dinner; closed in September. Reservations recommended. Villa Beach. 458.4972

20 Aquatic Club A live band usually hits the stage Saturday nights at this club, a favorite of locals and tourists alike. Otherwise the popular disco rocks with canned dance tunes until the wee hours. ♦ Admission. W-Sa (days and hours may change; call ahead). Indian Bay. 458.4205

20 Coconut Beach Inn $ This beachfront beauty has lovely views of Young Island and Bequia, a pool, piers, a dock, and 10 basic rooms. The open-air restaurant/bar serves local food and drinks by the sea. ♦ Indian Bay. 458.4900; fax 458.4900

20 Indian Bay Beach Hotel & Apartments $ Set in a white latticed complex trimmed with blue awnings, the accommodations here are basic, but conveniently located on the beach. The 12 air-conditioned 1- and 2-bedroom units offer kitchenettes and daily maid service. Breezy **Restaurant à la Mer** is known for West Indian cuisine and Friday night barbecues in season. ♦ Indian Bay. 458.4001, 800/74.CHARMS; fax 457.4777

20 Grand View Beach Hotel $$$ As the name implies, views of the Grenadines are indeed grand from this turn-of-the-century cotton plantation house, a cozy 19-room enclave set in 8 acres of tropical gardens overlooking a secluded beach. The family-operated complex also features a striking high-perched swimming pool, a fitness center, a tennis court, a squash court, water sports, and a panoramic dining room that serves hearty West Indian fare. Rates include full breakfast. ♦ Villa Point. 458.4811, 800/223.6510; fax 457.4174

20 Villa Lodge $$ A 5-minute walk from the beach, the 10 spacious air-conditioned rooms at this hostelry have full baths, mini-refrigerators, TVs, and terraces (some with views of Indian Bay). Extra beds are available for children. An open-air bar overlooks the harbor, and the restaurant serves seafood and steaks; meal plans are available. Originally built as a private home, this friendly hotel shares a pool with the **Breezeville Apartments** next door. ♦ Villa Point. 458.4641, 800/74.CHARMS; fax 457.4468

21 Young Island $$$$ Just 200 yards off St. Vincent, this private isle offers 35 acres of tropical gardens and "a smile of a beach." Accommodations are in 29 large Tahitian-style cottages cooled by ceiling fans and louvered walls that let in the tradewinds. The ambience is wild, yet luxurious: Interiors lined with stone and South American hardwoods blend with surrounding greenery, and tiled baths lead to outdoor showers shielded by ferns and tropical blooms. Three beachside cottages have private plunge pools. Meals are served in waterfront gazebos or a Polynesian pavilion terraced into the rocks. Paddlers can pause for a drink at the thatch-roofed **Coconut Bar** that floats just offshore, a short wade from the main bar on the beach. Sports facilities include a full diving operation (instruction available), Windsurfers, a saltwater pool, and a tennis court. Two yachts make day trips to Bequia and Mustique. Hammocks line the beach, and evenings are peaceful, though sometimes blessed by a little night music. Weekly cocktail parties on Ft. Duvernette, a tiny islet whose mountain steps are lit by torches, is the last word in Caribbean romance. Packages include crewed yacht cruises. ♦ Take the Young Island ferry from the Young Island Dock, Villa. 458.4826, 800/223.1108; fax 457.4567

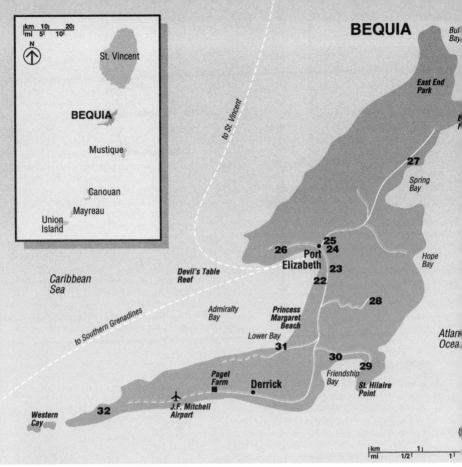

Bequia

Sun and rum are both very strong on Bequia, just five miles south of St. Vincent and the largest and northernmost of the Grenadines. Some 5,000 islanders populate these 7 square miles—mostly fishermen, sailors, and master boatbuilders. Today the descendants of the determined Scottish whalers of the mid-1800s still hunt in sailboats with hand-hurled harpoons, bringing in a catch of less than one humpback per year—all of which is eaten, with the approval of environmental authorities.

The main point of entry is picturesque **Port Elizabeth** on the shore of **Admiralty Bay**. Stop by the **Bequia Tourist Bureau** on the main wharf (458.3286) for directions or to hook up with a driver/guide. Good beaches dot the island, and beyond the last whalers' village at **Paget Farm** lies an unusual, but stunning, settlement of "cave dwellers," whose stone homes (no electricity, no glass in the windows) are worked into the cliffs at **Moonhole**.

22 Plantation House $$$ Often still called the **Sunny Caribbee** (its former name) by locals, this stately peach-and-white great house, surrounded by a wraparound porch, holds five guest rooms and the **Plantation House Restaurant** overlooking Admiralty Bay. In addition there are 17 1- and 2-bedroom cottages graced with small private verandas,

and a 3-bedroom beachfront unit, all scatter across 10 manicured acres of palm trees, hibiscus, and frangipani. Other bright spots include a lighted tennis court, a small pool, water sports, and full diving facilities. The waterside bar/grill presents live soca and reggae Tuesday nights (in season) and a beach barbecue on Friday. ♦ Port Elizabeth. 458.3425, 800/223.1108; fax 458.3612

22 Crab Hole Vibrant tropical-print cotton fabric is silk-screened in the back studio her and visitors are encouraged to view the process before they purchase the fabric or t original hats, totes, bikinis, *pareos* (sarongs and other garments created with it in a workshop upstairs. Custom designs are available. The bougainvillea-draped cottage also stocks mango chutney, exotic jams and jellies, and hand-crafted jewelry. ♦ M-Sa. P Elizabeth. 458.3290

22 Old Fig Tree ★$ Local produce stars in t West Indian fare served at the restaurant of the six-room **Old Fig Tree Guesthouse.** Conch, roti (fried dough filled with potatoes and meat, chicken, or conch), and rice and peas are recommended. Set dinners are a good deal. ♦ West Indian ♦ M-Sa breakfast, lunch, and dinner; Su brunch. Reservations recommended. Port Elizabeth. 458.3201

22 Maranne's Ice Cream Maranne offers delicious homemade ice cream, yogurt, and sorbets made from local exotica like soursops, mangoes, and papayas. ♦ M-Sa. Port Elizabeth. 458.3041

22 Hotel Frangipani $$ A family home turned public house, "the Frangi" was once home to James "Son" Mitchell, now SVG's prime minister. The shingle-sided main building, built in 1927 and converted to an inn in 1966, offers 5 simple rooms with shared cold-water baths. Viewless but more comfortable are eight garden units hand-crafted from local stone and wood, with private balconies and full baths. Thursday-night jump-ups in the open-air restaurant and bar are a must, with barbecue, steel-band music, and true local color. String bands play in the same venue on Monday nights. Windsurfing, a dive shop, and water sports are available next door. The hotel also maintains a phone/fax/mail center for yachties. ♦ Port Elizabeth. 458.3255; fax 458.3824

22 Mac's Pizzeria and Bake Shop ★★$$ Lobster pizza (when available) is the real novelty here—and much tastier than it sounds. Fish, pita sandwiches, and quiche are also served at this deservedly popular spot. Scrumptious banana bread, pineapple rolls, cookies, and brownies, all baked on the premises, are available to go. ♦ American/Caribbean ♦ Daily lunch and dinner. Reservations recommended. Port Elizabeth. 458.3474, takeout VHF 68

22 Melinda's One-of-a-kind hand-painted T-shirts star at this shop, whose inventory ranges from tennis shoes to silk robes. ♦ M-Sa. Port Elizabeth. 458.3895

23 Julie's Guest House $ Here's a friendly and inexpensive spot, where breakfast and dinner are included in the rate. Though small, the 19 rooms have private baths and balconies that overlook Admiralty Bay, about a block away. The dining room serves good West Indian food. Barbecues, beach picnics, water sports, and steel bands are part of the fun during high season. ♦ Port Elizabeth. 458.3304; fax 458.3812

24 Le Petit Jardin ★★$$$ An elegantly casual atmosphere and innovatively prepared French cuisine with a West Indian accent (including good seafood specialties) make for a pleasant dining experience at this chalet-style restaurant. ♦ French/Caribbean ♦ Daily lunch and dinner. Reservations recommended. Back St, Port Elizabeth. 458.3318

24 Local Color Ltd. Swimwear, T-shirts, beach accessories, jewelry, and decorative items hand-painted in vibrant hues are sold at this boutique, one of SVG's very best. ♦ M-Sa. Port Elizabeth. 458.3202

24 Solana's Boutique Batik items and local crafts share the shelves here with postcards, photo supplies, maps, and souvenirs. ♦ M-Sa. Port Elizabeth. 458.3554

25 Daphne Cooks It ★★$$ Whatever looks freshest when she goes to market each day Daphne cooks at this homey spot. There's no fixed menu, just solid West Indian fare from old family recipes, also available for takeout. ♦ Caribbean ♦ Daily lunch and dinner. Dinner reservations recommended; no credit cards accepted. Port Elizabeth. 458.3271

25 Mauvin's Model Boat Shop Order a replica of your own yacht, or cruise the brightly colored collection of Bequia whaleboats and schooners. Mauvin Hutchins has made model boats by hand for more than a quarter of a century. ♦ M-Sa. Port Elizabeth. 458.3669

26 Sargeant Bros. Model Boat Shop A staff of 12 produces detailed scale models of boats, including the famous Bequia whalers. The company created a model of the royal yacht for Queen Elizabeth II. ♦ M-Sa. Point Bay (just west of Port Elizabeth). 458.3344

Spring on Bequia

27 Spring on Bequia $$$ This romantic hillside getaway is part of a 200-year-old working plantation carpeted with fields of citrus, banana, and mango trees. Guests stay in 10 cool stone units in 3 hillside buildings, with natural rock showers and purple heartwood trim. The dining room and bar in the main house overlook the pool, and the Sunday curry buffet should not be missed. Also on the tranquil grounds are a tennis court and a secluded beach. ♦ Spring Bay. 458.3414, 612/823.1202; fax 457.3305

28 The Old Fort Country Inn $$ On a clear day you can see Grenada from this French fort perched atop Mount Pleasant. It was rebuilt with local stone and hardwood by world traveler Otmar Schaedle, a German music professor turned hotelier. Now a unique inn, the fort houses six airy apartments with private baths and "the best view and coolest climate on the island, with no mosquitoes." Breakfast, lunch, and dinner are available at the open-air restaurant. ♦ Mount Pleasant Rd (east of Admiralty Bay). 458.3440; fax 458.3824

29 Friendship Bay Hotel $$ Sprawling along the beach at Friendship Bay, 27 simple but cheerful rooms have terraces and panoramic

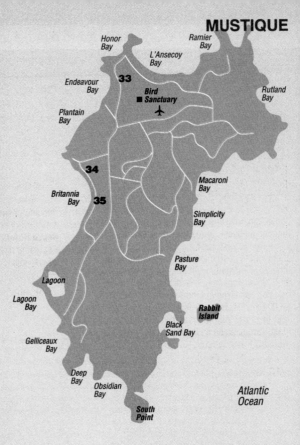

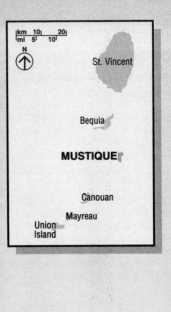

MUSTIQUE

sea views. Guests at this charming property can parasail, windsurf, dive (full facilities and instruction are available), sail to Mustique, play on the tennis court, and dine on fresh seafood and West Indian dishes outdoors or in. The congenial beach bar hosts lively Saturday night jump-ups, which include West Indian barbecue and live reggae and rock music. ♦ Friendship Bay. 458.3222; fax 458.3840

30 Blue Tropic Hotel $ Overlooking Friendship Bay, these 10 roomy beachside apartments have kitchens and balconies. The garden terrace of the **Flame Tree Restaurant** draws both residents and visitors, especially for Wednesday night barbecues with local music. Room rates include breakfast. ♦ Friendship Bay. 458.3573; fax 457.3074

31 De Reef ★$ Hang out at this quintessential beach bar, where they'll find you on the beach (or afloat) when your seafood, chicken, or sandwich is ready. Showers and lockers are available and you can rent Windsurfers and snorkeling gear. Buffets with live entertainment are held some Saturdays (call ahead), and the whole island shows up Sunday afternoon. ♦ Seafood ♦ Daily lunch and dinner. Reservations recommended for dinner; no credit cards accepted. Lower Bay. 458.3447

31 Coco's ★★$$ The local color is as appealing as the food at this eatery, which overlooks the bay a short way up a steep hill. Calypso music and beer and drinks accompany the authentic West Indian fare. ♦ West Indian ♦ Daily lunch and dinner. Dinner reservations recommended. Lower Bay. 458.3463

31 Dawn's Creole Garden ★★$$ Another very Caribbean spot, this place is surrounded by foliage and serves mouthwatering chicken, goat, and mutton dishes. ♦ West Indian ♦ Daily breakfast, lunch, and dinner. Dinner reservations recommended; no credit cards accepted. Lower Bay. 458.3154

31 Theresa's ★★$$ A tiny indoor-outdoor beachside bar and restaurant, it offers international (Greek, Indian, etc.) buffet dinners on Monday nights and hearty, local dishes the rest of the week. Even if the food weren't as good as it is, the atmosphere would be worth the trip. ♦ West Indian ♦ Daily lunch and dinner. Dinner reservations recommended; no credit cards accepted. Lower Bay. 458.3802

32 Moonhole Huge private homes that look like free-form rock caves dot the cliffs on the island's western end. Residents Jim and Sheena Johnston give group tours of these amazing dwellings; groups must have between 4 and 20 people. ♦ Fee. By appointment. Reservations necessary, with 24 hours notice. West of Derrick. 458.3038 or VHF Channel 06

Mustique

Exclusive in every sense of the word, the island of Mustique attracts very rich and often famous (Princess Margaret, Cher, Mick Jagger) vacationers who can frolic here without being bothered by autograph seekers. With no town and few activities, Mustique has been called "a house party, to which, if you have not been invited, it might be best not to come," though day-trippers are welcome and enjoy great snorkeling. Just two by three miles, Mustique's wooded hills and valleys are surrounded by white-sand beaches and numerous coves.

The single hotel and guest house on the island often function as guest rooms for local homeowners. But if you have the cash (and the references), you can stay at one of the posh mansions when the owners are otherwise engaged. High-season prices start at about $2,500 per week for a 2-bedroom villa with staff and car. You can sleep in Meg's home for less than $7,000 a week; Mick rents his Japanese-style digs for slightly more, but off-season rates are lower. Most rentals are handled by the **Mustique Company, Ltd.** (458.4621 in Mustique, 457.1531 in St. Vincent, 800/557.4255 in the US; fax 456.4565).

33 Cotton House $$$$ Once part of a working plantation, Mustique's only hotel is set in an 18th-century manor built of native stone and coral and decorated with English and Caribbean antiques. Recently renovated, the main building is surrounded by wide verandas, and rooms are graced with cedar shutters and louvered doors. Guest accommodations include 13 cottages (3 poolside) and 7 suites. All have air-conditioning, private patios, mini-bars, and telephones. Water sports (sailing, surfing, snorkeling) on Macaroni Beach are free to hotel guests, who also have access to horseback riding, a tennis court, and a hilltop swimming pool. Evenings are a bit dressy here, though no jackets are required for men. There's free van transportation. Room rates include meals. ♦ Endeavour Bay. 456.4777, 800/447.7462, 800/223.1108; fax 456.4777

34 Basil's Bar ★★$$$$ You could sit next to a viscount or a deckhand, Prince Andrew or David Bowie, especially during high season, when bands heat up the joint on Wednesday nights. Mustique's answer to *Casablanca*'s Rick is entrepreneur Basil Charles, whose wicker-and-wood complex is the only game in town. The restaurant serves fresh fish, lobster, and a wide choice of wines; lighter meals and snacks (including homemade ice cream) are also available. Two boutiques next door sell Balinese batiks, gifts, and resortwear. ♦ Seafood ♦ Daily breakfast, lunch, and dinner. Reservations recommended. Britannia Bay. 458.4621 ext 350; VHF 68

35 Firefly Guest House $$$ Owner Billy Mitchell sailed the world for 19 years before settling down on this verdant isle. Mistress of the island's first house (it sits on a hill overlooking Britannia Bay), she lodges guests in four charming rooms with private baths and terraces. All accommodations are equipped with refrigerators and picnic paraphernalia and are a short walk from the beach. There's no restaurant on the premises. ♦ Britannia Bay. 456.3414; fax 456.3514

Canouan

This quiet little island 25 miles south of St. Vincent remains unspoiled, visited mostly by yachting folk and Italians who frequent the 48-room **Tamarind Beach Hotel & Yacht Club,** the largest resort in SVG. Populated by fishermen and goatherds, the crescent-shaped isle (3.5 miles long) is surrounded by ribbons of white sand, wide shallows, and coral reefs.

36 Canouan Beach Hotel $$$$ On a long beach jutting into the Caribbean, this 43-unit French-managed resort offers a dive shop with a certified instructor, a marina, a shopping mall, snorkeling equipment, windsurfing, table tennis, volleyball, and day sails. The bright and charming complex includes 11 standard rooms in the main building and 32 airy bungalows with spacious verandas. The all-inclusive plan covers West Indian meals, drinks, and sports. A steel band plays Monday and Thursday. ♦ South Glossy Bay. 458.8888; fax 458.8875

37 Villa Le Bijou $$ Ten minutes up a steep hill from the beach (and taxis are hard to find), this *very* basic six-room guest house (no hot water, no private baths, no restaurant) offers spectacular views from its terrace. ♦ No credit cards accepted. Northeast of Friendship Bay. 458.8025, VHF 16

38 Tamarind Beach Hotel & Yacht Club $$$$ Three simple, gingerbread-adorned buildings offer 48 smallish, ceiling-fan-cooled rooms and a fabulous view of white-sand beach, bright turquoise water, and the southern Grenadines. Italian-owned and Italian-frequented, the hotel serves inventive Caribbean food and great pizza in a lovely garden setting. Guests can take advantage of complete water-sports and sailing facilities— if they can drag themselves off the beach. ♦ Grand Bay. 458.8044, 800/223.1108; fax 458.8851

Beware the machineel. The large, flat-leafed trees produce small green (or, at maturity, yellow) poisonous apples that cause blistering of the skin and mouth. DO NOT TOUCH OR EAT THEM! Don't touch the leaves either, or even stand under the trees during a rainstorm. Machineel trees are usually marked with a warning sign or a red stripe painted around the trunk.

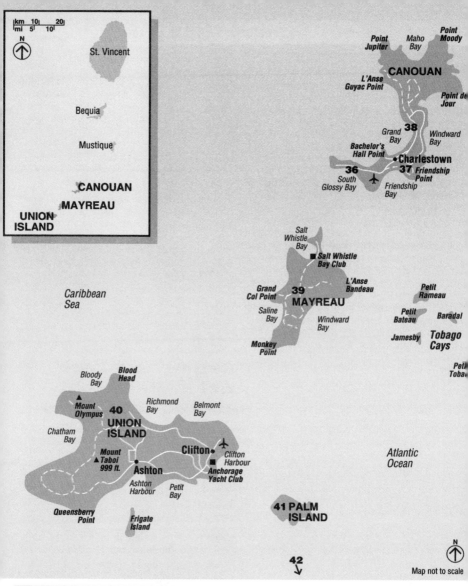

Other Grenadine Islands

39 Mayreau In the heart of the Grenadines, this 1.5-square-mile outpost can be reached by the mailboat or from Union Island. Most of the 182 locals live on top of Station Hill, and the cactus-y trek to the peak is worthwhile. If the gentle climb doesn't take your breath away, the great views will. Salt Whistle Bay is edged by one of the world's most magnificent beaches, and the curving sands of Saline Bay stretch for nearly a mile.

On Mayreau:

Salt Whistle Bay Club $$$$ This is the very definition of a barefoot hideaway: As you approach via its private launch (or your own sailboat), you can't even see the stone units of the resort, so well hidden are they behind palms and bushes. The informal South Seas–style retreat (no roads, no cars, no telephones) lies on the Caribbean's loveliest curving beach; here guests need never don more than a swimsuit and cover-up, even for dinner. Five widely-spaced, shaded, breeze-cooled two-room units share second-floor verandas. Activities (most included in the room rate) include water sports, table tennis, darts, volleyball, and board games. Dive, snorkeling, and boating excursions can be arranged. The beach bar/restaurant once had live music . . . until guests complained about the noise. ♦ Salt Whistle Bay. 458.8444, VHF 16; fax 458.8944

40 Union Island Dominated by mountains that dip into palm-lined sands along the shore, the approach to this southern entry port for the Grenadines reminds some travelers of Tahiti. Union Island is home to Mount Taboi, the highest peak in the archipelago. Great beaches are at Chatham Bay and Bloody Bay, and snorkelers will love spectacular Lagoon Reef.

Though only two miles by three miles, Union Island is a busy place. Small interisland planes frequent the airstrip and hundreds of yachts anchor here in winter. Union is also the connecting point for launches to nearby Mayreau, Petit St. Vincent, and Palm Island, as well as to the national water park that surrounds the uninhabited Tobago Cays. The **Union Island Tourist Office** (458.8350) at the airstrip is open daily.

On Union Island:

Anchorage Yacht Club $$$ Though it has a style of its own, this French-owned inn doesn't have the "yacht club" cachet the name implies. Still, it's popular with sailors, who come ashore to stay in one of the 10 comfortable rooms and bungalows and avail themselves of the French restaurant, water sports, day charters, and boutique. The bar is popular, and there's even a shallow shark pool, inhabited by sleepy (and harmless) sharks. Breakfast is included in the rate, and meal plans are available. ♦ Clifton. 458.8221; fax 458.8365

41 Palm Island Beach Club $$$$ After wisely changing its name from Prune to Palm, owners John and Mary Caldwell set about transforming their bald, deserted 130-acre islet into a lush, secluded resort. They drained a mangrove swamp, evicted land crabs, planted palm trees by the hundreds, and opened their doors to guests in 1967. Improvements have continued ever since: Now nestled among the palm, almond, and casuarina trees are 24 oceanfront cottages, blessedly free of telephones, TVs, and air-conditioning. (An additional seven apartments and six villas on the island, each with one to four bedrooms, are privately owned, but can be reserved through the hotel.) This informal hideaway has 5 beaches, a tennis court, jogging and walking trails, a 37-foot yacht ideal for catered day sails, and another boat for fishing trips. Windsurfing, snorkeling, and use of Sunfish are complimentary; scuba diving can also be arranged. All meals and afternoon tea are included in the room rate. The island is reached by a 15-minute launch ride from Union Island. The flight to Union Island is 55 minutes from Barbados, 10 minutes from St. Vincent. ♦ Palm Island. 458.8824, 800/999.7256, 212/242.4700,; fax 458.8804, 212/242.4768

42 Petit St. Vincent $$$$ If it's privacy you seek, drop anchor here; the entire 113-acre island is a single resort of 22 secluded villas with service that goes beyond discreet. You

need never see another human while you're here; for total seclusion, send a red flag up your own bamboo pole, and the staff will stay clear. If you need something, hoist a yellow flag, and tuck your request into a notch on the pole. Room service arrives by golf cart. Otherwise, everything is within easy reach: swimming, sailing, snorkeling, windsurfing, tennis, volleyball, croquet, and a fitness trail. If you're in the mood for company, nights bring live music, beach barbecues, and socializing with visiting yachties. Rates include all meals (meat is flown in from Julia Child's butcher) and all sports except scuba diving and boat charters. Many guests return because of what's *not* included: television, telephones, air conditioners, or even room keys. The villas, designed by noted Swedish architect **Arne Hasselquist**, are placed for maximum privacy; those on the hilltops have shielded terraces for nude sunbathing.
♦ Closed September through October. Petit St. Vincent. 458.8801, 513/242.1333, 800/654.9326; fax 458.8428

Getting Your Feet Wet in St. Vincent and the Grenadines

There's more to do in the islands beyond the beach. Here are outfits that can set you afloat:

Boating
Baleine Tours Baleine Bay, St. Vincent. 457.4089
Sunsports Bequia. 458.3577
S/Y Passion Bequia. 458.3884
S/Y Pelangi Bequia. 458.3255
S/Y Scaramouche Union Island. 458.8418
For bareboat and skippered charters, contact:
Barefoot Yacht Charters St. Vincent. 456.9526
Bequia Marina Bequia. 458.3272
Nicholson Yacht Charters St. Vincent. 460.1530

Snorkeling and Scuba Diving
Bequia Beach Club Bequia. 458.3248
Dive Anchorage Union Island. 458.8221
Dive Bequia Bequia. 458.3504
Dive Canouan Canouan. 458.8138
Dive St. Vincent Young Island Dock, Villa, St. Vincent. 457.4714
Grenadines Dive Union Island. 458.8138
St. Vincent Dive Experience St. Vincent. 457.5130

Windsurfing
Bequia Beach Club Bequia. 458.3248
De Reef Bequia. 458.3447

TOBAG[O]
For nos.
29-47, s
pg. 311

For nos.
1-15, see
pg. 306

Trinidad and Tobago

About 1.2 million residents season the melting pot of Trinidad with a cosmopolitan blend of African, British, French, Portuguese, Spanish, Chinese, and East Indian cultures. Just 20 miles to the northeast, serene Tobago (pop. 8,600) is pure West Indian—an oasis of quiet beaches, lush rain forests, and old plantations. Together the sister islands (which form one republic) offer visitors a fine mix of nature, sport, dining, and culture.

Port of Spain is Trinidad's busy capital, an architectural hodgepodge of modern buildings and gingerbread houses, Anglican cathedrals and Hindu temples, funky boutiques and street bazaars. Just before Ash Wednesday, the city's parks and streets are crammed with steel bands and spectacular masqueraders "playing mas" as part of one of the greatest shows on earth. Though Carnival is celebrated throughout the Caribbean, Trinidad is center ring of the circus, where spectators are as wild as the nonstop parades and parties. If you miss the main event, be sure to see the dazzling costume display at Port of Spain's **National Museum and Art Gallery.**

Over half of Trinidad's residents are East Indian, and their traditional holidays and cuisine contribute significantly to the island's multicultural appeal. In October, Hindus outline their houses and shrines with thousands of earthenware lamps for Divali (the Festival of Lights) and in June Moslems march with exquisitely detailed model mosques for their solemn celebration of Hosein.

The island offers both sophisticated international restaurants and mom-and-pop cafes serving spicy stuffed crab backs, Creole goulash, and "doubles," a spicy vegetarian sandwich. Nightlife thrives at jazz clubs, discos, British-style pubs, and theaters.

But Trinidad is not all bright lights and big crowds. Sea turtles nest on the golden shoreline, and interior tropical jungles are alive with parakeets, hummingbirds, 600 species of butterflies, and some 700 varieties of tropical plants. Flocks of scarlet ibis swoop across the mangroves and marshes at sunset to roost at the **Caroni Bird Sanctuary. Maracas Bay** is a picturesque palm-lined beach, and roads all over the world have been surfaced by the natural asphalt (bitumen) mined from the famous 90-acre **Pitch Lake** at La Brea.

If refineries and other industrial landmarks occasionally spoil the view, remember the petrochemical industry contributed another boon to the local economy: oil-drum lids. Carefully hammered to key, the lids were used as makeshift instruments by the original steel bands. The three Caribbean musical trademarks—steel bands, calypso, and limbo—were all born on this two-island republic.

Although new resorts continually open on Tobago, the landscape and atmosphere on the smaller island are calmer than on Trinidad. Soft sand beaches are fringed with palm and mango trees, and snorkelers explore the coral gardens and fish sanctuary of **Buccoo Reef.** This is the site of the oldest rain-forest preserve in the western hemisphere—14,000 acres protected since 1765—and the **Bird of Paradise Sanctuary**, home to red-billed tropic birds and royal terns. The capital, **Scarborough**, with some 12,000 citizens, is still guarded by the 18th-century battlements of **Fort King George.**

An independent member of the British Commonwealth since 1962, Trinidad and Tobago became a republic in 1976. Today the islands are home to a hard working yet fun-loving group of people who have invented a name for just enjoying each other's company—*liming*. If someone says "let's *lime*," just say yes.

Area code 868 unless otherwise noted.

Getting to the Islands

Airlines

Air Canada..........................664.4065, 800/776.3000

American............................664.4661, 800/433.7300

BWIA International Airways.....................627.2942,
....800/538.2942

Interisland Carriers

Air Caribbean 623.2500

LIAT (Leeward Islands Air Transport).......627.2942,
....800/468.0482

Airports **Piarco International Airport** (669.8048) in Trinidad is 16 miles east of Port of Spain. Tobago's **Crown Point Airport** (639.8547) is at the western tip of the island, eight miles from Scarborough.

Ferries and Interisland Cruises Two ferries, the *M.V. Tobago* and the *M.F. Panorama*, travel daily except Saturday between Trinidad and Tobago. Call the **Port Authority of Trinidad and Tobago** (625.3055, 639.2417) for schedule and fare information.

Getting Around the Islands

Buses On Trinidad, regularly scheduled buses link Port of Spain with cities around the island. The terminal is on **South Quay** in Port of Spain; there are fixed bus stops along the routes. Tobago's public buses, fairly modern and inexpensive to ride, make the trip from one end of the island to the other. The terminal is at **Gardenside Street** in Scarborough. For schedule information call 623.7872.

Car Rental

On Trinidad:

Auto Rentals..............................669.2277, 623.7368

Autocenter Car 625.4041

Econo-Car Rentals Ltd 622.8074

Kalloo's Auto Rental 669.5673, 622.9073

Singh's.....................................664.5417, 664.3860

Southern Sales and Service.......................669.2424

On Tobago:

Carlton James 639.8084

Hill Crest Car Rental Service Ltd 639.5208

Peter Gremli 639.8400

Driving The challenge here is driving on the left-hand side of the road with a right-hand mounted steering wheel. Gas usually costs less than in the US. An international driver's license is useful, but not required—a valid US or Canadian driver's license is acceptable for stays of up to two months.

Motorbikes

Island Bikes ....Bon Accord, Tobago 639.8587

Taxis

Piarco Airport Taxi Cooperative Society,
Trinidad..669.168

Quashie's Car Rental & Taxi Services, Tobago.......
....639.842

Southern Sales Corporate Car/Bus & Driver Service
Trinidad..633.CAR

Tours There are a number of tour operators on bo islands. Many offer excursions focused on specific interests or activities such as nature, history, divin or fishing. On Trinidad, try **Classic Tours and Trav Ltd.** (628.5714), **Coroni Tours** (645.1305), **Hummingbird Tours** (623.3300), or **Trinidad and Tobago Sightseeing Tours** (628.1051). Tour operators on Tobago include **Ansyl Tours** (639.4125), **Classic Tours and Travel** (639.9891), and **David Rooks Nature Tours** (639.4276).

FYI

Electricity The current is 110 or 230 volts/60 cycles AC. At hotels, check with the management before plugging in appliances. Most of the better properties provide in-room hairdryers and/or electrical adapters.

Entry Requirements Visitors must present a va passport and complete two separate entry forms.

Language The official language is English.

Money The local currency is the Trinidadian dolla (TT), but US dollars are universally accepted. Occasionally, purchases will cost less if bought wit TT dollars. Most banks are open Monday through Thursday from 8AM to 2PM, and Friday from 8AM 12PM and 3PM to 5PM.

Personal Safety Exercise reasonable precaution in both Trinidad and Tobago. Avoid downtown streets, parks, and beaches late at night and don't leave valuables unguarded on the beach or in an unlocked car. Don't wear expensive jewelry or carry large amounts of cash when walking around. Leave valuables such as airline tickets, passports, and cas in your hotel safe.

Publications The *Trinidad Guardian, Trinidad Express,* and *Newsday* are the local dailies. *Discove Trinidad & Tobago* is the official publication of the **Trinidad and Tobago Hotel and Tourism Association.** It's available free at local hotels, restaurants, and travel agencies.

Reservation Services and House Rentals

Tobago Bed & Breakfast Association.........639.392

Taxes A 15-percent tax is added to hotel bills. There's also a departure tax of TT\$85 (about US\$14) that must be paid in Trinidadian currency, so remember to bring some TT dollars to the airport.

Tipping Most of the larger hotels and restaurants automatically add a 10-percent service fee to your bill. Otherwise, tip between 10 and 15 percent, depending on the service.

isitors' Information Offices On Trinidad, the **urism and Industrial Development Company IDCO**; 10-14 Philipps St, between Kew Pl and aser St, Port of Spain, Trinidad, 623.1932, 3.1934; fax 623.3848) is open Monday through day during business hours. The visitors' center at **arco International Airport** (669.5196) is open daily til midnight.

bago's visitors' center (NIB Mall, Post Office and rdenside Sts, Scarborough 639.2125) is open nday through Friday during business hours; the ice at **Crown Point Airport** (639.0509) is open ly until the last scheduled flight arrives.

Phone Book

Ambulance	990
Directory Assistance	6411
Emergencies	999
Fire	990
Hospitals	
Trinidad	623.2951
Tobago	639.2551
Police	999
Post Office	625.2121

rinidad

1 Queen's Park Savannah Here's a good place to begin a walking tour of Port of Spain. A three-mile pathway encircles this magnificent park, known to locals as simply "the **Savannah**." Manicured lawns attract picnickers and joggers, while vendors sell coconut water, oyster cocktails, and other snacks. Formerly a sugar plantation called **Paradise Pasture,** today this public playground hosts everything from formal cricket matches to pick-up soccer games. ♦ Bounded by Queen's Park E and Maraval Rd, and Queen's Park W and Circular Rd, Port of Spain

2 Magnificent Seven Along the western edge of the **Savannah** stand seven colonial mansions that were built at the turn of the century by wealthy planters, each trying to outdo the others. The flamboyant structures range from the Scottish Gothic **Stollmeyer Castle** to the German Renaissance building that now houses **Queen's Royal College.** The Anglican bishop lives at **Haynes Court,** and rococo **Whitehall** is the office (and former home) of the prime minister. All are privately owned and are not open to the public. ♦ Maraval Rd (between Queen's Park W and Serpentine Rd), Port of Spain

3 Botanic Gardens Along the northern edge of the **Savannah,** 70 acres of a former sugar plantation were laid out as gardens in 1820 to showcase specimens from around the world. Exotica include Egypt's sacred lotus lilies and a holy peepul (the fig tree that shaded Buddha when he attained Nirvana). A lavish collection of tropical blooms ranges from orchids and frangipani to sausage trees and lipstick plants. The homes of the president and prime minister overlook the grounds. ♦ Free. Daily. Circular Rd (between St. Ann's and Lady Chancellor Rds), Port of Spain. 622.4221

Within Botanic Gardens:

Emperor Valley Zoo This zoo (named for the native blue butterflies) features excellent exhibits of wildlife and plants from both Trinidad and Tobago. ♦ Admission. Daily. 622.3530

4 Trinidad Hilton International $$$ In 1808, this lofty panoramic perch was the governor's mansion. Today it's the site of a 394-room hotel and the largest convention facilities on the island. The lobby is at the top, and guest rooms spill down the hillside. Accommodations are luxurious, particularly those on the three executive floors, where VIPs are coddled with perks that include pickup at the airport, daily newspapers, complimentary continental breakfast, and a special lounge with an open bar and hot hors d'oeuvres. Guests may dine at the hotel's two restaurants or at colorful poolside buffets, such as Monday night's Poolside Fiesta, which features local dishes and a steel band. There's dancing Friday and Saturday nights at the **Carnival Bar.** Amenities include two lighted tennis courts, two pools, and a two-level shopping arcade. ♦ Lady Young Rd (just east of St. Ann's Rd), Port of Spain. 624.3211, 800/HILTONS; fax 624.4485

5 National Museum and Art Gallery The exhibits cover a wide range of regional culture, from snakebite cures to paintings by Michel Jean Cazabon, Trinidad's great 19th-century artist. There are brilliant Carnival costumes, Amerindian relics, and ornate Spanish cannons, along with works by regional artists Francisco Cabral, Alfred Codallo, and John Newel Lewis. The 1923 structure is a perfect replica of the original museum, which was built in 1892 to commemorate the Jubilee of Queen Victoria and destroyed by fire in 1920. The museum is a bit worn and weary, but a fun ramble nonetheless. ♦ Free. Tu-Sa. 117 Frederick St (at Keate St), Port of Spain. 623.5941

6 Red House The Trinidad and Tobago Parliament meets in this red Neo-

Lamy St.

Emperor Valley Zoo

Botanic Gardens 3

Prada Rd.

Wild Flower Park

President's House

Serpentine Rd.

Circular Rd.

Whitehall

ST. CLAIR

Serpentine Rd.

Jackson Square

Flood St.

Lady Youn R.

Elizabeth St.

Alexandria St.

Gray St.

Hayes St.

2

Queen's Park East

King George V Park

Queen's Royal College

St. Claire Ave.

Queen's Park West

1 Queen's Park Savannah

Havelock St.

The Oval Cricket Ground

Sweet Briar Rd.

NEWTOWN

White St.

Siegert Square

Marli St.

Alcazar St.

Maraval Rd.

Picton St.

Woodford St.

Cipriani Blvd.

Charlott St.

Alberto St.

WOODBROOK

Rosalino St.

Luci St.

Alfredo St.

Carlos St.

Murray St.

Rust St.

Herbert St.

Warner St.

Queen's Park West

Memori Park

Albion St.

Dere St.

Keate St.

5

Tranquillity

Melville La.

Stranmore Ave.

Gordon St.

Tragarite Rd.

Victoria Ave.

Borde St.

Dundonald St.

New St.

Lord Harris Square

Oxford St.

Robert St.

Kitchener St.

Adam Smith Square

Ariapita Ave.

14

13

French St.

Buller St.

Gatacre St.

12

Fitt St.

Cornelio St.

Methuen St.

Cloville St.

Lapeyrouse Cemetery

Phillips St.

Fraser St.

Kew Pl.

St. Vincent St.

Abercromby St.

Pembroke St.

Frederick St.

Henry St.

McDonald St.

Park St.

Wrightson Rd.

Dock Area

Flament St.

Stone St.

Scott Busche St.

Victoria Square

Richmond St.

Edward St.

Duke St.

Knox St.

6

Woodford Square

Dock Rd.

Charles St.

Hart St.

7

Sackville St.

8

9   10

London St.

11

Ajax St.

Queen St.

Gulf of Paria

Independence Sq.

Chacon St.

South Quay

N

Beetham Hwy.

km

mi

1/4

1/2

1/8

1/4

Queen's Wharf

Renaissance building overlooking Woodford Square; the plaza is the island venue for protests and rallies and a favorite podium for orators. The building is not open to the public. ◆ Abercromby St (between Hart and Knox Sts), Port of Spain. 622.1131

7 Holy Trinity Cathedral Look inside this lovely Gothic church, built in 1823, to see statues honoring some of the islands' more prominent (and now deceased) citizens. Also note the choir stalls and the intricate carvings on the altar. ◆ Abercromby and Hart Sts, Port of Spain. 623.7217

8 Stecher's Regional handicrafts, as well as a staggering inventory of duty-free crystal, china, watches, jewelry, and other imported luxuries are offered at the main branch of this shop (there are seven on Trinidad). Famous names include Wedgwood, Waterford, and Lladró. Purchases may be delivered to the airport. ◆ M-Sa. 27 Frederick St (between Queen and Hart Sts), Port of Spain. 623.5912. Also at: numerous other locations throughout Trinidad, and 45 Carrington St, Scarborough, Tobago. 639.2377

9 Y. de Lima This is the main branch of a chain that has some 15 outlets islandwide. High-quality gold and silver jewelry, duty-free cameras, watches, and a wide selection of crystal and china are sold. ◆ M-Sa. 83 Queen St (between Frederick and Abercromby Sts), Port of Spain. 623.1364. Also at: numerous other locations throughout Trinidad

10 People's Mall There's a lively carnival atmosphere at this colorful maze of tiny stalls and shops, offering a wide selection of crafts, jewelry, belts, and clothing. Even if you're not in the mood to buy, take a walk through. ◆ M-Sa. Queen St (between Henry and Frederick Sts). No phone

11 Holiday Inn $$ A dependable choice in the heart of the city's business and commercial section, this property offers 225 comfortable, air-conditioned rooms. Amenities include a large pool, two all-weather tennis courts, a restaurant (see below), and nightly entertainment. ◆ Wrightson Rd (between Ajax and London Sts), Port of Spain. 625.3361, 800/HOLIDAY; fax 625.4166

Within the Holiday Inn:

La Ronde ★★$$$ The lights of the mountains and Port of Spain provide a spectacular backdrop for this revolving rooftop restaurant. The menu features seafood crepes, fish platters, and crab backs. Beef eaters can opt for panfried or grilled steak with a variety of sauces. ◆ Steak/Seafood ◆ Tu-Sa dinner. Reservations recommended. 625.3361

12 Mas Camp Pub One of Trinidad's favorite *liming* locations, this nightspot features live music, drinks, and lots of local color. The music ranges from steel band to ballroom—check in advance to see what's in store for the evening. ◆ W-Su 8PM-3AM. French St and Ariapita Ave. 623.3745

13 Le Chateau De Poisson ★★$$ Oyster cocktails, fresh lobster, baked sea snails, and crab backs are specialties at this charming restaurant in an 1899 gingerbread cottage. Dine outdoors on the porch amid a garden of tropical plants, or indoors under ceiling fans and stained-glass windows. ◆ Caribbean/Seafood ◆ M-F lunch and dinner; Sa dinner. Reservations recommended. 38 Ariapita Ave (at Cornelio St), Port of Spain. 622.6087

14 Il Colosseo ★★★$$ Arched ceilings, Roman columns, and soft candlelight create an elegant ambience in which to enjoy classic Italian cuisine created by chef Angelo Cofone. Try the fried calamari, wild mushroom ravioli, charcoal-grilled shrimp wrapped in bacon, or steak in cream brandy sauce. The triple-layer chocolate cake is rich and decadent. ◆ Italian/Seafood ◆ M-F lunch and dinner; Sa dinner. Reservations recommended. 47 Ariapita Ave (at Fitt St), Port of Spain. 623.3654

15 Kapok $$ Set in an upscale residential neighborhood, this hotel is conveniently located near **Queen's Park Savannah**, the zoo, and the **Botanic Gardens** (see page 305). It has 95 comfortable guest rooms, a rooftop Chinese/Polynesian restaurant (see below), an outdoor pool, an air-conditioned exercise room, and a 24-hour computer center. Public transport stops just outside. ◆ 16-18 Cotton Hill (at Saddle Rd), Port of Spain. 622.5765, 800/344.1212; fax 622.9677

Within the Kapok:

Tiki Village ★★$$ A pleasant eighth-floor restaurant features panoramic views of neighborhood homes and the Gulf of Paria. The menu is extensive, including shark's fin soup, sesame fish, South Sea curried shrimp, garlic lobster, steak samoa, and pimento chicken. ◆ Chinese/Polynesian ◆ M-F lunch and dinner; Sa-Su dim sum and dinner. Reservations recommended. 622.5765

Come Celebrate Carnival!

From New Orleans to Venice, Catholic communities around the world celebrate Carnival (from the Latin *carnivale*—"farewell to flesh")—their last chance for an all-out celebration before the bell tolls on Ash Wednesday, ringing in 45 somber days of Lent. This raucous season of parades, balls, and assorted bacchanals can last a few days or a few weeks, and the warm Caribbean islands are the perfect place for taking the festivities to the streets.

Trinidad is the center ring of the circus, a two-day explosion of color, music, and unbridled excess. Marching groups parade through the streets in dazzling plumed and sequined costumes; everyone, including spectators, is part of the show. Bands and masqueraders begin their preparations a year in advance (a good time for visitors to make hotel reservations), and **Port of Spain** is alive with concerts, balls, and other festivities from early January through Ash Wednesday in February or early March.

While **Trinidad** has the biggest celebration, **Carriacou** definitely holds the record for the strangest. In this tiny offshore dependency of **Grenada,** *paywos* dressed in well-padded costumes (long socks, lace petticoat, cloak lined with cement bags, and protective headdress) roam the streets. Each man carries a whip. When two meet up, they face off by reciting Shakespeare extemporaneously. If either errs, the other deals him loud wallops for his mistakes.

Meanwhile, masqueraders on **St. Lucia** dance to the annual battle of the calypso bands. **Dominica** comes alive with street "jump-ups" (parades of floats, bands, and dancers) and West African pageantry. **Puerto Rico**'s most vibrant display is in the city of **Ponce,** famous for its brightly painted horned masks.

On **Curaçao** the fun begins with a competition to select the year's best *tumba* (road march song), ushering in a few weeks of islandwide parties and concerts. It ends with the Farewell Grand Parade on Shrove Tuesday, when *Rey Momo* (the spirit of Carnival) is burned in effigy. Similar celebrations are held on **Bonaire** and **Aruba.** On **Jamaica,** Carnival features calypso and reggae bands, soca parties, street dancing, and road marches of vibrantly costumed locals, while on **St. Thomas** Carnival is a wild extravaganza of street music, "jump-ups" and parading stilt walkers—"Mocko Jumbies"—that tower 20 feet overhead.

Right about the time other Carnival revelers are filing into church to have their repentant foreheads daubed with ashes, the residents of **Martinique** and **Guadeloupe** are just warming up for the final and most frenzied day of their celebration. During *La Fête des Diablesses* (the Festival of the She-Devils) on Ash Wednesday, the streets are crowded with hundreds of masked and costumed demons. Only black and white are allowed—dark faces are smeared with pale ash, bodies are painted with phosphorescent skeletons, and huge African masks tower above the marchers. Similar, but much smaller, processions wind through **St-Barthélemy** and **St-Martin.**

Throughout the French West Indies, local papers publish death notices for *Vaval* (King Carnival), aka *Bois-Bois*. Work continues on his funeral pyre throughout the day and the street dances grow ever wilder as the fire burns down. When his coffin is finally buried at midnight, the crowds chant "*Au revoir Bois-Bois, adieu Vaval!*" and "*Vaval, pas quitte nous!*" (Carnival, don't leave us!)

That's it—until three weeks later, when everyone suits up and parades again for *Mi-Carême*, a sort of mid-Lenten break. Following 24 hours of serious backsliding, it's back to Lenten strictures. And then the spirit of Carnival is truly laid to rest for another year.

Meiling One of the top names in local design, owner Meiling Esau is known for her sophisticated women's clothing made with natural fabric (cotton and linen) in island pastels. ◆ M-Sa. 628.6205

16 Long Circular Mall Comfortably air-conditioned, this friendly, five-level mall offers specialty shops and restaurants. ◆ M-Sa. Long Circular Rd, St. James. 622.4925

Within Long Circular Mall:

El Alligator Luggage, handbags, belts, wallets, 24-karat gold necklaces in pre-Columbian designs, and small accessories (including a few alligator products) are featured at this boutique. ◆ M-Sa. 622.7817

Singho Restaurant ★★★$$ Chicken corn chowder, pepper shrimp, and lemon chicken are standouts at this attractive restaurant, popular with neighborhood residents. Friendly service and fine cooking make for an enjoyable dining experience. There's a Wednesday night buffet and occasional live entertainment. ◆ Chinese ◆ Daily lunch and dinner. Reservations recommended for dinner. 628.2077

Olayinka Here's a diverse and colorful collection of paintings, sculpture, tapestry, brass, and paper artwork from Africa, South America, and the Caribbean. ◆ M-Sa. 628.2276

17 Linda's Bakery Excellent breads and cakes are baked daily, using coconut, papaya, cassava, and other exotic ingredients. Trinidadians swear it's the best bakery on the island. ◆ M-Sa. 23 Saddle Rd, Maraval. 622.6475. Also at: numerous other locations throughout Trinidad

17 Monique's Guest House $ If you want to stay in an authentic Trinidadian inn, try this charming spot close to **St. Andrew's Golf Club** (see below) and other attractions. The 19 spacious and immaculate rooms have air-conditioning and cable TV; 1 accommodates guests with disabilities. Some rooms have kitchenettes. Breakfast and dinner are available. ◆ 114 Saddle Rd, Maraval. 628.3334; fax 622.3232

18 St. Andrew's Golf Club This 18-hole championship golf course is generally acknowledged to be the best tee-off spot on Trinidad. Temporary memberships are available to visitors, and the club is featured in several hotel packages. ◆ Fee. M-Sa. Golf Dr, Maraval. 629.2314

19 The Normandie $$ This 1920s-era hotel, owned by Anna and Fred Chin Lee, features 12 rooms with sleeping lofts and 41 standard rooms; all are air-conditioned and decorated in light wood. Some overlook a garden courtyard, others a swimming pool. The complex also features an eclectic group of shops offering everything from stylish clothes to paper goods. ◆ 10 Nook Ave, St. Ann's. 624.1181, 800/235.6510; fax 624.0108

19 The Batique Artist Althea Bastien invites batik lovers to browse the intimate shop in the garden of her lovely home. She batiks cotton and silk fabrics that are then sewn into one-of-a-kind island fashions. Choose from a colorful array of men's and women's clothing, beachwear, pillows, tote bags, and tablecloths. Bastien's work is also exhibited at local galleries. ◆ Call for shop hours and directions. 43 Sydenham Ave, St. Ann's. 624.3274

20 Maracas Bay One of Trinidad's most popular beaches is about 12 miles north of Port of Spain. Hugged by mountains, it has palm-shaded white sand, crystalline water, changing facilities, and snack bars. The drive from the capital is an attraction in itself—the road crosses the Saddle (a pass that divides the Santa Cruz and Maraval Valleys), climbs up to the northern mountain range, then heads down to the shoreline. The view from 1,000 feet up takes in a 100-mile sweep from Tobago to Venezuela. ◆ North Coast Rd

On Maracas Bay:

Maracas Bay Hotel $$ Escape from TV, radio, clocks, and telephones at Trinidad's only beach hotel. A quiet 2-story property with 40 no-frills rooms, this is a splendid spot for swimming, fishing, sunning, and walking on the beach. Rooms are air-conditioned, with private balconies overlooking Maracas Bay beach. The hotel's open-air dining room serves delicious fresh fruit, vegetables, fish, chicken, and beef; meals are included in the room rate. The dining room is also open to nonguests by reservation only. Golf, bird watching, horseback riding, and hiking are all nearby. ◆ 669.1914, 669.1643; fax 623.1444

The average temperature of the waters of the Caribbean are 75 degrees F.

Bartlett Deep, in Cayman Trench between Jamaica and Grand Cayman, is the Caribbean's deepest point; it is approximately 25,197 feet below sea level.

21 Las Cuevas Beach Just up North Coast Road from Maracas Bay, this beautiful beach has changing rooms, a snack bar, a lifeguard, and other signs of civilization. If you want privacy (and can live without showers or changing rooms) continue a few miles to **Blanchisseuse Beach.** ◆ North Coast Rd

22 Asa Wright Nature Centre, Spring Hill Estate One of the most beautiful retreats in the Caribbean is set in a northern mountain range just 24 miles from Port of Spain, but light-years from the cosmopolitan capital in atmosphere. Nature lovers are treated to glimpses of tufted coquettes, squirrel cuckoos, toucans, and hummingbirds; some 170 bird species live here. Overnight guests at the lodge (see below) can tour **Dunston Cave** to see the resident colony of guacharo, a nocturnal oilbird, and can also sign up for sunset and sunrise hikes. Make arrangements at least 2 days in advance (only 40 visitors are admitted to the nature center at a time), wear comfortable hiking clothes (long pants and sneakers or hiking boots), and bring insect repellent. ◆ Admission. Daily. Reservations required. Arima Blanchisseuse Rd (between Arima and Blanchisseuse). 667.4655

Within Asa Wright Nature Centre:

Asa Wright Nature Centre and Lodge $ Bird-watchers and naturalists will be comfortable at this congenial 24-room property. Some of the rooms are rather basic; for high ceilings and charm, request **Number 1** or **2.** Rates include all meals, afternoon tea (a treat in itself), and rum punch each evening. Day-trippers to the nature center are welcome to stop by the lodge for lunch, dinner, or afternoon tea on the scenic terrace. ◆ 667.4655, 800/426.7781; fax 667.4540

23 Lopinot Historical Complex Once home to a French count, the 19th-century house and gardens are now a plantation museum with period furnishings, pottery, and artifacts. The complex also features a cocoa-drying house, a picturesque Anglican church, and a pleasant park. The museum frequently hosts concerts of *parang* (rustic Spanish-style music), especially at Christmastime. If you want more information than a self-guided tour provides, call the tourist board (623.1932, 623.1934) or the **Forestry Division** (622.3217) for information about guided tours. ◆ Free. Daily. Lopinot Rd (north of Eastern Main Rd)

Tobago is thought to have been the setting of Daniel Defoe's *Robinson Crusoe*.

The local sugar industry was once so prosperous that "rich as a Tobago planter" became a popular expression.

24 Pax Guest House $ Under the devoted care of Gerard and Oda Ramsawak, Trinidad's oldest guest house is a peaceful oasis set high among 600 acres of rain forest and pine plantation on Mount St. Benedict. Airy verandas with rocking chairs overlook Port of Spain below, and hiking trails around the house are noisy habitats for hummingbirds, warblers, and flycatcher The 18 guest rooms, some furnished with European antiques, are all cozy, and the 1916 house is surrounded by flowers and exotic plants and has a delightful outdoor tea garden. The dining room serves deliciou homemade meals (ask Oda for a slice of her fabulous cake). Guests here have included bird-watchers, naturalists, international diplomats, those seeking a spiritual retreat, and even the Dalai Lama. Smoking is prohibited in the guest rooms. ◆ Mount St. Benedict, Tunapuna. 662.4084 fax 662.4084

25 The City of Grand Bazaar Opened in 199 this is the eastern Caribbean's largest shopping center. On 11.5 acres just 20 minutes east of Port of Spain, the low-rise til roof mall has a Neo-Colonial Spanish design and a Middle Eastern theme. More than 80 shops sell clothing, housewares, cards, books, gifts, groceries, liquor, leather goods, cosmetics, and travel services. Eateries vary from fine Indian and Italian restaurants to fas food outlets to Chinese take-out spots. Water fountains, playgrounds, and live entertain-ment make this a popular hangout for local families, especially on weekends. ◆ M-Sa; supermarket also open Su 2-7PM. Uriah Butler and Solomon Hochoy Hwys, Valsayn. 662.2282, 662.2007

Within The City of Grand Bazaar:

Apsara ★★★$ Terra-cotta walls decorate with beaded dolls from Rajastan, India, colorful upholstered banquettes, and soft sita music are a soothing backdrop for the delicious food at Trinidad's only formal restaurant serving authentic Indian cuisine. The menu provides a vast array of choices. Recommended dishes include tandoori lobster, beef curry, chicken biryani, and stuffed paratha. Served in tiny copper woks o coal warmers, the spicy fare stays hot throughout your meal. Service is attentive an the wait staff looks great in Indian kurther pyjamas and shalwar kamis. ◆ Indian ◆ M-Sa lunch and dinner. Reservations recommended. 662.1013

26 Caroni Bird Sanctuary Here you'll see one of Trinidad's most spectacular sights: Hundreds of blood-red scarlet ibis swooping into nesting grounds on the mangrove islands. Visitors from around the world come to witness this phenomenon from boats that tour the waterways daily at 4PM. The 450-acre sanctuary is about 7 miles southeast of Port of Spain; **Caroni Tours** (645.1305) offers 4-hour excursions. ♦ Admission. Daily. Reservations required. Gulf of Paria (southeast of Port of Spain). No phone

27 Wildfowl Trust Nature trails lead through the forest, past flowering lotus and artificial lakes, at this protected breeding ground for endangered waterfowl. An educational center showcases Amerindian relics and Tobago burial artifacts. The 60-acre preserve, located on the Trintoc oil-refinery property, is operated by a volunteer-staffed nonprofit organization. ♦ Admission. Daily. Reservations required. Pointe-à-Pierre. 637.5145, 662.4040

28 Pitch Lake Walk on the surface of the world's largest asphalt deposit, discovered in 1595 by Sir Walter Raleigh, who used it to caulk his ships. The lake covers 114 acres and is 250 feet deep in the middle. The crude oil, or bitumen, seeps through a fault line in the sandstone to produce a self-replenishing supply that is shipped worldwide at the rate of 300 tons a day. Objects sink and reappear years later, as the deposits are constantly (though imperceptibly) swirling. ♦ Admission. Daily. Just southwest of La Brea. 648.7697

Tobago

29 Botanic Gardens Amble through this 17-acre tropical paradise of trees, shrubs, and flowers. It's a spectacular collection of tropical plants in a serene and safe setting. ♦ Free. Daily. Claude Noel Hwy (between Northside and Wilson Rds), Scarborough. 639.3421 ext 273

29 Blue Crab ★$$ Dine on callaloo, curried goat, crab backs, and conch chowder on a veranda overlooking Rockly Bay. Homemade tropical ice cream and fruit wine are also served. ♦ Creole/Seafood ♦ M-F lunch; call ahead to see if dinner is being served. Reservations required by noon for dinner. Main and Robinson Sts, Scarborough. 639.2737

30 Fort King George Drive or walk to this historic landmark perched 430 feet above Scarborough. To best enjoy your visit, take a free tour with **Department of Tourism** guides, who recount how these battlements changed hands numerous times during colonial days. The cannon and larger structures have been restored; the **Military Hospital,** built in 1777, is now a **Fine Arts Center** exhibiting paintings, photos, and crafts from around the world. Browse the **Craft Market** for gifts. The views at sunset are glorious. ♦ Free. Daily. Bournes Rd (east of Scarborough). 639.3970

Within Fort King George:

Tobago Museum Pottery shards and ancient shells that date back to Amerindian

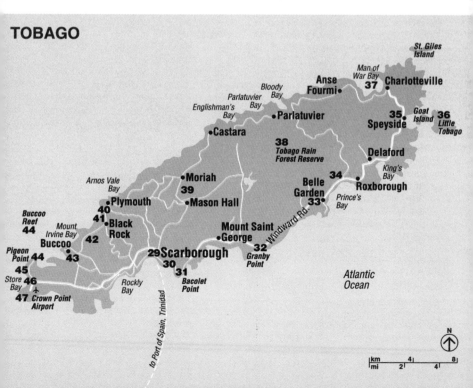

TOBAGO

times are displayed at this small museum, which also features exhibits on slavery and military relics. ♦ Admission. M-F. Barrack Guard House. 639.3970

31 Rouselle's ★★★$$ Located in a charming house decorated with island prints, this is one of Tobago's longtime favorite restaurants. Owner Bobbie Evans is a delightful hostess, greeting guests personally. Try callaloo soup, fresh lobster with mushrooms, and mango pie with homemade ice cream. Dine indoors or out on the veranda. ♦ Seafood/Caribbean ♦ Daily dinner. Reservations recommended. Old Windward Rd, Bacolet. 639.4738

31 Old Donkey Cart House $ Long known for its restaurant (see below), this 100-year-old French colonial home overlooking the beach has 11 guest suites. Rooms are modern, with refrigerators, TV sets, and telephones; some have stocked mini-bars and air-conditioning. There is also a large pool. The hotel is a good bargain, but guests may want to rent a car to get to the beaches and nature reserves. ♦ 73 Bacolet St, Bacolet. 639.3551; fax 639.6124

Within the Old Donkey Cart House:

Old Donkey Cart House Restaurant ★★ $$ Local seafood and imported meats and cheeses are complemented by a fine selection of German wines. Dine alfresco in the garden or indoors, where you'll still feel like you're under the sky—starlike lights illuminate the ceiling. ♦ Caribbean/Continental ♦ Daily dinner. Breakfast and lunch are served several days a week, call ahead for the schedule. Reservations recommended weekends and winter months. 639.3551

31 The Cotton House Shop owners Connie and Jimmy Young and a talented staff of local artists create an astonishing array of beautiful batik fabrics that are fashioned into the sundresses, bathing suits, sport shirts, and wall hangings sold here. The boutique is housed in what was originally Tobago's first hotel. Shoppers are invited to a free batik lesson and may take home their own creations. ♦ M-F; Sa 8AM-noon. Old Windward Rd, Bacolet. 639.2727, 639.2150

32 First Historical Café/Bar ★$ This funky West Indian–style cafe perched on a cliff's edge has breathtaking views of the Atlantic Ocean. Inside, walls are papered with handwritten posters detailing Trinidad's colorful history. The rest of the decor is colorful as well, with fruit-patterned tablecloths and green and gold bamboo. Enjoy a burger, salad, hot dog, or fruit plate served by proprietor Kenneth Washington or his daughter Sandra. ♦ American ♦ Daily breakfast, lunch, and dinner. Windward Rd (Mile 8), Studley Park. 660.2233

33 Richmond Great House $$ Serenity has always been the main attraction at one of Tobago's oldest great houses. Surrounded by tropical gardens and a working cocoa plantation, accommodations consist of 12 generous-size rooms with panoramic views of the countryside. Five rooms are in the great house, seven in a newer addition; none has air-conditioning, but some have ceiling fans. Ask for room **Number 2** in the old house, which has a gigantic bay window that seems to extend right into the surrounding forest. Public areas are adorned with African art from the collection of owner Hollis R. Lynch, a professor of African history at New York City's Columbia University. A pool and the good home cooking served at **Aburi Restaurant** (also open to nonguests) add to the appeal of this charming find. ♦ Belle Garden. 660.4467; fax 660.4467

34 Argyll Waterfall An easy 1.5-mile hike through rain forest ends at a rushing waterfall, with plenty of wildlife and natural beauty to be enjoyed along the way. Walk among lemon, papaya, mango, and bamboo trees and keep an eye out for great black hawks, humming-birds, and whistling frogs. Government-trained guides lead the way; ask for Lanville Toppin, who is especially knowledgeable. ♦ Admission. Roxborough. No phone

35 Speyside This pretty fishing village is a good spot for Atlantic views and a scenic drive along Windward Road, but the beaches are much better at Mount Irvine and Bacolet Bay. ♦ East coast

At Speyside:

Jemma's Sea View Kitchen/ Tree House ★★$$ Enjoy a meal in a dining room set in a centuries-old almond tree, soothed by cooling breezes and crashing surf. (The restaurant

Richmond Great House

building is next to the tree, and the veranda extends into the branches.) Jemma Sealey and her daughter Sherrene serve up tasty Caribbean cuisine in this unique setting. Try broiled kingfish, spicy shrimp, tanya (a root vegetable) fritters, and thirst-quenching fruit punch. ♦ Caribbean ♦ M-Th, Su breakfast, lunch, afternoon tea, and dinner; F breakfast, lunch, and afternoon tea. Reservations recommended. Speyside Main Rd. 660.4066

Blue Waters Inn $$ Divers love this beachside hideaway on the island's remote eastern edge, where snorkeling and windsurfing are superb. All 38 rooms have ocean views; some have air-conditioning and kitchens. There's an on-site dive facility, a tennis court, a restaurant, and a bar that's open almost around the clock (11AM-7AM). Scuba packages and meal plans are available. ♦ Batteaux Bay. 660.4341, 800.742.4276; fax 660.5195

Within Blue Waters Inn:

AquaMarine Dive Ltd. This full-service dive shop offers **PADI** instruction and scuba and snorkeling trips. Night dives are available as well. ♦ Daily. 660.4341, 660.4077; fax 639.4416

Speyside Inn $$ Everybody gets a good view at this rustic spot, where each of the nine rooms has its own private balcony and windows overlooking the sea.

Accommodations include two self-contained cabins with kitchens and wide verandahs. Breakfast is included in the rate. ♦ Windward Rd. 660.4852; fax 660.4852

Manta Lodge $$ From December through June giant manta rays, fondly called "Tobago taxis," frequent dive sites just minutes from this attractive 22-room lodge. Friendly service, comfortable rooms, and an on-site dive shop make this a good spot for underwater adventures. The pool set in a flower garden and fresh local cuisine add to the pleasant experience. ♦ Windward Rd. 660.5268, 800.544.7631; fax 660.5030

36 Bird of Paradise Sanctuary Bird-watchers flock to Tobago to explore this celebrated sanctuary on the offshore islet of Little Tobago. The 450-acre preserve is home to red-billed tropic birds, red-footed boobies, audubon shearwaters, and many other exotic species. The best viewing times are early morning and late afternoon. The **Blue Waters Inn** and the **Speyside Inn** (see above) run boats out to the islet for a fee. ♦ Free. Daily. Little Tobago. No phone

37 Man of War Bay A long sandy beach lines the south shore of the bay, one of the Caribbean's greatest natural harbors. After sunning and swimming, plan a picnic at the government-owned "rest house"—a covered pavilion on the beach. ♦ East end

On Man of War Bay:

Charlotteville Pigeon Peak, Tobago's highest point (1,890 feet), serves as the backdrop for this quaint and lovely fishing village, which rises up a hillside.

38 Tobago Rain Forest Reserve The oldest rain-forest preserve in the western hemisphere encompasses 14,000 acres that have been protected since April 1765. The

313

lush jungle, where towering trees are a tangle of hanging vines and exotic blooms, clings to the mountainous spine of the island's eastern half. Great blue herons and snowy egrets forage in the numerous wetland areas. Hikes through the preserve can be arranged with tour operators, including **Ansyl Tours** (Wilson Rd, Scarborough, 639.3865), **Good Time Tours** (Scarborough Port, 639.6816), and **Pioneer Journeys** (Charlotteville, 660.4327). Exploring the reserve without a guide is not recommended as the trails are not clearly marked and it's easy to get lost. ♦ Free. Daily. Parlatuvier Rd (between Roxborough and Bloody Bay)

39 Witch's Grave According to local legend, here lie the remains of Gang Gang Sara, a witch who flew to this mountain village from Africa several hundred years ago. She was unable to make the return trip (so the story goes) because she ate salt on the island—and eating or even seeing salt impairs witches' flying powers. ♦ Golden La (between Mason Hall and Moriah)

40 Mystery Tombstone "A mother without knowing it, and a wife without letting her husband know it, except by her kind indulgence to him" is the inscription on Betty Stiven's tombstone. The 18th-century marker's cryptic message has long mystified islanders and visitors. ♦ Plymouth

40 Cocrico Inn $$ A 5-minute walk from the beach, this pleasant motel-style property offers 16 rooms, a pool, and good food (see below) in the heart of Plymouth village. Paintings by local artist Anthony Lewis add style to the decor. ♦ Plymouth. 639.2961, 800/223.9815; fax 639.2014

Within Cocrico Inn:

Cocrico Inn Restaurant ★★$$
Authentic Tobagonian cuisine is served in this popular and picturesque dining room. The kitchen makes good use of local seafood. ♦ Caribbean ♦ Daily lunch and dinner. Reservations recommended. 639.2961

41 Great Courland Bay and Stone Haven Bay Local fishers cast their nets from the unspoiled sands that stretch along these two adjoining coves, where giant sea turtles lumber ashore during the nesting season (March through August). Though seas can be rough, this is a good destination for swimming and snorkeling. A few beachfront hotels offer water sports, restaurants, and nightly "turtle watches" in season. ♦ Grafton Rd (southwest of Plymouth)

At Stone Haven Bay:

Plantation Beach Villas $$$$ Nestled in a hillside are six two-story luxury villas, each with three air-conditioned bedrooms, fully equipped kitchens (you can arrange for your own cook), and sweeping verandas. In the true spirit of escape, there are no telephones or TV sets in the villas, but a pool and bar are on the premises. The resort's grounds are alive with various species of tropical birds and the nearby beach is a good spot for watching leatherback turtles nest from March through August. A three-day minimum stay is required; long-term rentals are available. ♦ 639.9377; fax 639.0455

41 Grafton Beach Resort $$$ Located right on the beach, this 3-story hotel is conveniently close to the 18-hole **Mount Irvine Golf Club** (see below). The complex offers 112 air-conditioned rooms, 2 squash courts, 2 restaurants, nightly entertainment, a pool with swim-up bar, and tennis nearby. For a two-hour rain-forest walk, ask the hotel concierge to introduce you to Curtis James, "The Parrot Man," who lives nearby in Bloody Bay Village. ♦ Grafton Rd, Black Rock. 639.0191, 800/223.6510; fax 639.0030

Within Grafton Beach Resort:

Tobago Dive Experience Headed by Sean Robinson and Derek Chung, this full-service dive shop offers **NAUI** and **PADI** certification courses, review courses, and dive and snorkeling trips. Equipment is available for rent. ♦ Daily. 639.0191

41 Le Grand Courlan $$$$ This plush modern 78-room hotel (under the same management as the adjacent **Grafton Beach Resort**) gives guests plenty of creature comforts. The spacious rooms have private balconies with ocean views, mini-bars, safes, cable television, and telephones. Eight units have outdoor hot tubs. Dine at the open-air seaside restaurant, **Pinnacle** (see below), swim laps in the beautiful pool with a swim-up bar, play on two lighted tennis courts, hit a few at the indoor squash court, or work out at the fully equipped gym. The spa offers facials, massage, and beauty services. The **Mount Irvine Golf Club** (see below) is nearby. ♦ Grafton Rd, Black Rock. 639.9667; fax 639.9292

Within Le Grand Courlan:

Pinnacle ★★$$$$ Continental and West Indian fare are featured at this pleasant restaurant overlooking the sea. Menu highlights include loin of lamb, steaks, seafood, and pasta with smoked chicken and duck. ♦ Continental/West Indian ♦ Daily breakfast, lunch, dinner. 639.0191

42 **Mount Irvine Bay Hotel and Golf Club**

$$$ A spectacular golf course is the centerpiece of this somewhat faded resort where guests are treated to discounts on greens fees and use of the clubhouse. Choose either a cottage with ocean or fairway views or a standard hotel room overlooking the attractive swimming pool; there are 105 units in all. Besides golf, amenities include two lighted tennis courts, four restaurants (including the **Sugar Mill,** below), and a beach with a water-sports center. Formerly part of an 18th-century sugar plantation, the property boasts tropical gardens and spacious lawns. ♦ Grafton Rd (southwest of Black Rock). 639.8871, 800/44UTELL, 800/221.1294; fax 639.8800

Within the Mount Irvine Bay Hotel and Golf Club:

Sugar Mill ★★$$ Set in a 200-year-old sugar mill, this casual eatery offers a buffet featuring local seafood and Creole dishes as well as à la carte selections. ♦ Seafood/Creole ♦ Daily breakfast, lunch, and dinner. Reservations recommended. 639.8871

Mount Irvine Golf Club One of the greatest courses in the West Indies, this 18-hole championship layout overlooks Tobago's famous Buccoo Reef. The palm-shaded fairways trace the Caribbean coastline (beware of falling coconuts), and the infamous Number 9 hole has raised more than a few scores (and tempers). A pro-am championship tournament is held here the third and fourth weeks of January. ♦ Fee. Daily. 639.8871

43 **Papillon** ★★★$$$ A longtime island fixture, Jakob Straessle's restaurant (the dining room of the 18-room **Old Grange Inn**) boasts one of the largest menus in Tobago, with entrées ranging from *boeuf Chez Jacques* (a French-style cubed steak) to baby shark marinated in lime and rum. This is the birthplace of many dishes that have become local mainstays—lobster crepes, seafood casserole with ginger wine, and conch stewed in coconut and rum. ♦ French/Seafood ♦ M-Sa lunch and dinner; Su dinner. Reservations recommended. Buccoo Crossing, Buccoo. 639.0275

Getting Your Feet Wet in Trinidad and Tobago

There's so much more to do in the islands beyond the beach. Here are a few outfits that can set you afloat:

Boating

Kalina Cats Scarborough, Tobago. 639.6304

Loafer Store Bay, Tobago. 639.7312

Sail with Chloe Mount Irvine Bay, Tobago. 639.2449

Trinidad & Tobago Yacht Club Bayshore, Trinidad. 633.7420

Snorkeling and Scuba Diving

AquaMarine Dive Ltd. Blue Waters Inn, Batteaux Bay, Speyside, Tobago. 660.4341, 660.4077

Tobago Dive Experience Manta Lodge, Windward Rd, Speyside, Tobago. 660.5268, 800/544.7631; Grafton Beach Resort, Grafton Rd, Black Rock, Tobago, 639.0191

Winston Nanan, Caroni Tours Port of Spain, Trinidad. 645.1305

Sportfishing

David Rooks Nature Tours Scarborough, Tobago. 639.4276

Winston Nanan, Caroni Tours Port of Spain, Trinidad. 645.1305

Windsurfing

Grafton Beach Resort Grafton Rd, Black Rock, Tobago. 639.0191, 800/223.6510

Mount Irvine Bay Hotel Grafton Rd (southwest of Black Rock), Tobago. 639.8871, 800/44UTELL, 800/221.1294

Rex Turtle Beach Hotel Grafton Rd, Black Rock, Tobago. 639.2851

Tips for Turtle Watchers

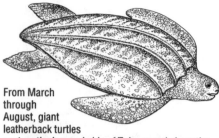

From March through August, giant leatherback turtles nest on the leeward side of Tobago and along the east coast of Trinidad. The largest species of marine turtle, usually weighing around 1,000 pounds (the largest on record weighed over a ton), these huge creatures only come to land during the reproductive season. The female turtles lumber up from the surf and use their flippers to dig nests in the sand just above the high water mark. Leatherback turtles lay eggs 4 or 5 times each season, depositing up to 125 white eggs on each trip. After an incubation period that ranges from 50 to 78 days, the little hatchlings emerge and make a mad dash for the sea.

The best time to view the egg-laying is from 7PM to 5AM, and the most accessible nesting grounds are on the Tobago beaches at **Stone Haven Bay** and **Great Courland Bay**. The **Grafton Beach Resort** (Grafton Rd, Black Rock, 639.0191), **Rex Turtle Beach Hotel** (Grafton Rd, Black Rock, 639.2851), and **Plantation Beach Villas** (Stone Haven Bay, Grafton Rd, Black Rock, 639.9377) all have nightly turtle watches in season.

Keep in mind that only 60 percent of the eggs will hatch, and, of those, only 1 or 2 turtles will ever reach maturity and return to make nests of their own. If you want to help them beat the odds, follow these important guidelines:

 Keep noise down—speak softly and turn off all radios.

 When turtles emerge from the sea, be very still. They will turn back if disturbed.

 Use minimal lighting and never shine flashlights at the turtles or their nests. Turn off all lights when the turtles are returning to the sea.

 Keep your distance (at least 15 yards) until the nest is prepared and the laying process has begun. This is the only time to take photographs; approach quietly and keep lights low.

 Never attempt to touch or ride the mother turtles. Be careful not to cave in the sides of the nest, and do not handle the eggs or the hatchlings.

43 La Tartaruga
★★★$$ Homemade pasta and seafood are the specialties in this homey dining room right across from the beach. The owner, Gabriele de Gaetano, prepares all dishes to order using only the freshest ingredients. Appetizers include fish pâté, seafood soup, focaccia, and pizza. Tagliatelle is made daily and served with a variety of sauces, and the 14-layer lasagna (vegetarian or with meat) is truly remarkable. The risotto with saffron and porcini mushrooms is another excellent choice, as is the catch of the day, served in wine sauce with capers or sage. Desserts range from Italian cheesecake to *affogato al caffè* (ice cream "drowned" in espresso). ♦ Italian/Seafood ♦ Tu-Sa dinner; lunch for groups available by arrangement. Reservations recommended. Buccoo Bay. 639.0940

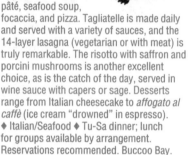

44 Buccoo Reef Yellow angelfish, purple damsels, and blue parrot fish thrive at this spectacular protected marine park. Daily two-and-a-half-hour glass-bottom boat tours (639.8519) include snorkeling at the reef, a swim in the **Nylon Pool** (a natural shallow area in the lagoon), and a visit to the brilliant **Coral Gardens**. The boats pick up passengers at the beach, Buccoo Point, and Store Bay. Each year during the last two weeks in July, the Tobago Heritage Festival is held on the dry-land portion of the park at Pigeon Point. It's a celebration of local history, with goat and crab races, folk dancing, and steel band competitions—there's even a (staged) traditional Tobago wedding. ♦ Fee for boat tours. ♦ West end

At Buccoo Reef:

 Pigeon Point Gorgeous beaches are the main attraction on Tobago, and this is the most celebrated of all. The clear green water is edged by a long stretch of gleaming coral sand, with thatch-roofed changing shelters, tables, benches, and lavatories. Fame has its price; visitors must pay to use this privately owned beach. ♦ Admission. 639.8141

45 Coco Reef $$$$ The 135 cheerful guest rooms of this hotel are decorated with wicker furniture and floral fabrics, and embossed bird paintings adorn the walls. Private balconies overlook a pretty private beach, where a crystal-clear lagoon is perfect for swimming, snorkeling, and sea kayaking. Dine on fresh snapper and fruit salads at beachside **Bacchanals Restaurant** or on Italian or French cuisine at **Tamaras**. The resort has two lighted tennis courts and several boutiques. ♦ Coconut Bay. 639.8571, 800/221.1294; fax 639.8574

46 Miss Esmie ★★$ Your bathing suit may be snug after a meal at this beachfront food stall, where you can enjoy an authentic island feast—dumplings, conch or crab, sweet potatoes, plantains, callaloo, a vegetable, and a soft drink—for as little as US$5. There are tables on the beach. ♦ Caribbean ♦ Daily lunch and dinner. Store Bay. No phone

47 Kariwak Village $$ Twenty-four rooms are divided among air-conditioned cottages that surround a lovely garden pool. The complex is a five-minute walk from the beach. ♦ Crown Point. 639.8442; fax 639.8441

Within Kariwak Village:

Kariwak Village ★★★$$ The bamboo dining room is a comfortable place to enjoy local dishes prepared with herbs, spices, and vegetables from the hotel's garden. The set dinner menu might include aromatic pigeon-pea soup, dolphinfish, and homemade ice cream. The Friday and Saturday night buffets feature jazz and regional music performed by a local band. ♦ Caribbean/Seafood ♦ Daily lunch and dinner. Reservations required. 639.8442

Bests

Edward Hernandez
Curator/Executive Trustee, Tobago Trust Museum

Goat and crab races: Over the past 50 years, Tobago has hosted one of the most peculiar events this side of the hemisphere. Every year on the Tuesday following Easter Sunday at the village of Buccoo—well known for its famous reef—the villagers put on an event called "The Buccoo Goat Races & Crab Races," a parody of horse racing. The goats have names, numbers, owners, trainers, and "jockeys," who run behind the goats with whips in hand. There are judges, rules and regulations, and handicaps, and the atmosphere is complimented with music and traditional foods. The crab races provide exciting entertainment for those who can get a vantage point outside the circled arena. The crabs have strings attached and are guided by female "jockeys" who keep them in line towards the finish.

"Sunday School": When you are invited to "Sunday School" in Tobago, it's not an invitation to church or school, but to an open air fete which is held every Sunday from early evening to past midnight at Buccoo Bay.

Joan Applewhite
Tobago Tourism Promotion Officer

Fort King George: Take a guided tour to Tobago's best-preserved historical site.

Tobago Museum: See a great display of early Tobago history, including Amerindian artifacts and military relics, maps, and documents from the colonial period.

Jemma's Sea View Kitchen/Tree House: Enjoy a glorious local meal in **Speyside**. Sample deliciously cooked meals in Creole style atop a tree overlooking the ocean.

Buccoo Reef: Nylon Pool is a protected marine park bounded by Tobago's most famous reef. Daily tours by glass-bottomed boats allow even non-swimmers to see the reef life.

Richmond Great House: Savor the elegance of a restored plantation great house dating from 1776, with early 20th-century furniture and a collection of African textiles and carvings.

Pigeon Point: Relax and enjoy yourself at Tobago's most famous beach. Turquoise-blue water surrounds you at this white-sand idyll. The entrance fee allows access to changing rooms, thatch-shaded seating areas, a restaurant, and a bar.

Store Bay Beach: This is Tobago's most popular beach with modern changing-room facilities. Tour boats leave from here for Buccoo Reef. Hearty local food is served in kiosks. There is also a spectacular craft market where vendors and craftsmen sell everything imaginable.

Speyside Reef: The various reefs off Speyside vary in depth. The shallow reefs are excellent for snorkeling, while the deeper reef areas are great for scuba diving.

Little Tobago Island: Have a fun-filled day on this small offshore island located just off the village of Speyside. It's one of the most important seabird sanctuaries of the Caribbean. See the red-billed tropic bird in its splendor from October to June.

Main Ridge Forest Reserve: The mountainous spine of Tobago supports the oldest protected forest reserve in the western hemisphere. Nature trails allow you to explore this tropical rain forest with its diversity of flora and fauna.

The maximum daily temperature on Caribbean islands ranges from the mid-80s F from December through April to the upper 80s F from May through November. Nighttime temperatures tend to be about 10 degrees F cooler.

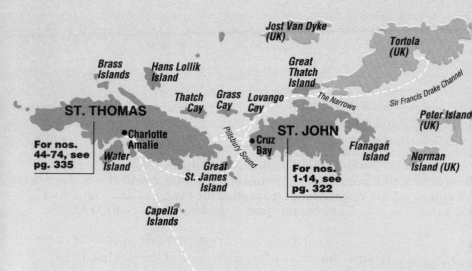

Jost Van Dyke (UK)

Tortola (UK)

Brass Islands

Hans Lollik Island

Great Thatch Island

ST. THOMAS

Thatch Cay

Grass Cay

Lovango Cay

The Narrows

Sir Francis Drake Channel

Peter Island (UK)

For nos. 44-74, see pg. 335

●Charlotte Amalie

Pillsbury Sound

●Cruz Bay

ST. JOHN

Flanagan Island

Norman Island (UK)

Water Island

Great St. James Island

For nos. 1-14, see pg. 322

Capella Islands

Caribbean Sea

British Virgin Islands

Puerto Rico

US VIRGIN ISLANDS

Anguilla

St-Martin/ St. Maarten

Barbuda

St. Kitts

Nevis

Antigua

Caribbean Sea

Guadeloupe

Dominica

Martinique

St. Lucia

N

|km_____300|
|mi_____180|

Buck Island

ST. CROIX
For nos. 15-43, see pg. 327

●Christiansted

●Frederiksted

N

|km_____10_____20|
|mi_____5_____10|

US Virgin Islands

Christopher Columbus named this cluster of more than 50 verdant islands and cays after the beautiful Saint Ursula and her legendary 11,000 martyred virgins. The islands sit in the middle of the Caribbean archipelago, surrounded by sapphire waters and cooled by trade winds blowing in from Africa. The stunning scenery has inspired all sorts of people—from infamous pirates like Blackbeard and Captain Kidd to modern dropouts seeking an unhurried lifestyle.

Like most Caribbean islands, these originally were inhabited by the Arawak and Carib peoples. Though spotted by Columbus in 1493, the islands were not settled by Europeans until Denmark planted its flag on **St. Thomas** in 1666. The territory was traded among England, Holland, Spain, and France (**St. Croix** was even ceded to the Knights of Malta in 1653) before the Danish took firm hold in 1733. Denmark ruled until World War I, when the US purchased the Virgin Islands (to protect the Panama Canal) for a cool $25 million in gold. They became part of the United States on 31 March 1917.

The islands are unincorporated territories of the US, so US currency is used and English is spoken. Amenities here match those of the mainland; the phone systems are as sophisticated as those in New York, and cable TV comes in so clearly you won't have to miss even one episode of your favorite soap opera. The three major islands—St. Thomas, St. Croix, and **St. John**—have a combined population of almost 102,000.

St. Thomas welcomes most visitors at the docks of **Charlotte Amalie**, the capital of the USVI and the most popular cruise port in the Caribbean. Here red-roofed buildings are set against a backdrop of deep green hills, and waterfront alleyways are lined with old Danish warehouses that have been transformed into a world-famous shopping center. The 38-square-mile island has been compared to the countryside of France, with winding roads leading through hills to pastures filled with grazing cattle. Visitors will also find sophisticated hotels, international restaurants, and a large fleet of charter yachts.

More tranquil and less well known than St. Thomas, St. Croix (pronounced *Saint Kroy*) is often referred to as "the other Virgin." Once the province of rich planters, its rolling hills and grassy valleys are dotted with ruins and restorations of more than a hundred sugar mills and great houses. St. Croix has a drier climate than her siblings; offshore are what locals call the "gardens of the Caribbean"—a vibrant underwater world filled with coral formations, giant sponges, and tropical fish. The island is home to the historic Danish towns of **Christiansted** and **Frederiksted**, which are also fine destinations for duty-free shopping. A low-key ambience prevails here, although the pace of life may soon change thanks to a 1995 law permitting casino gambling on the island. At press time, no casinos were yet in operation on St. Croix, although some hotel and casino complexes were in the planning stages.

St. John is the smallest of the chain, at 28 square miles, and is generally considered to be the most beautiful. Nearly two-thirds of the island is taken up by the **Virgin Islands National Park**, where woodland trails lead to panoramic plateaus, and unspoiled white beaches line the emerald cays and turquoise sea. In the small town of **Cruz Bay** visitors can stock up at the grocery stores, explore the craft shops, or help solve the problems of the world at a congenial pub.

Area code 340 unless otherwise noted.

Getting to the Islands

Airlines

American Airlines
  from the US Virgin Islands 800/474.4884
  from the US....................................800/433.7300
Continental........................777.8190, 800/231.0856
Delta 800/221.1212
USAirways 800/622.1015

Interisland Carriers

Air St. Thomas..................776.2722, 800.522.3084
American Eagle 774.6464, 800/474.4884
LIAT (Leeward Islands Air Transport).......778.9930
  on St. Croix 774.2313
  on St. Thomas................................800/468.0482
Seaborne Seaplane.....................................777.4491

Airports **Alexander Hamilton Airport** (778.1012) is about 10 minutes due east of Frederiksted, St. Croix, by car. At press time, the airport was slated for renovation, including the construction of a new $26-million passenger terminal. **Cyril E. King Airport** (774.5100) is about 10 minutes west of Charlotte Amalie, St. Thomas. In 1991 the air-conditioned state-of-the-art terminal extended its runways to attract more traffic to the island. **American Airlines, Delta,** and **USAirways** fly here nonstop from the US. Visitors to St. John, which has no airport, fly into **Cyril E. King Airport** and take a ferry or seaplane to the island.

Ferries The following ferries travel among St. Thomas, St. John, and the neighboring British Virgin Islands.

Dohm's Water Taxi.....................................775.6501
Inter-Island Boat Service...........................776.6597
Smith's Ferry Service 775.7292
Transportation Services of St. John 776.6282

Getting Around the Islands

Buses On St. Thomas, there's service throughout Charlotte Amalie; there's also connecting service between Charlotte Amalie and **Red Hook Bay,** and between Charlotte Amalie and **Fortuna.** For more information, call 774.5678. St. Croix has taxi vans that run between Christiansted and Frederiksted; for more information, call 778.1088. On St. John, open-air buses (called **Safari** buses) run from Cruz Bay to several points on the island. Contact the St. John tourist office by the ferry dock (776.6450).

Car Rental

On St. Croix:

Avis....................................778.9355, 800/331.1084
Hertz 778.1402, 800/654.3131
Olympic ....773.2208 (Christiansted),
....772.1617 (Frederiksted)

On St. John:

Courtesy Car/Jeep Rental 776.6650
St. John Car Rental....................................776.6103

On St. Thomas:

ABC Auto and Jeep Rental ....
....776.1222, 800/524.2080
Budget 776.5774, 800/626.4516
Dependable 774.2253, 800/522.3076
Sea Breeze 774.7200

Driving Driving is on the left side of the road. On St. Thomas, rush-hour traffic is as congested as in any major US city. Parking in Charlotte Amalie is difficult, and if you park where you're not supposed to, chances are you'll get a $25 ticket. Avoid the problem by parking in the large pay lot beside **Fort Christian.** Outside of the main towns, locals will sometimes stop in the middle of the road to chat a moment with a passing friend; be patient with them. Also, it's customary when going around a blind curve to give notice by beeping your horn a few times. The roads are paved and tend to be good on all three islands. However, beware the occasional mongoose, goat, or grazing donkey; they do not always yield the right of way. Most car-rental companies require drivers to be at least 25 years of age. Beyond that, all that's needed to rent a car is a valid US or Canadian driver's license and a major credit card.

Ferries and Interisland Cruises The following ferries provide regular service between St. Thomas (departing from Charlotte Amalie and Red Hook Bay) and St. John.

Dohm's Water Taxi.....................................775.6501
Inter-Island Boat Service...........................776.6597
Smith's Ferry Service 775.7292
Transportation Services of St. John 776.6282

In addition, a high-speed hydrofoil provides ferry service between Christiansted, St. Croix, and Charlotte Amalie, St. Thomas. Call **Katran** (776.7417).

A number of companies offer boat trips to various uninhabited isles. All types of craft are available, from sailboats to ferries, motor yachts, and party trimarans.

For full-day, half-day, snorkel, sunset, and moonlit sails, contact one of the following:

On St. Croix:

AristoCat 773.5086, 773.1453
Big Beard's Adventure Tours 773.4482
Blinda Charters...773.1641
Diva..778.4675
Teroro II 773.4041, 773.3161

On St. John:

Arawak Expeditions 693.8312
Sadie Sea 776.6330

On St. Thomas:

Daydreamer & Coconut Cruises 775.2584

Ike Witt Charters 779.1851

Nightwind Charters 775.4110

Treasure Isle Cruises....................................775.9500

The following companies on St. Thomas allow passengers to choose their own itineraries:

Dohm's Water Taxi..775.6501

High Performance Charters........................777.7545

Stormy Petrol 775.7990, 800.866.5714

Taxis The cabs are not metered, but fares are regulated by the Virgin Islands Taxi Commission. Fees vary according to the number of passengers and suitcases. All cabs are required to carry a copy of the official rates and to show it to passengers when asked. Local tourist guides also print the fares between popular destinations. Always agree on the fee before you start. It's not unusual for a taxi to pick up additional passengers headed in the same direction.

Tours **St. Croix Bike and Tours** (772.2343, 773.5004), **St. Croix Safari Tours** (773.6700), and **Travellers' Tours** (778.1636) offer good tours of St. Croix aboard open-air safari-style buses that seat 12 to 16 people. **St. Croix Heritage Tours** (778.6997) runs guided walking tours.

On St. Thomas, try **Tropic Tours** (774.1855, 800/524.4334), which offers two- to three-hour Safari bus tours. To view the islands from the air or to be dropped off on an uninhabited isle for the day, arrange a helicopter ride with **Air Center Helicopter Tours** (775.7335) or **Hill Aviation Helicopter Tours** (776.7880, 809/723.3385 in Puerto Rico).

The **Virgin Islands National Park** (776.6201) on St. John offers a variety of hiking, boat, and bus tours.

FYI

Electricity The current is 110 volts/60 cycles, the same as in the US and Canada.

Entry Requirements No passports or visas are required of US citizens. Canadian visitors must present either a current passport or other proof of citizenship (birth certificate, voter's registration card) plus a photo ID.

Language English is the official language.

Money The US dollar is used here. Banks are open Monday through Thursday from 9AM to 2:30PM, and Friday from 9AM to 2PM and from 3:30PM to 5PM.

Personal Safety Serious crime exists, even on laid-back St. John. Avoid deserted streets or alleys, and always keep your wallet in your front pocket or a zippered pocketbook. Lock car doors and don't leave your valuables in sight.

Publications St. Thomas's *Daily News,* St. Croix's *Avis,* and St. John's *Tradewinds* are the main island newspapers. *St. Thomas This Week* (which includes St. John information), *St. Croix This Week,* and the *Virgin Islands' Business Journal*'s *Quittin' Times Guide* publish news and listings of interest to tourists. *The San Juan Star* (Virgin Islands edition),

The New York Times, New York's *Daily News,* the *Wall Street Journal, The Miami Herald,* and *USA Today* are all available on newsstands daily.

Reservation Services and House Rentals

McLaughlin Anderson Vacations 776.0635,
....800/537.6246

Taxes An eight-percent tax is added to hotel bills. An airport tax is included in the price of your plane ticket.

Tipping Many hotels add a service charge of 10 to 15 percent, which covers the room maid, dining room waiters, and other staff; tips are expected for special errands or other extras. If there's no service charge, give the room maid $1 or $2 each day, waiters and bartenders 15 percent of the tab, bellmen and porters at least $1 per bag. Many restaurants add a 12- to 15-percent service charge to the tab, otherwise tip that amount. Tip cab drivers 15 percent of the fare.

Visitors' Information Offices St. Croix's tourist office is located in the **Scalehouse** at Christiansted Harbor (773.0495); it's open Monday through Friday from 8AM to 5PM. There's also an unstaffed facility offering brochures at **Alexander Hamilton Airport.**

On St. John, the tourist office is around the corner from the Cruz Bay ferry dock, next to the post office (776.6450). It's open Monday through Friday from 8AM to 5PM.

St. Thomas has tourist offices at the **Old Customs House** office in Charlotte Amalie (774.8784) and at **Havensight Shopping Mall,** near the cruise-ship pier (774.8784). Both are are open Monday through Friday from 8AM to 5PM. The **Old Customs House** also has a **Hospitality Lounge** (774.3519) where visitors may leave bags and luggage while they tour or shop; it's open Monday through Friday from 8AM to 5PM and Saturday from 10AM to 4PM. A small information booth operated by the Havensight Retailers Association dispenses maps and brochures at the **Havensight Shopping Mall** on weekends. There's also an unstaffed tourist information booth (brochures only) at the **Cyril E. King Airport.**

Phone Book

Ambulance 911

Directory Assistance 913

Diving Emergencies/Decompression Chambers

   St. Croix 776.2686

   St. Thomas..776.2686

Emergencies 911

Fire..911

Hospitals

   St. Croix 778.6311

   St. Thomas..776.8311

Police 911

Post Office 774.1950

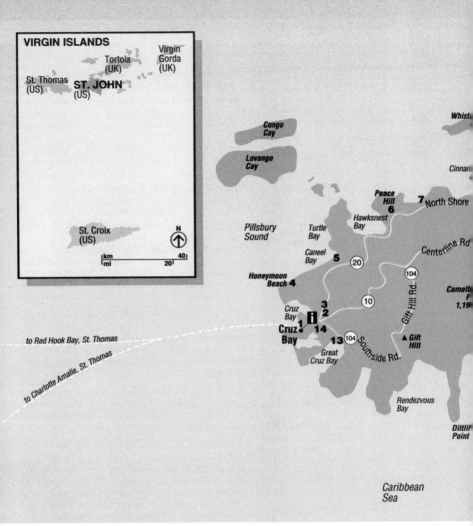

St. John

When Virgin Islanders want a vacation, they head over to St. John, nicknamed **Love Island** because locals say there's not much else to do there. But that's not *entirely* true. St. John's other lures include soaring mountains, curving white beaches, underwater coral gardens, and a slow pace of life. Furthermore, two-thirds of the land is a national park (donated to the US in 1956 by multimillionaire Laurance Rockefeller) that provides numerous walking trails through junglelike terrain. There are no airports, neon signs, late-night discos, or traffic lights. This one-village island caters to nature-loving escapists with thick wallets or a yen for camping.

1 **Cruz Bay** When St. Johnians say they're going into town, they mean this tiny seaside village. Small boutiques are filled with local handicrafts, and the cafes teem with people who come to browse, chat, gossip, argue politics, and watch the boats cruise into the harbor. Everyone is friendly—it's hard to stay strangers on an island this size, and it's rare to come across anyone in a rush. Two caveats:

It's against the "Keep St. John Beautiful" law to walk around town in a bathing suit; and, while slow-paced, the main streets can get congested with traffic generated by locals and day-trippers from St. Thomas. ♦ West coast

1 **Virgin Islands National Park Visitors' Center** The park takes up nearly two-thirds of St. John, so the visitors' center is a logical place to start. It's full of information on the park service's numerous hiking trails and educational programs. Lots of activities are free, including children's environmental workshops, bird-watching hikes, and a series of hour-long evening lectures on subjects that range from endangered animals to medicinal plants to coral-reef ecology. There's a charge for guided snorkeling, hikes, and historic bus tours to the east end of the island, but these excursions are worth every penny, as groups are led by park rangers who are well versed in local history, culture, and animal and marine life. Programs are held year-round, but more are scheduled during peak tourist months (January through April). Programs change

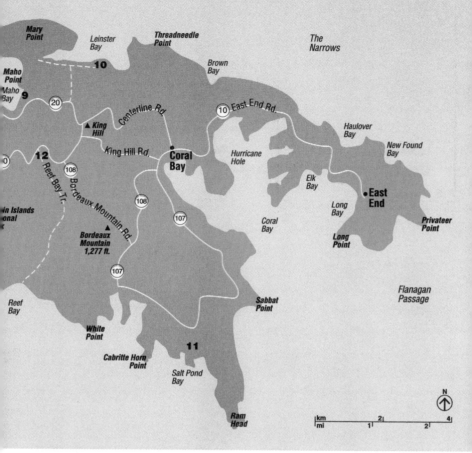

seasonally, so stop in for the latest trail maps, hiking advice, and list of activities. ♦ Daily. North Shore Rd, Cruz Bay. 776.6201

1 Wharfside Village An unusual group of original-art emporiums resides in this three-story mini-mall, where prints, paintings, pottery, and clothing are sold. You'll also find smaller outlets of the trendy St. Thomas duty-free shops that sell name-brand perfumes, watches, and jewelry, including **Jeweler's Warehouse** (693.7490) and **Blue Carib Gems** (693.8299). ♦ Daily. Just southwest of the ferry dock, Cruz Bay. 693.8210

2 Mongoose Junction This pleasant mix of shops and restaurants set in a complex built of native stone is the place to watch artisans at work and to buy one-of-a-kind crafts, pottery, fine art, resortwear, and even antique West Indian furniture. Look for batik, silk-screened, and hand-painted wall hangings, beach wraps, and bolts of material at the **Fabric Mill** (776.6194). The adjoining **Wicker, Wood & Shells** (776.6909) offers prints by local artists as well as cards, gifts, and straw

bags. Pottery and richly colored blown glass can be found at the **Donald Schnell Studio** (776.6420), and Caribbean crafts, folk art, and furniture are carried by **Bamboula** (693.8699). For hand-crafted silver and gold jewelry, stop by **R&I Patton Goldsmiths** (776.6548). ♦ Daily. North Shore Rd, Cruz Bay. 776.6267

Within Mongoose Junction:

Paradiso ★★$$$ This place is known for combining two favorite island activities: eating and people watching. The setting is a veranda, and the menu features pasta and veal. Stop by early and enjoy a drink at the bar. ♦ Northern Italian ♦ Daily lunch and dinner. Reservations recommended. 693.8899

3 North Shore Road From Cruz Bay, head north on this winding, well-paved road that hugs the hills overlooking the shoreline. Driving is on the left, and so are all the scenic overlooks. From different vantage points, you can see the islands of St. Thomas, Jost Van Dyke, and Tortola, to name a few. Drive carefully, as there are no traffic lights, and donkeys, goats, and mongooses don't know the road was built for people. ♦ Between Centerline Rd and Cruz Bay

4 Honeymoon Beach Just beyond the narrow crescent of white sand lies a unique experience: The tame manta rays in these shallow waters will eat out of your hand. Just wade out into the knee-deep water, swish some bread about, and wait. The small rays are usually hungriest from 11AM to 2PM, when they'll be happy to swim over for the free handout. There are no facilities. ♦ West of North Shore Rd

CANEEL BAY

5 Caneel Bay $$$$ Multimillionaire Laurance Rockefeller turned this sprawling wilderness into his dream resort, a place where privacy and peace prevail, crowds are unheard of, and the hassles of civilization are left outside the front gate. The managers, Rosewood Hotels & Resorts, have maintained the old-fashioned luxury here, responding to the severe damage done by Hurricane Marilyn in 1995 by totally refurbishing the entire property, even adding new handmade furniture in the guest rooms.

There's a beach for every day of the week here and an acre for each of the 166 rooms, spread out along the sandy shore or overlooking the gardens and 11 tennis courts. The atmosphere is a cross between an exclusive country club and a genteel island plantation; the meticulously kept grounds overflow with more than 2,000 varieties of trees, plants, shrubs, and exotic flowers. The rooms are comfortable and basic, many cooled by ceiling fans and tropical breezes flowing through louvered windows. But the rooms are not the focus here—the idea is to relax on the beaches or among the gardens, or to take advantage of the complimentary Windsurfers, snorkel gear, and day-sailers. Guests are invited to a weekly garden walk led by the grounds botanist, as well as evening movies, exercise classes, and marine slide shows. A fitness center features state-of-the-art equipment. For an extra fee, you can enjoy excellent scuba diving, an excursion to Virgin Gorda (in the British Virgin Islands), and both day and sunset cruises. Three outstanding restaurants (including **Caneel Bay Terrace,** see below) round out the picture. Children can participate in **Caneel Kids,** a program offering many activities. And for those who can't get completely away from it all, there's a business center with computers and cellular phones. ♦ Caneel Bay. 776.6111, 800/928.8889; fax 693.8280

Within Caneel Bay:

Caneel Bay Terrace ★★★$$$ The least formal of this elegant resort's eateries offers two superb dining experiences. On weekdays, order a personal pizza, custom-topped with delicacies like grilled veggies, goat cheese, and Italian sausages and cooked in a wood-burning oven. Come Sunday, settle down to brunch complete with a make-your-own Bloody Mary bar, a whole roast pig, and decorative and delicious tropical fruit desserts. A swim or snooze on the beach afterward makes for a perfect day. The restaurant is open to the public, as is the beach (although the chairs and water-sports facilities are reserved for hotel guests). ♦ Continental ♦ Daily breakfast, lunch, and dinner. 776.6111

6 Peace Hill This peak is one of the top spots for viewing the island. It's also the site of the oldest sugar mill on St. John. ♦ Just northwest of North Shore Rd, Hawksnest Bay

7 Trunk Bay *National Geographic* singled out this slice of brilliant white coral sand as one of the world's most beautiful beaches. Sunbathers who can drag themselves off the shore will find an underwater trail marked by a series of floats. Snorkelers can peer down at the written displays to read about reef life and watch the fish in action. The park service maintains the entire bay, including the picnic areas, snack bar, changing rooms, and showers. Lifeguards are on duty, and there's a shack that rents snorkel gear. ♦ North of North Shore Rd

8 Cinnamon Bay $ The locale is lovely, with 126 campsites hugging a long, scalloped beach. Managed by the **Caneel Bay** resort (see above), the accommodations here are spartan—cottages with two concrete and two screened walls and tent platforms. There's a snack bar, a commissary, and showers; bathrooms are communal. The park service runs snorkel tours here and several park service hikes begin at a point just across the road. Rangers also teach campers how to bake johnnycake and other native favorites in an outdoor wood-burning oven. Water sports are available. ♦ Reservations required almost a year in advance. Cinnamon Bay. 776.6330, 800/539.9998; fax 776.6458

MAHO BAY
St.John. U.S. Virgin Islands

9 Maho Bay Camps $ Surrounded by national park land and facing an unspoiled beach, this 14-acre hillside is planted with 114 tents raised on platforms like small canvas tree houses. Each offers an open sundeck, very basic furnishings (beds, linens, tables, chairs), and a kitchen area (ice chest, camp stove, place settings for four). Bathrooms are communal. Eco-friendly landscaping is crisscrossed by non-erosive boardwalks and pick-your-own herb gardens. Water sports are inexpensive and plentiful. Simple breakfasts and dinners are served at a rustic open-air restaurant, and groceries are available at the on-site commissary. Entertainment, which might be live music or a lecture on island lore, is scheduled most evenings during the winter season. A beautifully situated pavilion hosts weddings and meetings. Shuttle service connects the complex to Cruz Bay. Some campsites are reserved a year in advance, but be aware that this is no place for softies: You'll need plenty of insect repellent. ♦ Maho Bay. 776.6240, 800/392.9004; fax 776.6504

10 Annaberg Plantation The National Park Service has restored the stone ruins of this 18th-century Danish sugar mill, which include slave quarters, a sugar mill, and storage buildings. Park rangers offer tours on Wednesday at 9:30AM and Friday at 1PM; at other times visitors can take a self-guided tour. Several times a week St. Johnians present a morning of colonial crafts, cooking, and gardening demonstrations aimed at showing visitors what life was once like here; the days vary, so call ahead. ♦ Free. Daily. Leinster Bay. 776.6201

11 Estate Concordia $$ Nature lovers who crave a few creature comforts might prefer this place to **Maho Bay Camps** (see page 324), also a Stanley Selengut development. On the secluded south shore, the property features 10 spacious studios or suites with private baths and either a full kitchen or kitchenette. Rollaway beds are available for extra guests. All units have views of Salt Pond Bay, and there's a hillside swimming pool. The property has no restaurant, entertainment, or water sports, but the beach at Salt Pond Bay is within walking distance and a number of restaurants and bars (many with live music on weekends) are within a five-minute drive. Sun and wind provide the power at this ecologically-aware place. ♦ Salt Pond Bay. 693.5855, 800/392.9004; fax 693.5960

12 Reef Bay Trail This is the most popular hiking trail in the USVI, probably because it's all downhill. The 2.6-mile path offers a self-guided tour, with signs providing information about the island's history and the more than 100 species of birds and trees found here. Along the way, hikers can listen to the rattling pods of the tree known as mother-in-law's tongue, smell the foul stinking toe (a large bean-shaped pod), and laugh at the red and peeling tourist tree.

The walk also passes the ruins of four sugar estates that were home to early Danish settlers. About midway, look for a trickling waterfall and follow it to its base. Here, primitive "graffiti," said to have been carved by either the Arawak or Carib Indians, can be seen on the rocks alongside the placid pools.

The trail is just 1 of 12 maintained by the National Park Service, which offers guided tours on Tuesdays, Thursdays, and Saturdays for a small fee (check with the **National Parks Visitors' Center** in Cruz Bay for the latest schedule). As an added incentive, the park service will arrange a ride back to Cruz Bay from the bottom of the trail (it sure beats walking back up). ♦ Fee for guided tours. Between Reef Bay and Centerline Rd. 776.6330

13 Westin Resort, St. John $$$$ The 285 guest rooms, suites, and town houses at this modern resort, formerly the **Hyatt Regency St. John,** were fully refurbished after Hurricane Marilyn in 1995. All offer air-conditioning, color TVs, telephones, marble bathrooms, and private terraces or balconies. Be aware, though, that what you gain in luxury, you lose in ambience. The island feel is lost among the pink buildings and giant quarter-acre pool. Sure, there are lots of palm trees, and the beach is a dream, but you can never forget you're in a top-notch American resort dropped into a Gilligan's Island setting.

That said, there's lots to do. Sign the kids up for the **Westin Kids Club,** then take advantage of the fitness center and the free snorkeling, windsurfing, kayaking, and tennis (six lighted courts). There are three restaurants, nightly music, and a weekly comedy show. Wheelchairs are available for guests who might have trouble navigating the hills. Children under 18 stay free in their parents' room. ♦ Great Cruz Bay. 693.8000, 800/WESTIN-1; fax 779.4985

14 Elaine Ione Sprauve Library & Museum Pottery and tools made by the Arawak and Carib Indians line the shelves of this former plantation house that was once known as **Enighed.** Displays include old photographs from the island's past, a working windmill model, and a few colonial-era relics. Changing exhibits occasionally showcase the work of local artists and artisans. The small museum shares its home with the public library. ♦ Donation. M-F. Southside Rd (south of Centerline Rd), Cruz Bay. 776.6359

Restaurants/Clubs: Red   Hotels: Blue
Shops/ Outdoors: Green   Sights/Culture: Black

ST. CROIX

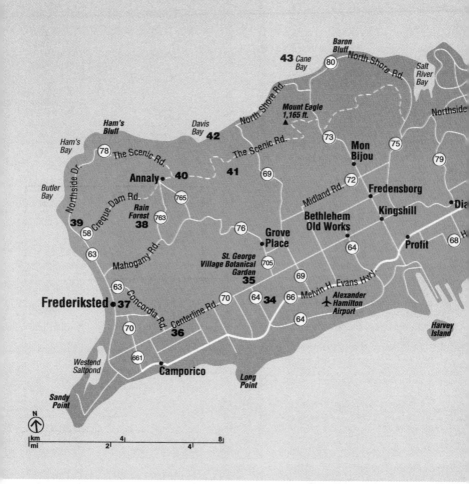

St. Croix

The offshore "gardens of the Caribbean" are busy with marine life, but hustle and bustle are virtually unheard of on St. Croix. What little action there is occurs in the island's two towns, **Christiansted** and **Frederiksted**.

Christiansted, one of the Caribbean's most charming towns, offers a mixture of Danish and Caribbean architecture in an array of pastel colors. Narrow, mostly one-way streets make driving difficult, so your best bet is to take a cab to town and start your own walking tour at **Fort Christiansvaern**.

The town is also a destination for duty-free shopping. Boutiques filled with resortwear, crafts, and duty-free cameras, perfumes, watches, and jewelry can be found at the **Caravelle Arcade**, **King's Wharf**, **King's Alley Walk**, **Market Square Mall**, and the **Pan Am Pavilion**. (Note: Store entrances on the main streets are often up or down a few steps; those with physical disabilities will find shopping easier at the small malls.)

15 Fort Christiansvaern This is the best preserved of the five remaining Danish forts the Virgin Islands and a prime example of 18th-century Danish colonial military architecture. The color comes from the yello bricks used in its construction. An exhibit on local military history is displayed in the **Commandant's Quarters** on the second floo and interesting tours are available on reques Park at King's Wharf. ◆ Admission; senior citizens, children under 16 free. Daily. Hospital and Company Sts, Christiansted. 773.1460

16 Steeple Building Built by the Danes in 1753 as a Lutheran church, this handsome structure was subsequently used as a military bakery, hospital, and school.

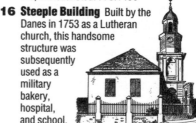

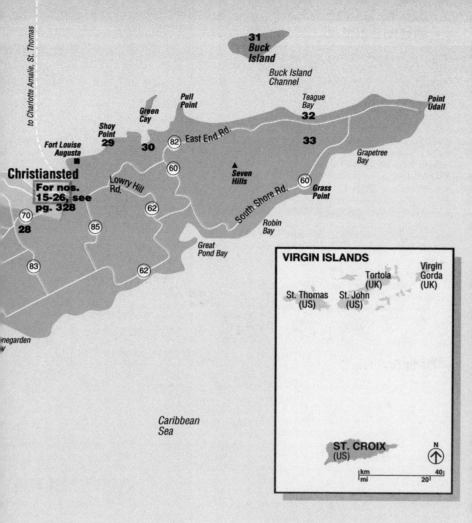

Today it houses the **National Park Museum**, with exhibits on island archaeology, African-Caribbean history, and Danish architecture. ♦ Admission. M-F. Hospital and Company Sts, Christiansted. 773.1460

17 Quin House Galleries Handcrafted mahogany furniture, both originals and authentic reproductions, is sold here. Pieces range from four-poster beds to tiny desk accessories. Distinctive china and ceramics, works by local artists, and hand-woven baskets are also available. ♦ M-Sa. Quinn House Complex, Company and King Cross Sts, Christiansted. 773.0404

17 Kendrick's ★★★$$ Consistently good food and top-notch service distinguish this elegant second-floor restaurant, which is filled with antiques. The menu features continental food with French touches; try the sautéed shrimp with mustard greens or the rack of lamb with thyme sauce. Pizza, burgers, and shrimp cocktail can be ordered at the bar. ♦ Continental/French ♦ M-F lunch and dinner;

Sa dinner. Reservations recommended. Quinn House Complex, Company and King Cross Sts, Christiansted. 773.9199

18 Top Hat Restaurant ★★★★$$$ The husband-and-wife team of Bent and Hanne Rasmussen serve true Danish food in a historic Danish town house. Come early for drinks and gawking, as the bar's walls and ceiling are plastered with hundreds of photographs of the famous and not-so-famous faces that have been fed here. The menu features lots of meat dishes; Danish specialties to try include herring, housemade sausages, and roast duck with apples, prunes, and red cabbage. ♦ Danish ♦ M-Sa dinner; closed May through July. Reservations required. 53 Company St (between Queen Cross and King Cross Sts), Christiansted. 773.2346

19 Little Switzerland Part of a chain of stores throughout the Caribbean, this shop features a wide variety of imported china, crystal, jewelry, and figurines. ♦ M-Sa. 1108 King St (at King's Alley), Christiansted. 773.1976. Also at: Main St and Nye Gade, Charlotte Amalie, St. Thomas; Norre Gade, Charlotte Amalie, St. Thomas. 776.2010 for both St. Thomas locations

20 King's Alley Walk Built in 1997, this airy mall with atrium skylights leads from Christiansted Harbor to King Street. Among the 20 stores here are the **Caribbean Bracelet Company** (773.9110); **King's Alley Jewelry** (773.4746), where owner Brian Bishop handcrafts gold jewelry; **St. Croix Watch Factory Outlet** (773.7882); and **The White House** (773.9222), specializing in all-white clothing and accessories for women. Among the eateries in the mall are **King's Alley Cafe** (773.9400) and the **St. Croix Chophouse and Brewery** (773.9820). ♦ King's Alley (northwest of King St), Christiansted. 773.0130

20 King's Alley Hotel $$ On the harbor, next to **King's Alley Walk,** this old hotel underwent a face-lift in 1996, giving its 23 rooms a pastel-colored makeover and new mahogany furniture, and sprucing up the pool area. The atmosphere is convivial, the staff is friendly, and there's plenty of activity—day-trippers from St. Thomas arrive in the waters in front of the hotel aboard the **Seaborne Seaplane**

and make their way to the **King's Landing Yacht Club and Marina,** the hotel's lively restaurant/bar. The hotel also manages 12 new 1-bedroom suites on the 2nd floor of the adjacent **King's Alley Walk.** ♦ King's Alley (northwest of King St), Christiansted. 773.0103, 800.843.3574; fax 773.4431

⊠Club Comanche

21 Club Comanche $$ This town house, more than 250 years old, is said to have been the boyhood home of Alexander Hamilton, who moved here with his mother from Nevis, where he was born. Today it houses 36 cozy, antiques-filled rooms, some with four-poster beds. The hotel, conveniently located near the harbor and the shopping district, also has a saltwater pool and a highly regarded restaurant (see below). ♦ Comanche Walk and Strand St, Christiansted. 773.0210, 800/524.2066; fax 773.0210

Within Club Comanche:

Comanche Restaurant ★★★$$$ This second-floor eatery is one of the most popular in town. The decor has a nautical touch—note the canoe from Surinam hanging from the ceiling. The menu features seafood, lamb chops, and baby-back ribs, but try the steaks

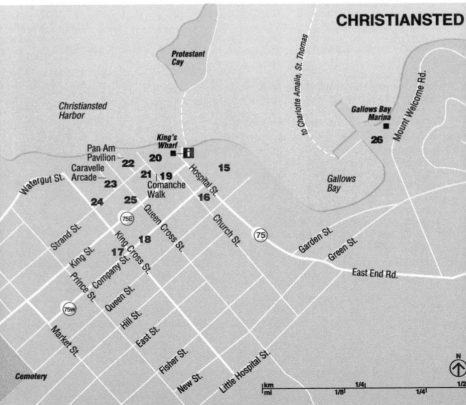

CHRISTIANSTED

for a real treat. There's live piano music nightly. ♦ Seafood/Continental ♦ M-Sa lunch and dinner. 773.0210

22 Many Hands Seashells, spices, jams, cards, and interesting arts and crafts are offered at reasonable prices. Don't miss the imaginative Christmas ornaments. ♦ M-Sa. Pan Am Pavilion (northwest of Strand St), Christiansted. 773.1990

22 Steele's Smokes & Sweets Premium cigars, pipes, tobacco, and Dunhill lighters share space with culinary creations like homemade fudge and hand-formed chocolates. ♦ M-Sa. Pan Am Pavilion (northwest of Strand St), Christiansted. 773.3366

23 St. Croix Aquarium On the list of sights to see is this aquarium, an educational marine center with hundreds of tropical fish. Guided tours are informative and entertaining. ♦ Admission. Tu-Sa. Caravelle Arcade (northwest of Strand St), 773.8995

23 Violette Boutique Perfumes, cosmetics, and leather goods at discount prices are featured in this two-story boutique. ♦ M-Sa. Caravelle Arcade (northwest of Strand St), Christiansted. 773.2148, 800.544.5912

24 Royal Poinciana Here the aromas of spices, coffees, teas, Caribbean condiments, tropical perfume, and soaps fill the air. ♦ M-Sa. 38 Strand St (between Caravelle Arcade and King Cross St), Christiansted. 773.9892

25 From the Gecko Here's an eclectic collection of tropical clothing and accessories for men, women, and children. Check out hand-painted clothing by Sloop Jones, Yemaya's original silk creations, unique jewelry from various designers, and the largest sarong selection on the island. ♦ M-Sa; open Su when a cruise ship is in port. 43 Queen Cross St (between King and Strand Sts), Christiansted. 778.9433

26 Rare Finds Choose something old or something new—there's a wonderful assortment of one-of-a-kind gifts and collectibles to suit every taste and budget

here. ♦ F-Sa. Gallows Bay Marketplace, Mount Welcome Rd (north of Garden St), Christiansted. No phone

27 Cormorant Beach Club $$$ Thoughtful extras set this property apart: The longtime staff quickly learns your name, beverages are kept in a cooler by the tennis courts, morning coffee and tea are delivered to your room gratis, and complimentary afternoon tea and pastries are served in the lobby. The 34 beachfront rooms and 4 penthouse suites are all air-conditioned and tastefully furnished. It's the perfect place to relax, lounging in one of the hammocks or chaises that dot the pristine palm-shaded beach. For the more energetic, snorkel gear is provided and the reef starts right offshore (wear booties, as the bottom here is a bit rocky). Swimmers and splashers will fare better in the free-form pool with its massaging waterfall. There are two tennis courts and a video/game room as well. The resort has a restaurant (see below) and a casual beach bar that serves burgers. Two meal plans are offered, but with so many dining establishments on St. Croix, you may not want to lock yourself into eating only here. The adjacent high-rise **Cormorant Cove** has six luxury condominium units, each with a deluxe kitchen and some with marble baths and Jacuzzis, plus its own freshwater pool. No children under six are allowed at the **Cormorant Beach Club,** but families with young children may stay in the **Cormorant Cove** condo units. ♦ 4126 La Grande Princesse (north of Northside Rd). 778.8920, 800/548.4460; fax 778.9218

Within the Cormorant Beach Club:

Cormorant Beach Club Restaurant ★★ $$$ Dine formally in the enclosed restaurant or more casually at the open-air tables. Choices include island seafood chowder, chicken Athena (chicken breast filled with spinach, feta cheese, and dried apricots), and filet mignon with mushroom compote. Thursday nights feature a Caribbean buffet and live steel-pan music; on Friday there's jazz. ♦ Continental ♦ M-Sa breakfast, lunch, and dinner; Su brunch and dinner. Reservations recommended. 778.8920

When 8,000 slaves gathered outside of St. Croix's Fort Frederik to protest the Danish king's decision that they would not be freed before serving a 20-year apprenticeship, Danish governor-general Peter von Scholten kept the peace by announcing, "All unfree in the Danish West Indies are from today emancipated." Although he was returned to Copenhagen for acting without authority, his 1848 proclamation was honored. But he never got to see the islands again, nor the former slave who became his mistress after his Danish wife deserted him.

28 Hilty House $$ Set atop a hill above Christiansted, this guest house has garnered rave reviews as *the* bed-and-breakfast on the island. Owners Hugh and Jacquie Hoare-Ward (natives of Britain and Lebanon, respectively) set up shop in this gracious estate, which was once part of a sugar plantation; the current great house was the rum factory. Hand-painted Florentine tiles adorn the floors of the five guest rooms, and crystal chandeliers (salvaged from the original property) hang in three of the six bathrooms. There are also two one-bedroom cottages, available by the week or month. Amenities are plentiful, but likely to appeal to those in search of a peaceful retreat: quiet grounds filled with wild mango, tamarind, lime, and papaya trees; a swimming pool; and a sundeck. Those who can't survive without the nightly news will find a TV and VCR in the library. Everything is geared toward adults, with no scheduled activities. Breakfast is the only meal provided, so you'll need a car to drive to area restaurants. ♦ Questa Verde Rd, Herman Hill. 773.2594; fax 773.2594

29 The Buccaneer $$$$ This full-service resort is one of the island's top properties. Three beaches and a spread of 240 acres provide the backdrop for a variety of accommodations, ranging from basic rooms to tennis villas and super deluxe oceanfront suites. All 150 units are air-conditioned and have TV sets. Golfers are lured here by the 18-hole, par-71 course. Parents can play at ease while their children enjoy a supervised program offering arts and crafts, sand-castle building, snorkel parties, and other fun. A comprehensive water-sports program, including lessons, is offered by the **Beach Shack,** and pros offer tennis instruction on eight Laykold courts. There are 2 pools, 4 restaurants (be sure to check out **Terrace**—the view of Christiansted is fabulous), an 18-station exercise path, day and evening cruises, and a shopping arcade. The health salon offers massages, seaweed wraps, and reflexology. The property is owned and run by the Armstrong family, which has lived on St. Croix for nine generations. Elizabeth Armstrong, granddaughter of the original owners, leads free weekly nature walks, pointing out exotic flowers and plants

while enchanting guests with stories of the resort's history. Rates range from "room only" to the "Treasures" program, a package covering meals, water and land sports, several tours, airport transfers—essentially everything except drinks and tips. ♦ Shoys. 773.2100, 800/255.3881; fax 773.0010

30 The Galleon ★★★$$$ This local favorite offers traditional French and Northern Italian cuisine along with wonderful live piano music. Of special note on the menu are the foie gras, bouillabaisse, and rack of lamb for two. Oenophiles will appreciate the large selection of fine wines available by the glass. ♦ Continental ♦ M-Sa dinner. Reservations required. Green Cay Marina (north of East End Rd). 773.9949

31 Buck Island This reef-encircled isle only one mile off St. Croix is a snorkeler's paradise. The reef lies just beneath the water's surface, at an average depth of 13 feet. The underwater trail is very clearly marked, with angelfish, parrot fish, and groupers feeding near the signs. As you swim along, schools of iridescent blue tangs part to let you pass.

The reef is alive with color and filled with elkhorn, brain, and finger coral in formations that would make a sculptor blue-green with envy. Your best bet is to go during the week, as on weekends the island gets crowded with Crucians basking on the powder beaches and lolling in the aquamarine lagoon. The island is protected by the National Park Service; souvenir collecting of sea creatures living or dead (including shells, sea fans, and coral) will net a severe fine. Trips to the island are offered by **Teroro II** (Green Cay Marina, north of East End Rd, 773.4041, 773.3161) and **Big Beard's Adventure Tours** (Pan Am Pavilion, northwest of Strand St, Christiansted, 773.4482). ♦ Off the northeast coast

32 Duggan's Reef ★★$$ Overlooking the beach and Buck Island—and popular with locals and tourists in the know—this informal restaurant serves the best conch fritters on St. Croix. Owner Frank Duggan keeps both the service and the smiles flowing. Try the Creole-style flying fish for lunch, or feast on veal *piccata* or fresh lobster pasta at dinner. ♦ American/Seafood ♦ Daily lunch and dinner. Reservations recommended for dinner. Reef Beach (just north of East End Rd), Teague Bay. 773.9800

Island Smorgasbord:
From Bull's Feet to Goat Meat

Some of the most exotic dishes in the world come from the Caribbean. After whetting your appetite in the sun, consider trying some of the local dishes; they're unlike any you'll come across on the mainland. Here are a few US Virgin Islands favorites:

Bullfoot soup As the name implies, these are bull's feet boiled with a medley of vegetables and dumplings.

Callaloo These spinachlike (at least insofar as texture is concerned) greens are served in a soup accompanied by pork or crabmeat.

Caribbean lobster Unlike its North American cousin, this shellfish has no claws. Most of the meat is in the tail, and it's served broiled or mixed with other seafood in a variety of dishes.

Conch This mollusk, which resides in large shells like those sold at roadside stands, is high in protein and low in cholesterol and calories—the perfect diet food. Try yours pan-sautéed, breaded and broiled, curried, or in a spicy soup called conch chowder. Or you can delve into the hypercaloric but delicious breaded and fried conch fritters. After many years of

steady fishing, the conch has become a threatened species.

Fungi This mildly spiced cornmeal mush is usually served as a side dish, but it's sometimes added as a thickener for callaloo soup as well. It is the islands' equivalent of potatoes.

Goat-water soup Goat meat (what else?) is this stew's main ingredient.

Johnnycakes This unleavened, deep-fried bread is fattening, but tasty.

Pates Palm-sized turnovers stuffed with meat and vegetables or salted fish. They are usually sold at roadside stands.

Roti A tortilla-type shell stuffed with curried meat or seafood, this inexpensive and filling dish is the local answer to a Big Mac.

Souse It's a stew made from leftover pig parts: the head, tail, and feet. Spices and fresh lime juice add flavor.

33 Villa Madeleine $$$$ Nestled in a ridge atop a large hill on the east end of the island is this elegant gem with views of the sea from both sides. Forty-three lemon-colored one- and two-bedroom villas are terraced along the hill below the main house, which is home to an outstanding restaurant (see below). Designer-decorated and air-conditioned, the units offer plush living rooms with color TVs and VCRs; oversize pink marble showers; his and hers closets; modern kitchens with microwave ovens, dishwashers, and refrigerators (stocked at your request); and four-poster beds. French doors open onto private pools, patios, and sun terraces. The overall effect is a slice of Mediterranean luxury. Borrow a book from the library, shoot pool in the billiards room, or play tennis on the single court. The nine-hole **Reef Golf Course** (773.8844) is just down the hill. This property is geared toward couples or families

traveling with older children. ♦ South of East End Rd, Teague Bay. 773.7377, 800/548.4461; fax 773.7518

Within the Villa Madeleine:

Great House at Villa Madeleine

★★★★$$$$ This fine restaurant, housed in the West Indian–style main building high above Teague Bay, is expensive—and worth every penny, for both the incredible sea views from the canopied terrace and the mouthwatering Italian cuisine. Those who have had their fill of the outdoors can enjoy their meal in the air-conditioned dining room, with its ceiling draped in a floral-print fabric chosen by former White House decorator Carleton Varney. The creative menu changes frequently but always relies heavily on fresh pasta, fish, and meats. Leave room for the devastating "chocolate blackout" dessert. This is currently considered the best restaurant on the island, so make your reservations early. ♦ Italian ♦ Tu-Sa dinner; Su brunch and dinner. Reservations required. 778.7377

34 Cruzan Rum Factory When you order a rum punch in these parts, here's what gives it the "punch." The factory offers tours of the distillery, followed by tastings. ♦ Admission. M-F. Rte 64 (between Melvin H. Evans Hwy and Centerline Rd). 692.2280

35 St. George Village Botanical Garden

Ask for the guidebook that follows the brown-and-white signs identifying some of the property's 350-plus species of trees, flowers, vines, and shrubs. You'll see the mother-in-law tree, so named because its brown pods make a chattering noise when the wind blows. There's also the soaring kapok tree, the quarter-sized plumbago blossom, and the endangered touch-me-not tree. The sticky gel from the nut of the tamarind tree is used in jams and jellies. ♦ Admission. Tu-Sa. Just north of Centerline Rd (west of Rte 705). 692.2874

36 Whim Plantation Estate The name has inspired lots of theories, including one that the man who bought the plantation in the mid-1700s was so rich he purchased it on a whim. Perhaps, but certainly the great house is whimsical: oval-shaped, and surrounded by an "air" moat and limestone walls three feet thick. The unknown architect was ahead of his or her time: The moat makes sense, allowing air to flow around and through the basement, and the thick walls have withstood every storm and hurricane to hit the island. Sugar was once milled on the grounds, and if wind power didn't suffice, donkeys were harnessed to the churn. Later, the mills were steam-powered. Today, all three styles of sugar mill can be seen on the grounds.

Inside, the house has been restored to its original French Neo-Classical decor and colonial furnishings, including several Duncan Phyfe pieces. Guided tours are led throughout the estate, and interesting stories are told of the "courting" chair and the "planter's" chair. There's even a johnnycake lady who makes the island specialty the old-fashioned way. ♦ Admission. M-Sa. Centerline Rd (between Rtes 703 and 63). 772.1539

37 Frederiksted Rich in history and anecdotes, but limited in actual sights, this second town is the reason Virgin Islanders refer to St. Croix as the "tale of two cities." Cruise ships dock here, and walking about is a time-honored tradition. Stop in for a map at the **Tourist Board** (772.0357), located in the **Port Authority** building at the entrance to the pier.

Several of the town's churches were built in the early 1800s, while the **Market Place** dates back to 1751. Vendors still use the spot at Queen and Market Streets to sell fresh fruits and vegetables from Monday through Saturday.

During the winter months, turn toward the sea at sunset to look for the "green flash." When atmospheric conditions are just right, a green streak can be seen on the horizon for a brief moment as the sun drops below the sea. ♦ West coast

Within Frederiksted:

Fort Frederik This fort, built under Danish rule in 1752, has been restored to its original appearance. Visitors can browse through the parade grounds, the barracks, and the command building. ♦ Free. M-F. King St (between Custom House St and Northside Dr). 772.2021

38 Rain Forest While not a true rain forest, it's so called because it's the wettest and greenest area on the island. The road that passes through this forest is canopied by tree boughs, including those of the *saman,* which looks like an enormous bonsai tree. White flowers grow atop the *yaki yaki* tree, while the flamboyant tree is awash in brilliant red blossoms. ♦ Northwest interior

Within the Rain Forest:

St. Croix LEAP Shop In this enormous workshop deep in the Rain Forest, local artisans produce magnificent furniture, carvings, and kitchen items from the wood of mahogany, *saman,* and Tibet trees. A film of sawdust covers everything, including the satin-smooth coffee tables, free-form wall clocks, wind chimes, bookends, and cutting boards for sale. Purchases can be shipped to the US. ♦ Daily. Mahogany Rd (between Rtes 765 and 763). 772.0421

39 Paul and Jill's Equestrian Center Jill Hurd, born and raised on St. Croix, conducts the trail rides, entertaining visitors on horseback with a combination of tall tales and facts; her husband, Paul, takes care of the business end of the operation. The excursions cut through the Rain Forest, past streambeds and Danish ruins, and over the hills of the west end. Tour guides point out termite nests, grazing cattle, and the infamous mongooses, brought to the island in its sugarcane heyday to kill rats. (The strategy didn't work; mongooses are day-loving creatures, while rats prefer the night.) Hurd also offers sunset rides into the hills, and full-moon rides through the forest. All levels of riders are accommodated, but children under eight are not allowed. Long pants are a must, and you'll

be disappointed if you forget your camera.
♦ Admission. Daily; call in advance for sunset and moonlight ride schedules. Reservations recommended at least three days in advance. Sprat Hall Plantation, Rte 63 and Creque Dam Rd. 772.2880.

40 Scenic Road Partially paved and partially dirt, this one-lane road meanders through some of St. Croix's loveliest scenery, from Ham's Bay near Frederiksted through Caledonia Valley, then over the hills of Annaly to Mount Eagle. On the way, it passes through the Rain Forest. Your best bet is to go in a four-wheel-drive vehicle. Watch out for darting mongooses! ♦ Between North Shore Rd and Ham's Bay

CaRaMBOLa

41 Carambola Golf Club Laurance Rockefeller hired Robert Trent Jones Sr. to design this outstanding 18-hole course. Coconut markers once lined the fairways; today they are edged with palm trees. A challenging and scenic course, a restaurant, and an extensive pro shop lure avid golfers. ♦ Fee. Daily. West of Rte 69 (between Rte 72 and Scenic Rd). 778.5638

42 Westin Carambola Resort $$$ This 46-acre property offers 151 rooms and suites in a villa-style complex with an immaculate white-sand beach, a pool, 2 Jacuzzis, and 4 tennis courts. There's a shuttle service to the 18-hole **Carambola Golf Club**, and golf packages are available. The decor was inspired by the great plantation houses of St. Croix, with Brazilian walnut furnishings. Rooms on the upper floor of the two-story villas have vaulted wood ceilings, and spacious bathrooms feature Mexican tiles. All rooms are equipped with air-conditioning, telephones, and cable TV. Horticultural tours are provided by the staff—the grounds have more than 89 different kinds of palm trees, many of them imported. Three restaurants offer good mealtime variety, from casual deli fare to continental dining. Water sports—including deep-sea fishing and scuba diving—can be arranged. ♦ Davis Bay. 778.3800, 800/228.3000; fax 778.1682

43 Cane Bay/St. Croix Wall Experienced scuba divers will smile for weeks, for there are not many other places in the world where you can wade into the surf off the beach, slip into your dive gear, and within 80 yards free-float over a coral wall that drops two miles straight down. The reef starts at the beach and gently slopes down until you're in 30 feet of water. Below, purple sea fans undulate, and iridescent fish dart past. A minute later, the reef has disappeared down the sheer ledge, and you're surrounded by the bluest water imaginable. The wall stretches along four miles of St. Croix's north coast. **Cane Bay Dive Shop** (773.9913) at Cane Bay and **Waterworld Divers Ltd.** (773.3434) in

Christiansted offer wall and other dives, resort courses, certification courses, and equipment rental.
♦ Northwest coast

St. Thomas

With a bustling port city and a deep harbor where one or more cruise ships are often docked, St. Thomas is the most developed and commercialized of the US Virgin Islands. Good roads wind through its green mountains, leading visitors to a multitude of shimmering beaches, upscale resorts, and gourmet restaurants. Of the three sister islands, this is the one to come to for action, nightlife, and shopping.

Pastel homes dot the hills surrounding the capital city, **Charlotte Amalie** (pronounced Ah-*mahl*-yah)—and a city it is, with lots of traffic, honking cab drivers, and sidewalks busy with people. **Main Street** is lined with old-style Danish buildings and converted warehouses with typical early West Indian architecture: hipped roofs of corrugated metal, arcaded first floors with Moorish-arched doorways, heavy wood shutters, and second-story verandas. The major shopping action takes place here, and, as elsewhere in the USVI, visitors from the US are allowed to take $1,200 worth of merchandise home duty-free. Be forewarned that the street hawkers are extremely persistent and that some merchandise, especially electronics, can be found at the same or lower prices in the US.

44 Water Island It's called the "fourth Virgin Island." Ownership of 50 of this island's 200-plus acres was transferred from the US Interior Department to the USVI territorial government on 12 December, 1996. The US Army's **Fort Segarra** operated here back in the 1940s, but now a hotel is planned, along with concessions for Honeymoon Beach on the western side of the island, a five-minute walk from the ferry dock. A small public ferry makes several trips between the island and **Crown Bay Marina** daily. ♦ South of Crown Bay

45 Frenchtown This area was originally settled by fishing families who emigrated from St-Barthélemy, a small French island east of here. The colorful hamlet is filled with tiny, gaily painted wooden homes with red-tin roofs. There are several excellent restaurants too.
♦ South of Rte 30 (just west of Charlotte Amalie)

Within Frenchtown:

Craig and Sally's ★★★$$$ A beautiful mural of island scenes covers the walls of this restaurant known for its eclectic and ever-changing menu. Diners often get to choose from Caribbean, Italian, Chinese, and Thai dishes, including such creations as graham cracker–crusted pork tenderloin with a tamarind glaze, duck with a mango chutney, and fish cakes with Key lime mustard.
♦ International ♦ Daily dinner. 22 Honduras St. 779.9949

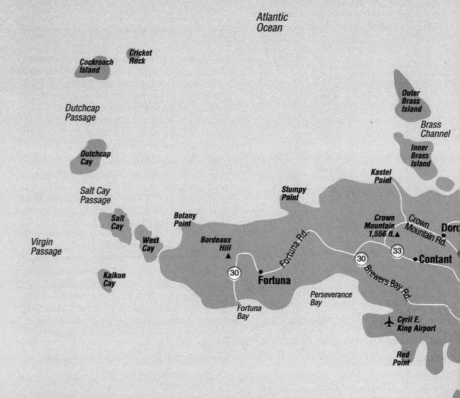

Atlantic
Ocean

Cockroach
Island

Cricket
Rock

Dutchcap
Passage

Outer
Brass
Island

Brass
Channel

Inner
Brass
Island

Dutchcap
Cay

Kastel
Point

Salt Cay
Passage

Stumpy
Point

Crown
Mountain
1,556 ft.▲

Crown
Mountain Rd.

Dorot

Salt
Cay

Botany
Point

Fortuna Rd.

Virgin
Passage

West
Cay

Bordeaux
Hill
▲

33

Contant

30

Kalkun
Cay

30

Fortuna

Brewers Bay Rd.

Fortuna
Bay

Perseverance
Bay

✈ Cyril E.
King Airport

Red
Point

Saba
Island

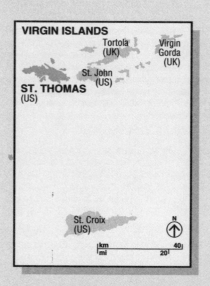

VIRGIN ISLANDS

Tortola
(UK)

Virgin
Gorda
(UK)

St. John
(US)

ST. THOMAS
(US)

St. Croix
(US)

N

km
mi

40
20

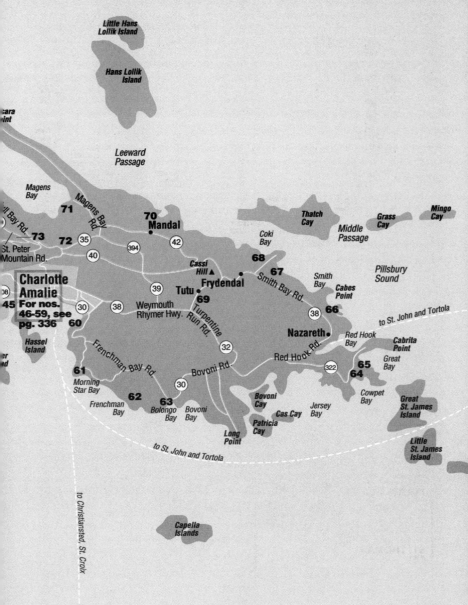

Little Hans
Lollik Island

Hans Lollik
Island

Leeward
Passage

Magens
Bay

71

Magens Bay Rd.

ll Bay Rd.

ara
int

73

72

35

St. Peter
Mountain Rd.

40

394

70 Mandal

42

Coki
Bay

Thatch
Cay

Middle
Passage

Grass
Cay

Mingo
Cay

Pillsbury
Sound

68

67

Smith Bay Rd.

Smith
Bay

Cabes
Point

Cassi
Hill ▲

Frydendal

39

Tutu

69

Weymouth
Rhymer Hwy.

Turpentine Run Rd.

38

38

66

to St. John and Tortola

**Charlotte
Amalie**
For nos.
46–59, see
pg. 336

08

45

30

38

Nazareth

Red Hook Rd.

Red Hook
Bay

Cabrita
Point

60

Hassel
Island

32

322

Great
Bay

65

64

r
d

61

Morning
Star Bay

Frenchman Bay Rd.

Bovoni Rd.

30

62

63

Frenchman
Bay

Bolongo
Bay

Bovoni
Bay

Bovoni
Cay

Cas Cay

Jersey
Bay

Cowpet
Bay

Great
St. James
Island

Patricia
Cay

Long
Point

Little
St. James
Island

to St. John and Tortola

to Christiansted, St. Croix

Capella
Islands

Caribbean
Sea

N

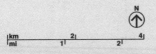

km
mi
1
2
2
4

46 Market Square Produce vendors hawk their wares in open-air stalls on the grounds of this former slave market. It's worth a stop for the color and bustle and a for taste of island-grown fruit. ♦ Daily. Strand Gade and Main St, Charlotte Amalie

47 Virgilio's/Virgilio's Wine Cellar & Bistro ★★★$$$ These two eateries both feature excellent Italian cuisine. Osso buco (veal shank marinated in a delicious sauce and served with fettuccine) is the specialty. The wine bar on the first floor of the newer wine cellar and bistro also offers oenophiles a choice of some 1,000 varieties. Traditional Danish archways lead the way into both of the two dining rooms, where paintings by local artists decorate the walls and stained-glass windows extend from the banquettes to the ceiling. Expect fine dining in an intimate setting with impeccable service. ♦ Northern Italian ♦ M-Sa lunch and dinner. Reservations recommended. 16-18 Main St (at Storetvaer Gade), Charlotte Amalie. 776.4920

48 Camille Pissaro Art Gallery Located in the birthplace of St. Thomas's most famous artist, this second-floor gallery offers a fine collection of original paintings and prints by local and regional artists as well as works by Pissarro himself. ♦ M-Sa. 14 Main St (between Trompeter and Storetvaer Gades), Charlotte Amalie. 775.5511

49 Synagogue of Beracha Veshalom Vegmiluth Hasidim Built in 1833, the third oldest Jewish temple in the Western Hemisphere (the oldest is in Curaçao, the ruins of the second-oldest are in St. Eustatius) takes the honors as the oldest synagogue in continuous use. The sand on the floor commemorates the biblical exodus of the Jews from Egypt. About 150 tourists stop in each day to see the Chair of Elijah, which is still used for circumcisions; the 900-year-old menorah from Cordoba, Spain; and two beautiful Torahs dating back 140 years. Visitors are welcome to join Shabbat services held Friday at 7:30PM and Saturday at 11:15AM. ♦ M-Sa. Crystal Gade (between Nye and Bjerge Gades), Charlotte Amalie. 774.4312

50 Blackbeard's Castle Get to the castle by climbing the **99 Steps** built by the Danes in the 1700s (trust us, there are more than 99 steps) or take the easy way and drive. The castle is actually a watchtower, purportedly built by pirate Edward Teach, the infamous Blackbeard, to scan the surrounding seas for ships to loot and plunder. Visitors are not allowed inside the watchtower (it's part of the **Blackbeard's Castle Hotel** complex, see below) but can enjoy unsurpassed views of Charlotte Amalie and its harbor from the

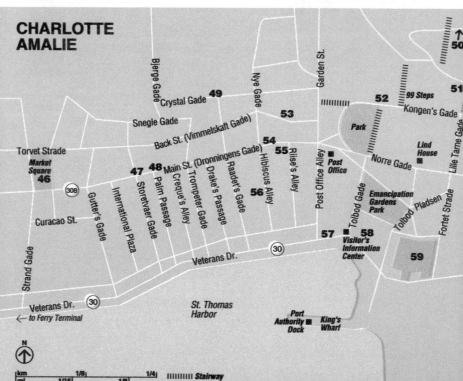

summit of the hill. ◆ Rte 35 (east of Store Tarne Gade), Charlotte Amalie

Within Blackbeard's Castle:

Blackbeard's Castle Hotel $$ This 17th-century Danish mansion is intimate and comfortable, with just 16 rooms and apartments and a simple decor. Amenities include an excellent restaurant (see below) and an Olympic-size pool. ◆ 776.1234, 800/344.5771; fax 776.4321

Within Blackbeard's Castle Hotel:

Café Lulu's ★★★★$$$ Live jazz and spectacular views of the city lights and docked cruise ships are stellar attractions at this lovely dining room atop Government Hill. Chef Patricia LaCorte creates Asian, Caribbean, and Mediterranean specialties like plantain-coated sea bass and goat cheese–filled filet mignon. Try the orange-mango mimosas and wasabi-spiced Bloody Marys at Sunday brunch. ◆ Continental ◆ M-Sa dinner; Su brunch. Reservations recommended. 714.1641

51 Seven Arches Museum An 18th-century house that once belonged to a Danish craftsman has been restored to its original style, complete with antique furnishings. Visitors can see how rain water was collected for household use in the original stone kitchen, which is separate from the main house. Note the gun slots in the walls around the house, indicating that it may have been used as a fort at some point in time. The balcony has a great view of the harbor, and guests are treated to a tropical drink. ◆ Admission. Tu-Su. Lille Tarne Gade (north of Norre Gade), Charlotte Amalie. 774.9295

52 Hotel 1829 $$ This charming pink building has long been a landmark in Charlotte Amalie. With its green awning and wrought-iron gate, plus a sunny courtyard, shady veranda, and small pool, the hotel evokes bygone days. There are 14 tastefully decorated guest rooms with refrigerators, and an excellent restaurant (see below) where hotel guests enjoy a complimentary continental breakfast. The beach is a 15-minute drive away. ◆ Kongens Gade (west of Lille Tarne Gade), Charlotte Amalie. 776.1829, 800/524.2002; fax 776.4313

Within Hotel 1829:

Hotel 1829 Restaurant ★★★★$$$$ Old World elegance reigns in this historic building overlooking Charlotte Amalie and the harbor beyond. Ask for a table on the terrace in order to take in the view, or stroll over the 200-year-old Moroccan floor tiles into the dining rooms to soak in the Moorish and Mediterranean ambience. With only 27 tables, the setting is intimate, romantic, and hedonistic—perfect for a last-night-of-vacation splurge. Start your meal with the wilted spinach salad, a house specialty prepared tableside, along with smoked Scotch salmon tartare. The fresh Anguillan rock lobster or the rack of spring lamb are excellent choices for a main course. There's also a prix-fixe three-course dinner menu that offers both elegance and (relative) economy. ◆ Continental ◆ Daily lunch and dinner. Reservations required. 776.1829

53 Bakery Square This old brick bakery now houses shops. At **Blue Carib Gems** (774.8525) you can tour the workshop and purchase gems, of course, and jewelry, too; it's even possible to design your own. ◆ M-Sa. Back St (between Garden St and Nye Gade), Charlotte Amalie

54 Little Switzerland Check out the 50-percent-off corner here; it features china, crystal, and figurines by Wedgwood, Lalique, and Lladró. ◆ M-Sa; Su when cruise ships are in town. Main St and Nye Gade, Charlotte Amalie. 776.2010. Also at: Norre Gade, Charlotte Amalie. 776.2010; 1108 King St (at King's Alley), Christiansted, St. Croix. 773.1976

55 A.H. Riise Print Gallery Pick up framed and unframed prints by local artists at this art gallery. ◆ M-Sa; Su when cruise ships are in town. Riise's Alley and Main St, Charlotte Amalie. 776.2303

56 Virgin Islands America's Cup Team Store Buying snappy nautical sportswear helps fund the USVI's bid for the Cup 2000 in New Zealand. ◆ West Indies Coffee Co., Hibiscus Alley (south of Main St), Charlotte Amalie. 774.9090

In 1997 and 1998 President Bill Clinton and his family spent a New Year's vacation on St. Thomas. The Clintons stayed in a private villa and the president played golf at Mahogany Run Golf course. In 1998, "first dog" Buddy, a Labrador puppy, took his first swim at Magens Bay Beach.

STORETVAER GADE

Star Jewelers	**The Crystal Shop**
jewelry, liquor **Sparky's**	
watches **Cartier Boutique**	**Imperial Jewelers**

TROMPETER GADE

electronics **Boolchand's**	
H. Stern Watches	**H. Stern** *jewelry*

RAADET'S GADE

jewelry **Gem Palace**	**Little Switzerland** *crystal, china*
electronics **Royal Caribbean**	
china, watches **Bolero**	**Colombian Emeralds** *jewelry*
A. H. Riise Liquor Store	**Diamonds International** *jewelry*
A. H. Riise Jewels Boutique	
jewelry, fragrances, cosmetics	
local art **Caribbean Print Gallery**	
jewelry **Bernard K. Passman**	**The Leather Shop** *handbags, belts*
jewelry **Cardow's Main Street**	**Cardow's Solid Gold** *jewelry*

(MAIN STREET runs vertically between the two columns above)

57 Down Island Traders Stop in for tropical spices and preserves, exotic teas, and Caribbean cookbooks. ◆ M-Sa; Su when cruise ships are in town. Veterans Dr and Post Office Alley, Charlotte Amalie. 776.4641

DOWN ISLAND TRADERS
TROPICAL DELICACIES & GIFTS
ORIGINAL SILK-SCREENED DESIGNS
DOWNTOWN ON THE WATERFRONT

58 Vendor's Plaza Folding tables shaded by a hodgepodge of umbrellas hold T-shirts, jewelry, shell art, prints, straw hats, and Caribbean (not necessarily local) handicrafts. Bargains may or may not be found, but it's always fun to cruise through and have a look. ◆ Daily. Veterans Dr (just east of Tolbod Gade), Charlotte Amalie. 776.4641

59 Fort Christian This national historic landmark was the first major building erected on St. Thomas (circa 1671). At various times in the past, the brick-colored fort has served as a jail, courthouse, church, rectory, and governor's residence. In its last incarnation, until 1982, it was a police station. Today it houses a museum with a fine collection of turn-of-the-century furniture, medicinal-plant exhibits, and a display of seashells. Graffiti engraved in the walls by prisoners is still visible in the narrow jail cells. Due to ongoing restoration, areas of the fort are occasionally closed. ◆ Free. M-F. 1 Fortet Strade (at Veterans Dr), Charlotte Amalie. 776.4566

60 Havensight Shopping Mall and Port of Sale Outlet Shops These side-by-side shopping centers, located right at the cruise-ship dock, are the epitome of convenience for cruise-ship passengers intent on shopping 'til they drop. Most of the major stores in town have satellite operations here, with the same prices. ◆ M-Sa; Su when a cruise ship is in town. Frenchman Bay Rd (just south of Charlotte Amalie). 774.5313

Impressionist painter Camille Pissarro was a native of St. Thomas.

Within the Havensight Shopping Mall:

Atlantis Submarines Next to scuba diving, this is as close as you can get to a deep natural reef. Just board the air-conditioned submarine and relax while it dives as many as 90 feet below the surface. Large portholes allow easy viewing of the teeming reef as the 46-passenger vessel cruises past brilliantly hued fish, vibrant sea fans, and giant purple and orange sponges. Occasionally a shark swims by, chasing off the cloud of curious yellowtail snappers that tend to drift over to investigate the sub. A guide narrates the hour-long journey. No children under 36 inches tall are allowed aboard. ◆ Admission. M-Sa. Building VI-L. Reservations 776.5650, information 776.0288.

FRENCHMAN'S REEF

61 Marriott's Frenchman's Reef Beach Resort $$$ There's a little bit of everything at this full-service resort, which was renovated in 1997. The establishment actually consists of two properties: **Marriott's Frenchman's Reef,** high on the hill, and the pricier, more upscale **Marriott's Morning Star Beach Resort.** Guests of either are welcome to use the facilities of both resorts, which include a comprehensive water-sports center, six restaurants, and free ferry service into town. There are also children's programs during the holiday season, but this resort is geared more toward adults than families.

Most of the action takes place at **Marriott's Frenchman's Reef** up on the hill, accessible by elevator from the beach. Here 293 deluxe rooms and 128 suites overlook the resort's pool complex (2 connecting pools and a waterfall), the harbor, or the sea. The free daily activities are well attended—not surprising, given that the workshops include rum tasting, water aerobics, and island cooking. Guests are encouraged to attend the free tennis, windsurfing, and snorkel clinics as well. There's even a wedding gazebo, where hundreds of couples have been married; the resort has a special wedding planner (800/FOR.LOVE) who arranges every detail, from the ceremony to the photos, and three wedding packages are available.

Marriott's Morning Star offers 96 luxury units right on a beach that's a vacationer's dream, with soft, clean, white sand and lots of palm trees. Rate plans at both properties range from "room only" to all-inclusive packages. ♦ Rte 315, Morning Star Bay. 776.8500, 800/524.2000; fax 774.3054

62 **Bluebeard Beach Villas** $$$ Set on a beautiful crescent-shaped beach, this resort offers 84 rooms with air-conditioning, cable TV, safes, and telephones. Amenities include a pool, two lighted tennis courts, and a restaurant. The resident iguanas are so tame they will eat red hibiscus blooms out of your hand. ♦ Frenchman Bay. 776.4770, 800/524.6599; fax 693.2648

63 **Bolongo Bay Beach & Tennis Club** $$$ This upscale beachfront hotel with 75 rooms (some with kitchenettes, all with ocean views) recently underwent a major overhaul. All rooms have air-conditioning, cable TV, safes, and telephones, and there's a wide array of activities to choose from, including scuba diving (an introductory lesson is included in the rate), tennis (there are four courts), day cruises, and frolicking in the pool, which has a swim-up bar. Two restaurants and **Iggies** piano and karaoke lounge round out the picture. Semi- and all-inclusive packages are available. ♦ Frenchman Bay Rd, Bolongo Bay. 775.1800, 800/524.4746; fax 775.3208

Within Bolongo Bay Beach & Tennis Club:

St. Thomas Diving Club Come here to book snorkeling or diving trips, including excursions to Buck Island near St. Croix or the wreck *HMS Rhone.* Certification courses are available. ♦ Daily. 776.2381

64 **Elysian Beach Resort** $$$ Smack on Cowpet Beach, this ultramodern resort has pink, low-rise buildings scattered around the landscaped grounds. The 175 air-conditioned units are as nice as your rich uncle's super-deluxe condo. They're furnished with four-poster beds, sleek bamboo and wicker furniture upholstered with thick cushions, remote-controlled color TV, limited-edition prints, stocked mini-bars, and balconies with views of the water.

Room rates include breakfast, an introductory scuba lesson, and some water sports, but an all-inclusive package is not available. There is, however, plenty to do, with tennis courts, a water-sports center, and a state-of-the-art health club. The beach is lovely, though not very large, and the view includes the sea and the anchored boats bobbing about in Cowpet Bay. The only drawback is the food at the two restaurants, which is mediocre at best. ♦ East of Rte 322, Cowpet Bay. 775.1000, 800/753.2554; fax 776.0910

65 **Ritz-Carlton, St. Thomas** $$$$ This delightful property—the most luxurious on the island—features Italian Renaissance–style architecture. Guests relax among marbled and tiled splendor in 152 rooms and suites, all with private balconies, cable TV, mini-bars, hair dryers, and in-room safes, among other amenities. Facilities include a 125-foot freshwater pool, a fitness center, and 4 lighted tennis courts; there's also a children's program. The poolside restaurant features Mediterranean fare at lunchtime, and a formal dining room offers breakfast and Caribbean cuisine at dinner. ♦ East of Rte 322, Great Bay. 775.3333, 800/241.3333; fax 775.4444

66 **Doubletree Sapphire Beach Resort & Marina** $$$$ This resort is geared toward fun-loving families and beach buffs. It sits on the beach, where the island's hottest bodies strut their stuff, and top-notch windsurfers make the sport look easy. On Sundays a lively steel band plays at the beach bar near the freshwater pool. Adults can take advantage of the complimentary Sunfish, day-sailers, snorkel equipment, tennis courts, and Windsurfers, while children under 12 enjoy 3 hours a day of free, supervised activities. (Kids 12 and under also stay and eat for free.) Baby-sitting service is available in the evening for a fee. Lodging is in 155 suites or villas with complete kitchens, air-conditioning, telephones, and TV sets. There are three restaurants. ♦ East of Smith Bay Rd, St. John Bay. 775.6100, 800/524.2090; fax 775.2403

67 **Agavé Terrace** ★★★$$$ This top island restaurant, part of the **Colony Point Pleasant Resort,** is situated on a breeze-cooled terrace overlooking the sea. While the resort is in need of a spruce-up, the restaurant's menu doesn't disappoint. Shellfish, fresh fish, and prime cuts of beef are prepared in delectably creative ways. Excellent choices include lobster on angel-hair pasta, and tuna or grouper with either a fresh dill or lobster cream sauce. Save room for the totally wicked peanut-butter cheesecake. For a truly memorable evening, book a table on a night when there's a full moon, then watch it rise high over the British Virgin Islands, which are visible in the distance. There's entertainment on full-moon nights and every Tuesday and Thursday. ♦ Continental/Caribbean ♦ Daily dinner. Reservations recommended. North of Smith Bay Rd, Water Bay. 775.4142

67 Eunice's Terrace ★★★$$ Conch fritters, boiled fish, *fungi* (cornmeal dumplings), rum cake, and soursop juice were President Clinton's favorites when he and the First Family dined here in 1997. Some say the cafe is overrated, but it's still one of the more popular places to sample local dishes. ♦ West Indian ♦ M-Sa lunch and dinner; Su dinner. 67 Smith Bay Rd (southeast of Rte 388). 775.3975

68 Coral World Underwater Observatory and Marine Gardens Re-opened in late 1997 after extensive hurricane damage, the fully rebuilt glass-enclosed marine observatory, which lies 20 feet below sea level, is more wondrous than ever. Think of it as a reverse zoo: You're in the cage, watching the reef fish, coral, and sponges going about their business in the open sea. Bring your postcards for the underwater mailbox—you can mail them from 14 feet below the surface. The **Reef Tank** is filled with moray eels, sharks, stingrays, and barracudas; each day at 11AM scuba divers feed these predators by hand. If you have only one day on the island, this is the number-one must-see attraction. ♦ Admission. Daily. Rte 388, Coki Point. 775.1555

69 Tillett Gardens Craft Studios Iguanas wander unhindered in this small artists' colony, where visitors can watch craftspeople silk-screening maps, hand-painting T-shirts, and goldsmithing  custom wedding bands in their studios. You can buy a painting or print in one stall and have it framed in another. Crafts fairs featuring the work of local artisans are held here three times a year, in April, August, and November. ♦ M-Sa. Rtes 38 and 382, Tutu. 775.1929

70 Mahogany Run Golf Course Designed by George and Tom Fazio, this 18-hole golf course is the only one on St. Thomas and it's a beauty. Holes 13 through 15, called the "Devil's Triangle," are especially picturesque. In 1996 the course was given a face-lift—the tee boxes were widened and the sand traps got new drainage systems. President Clinton played here during New Year's vacations in 1997 and 1998. ♦ Fee. Daily. Mandal Rd (just east of Mahogany Run Rd), Mandal. 777.6006, 800.253.7103

71 Magens Bay Beach This lovely horseshoe-shaped beach is written about in every guidebook and magazine article, yet the soft sands that border the calm bay, backed by a thick fringe of palm trees, are rarely crowded. The beach is worth seeing; it epitomizes everything you ever dreamed an island beach should be (though the snack bar is a bit rundown). ♦ Admission. Daily. Magens Rd (northwest of Mahogany Run Rd)

72 Drake's Seat Privateer Sir Francis Drake supposedly sat here, spyglass in hand, watching for passing enemy ships to plunder. The seat is a stone bench built into the hillside above Magens Bay. When the weather conditions are right, you can see as far as Jos Van Dyke and Tortola. It's a commercial spot, with several vendors selling souvenirs and trinkets. For a dollar, you can even have your photo taken alongside a donkey adorned with a crown of hibiscus. ♦ Rtes 40 and 35

73 Fairchild Park Arthur Fairchild, a longtime resident of St. Thomas, donated this park to the island in 1951. Seldom used, it's a perfect spot for an out-of-the-way picnic. Just bring everything you need, as there's only a bench in this tiny mountainside garden with views of both the Atlantic Ocean and Caribbean Sea. ♦ St. Peter Mountain Rd (west of Rte 37)

74 Mountain Top Legend has it that banana daiquiris were invented on this spot—formerly a hotel restaurant—more than 20 years ago. Now it's a one-story complex of small specialty shops, including **Tropic Spice** (Caribbean spices) and  **Paradise Remembered** (artwork and prints). It's situated at the highest point on St. Thomas, so the outdoor observation deck offers outstanding views. On a clear day you can see more than 20 islands and even part of St. Croix, 40 miles away. The air-conditioned shopping and cultural center also houses an aviary (the largest bird display on the island), an aquarium featuring fish caught off St. Thomas, a terrarium, and a snack bar that offers the famous drink. ♦ North of Rte 33 (between Rtes 37 and 40). 774.0909

Getting Your Feet Wet in the US Virgin Islands

There's so much more to do in the islands beyond the beach. Here are outfits that can set you afloat:

Boating

On St. Croix:

Green Cay Marina North of East End Rd. 773.1453

St. Croix Marina Mount Welcome Rd (north of Garden St), Christiansted. 773.0289

Salt River Marina North Shore Rd, Salt River Bay. 778.9650

On St. John:

Caneel Bay Caneel Bay. 776.6111, 800/928.8889

Cinnamon Bay Watersports Cinnamon Bay. 776.6330, 800/539.9998

Cruz Bay Watersports Cruz Bay. 776.6234

Low Key Watersports Wharfside Village (just southwest of the ferry dock), Cruz Bay. 693.8999

Maho Bay Camps Maho Bay. 776.6226

St. John Water Sports/Hinkley Charters Mongoose Junction, North Shore Rd, Cruz Bay. 693.9841

On St. Thomas:

Adventure Center Marriott's Frenchman's Reef, Rte 315, Morning Star Bay. 774.2990, 776.8500 ext. 445

American Yacht Harbor Red Hook Bay. 775.6454

Club Nautico Charters Red Hook Bay. 779.2555

V.I. Charteryacht League 774.3944

Snorkeling and Scuba Diving

On St. Croix:

Anchor Dive Center Christiansted. 778.1522, 800/532.3483

Cane Bay Dive Shop Cane Bay. 773.9913

Cruzan Divers Frederiksted. 772.3701, 800/352.0107

Dive Experience Christiansted. 773.3307, 800/235.9047

Waterworld Divers Ltd. Christiansted. 773.3434

On St. John:

Cinnamon Bay Watersports Cinnamon Bay. 776.6330, 800/539.9998

Cruz Bay Watersports Cruz Bay. 776.6234

Paradise Watersports Cruz Bay. 779.4999. 693.8690

On St. Thomas:

Aqua Action Secret Harbor, Jersey Bay. 775.6285

Chris Sawyer Diving Center American Yacht Harbor, Red Hook Bay. 777.7804

St. Thomas Diving Club Bolongo Bay Beach & Tennis Club, Frenchman Bay Rd, Bolongo Bay. 776.2381

Sportfishing

On St. Croix:

Fishaholic Services Green Cay Marina (north of East End Rd). 773.8988

Lisa Ann Charters Green Cay Marina (north of East End Rd). 773.3712

Ruffian St. Croix Marina, Mount Welcome Rd (north of Garden St), Christiansted. 773.7165, 773.0917 (evenings)

On St. John:

Caneel Bay Caneel Bay. 776.6111, 800/928.8889

Cruz Bay Watersports Cruz Bay. 776.6234

Low Key Watersports Wharfside Village (just southwest of the ferry dock), Cruz Bay. 693.8999

On St. Thomas:

Adventure Center Marriott's Frenchman's Reef, Rte 315, Morning Star Bay. 774.2990, 776.8500 ext. 445

American Yacht Harbor Red Hook Bay. 775.6454

Captain Al Petrosky East End Lagoon. 775.9058

Doubletree Sapphire Beach Resort and Marina East of Smith Bay Rd, St. John Bay. 775.6100, 800/524.2090

Windsurfing

Chenay Bay Beach Resort St. Croix. 773.2918

Hotel on the Cay Christiansted, St. Croix. 773.2035

St. Croix Water Sports Center Hotel on the Cay, Christiansted, St. Croix. 773.7060

Bests

L.H. Torre Newman

Manager, Hotel 1829

Magens Bay Beach on **St. Thomas** is a wonderful place to meet an international tourist or two. Also, very good food, especially the pizza. The most tranquil beach pick is **Secret Harbor,** on the east end, near **Red Hook.** For the perfect "I'm the only one on the beach" experience, take the time to get out to **Salt Pond,** on the east end of **St. John.** It's picturesque and usually deserted, so you must bring your own food and drinks. The wildlife here is abundant and friendly.

The best tour bargains in **Charlotte Amalie** are the self-guided walking tours of the three historic districts. The best way to see the island is one of the Safari bus tours from town; they're approximately two to three hours long and have lots of good stops. The Safaris are also the way to see St. John. Normally, you can get an island tour on your way to one of the beautiful north shore beaches.

Cut and uncut, set or unset, gem stones are abundant in Charlotte Amalie. Very competitive prices. My pick for "shinnies" is **Colombian Emeralds** or **H. Stern.** Gold is a bargain at all the jewelry stores. Without a doubt, the **Vendor's Plaza,** with its array of colors, people, and activity, is the place to choose the perfect T-shirt souvenir.

If one looks hard enough, they can find culture anywhere on St. Thomas and St. John. From the "Classics in the Garden" series at **Tillet Gardens Craft Studios,** to ballets, plays, and concerts, to the Carnival celebrations, art shows, and poetry readings, there are events and activities throughout the year. Somewhere, all the time, something is going on.

Carleton Varney

President, Dorothy Draper & Company (promotion and tourism)

Recommended places to visit on St. Croix:

Top Hat Restaurant. St. Croix's favorite restaurant— for the locals. Can be expensive, but worth it. The best bet on the menu is *frigadella* with a berry dressing. Cuisine is Danish, and Bent Rasmussen, husband of Hanne (the hostess), does the cooking.

The **Gallery** at **The Buccaneer.** A shop filled with art—including paintings by Sacha Tebo—and the most beautifully designed bead jewelry in the Caribbean. Louise Galembo is the proprietor and designer.

Whim Plantation Estate. The museum to visit on the island—a sugar plantation operated to show visitors what life once was.

Cruzan Rum Factory. Not to be missed—and they give samples, with a mixer of your choice.

St. Croix LEAP Shop. An institution on the island, where mahogany tables are made—and you'll enjoy the trip through the **Rain Forest** to get there.

The east end of the island. Stop for a cocktail at **Villa Madeleine.** A visit there will tell you why *Architectural Digest* chose the hotel for its cover. All villas have private swimming pools and great views.

Buck Island. A national underwater museum. A must must, must. See if you can arrange a day sail over to the whitest, sandiest beaches in the Caribbean.

The open-air market at **Market Square.** Vegetables and fruits, particularly island-grown sweet, finger-size bananas. You'll find spicy island sauces at the market too—they're very, very hot so be careful.

Carambola Golf Club. The prettiest golf course you've ever seen was created by Laurance Rockefeller, for everyone's enjoyment, and you can get a good meal there too. Rent a golf cart for the ride if you don't play golf.

The Buccaneer. The island's glamour hotel, in the plantation manor. You have to be a registered guest to enjoy the grotto pool, the golf course, and the health spa.

The Galleon—A fun spot for music, drinks and dinner at **Green Cay Marina.** The boats are fun to look at while dining, and the people at the piano bar are interesting to see and talk about also.

Leo Carty. St. Croix's best artist. I love his work. Also look at the works of Paul Youngblood. Paul's works are shown all over the world.

Duggan's Reef. A luncheon or dinner in this beachside restaurant on the East End is a must— particularly on Sunday for brunch. Bajan flying fish is a specialty, as is the cornbread.

Laura Davidson

President, Laura Davidson Public Relations

Magens Bay Beach. Beautiful crescent of beach for swimming and walking.

Charlotte Amalie. Shopping—when there are only one or two cruise ships, the bargains are better and no crowds.

Snorkel/sailing trip to **St. John's, Honeymoon Beach** or **Buck Island.**

Helicopter tour of the US and British Virgin Islands with **Air Center Helicopter Tours.**

See the islands by boat.

Check cruise-ship schedules on all tours and shopping sprees to avoid crowds!

Ask hotel staff for their favorite places.

In 1998 the US Virgin Islands commemorated the 150th anniversary of the emancipation of slaves on the islands with a week-long celebration. The celebration recognized the USVI as the first place slavery was abolished on what is now US soil.

History

Archaeologists believe the Caribbean islands once were populated by the Ciboney, the Taíno, the Arawak, and the namesake Carib Indians, who paddled their way in canoes north from South America as far as **Puerto Rico**. There is evidence of Amerindian settlements on **Trinidad** as early as 5000 BC. The Arawak were fishers and farmers who worshiped spirits of nature. Archaeologists have found carvings and cave paintings of these spirits on some islands, including **Aruba**. The Carib, for whom the region was named, were rumored to be cannibals.

1492 Christopher Columbus makes the first of four voyages to the New World, and wrecks his largest ship, the *Santa Maria*, off the shores of **Hispaniola** (now site of the **Dominican Republic** and Haiti).

1493 Columbus makes his second voyage to the Caribbean and sights too many islands to set foot on. The list includes what are now known as **Antigua**, the US and **British Virgin Islands, Dominica, Guadeloupe,** and **Puerto Rico** (which Columbus called San Juan). He does drop anchor on 1 November off the east coast of an island he names **St. Martin,** after the Bishop of Tours.

Columbus establishes the first permanent European settlement in the West Indies on Hispaniola and Spanish settlement expands to other islands in the **Greater Antilles** during the early 16th century. Columbus and his 12,000 to 15,000 men demand food, gold, spun cotton, and other goods from the Arawak people of Hispaniola. Those who refuse to comply are sent back as an example to their villages with their noses and ears cut off.

1494 Columbus declares **Jamaica** "the fairest island that eyes have beheld."

1495 The Spanish conquer the island of Hispaniola, enslaving or murdering many of the Arawak Indians.

1498 On his third trip to the New World, Columbus comes upon the island of **Grenada,** which he names **Concepción.**

1499 Amerigo Vespucci arrives at **Bonaire.** Alonso de Ojeda, one of Columbus's lieutenants, comes across **Curaçao.**

1503 Columbus reaches the mainland of South America, and later stops at the **Cayman Islands**.

1505 To replace the rapidly dying Indians of Hispaniola, Columbus's son Ferdinand initiates the trans-Atlantic African slave trade. (There may have been as many as 8 million Arawak people on the island in 1492; by 1516 some 12,000 remained; by 1555 they were all dead.)

1514 Work begins on the **Catedral de Santa María la Menor** (the oldest cathedral in the Western Hemisphere) in **Santo Domingo,** on Hispaniola.

1519 African and Indian slaves on Hispaniola band together for the first large-scale slave revolt, which will not be finally defeated by the Spanish for more than a decade.

1521 Juan Ponce de León moves the first settlement on the island of San Juan from its original site to the northern peninsula. With high hopes he dubs the new city Puerto Rico (rich port). He later switches the name, however, and the city now honors his patron saint, **San Juan.**

1536 Navigator Pedro a Campo of Portugal is the first European to come upon **Barbados.** The Portuguese stay a short while. After they leave, the British take over the island in 1627.

1571 English navigator Francis Drake sails through the passage between the British and United States Virgin Islands.

1586 Drake, a pirate as far as the Spanish were concerned, sacks and burns the Spanish colony of Santo Domingo.

1621 The Dutch West India Company is organized to increase trade and encourage privateering against the Spanish.

1623 The first English settlement is established on **St. Kitts and Nevis** by Sir Thomas Warner.

1627 British settlers come ashore at **Holetown** on Barbados, claiming the island for King James I of England. Antigua, St. Kitts and Nevis, and **Barbuda** are also taken under the "protection" of Great Britain.

1630 The Spanish leave St. Martin, and the French take over the island for a brief period.

1631 The Dutch, seeking outposts for their ever-expanding West Indian trade, settle again on St. Martin, already deserted by the French.

1633 The Spaniards return to St. Martin and drive the Dutch away.

1644 A Dutch fleet under the command of Peter Stuyvesant, the West India company director of Curaçao, arrives at St. Martin. During a three-week battle with the Spanish, Stuyvesant loses a limb and becomes "Pegleg Peter."

1648 On 23 March, an agreement between French and Dutch colonists on St. Martin is signed, dividing the island in half and naming it **St-Martin/St. Maarten.** The peaceful coexistence of the two sides of the island continues to this day.

1655 British forces capture Jamaica from Spain as Oliver Cromwell sets the stage for Britain's imperial role in the region.

1670 England formally takes control of Jamaica and the Cayman Islands.

1672 England annexes **Tortola** (now part of the British Virgin Islands).

1684 The number of slaves in Barbados's sugar trade increases from 5,680 in 1645 to 60,000. Slaves outnumber their owners three to one.

1692 More than half of **Port Royal,** Jamaica, Britain's infamous privateering base (which sent many a Spanish ship to the bottom), falls into the harbor when a severe earthquake hits the city.

1705 The French build **Fort George** on Grenada.

1732 The Jewish community on Curaçao (established in 1651) builds the **Synagoge Mikve Israel-Emanuel,** now the oldest in the Western Hemisphere.

1751 George Washington travels to Barbados for the healthy air with his half-brother, Lawrence, who suffers from tuberculosis. George comes down with smallpox.

1755 Alexander Hamilton is born on Nevis.

1763 Marie-Josèphe Rose Tascher de la Pagerie is born near **Les Trois-Ilets** on **Martinique.** She will become Napoleon's Empress Josephine.

1776 On 25 October, **Fort Frederik** on **St. Croix** in the Danish West Indies (now the US Virgin Islands) fires a salute to a privately owned merchant ship flying the Stars and Stripes. (Today locals call it the "first salute by a foreign nation to the flag of the United States of America.") On 16 November, **Fort Oranje** on **St. Eustatius** returns a salute to the US-owned and flagged warship *Andrew Doria.* (The island still celebrates the greeting, ordered by Dutch commander Johannes de Graaff, as the US's first *official* recognition by a foreign power.)

1784 French colonists on **St-Barthélemy** learn they are now Swedes—thanks to one of Louis XVI's ministers, who has traded away the island and its citizens for a single warehouse in Göteborg, Sweden.

Horatio Nelson takes command of the large naval installation located on **English Harbour** in Antigua.

1791 Slaves in northern Saint-Domingue/Haiti launch an uprising. Under the leadership of Toussaint Louverture, it spreads throughout the colony, turning into a revolution that will liberate Haiti and begin the abolition of slavery in the New World.

1793 Captain William Bligh finally succeeds in transporting Tahitian breadfruit trees to **St. Vincent.** (His first attempt brought about the famous "Mutiny on the Bounty.")

1794 As a result of the ongoing Haitian revolution, a decree on 4 February abolishes slavery in all French colonies. Complete emancipation, however, is not achieved until an act of the Second French Republic in 1848.

1796 French soldiers storm **Rendezvous Bay** in **Anguilla** in a futile attempt to reclaim the island from England. The island remains British, and in 1825 becomes a single crown colony, along with St. Kitts and Nevis.

1797 Sir Ralph Abercromby attempts to conquer San Juan, Puerto Rico. The British soldiers turn tail when they mistake a religious procession for Spanish reinforcements. The cannons they leave behind are melted down and forged into a statue of Juan Ponce de León.

1800 The Jamaican population reaches a high of 20,000 whites and 300,000 African slaves.

1803 After more than 30 changes of ownership in 300 years, **Tobago** falls to the British, who finally overpower the French government *du jour* and bring lasting peace.

1812 The Dutch gain final control of **Saba** after it has changed hands 12 times.

1825 Over 300 years after conquistadores began searching for gold in the West Indies, a young shepherd stumbles across a vein on **Aruba**'s north coast, prompting the birth of the island's first industry. Within months, more than 25 pounds of gold are collected. Mining operations last until 1916.

1833 The Emancipation Act ends slavery throughout the British Empire, including all island holdings. After five years of red tape, all slaves in the **British West Indies** are finally set free in 1838.

1834 Former slaves on Barbados become "apprentices" who work for their masters for the next four years.

1844 The Dominican Republic declares independence from Haiti under Juan Pablo Duarte's La Trinitaria movement. Except for a brief return to Spanish control in the early 1860s, it has been an autonomous nation ever since.

1845 The first indentured servants from India arrive on Trinidad.

1872 Smelting begins at the Aruba Inland Gold Mining Company on the island's north coast. Another smelting company opens at **Balashi** in 1899. The Netherlands government sends troops to Aruba to guard the fields and dry creeks.

1878 Ownership of St-Barthélemy is returned to France.

1887 Artist Paul Gauguin paints at **Le Carbet** on the western coast of Martinique.

1898 The United States acquires Puerto Rico after the Spanish-American War.

1902 Mount Pelée erupts and its gases and volcanic lava wipe out stately St-Pierre, Martinique's principal city. Within minutes, 30,000 people are dead; the only survivor is a prisoner locked in a dungeon. Villas and mansions banked by gardens are destroyed, and more than 40 ships sitting in the bay sink in the disaster.

1903 After centuries of fighting against foreign invaders, the Carib Indians of Dominica submit to British demands and are forced onto a reservation near the island's eastern coast, where their descendants still live today.

1917 The United States grants full citizenship rights to Puerto Ricans.

The US pays Denmark $25 million for St. Croix, St. John, and **St. Thomas.** The Danish West Indies thereafter are known as the US Virgin Islands.

1930 Generalíssimo Rafael Leónidas Trujillo takes control of the Dominican Republic, establishing a dictatorship that lasts more than 30 years.

1948 Severe fires destroy many of the early French and British buildings in **Castries, St. Lucia.** A second wave of conflagrations finishes the job in 1951. The capital is later rebuilt, the new capital buildings feature modern low-rise architecture.

1949 The Hilton hotel chain opens its first Caribbean outpost, the **Caribe Hilton,** in San Juan, substantially boosting tourism in the Puerto Rican capital.

Amber mining and jewelry production develop into serious business in the Dominican Republic.

1951 Puerto Rico elects its first native-born governor, Luis Muñoz Marín.

1955 The colonial status of the **Netherlands Antilles** (Aruba, Bonaire, Curaçao, Saba, St. Eustatius, and St. Maarten) is abolished, creating autonomous island territories that are administered through the capital of **Willemstad,** Curaçao. Aruba chooses independence from the other five islands but remains within the Dutch realm.

1956 The two-island nation of Trinidad and Tobago becomes a republic. The (US) **Virgin Islands National Park** is established on St. John, preserving 5,650 offshore acres and 9,000 acres of land—nearly two-thirds of the island's area.

1958 Jamaica joins the Federation of the West Indies. The Federation is comprised of a group of Caribbean islands that form a unit within the Commonwealth of Nations, an association of Great Britain and its past and present dependencies.

1961 The Dominican Republic dictatorship of Generalíssimo Rafael Leónidas Trujillo ends when he is assassinated. Many of the alleged assassins are later captured and executed.

1962 Jamaica secedes from the Federation of the West Indies and becomes an independent member of the Commonwealth of Nations.

1966 Barbados becomes an independent state within the Commonwealth of Nations. (Unique in the West Indies, the island has not changed ownership since the British originally settled here in the early 1600s.)

1974 Grenada declares independence from Great Britain.

1978 Bonaire proclaims its entire coastline—to a depth of 200 feet—the **Bonaire Marine Park.** Boaters, divers, and swimmers are forbidden to take anything—dead or alive—from the coral reefs.

1979 **St. Vincent and the Grenadines** declare total independence from Great Britain. St. Lucia (a self-governing British state since 1967) is granted full sovereignty as a full-fledged member of the Commonwealth of Nations.

1981 Antigua becomes an independent state within the Commonwealth of Nations.

1983 The independent nation of St. Kitts and Nevis withdraws from the United Kingdom.

US forces stage a six-day invasion of Grenada to help control civil unrest following the assassination of the leftist prime minister Maurice Bishop.

1986 Aruba becomes a separate entity within the Kingdom of the Netherlands.

1987 Saba establishes the underwater **Saba Marine Park,** a national preserve that protects pristine marine life surrounding the island and two offshore seamounts.

1988 Hurricane Gilbert hits Jamaica, causing hundreds of millions of dollars of damage. It takes two years for tourism to get back on track.

1989 Hurricane Hugo devastates St. Croix in the US Virgin Islands (it takes three years for the island recover). Puerto Rico is spared when **El Yunque** rain forest takes the brunt of the storm's force.

1991 The 500,000th visitor arrives on Aruba.

Sandals, the first couples-only resort in the Caribbean, opens on Jamaica.

In **Place de la Savane,** the central park of **Fort-de-France** in Martinique, the 1859 statue of Napoleon's Josephine is beheaded in an act of vandalism. Some locals are not outraged, noting that the island's most famous native campaigned for the continuation of local slavery (on behalf of her family's sugar interests) long after it was outlawed in other French possessions.

1992 The **Faro a Colón** (Columbus Lighthouse), commemorating the 500th anniversary of Christopher Columbus's first voyage of discovery, opens on the Dominican Republic.

1993 A possible *mikvah* (ritual bath) and synagogue dating back to the early 1650s are discovered in Charlestown, Nevis. Archaeologists continue to explore the site to determine their authenticity.

1994 On 7 January, the *USS Morris Bergman* spills 500,000 barrels of oil in the sea near San Juan, Puerto Rico. The damage is cleaned up by mid-March.

1995 In August, **Montserrat**'s long-dormant Soufrière Hills volcano awakes and starts spewing ash and steam. Residents of the southern and eastern parts of the island are evacuated several times the rest of the year, returning to their homes each time the volcano's activity quiets.

On 4 and 5 September, Hurricane Luis hits Anguilla, Antigua, St. Barts, and St-Martin/St. Maarten, causing widespread damage. Luis is also felt on Montserrat, Saba, St. Eustatius, St. Kitts, and some of the British Virgin Islands, but the devastation is not as severe.

On 15 September, Hurricane Marilyn blasts the US Virgin Islands, causing heavy losses on S t. Thomas and St. John.

The first Trinidad and Tobago prime minister of East Indian ancestry, Basdeo Panday, takes office on 9 November.

1996 A new political era begins in the Dominican Republic on 31 June, when Leonel Fernández is elected to replace longtime leader Joaquín Balaguer, president on and off since 1960.

Hurricane Hortense hits Puerto Rico on 10 September, causing $200 million worth of damage.

1997 Eruptions of Monserrat's Soufriere Hills volcano beginning in late June result in massive devastation and a number of deaths. By August nearly two-thirds of the island's population has been evacuated and the remaining residents are living in the designated safety zone in the northern quarter of the island. More than half of the island is declared off-limits to everyone but scientists. The US Department of State issues a warning advising against travel to the island.

1998 Monserrat's Soufriere Hills volcano continues to be active and much of the island is still in a restricted danger zone. (At press time a US State Department travel warning remains in effect.)

Tourists, scientists, and New Agers converge on the Caribbean on 26 February to view the Western Hemisphere's last total eclipse of the sun this century.

Paseo de la Princesa, Puerto Rico

Index

Restaurant Ratings

Only restaurants with star ratings are listed in the restaurant indexes below. All restaurants are listed alphabetically in each area's main index. Always call in advance to ensure a restaurant has not closed, changed its hours, or booked its tables for a private party. The restaurant price ratings are based on the average cost of an entrée for one person, excluding tax and tip.

★★★★ An Extraordinary Experience
  ★★★ Excellent
    ★★ Very Good
     ★ Good
  $$$$ Big Bucks
   $$$ Expensive
    $$ Reasonable
     $ The Price Is Right

Hotel Ratings

The hotels listed in the hotel indexes below are grouped according to their price ratings; they are also listed in each area's main index. The hotel price ratings reflect the base price of a standard room for two people for one night during the peak season.

  $$$$ Big Bucks
   $$$ Expensive
    $$ Reasonable
     $ The Price Is Right

Anguilla

Airlines **14**
Airport **14**
Anguilla **12** (chapter and map)
Anguilla Great House $$$ **15**
Arlo's Place ★★★$$ **17**
Bicycles **14**
Blanchard's ★★★★$$$$ **16**
Cap Juluca $$$$ **15**
Car rental **14**

Antigua Restaurants

Antigua Hotels

Index

Bonaire Restaurants

Bonaire Hotels

British Virgin Islands

British Virgin Islands Restaurants

Dominican Republic Restaurants

Dominican Republic Hotels

Grenada

Puerto Rico Restaurants

Puerto Rico Hotels

St-Barthélemy Restaurants

St. Lucia Restaurants

St. Lucia Hotels

St-Martin/St. Maarten

Index

St. Vincent and the Grenadines Restaurants

St. Vincent and the Grenadines Hotels

US Virgin Islands Restaurants

US Virgin Islands Hotels